READING FOR THINKING

Reading for Thinking

Fifth Edition

Laraine E. Flemming

Ann Marie Radaskiewicz
Contributing Writer

HOUGHTON MIFFLIN COMPANY
New York   Boston

Publisher: Patricia A. Coryell
Senior Sponsoring Editor: Lisa Kimball
Senior Development Editor: Judith Fifer
Senior Project Editor: Tracy Patruno
Senior Manufacturing Coordinator: Marie Barnes
Senior Marketing Manager: Annamarie Rice
Marketing Assistant: Andrew Whitacre

Cover image: © Richard Kolker/Photonica

Credits appear on pages 641–642, which are considered an extension of the copyright page.

Printed in the U.S.A.

Library of Congress Control Number: 2004115428

ISBN: 0-618-52869-5

123456789-CRW-09 08 07 06 05

CONTENTS

Chapter 4   Understanding and Outlining Longer Readings   *181*

Chapter 5   Summarizing and Synthesizing: Two More Strategies for In-Depth Learning   237

Chapter 6   Reading Between the Lines: Drawing Inferences and Conclusions   291

Chapter 7 Defining the Terms *Fact* and *Opinion* 358

 Chapter 8 Identifying Purpose and Tone 395

Chapter 9   Recognizing and Evaluating Bias   444

**Chapter 10   Understanding and Evaluating
               Arguments**   484

PREFACE

As the author, I am obviously happy to announce that the fourth edition of *Reading for Thinking* was enthusiastically received by both students and instructors. Teachers appreciated the careful sequence and liked how the book moved step by step from a review of comprehension skills to a detailed discussion of critical thinking skills and how to apply them. Students liked the stimulating readings and the varied exercises.

However, I don't mean to suggest that the previous edition could not be improved upon. On the contrary, I like to think that the new features listed below have made a good book even better.

New to the Fifth Edition

Comprehensive Review Tests   New to this edition are the *Taking Stock* tests, appearing at the end of Chapters 3 through 10. Like the questions concluding the end-of-chapter Digging Deeper readings, these tests review new material along with skills covered in previous chapters.

Drawing Conclusions   *Reading for Thinking* has always given a lot of attention to inferring main ideas. This is the first time, though, that the book deals with inferences, or conclusions, not necessarily intended by the author but still suggested by the reading. In Chapter 6, "Reading Between the Lines," students are asked to make inferences about the author's attitude toward an issue or event not specifically mentioned in the reading but in some way related to its message. They are also asked to infer how people or groups referred to in the reading might respond to similar or related issues. In other words, students learn how to draw logical conclusions that are grounded in explicit evidence, a skill essential to academic success and, for that matter, to daily life.

Supporting Detail Diagrams   Exercises in which students have to diagram major and minor details have been extremely popular with users of *Reading for Results*. Thus I decided to include a similar exercise in this edition of *Reading for Thinking*.

 New Icons for CD-ROM and Web Connections   Special icons point to where students can find additional help, including exercises, quizzes, and self-tests found on **Getting Focused,** the companion CD-ROM, or on the website **laflemm.com** that supports *Reading for Thinking.*

Emphasis on Ethical Decision Making   Many of the readings and some of the follow-up assignments focus on situations that require an ethical decision. Because this topic seems particularly timely in today's society, I thought it the perfect way to make students see how relevant critical thinking is to everyday life.

Improved Sequence of Exercises   Throughout the text, the number of multiple-choice answers moves from two possibilities, to three, and finally to four. Increasing the level of difficulty in this slow and steady way should keep students' performance anxiety at a minimum.

More Attention to Reading Flexibility   The selections in the final section of *Reading for Thinking,* "Putting It All Together," all begin with different suggestions for pre-reading and reading the material. The point of these varied suggestions—as opposed to the fourth edition's reliance on focus questions—is to make students realize that the material should generally dictate their choice of reading strategies, and no one strategy or set of strategies is appropriate to every reading.

Increased Coverage of Organizational Patterns   Reviewers requested more attention be paid to identifying organizational patterns, and that's precisely what I've done in Chapter 3, "Reviewing Paragraph Essentials." New exercises, tips, and tests will make it easier for students to identify organizational patterns.

New Tests   The fifth edition offers several new tests of key skills such as paraphrasing main ideas and differentiating between facts and opinions.

Pointers on Paraphrasing   Paraphrasing isn't something students automatically know how to do once they are told it's important. They need specific directions as to how they should go about paraphrasing when they read or write. This edition of *Reading for Thinking* provides these directions in an easy-to-read chart.

New Discussion of Web Research   This edition contains two new sections that describe how websites can and should be evaluated for accuracy.

Numerous New Readings   This edition includes a large percentage of new readings. As always, the readings were carefully selected to arouse students' interest and at the same time enlarge their knowledge of key historical events and current trends. Among the new topics addressed are identity theft, lawsuits against fast food companies, the history of Cape Canaveral, the popularity of reality TV, and the need for boxing reform.

Emphasis on Cultural Difference   Several of the readings deal with cultural differences and how they affect communication, behavior, and ethics. The choice of topic is intentional since, despite our living in a culture composed of different races and ethnic groups, we sometimes forget that Americans' view of how the world can or should work is not always shared by others. This seems a particularly important time to make students aware of that fact.

Longer Textbook Selections   I'd be the first to admit that I believe in giving students colorful, controversial readings to excite their interest in reading. However, students also need practice with textbook material. Thus this edition has included more selections drawn from textbook sources, and some of the selections are quite lengthy. The length is intentional, giving students additional chances to practice the study skills introduced early in the book.

Since my goal has always been to encourage students to see reading as an act of discovery, I have been careful to select textbook readings that I personally find quite interesting. I think they will help contradict or diminish students' oft-stated belief that textbooks are by nature filled with boring information.

 The open textbook icons appearing throughout *Reading for Thinking* identify selections that have been excerpted from college texts.

Many Thanks to Reviewers

My thanks to the following reviewers: Terry Bratcher of Lindsey Wilson College; C. H. Charlton of Northeast State Technical Community College; Dawn Sedik of Valencia Community College; B. Jean Sieffert of Hillsborough Community College; and Bryan J. Spann of Northeastern Technical College, all of whom offered excellent suggestions for improving *Reading for Thinking*.

Also Available in the Same Series

Reading for Thinking is the third and highest-level text in a three-part series. The two lower-level texts offer the same step-by-step approach combined with lively readings and clear explanations. *Reading for Results* concentrates mainly on comprehension skills and includes one chapter on critical thinking. The perfect precursor to *Reading for Thinking, Reading for Results* lays the groundwork for all of the skills introduced in its more advanced sister text. Instructors teaching a basic reading course, however, might prefer to start with *Reading Keys,* which offers more abbreviated explanations along with greater repetition. It also lets students master both concepts and skills in small, incremental bites.

Accompanying Software

Created by Ulrich and Laraine Flemming to accompany this series, the *Getting Focused* CD-ROM introduces both comprehension and critical reading skills in a carefully sequenced program of tutorials and tests. Like the texts, the software features the author's twin trademarks: lively readings and clear explanations.

Website Resources

In addition to easy-to-navigate and graphically engaging software—free to users of any Flemming text—the author's website (**laflemm.com**) offers suggestions for teaching each chapter and a 5th edition syllabus along with additional exercises and tests to be used in class and online exercises for students who want to work independently on vocabulary, comprehension, and critical reading. Chapters covering skills also included on the website conclude with a boxed description of where students can find similar exercises and tests on the companion website.

Students and instructors can also visit Houghton Mifflin's developmental English website, **http://college.hmco.com/devenglish** (select Developmental Reading, and then select Laraine Flemming's *Reading for Thinking* site), where they will find a variety of online tests covering vocabulary and comprehension skills.

Additional Online and Electronic Supplements

Eduspace With Houghton Mifflin's online learning tool powered by Blackboard, students get exercises with immediate feedback, chat rooms and discussion boards that encourage interaction, and 24-hour access to all assignments. Instructors receive a classroom management system that allows them to assign, distribute, track, and grade student assignments all online as well as post additional class assignments, announcements, and syllabi. Go to **www.eduspace.com** for additional information.

Reading Space This Web-based program fosters improved reading comprehension through a progressive sequence of Pre-, Practice, and Mastery Tests.

HM Reading CD-ROM Three diagnostic tests cover a total of 180 questions, as well as additional practice exercises. Each question focuses on one of twelve reading skills areas.

HM Vocabulary CD-ROM The CD features 800 questions comprising eighty drills. Four types of drills (matching, multiple-choice, fill-in-the-sentence, and fill-in-the-paragraph formats) ensure students have ample opportunities to practice new terms.

VEER Vocabulary Enrichment Exercises for Reading CD-ROM Eighty tests include matching, multiple-choice, fill-in-the-sentence, and fill-in-the-paragraph. The program features two modes, Practice and Test, so students can choose to either build their skills or gauge their progress.

Expressways 5.0 CD-ROM Expressways is a self-paced paragraph- and essay-level writing tutorial that provides students with extra practice on the writing process. Fourteen modules each include sections on pre-writing and drafting, revising, analyzing a reading, and a writing lab with three additional topics drawn from the earlier reading.

Additional Print Supplements

Houghton Mifflin Guide to Reading Textbooks, **Second Edition** This guide helps students develop their reading skills, specifically for textbook reading in an academic environment.

The American Heritage College Dictionary, **Fourth Edition** With 7,500 new words and meanings, along with 2,500 new illustrations, the Fourth Edition is the most up-to-date college dictionary available.

The American Heritage ESL Dictionary The first ESL dictionary of its kind to be based on one of the most respected and authoritative American language dictionaries available, this resource is specially designed to meet the needs of ESL students.

Words Count Also written by Laraine Flemming, this is a basic vocabulary book using a contextual approach to vocabulary building. Each chapter links new words together according to shared themes such as money, marriage, or friendship.

A Final Note

As contributing writer, Ann Marie Radaskiewicz has proven herself invaluable. She has an uncanny gift for ferreting out stimulating topics that also have practical value for students still learning the ways of the world. Mary Schnabel continues to catch my errors and make terrific suggestions about how best to organize material and highlight key features. As always, Nancy Benjamin and Books By Design see to it that my messy, sometimes illegible manuscript is turned into a readable book. A special thanks to Professor Dawn Sedik of Valencia Community College, who made me think more carefully about how inferring main ideas could be distinguished from drawing logical conclusions, and Professor Joan Hellman of The Community College of Baltimore County–Catonsville, whose comments on ethical thinking made an enormous contribution to this revision. And finally, thanks to Michel Laurie of North Branford High School, whose own use of case studies and realistic scenarios inspired me to try for a more innovative method of teaching students how to draw conclusions.

Best wishes and great success,
Laraine Flemming

C H A P T E R   1

Getting a Head Start on Academic Success

 In this chapter, you'll learn

- **how to use a proven study technique called *SQ3R*.**

- **how to use word parts and context clues to define unfamiliar words.**

- **how to read and answer multiple-choice questions.**

- **how to read and respond to essay questions.**

By the time you finish this book, you'll possess all the reading skills necessary to achieve academic success. Still, like most students, you probably want to improve your academic performance immediately. The good news is that you can. Put into practice all the pointers and tips introduced

in Chapter 1, and you'll be a better student in just a matter of weeks.

 # SQ3R: A System for Reading Textbooks

Textbooks aren't the same as novels. You can't just open up a textbook and start reading. Well, technically you can. But if you do, you won't understand and remember as much as you could if you use a study system like *SQ3R*.

Developed more than fifty years ago by teacher and researcher Francis Robinson, *SQ3R* has stood the test of time, with numerous studies indicating that it improves comprehension. The letters *S-Q-R-R-R* stand for *survey, question, read, recite,* and *review.* Following each of these five steps when you read textbooks will help you learn with greater speed and efficiency. So, without further ado, here's a brief explanation of each step.

S: Survey Before You Begin Reading

Survey a chapter before you begin reading it. Read only the title, the introduction, and the last page. Look carefully at all headings, captions, illustrations, and anything printed in the margins. Pay special attention to words printed in boldface or italics. Use this step to get a general sense of the chapter's content and to gauge how long it should take you to read it.

Q: Questions Help You Get Focused

To give your reading focus or purpose, use words like *why, what,* and *how* to transform headings into questions, such as "Why do glaciers grow and then retreat?" or "How do fossils of sea creatures end up on mountaintops?"

In addition to turning headings into questions, be sure to draw on your personal knowledge and ask questions like "What do I know about this topic?" and "Do I agree with the author's point of view?" Questions like these also will help you focus your attention and maintain concentration while you read.

Raising and answering questions strengthens your motivation. Each time you can answer one of your own questions, you'll feel a sense of accomplishment. The more successful you feel, the more likely you are to keep reading.

R-1: Read

The first *R* in *SQ3R* stands for *read*. However, that doesn't mean you should read a textbook chapter in the same way you might read a novel or a magazine. Instead, use some or all of the following strategies to make sure you thoroughly master the material.

Break the Assignment into Chunks

Don't read a chapter straight through from beginning to end. Read it in manageable chunks of fifteen or twenty pages at the most, even if that means you read an assignment over three consecutive nights.

Pose Questions and Make Predictions to Maintain Focus and Concentration

Each time you begin a chapter section, raise questions based on the heading. Whenever possible, predict how you think the author's train of thought will continue. For example, if you see the heading *Differences Between Broadcast and Print Media*, mentally make a prediction and pose a question: "The author will probably point out several differences between television and newspaper journalists. What exactly could those differences be?"

Even if you have to revise them when you finish reading a chapter section, those questions and predictions will serve their purpose. They will keep you focused on the material and alert you to differences between what you expected to read and what the author actually said.

Review After Each Chapter Section

Each time you finish a chapter section, review it by asking what message the author wanted to convey. Then ask yourself how you could explain that message to someone else. See whether you can recall some facts, reasons, or statistics the author used to describe, explain, or support a position or point.

Underline and Write While You Read

Want to make sure you are really reading your assignment and not just letting your eyes glide across the page? Then get into the habit of underlining and writing. While you are reading, underline key words in pencil, and jot main points and questions in the margins. When you go back for review, erase whatever seems less important the second time around and rewrite or add the rest in pen. Underlining and writing while reading forces you to maintain your concentration and really dig into the material. The close attention required to underline and write is what makes the difference between real reading and just letting your eyes drift across the page.

Annotate Pages

Like underlining, annotating (making marginal notes) while reading has a twofold reward. It will help you stay focused on the task at hand. It will also help you remember what you read, particularly if you are careful to **paraphrase** the author's language—use your own words whenever you can. By forcing you to re-create meaning with different words, paraphrasing gives your mind a chance to mull over the material. That's a major key to remembering.

You should also mark difficult or hard-to-understand passages for a second reading, using symbols like *X2* or *RR.* That way, you can return to the sections you marked after you finish. Often, because you now have the whole assignment to provide context, you will more readily understand what you did not grasp before. This is particularly true if you take some time and make your second reading slower than the first. Slowing down your speed will allow you to do a **close reading** so that you can think about the relationships between sentences and how they work together to create meaning.

R-2: Recite at the End of Each Chapter Section

Each time you finish a chapter section, you should recite the key points and any answers to questions you posed while surveying. Reciting will help you monitor, or check, your understanding of what you've read. Then you can decide if you need to reread the section. To recite, just ask yourself: "What were the key points in this reading?" Then see whether you can come up with some or all of those points. Next, try to answer your original questions. If you can't recite any key points or answer your own questions, reread the entire chapter section immediately or mark it for a later rereading with the letters *RR.*

Write Out the Answers

If the reading assignment is especially difficult or particularly important, it's a good idea to write out the answers to your questions. When you write answers, you can't fool yourself into thinking you've understood material that is actually vague or unclear in your mind.

R-3: Review After You Finish Reading the Chapter

When you finish the assignment, go back over the chapter and look at the headings. For each heading, try to mentally recite a few of the author's key points. Even better, ask a friend to quiz you on each of the headings.

Yes, using *SQ3R* and the strategies described in this section will take extra time. Simply reading a chapter straight through without surveying or reciting is a quicker method of studying. Unfortunately, it's not particularly effective. Thus, it's very much worth your while to make *SQ3R*—or some similar method—a regular study habit.

CHECK YOUR UNDERSTANDING

Describe each step in *SQ3R* without looking back at this chapter. When you finish, compare what you've written with the actual descriptions to see how complete your answers are. *Note:* You probably won't remember all the steps. Don't get discouraged. You will in time.

S: _____

_____

_____

_____

_____

_____

_____

Q: _____

_____

_____

_____

_____

_____

R-1: _____

_____

_____

_____

_____

_____

R-2: _____

_____

_____

_____

_____

_____

R-3: _____

_____

_____

_____

_____

_____

Adapting *SQ3R* to Shorter Readings

You can adapt *SQ3R* to all kinds of reading. If, for example, an author uses questions between chapter sections, those questions can easily become part of your survey as well as part of your reading. Similarly, if you are assigned a much shorter reading in a magazine or a journal, you don't have to abandon *SQ3R*. Merely adapt your survey, making it include some or all of the following:

---

1. Read the title. If you can, turn it into a question. If a brief overview appears right underneath the title, as is often the case in journal articles, read that as well. Notice, too, whether the title expresses a complete thought. If it does, that thought may be the reading's main idea. Assume that it is until the reading proves your prediction incorrect.

2. Read the first paragraph. If the article seems technical or complicated, read the second paragraph as well.

3. Pose a question or two about the author's main point.

4. Read the first line of every paragraph. If the writing style is difficult or the content is unfamiliar, read the first and last sentence of every paragraph.

5. Look at any visual aids.

6. Read the last two paragraphs.

7. Ask yourself why your instructor assigned the reading. Try to figure out how it connects to your textbook assignments and classroom lectures.

Purpose Is the Key

Generally speaking, the steps in your survey depend mainly on your reading purpose. If you need to get a detailed understanding of the ideas or events mentioned in your text, include more steps in your survey. If, however, you want only a general understanding of the author's argument, pare down the steps you use.

The following exercise will give you a chance to adapt *SQ3R* to a reading shorter than a chapter.

■ EXERCISE 1

DIRECTIONS *Survey* the following selection using the steps listed below. When you finish, answer the questions in Part A on page 11. Then go back and *read* the selection from beginning to end, making sure to underline and annotate. When you are done, answer the questions in Part B.

Survey Steps

1. Read the title and ask yourself, "What does the author want to tell readers about wartime Hawaii?"
2. Read the first paragraph and ask yourself, "What point does the author want to make in the reading?"
3. Read the headings and turn them into questions.
4. Read the first sentence of every paragraph.
5. Read the last paragraph.
6. Ask yourself whether you already know anything about wartime Hawaii that might enhance your understanding of this reading.

Wartime Hawaii

Much as the war came to the United States initially and most dramatically at Pearl Harbor, the outlines of an increasingly multicultural United States emerging from the Second World War could be seen first and most clearly in Hawaii. The nearly one million soldiers, sailors, and marines stopping in Hawaii on their way to the battlefront, as well as the more than one hundred thousand men and women who left the mainland to find war work on the islands, expected the Hollywood image of a simple Pacific paradise: blue sky, green sea, and white sand; palm trees and tropical sunsets; exotic women with flowers in their hair. They found instead a complex multiracial and multiethnic society. The experience would change them, as they in turn would change the islands.

Hawaii's Multiracial Society

Before December 7, 1941, few Americans knew where Pearl Harbor was or even that Hawaii was a part of their country, a colonial possession, a territory annexed by the U.S. government in 1898.

Few realized that Honolulu, a tiny fishing village when Captain James Cook sailed by the difficult entrance to its harbor in 1778, had subsequently become the major maritime center of a kingdom, the seat of a territorial government, and a gritty port city that would serve as the major staging ground for the war to be waged in the Pacific. And few knew that this American outpost, as a result of successive waves of immigration beginning in the 1870s by Chinese, Portuguese, Japanese, and Filipinos, had a population in 1940 in which native Hawaiians and white Americans (called *haoles,* which in Hawaiian means "strangers") each constituted only 15 percent of the islands' inhabitants.

The Nisei and Issei

The approximately 160,000 Hawaiians of Japanese ancestry—including some 100,000 second-generation Japanese, or *Nisei,* who had been born in Hawaii and were therefore U.S. citizens—composed Hawaii's largest ethnic group, more than a third of the population. Japan's attack on Pearl Harbor immediately raised fears of sabotage or espionage by Hawaiians of Japanese descent. Rumors flew of arrow-shaped signs cut in the sugarcane fields to direct Japanese planes to military targets and of *Nisei* women waving kimonos to signal Japanese pilots.

But in stark contrast to the wholesale incarceration of the Japanese in the Pacific coast states, where the dangers of subversive activities were slight in comparison to Hawaii, official military and administrative policy in the islands was to maintain traditional interracial harmony throughout the war, and to treat all law-abiding inhabitants of Japanese ancestry justly and humanely. "This is America and we must do things the American way," announced Hawaii's military governor. "We must distinguish between loyalty and disloyalty among our people." There was no mass internment of the *Nisei* and *Issei* (those who emigrated from Japan) as there was on the mainland.

For the *Issei,* loyalty to the United States had become an obligation, a matter of honor. To eliminate potential associations with the enemy, they destroyed old books, photographs of relatives, and brocaded *obi* (kimono sashes) and replaced portraits of the Japanese emperor with pictures of President Roosevelt. A burning desire to prove that they were true Americans prompted many of their Hawaiian-born children, often referred to as AJAs (Americans of Japanese ancestry), to become "superpatriots." AJAs contributed heavily to war-bond drives and sponsored their own "Bombs on Tokyo" campaign; they cleared areas for new military camps; and they converted the halls of Buddhist temples,

Shinto* shrines, and Japanese-language schools (all closed for the duration and reopened after the war) into manufactories of bandages, knit socks, sweaters, and hospital gowns (the latter sewn for the Red Cross and Office of Civil Defense). Their newly expanded contact with other Hawaiians, including *haoles,* hastened their assimilation into the larger Hawaiian society. In addition, AJAs served in the military campaigns in the Pacific as interpreters—translating, interrogating, intercepting transmissions, and cracking enemy codes; and they fought in Europe with the all-*Nisei* 442d Regimental Combat Team, the most highly decorated organization in the U.S. Army. These contributions gave the Japanese in Hawaii, as it did other ethnic groups, a new sense of their worth and dignity. The war experience aroused expectations of equal opportunity and treatment, of full participation in island politics, of no longer accepting a subordinate status to *haoles.*

Changing Attitudes Toward Haoles
Additionally, the attitudes of many Hawaiians toward *haoles* changed as native islanders witnessed a large number of whites doing manual labor for the first time. Their view that whites would always hold superior positions in society—as bosses, plantation owners, business leaders, and politicians—was turned topsy-turvy by the flood of Caucasian mainland war workers. The hordes of white servicemen crowding into Honolulu's Hotel Street vice district for liquor, for tattoos, for posed pictures with hula girls in grass skirts, for three-dollar sex at the many brothels,* and then for treatment at prophylaxis* stations to ward off venereal diseases also tarnished traditional notions of white superiority.

The Majority Becomes a Minority
Most of the whites who had come to Hawaii had never lived where whites did not constitute a majority and where *they* were the ones who were different. Most had never before encountered or conversed with those of African or Asian ancestry. Suddenly, they were in the midst of a mixture of ethnic and racial groups unmatched anywhere in the United States, in the midst of a society of people of diverse cultures working together for a common cause. So also were the nearly thirty thousand African-American servicemen and workers who arrived in the islands before the war's end. Having experienced nothing like the fluid and relaxed

*Shinto: a religion native to Japan characterized by worship of nature and ancestors.
*brothels: houses of prostitution.
*prophylaxis: preventive treatment for diseases.

racial relations of Hawaii's multiethnic society, blacks discovered an alternative to the racist America they knew. Some chose never to go back to the mainland. Others returned home to the States to press for the rights and freedoms they had first tasted in Hawaii. In so many ways, wartime Hawaii, termed "the first strange place" by historians Beth Bailey and David Farber, would anticipate the "strangeness" of U.S. society today. (Adapted from Boyer et al., *Enduring Vision*, pp. 779a–b.)

Part A: Surveying

DIRECTIONS Answer the following questions by filling in the blanks or circling the correct response.

1. The soldiers and wartime workers who came to Hawaii expected to find _____. But instead, they found _____.

2. Who composed Hawaii's largest ethnic group? _____

3. *True* or *False*. Unlike the mainland, Hawaii maintained interracial harmony throughout the war.

4. In wartime Hawaii, whites who lived there suddenly discovered what it was like to be _____.

5. In wartime Hawaii, African-Americans discovered _____.
_____

Stop! Now go back and read the article from beginning to end. When you finish, answer the questions in Part B.

Part B: Reading

DIRECTIONS Answer the following questions by filling in the blanks.

6. What general point about wartime Hawaii does the author make?
_____

7. The *Nisei* had been born in _____, whereas the *Issei* were born in _____.

8. Why did the Hawaiian-born Japanese become superpatriots?

_____.

9. Explain how the Hawaiian attitude toward *haoles* changed during wartime.

_____.

10. Give two reasons for that change.

_____.

_____.

Building Your Academic Vocabulary

In addition to a system for reading academic assignments, you need a system for mastering the academic vocabulary of college textbooks, readings, and lectures. As you might guess, the first step toward mastery is making sure you recognize the right words and terms. So let's start there.

Recognizing Key Words and Terms

Anxious for you to learn the specialized vocabulary of their subject matter, authors of textbooks usually provide an explicit definition right before or right after they introduce a key term. Thus you need to pay close attention to any words highlighted in boldface, italics, or colored ink *and* followed or preceded by a definition. Such words are bound to belong to the specialized vocabulary of the subject you're studying. Look, for example, at the way the author of a textbook on management defines the term *corporate culture*.

Corporate culture is made up of shared values, symbols, myths, rituals, and language that shape the world of work.

Organizations develop unique internal cultures. Within the last decade, much attention has been focused on the relationship between a corporation's culture and its success. **Corporate culture** consists of the shared values, symbols, stories or myths, rituals, and language that shape an organization's work patterns. (Bulin, *Supervision*, p. 5)

With a passage like this one, you should pause a moment to study the boldface term and its definition, both of which appear within the text itself as well as in the margin. Write the word and definition on an index card or in a vocabulary notebook so you can file it away for later review.

Boldface, colored ink, and marginal annotations are the most popular methods of highlighting textbook vocabulary, but italics, brackets, parentheses, and dashes are also widely used. Whenever you start an assignment, take a second or two to determine the method or methods an author uses to make specialized vocabulary jump out at the reader. These are the words that should become part of your vocabulary.

Breaking Words into Parts

Many English words—particularly those in textbooks—include parts of other words drawn from other languages, in particular Greek and Latin. Thus if you learn some of the frequently appearing prefixes and roots* (see pages 14–15), you can unlock the meanings of many, many different words.

While the meaning you derive from analyzing word parts may not be the exact same meaning you'd find in a dictionary, it will be close enough so that you can keep reading and not lose sight of the author's meaning. Take, for example, the word *intervention*. It's made up of the Latin prefix *inter* meaning "between" and the Latin root *ven* meaning "come." If you didn't know what the word *intervention* meant in the following sentence, you could figure it out from your knowledge of the two parts, *inter* and *ven:* "The intervention of Swedish diplomat Raoul Wallenberg saved thousands of Hungary's Jews from certain death at the hands of Hitler's supporters." According to this sentence, Raoul Wallenberg came between or interfered with plans to execute Hungary's Jews.

A knowledge of Greek prefixes and roots is particularly valuable when taking science courses. For example, the Greek prefix *peri* means "around." Armed with that information, you can probably figure out definitions for the italicized word in this sentence: "The *periphery* of the volcano clearly showed signs of a recent eruption." If you guessed that *periphery* means "area around," you would be absolutely right.

In addition to figuring out word meanings, you can usually remember a word's meaning more easily if you know something about its prefix or root. For example, if you know that *cardia* comes from *kardia,* the Greek word for "heart," you should have no trouble remembering that the *pericardium* is a fluid sac that encloses, or goes around, the heart.

---

*roots: the core parts that carry a word's meaning.

Prefixes

Prefix	Meaning	Examples		
A	away	anemia	aversion	
A, AN	not	agnostic	asexual	antagonist
AB	away from	abnormal	absent	
AD, AS	to, toward	adhere	advertisement	associate
ANTE	before	antecedent	antedate	anteroom
ANTI	against	antidote	antiseptic	anticlimax
CIRCUM	around	circa	circumference	circumstantial
COM, CON	together with	complete	compulsion	collect
CONTRA	against	contradict	contrast	controversy
DE	down from, away	decline	dethrone	depression
DIA	through, across	diagram	diameter	diagonal
DIS	apart from	distort	dissolve	disrupt
EX, EF, E	out of	exclude	efficient	event
IN, IM, IL	into	incline	immerse	impose
IN, IM, IL, IR	not	incorrect	informal	immoral
INTER	between	intercede	interfere	interstate
MONO	one, alone	monotone	monarch	monopoly
NON	not	nonstop	nonconformist	
PARA	beside, beyond	parallel	paraphrase	parasite
POLY	many	polygamy	polytechnic	
POST	after	postpone	postwar	postseason
PRE	before	predict	preheat	prepare
PRO	forward, in place of	progress	propel	pronoun
PRO	before	proposal	prologue	prophet
RE	back	refer	reflex	revoke
SUB, SUC, SUF, SUP, SUS	under	submerge	suffer	support
SUPER	above, over	supervise	superman	supernatural
SYN	with, together	sympathy	symphony	synagogue
TRANS	across, beyond	transmit	transit	transfer

Roots

Root	Meaning	Examples		
ANTHROP	man	anthropology	philanthropy	
ARCH	chief	monarch	architect	archangel
BIBL	book	bibliography	Bible	
CAPIT	head	capital	captain	decapitate
CED	move, yield	exceed	proceed	succeed
CHRON	time	chronology	chronicle	
CIV	city	civic	civilize	citizen
CORD	heart	cordial	accord	discord
DIC	speak	dictate	diction	dictaphone
FID	faith	fidelity	confide	infidel
FIN	end, finished	final	finite	confine
FLOR	flower	florist	flourish	florescence
GAM	marriage	monogamy	polygamous	bigamist
GRAPH, GRAM	write, written	photography	grammar	graphic
HOMO	same	homosexual	homonym	
LOC	place	location	local	allocate
LOG, OLOGY	speech, study	dialogue	geology	biology
MEMOR	memory	memorial	memorize	memorabilia
MIT	send	admit	commit	permit
MO	set in motion	move	remove	moment
ORD	order	ordinary	ordinance	ordain
PATH	feeling, suffering	pathetic	sympathy	antipathy
PHIL	love	philosopher	philanthropy	
PON	place, put	postpone	opponent	proponent
POPUL	people	popular	population	depopulate
PORT	carry	portable	porter	deportment
REG	straighten, rule	regular	regal	rectangle
SEQU	follow	sequence	persecute	pursue
SPEC	look	specimen	spectacle	spectator
THE	god	theology	atheism	monotheism
VEN	come	intervene	invent	prevent
VID	see	vision	visualize	visit

EXERCISE 2

DIRECTIONS Read the list of word parts and their meanings. Then use your knowledge of word parts to determine the meanings of the italicized words in the sentences that follow.

mer	Latin root	deserve, achieve
port	Latin root	carry
pend, pond	Latin root	hang, weigh
cracy	Greek suffix*	rule
pluto	Greek prefix	wealth
philo	Greek prefix	love
anthrop	Greek root	human, humanity
miso	Greek prefix	hatred

1. Next time you visit the office of a doctor or a lawyer, look at the awards, diplomas, or trophies on the wall. They have been placed there intentionally to indicate that the person inhabiting the office has accomplished tasks that *merit* approval or establish worth.

   Merit means ⎯⎯⎯⎯⎯⎯⎯⎯⎯⎯⎯⎯⎯⎯⎯⎯⎯⎯⎯⎯⎯⎯

2. There are those who claim that what we have in the United States is not a democracy but rather a *plutocracy*.

   Plutocracy means ⎯⎯⎯⎯⎯⎯⎯⎯⎯⎯⎯⎯⎯⎯⎯⎯⎯⎯.

3. Nowadays, the great industrialists and oil barons of the late nine-teenth century are famous for their *philanthropy;* but there was a time when they were considered immoral plutocrats, consumed by the pursuit of money, not the love of humankind.

   Philanthropy means ⎯⎯⎯⎯⎯⎯⎯⎯⎯⎯⎯⎯⎯⎯⎯⎯.

4. Some philosophers have argued that we would all be better off if we were led by a *meritocracy*.

   Meritocracy means ⎯⎯⎯⎯⎯⎯⎯⎯⎯⎯⎯⎯⎯⎯⎯⎯.

5. The heavy, *pendulous* leaves of the plant were covered in a dark, slimy mold.

   Pendulous means ⎯⎯⎯⎯⎯⎯⎯⎯⎯⎯⎯⎯⎯⎯⎯⎯.

⎯⎯⎯⎯⎯⎯
*suffix: word ending.

6. The antihero of the French play is a *misanthrope* whose mean-spirited nature is only made tolerable by wit.

   Misanthrope means _____.

7. Her *deportment* during her slain husband's funeral was incredibly brave.

   Deportment means _____.

8. As a scholar, she had written many *ponderous* articles about English morals and manners, but she made her fortune as a best-selling novelist writing lightweight mysteries.

   Ponderous means _____.

9. A long-time *Francophile,* he finally decided to return to the United States, but he was surprised to find that he was speaking English with just the hint of a French accent.

   Francophile means _____.

10. Try to *comport* yourself with a little more dignity when the queen arrives. This is a serious occasion.

    Comport means _____.

Using Context Clues

Like word parts, **context**—the sentence or passage in which a word appears—can give you an *approximate meaning* for an unfamiliar word. Although that meaning may not be exactly the same as the one in the dictionary, it will be close enough so that you can continue reading without interruption.

The following sections illustrate four of the most common context clues: contrast, restatement, example, and general knowledge.

Contrast Clues

Sentences containing contrast clues include **antonyms**—words or phrases opposite in meaning to the words you don't know. For example, suppose you were asked what the word *ostentatious* means. You might not be able to define it. After all, the word doesn't turn up that often in everyday conversation. But suppose that word had a context, or setting, as in the following passage:

Contrary to what many of us assume, the very rich are seldom *ostentatious* in their dress; they do not need to wear showy clothes to impress others. Secure in their wealth, they can afford to look plain and unimpressive.

In this case, the context of the word *ostentatious* provides contrast clues to its meaning. The words *plain* and *unimpressive* are antonyms for *ostentatious*. Using the contrast clues, you could **infer,** or read between the lines and figure out, that *ostentatious* means "being showy" or "trying to impress."

Restatement Clues

For emphasis, authors sometimes deliberately say the same thing two different ways. Look, for example, at the following passage:

Caffeine may well be bad for you. But without a cup of coffee in the morning, I get very *cantankerous*. My son says that on coffeeless days, I give new meaning to the words *cranky* and *ill-tempered*.

Here, the author announces that she becomes *cantankerous* in the morning if she doesn't have a cup of coffee. Then, to emphasize that point, she offers a restatement clue—two **synonyms,** or words similar in meaning, to the word *cantankerous: cranky* and *ill-tempered*. Thanks to that restatement, you can easily infer the meaning of *cantankerous*—"to be cranky and ill-tempered."

Example Clues

Be alert to passages in which the author supplies an example or an illustration of an unfamiliar word. Examples of the behavior or thinking associated with a word can often give you enough information to approximate a good definition.

The captain had a *dour* personality. He never laughed or smiled. He always prepared for the worst and seemed disappointed if the worst didn't happen.

You might infer from the examples in this passage that *dour* means "gloomy and depressed," and you would be absolutely correct.

General Knowledge Clues

Although contrast, restatement, and examples are common context clues, not all context clues are so obvious. Sometimes you have to base your inference solely on your familiarity with the experience or situation described in the text, as in the following example:

> As soon as I asked Magdalena to drive, I knew I had made a mistake. She was an excellent driver but always took the most *circuitous* route in order to enjoy the scenery. By the time we arrived at the restaurant, waiters were clearing the tables, and the restaurant was closed until dinnertime.

This passage does not contain any contrasts, restatements, or examples. But you can still figure out that *circuitous* means "indirect or roundabout." After all, the driver *chose* to take the route, so *circuitous* cannot mean "wrong." Because they arrived too late for lunch, the word must mean that the route was not direct.

CHECK YOUR UNDERSTANDING

Make up your own example of each context clue.

Contrast: _____

_____

Restatement: _____

_____

Example: _____

_____

General knowledge: _____

_____

![logo] **Turning to the Dictionary**

As the preceding examples show, the sentence or passage in which a word appears can help you infer approximate meaning. Sometimes, however, context does not give you a definition that seems appropriate, and you won't be able to make sense of the passage without knowing what the word means. In that case, you should look up the word before you continue reading.

Using context to derive meaning is valuable because it allows you to read without constantly referring to a dictionary. However, after you finish reading, you should still compare the definitions you inferred with those in a dictionary to be sure you are correct.

EXERCISE 3

DIRECTIONS Use context to define the italicized words in the following sentences. Then identify the type of context clue that helped you infer your definition: *C* (contrast), *R* (restatement), *E* (example), or *G* (general knowledge).

EXAMPLE In *flagrant* disregard of the rules, she passed on the right and exceeded the speed limit by at least twenty miles an hour.

Definition *open, obvious*

Type of Clue *E*

EXPLANATION The examples of flagrant disregard—speeding, passing on the right—both suggest definitions like "open" and "obvious."

1. The surprise party was a complete *fiasco;* she had never before given a party that was such a failure.

Definition _____

Type of Clue _____

2. As a child he had been the most *gregarious* kid on the block, but as an adult, he became a loner who found it difficult to bear the company of others.

Definition _____

Type of Clue _____

3. When the author stood at the podium to speak, there were no signs of her previous *trepidation*. In contrast to her earlier mood, she was remarkably relaxed and calm. Her voice did not break, her hands did not shake, and she seemed totally in command of the situation.

Definition _____

Type of Clue _____

4. That kind of *vituperation* has no place in a political campaign; he should be explaining his positions, not spewing insults.

Definition _____

Type of Clue _____

5. When it comes to publicity, the *incumbent* president obviously has more access to the press than other candidates. As the person already holding the office, the president is automatically followed everywhere by the press.

Definition _____

Type of Clue _____

6. He had come from an extremely *affluent* home where money was no object. But he gave it all up to live a life of poverty and serve those needier than himself.

Definition _____

Type of Clue _____

7. Although she wanted to, there was no way to *mitigate* the harshness of her criticism.

Definition _____

Type of Clue _____

8. The bulldog was remarkably *tenacious*. He wouldn't let go of the robber's leg even when the man rained blows down on his head. He let go only when his master yelled, "Stop!"

Definition _____

Type of Clue _____

9. Books on time management are popular primarily because *procrastination* is so common. After all, how many of us can honestly say we have never put off or postponed something we didn't want to do—washing the dog, writing a paper, cleaning the house—until the very last possible minute?

Definition _____

Type of Clue _____

10. After saving his mother from drowning, the twelve-year-old boy was *inundated* with letters praising him for his heroism.

Definition _____

Type of Clue _____

▶▬◀ Reading and Responding to Multiple Choice

Currently, multiple-choice questions are the most popular type of exam question. Easy to correct, they also let teachers test a wide range of knowledge. It makes sense, therefore, for you to learn how skillful test takers read and respond to multiple-choice questions.

Understand the Purpose and Prepare Accordingly

For the most part, multiple-choice questions directly or indirectly rely on seven words: *who, what, where, why, when, which,* and *how.* These words readily lend themselves to brief questions that can be easily incorporated into multiple-choice answers, or options, like the ones listed here.

*1. Which of the following British colonies was founded last?

   a. Plymouth

   b. Pennsylvania

   c. Georgia

   d. Massachusetts Bay Colony

   e. Jamestown, Virginia

2. Who discovered the law of universal gravitation?

   a. Johannes Kepler

   b. Sir Isaac Newton

   c. Galileo

   d. Aristotle

   e. Tycho Brahe

To study for multiple-choice tests, scour your textbook and lecture notes for references to famous figures, significant dates, crucial events, and major theories. Then review and reduce your notes until you have a collection of 3×5 index cards that show the name, date, event, or theory on one side with a brief description or explanation on the other. In the last day or two before the exam, rely primarily on your index cards for reviews.

Be Familiar with the Format

Just as understanding the structure of a paragraph makes you a better reader, understanding how multiple-choice questions are set up can make you a better test taker.

Type 1: Incomplete Sentence

The most common type of multiple-choice question starts with a partial or incomplete statement called the "stem." The test taker's job is to circle the letter of the ending that correctly completes the stem. Here's an example:

One of the chief reasons Americans were willing to join the peacetime North Atlantic Treaty Organization was because of the

---
*(*Answers*: 1.*c*; 2.*b*)

a. Cuban Missile Crisis.

b. Hungarian Revolution.

(c.) Berlin Blockade.

d. Berlin Wall.

e. Bay of Pigs.

From a test-taking perspective, multiple-choice questions that open with an incomplete sentence can sometimes help you eliminate an option. When you're stuck on a question, you should always read the stem followed by each possible answer. If you're lucky, one or even two options might not grammatically fit the opening portion of the sentence quite as well as the other answers, and you can cross them out as potential answers. Look, for example, at the following:

Johannes Kepler was an

a. astronomer.

b. astrologer.

c. physicist.

d. anthropologist.

e. paleontologist.

In this case, you could immediately eliminate options *c* and *e* because the article *an* is almost always followed by words beginning with the vowels *a, e, i, o,* or *u.* Although grammatical errors that make an option and the stem incompatible are not likely to appear in standardized tests created by an organization, they are possible in teacher-made tests. Your poor, overworked instructor has to create three different exams in one week. Under this type of pressure, it's easy for grammatical incompatibility to creep into a multiple-choice question and answer.

Type 2: Complete Sentence

Less common but still popular is a complete question followed by several answers:

From what source did the American Transcendentalists* find inspiration?[1]

---

*Transcendentalists: people like Henry David Thoreau, Margaret Fuller, and Ralph Waldo Emerson who turned to nature for inspiration.
[1]Adapted from William C. Kellogg, *AP United States History*, New York: Barron's Educational Service, 1999, p. 198.

a. the Bible
b. political leaders
c. nature
d. Buddhism

If you're stuck on a multiple-choice question with this format, start by reading the question with each separate answer. Sometimes one of the answers will jog your memory and help you make the correct choice.

Do the Easy Ones First

Whatever the format used on a multiple-choice exam, your first response should be to quickly read through all the questions, looking for those you can answer immediately. But even this first quick reading needs a method, so here's one that works for many successful test takers.

Anticipate the Answer, Then Read the Options

In your first reading of the entire exam, read each stem or question and see whether an answer comes to mind. Then quickly skim the options, checking to see if an answer that closely resembles yours is there. *Make sure you read all the options.* You don't want to circle *a* without looking at *b* and then discover when you get the test back that *b* was really the better answer.

At this stage, it's important not to dawdle. If the options provided don't resemble the answer you came up with, don't read into the question and force words to assume meanings they don't normally possess. Instead, mark the question and go back to it once you have looked over the entire exam.

Look for Key Words

If, on your second reading of a multiple-choice question, the answer still doesn't spring to mind, try to identify the names, events, or terms that are essential to the meaning of the stem or question. Underline or circle them. Often, key words or phrases will help you eliminate wrong answers and make it easier for you to determine the right one. Take, for example, the following test question. What word or phrase do you think might help you select an answer? Put a circle around it.

In what century did the Protestant Reformation begin?

a. sixteenth

b. nineteenth

c. eighteenth

d. seventeenth

If you circled the phrase "Protestant Reformation," you are on the right track and ready to start the process of elimination.

Use What You Know to Eliminate Wrong Answers

Let's say you studied hard but still drew a blank on the preceding question about the Protestant Reformation. Is it time to give up and go on to the next question? Absolutely not. Instead, try to call up what you know about the Protestant Reformation. Then test each option in light of that knowledge.

For example, you may not know exactly when the Protestant Reformation began. However, when you look at each possible answer, you might know immediately that it occurred way before the eighteenth or nineteenth centuries. Good, now there are only two answers to choose from.

At this point, you may remember that Martin Luther, the leader of the Protestant Reformation, was born in 1483. Based on common sense, you wouldn't assume that Luther led a religious revolution before the 1500s. After all, he was still a teenager. And if Luther led the Reformation as an older adult, then—thanks to the process of elimination—you have your answer: The Protestant Reformation began in the sixteenth century, also known as the 1500s.

Look for the Option "All of the Above"

Sometimes when you look over the options, you'll notice that two or even three answers seem to be correct. Study those choices carefully to see if there is a word or phrase that might eliminate one of them. If there isn't and one option says "all of the above," that's probably the correct answer.

Watch Out for the Words *Not* and *Except*

Whenever you see the word *not* or *except* in the stem of a question, circle it to make it stand out. That way you'll be sure to take the word into consideration when choosing your answer. Consider, for example, the following question. Ignore the word *not* and you are bound to choose the wrong answer.

Which scientist was not involved in the making of the hydrogen bomb?

a. J. Robert Oppenheimer

b. Edward Teller

(c.) Werner von Braun

d. John von Neumann

Be Willing to Guess

Unless there's a penalty for a wrong answer, don't be afraid to guess as a last resort. If you are really stumped and just aren't sure which answer is right, circle the one you think most plausible, keeping in mind the following pointers. They can help you make an "educated" guess.

Making an Educated Guess

1. The correct answer is sometimes longer and more detailed than the wrong answer.

2. The incorrect options are sometimes very similar and the correct answer is the one option that is quite different.

3. Words like *all, never,* and *always* frequently signal wrong answers, whereas words like *sometimes, usually,* and *generally* are more likely to be included in correct answers.

4. If two options seem equally correct and there's no option for "all of the above," choose the option that comes later in the list of answers. Test makers frequently put the wrong answer first because they know that some students are quick to choose the first seemingly correct answer they see.

5. Silly or foolish answers are not there to trick you. They really are wrong.

Don't Get Bogged Down

When you get your test, figure out generally how much time you can spend on each question. If you don't know the answer to a question and find yourself going way over your time limit, circle the question number and go back to it after you have answered all the others.

Avoid Overanalyzing

When answering multiple-choice questions, don't overinterpret or overanalyze either the stem or the options. Assign words their conventional, or common, meanings. Don't assume unlikely or rare meanings in an effort to discover where the instructor is trying to dupe you into choosing the wrong answer. Yes, your instructor wants to test your knowledge *and* your ability to read closely and carefully. But he or she does not want to mislead you with impossibly tricky questions or answers. So relax and take the language of the exam at its face value. There are no complicated, hidden meanings requiring you to wrench the language from its usual context.

EXERCISE 4

DIRECTIONS For each question, circle the letter of the correct response.

1. Multiple-choice questions are
   a. used primarily in science and history tests.
   b. not as popular as they once were.
   c. inferior to essay questions.
   d. the most popular types of test question.
   e. never used to test mathematical knowledge.

2. Multiple-choice questions rely heavily on the
   a. words *define, explain*, and *illustrate*.
   b. reader's ability to read between the lines.
   c. words *who, what, why, where, when, which*, and *how*.
   d. test taker's vocabulary.
   e. words *analyze, evaluate, annotate, synthesize, compare*, and *contrast*.

3. The incomplete portion of a multiple-choice test is called the

   a. stalk.

   b. stem.

   c. base.

   d. root.

   e. core.

4. When you first look at the exam, you should read

   a. every second question.

   b. only the answers.

   c. only the questions that look difficult.

   d. all the questions.

   e. only the questions that look easy.

5. When answering multiple-choice questions, you should

   a. never assume that words refer to their usual meanings.

   b. assume the instructor is trying to trick you.

   c. avoid overinterpreting or overanalyzing.

   d. interpret the stem more carefully than the options.

   e. interpret the options more carefully than the stem.

 # Reading and Responding to Essay Questions

If multiple-choice questions are the most popular exam question, essay questions are probably the most feared. Not only do they require a good deal of preparation on the test taker's part, but they also require a close reading. Yet unfortunately, many anxious students skim the essay question itself and plunge right into writing what they think is the correct answer. All too often, they end up answering a question that wasn't asked. To do well on essay exams, test takers need to do the kind of close and careful reading described in the pages that follow.

Identifying the Topic and the Requirements

Your goal in analyzing an essay question is to discover the two essential elements of every essay question: the topic and the requirement or requirements. The topic of an essay question is the specific subject you need to discuss. The requirements tell you how to approach or handle the topic.

Defining the Topic

Look at the following essay question. As you read it, ask yourself, "What word or phrase most effectively sums up the topic?"

On occasion, Mark Twain's novel *Huckleberry Finn* has been criticized for its supposed racism. Yet according to Twain expert Mark Fischer, Twain's novel is actually an attack on the institution of slavery, and the true hero of the novel is *not* Huck, but Jim. Begin your essay by summarizing Professor Fischer's argument. Then explain why you do or do not agree with it. Be sure to use evidence from the text to argue your position.

What is the topic of the question: (1) Mark Twain's novel *Huckleberry Finn*, (2) Mark Fischer's view of *Huckleberry Finn*, or (3) racism in the work of Mark Twain? If you chose topic 2, you're absolutely right. The sample essay question does not ask for a general discussion of the novel—its setting, characters, and themes. Nor does it ask you to go beyond *Huckleberry Finn* and look for evidence of racism in Twain's other works. The topic of the question is narrower than that. It focuses on Mark Fischer's defense of *Huckleberry Finn*. Your answer to the question should do the same.

Understanding the Requirements

Every essay question has one or more requirements, or necessary tasks, that your answer must fulfill. Let's look again at that sample essay question about Mark Twain. How many requirements does it have? In other words, how many tasks must you complete in your answer to get full credit: one, two, or three?

On occasion, Mark Twain's novel *Huckleberry Finn* has been criticized for its supposed racism. Yet according to Twain expert Mark Fischer, Twain's novel is actually an attack on the institution of slavery, and the true hero of the novel is *not* Huck, but Jim. Begin your essay by summarizing Professor Fischer's argument. Then explain why you do or do not agree with it. Be sure to use evidence from the text to argue your position.

This essay question has three requirements: (1) summarize Professor Fischer's position, (2) explain why you agree or disagree, and (3) use evidence from the text. If you failed to do any one of these, your exam score would suffer. That's why reading closely to determine all the requirements of an essay question is so important.

Key Words Help Identify Requirements

To determine exactly how many requirements you need to fulfill, pay close attention to words like *who, where, why, when, which,* and *how.* They frequently introduce a specific requirement of an essay question, often one that asks you to recall an important fact before you express an opinion or take a stand.

However, you should also familiarize yourself with the words listed below. Words like *argue, describe,* and *summarize* frequently introduce the individual requirements in an essay question.

	Key Words on Essay Exams	
Analyze	Divide or break a large whole into parts and comment on one or more of the parts, showing how it relates to the whole or reveals an underlying meaning.	*Analyze* the following excerpt from James Madison's *Federalist Papers* and show how it reveals his bias in favor of landowners.
Apply	Show how a principle or theory is illustrated in a particular instance or process.	*Apply* the Doppler effect to the behavior of light and sound waves.
Argue	Express a definite point of view and make it convincing through specific reasons, illustrations, and studies.	*Argue* the positive or negative effect of the *Miranda* decision on the American legal system.

Compare and Contrast	Describe how two topics are both similar and different. *Note:* Some essay questions may use only the word *compare,* but that almost always means point out similarities *and* differences.	*Compare and contrast* the leadership roles played by Grant and Lee during the Civil War.
Criticize	Explain the positive and negative effects of a particular decision, argument, or stand. *Note:* Sometimes instructors use the word *criticize* to ask for a summation of negative effects. If the meaning is not clear from the context, clarify it with your instructor.	*Criticize* the current regulations governing the use of pesticides in agriculture.
Define	Give a full and complete meaning, preferably one that includes an example or two, and some history of how the term came into being.	*Define* "Manifest Destiny" and explain its effect on the American West.
Describe	Tell how something looks or happens; supply specific details.	*Describe* how Benjamin Franklin came to develop his theory of positive and negative charges.
Discuss	Give the details of a situation, stand, or decision. Then explain the consequences.	*Discuss* the role of California governor Earl Warren in the government's decision to intern

		Japanese-Americans during World War II.
Evaluate	Explain the pros and cons of a situation or point of view and take a stand based on your evaluation.	*Evaluate* Richard Nixon's role in the shaping of U.S. policy toward China.
Illustrate	Give examples that clarify a point or show how something works.	*Illustrate* the different ways in which lasers have revolutionized the treatment of heart disease.
Interpret	Explain the meaning of a statement and give examples.	*Interpret* Edward L. Bernays's claim that "propaganda is only another word for education."
Show	Give examples. *Note:* This verb is usually used in combination with one of the other words listed here.	*Trace* the highlights of Lenny Bruce's career and *show* how he affected the next generation of American comedians.
Summarize	Cover the most essential points of a theory, discovery, or event.	*Summarize* the results of the Kefauver hearings on organized crime.
Trace	Step by step, explain how something happened (or happens) over a period of time.	*Trace* the chain of events that led to the Clean Air and Water Act.

What If the Question's Not a Question?

In the best of all possible worlds, essay requirements would always be neatly and clearly stated, as they are in the following example.

Define the term "republicanism"* and explain why the framers of the Constitution chose it over "direct democracy."

---

*republicanism: form of government in which decisions are made by elected officials.

This question asks you to do two things: (1) define the term "republicanism" and (2) explain why the framers of the Constitution chose republicanism over "direct democracy." For an essay question, the requirements are pretty clear-cut. But what about this next question: Does it also neatly spell out its requirements?

> Compare the use of participant and nonparticipant observation in sociological research.[2]

This kind of vaguely formulated essay question really benefits from a slow, word-for-word reading that teases out its hidden questions: (1) What do the terms *participant* and *nonparticipant observation* mean? (2) In what ways are they different or similar?

If an essay question is vague, don't just answer it without analysis and hope for the best. Instead, do a close reading to infer the question or questions implied.

CHECK YOUR UNDERSTANDING
What two key elements should you look for in every essay question?
_____

EXERCISE 5

DIRECTIONS Read each essay question and then answer the questions by filling in the blanks or circling the letter of the correct response.

EXAMPLE In the 1952 election, Dwight D. Eisenhower was the first presidential candidate to make effective use of television as part of his campaign. In your essay, identify the media adviser Ike relied on and explain how and why he needed television to promote his candidacy.

1. The topic of this essay question is
   a. Dwight D. Eisenhower.
   b. Dwight D. Eisenhower's use of television in the 1952 presidential campaign.
   c. the media's role in the shaping of presidential candidates.

---

[2]Example comes from Gregory S. Galica, *The Blue Book*, New York: Harcourt Brace, 1991, p. 40.

2. How many requirements are there? __*3*__

3. List each one separately.

a. *Identify Ike's media adviser.*

b. *Explain how Ike used television.*

c. *Explain why Ike needed television.*

_____

EXPLANATION In this case, you are not being asked to discuss the life and times of Dwight D. Eisenhower or the role of the media in presenting candidates to the public. The focus of the question is a good deal more specific. You're being asked to discuss Dwight D. Eisenhower's use of television during the 1952 presidential campaign—topic b.

1. Identify the historical event that provoked the internment of Japanese-Americans during World War II and describe the arguments used to justify that policy. Outline the Supreme Court decisions that first justified and then criticized the policy of internment.

    1. The topic of this essay question is

        a. the role of Japanese Americans during World War II.

        b. hysteria during World War II.

        c. the internment of Japanese-Americans during World War II.

    2. How many requirements are there? _____

    3. List each one separately.

_____

_____

_____

_____

2. Name and describe the four theories of motivation commonly used to explain behavior.

    1. The topic of this essay question is

        a. studies of motivation.

        b. the four theories of motivation.

        c. behavior modification.

   2. How many requirements are there? _____

   3. List each one separately.

   _____

   _____

   _____

   _____

3. Writer Gabriel García Márquez has been called a *magical realist.* Define that term and provide at least three examples of it from García Márquez's most famous work, *One Hundred Years of Solitude.*

   1. The topic of this essay question is

   a. Gabriel García Márquez's effect on Latin American literature.

   b. Latin American literature in the twentieth century.

   c. magical realism in the work of Gabriel García Márquez.

   2. How many requirements are there? _____

   3. List each one separately.

   _____

   _____

   _____

   _____

4. Identify and define the five different styles of responding to conflict. Give a brief illustration of each one and explain both the advantages and disadvantages of each response.

   1. The topic of this essay question is

   a. conflict.

   b. styles of conflict.

   c. response theory.

   2. How many requirements are there? _____

   3. List each one separately.

   _____

   _____

_____

_____

5. Describe William James's theory of the emotions. Then compare and contrast it with James Cannon's theory of emotional response.

   1. The topic of this essay question is
      a. William James.
      b. William James's theory of emotions.
      c. Cannon's theory of emotional response.

   2. How many requirements are there? _____
   3. List each one separately.

_____

_____

_____

_____

■ **DIGGING DEEPER**

LOOKING AHEAD Earlier in this chapter, you were told how important it is for college students to learn some Greek and Latin word parts. The following reading by *Time* journalist Mike Eskenazi suggests that Latin, in particular, should be making a comeback—not just in college, but already in elementary school.

THE NEW CASE FOR LATIN

1 Amy High is decked out in the traditional pink dress and golden stole of ancient Rome. She bursts into a third-grade classroom and greets her students: "Salvete, omnes!" (Hello, everyone!) The kids respond in kind, and soon they are studying derivatives. "How many people are in a duet?" High asks. All the kids know the answer, and when she asks how they know, a boy responds, "Because duo is 'two' in Latin." High replies, "Plaudite!" and the fourteen kids erupt in applause. They learn the Latin root *later*, or side, and construct such English words as *bilateral* and *quadrilateral*. "Latin's going to open up so many doors for you," High says. "You're going to be able to figure out the meaning of words you've never seen before."

2   High teaches at Providence Elementary School in Fairfax City, Virginia, which has a lot riding on the success of her efforts. As part of Virginia's high-stakes testing program, schools that don't boost their scores by the year 2007 could lose state funding. So Fairfax City, just eighteen miles southwest of the White House, has upgraded its two crumbling elementary schools with new high-tech television studios, computer labs, and one very old feature—mandatory Latin.

3   Here lies one of the more counterintuitive developments of the standardized-testing movement: Though some critics complain that teachers are forced to dumb down their lessons and "teach to the test," some schools are offering more challenging course work as a way of engaging students. In the past three years, scores of elementary schools in high-stakes–testing states such as Texas, Virginia, and Massachusetts have added Latin programs. Says Allen Griffith, a member of the Fairfax City school board: "If we're trying to improve English skills, teaching Latin is an awfully effective, proved method."

4   This is not your father's Latin, which was taught to elite college-bound high schoolers and drilled into them through memorization. Its tedium and perceived irrelevance almost drove

Latin from public schools. Today's growth in elementary school Latin has been spurred by new, interactive oral curriculums, enlivened by lessons in Roman mythology and culture. "One thing that makes it engaging for kids is the goofy fun of investigating these guys in togas," says Marion Polsky, author of *First Latin: A Language Discovery Program,* the textbook used in Fairfax City.

5   Latin enthusiasts believe that if young students learn word roots, they will be able to decipher unfamiliar words. (By some estimates, 65 percent of all English words have Latin roots.) Latin is an almost purely phonetic language. There are no silent letters, and each letter represents a single sound. That makes it useful in teaching reading. And once kids master the grammatical structure of Latin—which is simple, logical, and consistent—they will more easily grasp the many grammatical exceptions in English.

6   In the 1970s and '80s, the U.S. government funded Latin classes in underperforming urban school districts. The results were dramatic. Children who were given a full year of Latin performed five months to a year ahead of control groups in reading comprehension and vocabulary. The Latin students also showed outsize gains in math, history, and geography. But Congress cut the funding, and nearly all the districts discontinued Latin.

7   Some curriculum experts have examined the evidence and still favor modern languages instead of Latin. John Chubb, chief executive of the Edison charter schools, said the company decided to make Spanish, not Latin, mandatory in its elementary schools because "we want our kids to be socialized to the outside world."

8   Still, Griffith, the Fairfax City school board member, believes that "so far, the Latin looks like a good investment." He took encouragement from the confident smiles of Amy High's students each time they correctly responded to a question. "They're so receptive," says High. "They don't even know they're learning."

Sharpening Your Skills

DIRECTIONS Answer the following questions by filling in the blanks or circling the letter of the correct response.

1. Which of the following statements sums up the author's message?

   a. In Virginia, a lot is riding on the elementary schools' new Latin program.

   b. Although a few teachers think Latin should make a comeback, most believe that Spanish should be the mandatory language in elementary schools.

    c. In the hopes of improving vocabulary and language skills, many elementary schools have begun to add Latin to their curriculums.

    d. Latin should be taught in elementary school because kids at that age will be receptive, or open, to it.

2. Supporters of Latin instruction claim that once students learn the simple, logical, and consistent grammar of Latin, they will have an

   easier time learning _____.

3. At the core of the word *mandatory,* which appears in paragraph 2, is the root *mand,* meaning "to order." Based on context and your knowledge of that root, what's a good approximate meaning for *mandatory?*

   _____

   _____

4. In paragraph 5, the author says, "Latin is an almost purely phonetic language." Based on the context, what's a good approximate definition of the word *phonetic?*

   _____

   _____

WORD NOTES: ONE PREFIX, MANY MEANINGS

Mal is a prefix meaning "bad" or "badly." Using that knowledge, along with the context, write definitions for the italicized words below.

1. In an attempt to win the election, each opponent *maligned* the other.

    Maligned means _____.

2. The vampire's *malevolent* smile sent chills up and down her spine; she felt as if she had looked into the face of evil.

    Malevolent means _____.

3. On her deathbed, she issued a *malediction* against all who had defamed her.

    Malediction means _____.

4. My aunt is a chronic *malcontent;* nothing ever pleases her.

    Malcontent means _____.

5. The ancient Persians treated all *malefactors* harshly, assigning them severe punishments for small crimes like stealing fruit from the market.

    Malefactors means _____.

Students who want to review context clues with the help of **Getting Focused,** the companion software accompanying this text, should look at the CD's introductory section, titled "Context Clues."

For additional practice using context clues, go to **laflemm.com** and click on "Reading for Thinking: Online Practice." Practice 1 covers context clues. For vocabulary building, click on "Words Matter: Online Practice."

Test 1: Reviewing the Key Points

DIRECTIONS   Answer the following questions by filling in the blanks or circling the correct response.

1. *True* or *False*. A good survey always has six separate steps.

2. What words will help you transform headings into questions?

   _____

3. How can you make sure that you are really reading and not just letting your eyes glide across the page?

   _____

4. What are the benefits of underlining and paraphrasing while you read?

   _____

   _____

5. Why is recitation an important part of reading?

   _____

6. How do authors make specialized vocabulary stand out?

   _____

7. Identify the four common types of context clues.

   _____

8. *True* or *False*. An approximate definition should exactly match the dictionary definition of a word.

9. The most common multiple-choice questions start with _____

   _____

10. Test takers need to read essay questions very carefully in order to

    identify the _____ and the _____ of the question.

To correct your test, turn to the answer key on page 641.

Test 2: Using *SQ3R*

DIRECTIONS Survey the following selection using the steps listed below. When you finish, answer the questions in Part A on page 45. Then go back and read the selection from beginning to end. When you are done, answer the questions in Part B on page 46.

Survey Steps

1. Read the first and last paragraphs.
2. Use the title to pose a question.
3. Read the headings and the marginal note.
4. Read the first sentence of every paragraph.
5. Read through the questions on pages 45–46.

How the Need for Achievement Spurs Motivation

need achievement A motive for action influenced by the degree to which a person establishes specific goals, cares about meeting those goals, and experiences feelings of satisfaction by doing so.

Many athletes who hold world records still train intensely; many people who have built multimillion-dollar businesses still work fourteen-hour days. What motivates these people? A possible answer is a motive called **need achievement** (H. A. Murray, 1938). People with a high need for achievement seek to master tasks—such as sports, business ventures, intellectual puzzles, or artistic creations—and feel intense satisfaction from doing so. They work hard at striving for excellence, enjoy themselves in the process, take great pride in achieving at a high level, and often experience success.

Individual Differences How do people with strong achievement motivation differ from others? To find out, researchers gave children a test to measure their need for achievement and then asked them to play a ring-toss game. Children scoring low on the need-for-achievement test usually stood so close or so far away from the ring-toss target that they either could not fail or could not succeed. In contrast, children scoring high on the need-for-achievement test stood at a moderate distance from the target, making the game challenging but not impossible (McLelland, 1958).

Experiments with adults and children suggest that people with high achievement needs tend to set challenging, but realistic, goals. They actively seek success, take risks as needed, and are intensely satisfied with success. Yet if they feel they have tried their best, people with high achievement motivation are not too upset by failure. Those with low achievement motivation also like to succeed, but success tends to bring them not joy but relief at having avoided failure (Winter, 1996).

People with strong achievement motivation tend to be preoccupied with their performance and level of ability (Harackiewicz & Elliot, 1993). They select tasks with clear outcomes, and they prefer feedback from a harsh but competent critic rather than from one who is friendlier but less competent (Klich & Feldman, 1992). They like to struggle with a problem rather than get help. They can wait for delayed rewards, and they make careful plans for the future (F. S. Mayer & Sutton, 1996). In contrast, people who are less motivated to achieve are less likely to seek or enjoy feedback, and they tend to quit in response to failure (Graham & Weiner, 1996).

Development of Achievement Motivation Achievement motivation tends to be learned in early childhood, especially from parents. For example, in one study young boys were given a very hard task, at which they were sure to fail. Fathers whose sons scored low on achievement motivation tests often became annoyed as they watched their boys work on the task, discouraged them from continuing, and interfered or even completed the task themselves (B. C. Rosen & D'Andrade, 1959). A different pattern of behavior emerged among parents of children who scored high on tests of achievement motivation. Those parents tended to (1) encourage the child to try difficult tasks, especially new ones; (2) give praise and other rewards for success; (3) encourage the child to find ways to succeed rather than merely complaining about failure; and (4) prompt the child to go on to the next, more difficult challenge (McClelland, 1985).

Cultural influences also affect achievement motivation. Subtle messages about a culture's view of the importance of achievement often appear in the books children read and the stories they hear. Does the story's main character work hard and overcome obstacles, thus creating expectations of a payoff for persistence? Or does the main character loaf around and then win the lottery, suggesting that rewards come randomly, regardless of effort? And if the main character succeeds, is it the result of personal initiative, as is typical of stories in individualist cultures? Or is success based on ties to a cooperative and supportive group, as is typical of stories in collectivist cultures? Such themes appear to act as blueprints for reaching one's goals. It is not surprising, then, that ideas about achievement motivation differ from culture to culture. In one study, individuals from Saudi Arabia and from the United States were asked to comment on short stories describing people succeeding at various tasks. Saudis tended to see the people in the stories as having succeeded because of the help they got from others, whereas Americans tended to attribute success to the internal characteristics of each story's main character (Zahrani & Kaplowitz, 1993).

Achievement motivation can be increased in people whose cultural training did not encourage it in childhood (McClelland, 1985). For example, high school and college students with low achievement motivation were helped to develop fantasies about their own success. They imagined setting goals that were difficult but not impossible. Then they imagined themselves concentrating on breaking a complex problem into small, manageable steps. They fantasized about working hard, failing but not being discouraged, continuing to work, and finally feeling great about achieving success. Afterward, the students' grades and academic success improved, suggesting an increase in their achievement motivation (McClelland, 1985). In short, achievement motivation is strongly influenced by social and cultural learning experiences and by the beliefs about oneself that these experiences help to create. People who come to believe in their ability to achieve are more likely to do so than those who expect to fail (Butler, 1998; Dweck, 1998; Wigfield & Eccles, 2000). (Bernstein and Nash, *Essentials of Psychology*, pp. 274–276.)

Part A: Surveying

DIRECTIONS Answer the following questions by filling in the blanks or circling the correct response.

1. Throughout the reading, what question is the author trying to answer?

   _____

2. *True* or *False*. People with high achievement needs tend to set themselves impossible goals.

3. *True* or *False*. Achievement motivation is learned during adolescence.

4. *True* or *False*. Culture affects achievement motivation.

5. *True* or *False*. Once established, a person's level or degree of achievement motivation cannot be changed or altered in any way.

Part B: Reading

DIRECTIONS Answer the following questions by filling in the blanks or circling the letter of the correct response.

6. How do people with high achievement motivation respond to failure?

   a. They get outraged and give up.

   b. They criticize the person in charge for causing their failure.

   c. If they've tried their best, they don't get too upset by failure.

   d. They refuse to quit even when everything is against them.

7. Which of the following does *not* characterize people with high achievement motivation?

   a. They prefer to get feedback from someone who won't hurt their feelings.

   b. They like to struggle with a problem.

   c. They tend to make careful plans for the future.

   d. They select tasks with clear outcomes.

8. What was the difference when individuals from Saudi Arabia and the United States were asked to comment about people in stories succeeding at various tasks?

   _____

   _____

9. Which of the following does *not* characterize the parents of children with high achievement motivation?

   a. They encourage their children to try difficult tasks, especially new ones.

   b. Even if their children perform a task poorly, the parents give high praise in an effort to bolster their children's self-esteem.

   c. They encourage their children to find ways to succeed rather than merely complaining about failure.

   d. Once their children succeed at a task, the parents encourage them to go on to the next, more difficult challenge.

10. *True* or *False*. People who believe in their ability to achieve are more likely to succeed than people who expect to fail.

Test 3: Using Context Clues

DIRECTIONS Use context to define the italicized word in each sentence. Then circle the letter of the context clue you used to infer your definition.

1. When the storm began, we decided to wait for a more *auspicious* moment; no one in the group wanted to go on a picnic under such unfavorable conditions.

   Auspicious means _____

   _____.

   Context Clue a. contrast

   b. example

   c. restatement

   d. general knowledge

2. I can't accept that *spurious* $100 bill; it has George Washington's face where Benjamin Franklin's should be.

   Spurious means _____

   _____.

   Context Clue a. contrast

   b. example

   c. restatement

   d. general knowledge

3. Because of its harsh policies, the government is in a very *precarious* position; and because it is so insecure, the World Bank is unwilling to extend the term of the country's loans.

   Precarious means _____

   _____.

   Context Clue a. contrast

   b. example

   c. restatement

   d. general knowledge

4. The expression "Have a nice day" has been repeated so often, it has become *perfunctory*.

   Perfunctory means _____

   _____

Context Clue a. contrast

   b. example

   c. restatement

   d. general knowledge

5. As a result of the high altitude, his brain had been deprived of oxygen and he was *incoherent*. Because he wasn't making any sense, his fellow climbers couldn't understand his warnings.

   Incoherent means _____

   _____ .

Context Clue a. contrast

   b. example

   c. restatement

   d. general knowledge

6. The snowstorm *obliterated* all traces of the wolf's tracks.

   Obliterated means _____

   _____ .

Context Clue a. contrast

   b. example

   c. restatement

   d. general knowledge

7. For half a semester, her professor had preached about the importance of *cohesion*. But in her haste, the student produced a paper that was poorly organized and lacking in unity.

   Cohesion means _____

   _____ .

Context Clue a. contrast

   b. example

c. restatement

d. general knowledge

8. Having discovered that he had invented the details of his past, Frank's friends were appalled by his *duplicity.*

Duplicity means ⎯⎯⎯⎯⎯⎯⎯⎯⎯⎯⎯⎯⎯⎯⎯⎯⎯⎯⎯⎯⎯⎯

⎯⎯⎯⎯⎯⎯⎯⎯⎯⎯⎯⎯⎯⎯⎯⎯⎯⎯⎯⎯⎯⎯⎯⎯⎯⎯⎯⎯⎯⎯⎯.

Context Clue   a. contrast

b. example

c. restatement

d. general knowledge

9. Try as she might, she couldn't get any *purchase* on the mountain. Every time she tried to take a step, she would slide backward.

Purchase means ⎯⎯⎯⎯⎯⎯⎯⎯⎯⎯⎯⎯⎯⎯⎯⎯⎯⎯⎯⎯⎯⎯

⎯⎯⎯⎯⎯⎯⎯⎯⎯⎯⎯⎯⎯⎯⎯⎯⎯⎯⎯⎯⎯⎯⎯⎯⎯⎯⎯⎯⎯⎯⎯.

Context Clue   a. contrast

b. example

c. restatement

d. general knowledge

10. Having been a hard-working, no-nonsense realist all his life, he decided it was time to indulge in some more *quixotic* pursuits.

Quixotic means ⎯⎯⎯⎯⎯⎯⎯⎯⎯⎯⎯⎯⎯⎯⎯⎯⎯⎯⎯⎯⎯⎯

⎯⎯⎯⎯⎯⎯⎯⎯⎯⎯⎯⎯⎯⎯⎯⎯⎯⎯⎯⎯⎯⎯⎯⎯⎯⎯⎯⎯⎯⎯⎯.

Context Clue   a. contrast

b. example

c. restatement

d. general knowledge

Test 4: Using Context Clues and Word Parts

DIRECTIONS Use context clues and the word parts in the list below to define the italicized word in each sentence.

cred	belief
string, strict	draw or bind
solv	loosen, free
clam, claim	cry out

1. The *clamorous* crowd suddenly grew quiet once the speaker appeared.

   Clamorous means _____

   _____.

2. The rules of behavior in the nursery school were far too *stringent* for such young children.

   Stringent means _____

   _____.

3. You can't give any *credence* to her story; she has a hard time knowing the difference between fact and fiction.

   Credence means _____

   _____.

4. In all that *clamor,* it was difficult to follow the conversation for more than a few minutes.

   Clamor means _____

   _____.

5. He's innocent and somewhat *credulous,* but he's nobody's fool.

   Credulous means _____

   _____.

6. She followed all of the religion's *strictures* faithfully, but she did so more out of fear than belief.

   Strictures means _____

   _____ .

7. His financial *insolvency* made him a bad risk to most mortgage officers.

   Insolvency means _____

   _____ .

8. The look of *incredulity* on her face spoke volumes. She didn't believe a word he said.

   Incredulity means _____

   _____ .

9. After so many years of being in debt, he had finally become financially *solvent.*

   Solvent means _____

   _____ .

10. The *constricted* feeling in her throat only grew stronger as the plane rose higher, and she knew it would not go away until the flight ended.

    Constricted means _____

    _____ .

C H A P T E R   2

Power Tools for Learning: Annotating and Paraphrasing

In this chapter, you'll learn • how to effectively annotate pages while you read. • how to paraphrase. • how to tell the difference between accurate and inaccurate paraphrases.

Chapter 1 emphasized the importance of annotating and paraphrasing while you read. Chapter 2 looks more closely at these two reading strategies so critical to academic success.

Annotating Pages

When done right, annotating pages—making notes in the margins—can improve both concentration and comprehension. Marginal annotations can also ensure that you remember more of what you read. However, annotations are useful only if you make the right kind. Comments like "Boy, this is boring" or "Say what?" won't produce a big learning bonus. When annotating, don't waste space on trivial comments. Instead, you should: (1) identify key points, (2) connect the author's words to your own experience, and (3) predict test questions.

Identify Key Points

To check your understanding, get a head start on your notes, and prepare for exam reviews, it's a good idea to jot in the margin the main point of a chapter section or article. If there's enough space, you should add some of the reasons, studies, or examples used to clarify or prove that point. Still, if there are several different reasons, examples, studies, or statistics cited in support of the author's main idea, you can't possibly note them all in the margins. The result would be a cluttered, hard-to-read page. A better idea is to use lines, arrows, numbers, or any other symbols you choose to indicate how the author explains and supports the central or key point of a passage.

Compare the following selections. Both are correctly underlined and annotated but in different ways. Still, each set of annotations makes the main idea and the supporting details stand out for easy access. The two excerpts illustrate a key point about annotating pages: We all have our own individual method or style.

Long Prison Terms

How many times have you heard the expression "Lock 'em up and throw away the key"? It captures the frustration law-abiding people feel about the problem of crime in America. It reflects a belief that society is best off when criminals are housed in prisons for long periods. This strategy has an obvious appeal—locking up offenders prevents them from committing additional crimes in the community, at least during the course of their confinement. Yet, according to some scholars, long prison sentences may be unjust, unnecessary, counterproductive,* and inappropriate.

Some scholars think long prison sentences aren't effective or fair.

*counterproductive: tending to hurt rather than help.

4 reasons why ────→ • <u>Unjust</u> if <u>other offenders</u> who have <u>committed</u> the <u>same crime</u> receive <u>shorter sentences</u>.

• <u>Unnecessary if</u> the <u>offender</u> is <u>not likely</u> to <u>offend again</u>.

• <u>Counterproductive</u> <u>whenever</u> <u>prison increases</u> the <u>risk</u> of sub-sequent or habitual <u>criminal behavior</u>.

• <u>Inappropriate if</u> the offender has committed an <u>offense entailing</u> <u>insignificant harm</u> to the community. (Adler, Mueller, and Laufer, *Criminal Justice,* p. 349.)

In this case, the main idea—"Some scholars think long prison sentences aren't effective or fair"—is noted in the margin. The major details—the reasons why scholars don't think long sentences are effective—are highlighted by means of an arrow and the annotation "reasons why." The key words in each reason are also underlined, paving the way for later note taking.

Here's another example of how the passage might be annotated.

Long Prison Terms

Some scholars think long prison sentences are unfair and don't work.

How many times have you heard the expression "Lock 'em up and throw away the key"? It captures the frustration law-abiding people feel about the problem of crime in America. It reflects a belief that society is best off when criminals are housed in prisons for long periods. This strategy has an obvious appeal—locking up offenders prevents them from committing additional crimes in the community, at least during the course of their confinement. Yet, according <u>to</u> some <u>scholars</u>, long <u>prison sentences may be unjust</u>, unnecessary, <u>counterproductive</u>, and inappropriate.

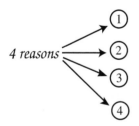

• <u>Unjust</u> if <u>other offenders</u> who have <u>committed</u> the <u>same crime</u> receive <u>shorter sentences</u>.

• <u>Unnecessary</u> if the <u>offender</u> is <u>not likely</u> to <u>offend again</u>.

• <u>Counterproductive</u> <u>whenever</u> <u>prison increases</u> the risk of sub-sequent or habitual <u>criminal behavior</u>.

• <u>Inappropriate if</u> the <u>offender</u> has committed an offense entailing <u>insignificant harm</u> to the community. (Adler et al., *Criminal Justice,* p. 349.)

In this instance, a slightly different paraphrase of the main idea appears in the margin. The four reasons that support the main idea get both a label and numbered arrows.

Exactly how you annotate is up to you. Each person has his or her own method. Also, different kinds of textbook material require different kinds of annotations. You might use more arrows or even diagrams in a science text or circle more dates in a history book. What's important is that you make annotating a habit. Once you do, you'll be surprised at your increased ability to concentrate, understand, and remember.

Symbols for Underlining and Annotating

The following chart lists symbols for underlining and annotating pages. Feel free to adapt the symbols listed here to better suit your particular needs. You can even make up your own symbols if you wish. Whichever symbols you choose, be sure to use them consistently so that you will remember exactly what each one represents.

Symbols for Underlining and Annotating Pages	
≡ ≡ ≡	**Double underlining** to highlight the main idea of the entire reading
— — —	**Single underlining** to highlight main ideas in paragraphs
=	**Equals sign** to signal a definition
1, 2, 3, 4	**Numbers** to itemize and separate a series of supporting details
(1830)	**Circles** to highlight key points, specialized vocabulary, key terms, statistics, dates, and unfamiliar words
?	**Question marks** to indicate confusion
!	**Exclamation points** to indicate your surprise at the author's statements

↗	**Arrows** to identify cause and effect relationships
‖	**Vertical lines** to emphasize key passages longer than a sentence or two
:	**Colon** to signal restatement
★★★	**Stars** to identify a crucial piece of information
RR	Symbol to indicate passages in need of a second reading
RP	Symbol to identify ideas for research papers
TQ	Symbol to identify the possible source of a test question
See p. 27 or Compare p. 27	**Cross-reference notes** to compare closely related statements in the text
Charles Darwin	**Boxes** to highlight names you need to remember

EXERCISE 1

DIRECTIONS Read, underline, and annotate the following passage. *Note:* Try your hand at using some of the symbols introduced in the preceding chart.

Rebellion in a Small Texas Town

The Mexican-American movement was a local one, born of poverty and oppressive segregation. Reflecting the grassroots character of the movement was the important role that youths played. Many Mexican-American teens and young adults adopted the term **Chicano** to stress their unwillingness to accept the dictates of Anglo society and to distinguish themselves from the more **accommodationist*** Mexican-Americans they called *Tio Tacos*.

In the small south Texas town of Ed Couch-Elsa, where the average educational level for Mexican-Americans was 3.5 years of

---

*accommodationist: someone ready to adapt to existing conditions.

schooling, Mexican-American students walked out of the high school in November 1968. Supported by their parents and most of the Mexican-American community, the students demanded dignity, respect, and an end to "blatant discrimination against Mexican-American students in the schools." For one thing, corporal punishment in the form of spankings was common for speaking Spanish on school grounds outside of Spanish class, and students wanted it stopped. The school board, blaming "outside agitators" for the unrest, suspended over 150 students and finally expelled 20. But changes took place. The board agreed not to discourage the speaking of Spanish and to incorporate a Mexican-American heritage program into the curriculum.

An extremely poor school district, Ed Couch-Elsa was limited in its efforts to improve the curriculum or educational environment, but under pressure from the Mexican-American community, other school districts, including Los Angeles, implemented Mexican-American studies and bilingual programs, hired more Mexican-American teachers and counselors, and adopted programs to meet the special needs of migrant farm worker children who moved from one school to another during picking season. By the 1970s, calls for bilingual education had become an important educational reform focus for the Latino community. (Berkin et al., *Making America*, p. 945.)

Make Connections to What You Know

Research on learning shows that reading scores improve when students make connections between what they already know and what they read. For an illustration of how to connect your personal knowledge to your reading, look at how the following passage has been annotated. Yes, the paraphrased main idea appears in the margin along with one or two supporting details, but so too do some comments based on the reader's personal experience. Those comments appear in boldface.

When cancer attacks, people do risky things like turn to quacks—multimillion-dollar business.
Aunt Mary

Cancer Quackery

Cancer quackery is a multimillion-dollar industry in the U.S. alone each year. When cancer strikes, many people do foolish, irresponsible, or dangerous things. One of the things they do is turn to "quacks," practitioners who offer the cancer patient hope in the form of "secret" cures. The person with cancer is desperate, so the practitioner who makes these offers has appeal. Quacks

May be prof. educated, but also may not.

Quack treatments are particularly risky in cancer's early stages. ***Aunt Mary almost died because she went to a quack who treated her with apricot pits.***

Quacks aren't easy to recognize. ***Aunt Mary's doctor seemed like an old sweetheart—Ha!***

may be professionally educated physicians; however, many times they have no degree and no medical education whatsoever.

Quack treatments can be especially dangerous to the patient who has cancer in its early stages. Trying useless gadgets or therapeutically worthless drugs is costly and wastes valuable time. Quacks may have no conscience about telling patients that they have cancer when in fact they do not. After a series of worthless but expensive "treatments," the patient is declared "cured." The practitioner takes the credit, which opens the door for the testimonial and exploitation of more people. Quacks are smart, friendly, and impressively attired. They provide warmth, act concerned and give assurance to patients who are filled with anxiety. (Adapted from Mullen et al., *Connections for Health*, p. 380.)

As this example shows, the reader did not confine her marginal annotations to rephrasing the author's main idea and supporting details. She also included personal comments that echo the author's thoughts. These comments anchor the author's ideas in memory by connecting them to a personal experience.

Anticipate Potential Test Questions

In addition to taking notes and jotting comments in the margins of your text, you should also jot down possible test questions (TQ).

As you read, give special attention to words and sentences that stand out because of repetition, italics, boldface, or colored ink. All of these devices are used to emphasize key points and essential vocabulary. This is the kind of material likely to make its way into an exam. Once you've identified potentially test-rich material, use the words introduced in Chapter 1—*how, who, why, when, where, which*, and *what*—to formulate possible test questions. If you happen to know that your instructor favors essay exams, become familiar with the words likely to be used in essay exams (see the chart in Chapter 1 on pp. 31–33). Then you can use them to create test questions.

To illustrate, here's a sample passage accompanied by two possible test questions.

TQ: What is the function of the sympathetic nervous system?

TQ: Explain how the sympathetic nervous system prepares the body for fight or flight.

The $\boxed{sympathetic\ nervous\ system}$ prepares the body to deal with emergency situations. It prepares us for "fight or flight." The system speeds up the heart, sends blood to the muscles, and releases sugar from the liver for quick energy. It can be activated by threat or by sexual arousal. (Allgeier and Allgeier, *Sexual Interactions*, p. 143.)

The test questions you predict may well appear on the exam. Even if they don't, writing potential exam questions in the margins is worth the effort. After completing a chapter section, you can test your understanding and review what you've read by trying to answer your questions. When you try to answer potential test questions, you are simultaneously checking comprehension, aiding memory, and reviewing for exams—all of which make jotting test questions in the margins a highly effective study strategy.

EXERCISE 2

DIRECTIONS Read, underline, and annotate the following selection. Then circle the letters of two test questions (p. 60) that you think would be appropriate to jot in the margins.

Ethics in Journalism

Two studies, both published in 1996, give us some idea of the importance of the study of ethics to students in journalism and mass communications programs. A survey of seventy-three free-standing media ethics courses at universities across the country revealed that "classes are full. The number of courses, students, teachers, and materials are all on the growth curve." Another study noted that 44 percent of all the schools responding to its survey required students to take a journalism/mass communication ethics course. Media organizations have told educators that they value students who can think critically, solve problems, and who have developed a keen sense of ethics.

However, there are reasons for studying ethics that go beyond what potential employers want or expect. Proper behavior is a necessity for growth and order. If it is one of the objectives of an education to promote the growth and development of the individual, then the place to start is with one's own behavior. Developing a sense of what is right and wrong, or appropriate and inappropriate, will promote order, not only in the life of the individual but also in the structure of society at large. Think, for example, of the order required to move traffic on roads and highways. Speed limits are set, proper directions are indicated, and numerous suggestions are made—seat belts, for example—so that travel by automobile will be reasonably safe and efficient. Without the "rules" of the road, travel would be chaotic. Order is required if we are ever going to get anywhere. The same could be said of ethical behavior. It sets "rules" for proper human activity and as a result promotes growth, development, and order in our lives.

It should be noted, however, that ethics is not a panacea for every problem one encounters in the world. Not every problem is an ethical one, and even when an ethical problem does present itself, we sometimes make the wrong ethical decision, or we make the right ethical decision and it results in unforeseen negative consequences. Nevertheless, we must realize that without a large number of individuals "doing the right thing," most of us would not be doing much at all except fighting for survival and trying to figure out an increasingly chaotic world. Things are bad enough with ethics; think how bad they might be without them.

"Rather than accept the way things are, the ethical person asks how things ought to be." Ethics promotes not only a better individual but also a better society. Idealists might suggest that doing the right thing is a valuable end in itself, regardless of the degree to which it contributes to life or to the culture. Others see ethics as more practical, as a tool that can lead to positive personal and social outcomes.

The real test of ethics may be in "how we treat the stranger— whether we are able to recognize the humanity and dignity of the stranger. We are all prepared to acknowledge the dignity of those we think of as like ourselves and to treat them with respect. It is those we perceive as different that we are tempted to treat differently." (Leslie, *Mass Communication Ethics*, pp. 18–19.)

Test Questions

a. Give at least two reasons why the study of ethics is valuable.

b. Explain the origin of the word *ethics*.

c. Describe the "real test" of ethics.

d. Explain the difference between morality and ethics.

 # Good and Bad Paraphrasing

Like annotating, paraphrasing is a learned skill. It can be done well or poorly, and you need to know exactly what makes the difference. To begin that discussion, study the next three passages. The first is the original text, and it's followed by two possible paraphrases. Read each paraphrase and decide which one is better.

Original Video rental stores started out in the 1970s as locally owned mom-and-pop stores. But these small-scale operations didn't last very long after big national chains emerged and gobbled up most of the local markets.

Paraphrase a. In the 1970s, video rental stores were frequently small and locally owned. But many of these stores lost their market and went out of business when the huge national chains came to town.

Paraphrase b. In the late 1970s, video rental stores were wildly successful as small, locally owned businesses, but they couldn't compete with the huge national chains that charged less and drove smaller stores out of business.

Did you circle paraphrase *a?* If you did, you clearly know the difference between good and bad paraphrasing. *A good paraphrase finds new words to express the original meaning.* It changes the words but not the message. A bad paraphrase, like passage *b*, distorts the original meaning, adding (or deleting) details that never appeared in the original text. For instance, the original text never suggests the degree of success experienced by early video stores. We don't know if initially they were or were not "wildly successful." Paraphrase *b* suggests that we do.

The original text also doesn't say exactly why the locally owned video stores went out of business. Yet paraphrase *b* assumes price cutting was a factor. Maybe it was, but we don't know that from the original. In other words, *b* distorts the original meaning—the last thing you want to do when you paraphrase.

── EXERCISE 3

DIRECTIONS Identify the better paraphrase by circling the appropriate letter.

Original EXAMPLE Political campaigns vary in the effectiveness with which they transmit their messages via the news media. Effective tactics recognize the limitations of both the audience and the media. Many voters are not deeply interested in politics and as a result have trouble keeping track of multiple themes explained in dense detail. By the same token, television is not willing to air lengthy statements from candidates. (Adapted from Janda et al., *The Challenge of Democracy,* p. 305.)

Paraphrase a. Most political campaigns simply do not take into account voter limitations. Instead, candidates assume that the typical voter is deeply interested in political issues. The truth is that the typical voter cares more about a candidate's image than about the candidate's political positions.

(b.) Not all political campaigns use the news media with equal effectiveness. Those that are successful recognize that television is not willing to air long, detailed explanations and that a large portion of the voting public is not deeply interested in politics and therefore has difficulty understanding issues that are complex and detailed.

EXPLANATION In this case, paraphrase *a* is not correct. It says candidates assume that the "typical voter" is deeply interested in political issues. Yet the original says only that many voters are not deeply interested in politics. It makes no mention of what candidates do or do not assume. Paraphrase *a* also leaves out a key component, or element, of the original, which points out that "television is not willing to air lengthy statements." *Remember:* Accurate paraphrases retain all parts of the original meaning without adding new information.

Original **1.** Most Americans were taken by surprise when the second wave of feminism swept the nation in the 1960s. Women's rights had been considered a dead issue—in the words of *Life* magazine, feminism seemed "as quaint as linen dusters* and high-button shoes." Supposedly, it lost its relevance once women won the vote. (Davis, *Moving the Mountain,* p. 26.)

Paraphrase   a. By the 1960s, feminism was again a hot topic, and most people were taken by surprise. Many people thought that the battle for women's rights was over when women won the right to vote.

b. In the 1960s, to almost everyone's surprise, the feminist movement reappeared and became a force to be reckoned with. Surprisingly, no one realized at the time what consequences would result from the second wave of feminism.

Original **2.** When Italians created the opera around 1600, there were no soloists. The first great Italian composer, Claudio Monteverdi, basically used different parts of the chorus to express ideas and emotions. However, singers vied with one another for the spotlight, and gradually, soloists became prominent. (Gannon, *Understanding Global Cultures,* p. 322.)

_____
*dusters: long coats worn around the end of the nineteenth and beginning of the twentieth century.

Paraphrase a. Created by the Italians circa 1600, opera did not initially include soloists. Claudio Monteverdi, the first great composer, actually used sections of the chorus to communicate ideas and emotions to his audience. But as a result of singers competing for the spotlight, the soloist became part of opera.

b. Italian opera began in 1600 with the great composer Claudio Monteverdi, who was the first composer to include a soloist in his operas. Monteverdi was forced to include soloists because singers in the chorus were not happy being out of the spotlight.

EXERCISE 4

DIRECTIONS Read the original. Then circle the letter of the best paraphrase.

Original 1. For some women living in the rural parts of Afghanistan, self-immolation—setting oneself on fire—is preferable to hard work and constant beatings. Human rights groups have confirmed nearly forty recent cases of self-immolation. With the defeat of the Taliban,* life has improved for women who live in cities, but the customs in the countryside still condemn many women to a life of hard labor and physical abuse. (Source of information: Carlotta Gall, "For More Afghan Women, Immolation Is Escape," *New York Times*, March 8, 2004, p. A1.)

Paraphrase a. Women living in the cities of Afghanistan have nothing more to fear now that the Taliban have been defeated, but women living in the countryside are still confronted by customs that treat them as little more than slaves.

b. Under the reign of the Taliban, women in Afghanistan were forced to become almost invisible or risk beatings and worse; but with the defeat of the Taliban, some women have nothing more to fear. The ones still living in rural areas, though, have not benefited from the demise of the Taliban.

c. Human rights groups have confirmed that women in the countryside are not experiencing the freedom some hoped for when the Taliban was forced out of power in Afghanistan. Women in urban areas do have more rights and more freedom, but rural women are desperate enough to set themselves on fire rather than live as domestic slaves. There have been at least forty recent confirmed cases of women attempting self-immolation.

---

*Taliban: a group that practiced a particularly harsh and rigid version of Islam.

Original 2. Currently around a half million families across the country home-school their children. For many of these families, home schooling serves a religious purpose, and two-thirds of those who home-school are Evangelical Christians who want their children educated in a Christian atmosphere that emphasizes the importance of religious faith in every aspect of life.

Paraphrase   a. Among the families who home-school their children are Christians who do not want their children in public schools, where the children will be exposed to teaching that contradicts religious law.

b. Of the half million people who home-school their children, two-thirds are Evangelical Christians who prefer to teach their children at home rather than giving them a public school education that does not adequately stress the importance of religious faith.

c. Two-thirds of the people who home-school their children are Evangelical Christians who don't want their children exposed to the teachings of those who do not believe in God.

■ EXERCISE 5

DIRECTIONS Read the original and then circle the letter of the best paraphrase.

1. Over the last several decades, manufacturers have learned that they must "automate or evaporate." Companies that make everything from automobiles to Oreo Cookies know that adding robots to assembly lines allows the human employees to produce faster and more efficiently. However, robots also allow companies to avoid hiring more workers. When American workers aren't losing their jobs to countries that provide cheaper labor—a practice known as outsourcing—they are losing them to machines as businesses desperately seek to improve productivity. (Source of information: James M. Pethokoukis, "Meet Your New Coworker," *U.S. News & World Report,* March 15, 2004, p. E4.)

a. American manufacturers have always cared more about their profits than their employees. That's why they have replaced human workers with robots that make assembly lines move faster. Robots have certainly allowed companies to keep their personnel costs low, but they have also increased America's unemployment rate.

b. Modern manufacturers know that if they don't use robots on their assembly lines, they will surely go out of business. Robots have increased the productivity of human workers. However, automating manufacturing processes has also reduced the number of jobs available for workers or replaced them altogether.

c. American manufacturers are convinced that automation will keep them in business, and they are adding robots to the assembly line. Assembly line robots force human employees to work even faster so that companies don't have to hire more people. At the same time, companies are building more plants overseas, where wages are lower. Between automation and outsourcing jobs are disappearing.

d. American manufacturers are using robotic technology more than ever before. The automotive industry, in particular, has automated many assembly lines; in the General Motors plants, for example, robots even install parts and weld them together. Robots are faster and more accurate than human workers will ever be, so they are taking jobs away from people. Eventually, machines will do all the hard labor because they are much more productive.

2. One of the most important factors in the formation of friendships and romantic attractions is simply physical proximity.* As long as you do not form an initial dislike, your liking of a person tends to grow every time you see him or her. This happens because the more contact you have with someone, the more chances you have to get to know the person. Familiarity leads to increased fondness, which is known as the *mere exposure effect*. (Source of information: Bernstein et al., *Psychology*, 6th ed., pp. 662, 672.)

a. According to the *mere exposure effect*, if you want to have more friends and romantic relationships, you should try to be around other people as much as possible. The more a person sees you, the more he or she will like you. This happens because we all enjoy interacting with the familiar instead of the unknown. So increasing the physical closeness between you and another person will ensure that he or she will develop strong feelings for you.

b. When it comes to friendships and romantic relationships, the old saying "Out of sight, out of mind" turns out to be very true. Without physical proximity, it's virtually impossible to establish or maintain relationships. We can't get to know people unless we come into contact with them repeatedly, so we use the *mere exposure effect* to ensure that we don't end up alone.

---

*proximity: closeness.

c. The *mere exposure effect* explains why many friendships and romances are formed between people who come into contact with one another often. Because people tend to like those with whom they're familiar, our fondness for someone is likely to increase every time we interact with the person, unless we had already formed an initial dislike. Thus, physical proximity is important for the establishment of new relationships.

d. Some people say that "familiarity breeds contempt." In other words, the more you get to know someone, the more his or her faults will irritate you, leading to a breakup. However, the *mere exposure effect* has proved this notion to be false. Familiarity turns out to be responsible for the creation, rather than the destruction, of all relationships.

EXERCISE 6

DIRECTIONS Paraphrase each of the following statements.

Original   **EXAMPLE** About 25 percent of people are primarily *auditory*, learning and thinking through hearing; another 15 percent are primarily *kinesthetic*, learning by feeling, touch, and movement. (Adapted from Lofland, *Powerlearning*, p. 13.)

Paraphrase   *Around 25 percent of the population learns mainly through listening, whereas another 15 percent learns largely by touch or movement.*

EXPLANATION As it should, the paraphrase replaces most of the original language but retains the original meaning. *Note:* There may be times when there is no substitute for the original language; for example, in this case, *percent* would be a difficult word to replace.

Original **1.** Divorce lawyers all over the country are noticing a new phenomenon: Internet-sparked divorces. In other words, marriages are breaking up when one spouse or the other meets someone online in a chatroom and decides that that someone is a true soulmate. There actually have been cases of spouses abandoning their marriages and running off with people they had met only online and never even seen.

Paraphrase   _____

   _____

_____

_____

Original **2.** University of Tulsa psychologist Judy Berry studied seventy-three Oklahoma eighth graders who had taken a parenting course. For ten days, each student had to care for a ten-pound sack of flour as if it were a baby. Berry's research on her young subjects suggests the course worked: The teenagers in the study had a sounder sense of parental responsibility than they did before they took the course.

Paraphrase _____

_____

_____

_____

CHECK YOUR UNDERSTANDING

What is the cardinal, or key, rule of accurate paraphrasing?

_____

_____

_____

When Should You Paraphrase?

At this point, you know the purpose of paraphrasing. However, you may not be quite sure *when* to paraphrase. Actually, the answer to that question varies. If, for example, you are reading material that is both difficult and unfamiliar—say, chemistry or philosophy—then paraphrasing the key points of every paragraph—the main idea and major supporting details—may be your best bet. It will be slow going, but there's a bonus. You will probably need to read the material only once rather than over and over again.

If you are reading a sociology or health textbook, and are familiar with some of the concepts, or ideas, then paraphrase only the passages you don't readily understand. If you finish a paragraph and aren't quite sure of the author's meaning, it's time to check your understanding by paraphrasing. If you can't paraphrase, mark the paragraph for rereading (RR). Paraphrasing chapter sections when you finish them is also an excellent way to test your understanding and ensure long-term remembering.

Paraphrasing Guidelines

1. Change the words but don't tamper with the meaning.

Original: In *On Liberty,* the nineteenth-century philosopher John Stuart Mill strongly defends freedom of speech. He argues, in fact, that the content of the speech should *not* limit the freedom of expression.

Accurate Paraphrase: John Stuart Mill's *On Liberty* defends freedom of speech, to the point of arguing that freedom of speech should be allowed no matter what the content.

Inaccurate Paraphrase: In perhaps his most famous work, *On Liberty,* writer John Stuart Mill defends freedom of speech no matter what the cost, and for Mill, even hate speech is acceptable.

2. Abbreviate whenever possible (as long as you don't alter the meaning).

Original: There is a profound difference between an argument and an assertion. An argument puts forth the evidence for a conclusion, whereas an assertion puts forth a conclusion and hopes for acceptance from sympathetic readers or listeners.

Accurate Paraphrase: An argument supplies a conclusion along with support for that conclusion, that is, reasons or evidence. An assertion, in contrast, offers readers and listeners only a conclusion and relies on their goodwill for acceptance.

Inaccurate Paraphrase: An argument is always accompanied by evidence while an assertion can't be bothered with anything as tiresome as making a point.

3. Change the order of ideas.

Original: In his book *The Good, the Bad and the Difference,* writer Randy Cohen has collected some questions and answers that have made their way into his *New York Times Magazine* column on ethics. Cohen's book is one of the

---

many currently available on the subject of ethical thinking in everyday life.

Accurate Paraphrase: At the moment a number of books are on the market about how to be ethical in daily life. Among them is a collection of ethical questions and answers titled *The Good, the Bad and the Difference.* The book is based on Randy Cohen's ethics column, which appears in the *New York Times Magazine.*

Inaccurate Paraphrase: At the moment, bookstores are filled with best-selling books about how to be ethical in daily life. Among the better ones is *The Good, the Bad and the Difference,* based on Randy Cohen's ethics column.

4. Hold on to the specifics.

Original: In the spring of 2003, a military physician, Dr. Jiang Yanyong, became a Chinese folk hero when he told the truth about the number of cases of a serious flu-like disease called SARS. The government had been insisting that there were only a dozen cases, but Dr. Yanyong went public with the real number, more than 100.

Accurate Paraphrase: Dr. Jiang Yanyong, a doctor in a military hospital, became a national hero in the spring of 2003 when he announced the real number of patients suffering from a flu-like disease called SARS. While the government had been insisting that there were no more than twelve or so, Dr. Jiang Yanyong publicly announced that there were more than 100 cases.

Inaccurate Paraphrase: A military official became a Chinese folk hero when he admitted to the public that many people were suffering from a flu-like disease called SARS. The official's public statement openly contradicted the government's claim of only a few cases.

Paraphrasing and Plagiarism

When students write papers, they are often confused about the relationship between paraphrasing (rewording someone else's ideas) and plagiarizing (using someone else's ideas without attributing them, or mentioning their source). Some students assume they are not plagiarizing if they change the wording while leaving the meaning intact. This assumption is dead wrong. *Original ideas belong to the people who had them first.* If you use someone else's discovery or interpretation in a paper, you have to cite your source.

For instance, let's say you read the following passage while you were researching a paper on the nineteenth-century brothers William and Henry James:

> Studies of the brothers William and Henry James usually highlight the obvious differences. William, the philosopher-psychologist, is portrayed as clever, eloquent, and athletic, eager to explore the world around him. Henry, in contrast, is painted as the reclusive novelist—timid, watchful, sickly, and easily intimidated by his adventurous older brother. Yet, because they are wrapped up in pointing out the easy-to-see differences, authors of traditional studies have repeatedly missed an essential similarity: These famous nineteenth-century siblings chose to explore the same subject matter—the relationship between imagination and reality.

Having read that new interpretation, imagine now that you decided to paraphrase the author's point about the brothers' essential similarity in the introduction to your paper. The introduction might read like this:

Paraphrase
> On the surface, William and Henry were the most opposite of brothers. William loved sports, people, and ideas. Articulate and brilliant, he drew both men and women to him like a magnet. Henry—shy, nervous, and uncomfortable with people—could only view William with admiration. Yet to focus on the differences between the brothers is to miss a more essential similarity. Both were fascinated by the same subject matter: They wanted to explore the relationship between what we actually experience and how we imagine it in our minds.

This second passage includes a solid paraphrase of the first author's key point. As it should, the paraphrase changes the author's words yet maintains the original idea. Unfortunately, that careful paraphrase still represents an act of plagiarism. It's clear in the original passage that the author has come up with a new insight, one that differs from already existing points of view. Thus it can't be absorbed into a paper without attribution. You need to cite your source. If you don't, you're plagiarizing. Ideas original to the person who first put them on paper cannot and must not find their way into your work without a reference to where those ideas came from.

Paraphrasing Common Knowledge

Unfortunately, warning students about the danger of plagiarism often leads to another problem. Anxious about plagiarizing, they cite sources for information that is **common knowledge,** or found in any number of reference works or studies. For example, if you looked up William James in five different biographies and reference works, you would find information very similar to the following:

> **William James** (1842–1910) American philosopher and psychologist of the late nineteenth and early twentieth centuries. James was one of the first to suggest that humans, like other animals, possess instincts. He also argued that any view of the world is a compromise between external reality and personal desires. Turning away from abstract theories, verbal solutions, fixed principles, and pretended absolutes, he looked at concrete experience, facts, and actions. *Principles of Psychology* is the most complete expression of his theories about the mind and its workings. James's focus on the "stream of thought" also had a profound influence on fiction and helped inspire the "stream of consciousness" writing technique, which revolutionized modern literature.

Read about William James in several different sources and you are bound to find descriptions similar to this one. That means the information is common or general knowledge, and it can be paraphrased without a footnote. For the most part, anything expressed in a reference work is going to be common knowledge. In addition, any time you find the same point made in several different works, you can assume it falls under the heading of common knowledge.

To help you decide when you can or can't paraphrase without citing a source, keep in mind this rule of thumb: When a writer signals that he or she is offering a new opinion, reinterpreting existing facts, or challenging long-held opinions—as does the writer of the first passage about the James brothers (p. 70)—these ideas are not yours to freely paraphrase without mentioning where you got them. You need to cite your source.

CHECK YOUR UNDERSTANDING

1. Explain when it is acceptable to use information from a published source without mentioning where it came from.

   _____

   _____

2. Describe the kind of information that requires you to cite your source.

   _____

   _____

■ DIGGING DEEPER

LOOKING AHEAD On pages 59–60, you learned something about ethics in journalism, but as the title suggests, the author of the following reading takes a more general approach to the subject.

ETHICS IN AMERICA

1   Ethics is a hot topic in America. Pick up any newspaper or magazine or tune in any news program and you are sure to find an ethics story of some sort. Universities have rushed to set up ethics institutes; corporations have scheduled ethics workshops for their employees; federal, local, and state governments have established ethics commissions whose main task is to monitor the ethics of politicians and others in government service. Ethics courses have been added to educational curricula. Everywhere, it seems, there is a renewed interest in "doing the right thing."

Current Concerns

2   The last three decades of the twentieth century may come to be known to future generations as a period of ethical incongruities.* In the face of a renewed emphasis on ethics, major political, economic, social, and religious scandals were revealed. The alleged exploits of Wall Streeters Ivan Boesky and Michael Milken (insider trading and junk bond scams), religious leaders Jim and Tammy Bakker (using church money for personal perks) and the Reverend Jimmy Swaggart (soliciting a prostitute), Marine Colonel Oliver North (questionable arms-for-hostages deal with Iran), baseball's Pete Rose (betting on games), House Speaker Newt Gingrich (shady book deals and speaking fees), and President Bill Clinton (affair with a White House intern and possible perjury), as well as a host of others, dominated the news. The presidential election campaigns of 1992 and 1996 were said to be two of the most misleading and misdirected campaigns in recent memory. Questions were raised regularly about the fund-raising practices and advertising campaigns of many candidates for public office.

3   Ethical problems were not limited to public figures or to those in powerful positions. They also touched many aspects of our own daily lives. Résumé fraud continued to be a problem for many

---

*incongruities: things that don't fit together correctly.

employers. One survey reported a "stunning 80% of checked résumés included lies about applicants' job histories." More startling is the idea that "nobody expects job candidates to be totally candid*. . . a little gilding of the lily is understandable—and acceptable."

4   Early in 1997, residents of a poor Miami, Florida, neighborhood scooped up almost half a million dollars in cash and a quarter of a million dollars' worth of food stamps when a Brinks armored truck flipped on an overpass and spilled its cargo. Area residents made off with most of the cash and stamps. Appeals by Brinks to return the money, with no questions asked, went virtually unheeded. Two weeks after the accident, only two people had come forward to turn in a total of $20.38. Additional appeals were made, and within three weeks of the accident, almost $300 had been returned. When questioned, many area residents said they did not intend to return the money. "Finders keepers, losers weepers," many said.

5   Education had its share of ethical problems, too. A University of Virginia study found that when students talk to their mothers, "they lie about once in every two conversations" and that "they lie even more to strangers." A 1993 survey of undergraduates at the Massachusetts Institute of Technology revealed that 83 percent cheated, from collaborating on homework answers, to plagiarism, to copying on exams.

6   Plagiarism in scholarly writing continued generally unchallenged. At the time this . . . was being written, only one organization, the American Historical Association, had taken steps to improve the ethical behavior of its members; it discussed the possibility of disclosing the names of those who plagiarize or who are otherwise in serious violation of professional ethics.

7   Another survey, this one conducted in connection with the 1996 presidential campaign, noted that 65 percent of Americans do not believe character is important in deciding whom to support for president. If character is not an important quality in the president of the United States—the leader of the Western world—then for whom is it important?

8   There is much talk but little action when it comes to acting ethically. Why has all our talk resulted in so little behavioral change?

Ethics Defined

9 There are probably as many definitions of the term *ethics* as there are individuals asked to provide one. Nevertheless, most

---

*candid: direct, honest.

definitions are similar and none is all that complicated. The simplest and most straightforward definition is this one: *Ethics are
moral principles for living and making decisions.* There are, of
course, any number of other good definitions. Some might say
that ethics are the morals, beliefs, norms, and values that individuals and societies use to determine right from wrong. Others
might say that ethics are the moral guidelines one uses in living
and making decisions in a world of hard choices. A few might consider ethics to be a human mental construction that serves as a
basis for understanding what is right and what is wrong. As a
field of philosophical inquiry, ethics concerns itself with such concepts as good, right, wrong, duty, value, and responsibility,
among others.

10   The word *ethics* comes from the Greek *ethos,* which means
"character." As a practical matter, your ethical behavior is governed by the sort of person you are, as well as by the value or relative worth you assign to various activities or aspects of life. For
example, one person might see value in pursuing wealth and position in life and might aspire to own many valuable material goods,
such as jewelry, real estate, and the like. Another person might
value relationships the most, working to develop or enhance relationships with a spouse, children, friends, and significant others.
Still others might value travel, personal time, or recreational
activities.

11   There are no givens in terms of what a person may value. As
individuals, we may assign to the various aspects of our lives
whatever relative worth we deem appropriate. However, the
freedom to assign worth to any one or more of a number of
activities or aspects of life does not absolve us of the responsibility
of pursuing these goals in an ethically appropriate fashion, especially since our actions will most certainly involve others. We
must be careful in determining just what values will guide our
actions.

12   Morality is closely related to ethics, and the terms are often
used interchangeably. However, the word *morality* comes from
the Latin *moralis,* meaning "customs and manners." In this
respect, morality can involve issues that may go beyond the
individual to a larger society. Society is often seen as the arbiter
of proper behavior. One is encouraged to follow society's customs and manners, that is, society's view of the proper way of
doing things. Because concepts like good and evil, right and
wrong, and ethics and morality often have imprecise definitions,
many people are comfortable with leaving the whole issue of
ethical and moral behavior to others. However, "to the degree

that we get our ethical bearings only from the society around us, we remain as vulnerable as the citizens of Nazi Germany to . . . ethical distortions. We, too, can be led to commit atrocities and call it 'good.'"

13   Americans have always valued the freedom to choose certain things for themselves; it seems only natural that no one should dictate specific behaviors. Nevertheless, wrestling with ethical issues is difficult for some and impossible for many. A word of warning: Ethics should not be considered only in terms of the individual. One should not develop a private morality; it is dangerous to drift toward *moral relativism,* the notion that all ethical systems are equal and that we are free to choose our own regardless of how others might be affected. There are moral absolutes; not everything depends on the individual or the situation. The key to successful ethical decision making is developing a set of moral beliefs that serve not only the self but also the culture. Moral behavior is always important, regardless of what we value or what others value. Ethics, therefore, is applicable to all life situations and should not be discarded simply because there are differences in what individuals say or do in their lives. One must work through these differences—adjusting, modifying, improving, growing, both as an individual and as a member of society.

14   Many people are comfortable with a theory of behavior that is not an ethical theory at all but a legal one. *Moral legalism* is the notion that whatever is legal is ethical, and conversely, whatever is illegal is unethical. This legalistic approach is satisfactory to many. It may, in fact, be the "default" ethical philosophy in America—that is, the philosophy almost everyone follows in the absence of some other system that has been rationally developed and empirically* applied.

15   For many people, however, moral legalism is barely workable. Its most significant flaw is that many human behaviors that are not illegal—lying to a friend, for example—are clearly unethical. Other individuals see little value in allowing the criminal justice system to determine right and wrong, beyond the necessities of law and civil order. We need more than a set of legal principles for living and making decisions; we need a set of moral principles, too. (Adapted from Leslie, *Mass Communication Ethics,* pp. 15–19.)

---

*empirically: using observation or experiments.

Sharpening Your Skills

DIRECTIONS Answer the following questions by filling in the blanks or circling the letter of the correct response.

1. In your own words, how does the author feel about the current state of ethics in America?

   _____

2. Based on the context, how would you define the word *inquiry* in paragraph 9?

   a. study

   b. growth

   c. experts

   d. expression

3. Based on the context, how would you define the word *absolve* in paragraph 11?

   _____

4. Does the author think that the terms *ethics* and *morality* can always be used interchangeably? _____

   Explain your answer. _____

   _____

5. Based on your reading, which one of the following questions do you think would *not* appear on an exam?

   a. Define the term *moral relativism.*

   b. Explain the difference between the terms *moral legalism* and *moral relativism.*

   c. Using each word's etymology, or history, explain the difference between *morality* and *ethics.*

   d. Could the Greek philosopher Aristotle be classified as a moral relativist?

6. Do you think the author would agree or disagree with the following statement? _____

   Ethical questions have to be answered on an individual basis because no one system of ethics fits all people. By the same token, no ethical system can be judged better or worse than another.

Explain your answer. _____

_____

7. Which is the best paraphrase for this statement (paragraph 13)? "[I]t is dangerous to drift toward *moral relativism*, the notion that all ethical systems are equal and that we are free to choose our own regardless of how others might be affected. There are moral absolutes; not everything depends on the individual or the situation."

   a. *Moral relativists* believe that certain standards of conduct must be observed and cannot change with the individual or culture. They believe society needs moral absolutes.

   b. *Moral relativism* is at the heart of what's wrong with America today. Too many people believe that they can create their own rules or standards of conduct solely to suit themselves. They think being a moral person and being happy are one and the same.

   c. It's a mistake to embrace *moral relativism*, the belief that there are no enduring standards of moral conduct. Moral absolutes unaffected by person, place, or time are necessary.

8. Which is the best paraphrase for this statement (paragraph 14)? "*Moral legalism* is the notion that whatever is legal is ethical. . . ."

   a. *Moral legalism* is the belief that ethical actions do not necessarily coincide with legal ones.

   b. *Moral legalists* believe that the law should be used to define ethical behavior.

   c. *Moral legalists* think that the law can be used only to decide what's right or wrong in cases that involve a crime.

9. Would you need to footnote the following statement (paragraph 12) if you paraphrased it in a paper? "[T]he word *morality* comes from the Latin *moralis*, meaning 'customs and manners.'" _____

   Explain your answer. _____

   _____

10. In paragraph 11, the author says, "We must be careful in determining just what values will guide our actions." Briefly describe the values you use to guide your actions.

_____

_____

WORD NOTES: MORALS AND MORES

On page 75, you learned that the word *morality* comes from the Latin *moralis*, meaning customs and manners. Even though you probably didn't need to know the root to determine the meaning of *morality*, that same root would help you figure out the meaning of the word *mores* in the following sentence: "Unfamiliar with the social *mores* of the culture, he was constantly offending the very people he wanted to impress." Based on the context and your knowledge of the word's root, you would be right to say that *mores* are the customs of a particular social group. And there is no singular for the word because it is unlikely that any group would have only one custom.

   To test your understanding of the difference between these two words, fill in the blanks in these two sentences:

1. The judge's behavior was certainly legal; it was the

_____ of it her husband questioned.

2. The anthropologist wanted to discover if the group's

_____ had been affected by its newfound wealth.

Students who want to work on paraphrasing before completing the end-of-chapter tests should go to **laflemm.com** and click on "Reading for Thinking: Online Practice." Practice 2, "Paraphrasing Topic Sentences," will help you hone your skills.

Test 1: Reviewing the Key Points

DIRECTIONS Answer the following questions by filling in the blanks or circling the correct response.

1. Annotating pages while you are reading can help you improve

   _____ and _____.

2. *True* or *False*. All marginal comments are useful.

3. When you annotate, you should try to do the following:

   (a) _____

   (b) _____

   (c) _____

4. *True* or *False*. Readers vary in the way they annotate pages.

5. Annotation should make the _____ stand out for easy access.

6. The goal of paraphrasing is to _____

   _____.

7. With difficult material, you should paraphrase _____

   _____.

8. If the material is fairly familiar, then paraphrase _____

   _____.

9. Plagiarizing means _____

   _____.

10. Information considered common knowledge can be _____

    _____.

To correct your test, turn to the answer key on page 641.

Test 2: Recognizing an Accurate Paraphrase

DIRECTIONS Circle the letter of the most accurate paraphrase.

1. A *dialect* is language use—including vocabulary, grammar, and pronunciation—unique to a particular group or region. Audiences sometimes make negative judgments about a speaker based on his or her dialect. Such negative judgments are called *vocal stereotypes*. (Gronbeck et al., *Principles of Speech Communications,* p. 100.)

Paraphrase a. A dialect is a particular way of speaking. Unfortunately, people sometimes judge others based on the way they speak. Southerners, for example, rightfully complain about being stereotyped because of their accent.

b. The term *vocal stereotypes* refers to the negative judgments people sometimes make based on a person's dialect. A dialect is speech unique to a group or region, and it includes vocabulary, grammar, and pronunciation.

c. A *vocal stereotype* is a type of dialect, which includes certain vocabulary, grammar, and pronunciation. People who speak one particular dialect tend to be critical of those who speak other dialects.

2. Because China has banned them from selling their products door to door, vendors* for companies like Amway, Mary Kay, and Avon are not very happy with the Chinese government. According to the Chinese press, such door-to-door marketing tends to foster "excess hugging" and "weird cults." ("China Slams the Door on the Avon Lady," *Newsweek,* May 4, 1998, p. 49.)

Paraphrase a. The Chinese press has given an odd reason for the government's ban on door-to-door salespeople selling products from companies like Avon and Amway: It's been reported that the salespeople encourage "weird cults" and "excess hugging."

b. Amway, Mary Kay, and Avon have decided to stop selling their products in China because their salespeople have become the victims of too much hugging.

c. The Chinese government is angry with companies who use door-to-door marketing because it says that Amway, Mary Kay, and Avon do not really understand the Chinese people. People in China are different from Americans because they do not like to hug others or join cults.

---

*vendors: people who sell products.

3. During World War II, movies about Japan made little effort to develop a Japanese character or explain what Japan hoped to accomplish in the war. The Japanese remained nameless, faceless, and almost totally speechless. No attempt was made to show a Japanese soldier trapped by circumstances beyond his control, or a family man longing for home, or an officer who despised the militarists* even if he supported the military campaign. This was in sharp contrast to the portrayal of German soldiers, who were often shown as decent human beings altogether different from the Nazis. (Adapted from Clayton R. Koppes and Gregory D. Black, *Hollywood Goes to War.* Berkeley: University of California Press, 1998, p. 254.)

Paraphrase a. During World War II, Hollywood filmmakers were applauded for engaging in openly racist propaganda. The 1942 film *Wake Island,* for example, with its story of 377 Marines who resisted a Japanese invasion, was a smash hit despite its use of racial stereotypes to characterize Japanese soldiers. Today, however, such cinematic practices, even during wartime, would be sharply criticized.

b. Hollywood films made during World War II conveyed the idea that Japanese soldiers were like robots, who followed government orders without question. These films suggested that Japanese soldiers never experienced the kind of conflict felt by German soldiers, who did not always agree with their government's inhumane course of action. Indeed, Japanese soldiers always set aside their personal emotions in order to fulfill their duty to Japan.

c. During World War II, Hollywood filmmakers made propaganda movies that failed to distinguish between the Japanese government's war machine and the Japanese soldier caught in that machine.

4. Disco became the biggest commercial pop genre* of the 1970s—actually, the biggest pop music movement of all time—and in the end, its single-minded, booming beat proved to be the most resilient and enduring stylistic breakthrough of the last twenty years or so. (Mikal Gilmore, *Night Beat.* New York: Doubleday, 1998, p. 241.)

Paraphrase a. In the 1970s, disco challenged rock and roll's position as the music of the young. But thankfully, following the success of *Saturday Night Fever,* disco died a quick and well-deserved death.

---

*militarists: people devoted to war.
*genre: type or class; a category of literature, music, or art.

b. In the 1970s, disco was the hottest dance music around; over the last two decades, its pulsing beat has proved to have real staying power.

c. No other kind of music was more popular than disco in the 1970s, and rightly so. It is the freshest, most upbeat type of music ever created, so it's no wonder that people still love it as much as they did decades ago.

5. During the nineteenth and early twentieth centuries, the South American countries of Argentina, Uruguay, and Brazil had their own homegrown cowboys called *gauchos*. Derived from the Quechua* word *wáhcha*, the word *gaucho* usually referred to cowhands or horse handlers, but it could also refer to horse thieves and mercenaries.*

Paraphrase a. In the South American countries of Argentina, Uruguay, and Brazil, gauchos were considered romantic figures, and much like America's cowboys, they were the heroes of countless movies and novels. Among the most famous of these novels was *The Four Horsemen of the Apocalypse*, which also became a movie.

b. During the nineteenth and beginning of the twentieth centuries, American-like cowboys, called gauchos, worked the ranches of Uruguay, Argentina, and Brazil. Although the term *gaucho*—which comes from the Quechua word *wáhcha*—means "cowboy" or "horse handler," it could also be used to refer to horse thieves and soldiers of fortune.

c. Gauchos, the nineteenth- and early twentieth-century horsemen of Argentina, Uruguay, and Brazil, tended to be lawless robbers and guns-for-hire. At the same time their American counterparts were wreaking havoc in the Old West, these South American cowboys were causing trouble in their homeland.

*Quechua: language spoken by people belonging to the Incan Empire.
*mercenaries: soldiers for hire, soldiers of fortune.

Test 3: Recognizing an Accurate Paraphrase

DIRECTIONS Circle the letter of the most accurate paraphrase.

Original **1.** In 1960, researcher Jane Goodall went to Africa's Gombe National Park to study chimpanzees. No one before her had attempted to observe the animals in their natural habitat, and initially, the chimps ran from her. However, when Goodall didn't give up, the animals gradually became used to her, letting her watch them for hours every day. This pioneering fieldwork revolutionized primate research: Goodall was the first to observe that chimps eat meat, use tools, and engage in warfare. (Source of information: Dan Vergano, "Chimp Charmer Jane Goodall Returns to Gombe," *USA Today,* March 8, 2004, p. 8D.)

Paraphrase
    a. Jane Goodall, who studied chimpanzees in 1960 in Africa's Gombe National Park, was a better researcher than anyone who had previously studied the shy animals. Unlike earlier researchers, she got the chimps to accept her. Their acceptance gave her the opportunity to observe them in the wild for long periods of time. As a result, she found out that chimps are just like humans: They eat meat, use tools, and wage war.

    b. In 1960, Jane Goodall became the first person to study chimpanzees in their natural habitat of Africa's Gombe National Park. After patiently overcoming the chimps' initial resistance to her presence, Goodall significantly influenced primate research by witnessing and reporting on chimpanzee behaviors such as meat eating, tool use, and warfare, none of which had been documented before.

    c. If Jane Goodall hadn't gone to Africa's Gombe National Park in 1960, it's unlikely that we'd know today that chimpanzees are meat-eaters, use tools, and occasionally fight each other to the death. Jane Goodall had a special talent for working with the animals, and she was able to communicate to them that they need not fear her. The chimps allowed her to get close enough to make some astonishing discoveries about them.

    d. When Jane Goodall went to Africa's Gombe National Park in 1960, she did not know how difficult it would be to study chimpanzees in their natural surroundings. Initially, the animals would not let her get close to them. Goodall didn't give up, though. She kept trying, and eventually the chimps permitted her to watch them for long periods of time.

Original **2.** People can successfully perform two different activities simultaneously. However, one of the two has to be performed automatically and require little or no attention. For example, we are able to drive a car and converse at the same time because we can steer, brake, accelerate, and so on, without close attention to each individual action. The actions necessary to driving are practically automatic and require little thought once they have been thoroughly learned. We can also do two things at the same time if the tasks or activities involved require quite different kinds of attention. It's possible to read music and play the piano simultaneously because each activity requires a different mode of concentration. One forces us to pay attention to incoming stimuli; the other requires us to produce a response. It follows, then, that it is nearly impossible to have a conversation and read at the same time. Both activities rely on similar types of attention. (Source of information: Bernstein et al., *Psychology,* 6th ed., p. 177.)

Paraphrase a. To perform two activities at the same time, one of them has to be automatic. Driving, for example, is automatic, so we can usually drive while talking. When playing the piano, pressing the keys is an automatic response to reading the music. However, we cannot talk and read at the same time because we have to pay attention to both of these tasks. Neither one can be performed without thinking.

b. It is possible to do two different things at the same time. But one of those two things has to require little or no thought. It must be almost completely automatic. For instance, many people can drive while they talk because the motions of driving—steering, accelerating, braking, etc.—are so automatic they don't require close concentration. We can also do two things at the same time if the two tasks are quite different and thus require different types of concentration. We can, for example, read music at the same time that our fingers touch and make music with piano keys. Reading the music forces us to attend to incoming external stimuli. When we play the piano, in contrast, we are producing a response. However, we can't talk and read at the same time because those two tasks require similar kinds of attention.

c. If two tasks require different kinds of attention, then they can be performed at the same time. For example, you don't really have to pay attention when you drive a car, which leaves you free to talk to your passengers. Plus, you don't have to think about how your fingers are moving over the keyboard, so you can read music while playing a piano. But reading and talking both force you to pay attention to what you're doing. Therefore, they cannot be performed simultaneously.

d. Because the human brain allows us to divide our attention, we can often do two things at the same time. For example, we can drive and talk at the same time because one of the tasks (driving) is automatic. Also, we can read music while playing the piano because each task requires the same kind of attention.

Original **3.** Local television news directors have long known that their primary goal is to attract audiences for their advertisers. However, thanks to a large increase in media choices, competition for viewers has become fiercer. Because it's difficult to write catchy stories about politics and government, many news directors have given up trying to cover that kind of news. Instead, they concentrate on TV news programs that mix action stories—short clips about murders, robberies, rapes, fires, and car accidents—with weather, sports, human interest stories, and friendly banter between the anchors. (Source of information: Turow, *Media Today: An Introduction to Mass Communication,* pp. 423–424.)

Paraphrase a. Television news programmers know they have to draw big audiences if they are going to please their advertisers. Because audiences have many programs to choose from, local TV news directors try to attract viewers with action-oriented shows that mix stories about crimes, accidents, and disasters with news about sports and weather and the chipper chatter of the newscasters. Since it's hard to write snappy stories about government and politics, most news programs feature very little information about these kinds of topics.

b. Local TV directors know that viewers won't watch dull news programs. They also know they must provide viewers for their advertisers. For those two reasons, today's local news programs rarely include much information about boring subjects like government and politics. Instead, they tend to focus mostly on violent action. Tune in to a local TV news broadcast, and you're likely to see attractive and smiling anchormen and women introducing videotape of mangled cars, raging fires, and storm damage, all accompanied by interviews with teary victims.

c. Local TV news directors know they have to create action-packed shows to draw in advertisers. Consequently, they have stopped covering politics and government. Most people would rather see video footage of crimes, accidents, weather forecasts, and sports events, particularly if it is interspersed with friendly conversation between the newscasters. News directors can't really be blamed for giving people what they want.

d. Local TV news directors know that advertisers prefer to place their ads in action-oriented shows with large audiences. They have given up trying to make subjects like government and politics interesting, and they put together shows filled with reports of murders, robberies, accidents, sports highlights, and weather information. They know people are interested in those subjects.

Original 4. A *class-action suit* is a case brought into a court of law by a person who wishes to sue an organization not only for himself or herself but also on behalf of everyone who has been wronged in the same way by that organization. One of the most famous class-action suits was brought in 1954 by the National Association for the Advancement of Colored People (NAACP), which sued on behalf of Linda Brown, a black girl from Topeka, Kansas, who was denied admission to a white elementary school, as well as all other children who were forced to attend segregated schools. The resulting Supreme Court decision, *Brown v. Board of Education*, led to the desegregation of public schools. (Source of information: Wilson and DiIulio, *American Government: The Essentials*, 9th ed., pp. 419–420.)

Paraphrase a. Class-action suits are brought by people who want to sue an institution not only on their own behalf but also on behalf of anyone who might have been unfairly treated by the same institution. Perhaps the most famous class-action suit was brought by the NAACP, which sued in the name of Linda Brown, an African-American girl denied entry to an all-white elementary school. The suit also included the names of all other children excluded by the practice of segregation in the schools. This class-action suit, which the NAACP won, was the first step in the desegregation of all public schools.

b. The term *class-action suit* is applied to those cases where a group of people are suing one institution. The lawsuit that led to the desegregation of schools, *Brown v. Board of Education*, was a class-action suit filed by the NAACP.

c. The first and most famous class-action suit ever brought into court was *Brown v. Board of Education*, which was the first step in the desegregation of all public schools. The NAACP, fearing it could not win its case in the name of a single child, decided to sue on behalf of all the children who had ever been denied access to a local school because of the practice of segregation.

d. A class-action suit is brought by someone who wants to sue an institution not only in the name of himself or herself but also in the names of any others who might have been wrongly treated by the same institution. The famous lawsuit, which paved the way for desegregation, is probably the best example of a class-action suit that had important consequences not just for a single person but also for a host of people. This is typical of class-action suits brought by the NAACP.

Test 4: Paraphrasing with Accuracy

DIRECTIONS Paraphrase each of the following statements.

1. When things go wrong in a society, in a way and to a degree that can no longer be denied or concealed, there are various questions one can ask. A common one . . . is "Who did this to us?" (Bernard Lewis, *What Went Wrong?* New York: Oxford University Press, 2000, p. 94.)

   _____

   _____

   _____

   _____

2. In Colonial America, reading was not regarded as an elitist activity, and printed matter was spread among all kinds of people. (Neil Postman, *Amusing Ourselves to Death.* New York: Penguin Books, 1985, p. 35.)

   _____

   _____

   _____

   _____

3. Years ago, if there was major news, the public might see pictures of the event in their movie theaters a week or so later. But since we now expect to see live pictures from the scene almost immediately on TV, news departments compete with one another to be first in delivering pictures. (Neil Postman, *How to Watch TV News.* New York: Penguin Books, 1992, p. 45.)

   _____

   _____

   _____

   _____

4. In the late 1950s, union leaders Walter Reuther and George Meany battled over how to define American labor's role in the world. The liberal Reuther wanted unions to think of themselves as part of an international labor movement. The more conservative Meany insisted that American union members should concentrate on their own interests and let workers in other countries take care of themselves.

_____

_____

_____

_____

C H A P T E R 3

Reviewing Paragraph Essentials

In this chapter, you'll learn

- **how to identify topics.**
- **how to recognize main ideas.**
- **how to locate topic sentences.**
- **how to identify major and minor details.**
- **how to recognize organizational patterns.**

Overall, *Reading for Thinking* assumes you have a solid knowledge of how to read a paragraph. Still, it doesn't hurt to review paragraph essentials. A quick review of the essentials is precisely what Chapter 3 offers.

Starting with the Topic

Finding the topic is the first step toward discovering the main idea of a paragraph. The **topic** of a paragraph is the subject the author

91

chooses to discuss or explore. It's the person, place, object, event, or idea most frequently mentioned or referred to by the author. Usually, you can find the topic by posing one key question: Who or what is most frequently mentioned or referred to in the paragraph? To illustrate, let's use the following:

> The use of animals in scientific research is a controversial subject that provokes strong emotions on both sides. Animal rights activists define animals as sentient* beings who can think, feel, and suffer. They insist, therefore, that the rights of animals be acknowledged and respected. The more conservative animal rights activists argue that the use of animals in research should be strictly monitored, while the more radical activists insist that research using animals should be banned altogether. In response to these objections, research scientists who experiment on animals have reorganized their research to take better care of the animals involved. They argue, however, that research on animals is ethical and necessary because it saves human lives and alleviates* human suffering.

What's the topic of this paragraph? Is it "animal rights activists" or the "use of animals in research"? If you said it was the "use of animals in research," you are right on target. That is, indeed, the subject most frequently mentioned or referred to in the paragraph. The phrase "animal rights activists" is mentioned or referred to several times but not as frequently as the phrase "use of animals in research."

Another thing you should notice about the topic of the preceding paragraph is the number of words needed to express it—five, to be exact. Occasionally, you will be able to express the topic of a paragraph in a single word. However, much of the time you will need a phrase of two or more words to zero in on the precise topic. Look, for example, at the following paragraph. What's the topic?

> Although the fighting took place far from the United States, the Vietnam War* deeply affected the way Americans lived their lives. Military service became an important, life-changing experience for more than two million Americans. In the typical tour of duty, soldiers encountered racial tensions, boredom, drugs, and a widespread brutality against the Vietnamese. Even those Americans who did not fight were changed by the war. Millions of young men

---

*sentient: aware, possessed of consciousness.
*alleviates: relieves, eliminates.
*Vietnam War: a long civil war in Vietnam (1954–1975) that involved both the Soviet Union and the United States.

spent a substantial part of their late adolescence or young adult-hood wondering whether they would be drafted or seeking ways to avoid participation in the fighting. Far more men did not go to Vietnam than went, but the war created deep divisions among people of an entire generation. Those who fought in the war often resented those who did not, and people who did not go to Vietnam sometimes treated those who did with scorn, pity, or condescension. (Adapted from Schaller, Scharf, and Schulzinger, *Present Tense,* p. 301.)

Here again, no one single word could effectively sum up the topic. The word *Americans* won't do. Nor will the phrase "Vietnam War." To express the focus of the paragraph, we need a phrase like "the effect of the Vietnam War on American life." Note, too, that the words in the topic don't appear next to each other. This topic was created by combining words from different parts of the paragraph and adding the word *life.*

The point of this is that identifying the topic often requires you to do a good deal more than simply look for a word or two. On the contrary, frequently you have to figure out how to piece together a topic to effectively help you unlock paragraph meaning. To be effective, the topic you create should be general enough to include everything discussed in the paragraph and specific enough to exclude what isn't.

EXERCISE 1

DIRECTIONS Read each paragraph. Then circle the letter of the correct topic.

1. According to the attachment theory of love, adults are character-ized, in their romantic relationships, by one of three styles. *Secure lovers* are happy when others feel close to them. Mutual dependency in a relationship (depending on the partner and the partner's depending on you) feels right to them. Secure lovers do not fear abandonment. In contrast, *avoidant lovers* are uncomfortable feeling close to another person or having that person feel close to them. It is difficult for avoidant lovers to trust or depend on a partner. The third type, *anxious-ambivalent lovers,* want desperately to get close to a partner but often find that the partner does not recipro-cate the feeling, perhaps because anxious-ambivalent lovers scare away others. They are insecure in the relationship, worrying that the partner does not really love them. Research on the attachment theory shows that about 53 percent of adults are secure, 26 percent are avoidant, and 20 percent are anxious-ambivalent.

Topic a. mutual dependency in a relationship

b. attachment theory of love

c. secure lovers

2. Among the explanations of our nation's high divorce rate and high degree of dissatisfaction in many marriages is that we have such strong expectations of marriage. We expect our spouse to simultaneously be a lover, a friend, a confidant, a counselor, a career person, and a parent, for example. In one research investigation, unhappily married couples expressed unrealistic expectations about marriage (Epstein and Eidelson, 1981). Underlying unrealistic expectations about marriage are numerous myths about marriage. A myth is a widely held belief unsupported by facts. (Santrock, *Life-Span Development*, p. 445.)

Topic a. marriage

b. expectations about marriage

c. myths about marriage

3. Surveys show that about three out of four U.S. corporations have **ethics codes**. The purpose of these codes is to provide guidance to managers and employees when they encounter an ethical dilemma. A typical code discusses conflicts of interest that can harm the company (for example, guidelines for accepting or refusing gifts from suppliers, hiring relatives, or having an interest in a competitor's firm). Rules for complying with various laws, such as antitrust, environmental, and consumer protection laws, also are popular code provisions. The most effective codes are those drawn up with the cooperation and widespread participation of employees. An internal enforcement mechanism, including penalties for violating the code, puts teeth into the code. A shortcoming of many codes is that they tend to provide more protection for the company than for employees and the general public. They do so by emphasizing narrow legal compliance*—rather than taking a positive and broad view of ethical responsibility toward all company stockholders—and by focusing on conflicts of interest that will harm the company. (Frederick et al., *Business and Society*, p. 94.)

Topic a. U.S. corporations

b. ethics codes

c. penalties for violations of ethics codes

---

*compliance: obedience.

4. Throughout the seventeenth and eighteenth centuries, the rulers of Russia allowed most Russians to live in miserable poverty. But in 1855 a new emperor, Alexander II, came to the throne. Unlike his predecessors, he was determined to improve the lot of the people. Alexander II relaxed press censorship and permitted Russians to travel abroad more freely. Under his rule, minorities in the empire were treated better, and the courts were reorganized so that criminals might have a trial by jury. Alexander's greatest achievement was his decision to free the serfs—poor men and women who had been the slaves of the rich landowners.

Topic a. the suffering of the Russian people

      b. the achievements of Alexander II

      c. the rulers of Russia

5. Conjoined twins are usually classified into three basic categories depending on the point where they are joined. Twins of the first type are conjoined in a way that never involves the heart or the midline of the body. For example, about 2 percent of all conjoined twins are attached at the head only, and about 19 percent are joined at the buttocks. Twins of the second type are always joined in a way that involves the midline of the body. Many twins joined at the midline share a heart. Around 35 percent are fused together at the upper half of the trunk. Another 30 percent are joined at the lower half of their bodies. Finally, the third major type of conjoined twins includes the very rare forms. In this category are those in which one twin is smaller, less formed, and dependent on the other, as well as the cases involving one twin born completely within the body of his or her sibling.

Topic a. twins who share a heart

      b. twins

      c. conjoined twins

From Topic to Main Idea

Once you know the topic of a paragraph, the next logical step is to determine the main idea. The **main idea** is the central point or message of the paragraph. The main idea is what unites, or ties together, all the sentences in the paragraph.

To discover the main idea of a paragraph, you need to ask two key questions: (1) What does the author want to say *about* the topic? and (2) What one idea is developed throughout most of the paragraph?

To illustrate how these questions can help you determine the main idea, let's look at two different paragraphs. Here's the first one.

For a period of about seventy-five years (1765–1840), the Gothic novel, an early relative of the modern horror story, was popular throughout Europe. Many of the most popular novels—those written by Horace Walpole, Ann Radcliffe, and Monk Lewis—were sold by the thousands, quickly translated, and frequently plagiarized. The stories were the object of fascination because they described a world where mysterious happenings were a matter of course, and ghostly, hooded figures flitted through the night. Gothic novels were read and discussed by men and women of the upper classes, and publishers, ever alert to a ready market, made sure that copies of the books were available at bargain prices. Thus, even the poorest members of the working class could afford to pay a penny to enter the Gothic world of terror, and they paid their pennies in *astonishing numbers.*

In this example, the opening sentence announces that the Gothic novel enjoyed great popularity for almost a century. The remaining sentences either give specific examples of how popular the novels were or explain the source of their popularity. Because the author repeatedly returns to the idea that the Gothic novel was very popular, we can say that this is the main idea of the paragraph.

Now try to determine the main idea in another paragraph. As you read the following example, look for the topic—the subject repeatedly mentioned or referred to—and keep asking yourself, "What does the author want to say about that topic?" and "What one idea is developed throughout most of the paragraph?"

In the very near future, the world will face an energy shortage of extraordinary proportions. By the year 2040, the total population on Earth is expected to double to about 10 billion people. With the continued industrialization of Asia, Africa, and the Americas, world energy consumption is expected to triple. At that rate of consumption, the world's known oil supply will be depleted in about sixty years. The supply of gas will be depleted in about 100 years. If we are to maintain an acceptable quality of life, we must find new sources of energy that will make up for the shortages that are bound to occur in the coming decades.

The topic of this paragraph is "the energy shortage." That's the subject repeatedly mentioned or referred to. However, we still need to figure out what the author wants to say about that topic. We need to discover the one idea that is developed, not just in a single sentence, but throughout the paragraph.

If you go through the paragraph sentence by sentence, you'll see that each one further develops the point made in the first sentence: We're facing an energy shortage that's likely to arrive very soon. This main idea is developed not just in the opening sentence but throughout the entire paragraph.

CHECK YOUR UNDERSTANDING

Explain the difference between the topic and the main idea of a paragraph.

_____

_____

_____

EXERCISE 2

DIRECTIONS Read each paragraph. Then circle the letters that identify the topic and the main idea.

1. Impatient for victory as World War II dragged on, American leaders began to plan a fall invasion of the Japanese islands, an expedition that was sure to incur high casualties. But the successful development of an atomic bomb by American scientists provided another route to victory in World War II. The secret atomic program, known as the Manhattan Project, began in August 1942 and cost $2 billion. The first bomb was exploded in the desert near Alamogordo, New Mexico, on July 16, 1945. Only three weeks later, on August 6, the Japanese city of Hiroshima was destroyed by a bomb dropped from an American B-29 airplane called the *Enola Gay*. A flash of dazzling light shot across the sky; then, a huge purplish mushroom cloud boiled 40,000 feet into the atmosphere. Dense smoke, swirling fires, and suffocating dust soon engulfed the ground for miles. Much of the city was leveled almost instantly. Approximately 130,000 people were killed; tens of thousands more suffered severe burns and nuclear poisoning. On August 9, another atomic bomb flattened the city of Nagasaki, killing at least 60,000 people. Four days later, the Japanese, who had been sending out peace feelers since June, surrendered. Formal surrender ceremonies were held September 2 on the battleship *Missouri*. (Norton et al., *A People and a Nation*, p. 827.)

Topic a. the invasion of Japan

b. the atomic bomb

c. World War II

Main Idea a. Desperate for a victory, American leaders planned an invasion of the Japanese islands.

b. The atomic bomb gave the American forces another way to bring World War II to an end.

c. The question of whether or not the United States had to use the atomic bomb to end World War II is still the subject of debate.

d. Rather than dropping the atomic bomb, the United States should have invaded Japan.

 2. People have many different reasons for wanting children. Some really like children and want an opportunity to be involved with their care. Some women strongly desire the experience of pregnancy and childbirth. Many young adults see parenthood as a way to demonstrate their adult status. For people coming from happy families, having children is a means of reliving their earlier happiness. For those from unhappy families, it can be a means of doing better than their parents did. Some people have children simply because it's expected of them. Because society places so much emphasis on the fulfillment motherhood is supposed to bring, some women who are unsure of what they want to do with their lives use having a child as a way to create an identity. (Seifert et al., *Lifespan Development*, p. 484.)

Topic a. childhood

b. reasons for having children

c. parenting and past experience

Main Idea a. Some people have children to recreate the happiness they themselves experienced growing up.

b. There are several reasons why people have children.

c. Most people don't know why they have children; they just do what's expected of them.

d. Society places too much emphasis on the fulfillment motherhood is supposed to bring.

 3. *Fiber* is generally defined as that part of plants (cell wall material) that is essentially indigestible. Though not a direct source of nutrition, dietary fiber serves at least two vital functions in the body. It speeds the passage of food waste through the colon, allowing less time for absorption of dietary cholesterol and less tissue exposure to potential cancer-producing substances in the feces. In addition, some high-fiber foods (especially vegetables such as cabbage, cauliflower, and broccoli) may stimulate the production of cancer-fighting enzymes in the intestinal tract. (Williams and Long, *Manage Your Life*, p. 70.)

Topic a. nutrition

b. cancer-producing substances

c. fiber

Main Idea a. Fiber is the indigestible portion of plants.

b. Fiber has no nutritional value.

c. Fiber serves the body in two important ways.

d. Fiber in the diet speeds up digestion.

4. Almost half the world's population speaks an Indo-European language. The various languages in this family, which developed largely in the area from Europe to India, hence the name, share some characteristics in vocabulary and grammar, so linguists believe they all descended from one common tongue. Indo-European languages are further classified into different subfamilies, among them the Germanic, Indo-Iranian, Italic, and Slavic. The Germanic subfamily includes Danish, Swedish, German, Yiddish, and English, among others. The Indo-Iranian language subfamily includes Sanskrit, Hindi, Punjabi, and Persian. The Italic languages include Latin, Italian, French, and Spanish. The Slavic languages are those such as Russian, Czech, and Polish.

Topic a. Indo-European languages

b. Germanic languages

c. language study

Main Idea a. The Germanic languages include Danish, Swedish, German, Yiddish, and English.

b. The Indo-European languages share a common vocabulary.

c. Millions of people in the world speak an Indo-European language.

d. Linguists now know that all languages descended from one common tongue.

5. Sports have become an increasingly integral part of American culture. Thus it is not surprising that more and more children become involved in sports every year. Yet participating in sports can have both positive and negative consequences. Children's participation in sports can provide exercise, opportunities to learn how to compete, increased self-esteem, and a setting for developing peer relations and friendships. However, sports can also have negative consequences for children: too much pressure to achieve and win,

physical injuries, a distraction from academic work, and unrealistic expectations for an athlete. Few people challenge the value of sports for children when conducted as part of a school education or intramural program, but some question the appropriateness of highly competitive, win-oriented sports teams in schools. (Adapted from Santrock, *Life-Span Development*, p. 276.)

Topic   a. sports and self-esteem

b. the benefits of school intramural sports programs

c. positive and negative effects of sports in schools

Main Idea   a. For children, participating in sports can have both advantages and disadvantages.

b. School sports programs should not put so much emphasis on competition.

c. Playing sports can teach children important lessons about life.

d. Playing sports builds character.

 # Recognizing Topic Sentences

Topic sentences are general sentences that put into words the main idea of a paragraph. If someone were to ask you what a paragraph was about, you could use the topic sentence to sum it up. Although not all paragraphs contain topic sentences, a good many do. Particularly in textbooks, writers favor topic sentences because they aid communication between reader and writer. They make it easier for the reader to follow the writer's train of thought without getting confused.

As you might guess, experienced readers are always on the lookout for topic sentences. They consciously search, that is, for general sentences that (1) are explained in more specific detail and (2) could be used to sum up the paragraph. Be forewarned, however: The first sentence of a paragraph is not always the topic sentence. Yes, topic sentences are more likely to open than to close a paragraph, but they can and do appear anywhere—beginning, middle, or end.

Topic Sentence in First Position

Authors often begin a paragraph with a topic sentence that sums up the main idea. The sentences that follow then go on to develop or prove the main idea expressed in the opening topic sentence. Here's an example of a paragraph with the topic sentence in first position.

Topic Sentence

<u>In the last few years, Judge Howard Broadman has become the center of controversy over what supporters and critics alike have come to call "creative sentencing."</u> The term refers to the judge's penchant* for offering defendants what he considers acceptable alternatives to a jail sentence. For example, one defendant had to wear a T-shirt that announced his status as a criminal on probation. In another case, an abusive husband had to donate his car to a shelter for battered women. In perhaps his most publicized case, Judge Broadman gave a woman found guilty of child abuse a chance to avoid four years in jail if she would voluntarily allow Norplant, a form of birth control, to be implanted in her arm.

In this example, the topic sentence introduces the term "creative sentencing," and the rest of the paragraph gives examples of what that means.

Introductory Sentences Pave the Way for Topic Sentences

Sometimes authors begin a paragraph with one or two introductory sentences that provide background and pave the way for the topic sentence. For an illustration, read the following paragraph.

Topic Sentence

[1]The letters and journals of America's early Pilgrims are filled with complaints about food or, more precisely, about the lack of it. [2]<u>The first settlers, so adventurous when it came to travel, were amazingly slow to recognize that seventeenth-century America offered almost every kind of food imaginable; it just wasn't the exact same food they were used to eating at home.</u> [3]No, there wasn't much mutton, or lamb, to be had, but there were lobsters in abundance, along with oysters, duck, salmon, scallops, clams, and mussels. [4]There were also sweet and white potatoes, peanuts, squash, green beans, strawberries, and tomatoes. [5]Luckily for the settlers, the Indians in the New World grew and relished all of these foods, and they taught the Pilgrims to do the same. [6]But it took a while for the Pilgrims to catch on. [7]For example, during their first years in New England, the English settlers refused to eat clams or mussels. [8]They hadn't eaten them in the Old World,

---

*penchant: leaning, tendency.

so in the new one, they fed them to the pigs. [9]No wonder their Native American neighbors often looked on in amazement or maybe even amusement.

In this paragraph, the first sentence is an **introductory sentence.** The sentence is not developed in the remainder of the paragraph. Instead, it offers a partial introduction to the topic: the early Pilgrims and their attitude toward food in the New World. The real point of the paragraph comes in the second sentence, where we learn that the early Pilgrims took an incredibly long time to recognize the wonderful selection of foods at their disposal in the New World. The second sentence is the topic sentence because it expresses the main idea developed by the rest of the paragraph.

A Transition Can Reverse the Introduction

Here now is a variation on paragraphs opening with an introductory sentence or two. Once again, the introductory sentence paves the way for the topic sentence. The main difference between this paragraph and the preceding one is that the topic sentence begins with the contrast transition *However,* which reverses the opening statement.

Topic Sentence

Transition

[1]Most of us, males and females alike, love weddings. [2]*However,* *a good deal of evidence in the English language implies that* *weddings are more important to women than to men.* [3]A woman cherishes the wedding and is considered a bride for a whole year, but a man is referred to as a groom only on the day of the wedding. [4]The word *bride* appears in *bridal attendant, bridal gown, bridesmaid, bridal shower,* and even *bridegroom.* [5]Groom comes from the Middle English *grom,* meaning "man," but that meaning of the word is seldom used outside the context of the wedding. [6]With most pairs of male/female words, people habitually put the masculine word first—*Mr. and Mrs., his and hers, boys and girls, men and women, kings and queens, brothers and sisters, guys and dolls,* and *host and hostess*—but it is the *bride and groom* who are talked about, not the *groom and bride.* (Adapted from Nilsen, *About Language,* p. 251.)

As you probably guessed, **contrast transitions** are words and phrases such as *but, however,* and *yet in reality.* These transitions signal to the reader that the author is about to contradict or modify a point previously made.

Common Contrast Transitions	
but	nonetheless
contrary to	on the contrary
despite the fact	on the other hand
even so	still
however	unfortunately
in contradiction	yet
in opposition	yet in fact
just the opposite	yet in reality
nevertheless	

Topic Sentence in the Middle

Sometimes authors postpone introducing the topic sentence until the middle of the paragraph. Look, for instance, at the one that follows. The topic sentence appears smack in the middle of the paragraph. Notice, too, the use of a contrast transition. Here again, the transition signals that the author is about to change direction.

Topic Sentence

[1]In general, bats have a varied diet. [2]Flowers, insects, and fish are among their favorite foods. [3]Some bats, however, really are like the bats in horror movies. [4]They do, indeed, dine on blood. [5]<u>Contrary to their onscreen image, however, these so-called vampire bats don't attack and kill humans</u>. [6]They get their dinner from sleeping livestock. [7]Under the cover of darkness, they make small, pinprick incisions with their razor-sharp teeth. [8]Then they drink their fill from their sleeping prey. [9]Vampire bats are so skillful at getting their dinner they usually don't even wake the sleeping animals.

In this paragraph, the author uses several sentences to introduce the topic—vampire bats—and the paragraph's real point comes in sentence 5.

Topic Sentence at the End

Sometimes authors develop a paragraph with a series of specific facts, examples, or studies. Then, in the last sentence, they state the main idea. It's not the most common pattern, but it certainly does exist, as the following paragraph illustrates.

Topic Sentence

¹Researchers have discovered that body fat produces proteins that trigger inflammation, thus contributing to the development of heart disease, stroke, and diabetes. ²In fact, gaining just 10 pounds increases one's risk of heart disease and stroke considerably. ³And gaining 11 to 18 pounds actually doubles an individual's risk of developing diabetes. ⁴Fat cells also secrete estrogen, a hormone that may contribute to the development of breast cancer. ⁵Research has shown that women who gain more than 20 pounds double their risk of getting breast cancer. ⁶Weight gain also increases the risk of developing colon, kidney, and gallbladder cancer. ⁷Clearly, fat does not just lie inert in the body. ⁸<u>On the contrary, fat cells pump out substances that alter the body's chemistry, affect major organs, and contribute to disease</u>. (Source of information: Nancy Shute, "Why That Beer Belly Is a Killer," *U.S. News & World Report*, February 9, 2004, p. 55.)

Topic Sentence in Two Steps

Much of the time, the main idea in a paragraph can be summed up in a single sentence. Still, you need to be prepared for a fairly common alternative: the two-step topic sentence. Here's an illustration of one.

Two-Step Topic Sentence

¹<u>Movie director George Romero has made a number of horror films. ²But none of his films has ever matched the fame won by *The Night of the Living Dead*</u>. ³Made on a low budget with inexperienced actors, the film tells the story of technology gone wrong. ⁴Radiation in the atmosphere has caused the dead to come back to life and attack the living. ⁵Not only have the dead come back to life, they have become cannibals as well. ⁶Even worse, the living corpses are practically indestructible. ⁷Only a bullet through the head can stop them, a discovery not made until the film is half over and the audience has been properly horrified. ⁸Not surprisingly, Romero's film has become a cult classic, and true horror fans know the dialogue by heart.

In this paragraph, sentences 3 through 8 tell readers more about a film called *The Night of the Living Dead*. So at first glance, it would seem likely that sentence 2 is the topic sentence. But sentence 2, with its reference to "his films," requires the help of sentence 1 to effectively sum up the paragraph. "None of movie director George Romero's films has ever matched the fame won by his classic horror film, *The Night of the Living Dead*." Yes, writers do usually sum up main ideas in a single sentence, but not always. So be prepared to give them a little help by **synthesizing,*** or combining, two sentences into one complete topic sentence.

Question-and-Answer Topic Sentence

Particularly in textbooks, authors are likely to make the first or second sentence the topic sentence. However, they are also fond of opening a paragraph with a question. The answer that follows is often the topic sentence.

Topic Sentence What is genetics? <u>In its simplest form, genetics is the study of heredity</u>. It explains how certain characteristics are passed on from parents to children. Much of what we know about genetics was discovered by the monk Gregor Mendel in the nineteenth century. Since then, the field of genetics has vastly expanded. As scientists study the workings of genetics, they've developed new ways of manipulating genes. For example, scientists have isolated the gene that makes insulin, a human hormone, and now use bacteria to make quantities of it. (Magliore, *Cracking the AP Biology Exam,* p. 105.)

Questions for Analyzing Paragraphs

1. **To find the topic,** ask "Who or what is repeatedly mentioned or referred to in the paragraph?"

2. **To discover the main idea,** ask "What does the author want to say *about* the topic? What idea is developed throughout most of the paragraph?"

3. **To locate the topic sentence,** ask "Which sentence or sentences could I use to generally sum up the contents of the entire paragraph?"

EXERCISE 3

DIRECTIONS Read each paragraph and then write the number or numbers of the topic sentence in the blank.

1. [1]Compared with a corporate executive or a military officer, a teacher may not appear to have a great deal of power. [2]But teachers have a

---

*For more on synthesizing, see pp. 258–259.

special type of power. [3]Henry Adams* caught the sense of the teacher's *long-term* power in the words "A teacher affects eternity: No one can tell where his influence stops." [4]The teacher's powerful influence arises from the fact that he or she has an impact on people when they are still at a very impressionable stage. [5]Teachers take "a piece of living clay and gently form it, day by day." [6]Many careers are open to you, but few offer such truly inspiring power. (Adapted from Ryan and Cooper, *Those Who Can, Teach*, p. 148.)

Topic Sentence _____

2. [1]Before the collapse of the Communist party in Eastern Europe, the East German secret police, the *Staatsicherheit* (or Stasi), was an enormous bureaucracy that reached into every part of society. [2]It had 85,000 full-time employees, including 6,000 people whose sole task was to listen in on telephone conversations. [3]Another 2,000 steamed open mail, read it, resealed the letters, and sent them on to the intended recipients. [4]The Stasi also employed 150,000 active informers and hundreds of thousands of part-time snitches. [5]Files were kept on an estimated 4 to 5 million people in a country that had a total population, including children, of just 17 million. [6]Although East Germany had a large standing army, the Stasi kept its own arsenal of 250,000 weapons. (Adapted from Janda et al., *The Challenge of Democracy*, p. 452.)

Topic Sentence _____

3. [1]What causes plants to bloom? [2]Although you may think that plants flower based on the amount of sunlight they receive, they actually bloom according to the amount of uninterrupted darkness; this principle of plant bloom is called *photoperiodism*. [3]Plants that bloom in late summer and fall, like asters and sedum, are called short-day plants. [4]They require long periods of darkness and only short periods of light. [5]Plants that flower in late spring and early summer, such as daisies and poppies, are called long-day plants. [6]They need only short periods of darkness to blossom.

Topic Sentence _____

4. [1]When most of us consider where to go on a vacation, outer space is not one of the obvious places that comes to mind. [2]Yet in 2001, sixty-year-old California multimillionaire Dennis Tito became the very first space tourist. [3]Tito paid the Russians $20 million for a

_____
*Henry Adams: American historian (1838–1918).

seat aboard their *Soyuz* spacecraft. [4]Then he prepared for the trip by spending eight months at a Russian cosmonaut training facility. [5]On April 28, 2001, Tito and other cosmonauts blasted off from a launch pad in Kazakhstan. [6]On April 30, the spacecraft docked with the International Space Station. [7]They spent five days aboard the station, where Tito spent most of his time gazing out the windows and taking photographs. [8]On May 6, the *Soyuz* capsule returned Tito and the rest of the crew back to Earth. Tito said he was happy he had achieved a life-long dream of visiting outer space.

Topic Sentence _____

5. [1]On the surface, effective listening might seem to require little more than an acute sense of hearing. [2]But, in fact, there's a big difference between hearing and listening. [3]*Hearing* occurs when sound waves travel through the air, enter your ears, and are transmitted by the auditory nerve to your brain. [4]As long as neither your brain nor your ears are impaired, hearing is involuntary. [5]It occurs spontaneously with little conscious effort on your part. [6]*Listening*, in contrast, is a voluntary act that includes attending to, understanding, and evaluating the words or sounds you hear. [7]If you sit through a lecture without making an effort to listen, there's a good chance that the speaker's words will become just so much background noise. (Flemming and Leet, *Becoming a Successful Student*, p. 93.)

Topic Sentence _____

6. [1]When we are extremely fearful or angry, our heartbeat speeds up, our pulse races, and our breathing rate tends to increase. [2]The body's metabolism accelerates, burning up sugar in the bloodstream and fats in the tissues at a faster rate. [3]The salivary glands become less active, making the mouth feel dry. [4]The sweat glands may overreact, producing a dripping forehead, clammy hands, and "cold sweat." [5]Finally, the pupils may enlarge, producing the wide-eyed look that is characteristic of both terror and rage. [6]In effect, strong emotions are not without consequences. [7]They bring about powerful changes in our bodies. (Rubin et al., *Psychology*, p. 370.)

Topic Sentence _____

7. [1]Every human body ages over time. [2]Scientists believe that the probable maximum human life span is about 150 years; the record of the oldest person to date is Shigechiyo Izumi (1865–1986) of Japan, who lived to be 120 years and 237 days. [3]There are two theories as to why all living things grow old and die. [4]The *free-radical theory* states that free radicals, certain chemicals produced as a by-product of biological activity, are particularly harmful to healthy cells. [5]As a person ages, free radicals gradually destroy cells until they can no longer function properly, causing the entire body (especially whole organ systems such as the kidneys or heart) to break down and die. [6]The *programmed senescence theory* suggests that the rate at which we age is predetermined, and that our genetic makeup controls the aging and death of the cells. [7]After enough of the cells die, the organs cease to function and death occurs. (Barnes-Svarney, ed., "Theories on Aging," *New York Public Library Science Desk Reference,* p. 161.)

Topic Sentence _____

8. [1]On May 28, 1934, Elzire Dionne gave birth to five daughters who became famous as the Dionne Quintuplets. [2]Their birth made immediate headlines and was celebrated as a medical and maternal miracle. [3]Unfortunately, the little girls' fame was their downfall; almost from the moment of their birth, they were exploited by everyone around them. [4]Their parents were poor and didn't know how to support their family, which already included six children. [5]Confused and desperate, they agreed to put their five daughters on display at the Chicago World's Fair. [6]For a brief moment, it seemed as if the girls were saved from a miserable fate when the family physician, Dr. Allan Roy Dafoe, stepped in and insisted the girls were too frail to be on exhibit. [7]But after Dafoe took control of the girls' lives, he made himself rich by displaying the quintuplets to tourists and collecting fees for product endorsements.

Topic Sentence _____

9. [1]George W. Bush is only the second man in history to follow in the footsteps of his father and serve as president of the United States. [2]The first was John Quincy Adams, America's sixth president and the son of second president John Adams. [3]As a matter of fact, the elder George Bush calls his son "Quincy." [4]George W. Bush and John Quincy Adams share other similarities, too. [5]Both men are their fathers' oldest sons. [6]Both men held public office before being elected president. [7]Adams was a U.S. senator and served as secretary of state, while Bush was governor of Texas. [8]Both men were in their fifties when they successfully ran for president. [9]Both men also achieved the presidency in a contested election because neither of them had won the popular vote. [10]Perhaps more than any other pair of presidents, George W. Bush and John Quincy Adams share a remarkable number of similarities.

Topic Sentence _____

10. ¹First Lady Edith Wilson has been called the "secret president," the "first woman president," and the "28ᵗʰ and a half president." ²In 1919, her husband, President Woodrow Wilson, was serving his second term in office. ³In September of that year, he suffered a near-fatal stroke, which left him partially paralyzed and nearly blind. ⁴The president's doctors told Edith that her husband would recover faster if he stayed in office rather than resigning. ⁵For more than six months, Edith concealed the seriousness of his condition by running the country for him. ⁶She read all of his documents and made decisions about which matters would be brought to his attention. ⁷When the president seemed too ill to concentrate, she made decisions for him and communicated those decisions to his staff. ⁸Wilson never fully recovered, and in 1921, at the end of his presidential term, Woodrow and Edith retired. ⁹In 1924, after living three more years in virtual seclusion, President Wilson died. ¹⁰Edith lived to be eighty-nine years old and died in 1961.

Topic Sentence _____

CHECK YOUR UNDERSTANDING

Define the terms *topic*, *main idea*, and *topic sentence*.

Topic: _____

Main idea: _____

_____

Topic sentence: _____

_____

The Function of Supporting Details

Once you've determined the main idea of a paragraph, you've identified the author's reason for writing the paragraph. However, paragraphs include more than a main idea. To clarify their main ideas and make them convincing, writers also include major and minor supporting details. The **major supporting details** are the examples, reasons, studies, statistics, facts, and figures that explain, develop, or prove an author's main idea or point. **Minor supporting details** further explain major details. They add an interesting fact, tell a story, or use repetition for emphasis.

Because topic sentences are general sentences that sum up or interpret a variety of events, facts, examples, or experiences, they are subject to misunderstanding. Writers, therefore, use supporting details to avoid being misinterpreted or misunderstood. Supporting details are the author's way of saying to readers, "I mean this, not that."

For an illustration of supporting details at work, look at the following sentence: "Most people who have survived near-fatal automobile accidents tend to behave in the same fashion." Given only this one sentence, could you be sure you understood the author's message? After all, that sentence could mean different things to different people. Perhaps survivors have nightmares or fears about their health. Maybe they are just very slow and careful drivers.

Look now at the following paragraph. Note how the addition of supporting details clarifies the author's meaning.

> Most people who have survived near-fatal automobile accidents tend to behave in the same fashion. They are fearful about driving even a mile or two over the speed limit and flatly refuse to go faster than the law allows. If they are not at the wheel, their terror increases. As passengers, they are extremely anxious and are prone to offering advice about how to take a curve or when to stop for a light.

In this instance, the supporting details illustrate the three types of behavior that the author has in mind. Those illustrations are the author's way of answering questions such as "What does 'behave in the same fashion' mean?"

Types of Supporting Details

Supporting details can range from reasons and examples to statistics and definitions. The form they take depends on the main idea they serve. Look, for example, at the following paragraph. Here the writer wants to convince readers that a book defending the right to be fat is very much worth reading.

> [1]Marilyn Wann's book *Fat! So?* deserves a large and appreciative audience, one that does not consist solely of those who are overweight. [2]For starters, Wann is refreshingly unembarrassed about being fat (she tips the scales at 270), and that takes courage in a culture as obsessed as ours is with being thin. [3]If anything, the author encourages her readers—in the chapter titled "You, Too,

Can Be Flabulous"—to embrace the word *fat* and use it in favorable contexts, such as "You're getting fat; you look great." [4]Still, despite her lively, and often humorous, style, Wann is good at describing the real misery society inflicts on fat people. [5]Her chapters on the suffering endured by overweight teenagers are particularly moving; and they make a strong case for the need to attack, and attack hard, the tendency to treat the overweight as second-class citizens. [6]The book is also filled with sound advice about healthy eating habits. [7]Clearly, the author is not encouraging her readers to go out and gorge themselves on pizza and beer. [8]What she is suggesting is that they eat right to get fit, rather than thin. [9]Insisting that some people can, because of heredity, never be anything but overweight, Wann argues that they should not suffer for the genetic hand they've been dealt. [10]On the contrary, they should learn how to flaunt* their excess poundage and make society accept them just as they are.

In this paragraph, the major details all give reasons why Marilyn Wann's book deserves a wide audience. The minor details, in turn, flesh out and emphasize the major ones. Note, too, that at least two of the minor details are as important as the major detail they develop. In sentence 6, the author suggests that Wann's book is good because it offers sound advice about healthy eating. But without the presence of the minor details that follow, it would be hard to understand how a book celebrating fat could also provide tips on healthy eating. Minor details in 7 and 8 help explain this seeming contradiction: Wann's advice focuses on eating to be fit rather than thin.

Minor Details Can Be Meaningful

The previous discussion of major and minor details working together raises a key point: Readers shouldn't be fooled by the labels *major* and *minor*. Sometimes minor details can be as meaningful as major ones, so you need to judge them in terms of what they contribute to the major details they modify. If a minor detail simply adds a personal note or provides repetition for emphasis, you don't need to think about it much, and you certainly don't need to include it in your notes. But if a major detail doesn't make much sense without the minor one that follows, then both details are equally important.

---

*flaunt: to show off.

CHECK YOUR UNDERSTANDING

Explain the difference between major and minor details.

_____

_____

EXERCISE 4

DIRECTIONS Identify major and minor details by writing the appropriate sentence numbers in the boxes of the accompanying diagram.

EXAMPLE [1]Twins can be either identical or fraternal. [2]Identical twins are formed from one fertilized egg that splits in two, resulting in two children of the same sex who look very much alike. [3]One-third of all twins born are identical. [4]Fraternal twins are formed from two different fertilized eggs; these twins can be of different sexes and look quite different from one another. [5]Two-thirds of all twins are fraternal.

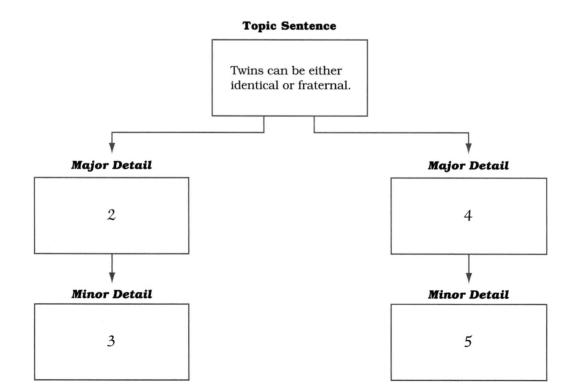

Topic Sentence

Twins can be either identical or fraternal.

Major Detail

2

Major Detail

4

Minor Detail

3

Minor Detail

5

EXPLANATION In this example, each major detail fleshes out the two terms introduced in the topic sentence, identical and fraternal. Each major detail is followed by a minor one that gives you an additional piece of information about the different kinds of twins. *Note:* Although this paragraph neatly balances major and minor details, this is not necessarily the case and major details may or may not be followed by minor ones. It's also possible for one major detail to be followed by two minor ones.

1. [1]Nightclub acts that use lions and tigers to entertain are a disgrace. [2]Making these animals learn tricks forces them to ignore their natural instincts. [3]Even worse, using lions and tigers for entertainment means that these proud creatures spend most of their lives in cages rather than roaming free in their natural habitat. [4]Club performances that feature lions and tigers are also bad because they are unsafe for both handlers and spectators. [5]These powerful beasts are fundamentally wild, and no amount of training can guarantee they will not suddenly turn and attack. [6]The horrific attack that took place on trainer Roy Horn of the duo Siegfried and Roy is a tragic illustration of that reality. [7]Horn had thirty years of training performing tigers, but all that experience did not prevent him from being attacked and severely injured by a tiger.

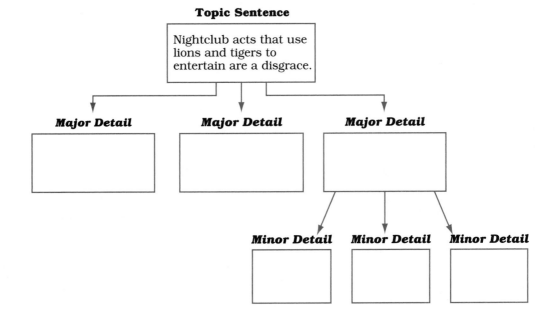

2. ¹Students who complete their first two years of higher education at community colleges reap definite benefits. ²Community colleges are less expensive. ³Courses usually cost only a fraction of what they do at four-year universities, allowing students and their parents to save thousands of dollars. ⁴A second benefit of community colleges is their location. ⁵They are generally close to students' homes, so they not only are convenient to access but also allow students to live at home instead of moving to a dorm or off-campus apartment. ⁶Yet another benefit is the more personalized instruction offered by community colleges. ⁷Classes tend to be smaller than those at universities, so students can get more attention and more help from their instructors.

Topic Sentence

Students who complete their first two years of higher education at community colleges reap definite benefits

Major Detail

Major Detail

Major Detail

Minor Detail

Minor Detail

Minor Detail

3. ¹According to the National Association for the Education of Young Children, media violence is having profound effects on our kids. ²Long-term viewing of media violence appears to desensitize children to the pain and suffering of others. ³It also seems to make children more aggressive. ⁴After they watch violent television programs, children often replicate the actions they have just seen on TV. ⁵Finally, media violence often makes young children more fearful of

the world around them. [6]They cannot distinguish between fantasy and reality, so watching violent TV shows makes them believe that the world is a scary place. (Source of information: ACT Against Violence, www.actagainstviolence.org/.)

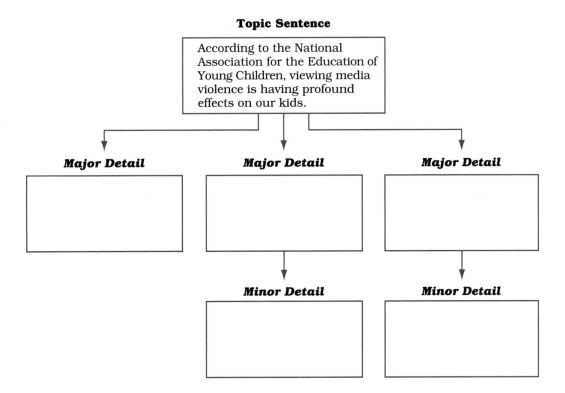

Topic Sentence

According to the National Association for the Education of Young Children, viewing media violence is having profound effects on our kids.

Major Detail

Major Detail

Major Detail

Minor Detail

Minor Detail

4. [1]When Hewlett-Packard decided to turn its instrumentation and measurement division into a separate company, there was a good deal of work to be done. [2]Among other things, new management had to be hired and shareholders had to be notified. [3]But the truly difficult task at hand was finding a name for the new company, which turned out to be a costly and complicated procedure. [4]First, Hewlett hired Landor Associates, the identity firm that had come up with the name for AT&T's spinoff company Lucent Technologies. [5]Then to get at precisely what image the new company was meant to project, Landor executives interviewed people at the highest levels of Hewlett management. [6]The goal of the interviews was to discover what the name of the new company was meant to reflect. [7]To help them in their quest for understanding, Landor interviewers would show Hewlett people pictures of things like ocean waves and chain-link fences and ask them, "Is this how you want to be, strong like

an unstoppable force of nature or strong yet capable of breaking?" [8]The use of interviews, pictures, and free association went on for four months until Hewlett settled on the name for its new company—"Agilent." [9]By that time Hewlett-Packard had spent over a million dollars, yet the search committee claimed to be delighted with the result: When the name Agilent was announced to top Hewlett executives, it got a standing ovation.

Topic Sentence

> But the truly difficult task at hand was finding a name for the new company, which turned out to be a costly and complicated procedure.

Major Detail

Major Detail

Major Detail

Major Detail

Minor Detail

Minor Detail

EXERCISE 5

DIRECTIONS Read each paragraph and write the number or numbers of the topic sentence in the first blank. Then answer the questions that follow by circling the correct response or filling in the blanks.

EXAMPLE [1]What makes an effective leader? [2]To be sure, no one characteristic or trait defines an effective leader. [3]It is true, however, that the most effective leaders hold group members to very high standards of performance. [4]Setting such standards increases productivity because people tend to live up to the expectations set for them by superiors. [5]This is called the *Pygmalion** effect, and it works in a subtle, almost unconscious way. [6]When a managerial leader believes that a group member will succeed, the manager communicates this belief without realizing that he or she is doing so. [7]Conversely, when a leader expects a group member to fail, that person will not usually disappoint the manager. [8]The manager's expectation of success or failure becomes a self-fulfilling prophecy. [9]The manager's perceptions contribute to the success or failure. (DuBrin, *Leadership*, p. 85.)

a. Topic sentence: _3_

b. The major details help answer what question or questions about the topic sentence? *Why do effective leaders set such high standards?*

c. *True or* (False:) Sentence 5 is a major supporting detail. Explain your answer. *This supporting detail further explains the previous one, making it a minor but far from unimportant detail.*

d. *True or* (False:) Sentence 9 is also a major supporting detail. Explain your answer. *The point made in sentence 9 was already clear from previous statements in the paragraph, so this supporting detail adds little more than repetition.*

EXPLANATION Sentence 3 is the only sentence that can effectively sum up the paragraph. Explanations for the *true* and *false* answers already appear in the blanks above.

1. [1]Despite its rapid spread, Islam is not a religion for those who are casual about regulations. [2]On the contrary, adhering to its rules takes effort and discipline. [3]One must rise before dawn to observe the first of five prayers required daily, none of which can take place

---

*Pygmalion: According to myth, Pygmalion, the king of Cyprus, carved and then fell in love with the statue of a woman who was transformed into a human being. The phrase *Pygmalion effect* reflects the myth's suggestion that wishing or believing something can make it happen.

without first ritually cleansing oneself. [4]Sleep, work, and recreational activities take second place to prayer. [5]Fasting for the month of Ramadan,* undertaking the pilgrimage to Mecca at least once in a lifetime, paying tax for relief of the Muslim poor, and accepting Islam's creed require a serious and energetic commitment. [6]On the whole, the vast majority of Muslims worldwide do observe those tenets.* (Adapted from Goodwin, *Price of Honor,* p. 29.)

a. Topic sentence: _____

b. The major details help answer what question or questions about the topic sentence?

_____

_____

c. *True* or *False:* Sentence 4 is a major supporting detail.

Explain your answer. _____

_____

d. *True* or *False:* Sentence 5 is also a major supporting detail.

Explain your answer. _____

_____

2. [1]The orchestra conductor Arturo Toscanini was born with a phenomenal memory that served him well throughout his career. [2]For example, Toscanini could remember every single note of every musical score he had ever studied. [3]Once, when he couldn't find a musical score for a performance, he simply wrote it down from memory. [4]When the score was finally found, it was clear that Toscanini had not made one single error. [5]When his eyesight failed him late in life, Toscanini conducted all of his concerts from memory. [6]Audiences agreed that his lack of sight did not in any way hinder the conductor's performance.

a. Topic sentence: _____

b. The major details help answer what question or questions about the topic sentence?

_____

_____

_____
*Ramadan: Muslim holy month.
*tenets: rules; principles.

c. *True* or *False:* Sentence 3 is a major detail.

Explain your answer. _____

d. *True* or *False:* Sentence 6 is a minor detail.

Explain your answer. _____

_____

3. [1]Those cuddly toys known as teddy bears seem to have been around forever. [2]But actually the first teddy bears came into being when President Theodore "Teddy" Roosevelt showed himself too much of a sportsman to shoot a staked bear cub. [3]In 1902 Roosevelt visited Mississippi to settle a border dispute, and his hosts organized a hunting expedition. [4]To make sure that the president would remain in a good mood, they staked a bear cub to the ground so that Roosevelt couldn't miss. [5]To his credit, Roosevelt declined the offer to shoot the bear. [6]When the incident was publicized, largely through political cartoons, a Russian candy store owner named Morris Mitchom made up a toy bear out of soft, fuzzy cloth and placed it in his shop window with a sign reading "Teddy's Bear." [7]The bear was a hit with passersby, and teddy bear mania spread rapidly throughout the country.

a. Topic sentence: _____

b. The major details help answer what questions or questions about the topic sentence?

_____

_____

c. *True* or *False:* Sentence 4 is a minor detail.

Explain your answer. _____

_____

d. *True* or *False:* Sentence 6 is a major detail.

Explain your answer. _____

_____

4. [1]Did you ever ask yourself just how much truth there is to the eerie legend of Count Dracula? [2]You may be surprised to discover that centuries ago there did exist a Prince Vlad, said to be the source of the Dracula legends. [3]Prince Vlad, however, did not spend his time seeking out fresh young victims; instead, he had disobedient members of the villages he ruled brought to his castle, where they would be executed before his eyes. [4]On one occasion, Vlad became furious

because some visiting Turkish diplomats failed to remove their turbans. [5]They meant no disobedience; it was simply not their custom to do so. [6]As punishment for this supposed insult, Vlad had the turbans nailed to their heads.

a. Topic sentence: _____

b. The major details help answer what question or questions about the topic sentence?

_____

_____

c. *True* or *False:* Sentence 4 is a minor detail.

Explain your answer. _____

_____

d. *True* or *False:* Sentence 5 is a major detail.

Explain your answer. _____

_____

5. [1]Many people don't know the difference between a patent and a trademark. [2]But there is a difference. [3]Usually granted for seventeen years, a patent protects both the name of a product and its method of manufacture. [4]In 1928, for example, Jacob Schick invented and then patented the electric razor in an effort to have complete control over his creation. [5]Similarly, between 1895 and 1912, no one but the Shredded Wheat company could make shredded wheat, because the company had the patent. [6]A trademark is a name, symbol, or other device that identifies a product and makes it memorable in the minds of consumers. [7]*Kleenex, Jell-O,* and *Sanka* are all examples of trademarks. [8]Aware of the power that trademarks possess, companies fight to protect them and do not allow anyone else to use one without permission. [9]Occasionally, however, a company gets careless and loses control of a trademark. [10]*Aspirin,* for example, is no longer considered a trademark, and any company can call a pain-reducing tablet an aspirin.

a. Topic sentence: _____

b. The major details help answer what question or questions about the topic sentence?

_____

_____

c. *True* or *False:* Sentence 3 is a minor detail.

Explain your answer. _____

_____

d. *True* or *False:* Sentence 5 is a major detail.

Explain your answer. _____

_____

 # Recognizing Patterns of Organization

Discovering the topic and the main idea of a paragraph will most definitely help you understand the author's message or meaning. But you can deepen and enhance that understanding by checking to see if the paragraph is organized according to one of the following patterns: (1) definition (2) classification, (3) time order, (4) comparison and contrast, or (5) cause and effect. Each of these patterns has specific characteristics, and knowing these characteristics can help you decide what to underline or what to include in your notes. As an additional bonus, your knowledge of paragraph patterns can help you formulate potential test questions. In other words, the ability to spot organizational patterns is a reading skill definitely worth having.

Pattern 1: Definition

Textbook authors are fully aware that their student readers need to master the vocabularies of various courses. Thus, they frequently employ the definition pattern of organization to make sure that students get the full meaning of a key term. Ninety percent of the time, the definition pattern begins with an explanation of the term. As you learned in Chapter 2, the term is usually highlighted in some way—boldface, italics, or colored ink—and it's followed by a detailed definition. Often, the author may also give a bit of the word's history, contrast it with a similar term, offer an example of the activity or behavior associated with the word, describe the conditions under which it comes into play, and/or define related terms.

Once they recognize the definition pattern, skillful readers know they have to make the paragraph's key characteristics stand out for future review. Look, for example, at the way the following definition paragraph has been underlined and annotated to make the central characteristics of the pattern as visible as possible.

TQ: What is product modification?

TQ: What conditions must be met for product modification to take place?

Product modification refers to changing one or more of a product's characteristics. For this approach to be effective, several conditions must be met. First,[1] the product must be modifiable. Second,[2] existing customers must be able to perceive that a modification has been made. Third,[3] the modification should make the product more consistent with customers' desires. (Pride et al., *Business*, p. 396.)

When you see an entire paragraph devoted to defining a key term, your best bet is to write a test question (TQ) that asks you to recall some aspect of the definition. As you can see, that's the focus of the test questions shown in the preceding marginal annotations.

Typical Topic Sentences

Topic sentences like the ones that follow are frequent clues to the definition pattern. This is particularly true if the word being defined appears at the beginning of the paragraph and is printed in boldface or italics.

---

1. Originating in Latin America, *Liberation Theology* is a Roman Catholic movement that stresses social and political action on behalf of the poor.

2. The **great man** theory of history assumes that special people are needed to change the world.

3. *Perestroika* (Russian for "restructuring") was a program of economic and political reform introduced by Soviet leader Mikhail Gorbachev in 1984.

4. In the early nineteenth century, the label *muckrakers* referred to journalists and artists intent on exposing political corruption and corporate wrongdoing.

5. The "Pygmalion effect" refers to the influence of expectations on performance.

Pattern 2: Classification

Particularly in business and science textbooks, authors are likely to outline a system of classification. Paragraphs devoted to classification start by explaining how some large group can be divided into smaller categories or subgroups. Then they identify and describe the specific characteristics of each subgroup. An example follows. Again, check out the underlining and annotations accompanying the paragraph.

Hippocrates classified people according to the four fluids in their body.

TQ: Explain Hippocrates' system of classification.

Like his contemporaries,* the <u>Greek physician Hippocrates believed</u> that the human <u>body consisted of four *humors*</u>, or <u>fluids: black bile, yellow bile, blood, and phlegm.</u> <u>Hippocrates' contribution</u> was to <u>classify human beings according</u> to the <u>predominant fluid</u> in their bodies. Persons with an <u>excess</u> of <u>black bile</u> were classified as ① *melancholic* and were presumed to be <u>depressed and pessimistic</u>. The ② *choleric,* possessing <u>excess yellow bile</u>, were considered <u>quick-tempered and irritable</u>. Persons with a <u>predominance of blood</u> were classified as ③ *sanguine.* They were usually <u>cheerful and optimistic</u>. The ④ *phlegmatic,* possessing <u>excess phlegm</u>, were thought to be <u>slow, unemotional</u>, and <u>uninvolved</u> with the world at large. While this classification <u>theory</u> has long since been <u>discarded</u>, the <u>terms used to describe personalities persist</u>.

As soon as you realize that an author is intent on outlining a system of classification, jot a test question like the one above in the margin.

Classification Topic Sentences

Topic sentences like those below are clues to the classification pattern. Note that some topic sentences name the categories while others identify only the number of groups to be described.

1. Stage actors claim that audiences fall into three distinct groups.
2. In his book *The Miracle Detective*, journalist Randall Sullivan divides the faithful into two groups, traditionalists and liberals.
3. Beginning in the nineteenth century, three distinct Jewish communities developed with divergent views on the importance of tradition: Orthodox, Reform, and Conservative.
4. There are five different kinds of listening.

*contemporaries: people born during the same time period.

Pattern 3: Time Order (Process and Sequence of Dates and Events)

The time order pattern frequently turns up in business, history, and science texts, where authors need to explain, step by step or event by event, how something works or developed over a period of time.

Process

When using the time order pattern to describe a process, writers list, according to their order in real time, the steps or stages necessary to explain how something functions or works. Here to illustrate is a time order pattern used to describe the digestion process.

Digestive system prepares food to be turned into energy.

TQ: Explain the process of digestion.

In the human body, the ⬚ digestive system ⬚ breaks down food so that it can be used for energy. As [1]food enters the mouth, chewing, along with enzymes in the saliva, break it down into small pieces. [2]Next the esophagus contracts and pushes the food into the stomach, where muscles, enzymes, and digestive acids turn the food into a thick liquid. That [3]liquid is emptied into the small intestine, where most of its nutrients are absorbed. [4]What remains travels to the large intestine, where water is removed from digested food and turned into waste. (Adapted from Barnes-Svarney, *The New York Public Library Science Desk Reference,* p. 166.)

If you recognize the process pattern, jot down a test question that asks you to remember the sequence of stages or steps in the process described. Not only is this a likely test question, but answering it is also a sure-fire means of review.

Clues to Time Order

Words like *steps, stages, phases, procedure,* and *process* are all signs that you are dealing with a process pattern. So too are the transitions in the following list.

Transitions That Identify a Sequence of Steps	
Afterward	In the final stage
At this point	In this stage
By the time	Next
Finally	Then
First, second, third	Toward the end

Time Order Topic Sentences

Sentences like these are typical of the process pattern:

---

1. Soil erosion can proceed at a rapid pace.
2. The bestowing of sainthood is an extremely complex process.
3. Energy can be converted from one form to another.
4. Storing information in long-term memory requires several steps.
5. The weathering of rocks takes place over an extended period of time.

Sequence of Dates and Events

Authors who write about history and government frequently use a sequence of dates and events to explain or argue their claims. In this form of the time order pattern, the supporting details present a series of dates and events listed according to the order in which they occurred. Here's an example.

TQ: What are the dates of the Mexican-American War?

TQ: What event helped encourage a war with Mexico?

TQ: What was the name of the treaty that ended the Mexican-American War?

The Democrat James Polk became president of the United States in ⟨1844⟩. From the very beginning of his presidency, Polk made it clear that he intended to expand the boundaries of the United States. In ⟨1846⟩, he ordered General Zachary Taylor to take troops into Mexican territory. On ⟨April 25⟩ of the same year, the Mexican military fired on Taylor's troops and war between the United States and Mexico began, even though Congress had not yet officially declared it. By ⟨1847⟩, U.S. troops had arrived in Mexico City and were claiming victory. (The opening phrase in the Marines' anthem—"From the Halls of Montezuma"—is a reference to the arrival of those troops in Mexico's capital.) In ⟨1848⟩, Mexico and the United States signed the Treaty of Guadalupe Hidalgo, which ceded a portion of Mexican land that today includes Arizona, Utah, Nevada, and New Mexico to the United States. Polk had his wish: He had expanded and redefined U.S. borders. But in an effort to assuage* the war's critics—and there were many who considered the war with Mexico unjust—the U.S. government paid the Mexican government $15 million.

---

*assuage: calm, soothe.

If you recognize a sequence of dates and events pattern in a paragraph, use your knowledge of the pattern to create test questions that focus on the significance of particular dates or the sequence of events that led up to some important happening or achievement.

Typical Topic Sentences

Numerous dates and events are obvious clues to this pattern. But so, too, are topic sentences like those you see here.

1. From 1753 to 1815, Native Americans cooperated, fought with, or tried to avoid the Spanish, French, British, and Anglo-Americans who intruded on their homelands. (Boyer et al., *Enduring Vision*, p. 168.)

2. British children's writer Frances Hodgson Burnett started her career in 1849 at the age of four by telling stories to her siblings; by the time she died in 1924 she had written fifty-two books and thirteen plays.

3. For twenty years, between 1776 and 1796, the Anglo-American revolutionary Thomas Paine was intensely productive as both writer and theorist.

4. In the sixteenth and seventeenth centuries, Calvinist Protestants tried to purify English religion and society.

5. The young Latina singer Selena had a brief but enormously influential career.

Common Transitions

The following transitions are additional clues to the dates and events pattern.

Time Order Transitions That Accompany Dates and Events

After	From ____ to ____
At that point	In ____
A year later	In the years
Before	In the following years
Between the years ____ and ____	In the years that followed
During the years	Previously
Finally	Then
Following	

Pattern 4: Comparison and Contrast

In all kinds of textbooks, authors are likely to compare (discuss similarities) and contrast (cite differences). Sometimes, in fact, writers devote an entire chapter section to pointing out the similarities and differences between two topics, but more often the comparison and contrast pattern is confined to a single paragraph. Here is an example.

TQ: Explain the difference between assertive and aggressive behavior. Give examples for each type.

My Uncle Ralph always keeps cool.

My ex-wife is a good example.

Assertive behavior involves standing up for your rights and expressing your thoughts and feelings in a direct, appropriate way that does not violate the rights of others. It is a matter of getting the other person to understand your viewpoint. People who exhibit assertive behavior skills are able to handle conflict situations with ease and assurance while maintaining good interpersonal relations. In contrast, aggressive behavior involves expressing your thoughts and feelings and defending your rights in a way that openly violates the rights of others. Those exhibiting aggressive behavior seem to believe that the rights of others must be subservient to theirs. Thus they have a difficult time maintaining good interpersonal relations. They are likely to interrupt, talk fast, ignore others, and use sarcasm or other forms of verbal abuse to maintain control. (Adapted from Reece and Brandt, *Effective Human Relations in Organizations,* pp. 350–353.)

A paragraph like this one with its two topics—assertive behavior and aggressive behavior—and its emphasis on the difference between them has comparison and contrast written all over it. It just about cries out for you to predict a test question that asks for a description of how the two topics are similar or different.

Typical Topic Sentences

Sentences like the ones that follow are clues to the comparison and contrast pattern. Note the consistent presence of two topics.

1. Spartan society was very different from Athenian society.

2. In the days of the Wild West, the life of a cowboy was not all that different from that of a cowgirl, as the life of Calamity Jane well illustrates.

3. Although Carl Jung began as a disciple of Sigmund Freud, the two men eventually diverged in their thinking.

4. Like his Persian predecessor, philosopher and physician Ibn Sina (980–1037), the Spanish-Arab philosopher Ibn Rushd (1126–1198) believed that the universe is eternal and the individual mortal.

5. Unlike former Secretary of State Henry Kissinger, Secretary of State Colin Powell (2000–2004) did not have much influence in the administration.

Common Transitions

In addition to topic sentences like those above, the following transitions are also clues to the comparison and contrast pattern.

Transitions That Signal Similarity

Along the same lines	Just as
By the same token	Just like
In like manner	Likewise
In much the same vein	Similarly
In the same manner	

Transitions That Signal Difference

And yet	In opposition	On the one hand
But	In reality	On the other hand
Conversely	Nevertheless	Still
Despite that fact	Nonetheless	Unfortunately
However	On the contrary	Whereas
In contrast		

Pattern 5: Cause and Effect

Because connecting cause to effect is so basic to our thinking, you will encounter cause and effect paragraphs in every type of textbook. No matter what the subject matter, authors need to explain how one event (the cause) produced another event (the effect).

Ultraviolet radiation is harmful

TQ: What are some of the effects of ultraviolet radiation?

Effects

The ultraviolet radiation from the sun that reaches the Earth's surface is a health threat. At the very least, it causes [1]aging and wrinkling of the skin. At the very worst, it is responsible for [2]cataracts, [3]sunburn, [4]snowblindness, and [5]skin cancer, which claims around 15,000 lives each year in the United States alone. Exposure to UV radiation also [6]suppresses the immune system, enabling cancers to become established and grow. In addition, [7]radiation slows plant growth, [8]delays seed germination, and [9]interferes with photosynthesis.* (Adapted from Kaufman and Franz, *Biosphere 2000,* p. 266.)

Cause and effect paragraphs are a likely source of test questions. When you encounter such paragraphs in your reading, make sure you can easily identify both cause (or causes) and effect (or effects). Then turn that information into a question like the one that appears in the margin above.

Typical Topic Sentences

Topic sentences like these are typical of the cause and effect pattern.

> **1.** Thanks to the newly invented telescope, Galileo Galilei (1564–1642) was able to detect lunar mountains.
>
> **2.** Teacher and writer Paolo Friere (1921–1997) knew that poverty can create a "culture of silence"—a sense that talking about one's misery is useless.
>
> **3.** Liberation Theology has spread beyond Catholicism and inspired other social-change movements throughout the world.
>
> **4.** The social and political program known as *perestroika* stemmed from Mikhail Gorbachev's recognition that socialism in the Soviet Union had been an economic and political disaster.
>
> **5.** The "great man" theory of history resulted from historians' attempt to explain the French Revolution and the rise of Napoleon Bonaparte.

*photosynthesis: process by which plants use sunlight to create food.

Common Transitions and Verbs

In addition to topic sentences like those listed above, the following transitions and verbs frequently make their way into paragraphs employing the cause and effect pattern.

Transitions That Signal Cause and Effect	
As a result	In reaction
Consequently	In response
Hence	Therefore
In the aftermath	Thus

Verbs That Connect Cause and Effect	
brings about	leads to
causes	produces
creates	results in
engenders	sets off
evokes	stems
fosters	stimulates
generates	triggers
initiates	

Mixed Patterns

As you might expect, writers don't necessarily restrict themselves to a single paragraph pattern. If their material calls for it, they combine patterns. When you recognize two or more patterns in a paragraph or reading, see if you can generate a test question for each pattern. For an illustration, see the annotations that follow.

TQ: Define the term "scientific method."

TQ: Explain each step in the scientific method.

Examples of research questions.

Example of hypothesis.

All <u>research studies</u> of human development <u>follow some form of</u> scientific method, or <u>set of procedures</u> designed to <u>ensure objective observations</u> and <u>interpretations</u> of observations. Even though it is not always possible to follow these procedures perfectly, they form an ideal to which psychological research tends to aspire (Cherry, 1995; Levine & Parkinson, 1994). The procedures or steps in the scientific method are as follows: (1) *Formulating research questions.* Sometimes these questions refer to previous studies, such as when a developmental psychologist asks, "Are Professor Deepthought's studies of thinking consistent with studies from less developed countries?" Other times they refer to issues important to society, such as "Does preschool education make children more socially skilled later in childhood?" (2) *Stating questions as hypotheses.* A hypothesis is a statement that expresses a research question precisely. In making a hypothesis out of the preschool education question above, a psychologist would further define the terms *preschool education* and *socially skilled:* "Do children in day care learn to share toys with other children at an earlier age than children cared for at home?" (3) *Testing the hypothesis.* Having phrased a research question as a hypothesis, researchers can conduct an actual study of it. The choice of study method usually depends on convenience, ethics, and scientific appropriateness. (Seifert and Hoffnung, *Child and Adolescent Development*, pp. 16–17.)

In this paragraph, the authors combine two patterns—definition and time order (process)—to make their point. What are two likely test questions based on this passage? Well, the two shown in the margin above are definite possibilities.

Common Combinations

It is not unusual for writers to combine definition and time order (process) patterns. These two patterns often work together because an author needs to define the key terms essential to understanding a particular process or sequence of steps. Some of the other patterns likely to be combined are time order (process) with cause and effect, classification with comparison and contrast, and definition with classification. All of which suggests one simple tip: If you recognize one member of a common combination, you should check for its likely companion.

Common Combinations

Time Order (Process) with Cause and Effect and/or Definition

Classification with Comparison and Contrast

Time Order (Sequence of Dates and Events) with Cause and Effect

---

EXERCISE 6

DIRECTIONS Circle the appropriate letter or letters to identify the organizational pattern or patterns used in each paragraph.

1. The ethnic and racial classifications differed in the 1990 and 2000 U.S. Census questionnaires. In 1990, Americans were asked to identify themselves as one of two ethnic categories. One category was Hispanic Origin; the other was Not of Hispanic Origin. In the 2000 census, there were again just two ethnic categories, but the categories were slightly expanded. The first category was Hispanic or Latino, and the second was Not Hispanic or Latino. The racial classifications underwent a more significant change. In 1990, Americans were asked to identify themselves as belonging to one of five different racial categories: American Indian or Alaska Native, Asian or Pacific Islander, Black, White, or Some Other Race. The 2000 census expanded and reorganized this classification to include six categories: American Indian or Alaska Native, Asian, Black or African American, Native Hawaiian or Other Pacific Islander, White, or Some Other Race. Furthermore, respondents were permitted to select more than one category if they self-identified with two or more different races.

Patterns a. definition

b. classification

c. time order (process)

d. time order (sequence of dates and events)

e. comparison and contrast

f. cause and effect

2. Economists have classified resources into three general categories: land, labor, and capital. **Land** includes all natural resources, such as minerals, timber, and water, as well as the land itself. **Labor** refers to the physical and intellectual services of people and includes the training, education, and abilities of the individuals in a society. **Capital** refers to products such as machinery and buildings that are used to produce other goods and services. You will often hear the term *capital* used to describe the financial backing for some project to finance some business. Economists refer to funds used to purchase capital as **financial capital.** (Boyes and Melvin, *Fundamentals of Economics,* p. 4.)

Patterns a. definition

b. classification

c. time order (process)

d. time order (sequence of dates and events)

e. comparison and contrast

f. cause and effect

3. On April 26, 1986, the worst accident in the history of nuclear power took place at the Chernobyl plant about 110 km north of Kiev in the Ukraine. At Chernobyl, the uranium was contained in fuel rods surrounded by graphite bricks, which served to moderate the nuclear reaction. (In the United States, commercial generating plants do not use graphite and have a containment dome.) The accident occurred when engineers turned off most of the reactor's automatic safety and warning systems to keep them from interfering with an unauthorized safety experiment. At this point, cooling water was one of the safety systems turned off. Unfortunately, the remaining water in the reactor then turned to steam, and the steam reacted with the nuclear fuel and the graphite bricks. An explosive mixture of gases formed and ignited. The reactor was destroyed, the roof blew off the building, and the graphite bricks caught fire. Soviet officials claimed the fire was extinguished on April 29. According to Soviet reports, 500 people were hospitalized and the acknowledged death count stood at 31. Incidences of thyroid cancer, leukemia, and other radiation-related illnesses are high among people who were living near the power plant. More ominously, the radioactive particles produced by the explosion were dispersed all over the planet by the natural circulation of air. It will be years before all of the effects of the Chernobyl disaster can be assessed. (Adapted from Sherman et al., *Basic Concepts of Chemistry,* p. 484.)

Patterns a. definition

           b. classification

           c. time order (process)

           d. time order (sequence of dates and events)

           e. comparison and contrast

           f. cause and effect

4. Viral marketing* is a highly successful sales technique that sold $7.7 billion of merchandise in 1999. Using this strategy, companies actually get their customers to sell products via word-of-mouth advertising. In exchange for products, a current customer agrees to host a home party. This host or hostess then invites his or her friends, relatives, neighbors, and coworkers to come to the party to see the products, watch demonstrations, and tell stories about how the products are or can be used. In this friendly, fun, and sociable atmosphere, people are eager to buy and sell the products to one another. For instance, viral marketing has been used to sell millions of dollars of Tupperware plastic containers, Pampered Chef kitchenware, and Longaberger baskets.

Patterns a. definition

           b. classification

           c. time order (process)

           d. time order (sequence of dates and events)

           e. comparison and contrast

           f. cause and effect

5. During the process of labor, the mother's uterus contracts rhythmically and automatically to force the baby downward through the vaginal canal. The contractions occur in relatively predictable stages. The **first stage of labor** usually begins with relatively mild and irregular contractions of the uterus. As contractions become stronger and more regular, the *cervix* (the opening of the uterus) dilates, or widens, enough for the baby's head to fit through. Toward the end of this stage, which may take from eight to twenty-four hours for a first-time mother, a period of **transition** begins. The cervix nears full dilation, contractions become more rapid, and the baby's head begins to move into the birth canal. Although this period generally lasts for only a few minutes, it can be extremely painful because of the increasing pressure of the contractions. The

---

*Yes, the term does come from the expression "It spreads like a virus," which suggests speed.

second stage of labor includes complete dilation of the cervix to the actual birth. It usually lasts between one and one-and-one-half hours. During the **third stage of labor,** which lasts only a few minutes, the afterbirth (the placenta and umbilical cord) is expelled. (Adapted from Seifert and Hoffnung, *Childhood and Adolescent Development,* pp. 131–132.)

Patterns   a. definition

            b. classification

            c. time order (process)

            d. time order (sequence of dates and events)

            e. comparison and contrast

            f. cause and effect

EXERCISE 7

DIRECTIONS Circle the appropriate letter or letters to identify the organizational pattern or patterns used in each paragraph. Then circle the letter of the one test question you would *not* be likely to predict, based on the paragraph.

1. Two small lakes in a remote part of Cameroon, a small country in central Africa, made international news in the mid-1980s when deadly clouds of carbon dioxide (CO_2) gas from deep beneath the surface of the lakes escaped into the surrounding atmosphere, killing animal and human populations far downwind. The first gas discharge, which occurred at Lake Monoun in 1984, asphyxiated* thirty-seven people. The second, which occurred at Lake Nyos in 1986, released a highly concentrated cloud of CO_2 that killed more than 1700 people. The two events have similarities other than location: Both occurred at night during the rainy season; both involved volcanic crater lakes; and both are likely to recur unless there is some type of technologic intervention.*

Patterns   a. definition

            b. classification

            c. time order (process)

            d. time order (sequence of dates and events)

            e. comparison and contrast

            f. cause and effect

---

*asphyxiated: killed by loss of air.
*intervention: interference.

Test Questions a. What caused the disasters at Lake Monoun and Lake Nyos?

    b. In what ways were the disasters at Lake Monoun and Lake Nyos similar?

    c. How did the people of Cameroon react to the Lake Monoun and Lake Nyos disasters?

2. In 1862 Congress passed the **Homestead Act.** This measure offered 160 acres of land free to any American citizen who was a family head and over twenty-one. The only conditions were that the settler live on the land for five years and make improvements to it. In the well-watered East, 160 acres was a sizable farm. Yet in the semi-arid West, it was barely enough to support a family. To prosper, a farmer needed at least twice that amount. Despite these risks, the Homestead Act produced an explosion of settlement. Within a half century after the passage, all western territories had gained enough settlers—at least 60,000—to become states. As a result of the Homestead Act, most western areas experienced enormous population growth. (DiBacco et al., *History of the United States*, p. 315.)

Patterns a. definition

    b. classification

    c. time order (process)

    d. time order (sequence of dates and events)

    e. comparison and contrast

    f. cause and effect

Test Questions a. In what year did Congress pass the Homestead Act?

    b. What was the Homestead Act and what effect did it have?

    c. Explain why the Homestead Act was considered a failure.

3. A **tsunami** is a very long ocean wave that is generated by a sudden displacement of the sea floor. The term is derived from a Japanese word meaning "harbor wave." Tsunamis are sometimes referred to as **seismic sea waves** because submarine and near-coast earthquakes are their primary cause. They are also popularly called "tidal waves," but this is a misnomer;* tsunamis have nothing to do with tides. Tsunamis can occur with little or no warning, bringing death and massive destruction to coastal communities. (Murck et al., *Environmental Geology*, p. 131.)

Patterns a. definition

    b. classification

———————
*misnomer: inappropriate name.

    c. time order (process)

    d. time order (sequence of dates and events)

    e. comparison and contrast

    f. cause and effect

Test Questions a. Tsunamis are caused by _____.

    b. Describe how a tsunami affects ocean life.

    c. What is the meaning of the word *tsunami* and what is its origin?

4. Watergate,* the scandal that rocked the nation, began on June 17, 1972, when five men were caught trying to burglarize the offices of the Democratic National Committee. The arrest of the five led to an investigation that uncovered a White House plan of systematic espionage* against political opponents. Deeply involved in that plan were the two top aides to President Richard Nixon, John Erlichman and H. R. Haldeman. On April 30, 1973, Attorney General Elliot Richardson appointed a special prosecutor, Harvard Law School professor Archibald Cox, to conduct a full-scale investigation of the break-in at the Watergate Hotel. On May 20, 1973, the Senate Committee on Presidential Activities opened hearings, and on July 16 White House aide Alexander Butterfield told the committee that President Nixon had taped all of the conversations that occurred in his office. However, Nixon refused to turn the tapes over to the investigating committee, and on October 20 he ordered the dismissal of prosecutor Cox. After a storm of public protest, Nixon agreed to turn over the tapes in June of 1974. Once members of the committee had examined the tapes, they discovered that eighteen-and-one-half minutes had been mysteriously erased. By July 30, the House Judiciary Committee had approved three articles of impeachment. Rather than face almost certain disgrace, Richard Milhous Nixon resigned on August 9, 1974.

Patterns a. definition

    b. classification

    c. time order (process)

    d. time order (sequence of dates and events)

    e. comparison and contrast

    f. cause and effect

---

*The Watergate, the origin of the scandal's name, is a hotel-apartment-office complex in Washington, D.C., where the DNC's offices were located.
*espionage: spying.

Test Questions a. What was the public's response to the resignation of Richard Nixon?

b. Outline the chain of events that began with the break-in at the Watergate and ended with the resignation of Richard Nixon.

c. How did the scandal known as Watergate affect the U.S. government?

5. Manners and morals are terms that overlap, sometimes confusingly, but here I am using the two words in senses that are easier to distinguish. *Manners* would be the standards of conduct that prevail in a group, large or small, and hence they would change from group to group and year to year. *Morals* would be defined as the standards that determine the relations of individuals with other individuals, one with one—a child with each of its parents, a husband with his wife, a rich man with a poor man (not *the* rich with *the* poor)—and also the relations of any man with himself, his destiny, and his God. They are answers found by individuals to the old problems of faith, hope, charity or love, art, duty, submission to one's fate . . . and hence they are relatively universal; they can be illustrated from the lives of any individuals, in any place, at any time since the beginning of time. (Cowley, *New England Writers and Writing*, p. 238.)

Patterns a. definition

b. classification

c. time order (process)

d. time order (sequence of dates and events)

e. comparison and contrast

f. cause and effect

Test Questions a. How does Cowley apply the distinction between manners and morals to the work of Nathaniel Hawthorne?

b. According to Cowley, morals are _____.

c. Explain the difference between manners and morals.

EXERCISE 8

DIRECTIONS Circle the appropriate letter or letters to identify the organizational pattern or patterns used in each paragraph.

1. "Cloud seeding" is a process used by several western state governments and private businesses, such as ski resorts, to increase the amount of rainfall or snow over a certain area. First, meteorologists

use radar, satellites, and weather stations to track storm fronts. Then they measure a storm's clouds for temperature, wind, and composition. When the meteorologists determine that conditions are right, pilots are sent to "seed" the clouds with dry ice (frozen carbon dioxide). An aircraft flies above the clouds and dry ice pellets are dropped directly into them. Almost immediately, the dry ice begins attracting the clouds' moisture, which freezes to the dry ice's crystalline structure. Finally, precipitation drops from the clouds to the earth in the form of rain or snow. (Source of information: North Dakota State Water Commission Atmospheric Resource Board, "Summer Cloud Modification," 1997; www.swc.state.nd.us/arb/graphics/cloudmod.pdf.)

a. definition

b. classification

c. time order (process)

d. time order (sequence of dates and events)

e. comparison and contrast

f. cause and effect

2. More than thirty years after its birth, breakdancing is still alive and well. In 1969, breakdancing began when singer James Brown's performance of the song "Get on the Good Foot" encouraged energetic, athletic dance moves. Throughout the 1970s, the new style continued to develop as African-American and Hispanic young people incorporated movements from the martial arts, gymnastics, and acrobatics into their dancing. In the late 1970s, breakdancing was a feature of urban block parties in the Bronx, New York. During this time, a famous group of talented young performers known as Rock Steady Crew added amazingly difficult moves, including the "windmill" from the Chinese martial arts and the "flare" from men's gymnastics. In the 1980s, films like *Beat Street, Breakin'*, and *Flashdance* led to breakdancing's entry into mainstream popular culture. The media lost interest in the craze by the late 1980s. As a result during the 1990s, much of America assumed that it was a fad of the past. In the late twentieth and early twenty-first centuries, though, breakdancers began to reappear in television commercials, music videos, and competitions, with moves even more powerful and complex than before. Now a new generation of young breakdancers is flipping, spinning, and kicking to the beat. (Source of information: Tonya Jameson, "Breaking Out," *The Charlotte Observer*, July 27, 2003, pp. 1H, 8H.)

a. definition

b. classification

    c. time order (process)

    d. time order (sequence of dates and events)

    e. comparison and contrast

    f. cause and effect

3. Social drinking differs significantly from alcoholism. Social drinkers usually drink in moderation and can limit the amount of alcohol they consume. Alcoholics, conversely, drink ever-increasing amounts. Often they do not stop until they pass out. Social drinkers sip drinks, while alcoholics gulp them. Social drinkers drink to have more fun at social gatherings, while alcoholics will also drink alone, often to relieve stress or avoid confronting problems. Social drinkers don't usually think or talk about drinking; alcoholics, however, are preoccupied with how and when they will drink again. Finally, social drinkers do not experience physical, psychological, or job-related problems caused by their drinking. Alcoholics, in contrast, often let drinking damage their health, harm their relationships with others, and destroy their careers. (Source of information: Bernstein et al., *Psychology*, 6th ed., p. 597.)

    a. definition

    b. classification

    c. time order (process)

    d. time order (sequence of dates and events)

    e. comparison and contrast

    f. cause and effect

4. There are four major kinds of exercise, and each one offers different benefits to the body. The first type of exercise includes those that are *aerobic*. Aerobic means "with oxygen"; this kind of exercise—activities like jogging, walking, bicycling, and swimming—requires the lungs and heart to provide a steady supply of oxygen. As a result, these exercises strengthen the cardiovascular system, which in turn lowers the risk of heart disease. Aerobic exercise also helps reduce body fat and can relieve stress and feelings of depression. The second type of exercise is *anaerobic*, meaning "without oxygen." The exercises in this group draw on energy already stored in the body's muscles, so engaging in them does not require additional oxygen. Anaerobic activities, such as sprinting and lifting heavy weights, require short bursts of power that improve speed and muscle strength, so they tend to boost athletic performance. Lifting or resisting the force of lighter weights falls into the third category of exercise, *strength training*. Exercises in this category include working out on weight machines or performing calisthenics like push-ups and sit-ups to tone and strengthen muscles. The final type, *flexibility exercise*, lengthens the muscles and increases the range of motion. This category includes exercises like yoga and Pilates, both of which improve posture, maintain mobility, prevent injury, and encourage mental and physical relaxation. (Source of information: Aetna InteliHealth, Inc., "Types of Exercise," www. intelihealth.com/IH/ihtIH/WSIHW000/325/8914/36127.html.)

a. definition

b. classification

c. time order (process)

d. time order (sequence of dates and events)

e. comparison and contrast

f. cause and effect

5. According to experts, if you want to gauge how healthy the economy is, find out how much lipstick is being sold. Economists have discovered that lipstick sales go up when the economy is bad and down when the economy is good. Why? When the economy is good and women feel confident, they tend to indulge by purchasing more expensive items, such as shoes and spa treatments. When the economy is poor, they treat themselves with less expensive perks, such as a new shade of lipstick. In 2000, for example, when the economy was still booming, lipstick sales totaled $600 million. During 2001, while the economy grew steadily worse, lipstick sales rose 7.5 percent, to $647 million. At the beginning of 2002, sales peaked at about $700 million. Throughout 2003, as the economy improved, lipstick sales dropped by 3 percent. Although this news was not good for cosmetic companies, it indicated that female consumers were feeling better about spending their money on more expensive items. (Source of information: Paul J. Lim, "Here's How to Read the Tea Leaves Like Alan Greenspan," *U.S. News & World Report,* January 12, 2004, p. 34.)

a. definition

b. classification

c. time order (process)

d. time order (sequence of dates and events)

e. comparison and contrast

f. cause and effect

EXERCISE 9

DIRECTIONS Identify and circle all the transitions in each paragraph. Then identify the pattern suggested by those transitions.

1. You can save the life of a choking victim by performing the Heimlich maneuver. If a person suddenly cannot breathe, cough, or speak, the person's airway is probably blocked by something that needs to be removed. To perform the Heimlich maneuver, stand behind the victim and make a fist with one hand. Then reach your arms around the victim from behind. Place your fist against the person's belly just above the bellybutton and below the rib cage. Next, cover your fist with your other hand and press into the person's belly with a quick, upward thrust. If the object that was in the person's throat does not come flying out of his or her mouth, perform another thrust. Repeat thrusts over and over until you dislodge the object. At the same time, yell for help and get someone to call 911.

   Organizational pattern: _____

2. Although Judaism and Christianity share some similarities, there are several important differences between the two religions. Christians view God as a trinity made up of three parts: God the Father, God the Son, and God the Holy Spirit. On the contrary, Judaism's followers believe that such a division is impossible, so they worship one, unified God. The religions also differ in their beliefs about Jesus. Christians contend that Jesus was the Son of God and, therefore, divine. Jews believe that, although Jesus was a wise, ethical teacher, he was human and not divine. These two faiths differ, too, in their ideas about the nature of human beings. Those who follow the Christian faith believe that all people are born sinful and that the only way to achieve salvation is to accept Jesus' sacrificial death. In contrast, those who follow Judaism reject the idea of "original sin"; they believe that humans are not born good or bad. This faith stresses moral, ethical living as the path to God's salvation. (Source of information: "The Differences Between Judaism and Christianity," www.convert.org/differ.htm.)

   Organizational pattern: _____

3. Historians have rightly called the era spanning the early fifteenth century to the early sixteenth century the "Age of Discovery" or the "Age of Exploration." In 1419, Portugal's Prince Henry the

Navigator* began funding the efforts of mapmakers, shipbuilders, and instrument makers, and by the mid-1400s, Portuguese sailors were traveling down the West African coast. In the 1490s, explorer Vasco da Gama* sailed around Africa's Cape of Good Hope and as far as the Indian Ocean. For the next twenty-five years, Portugal invested in sending thousands of sailors to sea in an effort to establish trading outposts from West Africa to China. By 1500, the Portuguese had become the first Europeans to reach Brazil. Around the same time, inspired by Portugal's success, the Spanish began aggressively exploring new lands with the express purpose of conquest and colonization. Between 1492 and 1504, Christopher Columbus, financed by the Spanish king and queen, became the first European to reach the Bahamas along with several other Caribbean islands and Central America. In 1519, Ferdinand Magellan left Spain to claim undiscovered lands for the Spanish crown. He also located and traveled around the tip of South America to the Pacific Ocean. Although Magellan was killed in the Philippines in 1521, the following year his ship became the first to circumnavigate the globe. From 1519 to 1531, Spaniards Hernando Cortés and Francisco Pizarro explored Central and South America, conquering the Aztec and Incan civilizations to claim the lands as Spain's. (Source of information: Steven Kries, "Lecture 2: The Age of Discovery," *The History Guide*, April 15, 2003, www.historyguide.org/earlymod/lecture2c.html.)

Organizational pattern: _____

4. Many industrial processes, like those involving the burning of coal, release mercury into the air. The mercury, a dangerous pollutant, then falls directly onto waterways or is washed by rain from the land into the water. Bacteria in the water chemically alter mercury so that it becomes highly toxic. As a result, the fish—especially shark, swordfish, and mackerel—become contaminated too. Catching and eating mercury-poisoned fish has, consequently, become the primary cause of mercury exposure in the United States. Studies have shown that mercury can negatively affect the developing brain of a fetus and can lead to impairment of an infant's motor skills or mental abilities. Therefore, public health researchers advise pregnant women to limit their intake of fish to avoid the dangers of mercury. (Sources of information: Charles Lee, "EPA Report

---

*Prince Henry the Navigator (1394–1460): A nobleman of English, French, and Spanish ancestry, Prince Henry sponsored voyages of exploration in an effort to serve his king.
*Vasco da Gama (1460–1524): Portuguese explorer who found a route from Portugal to the East.

Analyzes Child Health Problems," *The Daily Californian,* March 5, 2003, www.dailycal.org/article.php?id=11150; U.S. Environmental Protection Agency, "EPA National Advice on Mercury in Freshwater Fish for Women Who Are or May Become Pregnant, Nursing Mothers, and Young Children," November 18, 2003, www.epa.gov/waterscience/fishadvice/advice.html.)

Organizational pattern: _____

5. Chimpanzees are remarkably similar to humans. For example, the physical proportions for the body parts of both humans and chimpanzees are relatively the same. Both species also have similar hands, feet, legs, and facial features. In fact, the DNA of humans and chimpanzees is 98.4 percent identical. In addition to these physical similarities, chimpanzee societies parallel human ones in a variety of ways. Human beings establish political systems and fight each other. Likewise, groups of chimpanzees form hierarchies with high-ranking and low-ranking chimps, and they too engage in warfare against other groups. Moreover, observation of chimps in the wild has indicated that chimpanzees experience and display humanlike emotions. Humans grieve for lost loved ones, and chimps appear to do the same. In one case, a healthy young chimp seemed to fall into a severe depression after his mother's death, stopped eating, and died. Research on the brain suggests that emotions like grief arise from ancient parts of the brain that are found in both species. (Source of information: "Are Chimpanzees Capable of Understanding and Recognizing Emotions?" www.whozoo.org/AnlifeSS2001/serishoo/Are%20Chimpanzees%20Capable%20of.htm.)

Organizational pattern: _____

CHECK YOUR UNDERSTANDING

Name and describe each of the patterns introduced on pages 121–130.

1. _____.

2. _____.

3. _____.

4. _____.

5. _____.

■ DIGGING DEEPER

LOOKING AHEAD The paragraph on page 125 suggests that U.S. President James Polk encouraged a war with Mexico in an effort to expand U.S. boundaries. What's the first tip-off that the authors of the following reading seem to agree wholeheartedly with this point of view?

MR. POLK'S WAR

1   In early 1846, President James K. Polk ordered American troops under "Old Rough and Ready," General Zachary Taylor, to march south into Mexico and defend the contested border of the Rio Grande across from the town of Matamoros. Polk especially desired California as the prize in his expansionist strategy, and to that end he attempted to buy from the angry Mexicans a huge tract of land extending to the Pacific. When the effort failed, Polk waited for war. Negotiations between troops on the Rio Grande were awkwardly conducted in French because no American officer spoke Spanish and no Mexican spoke English. After a three-week standoff, the tense situation came to a head. On April 24, 1846, Mexican cavalry ambushed a U.S. cavalry unit on the north side of the river; eleven Americans were killed and sixty-three taken captive. On April 26 Taylor sent a dispatch overland to Washington, D.C., which took two weeks to arrive, announcing: "Hostilities may now be considered as commenced."

2   Polk now drafted a message to Congress: Mexico had "passed the boundary of the United States, had invaded our territory and shed American blood on American soil." In the bill accompanying the war message, Polk deceptively declared that "war exists by the act of Mexico itself" and summoned the nation to arms. Two days later, on May 13, the House recognized a state of war with Mexico by a vote of 174 to 14, and the Senate by 40 to 2, with numerous abstentions.* Some antislavery Whigs* had tried to oppose the war but were barely allowed to gain the floor of Congress to speak. Since Polk withheld key facts, the full reality of what had happened on the distant Rio Grande was not known. But the theory and practice of Manifest Destiny had launched the United States into its first war on foreign territory.

---

*abstentions: refusals to vote.
*Whigs: A nineteenth-century political group formed to oppose the Democratic party, the Whigs favored a loose interpretation of the Constitution.

3   The war spawned an outpouring of poetry, song, drama, travel literature, and lithographs that captured the popular imagination and glorified the war. New lyrics to the tune "Yankee Doodle" proclaimed: "They attacked our men upon our land/and crossed our river too sir/now show them all with sword in hand/what Yankee boys can do sir." Most of the war-inspired flowering in the popular arts was patriotic. But not everyone cheered. The abolitionist James Russell Lowell considered the war a "national crime committed in behoof of slavery, our common sin." Ralph Waldo Emerson confided to his journals in 1847: "The United States will conquer Mexico, but it will be as the man swallows arsenic which brings him down in turn." (Adapted from Norton et al., *A People and a Nation*, pp. 361–366.)

Sharpening Your Skills

DIRECTIONS Answer the following questions by filling in the blanks or circling the letter of the correct response.

1. What does the title suggest about the war between the United States and Mexico?

   _____

2. On April 24, 1846, Mexican troops ambushed a U.S. cavalry unit. What had the United States done to initiate hostilities?

   _____

3. The authors do not explicitly define the term "expansionist strategy" in paragraph 1. But context suggests what meaning?

   a. Polk wanted to expand U.S. boundaries.

   b. Polk wanted to expand the power of the president.

   c. Polk wanted to increase his own personal wealth.

4. Based on the context, which definition for "Manifest Destiny" (paragraph 2) makes more sense?

   a. Manifest Destiny was the nineteenth-century belief in the right of the United States to take control of all land owned by Mexico.

   b. Manifest Destiny was the nineteenth-century belief in the right of the United States to expand westward.

   c. Manifest Destiny was the nineteenth-century belief in the power of good intentions.

5. In paragraph 2, the authors say that "Polk deceptively declared that 'war exists by the act of Mexico itself.'" What was deceptive about that statement?

_____

6. Paraphrase the last sentence of paragraph 2.

_____

7. What's the main idea in paragraph 3?
   a. The war against Mexico unleashed a flood of patriotism in the United States.
   b. The war against Mexico was not popular with abolitionists.
   c. The war against Mexico aroused mixed emotions.

8. What patterns of organization are at work in paragraphs 1 and 2?
   a. definition
   b. classification
   c. time order (process)
   d. time order (sequence of dates and events)
   e. comparison and contrast
   f. cause and effect

9. What pattern of organization is used in paragraph 3?
   a. definition
   b. classification
   c. time order (process)
   d. time order (sequence of dates and events)
   e. comparison and contrast
   f. cause and effect

10. In the final paragraph of the excerpt, the authors cite Emerson's quote comparing the U.S. victory over Mexico to a man swallowing arsenic. What point was Emerson trying to make with that comparison?
    a. Mexico will be the victor in the long run.
    b. The United States will be poisoned by Mexico's debts.
    c. In the long run, the United States will suffer from its victory over Mexico.
    d. War is a poison that infects the souls of men.

WORD NOTES: WORDS AND MYTHS

The expression "Pygmalion effect" (p. 122) was derived from the Greek myth of Pygmalion, the king who fell in love with his own creation. But the phrase "Pygmalion effect" is hardly the only word or phrase from mythology that has found a home in the English language. There are many others. Here are just a few:

1. **Mentor.** Mentor was the trusted friend and teacher of Odysseus. While Odysseus was away, a goddess came down to earth to protect the family of Odysseus. To do so, she disguised herself as Mentor and took over his role as teacher and counselor. Today we use the word *mentor* to mean someone we consider a teacher or an adviser.

   Sample Sentence My older brother has always been my *mentor* in life.

2. **Pandora's Box.** Zeus, the king of the Greek gods, wanted to punish mankind for accepting, without Zeus's permission, the gift of fire. To show his displeasure, Zeus ordered the creation of Pandora, the world's first woman, who carried with her a box packed with all manner of evil. Told not to open the box, Pandora was overcome by curiosity—as Zeus intended her to be—and she loosed a plague of evils on unsuspecting humanity. *Pandora's box* has become a common way of referring to the source of numerous evils or unpleasant consequences.

   Sample Sentence In her quest for the truth about her biological parents, Clara did not realize until too late that she was opening *Pandora's box.*

3. **Herculean.** Hercules was a Greek hero who possessed extraordinary strength. It was said that he could perform fantastic feats. Today when we use the word *Herculean,* we are referring to something that requires much effort or strength or someone who has a lot of strength.

   Sample Sentence Before she became vice president, she had to complete the *Herculean* task of reorganizing the entire office system.

4. Flora and fauna. Flora was the Roman goddess of flowers, and Faunus was the Roman god of nature and fertility. Today we use the expression *flora and fauna* to mean the plants and animals of a particular region.

Sample Sentence We spent three whole days studying the *flora and fauna* of New Zealand.

Other Forms of the Word florae *or* floras, faunae *or* faunas

5. Narcissism. Narcissus was a beautiful young man who loved no one until the day he saw his own reflection in a pool of water. From then on, he was in love with himself. Today when we talk about *narcissism,* we are talking about excessive love or admiration for oneself.

Sample Sentence Only his incredible *narcissism* allowed him to ignore all the insulting remarks directed his way.

Other Forms of the Word narcissist, narcissistic

Now fill in the blanks with one of the preceding words.

1. Most geography books contain a section listing the

_____ of different regions.

2. The candidate stayed away from the subject of campaign finance reform. She knew it was a politically charged _____ that could leave her explaining issues she herself did not understand.

3. She was more than a friend; she was my _____.

4. His excessive _____ endangered their marriage.

5. The champion weightlifter's _____ strength impressed the crowd.

Students who want to do a more in-depth review of paragraph essentials with the help of **Getting Focused,** the companion software accompanying this text, should look at "Question 2: What's the Topic?"; "Question 3: What Does the Author Say About the Topic?"; "Question 5: How Does the Author Support the Main Idea?"; and "Question 7: Has the Author Combined Patterns?"

To get more practice paraphrasing main ideas and recognizing paragraph patterns, go to **laflemm.com** and click on "Reading for Thinking: Online Practice." Complete and correct Practices 2 and 3.

Test 1: Reviewing the Key Points

Answer the following questions by filling in the blanks or circling the correct response.

1. _____ is the first step toward discovering the main idea of a paragraph.

2. *True* or *False*. You should always be able to express the topic in a single word.

3. To discover the main idea, you need to ask two questions. Those

   questions are _____ and _____.

4. The function of the topic sentence is to _____.

5. *True* or *False*. The first sentence of a paragraph is not necessarily the topic sentence.

6. Contrast transitions signal to the reader that _____

   _____.

7. Major details serve to _____.

8. Minor details serve to _____.

9. *True* or *False*. Minor details are never important enough to be included in your notes.

10. Recognizing the organizational pattern underlying a reading can help you decide what to underline and what to include in your notes.

    It can also help you _____.

To correct your test, turn to the answer key on page 642.

Test 2: Recognizing Topic Sentences

DIRECTIONS Write the number or numbers of the topic sentence in the blank.

1. ¹Throughout the 1950s, repeated attempts were made to unionize migrant farm workers. ²But because the workers had to follow the crops they picked, they were never in one place for very long and were hard to organize. ³However, in the 1960s, a Mexican-American farm worker named César Chávez succeeded against all odds at unionizing agricultural workers. ⁴Using the donations he had gathered from friends and supporters, Chávez traveled from farm to farm speaking to California's migrant workers, most of whom were Mexican Americans like himself. ⁵Used to union activists who came to their fields and talked down to them, the farm workers knew immediately that Chávez understood and respected them in a way other union organizers had not. ⁶One by one, they joined his organization, the National Farm Workers Association. ⁷In 1965, recognizing the power in numbers, Chávez persuaded union members to take part in a strike initiated by Filipino grape pickers. ⁸Then he went to the media and told the country that no one should eat grapes because the people who picked them were paid starvation wages and denied the right to toilet facilities while working in the fields. ⁹To the amazement of the grape growers, millions of people listened. ¹⁰The boycott lasted until 1970, and cost the growers millions of dollars. ¹¹César Chávez's National Farm Workers Association had become a force to be reckoned with. ¹²Farm owners had to recognize the union, which was renamed the United Farm Workers.

Topic Sentence _____

2. ¹The sinking of the luxury liner *Lusitania* by a German submarine helped propel the United States into World War I. ²Although initially it was claimed that the ship had been torpedoed for no reason except German viciousness, later evidence contradicted that story. ³In fact, the boat's cargo was almost completely contraband.* ⁴It was carrying fifty-one tons of shrapnel shells and five thousand boxes of bullets. ⁵Within eighteen minutes of being hit at 2:10 p.m. on the afternoon of May 6, 1915, the *Lusitania* sank beneath three hundred feet of water. ⁶Because there weren't enough crew members to man the forty-eight lifeboats, panic reigned and hundreds

---

*contraband: goods prohibited by law or treaty from being imported.

of people died—1,195 to be exact. [7]Furious at what was perceived to be German treachery, the American public began to support the idea of going to war against Germany.

Topic Sentence _____

3. [1]In 1987, Brazilian labor leader and environmentalist Francisco "Chico" Mendes was awarded the United Nations Global 500 Prize, along with a medal from the Society for a Better World. [2]Sadly, medals couldn't save his life when he took on a group of cattle ranchers in Acre, Brazil. [3]Determined to drive out rubber workers like the ones Mendes represented, the ranchers openly used threats and violence to do it. [4]Mendes, who had a public name and the respect of his fellow workers, was a special thorn in the ranchers' side, and they threatened his life. [5]Mendes took their death threats seriously but refused to give up his labor activities. [6]On December 15, 1988, he told a friend, "I don't think I'm going to live." [7]One week later, Mendes was shot in the chest as he stepped out of his house.

Topic Sentence _____

4. [1]The Underground Railroad was an informal network of routes traveled by a few thousand American slaves escaping to freedom between 1840 and 1860. [2]These routes included paths through woods and fields; transportation such as boats, trains, and wagons; and homes where runaways hid from slave owners and law enforcement officials. [3]In keeping with the idea of a railroad, slaves were referred to as "passengers," homes that took them in were "stations," and the people who assisted them were known as "conductors." [4]These conductors were abolitionists and included both free blacks and many sympathetic whites, particularly those who practiced the Quaker faith. [5]Abolitionists defied fugitive slave laws to shelter and feed runaways and to guide them along the safest routes out of the South to free states in the North. [6]Harriet Tubman, for example, liberated at least 300 black slaves after she herself had used the Underground Railroad to escape.

Topic Sentence _____

Test 3: Recognizing Topic Sentences and Evaluating Paraphrases

DIRECTIONS Read each selection paragraph and write the number or numbers of the topic sentence in the blank. Then circle the letter of the statement that best paraphrases the topic sentence.

1. ¹In the past, young adults who went off to college would earn their degrees, get jobs, and move out into their own homes or apartments. ²Today, however, twenty-something college graduates are more likely to return home for an extended period of time. ³As a matter of fact, one informal poll of college seniors revealed that 63 percent of them planned to move back home after graduation. ⁴This nationwide "back-to-the-nest" trend is the result of several factors. ⁵Because of the unstable economy, jobs are more scarce, so recent graduates are often unemployed. ⁶Even those lucky enough to find jobs are concerned about keeping them. ⁷Plus, young people with entry-level salaries are finding it difficult to afford their own place to live. ⁸In high-cost-of-living cities, such as New York, Boston, and San Francisco in particular, recent college graduates often do not make enough money to pay the exorbitant rents. ⁹Even in lower-rent areas, young people in their twenties who have student loans to repay or who plan to attend graduate school cannot afford to pay their bills and live on their own. (Source of information: "Back to the Nest: Welcome Home," *Newsday*, May 23, 2002, www.twentysomething.com/newsday.htm.)

Topic Sentence _____

Paraphrase a. An unstable economy is changing U.S. society in a number of ways.

   b. Many twenty-somethings are moving back home because they cannot handle financial responsibility.

   c. Today's young people know far more about handling money than their counterparts in a previous generation did.

   d. For several reasons, many college graduates are going back to their parents' home to live.

2. ¹What is the difference between a computer virus and a computer worm? ²Both can infect and damage computer systems. ³However, they differ in the way they reproduce and spread. ⁴A *virus*, which is short for "vital information resources under siege," is a program or code that secretly enters a computer by piggybacking on e-mail messages, files, or programs shared

between two different computer systems. [5]Then the virus infects its new host by attaching itself to the files within that computer and deleting or changing them or even overwriting entire programs. [6]Just like a biological virus in the human body, a computer virus replicates itself so that it will continue to be contagious when data is shared with another computer system. [7]In 2000, for example, the famous "Love Bug" virus, which traveled via e-mail messages, destroyed files in computers all over the world. [8]*Worms,* too, are malicious programs that reproduce and spread. [9]But unlike viruses, they do not need to attach themselves to other files. [10]They are programs that run independently and spread on their own through computer networks. [11]Thus they do not require human intervention to make their way from one computer to another. [12]The famous Internet worm of 1988, for example, copied itself across the Internet, destroying many computer systems as it went. [13]Currently, computer analysts are worried about the Sasser worm, which disabled computers in Britain, South Africa, and Taiwan.

Topic Sentence ———

Paraphrase a. Both computer viruses and worms are programs that damage computer systems.

b. Although computer viruses and worms can both do significant damage to computers, they replicate and spread in different ways.

c. Computer worms are far worse than computer viruses because they do not require human participation to spread.

d. Computer viruses must reproduce themselves in order to be a significant threat.

3. [1]In 1949, President Harry S. Truman decided to use Cape Canaveral in Florida as a testing site for missiles. [2]The Cape Canaveral location was so perfectly adapted to the job of missile launching that it became the site of the Kennedy Space Center, where not just missiles but also rockets and space shuttles are launched. [3]The site worked because Cape Canaveral is a rather remote area that is nevertheless accessible by roads and highways. [4]Thus it could be used as a place to build and launch missiles without endangering people living in the area. [5]Although over the years the Kennedy Space Center has expanded to cover 140,000 acres, it is still remote enough to ensure the safety of nearby communities. (Sources of information: Kennedy Space Center, "The Kennedy Space Center Story" (1991 edition), October 22, 2002, www-pao. ksc.nasa.gov/kscpao/kscstory/ch1/ch1.htm; Cliff Lethbridge, "The

History of Cape Canaveral," Spaceline.org, 2000, http://spaceline. org/capehistory.html.)

Topic Sentence ____

Paraphrase

a. Cape Canaveral became the site of the Kennedy Space Center because it turned out to be the perfect place for testing and launching missiles, rockets, and space shuttles.

b. Cape Canaveral was the only site in the United States where missiles, rockets, and space shuttles could be launched.

c. Cape Canaveral's remoteness led to its selection as America's missile and rocket launch site.

d. Harry S. Truman chose Cape Canaveral as the site of the Kennedy Space Center.

4. [1]Members of living history clubs are wildly passionate about history, so much so that they are not content to simply *read* about a particular era. [2]Instead, they seek to re-create life as it was lived in their favorite time period. [3]The 24,000 members of the Society for Creative Anachronism,* for example, study the European Middle Ages and Renaissance by re-creating the arts and skills of those eras. [4]Each participant makes and wears clothing from the period and creates a "persona," a person whom he or she would have liked to have been. [5]When the club's members gather at meetings, which may take the form of feasts or tournaments, they reenact the behaviors of those who lived during that era. [6]They might, for instance, practice sword fighting or learn a craft like brewing, weaving, or candle making. [7]Similarly, hundreds of Civil War buffs frequently dress as soldiers and reenact whole battles, often while a crowd of spectators looks on. [8]The reenactors spend weekends camping in canvas tents, eating foods that were available to their historical counterparts, and trying to capture what it was like to have lived during the nineteenth century. [9]Other living history groups around the country focus on re-creating the Roman Empire, the pirate era, or the Wild West. (Sources of information: Society for Creative Anachronism, www.ansteorra.org/regnum/hospitaler/ articles/fip.htm; Living History Society, www.livinghistorysociety.org.)

Topic Sentence ____

---

*anachronism: something that is out of its proper or appropriate order in time. For example, a play about ancient Rome would never have an actor looking at a watch because the watch is an *anachronism*.

Paraphrase   a. Many people are fascinated by a certain period of history.

b. The Society for Creative Anachronism is a group that reenacts the Middle Ages and Renaissance.

c. Historical reenactments of important events are often marred by clothing, furniture, or speech that does not fit the time period.

d. Members of living history clubs enjoy re-creating a particular historical era.

Test 4: Recognizing and Paraphrasing Topic Sentences

DIRECTIONS Read each paragraph and write the number or numbers of the topic sentence in the blank. Then paraphrase it on the lines that follow.

1. [1]The largest demographic* group in the United States, called "baby boomers," consists of those born between 1946 and 1964.[2]Because baby boomers are presently the segment with the greatest economic impact, they are the target for numerous products and services. [3]This includes cars, housing, foreign travel, and recreational equipment. [4]Boomers are also heavy consumers of banking and investment services. [5]They are the heaviest users of frozen dinners and are a growing market for movies, especially highly original ones with adult themes. [6]They are also the target of marketing efforts for children's products and services. (Hoyer and MacInnis, *Consumer Behavior,* p. 357.)

Topic Sentence _____

Paraphrase _____

_____

2. [1]Beavers, North America's largest rodents (they grow to more than two feet long), are delightful to watch for their industry and their family affection. [2]Yet few animals have been so relentlessly exploited as the beaver. [3]In the eighteenth and nineteenth centuries, beaver pelts were worth their weight in gold. [4]As a result, by 1896, at least fourteen American states—Massachusetts, Vermont, New Hampshire, New York, Rhode Island, Connecticut, Pennsylvania, New Jersey, Delaware, Maryland, Illinois, Indiana, West Virginia, and Ohio—had announced that all of their beavers had been killed. [5]By the beginning of the twentieth century, it looked as if the beaver was about to disappear from the face of the earth. [6]Fortunately, thanks to a beaver recovery program, which included trapping and relocating to protected areas, beavers have made an impressive comeback throughout the country. (Adapted from Montgomery, *Nature's Everyday Mysteries,* p. 99.)

Topic Sentence _____

Paraphrase _____

_____

*demographic: related to the characteristics of a population.

3. ¹Coral reefs are extremely important to the environment, and they perform many useful functions; above all, they provide a habitat for organisms that cannot survive elsewhere. ²Yet coral reefs all over the world are being threatened by human activities. ³Logging near the waters of Bascuit Bay in the Philippines has destroyed 5 percent of the coral reefs in the bay. Dynamite fishing around the world has not only killed large numbers of fish, it has also blown apart a significant number of coral reefs in Kenya, Tanzania, and Mauritania. ⁵Coral reefs have also fallen victim to the tourist industry. ⁶Coral and shells are hot tourist commodities, and they have been collected in large quantities for sale to souvenir-hungry tourists. ⁷Undoubtedly, the most violent assault on the reefs has come from nuclear testing. ⁸France, for example, has detonated* more than 100 nuclear devices in Polynesian waters once rich with coral reefs that are rapidly disappearing.

Topic Sentence _____

Paraphrase _____

_____

4. ¹Officials in countries such as Egypt, Afghanistan, and Greece are pressing European and American museums to return ancient art stolen from them long ago. ²However, the museums that now display these antiquities argue that they have good reasons for keeping them. ³Of course, some of the reasons are selfish. ⁴Museums fear, for instance, that returning treasures to their place of origin would result in the dismantling of their collections and the loss of revenue from museum visitors. ⁵But museum officials also insist that many of the antiquities are too fragile to move. ⁶London's British Museum, for example, says that the sculptures sawed off the Parthenon in 1801 are too delicate to transport from England back to Greece. ⁷Museum officials argue, too, that they are better equipped to preserve such priceless treasures and accuse some countries of not taking proper care of precious artifacts. ⁸Those on the side of the museums point out that in unstable or war-torn countries, where the looting and destruction of museums is still a very real possibility, antiquities are at greater risk. ⁹Plus, returning works of art to their place of origin often significantly reduces public access to them. ¹⁰Russia's Hermitage Museum, for example, reluctantly returned a rare copper bowl to Kazakhstan, and now the bowl is kept in a mosque where few visitors are allowed to go.

_____

*detonated: set off, caused to explode.

(Source of information: Betsy Carpenter with Gillian Sandford, "Who Owns the Past?" *U.S. News & World Report*, December 15, 2003, pp. 58–60.)

Topic Sentence ⎯⎯⎯

Paraphrase ⎯⎯⎯⎯⎯⎯⎯⎯⎯⎯⎯⎯⎯⎯⎯⎯⎯⎯⎯⎯⎯⎯⎯⎯⎯⎯⎯⎯

⎯⎯⎯⎯⎯⎯⎯⎯⎯⎯⎯⎯⎯⎯⎯⎯⎯⎯⎯⎯⎯⎯⎯⎯⎯⎯⎯⎯⎯⎯⎯⎯⎯⎯⎯

5. [1]Around 1950 agriculture in the United States underwent a profound change. [2]For one thing, agriculture became energy intensive, or, more specifically, fossil-fuel intensive. [3]In 1950, an amount of energy equal to less than half a barrel of oil was used to produce a ton of grain. [4]By 1985, the amount of energy needed to produce a ton of grain had more than doubled. [5]Searching for ways to increase the yield of the lands already in use, farmers also began to rely heavily on inputs of water, on inputs of chemical fertilizers and pesticides (many of which are petroleum-derived products), and on high-yield strains of crops. [6]In some areas, especially the drier regions of the Southwest, irrigation projects allowed dry lands to be cultivated. [7]In contrast to past agricultural practices, farmers began to concentrate on producing only one or two profitable crops as opposed to a variety of crops. (Adapted from Kaufman and Franz, *Biosphere 2000,* p. 182.)

Topic Sentence ⎯⎯⎯

Paraphrase ⎯⎯⎯⎯⎯⎯⎯⎯⎯⎯⎯⎯⎯⎯⎯⎯⎯⎯⎯⎯⎯⎯⎯⎯⎯⎯⎯⎯

⎯⎯⎯⎯⎯⎯⎯⎯⎯⎯⎯⎯⎯⎯⎯⎯⎯⎯⎯⎯⎯⎯⎯⎯⎯⎯⎯⎯⎯⎯⎯⎯⎯⎯⎯

▶️● **Test 5: Topic Sentences and Supporting Details**

Read each paragraph and write the number or numbers of the topic sentence in the blank. Then answer the questions that follow by circling the correct response or writing it in the blanks.

1. Most bilingual programs are considered purely transitional: They provide instruction for students in their native language until they can speak English well enough to function in classrooms where only English is spoken. [2]A typical bilingual program begins by teaching kindergarten students in their primary language and translating key words into English. [3]However, by the end of first or second grade, English is the primary language: Words are only occasionally translated into the students' native tongue. [4]For a while now, bilingual education has been a controversial topic, with critics arguing that the native language should be eliminated from the classroom as early as possible because it interferes with the learning of English. [5]But research does not support this claim (Hakuta & Garcia, 1989). [6]On the contrary, bilingualism seems to improve the thinking abilities of children. (Adapted from Santrock, *Life-Span Development*, p. 301.)

   a. Topic sentence: _____

   b. What question or questions about the topic sentence do the major details help answer?

   _____

   _____

   c. *True* or *False:* Sentence 3 is a major detail.

   Explain your answer. _____

   _____

   d. *True* or *False:* Sentence 4 is a minor detail.

   Explain your answer. _____

   _____

2. [1]Beliefs about maintaining ties with those who have died vary from culture to culture. [2]For example, maintaining ties with the deceased is accepted and sustained in the religious rituals of Japan. [3]Yet among the Hopi Indians of Arizona, the deceased are forgotten as quickly as possible and life goes on as usual. [4]In fact, the

Hopi funeral ritual concludes with a break-off between mortals and spirits. [5]The diversity of grieving is nowhere clearer than in two Muslim societies—one in Egypt, the other in Bali. [6]Among Muslims in Egypt, the bereaved* are encouraged to dwell at length on their grief, surrounded by others who relate similarly tragic accounts and express their sorrow. [7]By contrast, in Bali, bereaved Muslims are encouraged to laugh and be joyful rather than be sad. (Adapted from Santrock, *Life-Span Development*, p. 301.)

a. Topic sentence: _____

b. What question or questions about the topic sentence do the major details help answer?

_____

_____

c. *True* or *False:* Sentence 2 is a major detail.

Explain your answer. _____

_____

d. *True* or *False:* Sentence 4 is a minor detail.

Explain your answer. _____

_____

3. [1]In October 1871, a huge fire consumed three-and-one-third miles of Chicago real estate over the course of forty-eight hours. [2]To this day what came to be known as "The Great Chicago Fire" is attributed to one lone cow's misbehavior. [3]The lack of rain, a strong dry wind blowing the flames, and buildings made of timber produced conditions that allowed the blaze to spread rapidly. [4]In a short time, the fire was so hot that office buildings' iron beams and columns melted, producing molten ore that contributed to the fire's spread. [5]Before the flames were finally quenched, 300 people were dead, 100,000 were homeless, and almost $200 million in property had been destroyed. [6]The next month, the Board of Police and Fire Commissioners began an inquiry to determine the fire's cause. [7]Their investigation revealed that the disaster began in a barn owned by Mr. and Mrs. Patrick O'Leary. [8]The board was then compelled to determine if the fire started due to arson or an accident. [9]In its final report, however, the board admitted that it was unable to determine the fire's exact cause. [10]Nonetheless, even as the fire still

---

*bereaved: those suffering the loss of a loved one.

raged, the *Chicago Evening Journal* printed the rumor that it had been caused by a cow in the O'Leary's barn. [11]The newspaper story said the cow kicked over a lantern, which started the fire in a pile of straw. [12]That story eventually became a legend.

a. Topic sentence: _____

b. What question or questions about the topic sentence do the major details help answer?

_____

_____

c. *True* or *False:* Sentence 3 is a major detail.

Explain your answer. _____

_____

d. *True* or *False:* Sentence 4 is a major detail.

Explain your answer. _____

_____

4. [1]Research on attitude change suggests that people pay attention to messages that fit their established opinions and ignore those that don't. [2]Thus media such as radio, television, and newspapers tend to reinforce existing views rather than change them. [3]Faced with messages that challenge their beliefs, listeners, viewers, or readers often ignore anything that doesn't fit their existing worldview; this kind of selective perception* also accounts for what's called the *boomerang effect.* [4]Experiments have shown that those with strong beliefs are likely to misinterpret messages that challenge their opinions. [5]In other words, people ignore or distort evidence rather than be challenged by it. [6]The classic example of the boomerang effect was the popular television show *All in the Family.* [7]The show was meant—in the person of the lead character, Archie Bunker—to make bigotry* look laughable and silly. [8]Yet viewer surveys consistently discovered that those who shared Archie Bunker's wide-ranging prejudices thought of the character as a role model who helped confirm the rightness of their opinions.

a. Topic sentence: _____

---

*perception: way of seeing.
*bigotry: prejudice.

b. What question or questions about the topic sentence do the major details help answer?

_____

_____

c. *True* or *False:* Sentence 4 is a major detail.

Explain your answer. _____

_____

d. *True* or *False*: Sentence 5 is a minor detail.

Explain your answer. _____

_____

5. [1]**Trichotillomania** is a disorder characterized by an inability to resist the impulse to pull out one's own hair. [2]Although trichotillomania principally involves the hairs in the scalp, a person with this disorder may pull hair from other parts of the body, such as eyelashes, beard, or eyebrows. [3]The hair pulling is not provoked by skin inflammation, itch, or other physical conditions. [4]Rather, the person simply cannot resist the impulse, which begins with a feeling of tension that is replaced by a feeling of release or gratification* after the hair is pulled. [5]Initially, the hair pulling may not disturb the follicles, and new hair will grow. [6]In severe cases, new growth is compromised and permanent hair loss results. [7]One thirty-five-year-old woman entered therapy saying that she had a compulsion to pull the hairs from her head. [8]When asked to reveal the extent of her hair pulling, the woman took off her wig. [9]She was completely bald except for a few strands of hair at the back of her head. [10]There is no information on the prevalence of trichotillomania, although it is probably more common than currently believed and more common among women than men (Meyer, 1989). [11]About 1 to 2 percent of college students appear to have a past or current history of this disorder (American Psychiatric Association, 1994). (Sue et al., *Understanding Abnormal Behavior,* p. 247.)

a. Topic sentence: _____

b. What question or questions about the topic sentence do the major details help answer?

_____

_____

_____
*gratification: pleasure.

c. *True* or *False:* Sentence 3 is a minor detail.

Explain your answer. _____

_____

d. *True* or *False:* Sentence 4 is a minor detail.

Explain your answer. _____

_____

Test 6: Recognizing Organizational Patterns

DIRECTIONS Circle the letter or letters that identify the organizational pattern or patterns used in each paragraph.

1. A **cartel** is an organization of independent firms whose purpose is to control and limit production and maintain or increase prices and profits. A cartel can result from either formal or informal agreement among members. Like collusion,* cartels are illegal in the United States but occur in other countries. The cartel most people are familiar with is the Organization of Petroleum Exporting Countries (OPEC), a group of nations rather than a group of independent firms. During the 1970s, OPEC was able to coordinate oil production in such a way that it drove the market price of crude oil from $1.10 to $32.00 a barrel. For nearly eight years, each member of OPEC agreed to produce a certain limited amount of crude oil as designated by the OPEC production committee. Then in the early 1980s, the cartel began to fall apart as individual members began to cheat on the agreement. Members began to produce more than their allocation in an attempt to increase profit. As each member of the cartel did this, the price of oil fell, reaching $12 per barrel in 1988. Oil prices rose again in 1990 when Iraq invaded Kuwait, causing widespread damage to Kuwait's oil fields. But as repairs have been made to Kuwait's oil wells, Kuwait has increased production and oil prices have dropped. (Boyes and Melvin, *Fundamentals of Economics,* p. 109.)

   a. definition

   b. classification

   c. time order (process)

   d. time order (sequence of dates and events)

   e. comparison and contrast

   f. cause and effect

2. The Bermuda Triangle is, without a doubt, a strange and mysterious area of the Atlantic Ocean. During the last century, more than one hundred ships, boats, and airplanes have disappeared in this area. For example, the USS *Cyclops,* a Navy ship with 306 people aboard, disappeared there in 1918. Also lost without a trace was an entire squadron of five Navy torpedo bombers that took off from Fort Lauderdale, Florida, in 1945. In 1947, a United States C-54

---

*collusion: a secret agreement between parties for the purpose of illegal activities.

bomber disappeared near Bermuda and was never seen again. One year later, the same thing happened to the British airliner *Star Tiger*. And in 1968, the *Scorpion*, a nuclear submarine, vanished only to be found after a long search. It was finally located in the waters on the fringes of the Triangle, but none of its crew members were on board.

a. definition

b. classification

c. time order (process)

d. time order (sequence of dates and events)

e. comparison and contrast

f. cause and effect

3. Instinctive behavior is caused by specific signals from the environment. For example, stalking behavior in cats may be initiated by the sight of prey. In male ring doves, the sight of an adult female triggers the bowing associated with courtship. The environmental signals that evoke, or release, instinctive behavior are called **releasers**. A releaser may be only a small part of any appropriate situation. For example, fighting behavior in territorial male European robins can be released not only by the sight of another male within their territories, but even by the sight of a tuft of red feathers at a certain height. Such a response usually "works" because red feathers at that height within the territory are normally on the breast of a competitor. The point is that the instinctive act can be triggered by only certain parts of the total environmental situation. (Adapted from Wallace, *Biology*, p. 450.)

a. definition

b. classification

c. time order (process)

d. time order (sequence of dates and events)

e. comparison and contrast

f. cause and effect

4. Eighteenth-century assemblies bore little resemblance to twentieth-century state legislatures. Much of their business would today be termed administrative; only on rare occasions did assemblies formulate new policies or pass laws of real importance. Members of the assemblies also saw their roles differently from that of modern legislators. Instead of believing that they should act positively to improve the lives of their constituents, eighteenth-century assemblymen saw themselves as acting defensively to prevent encroachments on the people's rights. In their minds, their primary function was, for example, to stop the governors or councils from enacting oppressive taxes, rather than to pass laws that would actively benefit their constituents. (Norton et al., *A People and a Nation*, p. 111.)

a. definition

b. classification

c. time order (process)

d. time order (sequence of dates and events)

e. comparison and contrast

f. cause and effect

5. Earth's atmosphere is classified by temperature into four regions. The *troposphere*, the lowest level of the atmosphere, is heated to an average of 59°F. In the *stratosphere*, the layer above the troposphere, temperatures range from –76°F to near 32°F, while the temperature maximum is called the "stratopause." Temperatures in the *mesosphere* can drop much lower. They range from 32°F to –212°F. The *thermosphere* is the highest layer of the atmosphere and the temperature rises with altitude to extreme values of thousands of degrees. The meanings of these extreme temperatures, however, can be misleading. High thermosphere temperatures represent little heat. (Adapted from Rennie, *Scientific American Science Desk Reference*, p. 266.)

a. definition

b. classification

c. time order (process)

d. time order (sequence of dates and events)

e. comparison and contrast

f. cause and effect

Test 7: Recognizing Organizational Patterns

DIRECTIONS Circle the letter or letters that identify the organizational pattern or patterns used in each paragraph.

1. In general, people use three different methods of learning, and most rely more heavily on one method than another. **Visual learners** absorb new information best when they can see it. Thus they like to learn through reading and are likely to take detailed notes with many diagrams and symbols. If visual learners have a choice between learning from a book or learning from a lecture, they are inclined to choose the book. **Auditory learners** rely most on their sense of hearing to learn new material, preferring to learn from lectures, discussions, and tours. At museums, they are the first ones to sign up for guided tours or make use of guides on tape by purchasing headphones. **Kinesthetic learners** are at their best when they are physically active. Thus they are likely to gesture while reviewing new information, and they like to use learning techniques that require movement. For example, kinesthetic learners might jot notes on sticky pads and attach the notes to the pages of a textbook because this method allows for maximum physical involvement. In the same vein, they are also likely to build models and take things apart to see how they work. (Source of information: "Three Different Learning Styles," University of South Dakota, www.usd.edu/ trio/tut/ts/styleres.html.)

   a. definition

   b. classification

   c. time order (process)

   d. time order (sequence of dates and events)

   e. comparison and contrast

   f. cause and effect

2. Magazines and journals are both print publications; however, they differ in a number of ways. One major difference is purpose. The primary purpose of magazines is to entertain readers, promote particular viewpoints, and sell products. The main purpose of journals, however, is to report on new research in a specific field. For example, a professional journal, such as the *Journal of the American Medical Association,* contains information about recent medical research. The two types of publication differ, too, in terms of article length, authors, and audience. Magazine articles, which are generally short, are written by staff or freelance writers who use layman's terms to appeal to a wide audience. Journal articles, on

the other hand, are longer and generally written by experts who use specialized jargon that will be understood only by those with education or training in a particular field. Magazine articles usually do not provide much, if any, information about sources, but journal articles always include footnotes or endnotes, along with bibliographic information. Finally, the two publications differ in terms of their publishers and frequency of publication. The issues of a magazine, published by general or commercial presses, appear either weekly or monthly. Journals, though, are generally published by universities, professional societies, or scholarly presses, and many of them appear just quarterly or annually. (Source of information: Denise Woetzel, "What's the Difference Between Journals and Magazines?" Guilford Technical Community College, December 9, 2001, http://webster.gtcc.cc.nc.us/library/jourmag.html.)

a. definition

b. classification

c. time order (process)

d. time order (sequence of dates and events)

e. comparison and contrast

f. cause and effect

3. Bats and dolphins gather information about their surroundings by bouncing sound waves off objects in a three-step process. First, both animals send sound waves out into the atmosphere. Bats make high-pitched sounds by moving air past their vocal chords, and dolphins transmit clicking sounds from nasal sacs in their foreheads. Next, these sounds hit an object in the animal's vicinity, bounce off the object, and return in the form of echoes. In the third step, the animal hears and interprets the echoes. Its brain processes the information, assessing the object's size and shape to form a mental image of it. It is even possible for bats and dolphins to determine how far away the object is based on how long it takes the echo to return.

a. definition

b. classification

c. time order (process)

d. time order (sequence of dates and events)

e. comparison and contrast

f. cause and effect

4. When Louis Braille was just a teenager, he invented the system of reading and writing that blind people still use today. In 1812,

three-year-old Braille was playing in his father's leather-working shop when he injured his eye with a sharp tool. The eye became infected, and the infection spread. By the following year, the boy was completely blind. In 1819, Braille's parents sent their sightless but nonetheless bright child to the Royal Institution for Blind Youth in Paris, where the boy soon became frustrated with the slow system of running his fingers over the huge, raised letters in the few books available to him. In the 1820s, Braille learned about a code devised by a French army captain who wanted his soldiers to be able to read messages at night. The teenager began to think about how he could adapt this code for blind people. By 1829, he had come up with a system that uses different combinations of raised dots to represent each letter of the alphabet, and he published the first Braille book. In 1837, he expanded his system to include symbols used in math and music. In 1868, sixteen years after Braille's death, a group of British men affiliated with their country's Royal National Institute for the Blind began promoting the Braille reading and writing method. It quickly caught on. Today, Braille is used in almost every country in the world and has been adapted for many different languages.

a. definition

b. classification

c. time order (process)

d. time order (sequence of dates and events)

e. comparison and contrast

f. cause and effect

5. The television variety show known as the *Ed Sullivan Show* is usually credited with introducing the rock group The Beatles to the United States in 1963 and thereby sparking what came to be known as "Beatlemania." However, a fifteen-year-old girl named Marsha Albert is the one who really started the Beatles rage. A news report about the Beatles' popularity in England inspired Marsha to write a letter to a local radio disk jockey and ask, "Why can't we have music like that here in America?" This letter prompted the D.J. to get a copy of the song, "I Want to Hold Your Hand." Within a week, the record was on the radio, and requests for the song began flooding the station, causing other stations to want a copy. As a result of this explosive increase in demand, Capitol Records released the record to U.S. stores. Radio stations began playing the tune, and young people home from school for the holidays heard it over and over. As a result, the record sold one million copies in just three weeks. When Ed Sullivan presented The Beatles about two

months after Marsha wrote her letter, millions of Americans were excited about seeing the band, and an astonishing 40 percent of the population watched the show. Clearly, the phenomenon that began with a young girl's phone call was already in full swing. (Source of information: Edna Gundersen, "Search Has Been a Hard Day's Night," *USA Today,* January 16, 2004, p. E5.)

a. definition

b. classification

c. time order (process)

d. time order (sequence of dates and events)

e. comparison and contrast

f. cause and effect

Test 8: Taking Stock

DIRECTIONS Read each paragraph. Then answer the questions by circling the letter or letters of the correct response(s).

1. Although there is no equivalent English word for it, *schadenfreude* is the German term for the feeling of pleasure one gets when hearing of another's misfortune. The word comes from *schaden,* meaning "damage," and *freude,* meaning "joy." Psychologists say that we are expressing schadenfreude, for example, when we feel spiteful delight in watching celebrities fail. We're interested in court trials of the rich and famous because we are secretly—sometimes even openly—glad that the high-and-mighty have been brought down to a less-exalted position. Schadenfreude is the glee we experience when the pretty homecoming queen trips on her dress. And it's the satisfaction we get from watching rivals and enemies flounder. Historian Peter Gay, for instance, admitted to feeling schadenfreude when, as a Jewish child during the Nazi era, he watched German athletes lose competitions in the 1936 Olympic games. Some psychologists insist that it's perfectly normal to occasionally feel schadenfreude even toward people we love, like friends and family members, if they have achieved successes in the past that we wished for ourselves but did not achieve. Feelings of schadenfreude are considered abnormal only when they are constant or if they lead to attempts to make others fail so we can feel better about ourselves. (Sources of information: Kathleen McGowan, "Seven Deadly Sentiments," *Psychology Today,* January/February 2004, pp. 46–48; "Word of the Day: Schadenfreude," Dictionary.com, May 10, 2000, http://dictionary.reference.com/wordoftheday/archive/2000/05/10.html.)

1. What is the topic?

   a. German words

   b. psychology

   c. the meaning of the term *schadenfreude*

   d. schadenfreude and celebrities

2. Which sentence is the topic sentence?

   a. Although there is no equivalent English word for it, *schadenfreude* is the German term for the feeling of pleasure one gets when hearing of another's misfortune.

b. Psychologists say that we are expressing schadenfreude, for example, when we feel spiteful delight in watching celebrities fail.

c. We're interested in court trials of the rich and famous because we are secretly—sometimes even openly—glad that the high-and-mighty have been brought down to a less exalted position.

d. Schadenfreude is also the glee we experience when the pretty homecoming queen trips on her dress.

3. Which statement best paraphrases the topic sentence?

a. *Schadenfreude,* a word with no English equivalent, is the term Germans use to describe happiness sparked by someone's failure or setback.

b. We humans enjoy watching celebrities fail and make major mistakes.

c. Because we secretly dislike homecoming queens, we feel schadenfreude when we think about them.

d. Criminal proceedings against the wealthy and the well known make us happy because we like seeing the once rich and famous humbled and humiliated.

4. What pattern or patterns do you see at work in this passage?

a. time order

b. cause and effect

c. comparison and contrast

d. definition

e. classification

2. According to neuropsychologist Prathiba Shammi, the human brain has to complete a two-step process to comprehend humor. First, we have to realize that something surprising or unexpected has occurred. For example, consider a sign in a Hong Kong tailor's shop that reads "Please have a fit upstairs." If we are going to find this sign amusing, then our brain has to recognize that the tailor seems to be inviting us to come upstairs to display some kind of emotional outburst. That thought still won't seem funny, though, until our brain completes the second step and searches our working memory for a meaning that makes sense. In this case, our mind realizes that tailors "fit" clothes on people; that particular sense of *fit* was what the sign intended. After we complete both mental steps, we can see the humor. This same process occurs when we hear the punch line of some jokes. First, we feel surprise because for a split second the joke doesn't make any sense. Next, though, our mind searches for a meaning that *does* make sense and then we mentally put the two together in order to see why the joke is funny. (Source of information: Lee Dye, "Humor on the Brain," ABCNews.com, http://abcnews.go.com/sections/science/DyeHard/dye990414.html.)

1. What is the topic?

    a. the brain

    b. humor

    c. comprehending humor

    d. the elements of a funny joke

2. Which sentence is the topic sentence?

    a. According to neuropsychologist Prathiba Shammi, the human brain has to complete a two-step process to comprehend humor.

    b. First, we have to realize that something surprising or unexpected has occurred.

    c. That thought still won't seem funny, though, until our brain completes the second step and searches our working memory for a meaning that makes sense.

    d. This same process occurs when we hear the punch line of some jokes.

3. Which statement best paraphrases the topic sentence?

    a. Prathiba Shammi claims that your brain has to complete two mental steps in order to find something funny.

    b. Understanding the surprise or unexpected element of a joke is necessary to see the humor.

    c. Until your brain finds something in your memory that makes sense, a joke won't seem humorous.

    d. If your mind does not use an orderly thought process, you can't understand a joke's punch line.

4. What pattern or patterns do you see at work in this passage?

    a. time order

    b. cause and effect

    c. comparison and contrast

    d. definition

    e. classification

3. Do you want to own more stuff? Do you crave more clothes, jewelry, stereos, a big-screen TV, new appliances, a better computer, recreation and fitness equipment, a more expensive car, and a big house to put it all in? If so, like many Americans, you may be caught up in a cycle of acquisition, which begins with a desire to have more possessions. This desire causes us to buy all of the latest high-tech devices, gadgets, fashions, and so on. As the pile of new stuff grows, we realize that we need more space to put it all in, so we buy bigger and more expensive houses. The size of an average U.S. house, which is now 2,200 square feet, has increased 24 percent since 1985. Of course, a larger house means a larger mortgage payment. Thus, after we move all of our stuff into our bigger homes, we have to spend more time and energy making money to pay for it all. Consequently, we work more and more to be able not only to pay for what we already have but also to buy even more. In the end, we spend less and less time in the big houses that contain the stuff we already have because we have to go to work to earn the money to pay for all of it. And the cycle begins again. (Source of information: S. E. Gloger, "Home Sweet Cocoon: Hearthland Economics," *Future Magazine,* Winter 2003, www.phoenix.edu/students/future/oldissues/Winter2003/cocoon.htm.)

1. What is the topic?
   a. personal possessions
   b. big houses
   c. the cycle of acquisition
   d. making money in America

2. Which sentence is the topic sentence?
   a. Do you want to own more stuff?
   b. If so, like many Americans, you may be caught up in a cycle of acquisition, which begins with a desire to have more possessions.
   c. As the pile of new stuff grows, we realize that we need more space to put it all in, so we buy bigger and more expensive houses.
   d. Consequently, we work more and more to be able not only to pay for what we already have but also to buy even more.

3. Which statement best paraphrases the topic sentence?
   a. Americans own more stuff than people in any other nation.

b. Many Americans have become caught in a cycle of spending and working and spending.

c. In America, the size of houses continues to grow.

d. Americans work hard because they are very materialistic.

4. What pattern or patterns do you see at work in this passage?

a. time order

b. cause and effect

c. comparison and contrast

d. definition

e. classification

4. A recent Allstate Insurance survey revealed that there are five different types of American driving personalities. The company labeled the first type "Auto-Bahners." This group, which includes 17 percent of all drivers, contains those who describe themselves as "fast" and "aggressive" but also "good" drivers. These drivers consider driving exciting and often speed; the majority of them have driven more than twenty miles over the speed limit at least once. Most have been pulled over by the police, some even ticketed, within the last five years. The second group, the "Auto-Nomous," accounts for 21 percent of drivers. They, too, describe themselves as "good" drivers, but they tend to find driving more relaxing than exciting. These people, two-thirds of whom are male, describe themselves and their cars as "rugged" and "powerful." Not surprisingly, six in ten of them drive either a pickup truck or a sport utility vehicle. Another 23 percent of drivers are the "Auto-Matics." These people do not enjoy driving; almost two-thirds say that they dislike it or are indifferent to it. Of all drivers, Auto-Matics tend to be the least confident about their driving skills; nonetheless, they tend to like owning "trendy" and "attention-getting" vehicles. A fourth category of drivers are the "Auto-Pragmatics." Members of this group, 15 percent of all drivers, use words and phrases like "cautious," "economically conscious," and "environmentally friendly" to describe themselves and their vehicles. Predominantly female, these drivers are the most safety-conscious of all motorists. The majority of the last category, the "Auto-Pilots," is female. This group, another 15 percent of all drivers, includes many people who have children under eighteen living at home. Like the Auto-Pragmatics, they consider themselves to be safe drivers, but the type of vehicle they drive is not important to them. Of all drivers, Auto-Pilots are the most likely to drive a minivan. (Source of information: "What's Your Driving Personality?" *Road*

& *Travel,* August 8–23, 2003, Survey, www.roadandtravel.com/newsworthy/newsandviews03/allstatesurvey2.htm.)

1. What is the topic?

    a. Allstate Insurance

    b. driving in America

    c. types of Americans

    d. types of driver personalities

2. Which sentence is the topic sentence?

    a. A recent Allstate Insurance survey revealed that there are five different types of American driving personalities.

    b. The company labeled the first type "Auto-Bahners."

    c. This group, which includes 17 percent of all drivers, contains those who describe themselves as "fast" and "aggressive" but also "good" drivers.

    d. Of all drivers, Auto-Pilots are the most likely to drive a mini-van.

3. Which statement best paraphrases the topic sentence?

    a. The Allstate Insurance Company has identified five different kinds of drivers in America.

    b. One kind of driver is the "Auto-Bahner."

    c. Although the "Auto-Bahners" are good drivers, they tend to drive much too fast.

    d. Most minivan drivers are parents who don't care what kind of vehicle they drive.

4. What pattern or patterns do you see at work in this passage?

    a. time order

    b. cause and effect

    c. comparison and contrast

    d. definition

    e. classification

5. Generally speaking, the term *noise pollution* refers to any form of unwelcome or annoying sound, from the sound of a neighbor's barking dog to the rattle of a construction site jackhammer. However, the term noise pollution has long been difficult to accurately define because noise differs from other forms of pollution in several respects. For one thing, noise can completely disappear. Unlike chemicals and other kinds of pollutants, which remain in the air, water, or soil even after polluting stops, noise does not remain in the environment after its source ceases to generate it. Second, noise pollution cannot be measured as easily as can other forms of pollution. Scientists can analyze soil, water, and air samples to determine how many pollutants they contain and then decide if the amounts are unhealthy. However, it is more difficult to determine how much exposure to noise causes damage. Finally, the definition of the word *noise* is subject to individual opinion. To some people, the sound of loud music or the roar of a motorcycle engine may be pleasant or exhilarating while to others those same sounds seem grating and stressful. (Source of information: "The Noise FAQ," Right to Quiet, www.quiet.org/faq.htm.)

1. What is the topic?

    a. noise

    b. pollution

    c. noise pollution

    d. sound

2. Which sentence is the topic sentence?

    a. Generally speaking, the term *noise pollution* refers to any form of unwelcome or annoying sound, from the sound of a neighbor's barking dog to the rattle of a jackhammer at a construction site.

    b. However, the term *noise pollution* has long been difficult to accurately define because noise differs from other forms of pollution in several respects.

    c. For one thing, noise can completely disappear.

    d. To some people, the sound of loud music or the roar of a motorcycle engine may be pleasant or exhilrating while to others those same sounds seem grating and stressful.

3. Which statement best paraphrases the topic sentence?

    a. Noise pollution is defined as any sound that irritates people.

    b. Noise pollution differs from other kinds of pollution, so it's not easy to define the term.

    c. Noise comes and goes.

    d. Some people like loud noises, and some people don't.

4. What pattern or patterns do you see at work in this passage?

a. time order

b. cause and effect

c. comparison and contrast

d. definition

e. classification

C H A P T E R 4

Understanding and Outlining Longer Readings

In this chapter, you'll learn

- how to adapt what you know about paragraphs to longer, multiparagraph readings.

- how to recognize the *thesis statements* that put main ideas into words.

- how to locate major and minor supporting details.

- how to create informal outlines.

In Chapter 4, you'll be using some of the same skills you polished in Chapter 3, "Reviewing Paragraph Essentials." But this time, you'll apply those skills, with some modification, to readings a good deal longer than a paragraph.

Understanding Longer Readings

To thoroughly understand a paragraph, you need to answer three questions:

1. What's the topic?
2. What's the main idea?
3. Which supporting details are essential to understanding that main idea?

Fortunately, the same questions also apply to readings longer than a single paragraph. Still, that's not to say there are no differences between reading a single paragraph and reading longer selections. There are, in fact, six crucial differences you need to take into account.

The Main Idea Controls More Than a Paragraph

In longer readings, there is one main idea that unifies not just a single paragraph but all or most of the paragraphs in the selection. Because it controls the content of the other paragraphs, you can think of this main idea as the "controlling main idea." The controlling main idea gives all the other paragraphs a purpose. They exist to explain, clarify, and argue its meaning.

Several Sentences May Be Needed to Express the Main Idea

The main idea of an entire reading can often be summed up in a single sentence. But sometimes it requires several sentences, maybe even a paragraph. For that reason, many composition textbooks use the term **thesis statement** to talk about the stated main idea of a research paper or an essay. Following that tradition, we'll use the same term here to emphasize that the main idea of a reading cannot always be summed up in one single sentence.

Introductions Are Likely to Be Longer

In paragraphs, introductions are usually limited to only a sentence or two. However, in longer readings, introducing the main idea may require several paragraphs. While it's true that textbook authors are likely to present readers with the main idea in the first or second paragraph, don't assume that's the case with magazine or journal articles and essays. In these materials, writers sometimes include lengthy introductions in order to provide background or to stimulate reader interest.

Thesis Statements Don't Wander Quite So Much

Topic sentences can appear anywhere in a paragraph—at the beginning, middle, or end. Thesis statements, in contrast, are more fixed in their location. Yes, an author occasionally builds up to the main idea and puts the thesis statement at the very end of a reading. But that's not typical. Far more likely is the appearance of the thesis statement at the beginning of a reading. Thus the opening paragraphs in an essay, an article, or a chapter section deserve particularly close attention.

Major Supporting Details Can Take Up More Space

In longer readings, one supporting detail essential to the main idea can take up an entire paragraph. Thus longer readings require you to do a good deal more sifting and sorting of information as you decide which individual statements are essential to your understanding of a major detail.

Minor Details Can Occupy an Entire Paragraph

As they do in paragraphs, minor details in longer readings further explain major ones. They add colorful facts or supply repetition for emphasis. Like major details, minor details can also take up an entire paragraph. And just as in paragraphs, minor details may or may not be important.

Sometimes minor supporting details supply the more specific examples or explanations necessary for a clear understanding of a major detail. When this is the case, the minor details should be considered essential. But if they simply offer a colorful or humorous anecdote or just provide repetition for emphasis, you need not store them away in your long-term memory. Nor should you make an effort to include them in your notes.

Now that you know how reading a paragraph is different from reading a more extended piece of writing, it's time to put what you have learned into practice. Read the following selection.

Research on Leadership

Thesis
Statement

Topic Sentence

1   In business, managers have to be leaders. Thus it comes as no surprise that researchers have been studying the nature of leadership in business. <u>At the University of Michigan, researchers have found that leadership behavior among managers can be divided into two categories—job-centered and employee-centered.</u>

2   <u>Job-centered leaders closely supervise their employees in an effort to monitor and control their performance</u>. They are primarily concerned with getting a job done and less concerned with the feelings or attitudes of their employees—unless those attitudes and feelings affect the task at hand. In general, they don't encourage employees to express their opinions on how best to accomplish a task.

Topic Sentence   3   <u>In contrast, employee-centered leaders focus on reaching goals by building a sense of team spirit</u>. An employee-centered leader is concerned with subordinates' job satisfaction and group unity. Employee-centered leaders are also more willing to let employees have a voice in how they do their jobs.

Topic Sentence   4   <u>The Michigan researchers also investigated which kind of leadership is more effective</u>. They concluded that managers whose leadership was employee-centered were generally more effective than managers who were primarily job-centered. That is, their employees performed at higher levels and were more satisfied. (Adapted from Van Fleet and Peterson, *Contemporary Management*, p. 332.)

Having read "Research on Leadership," look closely at the thesis statement. Now look at the topic sentences of the remaining paragraphs. Can you see how those topic sentences clarify the thesis statement? This reading illustrates how thesis statements and topic sentences work together. The thesis statement introduces the author's general point. Then the topic sentences of each paragraph flesh out and clarify that point. Within each paragraph, the major details should always clarify the topic sentence; however, they may or may not directly support the thesis statement.

The following diagram expresses the relationship between the thesis statement and the topic sentences within a reading or an essay.

Thesis Statement

At the University of Michigan, researchers have found that leadership behavior among managers can be divided into two categories—job-centered and employee-centered.

Topic Sentence of Paragraph 2

Job-centered leaders closely supervise their employees in an effort to monitor and control their performance.

Topic Sentence of Paragraph 3

In contrast, employee-centered leaders focus on reaching goals by building a sense of team spirit.

Topic Sentence of Paragraph 4

The Michigan researchers also investigated which kind of leardership is more effective.

Before going on to Exercise 1, read the following selection and underline the thesis statement. Remember, the thesis statement shouldn't unify just one paragraph. It should unify the entire reading.

The Death Penalty Through the Ages

1 In the United States today, the federal government and 38 states—including Florida, Texas, New York, and North Carolina—have statutes allowing the death penalty for certain crimes. Still, capital punishment is now reserved almost exclusively for murderers, and nationwide, fewer than 100 criminals are executed every year.

2   In times past, though, the death penalty was imposed not only more often but also for more offenses, some rather trivial by modern standards. In ancient Babylon, for example, the Code of King Hammurabi allowed the death penalty for 25 different crimes that did not involve the taking of a life. Around 1500 BCE, the Egyptians imposed the death penalty for killing a cat, an animal they considered sacred. In the seventh century BCE, the Draconian* Code of Athens actually prescribed capital punishment for *every* crime committed. In the fifth century BCE, the Romans punished with death anyone who sang

*Draconian: Draco was a Greek leader whose laws were considered extremely harsh. Thus his name has become an adjective meaning "harsh and severe."

insulting songs, burned a stack of corn too close to a house, committed perjury, or disturbed the peace in the city at night. In 438, the Code of Theodosius designated more than 80 different crimes as punishable by death.

3   During the Middle Ages, the death penalty was used for a number of major as well as minor crimes. In Britain, for example, people were put to death for everything from stealing a loaf of bread to sacrilege* or treason. From 1509 to 1547, during the reign of Henry VIII, as many as 72,000 people were executed for various offenses. By the 1700s, the list of crimes punishable by death increased to 220 offenses. These offenses included stealing, cutting down trees, sending threatening letters, and producing counterfeit money.

4   English settlers in America initially brought with them to the New World the idea of severe punishments for crimes both large and small. In addition to executing murderers, the Capital Laws of New England, in effect from 1636 to 1647, punished with death anyone convicted of witchcraft, adultery, assault, blasphemy,* idolatry,* and perjury. In 1665, the New York colony imposed capital punishment on anyone found guilty of challenging the king's rights for striking a parent. Although these laws were relaxed for fear of discouraging new colonists, by 1780 the Commonwealth of Massachusetts was still executing those convicted of crimes such as burglary, homosexuality, and arson. As late as 1837, North Carolina required death for the crimes of assisting with arson, bigamy, encouraging slaves to riot, and hiding slaves with the intention of freeing them. (Sources of information: U.S. Department of Justice, Office of Justice Programs, Bureau of Justice Statistics, "Capital Punishment Statistics," www.ojp.usdoj.gov/bjs/cp.htm; Michael H. Reggio, "History of the Death Penalty," *PBS Frontline,* 1999, www.pbs.org/wgbh/pages/frontline/shows/execution/readings/history.html.)

Tempting as it might be to assume that the first paragraph of this reading contains the thesis statement, that assumption would lead you astray. Neither of the sentences in paragraph 1 is developed beyond the first paragraph. Therefore the first paragraph cannot possibly contain the thesis statement.

Look now at paragraph 2. The first sentence is the topic sentence. All of the sentences after the first one serve to illustrate the

*sacrilege: treating religious beliefs or objects with disrespect.
*blasphemy: using profane language, swearing.
*idolatry: excessive devotion to images of worship or false gods.

"rather trivial" offenses that once warranted the death sentence. However, the topic sentence of paragraph 2 also expresses the main idea of the entire reading: In other words, it is also the thesis statement of the entire reading. Both paragraphs 3 and 4—like the individual sentences in paragraph 2—identify some of the trivial offenses referred to in paragraph 2.

CHECK YOUR UNDERSTANDING

Without looking back at the text, describe how single paragraphs differ from longer readings. When you finish, compare your list to the original explanation.

1. _____

_____

2. _____

_____

3. _____

_____

4. _____

_____

5. _____

_____

6. _____

_____

EXERCISE 1

DIRECTIONS Underline the thesis statement in each reading.

EXAMPLE

Is Your Home Clean?

1 Surveys show that, overall, Americans scrub and wipe down their homes fairly often. A Bounty Home Care Council survey, for example, revealed that bathrooms are cleaned an average of five

times a month, and that 42 percent of people clean their bathrooms twice a week or more. However, environmental microbiologist Dr. Charles Gerba of the University of Arizona has shown that many clean homes just *look* clean. In reality, they are often breeding grounds for bacteria. <u>Indeed, the homes that seem the cleanest are often the ones teeming with the most disease-causing germs. This happens because cleaning tools and techniques not only don't kill the pathogens, they also spread the germs all over the place.</u>

Thesis Statement

2   Dr. Gerba's research has shown that a clean bathroom is often smeared with millions of harmful microorganisms. This is because about half the population uses sponges and rags to clean. Yet only 24 percent of Americans disinfect them after each use, about 40 percent rinse them only with water, and 16 percent just put the sponges and rags away after using them. Consequently, bathroom sponges and rags are filled with germs; the more they are used, the more microorganisms get spread around on surfaces.

3   Clean kitchens, too, often harbor more dangerous bacteria than messy kitchens. As a matter of fact, research has shown that even in the most spotless of homes, bacteria associated with fecal matter, such as *E. coli,* are regularly found in the sink and on countertops. These germs are spread by unwashed hands; raw meat; and the sponges, dishrags, and dish towels used to clean up. For example, a kitchen sponge that has been used for only two or three days is filled with millions of bacteria, so the more it's used to wipe surfaces, the more it spreads germs around.

4   Dr. Gerba's research has also shown that freshly laundered clothes are not truly clean either. In one study, he swabbed the inside of 100 household washing machines in Florida and Arizona and found that more than 60 percent tested positive for coliform bacteria, which comes from fecal matter, and 20 percent tested positive for *staphylococcus,* a major cause of food-borne illness. Swabs of dryers showed that even high-heat settings don't kill salmonella and another bacteria (*mycobacterium fortuitium*) that causes skin infections. Thus every time a new load of clothes or towels goes into either the washer or the dryer, these harmful germs get into the fabrics.

5   However, Dr. Gerba and other experts say that changing to different tools and techniques will help kill and stop the spread of germs. They recommend cleaning with sturdy paper towels and then throwing them away. They also suggest using bleach on surfaces and in the laundry, as well as putting rags, towels, and sponges in the microwave for at least one minute after each use. (Sources of information: Amanda Hesser, "Squeaky Clean? Not

Even Close," *New York Times*, January 28, 2004, p. F1; "Paper Towels Help Wipe Out Harmful Bathroom Germs," *PR Newswire*, November 2, 2000; Jo Werne, "Clean Kitchen Can Be a Hotbed of Germs," *Knight Ridder/Tribune News Services*, October 12, 1995; "Germs in the Laundry," Clorox Company, *PR Newswire*, June 4, 1999.)

EXPLANATION In this reading, the thesis statement consists of two sentences rather than one. The thesis statement tells readers that the author intends to explore two related points: (1) Clean homes are often not really clean at all, and (2) this is because improper cleaning tools and techniques can spread germs. Paragraphs 2, 3, and 4 then provide the supporting details that clarify both parts of this thesis statement.

1. Gender and Listening

1 Men and women learn different styles of listening just as they learn different styles for using verbal and nonverbal messages. Not surprisingly, these different styles can create major difficulties in opposite-sex interpersonal communication. According to Deborah Tannen in her best-selling *You Just Don't Understand: Women and Men in Conversation,* women seek to build rapport and establish a closer relationship and use listening to achieve these ends. Men, on the other hand, will play up their expertise, emphasize it, and use it in dominating the interaction. Women play down their expertise and are more interested in communicating supportiveness. Tannen argues that the goal of a man in conversation is to be given respect, so he seeks to show his knowledge and expertise. A woman, on the other hand, seeks to be liked, so she expresses agreement.

2 Men and women also show that they're listening in different ways. In conversation, a woman is more apt to give lots of listening cues such as interjecting "Yeah" or "Uh-uh," nodding in agreement, and smiling. A man is more likely to listen quietly, without giving lots of listening cues as feedback. Subsequent research seems to confirm Tannen's position. For example, an analysis of calls to a crisis center in Finland revealed that calls received by a female counselor were significantly longer for both men and women callers (Salminen and Glad 1992). It's likely that the greater number of listening cues given by the women encouraged the callers to keep talking. This same study also found that male callers were helped by "just listening," whereas women callers were helped by "empathic understanding."

3   Tannen argues, however, that men listen less to women than women listen to men. The reason, says Tannen, is that listening places the person in an inferior position, whereas speaking places the person in a superior position. Men may seem to assume a more argumentative posture while listening, as if getting ready to argue. They may also appear to ask questions that are more argumentative or that seek to puncture holes in your position as a way to play up their own expertise. Women are more likely to ask supportive questions and perhaps offer criticism that is more positive than men. Women let the speaker see that they're listening. Men, on the other hand, use fewer listening cues in conversation. Men and women act this way to both men and women; their customary ways of talking don't seem to change depending on whether the listener is male or female.

4   There is no evidence to show that these differences represent any negative motives on the part of men to prove themselves superior or of women to ingratiate themselves. Rather, these differences in listening seem largely the result of the way in which men and women have been socialized. (DeVito. *The Interpersonal Communication Book,* p. 122.)

2. Our Oldest Enemy: The Locust

1   In 2001, America, Russia, and China were invaded by vast armies bent on nothing less than total destruction. In early June of that year, the enemy entered these countries on foot, creeping along at just a mile an hour at first. But two weeks later, they had begun to take to the air, swooping in from the skies to plunder the land and covering hundreds of miles a day, obliterating everything in their path.

2   Specialized emergency teams went into action. Aircraft roared into the skies, flying only sixty-five feet above the ground in a skillful counterattack. The initial battle raged for a week; sporadic fighting continued until July, when the three countries finally declared themselves victorious. At war's end, the enemy dead numbered in the *billions*.

3   It had been no human invasion but a far more fearsome and rapacious* threat: locusts. Using chemicals sprayed from aircraft or importing hundreds of thousands of locust-eating ducks, humans wreaked havoc on these prodigiously* destructive pests. Nevertheless, throughout most of history, the reverse has been

---

*rapacious: greedy.
*prodigiously: enormously.

true. When a plague of locusts arrives, it has been people who have suffered more than the insects.

4　　The earliest written record of a locust plague is probably in the Book of Exodus, which describes an attack that took place in Egypt in about 3500 BCE: "They covered the face of the whole land, so that the land was darkened . . . ; not a green thing remained, neither tree nor plant of the field, through all the land of Egypt" (Exodus 10:12–15). Another biblical account, in the Book of Job, describes trees "made white" as locusts stripped even the bark from the branches.

5　　Locusts have always spelled disaster. In a single day, a typical large swarm (about 40 million insects) can eat 80,000 tons of corn, devouring a city's food supply for an entire year in just hours. In 125 BCE, locusts destroyed the grain crop in northern Africa; 80,000 people died of starvation. In 591 AD, a plague of locusts in Italy caused the death of more than a million people and animals. In 1613, disaster struck the French region of La Camargue when locusts ate enough grass in a single day to feed 4,000 cattle for a year. Between 1873 and 1877, locusts blackened the skies of the American West from California to Missouri, causing $200 million in crop damage. At the time, in fact, the U.S. government pronounced the locust to be "the most serious impediment to the settlement of the West." The Nile Valley suffered in 1889 when locusts so thoroughly destroyed crops over an estimated 2,000-square-mile area that even the mice starved in their wake. Between 1949 and 1963, locust swarms in Africa caused an estimated $100 million worth of damage annually. In 1988, the Ethiopian cereal crop was laid waste, leaving a million people without food. The 2001 invasion of America destroyed more than 12 million acres of farmland, forcing some areas, such as the state of Utah, to declare an agricultural emergency. (Sources of information: Adams and Riley, eds., "The Ravenous Millions," *Facts and Fallacies,* p. 50; June Southworth, "Day of the Locusts," *The Daily Mail* (London), June 20, 2001; Frithjof Voss, "Simply the Pest," *Geographical,* March 1, 2000, pp. 98–99.)

3. Killer Bees

1 Although their name makes them sound like something out of a horror film, killer bees really do exist. And while they are not quite so terrifying as their name implies, they are definitely not an insect—like the ladybug—that one should invite into the garden. On the contrary, both animals and humans would do well to avoid these sometimes ferociously angry bees.

2   Killer bees (officially called Africanized honeybees) originated in Brazil in 1956 as an experiment in mating the African honeybee with local bees. The breeders were hoping to get bees that would produce more honey. Instead, they produced extremely aggressive bees that have attacked—and in some cases killed—both people and animals. Each year the bees move about 350 miles (563 kilometers) north; in 1990, they crossed the U.S. border into Hidalgo, Texas.

3   Similar to the rumors that surround sharks, myths about African bees abound.* For example, it's not true that they fly faster than domestic honeybees. On the contrary, both types of bees average between 12 and 15 miles per hour. Also, the sting of the African bee actually has less, not more, venom than that of domestic honeybees. African bees are also a good deal smaller than domestic ones, not gigantic in size as has been rumored.

4   Still, African bees do have some features that make them an insect to avoid. When an African bee's body is crushed—from a swat, for example—it releases an odor that incites nearby bees to attack. Also, African bees vigorously and aggressively protect their hives. About ten times as many African bees as European bees will sting when their colonies are invaded. The good news is that scientists believe the African bees' aggressiveness will eventually diminish as they interbreed with the more peaceful European bees to the north.

4. Eat Garlic for Your Health

1 The ancient Egyptians believed that garlic could cure a wide variety of ills. In fact, early writings on the medical uses of herbs record close to thirty uses for the plant that the Romans used to call "the stinking rose." For example, it was claimed that garlic could heal wounds, cure stomach cramps, and chase away common colds. What's surprising about these claims is that modern science actually bears some of them out, and eating garlic seems to be remarkably good for your health.

2   In 1858 Louis Pasteur* discovered that garlic could kill bacteria. Since Pasteur's time, researchers have found that garlic also

---

*abound: exist in great supply.
*Louis Pasteur: (1822–1895) French microbiologist who invented pasteurization and developed a vaccine for rabies.

inhibits the growth of bacteria in the stomach. A diet rich in garlic actually inhibits the growth of the bacteria that cause ulcers. Some studies have also suggested that eating garlic can slow the growth of cancers in the colon, breast, and skin. Although research still needs to be done to prove conclusively* that garlic can help prevent or cure cancer, existing evidence suggests that it may well help us fight this deadly disease.

3   There are also indications that garlic can help prevent heart disease. A diet high in garlic seems to reduce the chance of blood clots. In addition, garlic may reduce hardening of the arteries, another known contributor to heart problems.

4   Because garlic has such a powerful—some would even say unpleasant—smell, many people are loath* to eat it. Instead, they consume deodorized garlic pills. Unfortunately, though the pills do confer some health benefits, they aren't as effective as raw garlic cloves. So if you want to eat garlic for your health, you might consider stocking up on breath mints as well.

 ## Major and Minor Details

Major details in longer readings directly explain the thesis statement. They answer potential questions readers might raise; further define any general words or terms; and, when necessary, offer proof of an author's claim. While major details in a paragraph consist of single sentences, in longer readings you may find that an entire paragraph is devoted to explaining one major detail. When this happens, you'll have to decide how much of the paragraph is essential to your understanding of that one detail.

As they do in paragraphs, minor details in longer readings further explain or flesh out major details; they also provide color or emphasis. But here again, you can't assume that minor details are automatically not essential to your understanding of the thesis statement. It all depends on what they contribute to your understanding of the major details they modify.

Read the following selection. As you do, think about which supporting details are essential to your understanding of the underlined thesis statement.

---

*conclusively: without a doubt.
*loath: unwilling.

Defining Love

Thesis
Statement

1 What is love? No one knows for sure. However, researcher R. J. Sternberg has a theory. <u>According to Sternberg, love consists of three separate ingredients, and each one is crucial either to falling in love or to staying in love.</u>

2   Passion is a feeling of heightened sexual arousal, and it's usually accompanied by a strong, romantic attraction. In the throes* of passion, each lover feels that life is barely worth living unless the other is present. Unfortunately, passionate feelings almost always diminish over time, although they are still essential to a loving relationship. Luckily, if there's a strong sense of intimacy between the partners, the loss or decrease of passion can be accepted and the love maintained.

3   Intimacy—feelings of closeness, sharing, and affection—is essential to staying in love. Both partners need to feel that they view the world in similar ways and can turn to one another in times of great sadness or joy. If the one you love is not the one you feel particularly close to, over time you may find that love doesn't last. Typically in a relationship, intimacy grows steadily at first and then levels off.

4   Commitment refers to a conscious decision to stay with a person both in good times and in bad. Like intimacy, a sense of commitment is essential to staying in love as time passes. But unlike intimacy, commitment frequently requires some hard work and determination. It seldom comes without effort.

    While reading the thesis statement in this selection, you probably wondered what three ingredients the author had in mind. Anticipating that question, the author defines all three. Those definitions are the major details that refer directly to the thesis statement. However, the minor details that expand on those major details cannot simply be ignored—not if you want to understand Sternberg's theory. Minor detail or not, it is important to remember that if intimacy is lacking, love doesn't last—at least that is R. J. Sternberg's point of view.

▶️ Thesis Statements and Major Details

    In trying to differentiate between major and minor details, it's important to use any and all clues provided by the thesis statement.

---

*throes: pangs, spasms.

For example, the thesis statement in the reading about love pointed out that love consists of "three separate ingredients." This phrase is a tip-off to the major details. It practically guarantees that each major detail will describe one of the three ingredients.

Key Words in Thesis Statements

Any time a thesis statement focuses on general words, such as *reasons, studies, groups, causes,* and *theories,* those words need to be further explained in order to be meaningful to readers. After all, if you know that there are three reasons for increased violence in the schools, this information doesn't help you much until you know what the reasons are. When you see words like *reasons, causes,* and so on in what you think is the thesis statement, check to see if the paragraphs that follow further explain those reasons or causes. If they do, you have gained on two fronts: (1) You have confirmed your guess about the thesis statement and (2) you have discovered a key to the major details.

Look now at the opening paragraph of a reading from a psychology text. Read it through and see if you can find a word or phrase that points the way to the major details.

In everyday life, requests for compliance are common. A stranger asks you to yield a phone booth so she can make a call. A salesperson suggests you buy a more expensive watch than the one you first asked to see. Or a coworker asks to borrow fifty cents in order to buy a danish during coffee break. Have you ever wondered what determines whether or not you say yes? Although many different factors come into play when we agree to a request, there are three essential strategies for inducing compliance.

Based on that paragraph, do you have the strong sense that the major details will describe the three strategies that encourage compliance? If you do, you are right. That is precisely the function of the major details that follow the opening paragraph. See for yourself:

1 One way of encouraging compliance is to employ the *foot-in-the-door strategy.* The name comes from a technique long used in the days when salespeople went door to door to sell their wares. As the saying went at the time, "If you can get your foot in the door, the sale is almost a sure thing." In psychological terms, the foot-in-the-door strategy means that if someone can get you to comply with some small request, you are very likely to

comply with a much larger demand. For example, if the committee to re-elect your local mayor wants you to put a huge sign in your front window promoting her candidacy, members of the committee might first ask you to display a bumper sticker. Once you agree to display the bumper sticker, they might ask you to wear a button. Once you've agreed to those two smaller requests, you would more than likely be ready to put that sign in your window.

2   Psychologists suspect that the foot-in-the-door strategy works because we observe our own behavior. Recognizing that we have agreed to a small request, we convince ourselves that the next, larger demand isn't all that different. Thus we're ready to comply.

3   The *door-in-the-face strategy*—the name was coined by psychologist Robert Cialdini—is a variation on foot-in-the-door, and it works like this: If you have flatly said no to a large and inconvenient request ("slammed the door in someone's face"), you're more likely to agree to a smaller bid for help. Say, for example, your neighbor comes by and asks you to pick up his daughter at school for the next week while he is working overtime. Chances are you will say no because it requires too big a chunk of your time. But if he comes back the next day and says he got a friend to handle Monday, Wednesday, and Friday, you are likely to agree to take over on Tuesday and Thursday.

4   This strategy works because it seems as if the person making the request is being reasonable and making a concession. For that reason, the person doing the favor feels that it is only fair to comply with the smaller request.

5   If you or someone you know has ever purchased a car, you will recognize the *low-ball* technique of encouraging compliance. In the context of car buying, the salesperson offers a "low-ball" price that is significantly less than that of the competition. Once the customer seems interested, the salesperson begins to bump up the price. In other words, the low-ball technique gets you to comply with a request that seems to cost little or nothing. Once you say yes, the person starts tacking on additional items. For example, your roommate asks for a ride to the local ticket office, where she hopes to get tickets to a hot concert. Since the ticket office is only five minutes away by car, you say, "Sure, no problem." It's at that point that your roommate tells you she has to be there by 5:00 in the morning because that's when the line starts forming. If you agree, you've just succumbed to the low-ball technique. (Source of information: Coon, *Essentials of Psychology,* p. 625.)

Particularly in textbooks, thesis statements frequently offer clues to major details in the form of phrases such as "three common factors," "four major reasons," or "five different categories." Generally speaking, every one of the factors, reasons, or categories is likely to be a major detail. Keep that in mind while you are completing your textbook assignments or doing research.

◾ EXERCISE 2

DIRECTIONS Read each selection and look carefully at the underlined thesis statement. Then answer the questions by filling in the blanks or circling the letter of the correct response.

EXAMPLE

The Ancient Roman Circus

Thesis 1 <u>Although nowadays we think of the circus as an amusing enter-
Statement tainment for kids, originally it was not quite such a harmless
event. To be sure, the first circus, like its modern counterpart,
included death-defying events. But there was one big difference.
In the early Roman circus, death was a very real possibility, and
circus spectators were accustomed to—and expected—bloodshed.</u>

2   The Roman Circus Maximus began under the rule of Julius Caesar, and it specialized in two big events—brutal fights between gladiators (or between gladiators and animals) and equally bloody chariot races. In most cases, both events ended in the death of either a person or an animal. If nobody died, the audience was likely to be disappointed. Even worse, the emperor would be displeased.

3   Not surprisingly, the circus event that was in fashion usually reflected the taste of the man in power. Julius Caesar, for example, favored aggressive chariot races. Because the charioteers were usually slaves racing to win their freedom, they drove their horses unmercifully, and serious accidents were an exciting possibility. In the hope of surviving, the charioteers wore helmets and wrapped the chariot reins around their bodies. They also carried knives to cut themselves free if necessary. Spills occurred more often than not, and the charioteers would be thrown from the chariot and dragged repeatedly around the ring by runaway horses. Knives and helmets notwithstanding, most did not survive, not that the screaming crowd cared.

4   During the reign of Augustus, from 27 BCE to 14 AD, a fight to the death between man and beast was the most popular circus

event, and more than 3,500 lions and tigers perished in the circus arena, taking hundreds of gladiators with them. Under the half-mad Emperor Nero, who ruled during the first century AD, the most popular circus spectacle was lion versus Christian, with the Christians the guaranteed losers. Fortunately for both Christians and the slaves who followed in their wake, this savage circus practice was outlawed in 326 AD by the Emperor Constantine.

5   Although the pitting of Christians against lions was staged in a special arena, most of the circus events that took place in Rome were staged in the largest arena of them all—the Colosseum. The capacity of this great stadium, completed in 79 AD, was enormous. It seated close to 50,000 people. In one Colosseum season alone, 2,000 gladiators went to their deaths, all in the name of circus fun.[1]

1. How would you paraphrase the thesis statement?

Unlike the modern circus, the ancient Roman circus was a good deal more deadly.

2. Which question about the thesis statement do the major supporting details help to answer?

a. What are the similarities between ancient and modern circuses?

b. How did early circus events all but guarantee death?

EXPLANATION As it should, the paraphrase restates the point of the thesis statement but alters the words. The most likely question raised by the thesis statement is *b*. The main idea of the entire reading is that ancient circuses were often deadly, and the reader needs to know why this was so.

1. The Five Languages of Love

1 According to relationship expert Dr. Gary Chapman, author of *The Five Languages of Love,* people not only have very different

Thesis Statement

personalities, they also express love in different ways. Chapman believes that every individual best expresses love—and prefers to receive love—through one of five different communication styles. He calls these styles "love languages."

———————

[1]Charles Panati, *Browser's Book of Beginnings.* Boston: Houghton Mifflin, 1984, pp. 262–264.

2   Some people feel that love is best expressed through **quality time** spent as a couple. Quality time, according to Dr. Chapman, does not mean simply being in the same room together; instead, it involves doing things as a couple and devoting attention to one another. People who prefer quality time as their love language feel loved when they are taken out on dates, or when their partners set aside time for them, even if it's just to chat for a few moments.

3   Other people, however, prefer **words of affirmation** as a way of giving or receiving love. These individuals like to be told that they are loved. They expect to hear "I love you" or "I appreciate you" often, and they like compliments, encouragement, and praise. They like to hear things such as "That dress looks great on you" or "You have a wonderful smile."

4   **Gifts** are yet another love language. People who use this language see presents as much more than material objects. For them gifts are symbols of love and signs of affection.

5   People who express love through **acts of service,** however, aren't impressed by gifts. They believe that helping others is the best expression of love. Voluntary acts of service are what makes them happy. Cooking, doing chores, changing the baby's diaper, and walking the dog are ways to make members of this group feel cared for and supported.

6   According to Chapman, **physical touch** is the fifth kind of love expression. People using this form of communication prefer to communicate their feelings for their partners by holding hands, kissing, hugging, or having sex. They feel secure and loved when they can touch and be touched in return.

7   Chapman believes that problems arise when two people involved in a romantic relationship have different styles of expression. If each person expresses him or herself in a language the other doesn't really understand or recognize, then expressions of affection may go unnoticed and undermine the relationship. For example, people who prefer expressing love through sharing quality time may doubt their partner's affection if the partner doesn't want to do lots of things as a couple. Similarly, people who need to hear words of affirmation will feel rejected if their partners don't tell them how much they care. But while it's true that speaking different love languages can lead to misunderstanding, there is still hope. If couples become aware of the different love languages and learn to give and receive affection in a partner's preferred stye, they can enhance, even revitalize, a romantic relationship. (Sources of information: Gary Chapman, *The Five Love Languages.* Chicago:

Moody Publishers; www.fivelovelanguages.com/thefivelove
languages/index.html; Family First, "The Five Love Languages,"
www.familyfirst.net/marriage/fivelovelang.html.)

1. How would you paraphrase the thesis statement?

_____

_____

2. Which question about the thesis statement do the major supporting details help to answer?

    a. What makes some love languages more effective than others?

    b. What are the five love languages?

    c. How can couples learn to use the same love language?

2. Taking Spam Off the Menu

Thesis Statement 1 Most computer users who have e-mail addresses are familiar with
spam—unwanted e-mail messages advertising a product or ser-
vice. Spam includes offers for everything from weight-loss aids to
get-rich-quick schemes. It's the electronic version of the "junk
mail" delivered to mailboxes or the online equivalent of a telemar-
keting phone call. Experts estimate that one in every ten e-mail
messages sent today is spam. The average Internet user receives
almost 1,500 junk messages each year.

2   Spam is a cheap form of advertising. That's why it's attractive
to marketers. A business can buy a list of consumers' e-mail
addresses from another company or compile its own list by
performing a sweep of the World Wide Web. Once the list is
composed, e-mail messages can be sent out instantly to thousands of possible customers. Sending ten messages or ten million
messages costs about the same.

3   Consumers, however, find spam extremely annoying. Determining which messages are spam and then deleting them is irritating
and time-consuming. Spam is also leading many individuals to be
more reluctant about using the Internet. They fear that going to a
chatroom or signing up for a mailing list will result in an ava-
lanche of new junk mail. As a result, unwanted e-mail is one of
the major complaints of subscribers to Internet service providers.

4   Employers dislike spam too. On the job, when workers spend
even a few minutes a day dealing with spam, the labor costs can
add up quickly. As a result, many companies are spending additional money on filters to screen out spam altogether. These filters

sometimes cause problems because they can block important, necessary messages from getting through.

5   Companies that choose to filter messages often purchase anti-spam software or hire a firm that specializes in blocking unwanted spam. Symantec's Brightmail is one successful anti-spam program. It maintains thousands of e-mail accounts that collect and identify sources of spam. Then it installs software on its clients' e-mail gateways, including those of many of the largest Internet service providers. When a known spam message tries to get through the gateway, the software blocks it.

1. How would you paraphrase the thesis statement?

_____

_____

2. Which question about the thesis statement do the major supporting details help answer?

a. Why is spam unwanted?

b. How does spam compare to junk mail?

c. Which software does the best job of blocking spam?

 # Outlining Longer Readings

For reading assignments that cover fairly familiar or uncomplicated material, you can probably prepare for class discussions or exams simply by reviewing your underlining and your annotations. However, if the material is at all complicated, you may want to take notes using an **informal outline.**

Like a formal outline, an informal outline signals relationships by aligning or indenting sentences, words, or phrases. With informal outlines, however, you needn't worry about using *all* sentences or *all* phrases, and you don't have to fuss over capital or lowercase letters. You can use whatever symbols seem appropriate to the material and combine letters, numbers, abbreviations, dashes, and so on, as you need them. In other words, informal outlines are not governed by a fixed set of rules. The main thing to keep in mind is the goal of your informal outline: to develop a clear blueprint of the author's ideas and their relationship to one another.

Here are some pointers for creating clear, concise, and complete informal outlines.

Start with the Title

The title of an essay, an article, or a chapter section usually identifies the topic being discussed. Sometimes it will identify the main idea of the entire reading. Thus your outline should usually open with the title.

Follow with the Thesis Statement

After the title comes the paraphrase of the thesis statement. Because indenting to show relationships is crucial to outlining, put your paraphrase at the left-most margin of your notepaper.

List the Major Details

Now's the time to read over the supporting paragraphs and sift out the major details. At this point, keep in mind that the major details you select have to be carefully evaluated in relation to the thesis statement, and minor details in a paragraph should be included only if they are essential to the major ones. Outlining, like underlining, requires conscious and consistent selectivity. Here's an outline of the reading from pages 197–198.

The Ancient Roman Circus

The first circus began in ancient Rome, but it was much bloodier than the circus we know today.

1. The first circus, Circus Maximus, originated under Julius Caesar.
2. Ancient circuses specialized in bloody events; emperor and spectators were upset if no one died.
3. Which event was featured depended on the emperor in power.
   a. Julius Caesar liked chariot races: slaves raced for freedom and risked their lives, often dying in the process.
      —dragged around the ring when they couldn't cut themselves free
   b. During reign of Augustus, hundreds of gladiators died, taking with them more than 3,500 lions and tigers.
   c. Under Nero, Christians were thrown to the lions.

4. Colosseum in Rome staged biggest circuses.

    a. It held 50,000 people.

    b. In one season, 2,000 gladiators went to their death.

Always Indent

As the sample outline illustrates, an outline is not a list. When you make an outline, you have to indent to indicate whether different ideas carry equal weight. Major details, for example, should all be aligned under one another to indicate that they are equal in importance. Similarly, if you are summarizing several different chapter sections, then the main ideas of each section should be aligned one underneath the other.

Be Consistent

Letters, numbers, dashes (—), stars (☆☆☆), or asterisks (**) can help you separate major and minor details. Whichever symbols you use, be sure to use them consistently within the outline. Don't switch back and forth, sometimes using numbers for major details and sometimes using letters. In the long run, this kind of inconsistency will only confuse you.

Be Selective

When you outline, reduce the content of the original text as much as possible. Try to retain essential details and eliminate nonessential ones. When adding supporting details to your outline, always decide what you need to include and what you can safely leave out.

EXERCISE 3

DIRECTIONS Read the following selection. Underline and annotate it. Then make a concise and complete outline.

EXAMPLE

World War II: Interning Japanese-Americans

1 Compared with previous wars, the nation's wartime civil liberties record during World War II showed some improvement, particularly where African-Americans and women were concerned. But

Not on WWII civil
rights record

there was one enormous exception: the treatment of 120,000 Japanese-Americans. The internment* of Japanese-Americans was based not on suspicion or evidence of treason; their crime was solely their race—the fact that they were of Japanese descent.

2   Popular racial stereotypes used to fuel the war effort held that Japanese people abroad and at home were sneaky and evil, and the American people generally regarded Japan as the United States's chief enemy. Moreover, the feeling was widespread that the Japanese had to be repaid for the bombing of Pearl Harbor. Thus, with a few notable exceptions, there was no public outcry over the relocation and internment of Japanese-Americans.

3   Yet there were two obvious reasons why internment was completely unnecessary. First and foremost, there was absolutely no evidence of any attempt by Japanese-Americans to hinder the American war effort. The government's own studies proved that fact beyond question. Thus it's not surprising that in places where racism was not a factor, in Hawaii for example, the public outcry for internment was much more muted.

4   Second, Japanese-American soldiers fought valiantly for the United States. The all Japanese-American 442nd Regimental Combat Team—heavily recruited from young men in internment camps—was the most decorated unit of its size in the armed forces. Suffering heavy casualties in Italy and France, members of the 442nd were awarded a Congressional Medal of Honor, several Distinguished Service Crosses, 350 Silver Stars, and more than 3,600 Purple Hearts. (Adapted from Norton et al., *A People and a Nation*, p. 795.)

Example of
Japanese-
American bravery

Title *World War II: Interning Japanese-Americans*

Main Idea *In World War II, the imprisonment of Japanese-Americans spoiled an otherwise creditable civil rights record.*

Supporting Details 1. *Racial stereotypes used to power the war effort encouraged people to see Japanese-Americans as the enemy.*

2. *General belief that the Japanese had to be paid back for bombing Pearl Harbor.*

---

*internment: imprisonment.

3. *Two reasons why internment unnecessary*

    1) *No evidence of wrongdoing, a fact proven by government*
       studies

    2) *Japanese-American soldiers fought bravely to defend the U. S.*
       —An all Japanese-American combat team was
          recruited largely from internment camps, and it was
          the most decorated of its size.

EXPLANATION Your outline of the same reading might have used letters instead of numbers and left out dashes altogether. Still, the content would have been fairly similar. Given the thesis statement in paragraph 1, you need to include the causes of internment as well as the reasons why the authors consider it an "enormous exception" to an otherwise creditable record on civil rights.

1. The Gains and Losses of Beauty

1 No doubt about it, extremely good-looking people have a significant social edge. They are less lonely; less socially anxious (especially about interactions with the opposite sex); more popular; more sexually experienced; and . . . more socially skilled (Feingold, 1992b). The social rewards for physical attractiveness appear to get off to an early start. Mothers of highly attractive newborns engage in more affectionate interactions with their babies than do mothers of less attractive infants (Langlois et al., 1995). Given such benefits, one would expect that the beautiful would also have a significant psychological advantage. But they don't. Physical attractiveness (as rated by judges) has little if any association with self-esteem, mental health, personality traits, or intelligence (Feingold, 1992b).

2 One possible reason why beauty doesn't affect psychological well-being is that *actual* physical attractiveness, as evaluated by others, may have less impact than *self-perceived* physical attractiveness. People who view themselves as physically attractive do report higher self-esteem and better mental health than those who believe they are unattractive (Feingold, 1992b). But judges' ratings of physical attractiveness are only modestly correlated* with self-perceived attractiveness. When real beauties do not see

_____

*correlated; related to.

themselves as beautiful, their appearance may not be psychologically valuable.

3   Physically attractive individuals may also fail to benefit from the social bias for beauty because of pressures they experience to maintain their appearance. In contemporary American society, such pressures are particularly strong in regard to the body. Although both facial and bodily appearance contribute to perceived attractiveness, an unattractive body appears to be a greater liability than an unattractive face (Alicke et al., 1986). Such a "body bias" can produce a healthy emphasis on nutrition and exercise. But it can sometimes lead to distinctly unhealthy consequences. For example, men may pop steroids in order to build up impressive muscles. Among women, the desire for a beautiful body often takes a different form.

4   Women are more likely than men to suffer from what Janet Polivy and her colleagues (1986) call the "modern mania for slenderness." This zeal* for thinness is promoted by the mass media. Popular female characters in TV shows are more likely than popular male characters to be exceedingly thin; women's magazines stress the need to maintain a slender body more than do men's magazines (Silverstein et al., 1986b). (Brehm and Kassin, *Social Psychology*, p. 180.)

Title _____

Main Idea _____

_____

_____

Supporting Details _____

_____

_____

_____

_____

_____

_____

_____

_____

_____
*zeal: strong desire.

_____

_____

_____

_____

_____

_____

_____

2. But If It's Natural, It Must Be Good For You

1 Depending on who's doing the estimating, Americans spend between $5 and $10 billion per year on herbal supplements with funny-sounding names like *echinacea, ginseng,* and *golden seal.* The production, marketing, and selling of herbal supplements is a serious and profitable business with countless people consuming a variety of herbal medicines in an effort to cure both minor and major health problems. Yet herbal medicines are not regulated by the Food and Drug Administration. In fact, few scientific studies are available to prove their curative powers. There are even fewer to detect the possibility that some herbal medications might cause harm.

2 Amazingly enough, American consumers don't seem to care that there is so little science backing up claims for herbal medicines. Generally, they don't even seem worried about the ill effects of ingesting herbs. The reigning assumption is that herbs are natural and anything natural can't hurt you. However, that assumption is misguided, even dangerous—just try ingesting a leaf of "natural" poison ivy. If they really want to take care of their health, consumers should demand more proof that herbal supplements can do what their makers claim. Even more to the point, consumers should wonder about the side effects of taking supplements that have not undergone much, if any, rigorous testing.

3 The herb widely known as *comfrey,* for example, is sold as a gel or ointment for treating minor cuts and burns. And comfrey does contain allantoin, a chemical that aids in skin repair. But comfrey is also sold as a treatment for ulcers and stomach upsets, even though there is no compelling evidence that it can help either condition. On the contrary, there is some evidence that it can destroy liver cells, so ingesting it might be extremely dangerous.

Still you are unlikely to find any warning label on a bottle of comfrey tablets, and the herb is a popular item in natural food stores.

4   It's been widely claimed that another herbal supplement, *ginseng*, can improve memory and mood while also boosting energy. In Germany, where there is a formal body that regulates the sale of herbal medicine, ginseng has undergone repeated testing, and the herb seems to live up to claims about its benefits. The problem with ginseng is less that the claims are exaggerated and more that authentic ginseng is hard to find and extremely expensive. Thus a bottle of tablets or powder labeled as ginseng may have very little of the herb but quite a few additives or fillers, and some of those additives might not be altogether harmless.

5   Additives were the problem with an herbal mixture called *Zhong gan ling*. Used for centuries in China as a cold medication, it has never been proven effective against the common cold. In fact, one California woman ended up being treated with a condition that resembled the blood disease leukemia. Test results showed that her body was responding to a veterinary painkiller that had been added to the herbal medicine she was taking, which just happened to be Zhong gan ling. Although the FDA immediately banned the particular mixture the woman had ingested, other forms of Zhong gan ling can still be found on the shelves of natural food stores.

6.   Anyone who thinks of herbs as "all natural" and therefore harmless should also recall what happened several years ago to some people who took an alleged weight-loss herb known as *ephedra* or *ma hung*. Ephedra contains ephedrine, a substance that acts as a stimulant to the body and seems to encourage weight loss. But the amount of ephedrine in each plant varies according to the conditions under which the herb was grown. If a particular batch of the herb contains extremely high levels of ephedrine, then ingesting the herb can cause both blood pressure and heart rate to soar. No wonder then that ephedra caused at least 800 people to have problems such as fluctuating blood pressure, dizziness, and heart palpitations. When ephedra was being marketed as one of the components of "herbal phen-fen," an allegedly miraculous, "all natural" diet drug, scores of people who used it suffered permanent heart valve damage. At least a dozen people died as a result of taking the dietary supplement, which is more proof that "all natural" is not synonymous with being safe for human consumption. (Source of information: Christian Millman, "Remedies: Natural Disasters," *Men's Health,* Vol. 14, April 1, 1999, pp. 90, 92, 94.)

Title _____

Main Idea _____

_____

_____

Supporting Details _____

_____

_____

_____

_____

_____

_____

_____

_____

_____

_____

_____

_____

_____

_____

_____

CHECK YOUR UNDERSTANDING

Describe the main goal of an effective informal outline.

_____

_____

_____

■ **DIGGING DEEPER**

LOOKING AHEAD In 1942, Franklin Delano Roosevelt—over the protests of his wife, Eleanor—signed Executive Order 9066. The selection that follows describes the misery and suffering Roosevelt's decision inflicted on Japanese-Americans. They were rounded up, forced to sell their possessions, and herded into miserable makeshift camps, where they were confined for the duration of the war despite the fact that there was no evidence of any wrongdoing on their part.

THE TRAGEDY OF JAPANESE INTERNMENT

1 On the morning of December 7, 1941, Japanese submarines and carrier planes launched an attack on the U.S. Pacific Fleet at Pearl Harbor. Two hundred American aircraft were destroyed, eight battleships were sunk, and approximately eight thousand naval and military personnel were killed or wounded. This savage attack and its horrifying consequences propelled the United States into World War II.

2   For people of Japanese descent living in the United States— both the American-born *Nissei* and the Japanese-born *Issei*—the attack on Pearl Harbor was doubly catastrophic. It was tragic enough that their adopted country was going to war with the land of their ancestors. But the attack on Pearl Harbor also unleashed a storm of fury and outrage against America's Japanese citizens. The result was *Executive Order 9066,* issued in February 1942. Signed by President Franklin Delano Roosevelt, the order condemned 120,000 Japanese-Americans—two-thirds of them native born—to be evacuated from their homes and interned in camps for the duration of the war. Even some Japanese-Americans who had volunteered to fight for the United States were viewed as potential spies. They were stripped of their uniforms and sent to relocation camps because they were considered too dangerous to go free.

The Reality of the Camps

3 In discussing the camps, government administrators favored euphemisms. The camps were temporary "resettlement communities"—"havens of refuge"* designed to protect the Japanese-Americans from those who did not trust them (Weglyn, 89). Comforted by words like *community* and *refuge,* few Americans

---

*refuge: safety.

were confronted by the reality of camp life. If they had been, there probably would have been a groundswell of public outrage.

4   Erected at breakneck speed, the camps were crude and flimsy. The "family apartments," as they were called, were tarpaper shacks surrounded by barbed wire. They usually measured twenty by twenty-four feet and housed anywhere from five to eight people. Furniture, except for that brought by residents, was almost nonexistent. The apartments contained cots, blankets, mattresses, and a light fixture—nothing more.

5   Because the buildings were shoddy, the weather created hardships. In the summer, residents of the Manazar Camp in California sweltered. The sun beating down on tarpaper roofs turned rooms into ovens. Occasionally, the asphalt floors melted (Weglyn, 80). Those living in colder climates, such as the Gila Relocation Center in Arizona or the Granada Center in Colorado, fared little better. They were exposed to freezing temperatures that turned their "homes" into iceboxes.

6   There were other hardships as well. Because walls would have added to building expenses, there were few of them. Camp residents had almost no privacy. They ate and showered together. Even the toilet facilities were communal. There was no way to be alone.

Economic Losses

7 Japanese-Americans also suffered terrible economic losses. Forced by the government to settle their affairs in a matter of days, they fell victim to the unscrupulous, who bought Japanese-owned property at the lowest possible prices. The property and possessions that couldn't be sold were stored, but no one seemed concerned with protecting what the Japanese-Americans left behind. Much of it was stolen or vandalized. In the end, the Japanese who were interned lost property valued at more than $500 million; they lost as well their leading position in the truck-garden, floral, and fishing industries.

Psychological Loss

8 But the tragedy of relocation was not limited to physical hardship and economic loss. For Japanese-Americans, the worst hardship was psychological. They had lost face in their adopted country. They had suffered the embarrassment and humiliation of being herded together and forced to live in poverty. For a proud people, it was a spiritual death sentence. Their family life was disrupted, and they felt themselves powerless. Although the young were able to bear up under such indignity, some of the old could not. One

elderly man committed suicide and was found holding an Honorary Citizenship Certificate in his hand (Weglyn, 78).

No Evidence of Espionage

9   Although many people seemed convinced that only a network of Japanese-American spies could account for the success of Japan's attack on Pearl Harbor, there was no evidence of such spying. On the contrary, there was a great deal of evidence affirming the loyalty of America's Japanese residents.

10   Two months prior to the attack on Pearl Harbor, Curtis B. Munson, a special representative of the U.S. State Department, conducted a study of Japanese-Americans. His objective was to find the degree of their loyalty to America. The results of Munson's research suggested that Japanese-Americans were deeply loyal to their adopted country. Their deepest affiliation* was to America rather than to the land of their birth. From Munson's perspective, they showed a "patriotic eagerness" to be Americans. There was, in fact, no Japanese-American threat: "There is no Japanese problem on the coast. There will be no armed uprising of Japanese" (Weglyn, 47).

11   Unfortunately, the Munson report became one of the war's best-kept secrets. As Eugene Rostow, one of America's foremost authorities on constitutional law, expressed it, "One hundred thousand persons were sent to concentration camps on a record which wouldn't support a conviction for stealing a dog" (Weglyn, 53).

12   Throughout the beginning of the twentieth century, anti-Japanese sentiment tended to swell and ebb with the economy. In times of economic expansion, evidence of prejudice diminished. But in times of recession, the Japanese were singled out for restriction and ostracism. Prevented by labor unions from working in the city, they moved to agricultural areas, where they became successful farmers. Their thrift and industry made them significant competitors, able to purchase several hundred thousand acres of land. But their success backfired when California passed the Alien Land Law preventing Japanese from purchasing land or leasing it for more than three years.

13   Japan's entry into World War I on the side of the United States temporarily curbed anti-Japanese sentiment in America. But it flared up again following the war, when Japan invaded Manchuria and China, withdrew from the League of Nations, and refused to limit naval arms. A threat to her neighbors, Japan was also perceived as a threat to America. As a result, the United States

---

*affiliation: connection, relationship.

passed the Japanese Exclusion Act of 1924, which specifically limited Japanese immigration. By the time Pearl Harbor exploded, the country was psychologically prepared to mistrust Japanese-Americans.

14 *Fear of the Unknown.*   Following their internment, Japanese-Americans tended to take the blame for their misfortunes. They blamed themselves for being too clannish, for trying to preserve Japanese customs, for being reticent* and reclusive when they should have been forward and open. Tragically, they had a point. "Because little was known about the minority which had long kept itself withdrawn from the larger community in fear of rebuff,* it was possible to make the public believe anything" (Weglyn, 36). Fed on vicious stereotypes about Oriental cunning and largely ignorant of Japanese customs, far too many Americans found it easy to believe the myth of Japanese conspiracy and sabotage.

15 *Government Secrecy.*   The decision to relocate the Japanese-Americans was hardly a public one. It was made by a few government officials who justified their actions in various ways. When General John L. DeWitt was questioned about evidence of Japanese-American treachery, he offered this logic: "The very fact that no sabotage has taken place to date is a disturbing and confirming indication that such action will take place" (Weglyn, 39). According to this argument, Japanese-Americans had to be imprisoned because they hadn't *yet* done anything wrong. From DeWitt's perspective, their failure to engage in any spying activities was proof that they would do so any day. From DeWitt's peculiar angle of vision, internment was a form of preventive medicine.

16   When members of humanitarian, religious, and civil liberties groups protested the internment, they were given another explanation. They were told that the camps were nothing more than "protective custody." The government allegedly needed to protect its Japanese-American citizens because Pearl Harbor had aroused so much anti-Japanese sentiment.

17   If friends and neighbors of Japanese-American citizens protested the relocation policy, yet another reason was proposed. Military officials insisted that Japanese-Americans were in possession of evidence that made internment a necessity. What this

---

*reticent: shy.
*rebuff: rejection.

evidence was, however, had to be kept top secret—government security was involved.

The Final Verdict

18 Amazingly, the U.S. Supreme Court initially upheld the government's internment policy. In 1943 (*Hirabayashi v. U.S.*), the Court claimed that "residents having ethnic affiliations with an invading enemy may be a greater source of danger than those of different ancestry" (Norton et al., 801). Similarly, in the 1944 *Korematsu* case, the Court approved the removal of Japanese-Americans from the West Coast. However, Justice Frank Murphy called the decision the "legalization of racism." In his anger, he echoed Circuit Court Judge William Denman, who had compared Japanese-American internment to the policies of the Nazis: "The identity of this doctrine with that of the Hitler generals . . . justifying the gas chambers of Dachau is unmistakable" (Norton et al., 802).

19   Thirty-eight years after these Supreme Court decisions, the government formed a special Commission on Wartime Relocation and Internment of Civilians. Not surprisingly, that commission did not share the earlier view of the Supreme Court justices. On the contrary, it recommended that victims of the internment policy be compensated for their suffering. In the view of the commission, they had been victimized by "race prejudice, war hysteria, and a failure of political leadership."

20   A year later, in 1983, the *Korematsu* case was overturned in a federal district court. The court ruled that Fred Korematsu had been the victim of "unsubstantiated facts, distortions, and misrepresentations." In clearing Fred Korematsu, the court also implicitly cleared the other men, women, and children who had shared his fate.

21   Reparations* have been paid to Japanese-Americans who suffered from the policy of internment. Although money can never make up for the humiliation and hardship they suffered, the reparations are a much-needed form of public apology. (Sources of information: Maisie Conrat and Richard Conrat, "Executive Order 9066." California Historical Society, *California History* 50 [1972]: 313–320; Audrie Girdner and Anne Loftis, *The Great Betrayal.* London: Collier-Macmillan, 1969; Norton et al., *A People and a Nation,* pp. 801–802; Michi Weglyn, *Years of Infamy.* New York: William Morrow, 1976.)

---

*reparations: something done or paid in compensation for past injury.

Sharpening Your Skills

DIRECTIONS Answer the following questions by filling in the blanks or circling the letter of the correct response.

1. Based on the context, how would you define the word *groundswell* in paragraph 3?

   _____

2. What euphemism appears in paragraph 4?

   _____

3. Which of the following most accurately paraphrases the main idea of the entire reading?

   a. The attack on Pearl Harbor shocked the United States and ended any indecision about the country's entry into World War II.

   b. The attack on Pearl Harbor caused a storm of outrage against people of Japanese descent living in the United States, and that outrage paved the way for Executive Order 9066, which treated all Japanese living in the U.S. as potential spies.

   c. Initially the Supreme Court did the unthinkable: It upheld the government's right to place Japanese-Americans in internment camps, but to its credit, the court eventually reversed its decision.

   d. For Japanese-Americans, the psychological suffering was worse than their material losses.

4. In your own words, what is the main idea of paragraph 4?

   _____

   _____

5. In paragraph 5, the details about the sun and freezing temperatures illustrate what main idea?

   _____

   _____

6. In paragraph 7, which is the topic sentence?

   a. sentence 1

   b. sentence 2

   c. sentence 3

7. Which statement best expresses the main idea of paragraph 14?

    a. In part at least, Japanese-Americans were themselves to blame for their internment during World War II.

    b. The tendency of Japanese-Americans to be clannish had a profound effect on how they were perceived by the American public.

    c. Because so little was known about Japanese-Americans, the general public found it all to easy to believe the worst during time of war.

    d. Always ready to believe the worst where foreigners were concerned, the American public did not question the government's need to intern Japanese-Americans.

8. Paragraphs 17–20 rely on which two patterns of organization?

    _____

9. Which statement best paraphrases the argument in favor of internment offered by General John L. DeWitt (paragraph 15)?

    a. The evidence of espionage by Japanese-Americans is everywhere, so much so that it has become invisible.

    b. Evidence of Japanese-American espionage must be kept top secret.

    c. An absence of any evidence is a sure sign that espionage by Japanese-Americans is going to take place in the future.

    d. Evidence of past espionage by Japanese-Americans suggests that the same thing will occur in the future.

10. How would you paraphrase the author's concluding point of view?

    _____

WORD NOTES: TWO COMMONLY CONFUSED WORDS

Recall that on page 193 some people were loath, or reluctant, to eat garlic because of the effect on their breath. Now that you know the adjective *loath*, you should also learn the related and commonly misused verb *loathe*, meaning "to hate or dislike." Although both *loath* and *loathe* are based on an Old English root *lath*, meaning "hateful," the two words are different in meaning and function. To show that you understand those differences, fill in the blanks in the following sentences. Then write two sentences of your own using *loathe* or *loath*.

1. The people of Chile quickly learned to _____ the policies of the military government.

2. Although she detested his behavior, the secretary of health

and human services was _____ to openly defy someone so powerful.

loathe: _____

_____

loath: _____

_____

To get more practice with longer readings, go to **laflemm.com** and click on "Reading for Thinking: Online Practice." Complete and correct Practice 15.

Test 1: Reviewing the Key Points

DIRECTIONS Answer the following questions by filling in the blanks or circling the correct response.

1. To understand the difference between paragraphs and longer readings, how many crucial differences do you need to take into account?

   _____

2. *True* or *False.* In longer readings, the main idea is sometimes expressed in several sentences.

3. *True* or *False.* Thesis statements are more fixed in location than are topic sentences.

4. *True* or *False.* In multiparagraph readings, the introduction is usually limited to a sentence or two.

5. Words like _____, _____, and

   _____ are clues to major details.

6. Outlines are appropriate for material that is _____.

7. Formal and informal outlines signal relationships by _____.

8. The goal of an informal outline is to _____.

9. *True* or *False.* Outlines should open with the title and the main idea.

10. *True* or *False.* In informal outlines, consistency of style is not important.

To correct your test, turn to the answer key on page 642.

Test 2: Underlining Thesis Statements

DIRECTIONS Underline the thesis statement in each selection.

1. **Marital Satisfaction in New Families**

1 Almost all studies that measure marital satisfaction before and after the birth of the first child have found that the birth of a child is a mixed marital blessing (Cowan & Cowan, 1988). Jay Belsky and Michael Rovine (1990) found that couples who were least satisfied with their marriages before the birth were most likely to report a decline in satisfaction after. Problems that existed before were likely to have been magnified by the additional stresses brought on by the birth.

2 Babies, however, do not appear to create severe marital distress where none existed before; nor do they bring couples with distressed marriages closer together. Rather, the early postpartum* months bring on a period of disorganization and change. The leading conflict in these first months of parenthood is division of labor in the family. Couples may regain their sense of equilibrium in marriage by successfully negotiating how they will divide the new responsibilities. Husbands' participation in child and home care seems to be positively related to marital satisfaction after the birth. One study found that the more the men shared in doing family tasks, the more satisfied were the wives at six and eighteen months postpartum and the husbands at eighteen months postpartum (Cowan & Cowan, 1988).

3 While many couples experience a difficult transition to parenthood, they also find it rewarding. Children affect parents in ways that lead to personal growth; enable reworking of childhood conflicts; build flexibility and empathy; and provide intimate, loving human connections. They also give a lot of pleasure. In follow-up interviews of new parents when their children were eighteen months old, Philip Cowan and Carolyn Cowan (1988) found that almost every man and woman spoke of the delight they felt from knowing their child and watching the child develop. They reported feeling pride for and closeness to their spouses, more adult with their own parents, and a renewed sense of purpose at work. (Adapted from Seifert et al., *Lifespan Development*, p. 488.)

---

*postpartum: following a birth.

2. Creating the Electoral College

1   The Framers of the American Constitution knew very well that the relations between the president and Congress and the manner in which the president is elected were of profound importance. They debated both at great length. The first plan was for Congress to elect the president. But if that were done, some delegates pointed out, Congress could dominate an honest or lazy president, while a corrupt or scheming president might dominate Congress.

2   After much discussion it was decided that the president should be chosen directly by voters. But by which voters? The emerging nation was large and diverse. It seemed unlikely that every citizen would be familiar enough with the candidates to cast an informed vote for a president directly. Worse, a direct popular election would give inordinate weight to the large, populous states, and no plan with that outcome had any chance of adoption by the smaller states.

3   The electoral college, whereby each of the states would select electors, seemed to offer a solution to these potential problems. Electors would meet in each state capital and vote for president and vice president. Many Framers expected that this procedure would lead to each state's electors' voting for a favorite son, and thus no candidate would win a majority of the popular vote. In this event, it was decided, the House of Representatives should make the choice, with each state delegation casting one vote.

4   The plan seemed to meet every test: large states would have their say, but small states would be protected by having a minimum of three electoral votes no matter how tiny their population. The small states together could wield considerable influence in the House, where, it was widely expected, most presidential elections would ultimately be decided. Of course it did not work out quite this way: the Framers did not foresee the role that political parties would play in producing nationwide support for a slate of national candidates.

5   Once the manner of electing the president was settled, the question of his powers was much easier to decide. After all, if you believe that the procedures are fair and balanced, then you are more confident in assigning larger powers to the president within this system. Accordingly, the right to make treaties and the right to appoint lesser officials, originally reserved for the Senate, were given to the president "with the advice and consent of the Senate." (Wilson and DiIulio, *American Government,* pp. 333–334.)

Test 3: Thesis Statements and Supporting Details

DIRECTIONS Underline the thesis statement. Then answer the questions by filling in the blanks or circling the letter of the correct response. *Note:* To decide if a detail is major or minor, you will probably need to look at the sentences in the context of the paragraphs where they appear.

 ## 1. Feminist Objections to Pornography

1 Beginning around 1978, some—though not all—feminists became very critical of pornography (e.g., Griffin, 1981; Lederer, 1980; Morgan, 1978). Why are feminists opposed to pornography? In general, there are three basic reasons for their objections.

2 First, they argue that pornography debases women. The milder, softcore versions portray women as sex objects whose breasts, legs, and buttocks can be purchased and then ogled.* This scarcely represents a respectful attitude toward women. Second, pornography associates sex with violence toward women. As such, it contributes to rape and other forms of violence against women and girls. Robin Morgan put it bluntly: "Pornography is the theory and rape is the practice" (1980, p. 139). Third, pornography shows, indeed glamorizes, unequal power relationships between women and men. A common theme in pornography is that of men forcing women to have sex, and so the power of men and subordination of women is emphasized. Consistent with this point, feminists do not object to sexual materials that portray women and men in equal, humanized relationships—what we would term *erotica*.

3 Feminists also note the intimate relationship between pornography and traditional gender roles. They argue that pornography may serve to perpetuate traditional gender roles. By seeing or reading about dominant males and submissive,* dehumanized females, each new generation of adolescent boys is socialized to accept these roles. (Adapted from Shipley Hyde, *Understanding Human Sexuality*, p. 524.)

1. Based on the title, what question should you use to guide your reading?

_____

---

*ogled; stared at.
*submissive: obedient.

2. In your own words, what is the main idea?

_____

_____

3. Based on the thesis statement, how many major details should you be looking for?

_____

4. Which of the following is *not* a major detail?

a. Pornography associates sex with violence toward women.

b. Feminists do not object to sexual materials that portray women and men in equal, humanized relationships.

5. Which of the following is a minor detail?

a. Feminists argue that pornography debases women.

b. Pornography glamorizes unequal power relationships.

c. A common theme in pornography is that of men forcing women to have sex.

2. The Meaning of Touch

1 Touching and being touched is an essential part of being human. However, the amount and meaning of touch changes with age, purpose, and location. Infants and their parents, for example, engage in extensive touching behavior, but this decreases during adolescence. The amount of touching behavior increases after adolescence as young people begin to establish romantic relationships. No matter how much we are touched, however, most of us want to be touched more than we are (Mosby, 1978).

2 Generally speaking, the meaning of touch varies with the situation, and there are five general categories of meaning. *Positive affective touches* transmit messages of support, appreciation, affection, or sexual intent. *Playful touches* lighten our interactions with others. *Control touches* are used to get other people's attention and to gain their compliance. *Ritualistic touches* are those we use during communication rituals such as greeting others and saying goodbye. *Task-related touches* are those that are necessary for us to complete tasks on which we are working. Touches also can fit into more than one category at a time. We can, for example, touch others as part of a ritual to express positive affection.

3 Age, sex, and region of the country also influence the amount people touch. To illustrate, people between eighteen and twenty-five and between thirty and forty report the most touching, while old people report the least (Mosby, 1978). Women find touching

more pleasant than men do, as long as the other person is not a stranger (Heslin, 1978). Finally, people who live in the South touch more than people who live in the North (Howard, 1985).

4   The United States is generally a noncontact culture. People do not engage in a great deal of touching. There are, however, situations in which people are likely to touch (Henley, 1977). People are more likely to touch, for example, when giving information or advice than when receiving information or advice. People are more likely to touch others when giving orders than when receiving orders, when asking for a favor than when granting a favor, or when trying to persuade others than when being persuaded. (Adapted from Gudykunst et al., *Building Bridges,* pp. 319–320.)

1. Based on the title, what question would you use to guide your reading?

_____

2. In your own words, what is the main idea of the entire reading?

_____

_____

3. Which of the following is a major detail?

   a. People who live in the South touch more than do people who live in the North.

   b. Age, sex, and region influence the amount people touch.

   c. People are more likely to touch, for example, when giving information or advice.

4. Which of the following is a major detail?

   a. Generally speaking, the meaning of touch varies with the situation and there are five general categories of meaning (paragraph 2).

   b. We can, for example, touch others as part of a ritual to express positive affection (paragraph 2).

   c. People between eighteen and twenty-five and between thirty and forty report the most touching (paragraph 3).

5. Which of the following is a minor detail?

   a. Women find touching more pleasant than men do as long as the other person is not a stranger (paragraph 3).

   b. The amount and meaning of touch change with age, purpose, and location (paragraph 1).

   c. Age, sex, and region of the country also influence the amount people touch (paragraph 3).

Test 4: Outlining Longer Readings

DIRECTIONS Read each selection. Then use the blanks to make an informal outline.

1. Phobias

1   **Phobias** are intense and irrational fears of everything from spiders to open spaces. Some of the more common phobias are fear of heights, blood, flying, dogs, and enclosed spaces. The key element that distinguishes a phobia from a normal fear is that a phobia is irrational, or not based on reason. For instance, someone who is phobic about spiders would be just as terrified by a harmless Daddy Long Legs as he or she would be by a deadly tarantula. In the United States, phobias are the most prevalent of the anxiety disorders. They affect 7 to 10 percent of adults and children (Kessler et al., 1994; Robins et al., 1984; U.S. Surgeon General, 1999).

2   Perhaps the most disabling phobia is **agoraphobia.** Agoraphobia is an intense fear of being away from a safe place like one's home; of being away from a familiar person, such as a spouse or close friend; or of being in a place from which departure might be difficult or help unavailable. For those who suffer from agoraphobia, attempts to leave home cause extreme anxiety. Thus agoraphobics are often severely house bound. For them, theaters, shopping malls, public transportation, and other potentially crowded places are particularly threatening. Most individuals who suffer from agoraphobia also have a history of panic attacks. In fact, their intense fear of public places starts partly because they don't want to go where they feel panicking would be dangerous or embarrassing.

3   **Social phobias** revolve around the anxiety of being negatively evaluated by others or acting in a way that is embarrassing or humiliating. This anxiety is so intense and persistent that it impairs the person's normal functioning. *Common social phobias are fear of public speaking or performance* ("stage fright"), fear of eating in front of others, and fear of using public restrooms (Kleinknecht, 2000). A *generalized social phobia* is a more severe form in that victims experience fear in virtually all social situations (Mannuzzi et al., 1995). Sociocultural factors can alter the form of social phobias. For example, in Japan, where cultural training emphasizes group-oriented values and goals, a common social phobia is *taijin kyofu sho*—fear of embarrassing those around

you (Kleinknecht, 1994). (Adapted from Bernstein et al., *Psychology*, 6th ed., pp. 566–567.)

Main Idea _____

_____

Supporting Details _____

_____

_____

_____

_____

_____

_____

_____

_____

_____

_____

_____

_____

 ## 2. Taking a Conversational Turn

1   Have you ever conversed with another person who wouldn't stop talking? If so, you may have wondered whether that person was either clueless, obnoxious, or just playing by a different set of cultural rules. Whatever the reason for such behavior, lopsided conversations usually remind us that turn taking is a fundamental part of the give and take we expect from others in our everyday interactions. Because most people don't verbalize intentions to speak or listen, learning to navigate conversational twists and turns can be a real challenge. The signals we use to regulate the flow of speech consist largely of verbal cues and gestures.

2   When we are speaking and want to continue speaking, we use signals that communicate our intention to listeners. It's a way of

preventing unwanted interruptions. Such signals include raising the volume of our voice, uttering *um*'s and *ah*'s, continuing to gesture, gazing away from the listener, and so on.

3   On the other hand, if we don't want to continue speaking, we can relinquish our turn by dropping the volume and pitch of our voice, slowing the tempo of our speech, pausing, not gesturing, making eye contact with a listener, or raising our eyebrows. These are **turn-yielding signals.** Some research shows that conversants are more inclined to take turns when speakers use these signals. (Duncan, 1972).

4   As listeners, we also use turn-taking signals. To express a desire to speak, we employ various **turn-requesting signals.** These signals include an open mouth, audible inhalations, a raised index finger or hand, forward body lean, eye contact, quickened or exaggerated head nods, and simultaneous speech (i.e., listener's speech overlaps with the speaker's). (Adapted from Remland, *Nonverbal Communications in Everyday Life*, pp. 255–256.)

Main Idea _____

_____

Supporting Details _____

_____

_____

_____

_____

_____

_____

_____

_____

_____

_____

_____

_____

Test 5: Thesis Statements and Supporting Details

DIRECTIONS Underline the thesis statement. Then answer the questions by filling in the blanks or circling the letter of the correct response. *Note:* To decide if a detail is major or minor, you will probably need to look at the sentences in the context of the paragraphs where they appear.

 ## 1. The Automobile and American Life

1 During the 1920s, the automobile profoundly changed Americans' way of living in both town and country. Rural residents, for example, benefited from automobiles in a number of ways. Highways built to accommodate automobiles significantly shortened travel time from rural areas to cities, reducing the isolation of farm life. When asked why her family had an automobile but no indoor plumbing, one farm woman responded, "Why, you can't go to town in a bathtub." Trucks allowed farmers to take more products to market more quickly and conveniently than ever before. Tractors significantly expanded the amount of land that one family could cultivate. Because the spread of gasoline-powered farm vehicles reduced the need for human farm labor, they stimulated migration to urban areas.

2 If the automobile changed rural life, it had an even more profound impact on life in the cities. The 1920 census, for the first time, recorded more Americans living in urban areas (defined as places having 2,500 people or more) than in rural ones. As the automobile freed suburbanites from their dependence on commuter rail lines, new suburbs mushroomed and streetcar use steadily declined. Most suburban growth was in the form of single-family houses. From 1922 through 1928, construction began on an average of 883,000 new homes each year. Home construction rivaled the auto industry as a major driving force behind economic growth.

3 As early as 1913, the automobile demonstrated its ability to strangle urban traffic, making driving both chaotic and dangerous. One response to this problem was the development of traffic lights. Various versions were tried, including the four-directional, three-color traffic light, which first appeared in Detroit in 1920. Although traffic lights spread rapidly to other large cities, traffic congestion nonetheless worsened. By 1926 during the evening rush hour, the more than 250,000 cars that entered Manhattan each day crawled along at less than three miles per hour—slower

than a person could walk. As a result, many commuters returned to using trains and subways. (Adapted from Berkin et al., *Making America*, 3rd ed., pp. 718–719.)

1. Based on the title, what question would you use to guide your reading?

_____

2. How would you paraphrase the thesis statement?

_____

_____

3. Which of the following sentences in paragraph 1 is a minor detail?

a. Trucks allowed farmers to take more products to market more quickly and conveniently than ever before.

b. When asked why her family had an automobile but no indoor plumbing, one farm woman responded, "Why, you can't go to town in a bathtub."

4. Which of the following sentences in paragraph 2 is a major detail?

a. If the automobile changed rural life, it had an even more profound impact on life in the cities.

b. Most suburban growth was in the form of single-family houses.

2. Commercialism's Effect on the Media

1 *Commercialism* is a term that describes the attitude or practice of placing a high value on the buying and selling of both goods and services. It's also a term frequently used to describe American society, and for some people America's embrace of commercialism is the source of numerous problems. Commercialism's detractors insist that our society's tendency to celebrate the pleasures of buying and selling has profoundly negative side effects. Their most important objections have to do with how commercialism affects the American mass media and their audience.

2 Critics of commercialism point out that advertisers are essential to the survival of the U.S. media, forcing media executives to take the needs of advertisers into account when making decisions about both content and audience. For example, if an advertiser sells products geared to young people, a fashion magazine running ads from that advertiser must include columns and covers to attract younger readers. In other words, every time people read a

magazine, watch a TV show, click on a website, or use any other ad-sponsored medium, they are entering a world that reflects close cooperation between media and advertisers.

3   Critics also argue that commercialism fosters censorship in much of the U.S. media. Because of their importance in funding the media, advertisers actually have a lot more power than government agencies do over the content of media in the United States.

4   What advertisers get from that power, say the critics, are programs that create a friendly environment for the consumers they are targeting as an audience. The rules are clear. TV programming executives are aware, for example, that some major advertisers won't fund content that involves too much violence or gays and lesbians. Newspaper editors understand as well that investigating local real-estate brokers (the sponsors of the papers' real-estate sections) is not an economically healthy activity. Magazines know that they will lose lucrative tobacco accounts if they publish too many articles about the hazards of cigarette smoking. Bluntly put, there is a lot at stake if media executives don't create environments that are friendly to marketers in general and to individual advertisers in particular.

5   Critics of commercialism believe, too, that the preoccupation of media with advertising and marketing often leads them to exploit children. Although you can find examples of media for children that do not carry ads, in general, children aged two through twelve are often treated like pintsize consumers. Ad people know all too well that children influence parental spending and, as they get older, have their own purchasing power from gifts and allowances. (Adapted from Turow, *Media Today: An Introduction to Mass Communication,* pp. 426–428.)

1. Based on the title, what question would you use to guide your reading?

_____

2. How would you paraphrase the thesis statement?

_____

_____

3. Which of the following sentences in paragraph 2 is a minor detail?

   a. Critics of commercialism point out that advertisers are essential to the survival of the U.S. media, forcing media executives to take the needs of potential advertisers into account when they make decisions about both content and audience.

b. In other words, every time people read a magazine, watch a TV show, go to a website, or use any other ad-sponsored medium, they are entering a world that reflects close cooperation between media and advertisers.

4. Which of the following sentences in paragraph 5 is a major detail?

a. Critics of commercialism believe, too, that the preoccupation of media with advertising and marketing often leads them to exploit children.

b. Ad people know all too well that children influence parental spending and, as they get older, have their own purchasing power from gifts and allowances.

Test 6: Taking Stock

DIRECTIONS Read the following selection. Then answer the questions by filling in the blanks or circling the letter of the correct response.

 ## 1. The Keys to Job Satisfaction

1   Everyone seems to have an opinion about the source of job satisfaction. Some say that money is the most important factor, others that working conditions are more important, and still others believe that employee participation in decision making is the critical ingredient. According to psychologists, though, four groups of characteristics or conditions are generally responsible for most people's job satisfaction.

2   The first category of contributing factors includes the job's characteristics. Research has indicated a consistent link between employees' perceptions of their jobs' characteristics and their level of job satisfaction. Employees who feel that their jobs provide them with autonomy, variety, significance, and feedback are more satisfied with their jobs than are employees whose jobs lack these elements. The *absence* of certain job characteristics is another factor in job satisfaction. Stress, for instance, contributes to employee dissatisfaction. Workers who report having to deal with unreasonable or unmanageable workloads or a high level of "daily hassles" report low levels of job satisfaction, while employees who experience low levels of stress tend to report higher job satisfaction.

3   The second set of factors affecting job satisfaction involves the characteristics of the individual performing the job. Research shows that most people seem to possess stable traits that predispose them to responding either positively or negatively to their work, even when they move from job to job. Studies have demonstrated that some individuals have a cheerful disposition that causes them to respond to the world in a favorable way, while others are predisposed to respond unfavorably. Some studies have looked at how genetic factors influence the way people respond to their work. One study in particular, which examined twins separated at birth, found that later in life, each twin had similar levels of job satisfaction, suggesting that genetic inheritance may well play a role in job satisfaction. Additional research has indicated, too, that individuals with high self-esteem tend to be satisfied with their jobs.

4   Social, or interpersonal, factors also appear to contribute to job satisfaction. For example, positive relationships between employees and their supervisors or coworkers usually increase job satisfaction. For most people, having coworkers who are seen as trustworthy, supportive, and likable usually raises job satisfaction. Clarity about one's role is another pertinent social factor. People tend to be uncomfortable with ambiguity; therefore, an individual who is uncertain about his or her role or function within an organization is prone to dissatisfaction. Employees also want to experience a sense of organizational justice or fairness. Workers who perceive their employers' policies, procedures, and treatments as fair and equitable for all tend to experience high job satisfaction.

5   One final factor affecting job satisfaction is opportunity for growth. When employees perceive a potential for advancement or promotion within an organization, they feel a higher level of satisfaction. A seven-year study of employees with a master's degree in business administration, for example, revealed that the more promotions these managers received, the more satisfied they were. (Adapted from Levy, *Industrial/Organizational Psychology*, pp. 281–282.)

1. What question based on the title would help you focus your reading?

_____

2. Based on the context clues in paragraph 4, how would you define the word *equitable*?

_____

3. Based on the context clues in paragraph 4, how would you define the word *ambiguity*?

_____

4. What is the topic of the entire reading?

   a. jobs

   b. employees

   c. job characteristics

   d. job satisfaction

5. Which statement best paraphrases the thesis statement?

   a. Employees who like their jobs differ in several ways from those who don't.

   b. Job satisfaction is determined by four main factors.

   c. Most workers prefer jobs that have certain characteristics.

   d. Satisfying jobs are getting harder to come by.

6. Which statement best paraphrases the topic sentence of paragraph 3?

   a. The characteristics of coworkers play a key role in job satisfaction.

   b. Some studies suggest that an individual's personality determines job satisfaction.

   c. The characteristics of the job determine satisfaction.

   d. Some people go from job to job and are never satisfied.

7. Which sentence best paraphrases the topic sentence of paragraph 4?

   a. Social factors affect an employee's satisfaction.

   b. Relationships with supervisors and coworkers determine job satisfaction.

   c. The characteristics of a job contribute to employee satisfaction.

   d. Most people prefer working with others to working alone.

8. Paraphrase the topic sentence in paragraph 5.

   _____

9. Is the last sentence of paragraph 3 a major or minor detail?

   a. major detail

   b. minor detail

10. What pattern or patterns do you see at work in the reading?

   a. time order

   b. cause and effect

   c. comparison and contrast

   d. definition

   e. classification

2. Types of Religions

1   Most religions in the world can be sorted according to how follow-ers feel about the nature of a deity, or god. Thus religious beliefs have generally been described as monotheistic, polytheistic, pan-theistic, or atheistic.

2   The word *monotheistic* contains the prefix *mono-*, meaning "one," and the root *theism*, meaning "belief in a god or gods"; therefore, monotheistic means "characterized by the belief in one single deity." Followers of monotheistic religions worship one omnipotent male deity as the creator and ruler of the universe. Christianity and Judaism are two major monotheistic religions. For both religions, the deity is God, written with a capital *G*. Islam, whose followers worship Allah, is another major monotheis-tic religion.

3   A second major type of religion is *polytheistic*, from the prefix *poly-*, or "many," and the root *theism*. Polytheistic religions are characterized by the worship of many gods. Hinduism, for exam-ple, is generally considered polytheistic. Although some Hindus revere Brahma as the supreme deity, or Creator, Hinduism recog-nizes many gods and goddesses such as Kali, goddess of time and death; Balrama, god of strength; Krishna, god of love; Shiva, the destroyer; and Vishnu, the preserver. Vishnu is said to have taken nine different bodily forms and led nine separate lives.

4   Pantheistic religions are a third major type. The word *panthe-ism* is made up of the prefix *pan-*, meaning "all," plus *theism*, so it literally means "belief in all gods." The term is used to describe those religions that see divinity as part of everything in existence, including humans, animals, and plants. Native-American reli-gions, for instance, are often described as pantheistic in their approach, for their followers believe that everything in the natural world is sacred. Thus they revere nature and believe that respect-ing Earth and its creatures is essential to spiritual well-being.

5   A fourth major type of religion is atheistic or nontheistic. The word *atheism* is derived from the prefix *a-*, meaning "without," and *theism*; therefore, atheists' religious beliefs do not include a god or gods. Contrary to popular belief, atheists don't necessarily believe in nothing. The term *atheism* can also refer to religious systems characterized by the belief that there is no divine being with a personality. Buddhism, for instance, has been described as an atheistic religion, because it does not include the worship of a god or gods; yet Buddhists do hold spiritual beliefs. They believe that an individual's essence, or spirit, can escape from the earthly cycle of birth, life, and death and attain freedom

from suffering by revering nature, cultivating virtue, and striving to be at one with the universe. Meditation and self-discipline are also central to the spiritual practices of Buddhists.

1. What question based on the title would help you focus your reading?

_____

2. The title would lead you to predict which pattern of organization?

_____

3. The prefix *omni* means "all." Based on the context clues in paragraph 2 and your knowledge of that word part, how would you define the word *omnipotent*?

_____

4. What is the topic of the entire reading?
   a. religion
   b. types of religions
   c. monotheistic religions
   d. religious belief in a deity.

5. Which statement best paraphrases the thesis statement?
   a. Humans have developed many different religious belief systems.
   b. There are different ways to classify religions.
   c. Most major religions can be classified according to how believers feel about a deity.
   d. The four different types of religions have similarities and differences.

6. Which sentence better paraphrases the topic sentence of paragraph 2?
   a. The monotheistic religions are those that worship one supreme God.
   b. Two monotheistic religions are Christianity and Judaism.

7. Is this sentence in paragraph 3 a major or minor detail: "Vishnu is said to have taken nine different bodily forms and led nine separate lives"?

   a. major detail

   b. minor detail

8. Is this sentence in paragraph 4 a major or minor detail: "Thus they revere nature and believe that respecting Earth and its creatures is essential to spiritual well-being"?

   a. major detail

   b. minor detail

9. What organizational relationship is suggested by the word *thus* in the last sentence of paragraph 4?

   _____

10. What patterns do you see at work in this reading?

    a. time order; cause and effect

    b. time order; comparison and contrast

    c. classification; definition; comparison and contrast

CHAPTER 5

Summarizing and Synthesizing: Two More Strategies for In-Depth Learning

In this chapter, you'll learn

- **how to compose summaries.**
- **how to adapt your summary to your purpose.**
- **how to create synthesis statements.**

At this point, you're ready to work on summarizing and synthesizing, two learning strategies that can markedly improve your mastery of college texts. To effectively summarize a chapter section or a journal article, you should reduce it to its bare essentials—the main idea and the supporting details. This process pays off in two ways: (1) If you can't figure out what essentials should go into a summary, you probably need to reread the material. In other words, summarizing is a good way to check your comprehension. (2) In analyzing a text in order to summarize it, you are also giving your mind a chance to focus on the author's ideas and store them in long-term memory.

Synthesizing is useful when you have two or more sources that deal with the same or a similar subject. When this happens, as it often does with textbook assignments and outside readings, you need to come up with synthesis statements that identify not only the authors' individual ideas but also their relationship to each other. Again, this kind of mental activity ensures both in-depth learning and long-term remembering.

 # Writing Chapter Summaries

If you are working your way through a chapter dense with details, facts, and figures, you should probably not use summary writing as a note-taking and review method. However, if you are reading a psychology or sociology text with familiar subject matter and rather general ideas, you might consider summary writing instead of or in addition to reciting after reading. Here are some general pointers to follow when writing summaries.

How to Write a Good Summary

1. Apply the One-Quarter Rule of Thumb

Generally speaking, try to reduce the original text to about one-quarter of its original length. You can usually accomplish this by including in your summary (1) the main idea of the entire reading and (2) the main idea of each supporting paragraph.

2. Underline and Annotate Before You Write

Thoroughly mark up your text before you write a summary. Circle important names and dates, underline key words, and write the main idea along with several supporting details in the margins. Then, by the time you start writing your summary, you will have already sifted out the nonessential material.

3. Make Distinctions Between the Essential and the Absolutely Essential

If the author uses an opening paragraph to describe the topic before introducing the main idea, don't summarize it. Instead, start right off with the main idea. Similarly, if the author uses three separate examples to explain or prove a point, decide which best illustrates the main idea and answers any questions it might raise. That's the example to include in your summary.

4. Include All Essential Details

However, if the author uses three reasons to support an argument or four categories to explain a system of classification, you need to include at least one sentence about each reason or category. Personal anecdotes, quoted material, and clever comments to the reader are the writer's way of giving the material audience appeal, but none of these things needs to be included in a summary.

5. Paraphrase

Paraphrasing will help you significantly condense the original text. Just keep in mind the key rule of paraphrasing: Change the wording but don't alter the meaning.

6. Make the Same Connections Between Ideas

If the author uses one of the organizational patterns identified in Chapter 3, you should maintain that pattern even while paraphrasing. In other words, if an author compares and contrasts the attitude of two different philosophers, say Plato and Aristotle, toward the role of virtue, then you should maintain that organizing pattern in your summary. Don't present ideas of the two philosophers as two seemingly independent summaries. If the writer makes it clear that her goal is to compare and contrast, then yours should be as well.

7. Don't Interpret or Evaluate

When you summarize, your purpose, or goal, is to inform. Even if you are convinced a writer is spouting nonsense, don't let that opinion make its way into your summary. Restrict your opinions to the margins. Particularly if you are using summaries for exam reviews, you don't want to make your ideas seem as if they were the author's.

8. Get the Format Right

If you need to turn in your summary to your instructor, make sure to include the author and title of the reading. Sometimes instructors want that information in a heading or a footnote, but often you'll be expected to weave it into the opening sentence. When you are assigned to write a summary, always find out how your instructor wants you to handle the author and title information.

Writing summaries requires you to combine information from different parts of the original text. As a result, sometimes connections between sentences can get lost. For that reason, it's important to read your summary aloud to check how your sentences flow together. If you can't figure out why one sentence follows another, you may need to add some transitions to connect the ideas. As you know from Chapter 3, transitions are verbal bridges that help readers move easily from one thought to another. Here's a list of the most common transitions.

Review of Common Transitional Signals

Transition Signal	*Common Terms*
To indicate addition to the original train of thought	also in addition first further furthermore last moreover second secondly* too
To indicate a change, challenge, or contradiction	although after all but by (in) contrast despite that fact however nevertheless on the other hand on the contrary rather regardless still yet
To point out similarities	likewise by the same token in the same vein similarly
To introduce examples and/or illustrations	for example for instance in other words specifically that is

---

*Many handbooks for college composition frown on the use of "secondly," so you should probably avoid using it. However, you will see it in print.

To introduce the effect of some cause	as a result consequently hence in response therefore thus
To help readers follow a time sequence	afterward after a while before finally in the meantime in time next of late soon then thereafter
To repeat a point made before	in brief in conclusion in other words in short in summary on the whole to reiterate to sum up to repeat

Putting the Pointers into Practice

Here is a selection that would lend itself nicely to summarizing. It's followed by a sample summary.

Museums' Dilemma*

Where do museums get the objects they put on display? Many of a museum's artifacts come from archaeological excavations sponsored by government or educational institutions. Sometimes, however, museums acquire ancient objects by buying them or accepting them as gifts from dealers or private collectors. In that case, museums don't always know the provenance, or origin, of

*dilemma: a situation where both choices have drawbacks.

the artifacts. They might have been stolen from archaeological sites or looted from other museums. It is not unusual during times of war or political upheaval, as recent wars in Afghanistan and Iraq have illustrated, for artifacts to be stolen and offered for sale to the highest bidder. During the Gulf War of 1991, for example, more than 2,000 objects were looted from Iraqi museums; only a handful have ever been recovered.

To avoid acquiring stolen artifacts, some museums—the British Museum and Chicago's Field Museum—have adopted strict policies that prevent them from accepting any object with questionable provenance. There are, however, curators who insist that adding questionable artifacts to museum collections is both necessary and right.

Some museum curators defend decisions to accept objects with uncertain origins on the grounds that they often come from legitimate sources. While museums obviously prefer clear proof of an artifact's origin, such documentation is not always available. Many unprovenanced objects have been in private collections for generations. Thus their exact sources cannot be traced when the objects finally become available for purchase or are donated. In other words, the lack of a centuries-old paper trail does not necessarily mean that an object was stolen.

Museum curators also argue that displaying only documented items would prevent them from exhibiting artifacts related to certain cultures. The Metropolitan Museum of Art in New York, for example, had to use several artifacts of unknown origin for its exhibit on the ancient country of Bactria, which was once located in present-day Afghanistan. If the museum had limited itself to objects with clear documentation, its exhibition about this particular civilization would have been incomplete.

As a result, many curators reason that banning artifacts of questionable provenance would prevent museums from fulfilling their mission—the imparting of knowledge about humanity's past. By not acquiring objects with uncertain origins, museums ensure that these objects will remain in private hands, where they are unavailable to scholars or to the general public. Thus the artifacts could never be used to reveal the secrets of the past. (Source of information: Betsy Carpenter with Gillian Sandford, "Who Owns the Past?" *U.S. News & World Report,* December 15, 2003, pp. 58–60.)

Sample Summary

While some museums refuse to accept any objects that have a questionable provenance, other museum directors insist that there are good reasons for accepting artifacts of unknown origin. Curators are, for example, reluctant to turn down artifacts that have been in private collections for several generations. They argue that a lack of paper documentation does not necessarily mean that those donating the artifacts got them by illegal means since it's difficult to hold on to paperwork for several generations.

Curators willing to display artifacts of uncertain provenance also insist that if they didn't do so, they wouldn't be fulfilling their function of providing the public with historical information about ancient cultures. The Metropolitan Museum of Art, for example, displayed artifacts of unknown origin during an exhibit of art objects from Bactria, an ancient country once located in what is now Afghanistan.

As it should, the sample summary reduces the original reading to essentials. Since the author's purpose, or intention, is to persuade readers that curators who use unsourced objects have a right to do so, the summary follows the writer's lead and focuses on the opinions put forth by some curators and their reasons for holding them. Except for the final example about the Metropolitan Museum of Art, all other details were eliminated. Because the point of the reading is to tell readers why some curators do not balk at displaying objects with unclear provenance, everything extraneous, or unessential— like the opening paragraph—was left out of the summary.

 # Reviewing Through Summary Writing

If you decide to include summarizing in your arsenal of reading and study strategies, there are two ways you can do it.

Method 1 After you finish a chapter section that you thought fairly easy to understand, see if you can summarize the overall main idea and a few essential details in writing. Don't look back at the text itself. Write your summary from memory. The ease with which you can summarize will tell you how well you have understood the material. A summary you have to struggle over suggests that you need to give the text a slow and thorough second reading. A summary that you can quickly dash off, however, suggests you probably don't need to do a second reading. When it comes time for exam review, you can just quickly reread the material you underlined.

Method 2 If you know that the chapter section you just completed was a bit hard to understand, write your summary with the text in front of you. That way you can evaluate each and every sentence. Pondering the material will deepen your understanding. It will also ensure remembering and make it easier for you to grasp the main point of what follows.

CHECK YOUR UNDERSTANDING

When is it a good idea to review through summary writing?

_____

When is it not a good idea to review through summary writing?

_____

— EXERCISE 1

DIRECTIONS Read each selection and then circle the letter of the most effective summary.

EXAMPLE

Going West

1   In nineteenth-century America, most migrants went west because the region seemed to promise a better life. Railroad expansion made remote farming regions accessible, and the construction of grain elevators eased problems of shipping and storage. As a result of population growth, the demand for farm products grew rapidly, and the prospects for commercial agriculture—growing crops for profit—became more favorable than ever.

2   Life on the farm, however, was much harder than the advertisements and railroad agents suggested. Migrants often encountered shortages of essentials they had once taken for granted. The open prairies contained little lumber for housing and fuel. Pioneer families were forced to build houses of sod and to burn manure for heat. Water was sometimes as scarce as timber. Few families were lucky or wealthy enough to buy land near a stream that did not dry

up in summer and freeze in winter. Machinery for drilling wells was scarce until the 1880s, and even then it was very expensive.

3   The weather was seldom predictable. In summer, weeks of torrid* heat and parching winds often gave way to violent storms that washed away crops and property. In winter, the wind and cold from blizzards piled up mountainous snowdrifts that halted all outdoor movement. During the Great Blizzard that struck Nebraska and the Dakota Territory in January 1888, the temperature plunged to 36 degrees below zero, and the wind blew at 56 miles per hour. The storm stranded schoolchildren and killed several parents who ventured out to rescue them. In the spring, melting snow swelled streams, and floods threatened millions of acres. In the fall, a week without rain could turn dry grasslands into tinder, and the slightest spark could ignite a raging prairie fire.

4   Nature could be cruel even under good conditions. Weather that was favorable for crops was also good for breeding insects. Worms and flying pests ravaged corn and wheat. In the 1870s and 1880s swarms of grasshoppers virtually ate up entire farms. Heralded only by the din of buzzing wings, a mile-long cloud of insects would smother the land and devour everything: plants, tree bark, and clothes. As one farmer lamented, the "hoppers left behind nothing but the mortgage." (Adapted from Norton et al., *A People and a Nation*, pp. 492–493.)

Summary (a.) During the nineteenth century, countless men and women went west in the belief that farming was a way to make money and improve their lot in life. Life on the farm, however, proved to be much harder and more rigorous than most expected. Essentials like lumber and water were hard to come by. The weather was both harsh and unpredictable. In winter, the temperature might plunge as low as 36 degrees below zero while the wind could blow at 56 miles per hour. In summer, scorching heat and drought would suddenly be followed by slashing rainstorms. Insects were an additional problem and plagues of them could devour entire farms.

b. In the nineteenth century, the American West seemed to be the land of opportunity. Many were convinced that farming was the way to make a fortune, but they were deeply disappointed upon their arrival. Lumber and water were hard to obtain. People were forced to build houses out of sod and burn manure to stay warm. Machinery was scarce and expensive, making farm labor backbreaking and discouraging. If that weren't enough, there

----
*torrid: intensely hot.

was the weather to contend with, and the heat and cold were intolerable. During the Great Blizzard that struck Nebraska and the Dakota Territory in January 1888, the temperature plunged to 36 degrees below zero and the wind blew at 56 miles per hour. The storm stranded schoolchildren and killed several parents who ventured out to rescue them. And in the spring, when streams melted, there were floods to contend with. It was a no-win situation, and it is not surprising that so many people gave up and went back east.

c. Throughout the nineteenth century, thousands of men and women decided to make their way west and try their hand at farming in the hope of earning a fortune. But that hope was quickly dashed upon their arrival. Life was hard in the west and it was easy to get discouraged and give up, particularly given the weather, which alternated between torrid heat and freezing cold. As if the unpredictable weather were not bad enough, there were floods and fires to contend with, along with plagues of locusts and bees. And the sound of buzzing wings was a warning of disaster. People who migrated west in the nineteenth century were badly fooled by the railroad agents who promised a land of milk and honey in exchange for the price of a ticket.

EXPLANATION Summary *a* is the most effective of the three paragraphs for two reasons. First, *a* sticks to the author's original ideas. Summaries *b* and *c* do not. Summary *b*, for example, ends with the explanation that difficulties out west made people go back east. This may be true, but that point is not made in the original, which means it shouldn't appear in the summary either. The same kind of error turns up in summary *c*. It's probably accurate to say that railroad agents tricked more than one would-be pioneer. But if the original didn't make that point, neither should the summary.

Summary *a* is also the most effective because it includes only the most essential details. A good summary includes only those details critical to fleshing out the main idea. In a personal essay, a detail like the "sound of buzzing wings" gives the reader a wonderful sense of atmosphere. But in the context of a summary, this detail, which appears in summary *c*, breaks a basic rule of summarizing: Include only those details essential to clarifying or proving the main idea.

1. Kinds of Salespersons

1 Because most businesses employ different salespersons to perform different functions, marketing managers must select the

kinds of sales personnel that will be most effective in selling the firm's products. Salespersons may be identified as order getters, order takers, and support personnel. A single individual can, and often does, perform all three functions.

2   An **order getter** is responsible for what is sometimes called creative selling: selling the firm's products to new customers and increasing sales to present customers. An order getter must perceive buyers' needs, supply customers with information about the firm's product, and persuade them to buy the product. Order-getting activities may be separated into two groups. In current-customer sales, salespeople concentrate on obtaining additional sales, or leads for prospective sales, from customers who have purchased the firm's products at least once. In new-business sales, sales personnel seek out new prospects and convince them to make an initial purchase of the firm's product. The real estate, insurance, appliance, heavy industrial machinery, and automobile industries in particular depend on new-business sales.

3   An **order taker** handles repeat sales in ways that maintain positive relationships with customers. An order taker sees that customers have products when and where they are needed and in the proper amounts. *Inside order takers* receive incoming mail and telephone orders in some businesses; salespersons in retail stores are also inside order takers. *Outside* (or *field*) *order takers* travel to customers. Often the buyer and the field salesperson develop a mutually beneficial relationship of placing, receiving, and delivering orders. Both inside and outside order takers are active salespersons and often produce most of their companies' sales.

4   **Support Personnel** Support personnel aid in selling but are more involved in locating *prospects* (likely first-time customers), educating customers, building goodwill for the firm, and providing follow-up service. The most common categories of support personnel are missionary, trade, and technical salespersons.

5   A *missionary salesperson,* who usually works for a manufacturer, visits retailers to persuade them to buy the manufacturer's products. If the retailers agree, they buy the products from wholesalers, who are the manufacturer's actual customers. Missionary salespersons are often employed by producers of medical supplies and pharmaceuticals to promote these products to retail druggists, physicians, and hospitals.

6   A *trade salesperson,* who generally works for a food producer or processor, assists customers in promoting products, especially in retail stores. A trade salesperson may obtain additional shelf space for the products, restock shelves, set up displays, and dis-

tribute samples. Because trade salespersons are usually order takers as well, they are not strictly support personnel.

7   A *technical salesperson* assists the company's current customers in technical matters. He or she may explain how to use a product, how it is made, how to install it, or how a system is designed. A technical salesperson should be formally educated in science or engineering. Computers, steel, and chemicals are some of the products handled by technical salespeople. (Pride et al., *Business,* pp. 402–403.)

Summary a. Most businesses employ different salespeople to perform different functions. Some salespeople are order getters, whereas others are order takers. Businesses also need salespeople who can act as support personnel. In some cases, one person can fulfill all three functions.

The order getter is responsible for what is called creative selling. The goal of creative selling is to get new customers or to increase the number of orders from old customers. Order getters accomplish this by figuring out a customer's needs and persuading that customer to fill those needs by buying products. Generally speaking, there are two kinds of order getting: (1) The salesperson convinces an existing customer to supply leads to new customers or to order more than the usual number of products, or (2) the salesperson seeks out new customers and writes up their orders for products. The second kind of order getting is especially important in the real estate, insurance, appliance, and automobile industries.

Order takers handle repeat sales and maintain positive relationships, whereas support personnel are more essential to locating prospects, educating customers, and building goodwill for the firm.

b. Sales personnel generally fall into three different groups: order getters, order takers, and support personnel. *Order getters* look for new customers and try to increase sales among existing customers. *Order takers* handle repeat sales and do their best to keep customers happy. An inside order taker handles calls in-house, whereas an outside order taker travels to the customer. *Support personnel* do sell, but they are more involved in finding customers or in maintaining the goodwill of existing customers.

Support personnel fall into three categories: (1) Missionary salespeople work for manufacturers and encourage retailers to buy products from wholesalers, who are the manufacturers' real customers. Medical and pharmaceutical companies often employ missionary salespeople. (2) Trade salespeople are most likely to work for food producers. These people try to get more shelf space for a particular product, create displays of products, and distribute samples. (3) As their name implies, technical salespeople show customers the technical ins and outs of a product. They are most likely to be employed by computer, steel, and chemical companies.

c. Sales personnel can be identified as order getters, order takers, and support personnel. Order getters are solely responsible for getting new customers. Order takers handle repeat sales, and support personnel are engaged in public relations.

2. Records and Students' Right to Privacy

1 In this age of information most of us probably have a personal history tucked away somewhere on computer disks. For students, the history may consist of school records, test scores, and ratings by teachers on everything from citizenship to punctuality. Teachers and other staff members judge a student's character and potential, and others use those judgments to decide whether the student should go to this school or get that job. Certainly we need some system of exchanging information about one another; otherwise, we would hire only our friends or attend only those schools where enough people knew us to vouch for us. However, the kind of information in school records may be very imperfect, and the danger that it will be misinterpreted or fall into the wrong hands is great.

2   In the early 1970s, a series of situations came to light in which information was poorly used or parents and students were denied access to records (for example, when a diagnosis was used to justify sending a child to a class for students with mental retardation). In response, Congress passed the Family Educational Rights and Privacy Act in 1974. The act, also known as the **Buckley amendment,** outlines who may and who may not see a student's record and under what conditions. A clear winner from this legislation is parents, who previously were kept from many of the officially recorded judgments that affected their children's futures. The amendment states that federal funds will be denied to a school if it prevents parents from exercising the right to inspect and review their children's educational records. Parents must receive an explanation or interpretation of the records if they so request.

3   However, the Buckley amendment does not give parents the right to see a teacher's or an administrator's unofficial records. For instance, a teacher's private diary of a class's progress or pri-

vate notes about a particular child may not be inspected without the teacher's consent.

4   Although the Buckley amendment has undoubtedly reduced the potential for abuse of information, it has had a somewhat chilling effect on teachers' and others' willingness to be candid* in their judgments when writing student recommendations for jobs or colleges. Because students may elect to see a teacher's letter of recommendation, some teachers choose to play it safe and write a vague, general letter that lacks discriminating judgments, pro or con, about the student. In effect, some faculty members and other recommenders have adopted the attitude "Well, if a student doesn't trust me enough to let me write a confidential recommendation, I'll simply write an adequate, safe recommendation." (Adapted from Ryan and Cooper, *Those Who Can, Teach,* pp. 434, 436.)

Summary   a. In 1974, Congress passed the Family Educational Rights and Privacy Act, also known as the Buckley amendment. Although the Buckley amendment does not give parents the right to see unofficial records such as a teacher's diary, it does grant them access to all official records. In fact, any school that denies parents that right can lose federal funding.

For parents, the act has been a blessing because now they can see the educational records that can powerfully affect their children's future. Teachers feel themselves less blessed by the Buckley amendment because they are now nervous about what they can say in student recommendations. Some simply won't take the risk of writing a candid recommendation. They would rather write a safe one that can't get them into trouble.

b. A student's history consists of records, test scores, and student ratings. For years that history was used to decide a student's future. But prior to 1974, neither students nor parents could view that history.

Then, in the early seventies, a number of situations involving poor use of student records made it clear that something had to change. At this time, for example, it was possible to assign a student to a class for the learning disabled without letting parents see the records on which such a decision was based. However, such assignments without full disclosure became impossible with the passage of the Family Educational Rights and Privacy Act in 1974. The act, also known as the Buckley amendment, outlines who may or may not view student records, and it allows

---

*candid: open, straightforward.

parents to see all official records. It further states that federal funds will be denied any school that prevents parents from exercising their right to access their children's records.

Parents have been understandably overjoyed at the act's passage, but teachers have been less so. Now when students ask for a recommendation, many are fearful about making any comments that might be considered negative. To protect themselves, teachers are prone to writing safe recommendations that won't get them into trouble.

c. It's difficult to imagine any piece of legislation that's done more harm than the Family Educational Rights and Privacy Act of 1974. Also known as the Buckley amendment, this legislation gives parents the right to view all student records. The result has been that teachers are now fearful of saying what they think in recommendations, and they say what's safe rather than what's true.

■ EXERCISE 2

DIRECTIONS Read and summarize the following passages.

EXAMPLE The search for a cheap, quick, and long-lasting insecticide was finally successful in 1939, when a Swiss chemist, Paul Müller, confirmed the bug-killing properties of dichlorodiphenyltrichloroethane (DDT). Used on everything from the potato beetle to disease-bearing lice and fleas (as well as during World War II to fumigate troops' bedding and clothing), DDT was heralded as a huge success for twentieth-century agriculture. But within twenty years, many insects developed strains resistant to the poison. Meanwhile, it wreaked havoc on the food chain by killing off insects beneficial to the environment. In the end, DDT was not a boon to the human race. If anything, it proved a disaster, the proportions of which are still becoming known.

Summary *When it was first introduced, DDT was considered a miracle chemical that could destroy pesky insects like lice, fleas, and beetles, but within twenty years it proved to be more disaster than miracle. Unfortunately, it killed off valuable insects as well as those that did harm.*

EXPLANATION As it should, this summary begins with the main idea of the original passage. In addition to the main idea, the sample summary includes a supporting detail that answers the potential question: How did the supposed miracle turn into a disaster?

1. The American family today is very different from a half century ago. In the fifties, husbands were usually considered the leaders of the family. They were the ones who made the major buying decisions and distributed income, in the form of an allowance, to their wives and children. The wife's main role was to take care of the home. But even here, she based her actions largely on what would please or help her husband. If, for example, he liked to eat dinner early so he could work in the evening, she would set the dinner hour accordingly. Nowadays, however, power and authority tend to be shared by husband and wife. Men have started taking responsibility for household chores. They also shop for groceries, toys, and cleaning products. Women today have a much greater voice in decisions about purchases and lifestyle. For instance, automakers have found that women constitute a large portion of their consumer market and have changed car designs accordingly. Although changes in the family have been rightly attributed to feminist demands for equality, there is another source for the marked shift in power relations. In the current economy, it's usually essential that both spouses work full-time, and wives who bring in half the family's income are far less willing to turn major decisions over to their husbands than were wives in the 1950s.

Summary _____

_____

_____

_____

2. Since 1928, the year penicillin was discovered, humans have significantly improved their health and longevity by using antibiotics to conquer infections. However, the misuse of antibiotics is reducing their effectiveness. Antibiotics are often prescribed and taken when they're not necessary. As a matter of fact, researchers estimate that as many as 50 percent of antibiotic prescriptions are inappropriate. Many people fail to take antibiotics correctly, and they often don't complete a full course of medication. When a course of medication is not finished, the bacteria that remain in the body can grow stronger. Antibiotics are also overused because they are injected into livestock and thus into our food. In addition, we put them into many soap products. Overexposure tends to eliminate weaker bacteria while it encourages

a growing number of antibiotic-resistant strains. As a result, some infections once curable with antibiotics are becoming deadly.

Summary _____

_____

_____

_____

_____

EXERCISE 3

DIRECTIONS Summarize each selection.

1. Negative Aspects of Internet Use

In spite of all its positive aspects, the Internet has its detractors. Some attack the use of the Internet as being time-consuming and addictive. In reality, research has shown that 90 percent of people who get on the Internet do what they need to do and then get off. It's the other 10 percent who are problem users. Early research stated that "although the new electronic media are frequently criticized for their so-called addictive qualities, little empirical evidence has been found to support the assertion that heavy media use is psychologically or physiologically addictive."

Newer findings indicate that **cyberaddiction**—compulsive preoccupied usage of the Internet, chatrooms, and the World Wide Web—can be a major negative aspect of Net usage. (Cyberaddiction is also called computer addiction, impulse control disorder, and Internet addictive disorder.) It is now believed that an Internet user can become addicted to the point of neglecting personal and work responsibilities, and becoming socially isolated. A study of college students, for example, found that 73 percent of students accessed the Internet at least once a week, and 13 percent of students indicated that their computer use interfered with personal functioning. Typically, computer addicts are bright, creative individuals who also feel lonely and isolated. They also can be bored, depressed, angry, or frustrated. In one study, "about 71 percent were diagnosed as suffering from bipolar disorder, commonly called manic depression."

The results of cyberaddiction can include lost jobs, college expulsions, emotional breakdowns, pedophiles stalking youngsters, marriages destroyed, domestic violence, unchecked deepening depression, heightened anxiety, mounting debts, broken trust, lies, and cover-ups.

Symptoms of cyberaddiction include lying about or hiding the level of Internet usage, being preoccupied with using the Internet, and neglecting everything else in one's life. It's like a craving that you continue to satisfy despite the problems it's causing. On the other hand, spending time online may be more positive than excessive time in front of a television or playing video games. The key question to ask might be, "Is your online time disrupting your face-to-face relationships, allowing you to hide from participating in face-to-face interactions, or forcing you to put other elements of your life on hold?" If you are an addict or think you are overdoing cyberconnectedness, ask yourself what you would do instead of spending so much time online. Learn how to control the computer so it doesn't control you, and set definite time limits to your computer use. Some people who are addicted may need mental health therapy. (Berko et al., *Communicating*, pp. 135–136.)

Summary _____

_____

_____

_____

_____

_____

_____

_____

_____

_____

_____

2. The New Individualism

Before the 1960s, individualism in the United States was largely confined to the political sphere. Freedom for individuals meant freedom to speak openly, freedom to worship as we wished, and freedom to live where we wanted. It did not mean freedom to operate outside the norms established by the community, family, and religion. A young man could go west to start his own business and enter politics; a young man could not leave his wife and kids to go west, and he couldn't open an X-rated movie theater once he got there. Among other things, the conformity* of the past was shaped by economic hardship. The struggle for basic sustenance dominated the lives of most Americans, and the struggle for physical survival also loomed large before the advent of modern medicine in the mid-twentieth century.

Powerful norms of self-sacrifice shaped people's values in this environment. You existed for your family, and you worked hard to contribute. There wasn't a lot of psychic space left over to focus on your own "needs" and "issues," as today's therapeutic culture uses these terms.

The 1960s famously changed all of that. Self-sacrifice and conformity were rejected and individual self-expression moved to the forefront of American culture, where it has remained ever since. The scholar Ronald Inglehart labeled the new values that emerged from this decade as "post-materialist," in that the triumph over economic adversity that occurred in America and other Western countries during the postwar era allowed people the freedom to turn to other concerns, such as self-expression in various forms—but also to things like environmental protection and animal rights. Daniel Yankelovich, whose research also tracked these changes, labeled this shift of values the "psychology of affluence."

Whatever you call it, the move away from an ethos of sacrifice to one of personal self-interest—to a "new society of individuals"—triggered a social earthquake in Western nations. It was a "psychological reformation as powerful and decisive as the religious reformation of the sixteenth century," according to one team of researchers.

The new individualism was a double-edged sword from the start. It fueled a long overdue assault on social conformity and helped Americans to finally realize the promise of personal freedom. But it also led many people to turn exclusively inward and elevate their own needs above other obligations. The pursuit of shared goals related to community, family, or political life often took a backseat to hedonism,* escapism, and endless self-analysis.

---

*conformity: obedience to tradition.
*hedonism: the pursuit of pleasure.

Individualism also thrived in a society where old institutions were on the defensive. Organized religion, especially the Catholic church, experienced widespread defections through the '60s and '70s. The traditional family was attacked as a patriarchic* tool for oppressing women. Government was discredited by war and scandal. Large corporations were derided as overly conformist and as the enemy of consumers and the environment. Community life in America was undermined by the growing mobility of Americans and the people's urge to escape small-town social strictures.

The rebels of the '60s talked of new humanistic values and institutions that would replace the old order. They imagined a society shaped by the ideals of cooperation and social responsibility. . . . It was a nice vision, and parts of it came true. Yet, in the end, many of the old institutions were not replaced by anything, and the new individualism emerged within a social order that did little to counterbalance its worst aspects. (Callahan, *The Cheating Culture,* pp. 109–110.)

Summary _____

_____

_____

_____

_____

_____

_____

_____

_____

_____

_____

*patriarchic: ruled by or in the interests of men.

Synthesizing Sources

Imagine your assignment is to read an account of President John Adams's* tenure in the White House and that the account emphasizes Adams's praiseworthy efforts to stop the country's undeclared war with the French. Now imagine as well that you are assigned an outside reading. The outside reading harshly criticizes Adams's role in bringing about passage of the Alien and Sedition Acts.* Having read about two different sides of the same subject, John Adams, how do you think you should proceed? Should you try to remember the main idea of each reading separately? Or should you look for a way to **synthesize,** or combine, the two different positions into one unified or connected piece of information?

If you said yes to the second choice, it may be because you already know a basic rule of memory: The human mind has an easier time storing connected pieces of information than unrelated ideas, theories, or facts. Thus whenever you read different authors who talk about the same subject, it pays to see if you can combine their ideas into a synthesis statement. **Synthesis statements** identify and clarify relationships between different sources that discuss the same topic.

Take the two readings just mentioned. Each one focuses on a different aspect, or side, of Adams's career. One reading notes a positive accomplishment, the other focuses on a more negative achievement. A synthesis statement like the following links the two readings and would help you remember the ideas in both: "Fans of John Adams like to point to his abilities as a peacemaker during the conflict with the French, but his critics can't forget that the Alien and Sedition Acts came into being during his presidency."

Taking the time to create synthesis statements based on two or even three different sources of information does more than improve your memory. It also deepens your understanding of individual viewpoints. To create a synthesis statement, you have to think long and hard about each reading and how it connects to the other reading or readings. This kind of prolonged processing of information is bound to improve your level of comprehension.

---

*John Adams: (1735–1826) the second president of the United States (1797–1801).
*Alien and Sedition Acts: acts that discriminated against the foreign born and blurred the distinction between political discussion and attempts to overthrow the government.

Useful Questions

When writers disagree, it's fairly easy to come up with a synthesis statement that emphasizes the authors' differences of opinion. Yet there will be times when the readings you want to synthesize are more similar than different. At those times, the following questions will prove useful. They will help you pinpoint the connection between or among the readings.

---

1. Do the authors express a similar point of view only in different forms, say poem and essay, fiction and nonfiction?

2. Does one author offer a general interpretation, whereas the other cites specific examples of the same interpretation?

3. Do the readings address the same topic or issue but from different time frames—say, past and present—or from the point of view of different groups—say, the elderly and the young, or the working person versus a corporation?

4. Does one author focus on the cause or causes of a problem while the other looks more closely at a solution?

5. Does one author zero in on the causes of an event while the other concentrates on the aftermath of that event?

6. Do the authors come from different schools of thought? Does one author, for example, concentrate on the psychological roots of an event while the other views it from an economic perspective?

7. Does one author offer an interpretation that is challenged by the other?

8. Did the ideas of one author influence the work of another?

9. Does one author offer a personal account of events that the other describes in more impersonal or objective terms?

CHECK YOUR UNDERSTANDING

Why are synthesis statements valuable?

_____

_____

EXERCISE 4

DIRECTIONS Read each group of passages. Then circle the number of the statement that more effectively synthesizes all three passages. *Note:* Keep in mind that an effective synthesis statement should not in any way contradict the passages it combines.

EXAMPLE

a. John Steinbeck's *Grapes of Wrath* movingly conveys the misery facing the migrant workers who, throughout the Depression, traveled Route 66 across the country searching for work. Steinbeck writes, "Route 66 is the path of people in flight, refugees from dust and shrinking land, from the thunder of tractors and shrinking ownership, from the twisting winds that howl up out of Texas, from the foods that bring no richness to the land and steal what little richness is there."

b. Statistics suggest the magnitude of the Great Depression's effect on the business world. The stock market crash in October 1929 shocked investors and caused a financial panic. Between 1929 and 1933, 100,000 businesses failed; corporate profits fell from $10 billion to $1 billion; and the gross national product was cut in half. Banks failed by the thousands. (Adapted from Norton et al., *A People and a Nation,* p. 754.)

c. As unemployment soared during the Great Depression, both men and women suffered homelessness. In 1932, a squad of New York City police officers arrested twenty-five in "Hoover Valley," a village of tents and crates constructed in Central Park. All over the country, people were so poor they lived in miserable little camps called "Hoovervilles," named in sarcastic honor of President Herbert Hoover, whose policy on the Depression was to pretend it didn't exist.

Synthesis Statement 1. During the Great Depression, no one suffered more than the men and women who earned their living as migrant workers.

2. The Great Depression took a terrible toll on people from all walks of life, from bankers to migrant workers.

EXPLANATION Passages *a, b,* and *c* all give specific examples of different groups that suffered as a result of the Great Depression. Statement 1 is incorrect because it puts the suffering of migrant workers above the suffering of the other groups, and none of the passages makes that point. Sentence 2 is a better synthesis statement because it combines the ideas in all three passages without adding any ideas that weren't there in the first place.

1. a. When World War II broke out in Europe on September 1, 1939, the United States was the only world power without a propaganda agency. Ever since World War I, Americans had been suspicious of the claim that propaganda could be used to good effect. Many believed that British propaganda had helped maneuver the United States into World War I. They also had not forgotten the bloody anti-German riots touched off by movies like America's own *Beast of Berlin* (1919). To most Americans, *propaganda* was simply a dirty word, no matter what its purpose.

   b. In 1939, as the world began to career into World War II, the president of the United States, Franklin Delano Roosevelt, applied pressure on Hollywood to make feature films that were little more than propaganda vehicles, but Hollywood producers were not so ready to give in. Committed to the doctrine of pure entertainment, pure profit, and above all to the need for America to stay out of the war, most balked at making films that reflected the horror engulfing Europe.

   c. The Japanese bombed Pearl Harbor on December 7, 1941. Astonished and outraged, the United States entered World War II. On December 17 of the same year, President Roosevelt appointed Lowell Mellett as head of the Hollywood propaganda office. Mellett's job was to make sure that Hollywood films aided the war effort, and for the most part, Hollywood was happy to cooperate by making films that celebrated the war effort and castigated* America's enemies.

Synthesis Statement

1. Up until the bombing of Pearl Harbor, the United States did not have an official propaganda office, a terrible mistake that produced unexpected and horrifying consequences.

2. Before the bombing of Pearl Harbor, Hollywood, like most of America, mistrusted propaganda. But after the bombing, propaganda became an acceptable part of the war effort and Hollywood embraced it.

2. a. The Egyptians revered Maat as the goddess of justice who weighed the hearts of the dead on a scale. The right balance guaranteed a happy afterlife; the wrong one promised torment.

---

*castigated: harshly criticized or punished.

b. The ancient Greeks worshipped Dike as the goddess of justice. When the Romans inherited her, they renamed her Justitia and represented her with a blindfold around her eyes to symbolize her lack of bias.*

c. With the arrival of Christianity and the rejection of the ancient gods, the goddess of justice was demoted to a saint and people apparently became suspicious of her ability to fairly deal out justice. Santa Justitia was often depicted holding an unevenly balanced scale. The implication was that the rich got different justice than the poor.

Synthesis Statement 1. Whereas the ancient Greeks and Romans held the goddess of justice in great respect, the early Christians seem to have been a bit more suspicious of how justice was meted* out.

2. The Christians refused to accept all of the ancient gods and goddesses, including Justitia, the goddess of justice.

3. a. In the 1992 election, political action committees (PACs) contributed more than $50 million to the various campaigns. The 1996, 2000, and 2004 elections saw even greater amounts of PAC money pour into campaign coffers. This sort of funding of the presidency puts a price tag on democracy: Whoever contributes the most money has the most access to the president.

b. In the name of campaign reform, there are those who would increasingly restrict the contributions of political action committees (PACs). Yet these contributions, no matter how high the sums, are nothing more than a legitimate form of free speech. Any group who wants to contribute to a political campaign as a show of support should have the right to do so.

c. Given the millions of dollars contributed to the last four presidential campaign funds, it's not hard to understand why enthusiasm for campaign reform has never been higher. Yet while outlawing all contributions by political action committees (PACs) seems extreme, it's clear that they have to be more closely monitored and accounted for.

Synthesis Statement 1. When it comes to the campaign contributions of political action committees, or PACs, there's a good deal of disagreement. But

---

*bias: prejudice in favor of one side or another. (For more on this subject, see Chapter 9.)
*meted: distributed.

on one point, no one disagrees: PACs have contributed huge sums to the presidential campaigns.

2. Political action committees (PACs) and their contributions to political campaigns may be controversial, but there is no proof of the claim that has so often been made—that they weaken the democratic process.

4. a. In 2003, many people objected to President Bush's decision to wage war on Iraq, and they used the Internet to organize huge demonstrations against the war.

b. In the campaign against the elimination of land mines* around the world, computers played a key role. Those who supported the elimination of the mines kept in touch and up-to-date via e-mail.

c. In 1998, activists fighting to make insurers extend hospital stays for breast cancer patients used the Internet to publicize their fight and collect signatures for petitions.

Synthesis 1. Because of the Internet, people who never found the time to
Statement write letters are managing to stay in touch.

2. Thanks to the Internet, it's become easier for political activists around the world to stay in touch.

5. a. With its brilliant and innovative techniques, D. W. Griffith's *The Birth of a Nation* dramatically changed the face of American movies forever. Before Griffith, movies contained neither close-ups nor fade-outs. It was Griffith who brought those two techniques to the screen. With the exception of Orson Welles and the film *Citizen Kane,* no other director and no other film have been as influential as Griffith and *The Birth of a Nation.*

 b. By 1910, motion pictures had become an art form, thanks to creative directors like D. W. Griffith. Griffith's most famous work, *The Birth of a Nation* (1915), an epic film about the Civil War and Reconstruction, used innovative techniques—close-ups, fade-outs, and battle scenes—that gave viewers heightened drama and excitement. Unfortunately, the film fanned racial prejudice by depicting African-Americans as a threat to white moral values. An organized black protest against it was

---

*land mines: explosive devices, usually laid below the surface of the ground, that explode if stepped on.

led by the infant National Association for the Advancement of Colored People (NAACP). (Norton et al., *A People and a Nation*, p. 583.)

c. Despite the film's famed innovations, it's nearly impossible for moviegoers to take pleasure in D. W. Griffith's *The Birth of a Nation*. Powered by racism, the film enrages more than it entertains, and it's no wonder that the NAACP picketed the film when it first appeared. Members of the group correctly feared that Griffith's film would revitalize the Ku Klux Klan.

Synthesis
Statement

1. D. W. Griffith was a famous film director who profoundly influenced the American film industry; in fact, Griffith changed the face of American film.

2. Although no one can deny the contribution that D. W. Griffith's *The Birth of a Nation* made to film history, many find it hard to overlook the racism that runs through the film.

EXERCISE 5

DIRECTIONS Read each set of statements. Then write a synthesis statement that links them together.

EXAMPLE

a. Even before the war, Nazi officials had targeted Jews throughout Europe for extermination. By war's end, about six million Jews had been forced into concentration camps and had been systematically killed by firing squads, unspeakable tortures, and gas chambers. (Norton et al., *A People and a Nation*, p. 843.)

b. To protest Hitler's treatment of the Jews during World War II, the philosopher Simone Weil went on a prolonged hunger strike. In the end, Weil starved to death rather than take food while the prisoners of concentration camps were being reduced to walking skeletons.

c. Born to a wealthy Swedish family, Raoul Wallenberg could easily have ignored the horror Adolf Hitler unleashed on the world. But he chose not to. Using his considerable daring, charm, and brains, Wallenberg saved the lives of thousands of Jewish refugees who would have died a horrible death without his help.

Synthesis *During World War II, the tragic plight of the Jews stirred*
Statement *people like Simone Weil and Raoul Wallenberg to extraordinary*
acts of heroism.

EXPLANATION All three passages focus on the plight of the Jews during World War II, and two of the passages describe how two people tried to stop or hinder what was happening. As you can see, the synthesis statement weaves together those two threads of thought.

1. a. Having studied the meditative states of monks and yogis,* researcher Elmer Green advocates and practices meditation. For him, it is a way of making the mind enter a deeper state of consciousness.

   b. In the 1960s and 1970s, the Essalen Institute at Big Sur was the center of what was then called the "human potential movement." At the heart of Essalen and the movement in general was Michael Murphy, who had cofounded the institute with his former classmate Richard Price. Although Murphy eventually moved away from the anti-intellectualism of Essalen's teachers, he remains committed to the daily practice of meditation. For him, the meditative state is a way to unlock human creativity.

   c. Although many exaggerated claims have been made for the benefits of meditation, research supporting those claims has not always been forthcoming. Much of the existing research consists of personal anecdotes, or stories, and many of the studies designed to test the effects of meditation have been poorly designed.

Synthesis _____
Statement _____

_____

2. a. Every society is concerned with the socialization of its children— that is, with making sure that children learn early on what is considered socially correct and morally ethical behavior.

   b. In Asian societies, the family is considered the most important agent of socialization.

―――――――

*yogis: people versed in meditation and focused more on the spirit than on the body.

c. In the last decade, a number of studies have suggested that in the United States, a child's peer group may be overtaking the family as the most powerful agent of socialization.

Synthesis Statement _____

_____

_____

3. a. No matter how far back in history we look, we find human beings making and listening to music. . . . At some point in our past, it was important enough that all human beings born, no matter whether Bengalese, Cruit, or Quechua, no matter whether blind, left-handed, or freckled, were not merely *capable* of making music; they *required* music to add meaning to their lives. (Diane Ackerman, *A Natural History of the Senses.* New York: Vintage Books, 1991, p. 210.)

b. The little girl would take no notice of anyone who entered the room. She seemed locked inside her own private world, unable or unwilling to leave it. But if her uncle played the piano, she would sit next to the piano bench, listening raptly,* a smile playing around her lips. As far as anyone knew, the music of the piano was the only sound that reached her.

c. Music doesn't just seem to soothe the spirit, it also appears to have a powerful effect on the body. In two different studies conducted at the University of Wisconsin, patients suffering from high blood pressure experienced a five- to ten-point decrease in their blood pressure readings after listening to the music of Mozart for a half hour.

Synthesis Statement _____

_____

_____

4. a. Anne Frank was a German-Jewish girl who hid from the Nazis with her parents, their friends, and some other fugitives in an Amsterdam attic from 1942 to 1944. Her diary covering the years of hiding was found by friends and published in 1947. Against the background of the mass murder of European Jewry, the book presents an impressive picture of how a group of hunted people found a way to live together in almost intolerable

_____
*raptly: intently.

proximity. It is also a stirring portrait of a young girl whose youthful spirit triumphs over the misery of her surroundings.

b. *The Diary of Anne Frank* has been read by millions. It has been made into a successful play and film. People are drawn to the story of Anne and her family because it reminds us that the human spirit has enormous resiliency* even in the face of terrifying evil.

c. In *Surviving and Other Essays*, psychologist and concentration camp survivor Bruno Bettelheim argued that the world had embraced Anne Frank's story too uncritically. For Bettelheim, Anne's fate demonstrated "how efforts at disregarding in private life what goes on around one in society can hasten one's destruction."

Synthesis
Statement _____

_____

_____

*resiliency: the ability to respond or to spring back.

■ DIGGING DEEPER: READING 1

LOOKING AHEAD   A number of passages in this chapter focus on events that took place during World War II. The two readings that follow evaluate the event that ended it, President Harry Truman's decision to drop the atomic bomb. Reading 1, drawn from a current history text, expresses doubts about the necessity of Truman's decision.

REEXAMINING TRUMAN'S MOTIVES

1   What motivated President Harry Truman to order the dropping of the atomic bomb? Truman explained that he did it for only one reason: to end the war as soon as possible and thus prevent the loss of one million American casualties in an invasion of Japan. An earlier generation of historians, writing in the aftermath of the war, echoed President Truman's explanation. But more recently historians have revised this interpretation: They argue that Japan might have surrendered even if the atomic bombs had not been dropped, and they dispute Truman's high estimate of casualties as being pure fiction and several times the likely figure. These revisionists* have studied the Potsdam Conference of July 1945 attended by Truman, Joseph Stalin, and Winston Churchill. In their research, they have demonstrated the value of diaries as historical evidence by consulting those kept by certain participants, notably Secretary of War Henry Stimson and Truman himself.

2   Scholars cite Stimson's diary as evidence that Truman's chief motivations included not only ending the war but also impressing the Russians with America's military might and minimizing the USSR's* military participation in the final defeat and postwar occupation of Japan. On July 21 Stimson reported to Truman that the army had successfully tested an atomic device in New Mexico. Clearly emboldened by the news, Truman said that possession of the bomb "gave him an entirely new feeling of confidence. . . ." The next day, Stimson discussed the news with British prime minister Churchill. "Now I know what happened to Truman," Churchill responded. "When he got to the meeting after having read this report he was a changed man. He told the Russians just where they got off and generally bossed the whole meeting."

---

*revisionists: people who challenge a long-standing view or theory.
*USSR: Union of Soviet Socialist Republics.

3   A few historians contend that the decision to drop the atomic bomb was partly racist. As evidence, they point to Truman's handwritten diary entry in which he discussed using the bomb against "the Japs," whom he denounced as "savages, ruthless, merciless and fanatic." Others cite these words to claim that Truman desired to avenge the Japanese attack at Pearl Harbor. It is clear that while personal diaries can help to settle some historical disagreements, they can also generate new interpretive disputes.

4   The deeply emotional question about the necessity for dropping the atomic bomb has stirred debates among the public as well as among historians. In 1995, for example, the Smithsonian Institution provoked a furor with its plan for an exhibit prompted by the fiftieth anniversary of the decision to drop the bomb. Rather than incur the wrath of politicians, veterans' groups, and other Americans outraged by what they perceived to be an anti-American interpretation of events, the Smithsonian shelved most of the exhibit. (Norton et al., *A People and a Nation*, p. 766.)

Sharpening Your Skills

DIRECTIONS Answer the following questions by filling in the blanks.

1. What's the main idea of this reading?

_____

2. According to the reading, why was Henry Stimson's diary important?

_____

3. In paragraph 2, the authors use the word *emboldened:* "Clearly emboldened by the news, Truman said that possession of the bomb 'gave him an entirely new feeling of confidence.'" Based on the context, how would you define *emboldened?*

_____

4. What pattern of organization is at work in paragraph 4?

_____

5. Write a summary of the reading.

Reexamining Truman's Motives

_____

_____

_____

_____

_____

_____

_____

_____

_____

_____

_____

■ **DIGGING DEEPER: READING 2**

LOOKING AHEAD This excerpt was taken from a textbook published in 1965. As you read it, compare this author's perspective with the one expressed in Reading 1.

TRUMAN'S CHOICE

1 Although many Americans have expressed contrition over exploding the first atomic bombs, it is difficult to see how the Pacific war could otherwise have been concluded, except by a long and bitter invasion of Japan. . . . The explosion over Hiroshima caused fewer civilian casualties than the repeated B-29 bombings of Tokyo, and those big bombers would have had to wipe out one city after another if the war had not ended in August. Japan had enough military capability—more than 5,000 planes with kamikaze*-trained pilots and at least two million ground troops—to have made our planned invasion of the Japanese home islands in the fall of 1945 an exceedingly bloody affair for both sides. And that would have been followed by a series of bitterly protracted battles on Japanese soil, the effects of which even time could hardly have healed. Moreover, as Russia would have been a full partner in these campaigns, the end result would have been partition of Japan, as happened to Germany.

2　Even after the two atomic bombs had been dropped, and the Potsdam declaration* had been clarified to assure Japan that she could keep her emperor and surrender was a very near thing, Hirohito* had to override his two chief military advisers and take the responsibility of accepting the Potsdam terms. That he did on 14 August, but even after that, a military coup d'état* to sequester* the emperor, kill his cabinet, and continue the war was narrowly averted.

3　. . . On 2 September 1945, General MacArthur, General Umezu, the Japanese foreign minister, and representatives of Great Britain, China, Russia, Australia, Canada, New Zealand, the Netherlands, and France signed the surrender documents on the deck of the battleship *Missouri*. (Morison, *The Oxford History of the American People*, pp. 1044–1045.)

---

*kamikaze: related to a suicidal air attack.
*Potsdam declaration: the result of the meeting described on page 268.
*Hirohito: the emperor of Japan.
*coup d'état: the sudden overthrow of government by a small group of persons previously in positions of authority.
*sequester: isolate.

Sharpening Your Skills

Answer the following questions by filling in the blanks or circling the letter of the correct response.

1. What question based on the title could help you focus your reading?

   _____

   _____

2. What's the main idea of this reading?

   _____

   _____

3. Based on context, how would you define the word *contrition* in the first sentence of paragraph 1?

   _____

   _____

4. Which of the following is *not* a supporting detail used to make the author's main idea convincing?

   a. The explosion over Hiroshima caused fewer deaths than bombing Japan would have caused.

   b. Long before the bombing of Nagasaki and Hiroshima, the Japanese were prepared to surrender.

   c. Russia would have been involved more and, therefore, been able to demand the right to control part of Japan.

5. Write a synthesis statement that connects this reading to Reading 1.

   _____

   _____

WORD NOTES: BORROWING FROM THE FRENCH

The reading on page 271 introduced the French term *coup d'état* (coo-day-tah) to describe the planned overthrow of Japanese emperor Hirohito. Here are three more words with French origins that you can add to your vocabulary.

1. Blasé (blah-zay). A person described as blasé is considered sophisticated and worldly wise, the kind of person who seems to have done and seen everything at least twice.

   Sample Sentence Born to parents of both wealth and taste, ten-year-old Seymour had traveled widely and already become a bit *blasé.*

2. Raison d'être (ray-zon det'ruh). This French expression means "reason for being" and refers to a person's main goal or purpose in life.

   Sample Sentence Now that his wife has left him, his young daughter has become his *raison d'être.*

3. Savoir faire (sav-wahr fair). This phrase describes the ability to get things done with skill, tact, and charm.

   Sample Sentence What the new CEO lacked in *savoir faire*, she made up for in determination and hard work.

Fill in the blanks with one of these words or phrases: *coup d'état, blasé, raison d'être, savoir faire.*

1. The generals were determined to regain their power even if it meant a _____

2. Even when he was an adolescent, earning money and getting rich was his _____.

3. Impressed by her surroundings but determined not to show it, the teenager tried to act as _____ as possible.

4. Even at seventy, he had the kind of _____ that made him a sought-after companion.

Test 1: Reviewing the Key Points

DIRECTIONS Answer the following questions by filling in the blanks or circling the correct response.

1. Generally speaking, when you summarize, your goal is to reduce the original material to about _____.

2. *True* or *False.* Introductions, personal anecdotes, and quoted material are especially important in summaries.

3. *True* or *False.* It's a good idea to underline and annotate before you write your summary.

4. *True* or *False.* Your personal opinion should not make its way into a summary.

5. *True* or *False.* Whether you are summarizing a chapter section for yourself or writing a summary for your instructor, the same rules or principles always apply.

6. *True* or *False.* When writing a summary, never fuss over transitions; they aren't necessary.

7. When you synthesize information from different sources that focus on the same topic, you need to create a statement that _____

_____.

8. *True* or *False.* Synthesis statements always pinpoint the differences between authors.

9. *True* or *False.* Synthesis statements are useful because the human mind is particularly good at storing unconnected pieces of information.

10. *True* or *False.* Synthesis statements are not effective if you are dealing with more than two sources.

To correct your test, turn to the answer key on page 642.

Test 2: Selecting the Better Summary

DIRECTIONS Read each selection. Then circle the letter of the summary that follows the pointers outlined in the box on pages 238–239.

1. The Triumph of American Movies

1 Moving pictures in America got their start in carnivals and sideshows. Cheap amusements, they were the poor person's substitute for live theater. Popular almost from the beginning, movies were still not considered quite legitimate in their early years between 1896 and 1910, and "nice" people didn't always admit to watching them. However, by the 1920s, the "picture shows" had become a popular and accepted form of entertainment. American movies had begun to take over the foreign market, and movies were America's fifth biggest industry.

2 It was in the twenties that American director Mack Sennett brought the Keystone Cops to the silver screen. Wildly popular with audiences, the Keystone Cops specialized in endless chases, scantily clad young women, and slapstick comedy of the pie-in-your-face variety. The 1920s also saw the rise of screen idols such as Mary Pickford and Rudolph Valentino. While Pickford played roles that celebrated the power of little-girl innocence, Valentino specialized in Latin lovers, whose handsome face and burning eyes made women swoon. Actors like Pickford and Valentino were the first movie stars to be so popular that they actually had fan clubs, a common enough occurrence today but not then.

3 However, it was the British-born Charlie Chaplin, in his role as "The Little Tramp," who truly won the world's heart. With his cane, bowler hat, and ragged, baggy pants, Chaplin breathed life into corny stories about a young man whose aspirations never matched his abilities and who rarely if ever won the heart of the girl he loved. Chaplin's genius was his ability to make audiences laugh and cry at the same time, and they loved him for it—not just in his adopted American home but abroad as well. Almost single-handedly, Chaplin won for the American movie industry an unrivaled mass audience that spanned the continents.

4 Only German moviemakers briefly competed with the Americans during the twenties. In films like *The Cabinet of Dr. Caligari*, German directors, such as F. W. Murnau, produced highly acclaimed Expressionist* dramas that specialized in heightened emotional states of horror and madness. But it wasn't long before

*Expressionist: a movement in the arts that focused on extreme states of mind.

American money had beckoned the Germans to Hollywood and consolidated America's domination of the picture industry.

Summary a. American movies started out in carnivals and sideshows. Movies were what poor people watched because they couldn't afford a ticket to the theater. But by the 1920s, the American movie industry was a virtual blockbuster: It was the fifth largest industry in the country. In the 1920s, America was also in heated competition with Germany for dominance over the world movie industry, but it wasn't long before the Germans were won over by American money, leaving the field clear for American domination. In addition, the Germans never produced movie stars as popular as Mary Pickford, Rudolph Valentino, and Charlie Chaplin. It was this trio that made the American film industry a powerhouse at home and abroad.

     b. By the 1920s, the American movie industry was garnering huge profits both at home and abroad. While stars like Mary Pickford and Rudolph Valentino were widely popular at home, it was Charlie Chaplin who really captured the international market with his portrayal of "The Little Tramp." True, the German movie industry briefly rivaled the American, but that rivalry didn't last long as the more gifted German directors, like F. W. Murnau, were lured to Hollywood by the promise of huge salaries.

2. Faces and First Impressions

1 People may not measure each other by bumps on the head, as phrenologists* used to do, but first impressions are influenced in subtle ways by a person's height, weight, skin color, hair color, eyeglasses, and other aspects of appearance (Alley, 1988; Bull & Rumsey, 1988; Herman et al., 1986). As social perceivers, we are even influenced by a person's name. For example, Robert Young and his colleagues (1993) found that fictional characters with "older generation" names such as Harry, Walter, Dorothy, and Edith are judged less popular and less intelligent than those with "younger generation" names such as Kevin, Michael, Lisa, and Michelle.

2   The human face in particular attracts more than its share of attention. For example, Diane Berry and Leslie Zebrowitz-McArthur (1986) have found that adults who have baby-faced

---

*phrenologists: people who claim to analyze character by touching the bumps on their subjects' heads.

features—large round eyes, high eyebrows, round cheeks, a large forehead, smooth skin, and a rounded chin—are seen as warm, kind, naive, weak, honest, and submissive. In contrast, adults with mature features—small eyes, low brows and a small forehead, wrinkled skin, and an angular chin—are seen as stronger, more dominant, and less naive. Thus, in small claims court, judges are more likely to favor baby-faced defendants accused of intentional wrongdoing, but they tend to rule against baby-faced defendants accused of negligence (Zebrowitz & McDonald, 1991). And in the workplace, baby-faced job applicants are more likely to be recommended for employment as daycare teachers, whereas mature-faced adults are considered to be better suited for work as bankers (Zebrowitz et al., 1991).

3   What accounts for these findings? There are three possible explanations. One is that human beings are genetically programmed to respond gently to infantile features so that real babies are treated with tender loving care. Another possibility is that we simply learn to associate infantile features with helplessness and then generalize this expectation to baby-faced adults. Third, maybe there is an actual link between appearance and behavior—a possibility suggested by the fact that subjects exposed only to photos or brief videotapes of strangers formed impressions that correlated with the self-descriptions of these same strangers (Berry, 1990; Kenny et al., 1992). Whatever the explanation, the perceived link between appearance and behavior may account for the shock that we sometimes experience when our expectations based on appearance are not confirmed. (Adapted from Brehm and Kassin, *Social Psychology*, pp. 83–84.)

Summary a. Like our names, our faces play an important role in making a first impression. Researchers Diane Berry and Leslie Zebrowitz-McArthur have shown, for example, that people with baby faces are frequently perceived, at first sight, to be innocent, naive, and helpless. In contrast, people with sharper, more mature, and more angular faces are often thought to be strong and domineering. No one really knows why this is so, but there are three theories. One theory is that human beings are genetically programmed to treat with care those who have childlike faces. Another theory says that we are used to treating babies in a certain way, and we then apply that same behavior to grownups who happen to have baby faces. And finally, there really may be a connection between how people look and how they behave.

b. We may no longer try to determine people's character by the bumps on their head—the way phrenologists used to do—but we are still influenced, it turns out, by a person's name. In 1993, researcher Robert Young found that characters with old-fashioned names like Harry, Dorothy, and Edith were assumed to be less popular and less intelligent than characters with more modern names like Kevin, Lisa, and Michelle. Our sense that appearance and behavior must be a match is probably one reason why we are so shocked when a person's behavior doesn't fit his or her appearance. We never seem to expect, for example, someone with a baby face to commit a violent crime. That's the kind of thing we would expect of someone who had a more mature and more angular face.

Test 3: Writing Summaries

DIRECTIONS Read and summarize each selection.

1. Interpreting Dreams

1 Sigmund Freud, the Austrian founder of psychoanalysis,* called dreams the "royal road to the unconscious." He therefore paid close attention to their content. Through his study of dreams, Freud identified four specific ways in which they disguise their underlying meaning. According to Freud, dreams make use of **condensation.** In other words, one dream figure or object might well represent several different real-life people or things. Thus, a person in a dream could look like your instructor yet speak and gesture like your father, which Freud, at least, would say was a condensed figure representing authority.

2 **Displacement** was another one of Freud's dream disguises. When displacement is at work in a dream, violent or angry actions, unacceptable in real life, are directed toward safe objects. For example, a teenager who goes to sleep furious at parents who are planning to divorce might dream of smashing a set of dishes rather than dreaming about being angry at the parents she loves.

3 In what Freud called "dream work," **symbolization** is often at play, and he believed that dream imagery should be interpreted in symbolic rather than real terms. A student who dreams of walking into class naked, for example, might well be motivated not by exhibitionist tendencies but by the fear of being weak and vulnerable.

4 **Secondary elaboration** involves not the dream itself but the memory of it. It was Freud's position that when remembering dreams, we elaborate on them, adding logical connections not originally present in the dream itself.

Summary _____

_____

_____

_____

_____

_____

_____

_____

*psychoanalysis: a theory of the human mind and its ills.

_____

_____

2. Technology and Modern Warfare

1 Technological innovations have changed the nature of warfare. For one thing, advances in technology have greatly increased the accuracy of bombs. During World War II, for instance, bomber crews were lucky to hit the right city, especially during night missions. Today, sophisticated radar, satellites, and spy planes can gather detailed information about intended targets. Strike aircraft with computer systems can then hit those targets with amazing precision. "Smart bombs," too, are guided by satellites or lasers to hit exact targets.

2 Technological advances in military communications have also had a profound effect on modern warfare. In twentieth-century conflicts, military commanders could never get enough information about their troops' movements and activities, let alone those of the enemy. These days ground forces use satellite communications gear and laptop computers to talk directly and instantly to pilots overhead. They also use new Information Age technologies to monitor the enemy's communications.

3 Innovations in weapons and communications have led to changes in the role of the foot soldier. During twentieth-century wars, including World War I and the Vietnam War, the foot soldier's mission was to get close enough to the enemy to kill him with whatever weapon he was carrying. That weapon might be a bayonet, a gun, or a grenade. Most battles occurred when the opposing forces were less than twenty-five yards apart. Today, the foot soldier's main function is to gather information about ground targets, mark them, and then call in fire from aircraft and missiles.

4 Together, all of these changes are eliminating the "fog of war," the uncertain outcomes caused by lack of accurate information. These innovations have also reduced the risk of death or injury to military personnel. Errors such as misfires, civilian casualties, and "friendly fire"* accidents are far less common today.

Summary _____

_____

_____

*friendly fire: fire from one's own side.

_____

_____

_____

_____

_____

_____

Test 4: Writing Synthesis Statements

DIRECTIONS Read each pair of passages. Then write a synthesis statement that links both parts together.

1. a. Eleanor Roosevelt (1884–1962) shattered the traditional, ceremonial role of the first lady and used her position and talents to make her own positive contributions to American society. She assisted her husband, Franklin D. Roosevelt, by traveling all over the country to gather information about the American people and their needs. However, she also took up her own causes. Eleanor worked hard to promote civil rights for African-Americans, and it was she who convinced her husband to sign a series of executive orders that prevented discrimination in the administration of his New Deal projects. She also devoted her considerable energies to many different organizations devoted to social reforms. In particular, she argued for equal rights and equal opportunities for women. She advocated women's right to work outside their homes and secured government funds to build childcare centers. She also used her gifts for public speaking, writing, and organizing to work toward the elimination of child labor. Throughout her years as first lady, Eleanor managed to transcend society's stereotypical views of presidential wives to effect, in her own right, many significant improvements in social justice and equality.

    b. As first lady, Hillary Rodham Clinton (1947–) used her intelligence and talents to improve the lives of people across the United States and all over the world. Before becoming first lady, she worked on issues affecting children and families. While in the White House, she published a book, *It Takes a Village,* in which she argued that all areas of society must work together to improve the lives of American children. Also during the two-term presidency of her husband, Bill Clinton, she headed a task force devoted to improving the health care system. In this position, she traveled all over the country, talking to health care professionals and American citizens about how the government could provide access to high-quality, affordable medical care. In addition, she visited many countries, serving as a goodwill ambassador for the United States and supporting human rights, women's rights, and health care reform. At the end of her term as first lady, she managed to do what none of her predecessors had done before: She established an independent political organization and successfully ran for the U.S. Senate.

Synthesis
Statement
_____

_____

_____

a. Somehow NASA* has convinced the world that it landed men on the moon. In reality, though, the entire Apollo space program was an elaborate hoax concocted by the U.S. government. Most people don't know it, but the government actually faked the whole series of landings. For one thing, NASA didn't possess the technical knowledge or equipment to get humans to the moon. In particular, there's no way the astronauts could have survived a trip through the Van Allen belt, a region of radiation trapped in Earth's magnetic field. This radiation would have penetrated the thin hulls of the spacecrafts and killed the men inside. NASA also can't explain the so-called landings themselves. The lunar landers' thrusters should have blasted craters into the moon's surface as they descended. Yet photographs of the landers show them sitting on undisturbed areas of what is supposedly the surface of the moon. Other photographs taken by the astronauts are just as suspicious. For instance, there are no stars in the photos' background. NASA apparently forgot to add them when it staged the settings for the photographs. Also, the actual photographers must not have realized that their studio had a slight breeze that rippled the American flag shown in the photos. Because there is no air on the moon's surface, a flag could not have waved. These glaring inconsistencies, and many others, prove that the Apollo program's moon landing was faked from beginning to end.

b. Surprising as it may seem, many people seriously believe that NASA's Apollo space program never really landed men on the moon. On the contrary, they claim that the moon landings were nothing more than a huge conspiracy, perpetrated by a government desperately in competition with the Russians and fearful of losing face. According to the theory, the U.S. government knew it couldn't compete with Russia in the race to space, so it was forced to fake a series of successful moon landings. As the television program "Conspiracy Theory: Did We Land on the Moon?" revealed, conspiracy theorists believe they have several pieces of evidence proving unquestionably that there was a cover-up. First of all, they claim that astronauts could never have safely passed through the Van Allen belt, a region of radiation trapped

---

*NASA: National Aeronautics and Space Administration.

in Earth's magnetic field. If the astronauts had really gone through that belt, they would have died, say those crying fraud. Scientists, however, have a twofold response to this argument. They point out that the metal hulls of the spaceship were designed to block radiation and that the spacecrafts passed so quickly through the belt that there wasn't time for the astronauts to be affected. Conspiracy theorists, however, are not impressed by this argument, preferring to believe their own version of events.

Conspiracy theorists also argue that the lander should have blasted a crater in the moon's surface when it descended. Photographs of the lunar surface, however, reveal no such craters. For some, this is clear proof of NASA's deception. They discount NASA's claims that the lander was purposely designed to land gently to disturb the moon's surface as little as possible.

Other photographs supposedly support the theory of a faked moon landing. These photographs do not show any stars. Supporters of a conspiracy insist, therefore, that the photos are fake. They refuse to acknowledge NASA's argument that the cameras were set to photograph bright objects like the astronauts' white suits. The faint light of the stars was not strong enough to register on the film.

Proponents of a conspiracy also want to know why the U.S. flag planted on the moon is rippling when it should be still because there is no air on the moon. They don't seem to grasp scientists' explanation that a flag can ripple in the vacuum of space. They also flatly don't believe the more commonsense explanation: The cloth of the flag rippled because the astronaut in the photograph was adjusting the rod that held it. They seem to consider this explanation just too simple to be true.

In other words, despite all proof to the contrary, conspiracy theorists are determined to believe that a hoax has been perpetrated on the American public. From their point of view, only a few wise souls like themselves have been smart enough to spot it. If the rest of us would only open our eyes to their "evidence," perhaps we would see the error of our ways. Yes, and if we would only let the scales drop from our eyes, we might also recognize the existence of the tooth fairy!

Synthesis
Statement _____

_____

_____

Test 5: Taking Stock

DIRECTIONS Read the following selections. Then answer the questions by circling the letter(s) of the correct response(s).

1. The Benefits of Sleep

1 In our modern society, it's difficult to get enough sleep. We lead busy, overworked lives and often have to forgo sleep to get everything done. Round-the-clock television shows tempt us to stay up late. And if we do manage to get a full night's sleep or grab a nap, we run the risk of being labeled "unmotivated" or "lazy" by the go-getters around us. Yet research suggests that those who insist on getting their rest are the wisest of all. Studies indicate that sufficient sleep is as important to health as regular exercise and a nutritious diet. It may even make us smarter.

2 First, adequate sleep is essential to warding off disease. Research has shown that when the body is sleep-deprived, the immune system does not fight infection as effectively. One University of Chicago study, for example, focused on volunteers who slept only four hours a night for six days in a row. The participants' metabolism and hormone production were not functioning efficiently after the six days, leading researchers to conclude that a chronic lack of sleep leaves the body vulnerable to serious diseases, from high blood pressure to obesity. Another study indicated that lack of sleep actually increases the risk of heart attack.

3 Getting sufficient sleep also seems good for our brains. Studies show that during sleep, the brain develops, checks, and expands its nerve connections. Thus sleep gives the brain a chance to strengthen itself, leading to clearer thinking when we're awake. This explains why babies and children sleep so much: Their brains are still developing, so they need a lot of sleep to improve their networks of brain cells. Sleep may also be necessary to purge the brain of sensation overload. During the day, our minds are bombarded with stimulation in the form of sensory experiences, thoughts, and feelings. Sleep gives the brain time to sift through all of this information and either store it or delete it. Without time to evaluate and reorganize, the brain could become overwhelmed and unable to remember anything.

4 Indeed, numerous studies reveal that sleep has a significant effect on memory. When people are deprived of sleep, they don't learn as well as when they have enough sleep. In one study, two

groups of students listened to a story. That night, one group was deprived of sleep and the other was allowed to sleep normally. The next day, each group was asked to recall some details about the story. The sleep-deprived group exhibited much poorer retention of the story than the group that had slept. Researchers therefore conclude that sleep deprivation reduces the ability to retain information.

5   Other studies support this conclusion. At Harvard University, for example, researchers found that people can improve their scores on memory tests simply by sleeping soundly for a minimum of six hours the first night after learning new information. In another study, Canadian researchers taught research subjects a game in the afternoon and then served some of them liquor before bedtime. The alcohol interfered with sleep, and the participants did not get adequate rest. The next day the sleep-deprived participants performed 40 percent worse than those who remained sober and got enough sleep. Additional studies at the University of California have shown that sleep-deprived people also have trouble learning new skills.

6   Clearly, we need to stop viewing a good night's rest as an unnecessary luxury. Sleep is crucial to good health and mental functioning. Instead of skimping on sleep, we should be finding ways to get more of it. (Source of information: Robert A. Stickgold et al., "You Will Start to Feel Very Sleepy . . . ," *Newsweek,* January 19, 2004, pp. 58–60.)

1. Which statement best paraphrases the thesis statement?

   a. Sleep has come to be stigmatized in modern society.

   b. Adequate sleep is crucial to good health.

   c. Getting enough sleep contributes to good health and facilitates learning.

   d. Many researchers are studying why we sleep.

2. Which statement best paraphrases the topic sentence of paragraph 3?

   a. The brain adjusts its network of nerve cells while we sleep.

   b. Babies and children need more sleep than adults do.

   c. Sleep prevents the brain from becoming overloaded by too much information.

   d. Sleep has positive effects on the brain.

3. Is this sentence in paragraph 3 a major or minor detail? "During the day, our minds are bombarded with stimulation in the form of sensory experiences, thoughts, and feelings"?

a. major detail

b. minor detail

4. What pattern or patterns do you see at work in the reading?

a. time order

b. cause and effect

c. comparison and contrast

d. definition

e. classification

5. Which of the following summaries best fulfills the criteria outlined on pages 238–239?

a. According to the latest research, sleep benefits us both physically and mentally. Recent studies indicate that adequate sleep enhances the functioning of the immune system, helping the body fight off major diseases and even heart attacks. In addition, sleep helps the brain function more effectively. Getting sufficient sleep gives the brain time to improve nerve connections and sort through all the thoughts and sensations it must handle during the day. Studies also indicate that sleep is important to building memory and aiding the learning process.

b. The latest scientific research indicates that a lot of sleep is good for us. People may criticize those who take naps or insist on getting eight or nine hours of sleep every night, for those who like to relax are considered to be less driven or ambitious. Those who love to sleep can now assure critics that the more we rest, the better off we are. For example, studies have shown that you learn better when you get plenty of sleep. Numerous experiments indicate that information-recall suffers when people do not get sufficient sleep while trying to learn new information or a new skill. So sleep is an essential component of clear thinking.

c. Studies are proving that sleep is essential to good health. Adequate sleep boosts the immune system, helping the body protect itself from all kinds of serious illnesses. It also protects us against heart disease. Research at Harvard University indicates that sleep helps us remember things better, too. Clearly, we have to stop working so much and watching so many late-night TV programs because these activities are interfering with our ability to get the rest we need.

2. Low-Fat versus Low-Carb Diets

1 Millions of Americans want to lose weight, and they know that in order to get rid of unwanted pounds, they'll have to change their eating habits. The two most popular options today are a diet that's low in fat or a diet that's low in carbohydrates. But is one more effective than the other? Advocates for each diet continue to debate which method is best. Thus when choosing between the two, most people evaluate the differences in food choices and short-term and long-term effectiveness, along with the health risks and benefits.

2 Both diets forbid the consumption of sugar and junk foods like potato chips; however, the allowed foods on each differ significantly. A low-fat diet includes high-carbohydrate foods like bread, pasta, fruit, and potatoes and shuns high-fat foods like bacon and mayonnaise. A low-carb diet is the complete opposite; it emphasizes protein, so dieters can eat as much meat and cheese as they want. However, avoiding bread, cereal, and other high-carbohydrate foods is a must. Dieters need to decide whether they'd rather go for long periods of time without bread or without meat. Depending on one's tastes and preferences, one diet may be more appropriate than the other. Meat lovers, for example, may find the low-carb diet more appealing.

3 Many dieters are willing to ignore their preferences, though, in exchange for short-term effectiveness; in this respect, the low-carb diet is clearly the better of the two. Several studies have shown that, over a six-month period, those who adhere to a low-carb diet tend to lose twice the weight as those who follow a low-fat diet. Plus, low-carb dieters can eat more calories than low-fat dieters and still lose weight. Consequently, those who are looking for quick results are more apt to choose the low-carb approach.

4 Yet research indicates that the low-fat diet may offer more long-term success. Although the low-carb diet results in faster initial weight loss, studies show that a year after dieting those who followed a low-carb plan had regained much more weight than those who chose a low-fat diet. Therefore, people who are determined to lose weight and keep it off may do better on a low-fat plan.

5   Those who are still undecided after considering the types of food and the effectiveness of each diet might want to consider one last point of comparison: the health benefits and risks. Although recent studies conclude that high-fat, low-carb diets do not raise artery-clogging cholesterol levels as was expected, many health professionals do not recommend a low-carb diet because its long-term health risks are still unknown. A low-fat diet, on the other hand, is thought to be nutritionally more sound because it permits one to consume a variety of essential nutrients.

1. Which statement best paraphrases the thesis statement?

   a. Millions of Americans need to lose weight.

   b. Low-fat and low-carb diets differ in essential ways, which makes it hard to decide which one is better.

   c. Because it keeps the weight off, a low-fat diet is better than a low-carb diet.

   d. A low-carb diet is healthier and more effective than a low-fat diet.

2. Which statement best paraphrases the topic sentence of paragraph 5?

   a. When choosing a diet plan, people should consider the potential risks.

   b. The health benefits are the most important factor in selecting the right diet option.

   c. People who are undecided might consider choosing one diet over the other based on each one's effects on health.

   d. Low-carb diets are not as unhealthy as people suspected they might be.

3. Is this sentence in paragraph 3 a major or minor detail: "Several studies have shown that, over a six-month period, those who adhere to a low-carb diet tend to lose twice the weight as those who follow a low-fat diet"?

   a. major detail

   b. minor detail

4. What pattern or patterns do you see at work in the reading?

   a. time order

   b. cause and effect

   c. comparison and contrast

   d. definition

   e. classification

5. Which of the following summaries best fulfills the criteria outlined on pages 238–239?

   a. America has become a nation of overweight and obese people; at any given time, millions of people are trying to follow either a low-fat or a low-carb diet. Unfortunately, though, both diets have major drawbacks. For example, both prohibit the consumption of certain kinds of popular foods. Thus people who choose the low-fat approach have to give up foods like cheese and mayonnaise, while those who try the low-carb approach can't eat even one slice of bread. The low-fat approach doesn't work very quickly, and the low-carb approach usually results in only temporary weight loss. In addition, the low-carb plan may increase long-term health problems; no one really knows for sure. Clearly, there's no one perfect diet.

   b. When choosing between a low-fat or a low-carb diet, most people usually examine four points of comparison. First, they consider the foods they could eat as part of each diet, for one emphasizes carbohydrates and the other emphasizes protein. A second point of comparison is short-term effectiveness; those who want to shed pounds quickly often select the low-carb method. A third important difference is long-term effectiveness, so those who desire permanent weight loss may get better results with a low-fat diet. Finally, dieters should compare the two diets' potential impact on health.

   c. It's obvious that a low-fat diet is better than a low-carb diet. Sure, you get to indulge in juicy meats swimming in rich cheese sauces if you choose the low-carb approach, but you might be sacrificing your long-term health while you do so. And you may shed a few pounds fast by not eating bread for a few months, but you'll probably gain all the weight back within a year. If you choose the low-fat approach, though, you'll be healthier and slimmer for life.

C H A P T E R   6

Reading Between the Lines: Drawing Inferences and Conclusions

 In this chapter, you'll learn

- **how to infer main ideas in paragraphs.**
- **how to evaluate your inferences.**
- **how to infer main ideas in longer readings.**
- **how to infer supporting details.**
- **how to draw logical conclusions.**

Chapter 6 shows you how to put into words what the author suggests but never says outright. In short, it teaches you the art of drawing inferences. And it's no accident

that this chapter bridges the gap between the comprehension and critical reading parts of this textbook. Essential to understanding an author's meaning, drawing appropriate inferences also lies at the heart of critical reading.

 # Inferring Main Ideas in Paragraphs

A good many paragraphs contain topic sentences. But not all of them do. Sometimes authors choose to imply, or suggest, the main idea. Instead of stating the point of the paragraph in a sentence, they offer specific statements that lead or guide readers to the implied main idea of the passage. Here's an example in which the main idea is implied rather than stated.

> The philosopher Arthur Schopenhauer lived most of his life completely alone. Separated from his family and distrustful of women, he had neither wife nor children. Irrationally afraid of thieves, he kept his belongings carefully locked away and was said to keep loaded pistols near him while he slept. His sole companion was a poodle called *Atma* (a word that means "world soul"). However, even Atma occasionally disturbed his peace of mind. Whenever she was bothersome or barked too much, her master would grow irritated and call her *mensch,* which is German for "human being."

In this paragraph the author makes specific statements about Schopenhauer's character and behavior: (1) he lived most of his life alone, (2) he distrusted women, (3) he always thought he was going to be robbed, (4) his only companion was a dog, and (5) he would call his dog a "human being" if she irritated him. However, none of those statements sums up the point of the paragraph. That means the paragraph lacks a topic sentence stating the main idea.

Instead, the paragraph implies a main idea like the following: "Schopenhauer did not care for his fellow human beings." Because this inference follows naturally from statements made in the paragraph, it qualifies as an effective inference.

Effective and Ineffective Inferences

Experienced readers know that main ideas aren't always expressed in sentences. Thus, if they can't find a sentence that sums up the paragraph, they read between the lines in an effort to infer a main idea that follows from the paragraph. However, they are always careful to draw an **effective inference,** one solidly based on the author's actual statements.

To recognize the difference between an effective and ineffective inference, imagine that we had inferred this main idea from the sample paragraph about Schopenhauer:

> Schopenhauer's miserable childhood made it impossible for him to have healthy relationships with other people.

Although the paragraph offers plenty of evidence that Schopenhauer did not have healthy relationships with people, it doesn't discuss his childhood. Because our inference is not based on what the author actually says, it is ineffective. In other words, it's likely to lead the reader in a direction the author never intended.

Even though common sense suggests that an adult who doesn't like people may have had a troubled childhood, we cannot rely mainly on common sense to draw inferences. To be useful, *inferences in reading must rely most heavily on what the author explicitly, or directly, says.* Inferences that lean more heavily in the direction of the reader's experience rather than the author's intent are often the cause of a communication breakdown between reader and writer.

Recognizing Effective and Ineffective Inferences

To evaluate your ability to distinguish, or see the difference, between effective and ineffective inferences, read the next paragraph. When you finish, look at the two inferences that follow and decide which one fits the paragraph and which one does not.

> In the West, the Middle Eastern country of Kuwait has a reputation for being more liberal than other Middle Eastern countries, at least where women's rights are concerned. Yet the majority of female students are not permitted to study abroad, no matter how good their grades. Similarly, female students almost never receive funding for international athletic competitions. Although the Kuwaiti government promised to give women the right to vote once the Gulf War of 1990–1991 was over, the women of Kuwait are still not allowed to participate in elections. Kuwaiti feminists, however, remain hopeful that the government will one day keep its promise.

Based on this paragraph, which implied main idea makes more sense?

1. It's clear that the government of Kuwait will never honor its promise to let women vote.

2. Despite Kuwait's liberal reputation, women are not treated as the equals of men in many key areas.

If you chose inference 2, you've grasped the difference between effective and ineffective inferences. Inference 2 is solidly backed by what the author says. The author's specific examples support the idea that women lack equality in key areas. Inference 2 is also not contradicted by anything said in the paragraph. That's important. If you infer a main idea that is undermined or contradicted by any of the author's statements, you need to draw a new inference.

Unlike inference 2, inference 1 is contradicted by the paragraph's last sentence. If Kuwaiti feminists still have hope, there's no reason to infer that the Kuwaiti government will *never* honor its promise to give women the vote.

Another problem with inference 1 is that the paragraph does not focus solely on voting rights. It also addresses funding for female athletes and travel privileges for female students. None of the statements addressing these issues can be used as the basis for inference 1, making it clear that this inference is ineffective.

Effective Inferences

1. are solidly grounded, or based on, specific statements in the passage.

2. are not contradicted by any statements made in the passage.

3. rely more heavily on the author's words than on the reader's background knowledge.

Ineffective Inferences

1. do not follow from the author's actual statements.

2. are contradicted by the author.

3. rely too heavily on the reader's personal experience or general knowledge rather than on the author's words.

EXERCISE 1

DIRECTIONS Read each passage. Then circle the letter of the better inference.

EXAMPLE Over the years, countless numbers of men and women have paid large sums of money for a treatment commonly known as *cell therapy*. Their reason was simple: They believed lamb cell injections could help them maintain their youth. These people either did not know or did not choose to believe that animal cells, when injected into the human body, are destroyed by the immune system. Others in pursuit of youth have tried *chelation therapy*, which is supposed to pull heavy metals like lead and mercury from the body. Proponents claim that the treatments improve cell function, inhibit the aging process, and prevent heart disease, all by eliminating toxicity from the body, yet researchers have never proved these effects. In fact, critics say that patients are not even "toxic" to begin with, so the therapy has nothing to treat. Other seekers of the fountain of youth have tried oral sprays of Human Growth Hormone. The sprays can supposedly accomplish everything from eliminating wrinkles to improving memory and concentration. However, not only have such treatments never been shown to work, but they also may produce side effects like increased risk of cancer and cardiovascular disease.

Implied Main Idea (a.) Therapies designed to keep people young generally do not work.

　 b. Therapies should be available for everyone, not just for those rich enough to afford them.

EXPLANATION Nothing in the paragraph suggests that therapies to maintain youth should be made available to everyone. On the contrary, most of the statements suggest that these therapies are useless against aging, making inference *a* the better choice for an implied main idea.

1. In all fifty states, the law protects the confidentiality of Catholics' confessions to priests. Even when a person reveals during confession that he or she has physically harmed another, priests are required to observe canon law* and withhold the information from law enforcement authorities. South Carolina and Oregon, for example, both protect the priest-penitent* privilege even when a confession reveals sexual abuse of children. However, other states—including New Hampshire and Kentucky—do not permit priests to offer confidentiality to child-abuse suspects, even when those suspects are in the darkness of the confessional. Other states distinguish between conversations inside and outside the confession box. While many

---

*canon law: a code of laws established by a church council.
*penitent: person confessing his or her sins.

states, such as New Jersey, still grant confidentiality to all priest-penitent conferences regardless of their setting, others are ruling that conversations outside the confession box may not always qualify as privileged communications. In Idaho, for example, a court ruled that an abusive father's confession to a hospital chaplain was not protected by canon law.

Implied Main Idea   a. Some states are limiting priest-penitent confidentiality in the interest of protecting the welfare of those who may be in danger.

b. All laws protecting the confidentiality of Catholic confessions should be stricken from the books.

2. The founding fathers based the Constitution of the United States on republican rather than democratic principles. In other words, laws were to be made by the representatives of citizens, not by the citizens directly. Yet whatever the intentions of the founding fathers may have been, eighteen U.S. states provide for legislation by *initiative.* In other words, voters can place legislative measures (and sometimes constitutional amendments) directly on the ballot as long as they get the required number of signatures on a petition. Forty-nine states allow *referendums,* a procedure which lets voters reject a measure adopted by the state legislature. Fifteen states permit *recalls.* If enough signatures can be collected, an elected official has to go before the voters, who may well vote him or her out of office. This is precisely what happened to Governor Gray Davis of California in 2003—a recall election propelled him out of office.

Implied Main Idea   a. Whatever the founding fathers had in mind, there are still a number of ways in which our country is governed by democratic rather than republican principles.

b. Over the years, U.S. citizens have consistently challenged the legality of the Constitution through initiatives, recalls, and referendums.

   3. On the one hand (if you can forgive the pun*), left-handers have often demonstrated special talents. Left-handers have been great painters (Leonardo da Vinci, Picasso), outstanding performers (Marilyn Monroe, Jimi Hendrix), and even presidents (Ronald Reagan, George H. W. Bush). (As these examples suggest, left-handedness is considerably more common among males than among females.) And left-handedness has been reported to be twice as common among

---

*pun: a play on words.

children who are mathematical prodigies as it is in the overall population (Benbow, 1988). On the other hand, left-handers have often been viewed as clumsy and accident-prone. They "flounder about like seals out of water," wrote one British psychologist (Burt, 1937, p. 287). The very word for "left-handed" in French—*gauche*—also means "clumsy." Because of such negative attitudes toward left-handedness, in previous decades parents and teachers often encouraged children who showed signs of being left-handed to write with their right hands. (Rubin et al., *Psychology*, p. 59.)

Implied Main Idea   a. Left-handed people tend to be more creative than right-handed people; nevertheless, the world has been organized to suit right-handers rather than left-handers.

b. Although some very gifted people have been left-handers, left-handed people have a reputation for being clumsy or awkward.

4. The topaz, a yellow gemstone, is the birthstone of those born in November. It is said to be under the influence of the planets Saturn and Mars. In the twelfth century, the stone was used as a charm against evil spirits, and it was claimed that a person could drive off evil powers by hanging a topaz over his or her left arm. According to Hindu tradition, the stone is bitter and cold. If worn above the heart, it is said to keep away thirst. Christian tradition viewed the topaz as a symbol of honor, while fifteenth-century Romans thought the stone could calm the winds and destroy evil spirits.

Implied Main Idea   a. There are many superstitions associated with the topaz.

b. The superstitions surrounding the topaz are yet another example of human stupidity.

EXERCISE 2

DIRECTIONS   Read each passage. Then circle the letter of the best inference.

1. The widely acclaimed singer and guitarist Buddy Holly died in a 1959 plane crash at age 22. Famed singer Otis Redding was only 26 when he was killed in a plane crash in 1967. At age 27, legendary rock guitarist Jimi Hendrix died from suffocation in 1970 after swallowing a mix of liquor and pills. Jim Morrison, lead singer of the popular rock band The Doors, was also only 27 when he died of mysterious causes in 1971. Just two weeks after Hendrix's death, rock-and-roll idol Janis Joplin died of a heroin overdose, also at the age of 27. In 1978, Sid Vicious, the 21-year-old

bass player of the influential Sex Pistols punk-rock band, took his own life. In 1994, Kurt Cobain, world-renowned lead singer for the band Nirvana, committed suicide; he was also only 27 years old.

Implied Main Idea   a. Plane crashes have taken the lives of many of rock's biggest stars.

b. Many celebrities have died when they were at the peak of their fame.

c. Many of rock's biggest stars died young.

2. Is chocolate good or bad for your health? In an attempt to answer this question, Dr. Norman Hollenberg of Harvard Medical School studied the Kuna Indians, an isolated group that lives on islands off the coast of Panama. The Kuna consume large quantities of locally grown cocoa, a plant that provides the raw material for chocolate. They also eat many foods high in salt, a diet that tends to produce high blood pressure. Yet most have normal blood pressure. However, when Kuna Indians move to a city and begin to eat a weaker, processed form of commercial cocoa, their blood pressure tends to rise. (Source of information: Randolph E. Schmid, "Scientists Explore Virtues of Chocolate," *The Charlotte* [NC] *Observer*, February 11, 2004, p. 18A.)

Implied Main Idea   a. A study of Kuna Indians indicates that eating unprocessed chocolate may help maintain normal blood pressure.

b. A study of Kuna Indians indicates that chocolate is bad for your health.

c. A study of Kuna Indians suggests that people who don't eat chocolate will probably have a heart attack.

3. A recent Harris Poll indicated that Americans, on average, believe that there is a 50 percent chance that they will be seriously hurt in a car accident. In reality, the chance of this is about 5 percent. The average woman believes that she has a 40 percent chance of getting breast cancer. However, the chance of this happening is actually only one in ten, or 10 percent. Women also believe that they have a 50 percent chance of having a heart attack, but the actual risk is just one in ten. The average man believes that he has about a 40 percent chance of getting prostate cancer, yet in reality the risk is also only one in ten. Although most people estimate their chance of getting HIV/AIDS to be about one in ten, the risk is actually about one in twenty, or 5 percent. (Source of information: Humphrey Taylor, "The

Harris Poll #7: Perceptions of Risks," HarrisInteractive, January 27, 1999, www.harrisinteractive.com/harris_poll/index.asp?PID=44.)

Implied Main Idea a. Most people underestimate their chances of developing many diseases or being hurt in an accident.

b. Most people overestimate their chances of developing many diseases or being hurt in an accident.

c. Most people accurately estimate their chances of developing many diseases or being hurt in an accident.

4. Cleveland child psychologist Sylvia Rimm interviewed 5,400 children in eighteen states about their worries, fears, relationships, and confidence. She also talked with another 300 children in focus groups. She discovered that overweight children feel less intelligent and less confident than their normal-weight peers. Overweight children also worry more than their slimmer peers. In addition, Rimm discovered that heavier children are lonelier and sadder than other kids, describing family relationships more negatively than average-weight children describe theirs. Unfortunately, most overweight kids are forced to endure their peers' hurtful taunts and ridicule much more often than normal-weight kids do. (Source of information: Nanci Hellmich, "Heavy Kids Battle Sadness Along with Weight," *USA Today,* March 29, 2004, p. 8D.)

Implied Main Idea a. According to Sylvia Rimm, average-weight children are very cruel to overweight children.

b. Sylvia Rimm's research indicates that negative emotions and problems lead children to overeat and, therefore, become overweight.

c. Sylvia Rimm's survey indicates that overweight children suffer more than their average-weight peers do.

◤ EXERCISE 3

DIRECTIONS Read each passage. Then circle the letter of the best inference.

1. For many years, studies have suggested that being married is beneficial to a woman's health because married women tend to have lower rates of heart disease and stroke than unmarried women. However, researchers wanted to find out whether this is true for both happily and *un*happily married women. In one study, psychologists followed 422 upper-middle-class women for twelve years, from their forties into their fifties. They checked the women's blood

pressure, blood fats, glucose levels, and abdominal fat because all these factors indicate the risk for heart disease and stroke. They discovered that women who were either unhappily married or divorced by fifty were twice as likely as single women or women who were happily married in their forties to be at risk for heart attacks and strokes. Other studies, too, are producing similar results. (Source of information: Marilyn Elias, "Marriage Taken to Heart," *USA Today,* March 5, 2004, p. 8D.)

Implied Main Idea   a. Research has shown that married women are healthier than unmarried women.

b. Studies suggest that while a happy marriage may be good for a woman's health, an unhappy marriage does not produce the same benefit.

c. According to recent studies, single women are actually healthier than married women.

d. Studies indicate that women who marry in their forties tend to be healthier than women who marry in their twenties.

2. After Reverend Martin Luther King Jr. and Robert F. Kennedy were assassinated in 1968, Congress banned mentally ill people from buying or owning guns. Today, however, anyone who does not reveal a *record* of mental illness when buying a gun will probably not get caught. Why? The answer is simple: Thirty-one states do not have access to the records of those committed to mental institutions. Only a handful of states provide mental-health information to the national database used to screen gun buyers. In fact, two-thirds of all states don't even compile such information. Furthermore, according to Americans for Gun Safety, fourteen states cannot search the records for people who have been convicted of domestic violence misdemeanors. Thus they cannot identify a would-be gun buyer with a history of domestic violence. Seven states cannot stop individuals who have been served with restraining orders from purchasing a gun. Fully one-fourth of all computerized records on convicted felons are inaccessible to those performing background checks of gun buyers. Federal immigration records are also very limited, so illegal aliens too can buy guns without being caught. (Sources of information: "History of Mental Illness Doesn't Prevent Gun Buys," *USA Today,* March 24, 2004, p. 12A; "Checks Are Spotty," *USA Today,* March 24, 2004, p. 12A.)

Implied Main Idea   a. Mentally ill people can easily buy guns.

b. Background checks on gun buyers are a waste of time; they do nothing to decrease the crime rate.

    c. The failure of states to share mental-health information diminishes the effectiveness of background checks.

    d. If all guns were banned, there would be no need for background checks.

3. Circulation of the tabloid newspaper *National Enquirer* far exceeds that of the *New York Times,* the *Los Angeles Times,* and the *Washington Post.* Online searches for information about singer Janet Jackson's breast exposure during the 2004 Super Bowl were twenty-five times greater than searches for information about the robot probe that was exploring the planet Mars. The average individual is more likely to know the name of superstar Michael Jackson's defense attorney than that of our nation's defense secretary. On the same day that Michael Jackson surrendered to police after being charged with child molestation, two terrorist bombings occurred in Turkey, President George W. Bush traveled to London, and 2,500 police officers had to use tear gas and pepper spray to quell a major protest in Miami. Yet the headlines that day—even from major, reputable news sources—focused on the pop singer's arrest. (Source of information: Lou Dobbs, "All the News That's Fit," *U.S. News & World Report,* February 23, 2004, p. 48.)

Implied Main Idea   a. Entertainers Janet and Michael Jackson have generated a lot of publicity recently.

    b. Celebrities usually know less than the average American citizen about significant world events.

    c. People tend to use multiple sources, including newspapers, the Internet, and television, to gather information about world events.

    d. The public and the media seem to be more interested in celebrity gossip than in serious news events.

4. In our busy society, many people *multitask,* or do several things at the same time. For example, they talk on cell phones while driving, cook dinner while cleaning, and surf the Internet while sending instant messages to friends. Are people who multitask more productive than people who do just one thing at a time? Researchers conducted four experiments in which young adults were asked to switch between different tasks like solving math problems or sorting objects. As subjects worked, researchers measured the speed at which they completed their tasks. The measurements indicated that subjects lost time whenever they had to shift their thinking to move from one task to another. The more complex or unfamiliar the tasks, the more time was lost as subjects shifted their attention and concentration. Even if each mental shift took only half a second, the time added up throughout the course of the experiment. (Source of information: Porter Anderson, "Study: Multitasking Is Counterproductive," CNN.com, August 5, 2001, www.cnn.com/2001/CAREER/trends/08/05/multitasking.study.)

Implied Main Idea   a. Multitaskers are more productive than people who do one thing at a time.

b. Multitaskers are not more productive than people who do one thing at a time.

c. Multitasking is effective at work but nowhere else.

d. Multitasking benefits employers but takes a negative toll on employees.

EXERCISE 4

DIRECTIONS Write a sentence that expresses the implied main idea of the paragraph.

EXAMPLE The plant known as kudzu was introduced to the South in the 1920s. At the time, it promised to be a boon* to farmers who needed a cheap and abundant food crop for pigs, goats, and cattle. However, within half a century, kudzu had overrun seven million acres of land, and many patches of the plant had developed root systems weighing up to three hundred pounds. Currently, no one really knows how to keep kudzu under control, and it's creating problems for everyone from boaters to farmers.

Implied Main Idea   *Intended to help farmers, kudzu has proven to be more harmful than beneficial.*

EXPLANATION At the beginning of the paragraph, the author tells readers that in the 1920s kudzu was viewed as a help to farmers. However, by the end of the paragraph, the author tells us what a pest the plant has become. Thus it makes sense that the implied main idea unites these two different perspectives on kudzu.

1. For football and baseball players, the mid-twenties are usually the years of peak performance. Professional bowlers, however, are in their prime in their mid-thirties. Writers tend to do their best work in their forties and fifties, while philosophers and politicians seem

---

*boon: benefit, favor.

to reach their peak even later, after their early sixties. (Adapted from Coon, *Essentials of Psychology,* p. 139.)

Implied Main Idea _____

_____

2. The webs of some spiders contain drops of glue that hold their prey fast. Other webs contain a kind of natural Velcro that tangles and grabs the legs of insects. Then, too, spiderwebs don't always function simply as traps. Some webs also act as lures. Garden spiders use a special silk that makes their intricate decorations stand out, and experiments have shown that the decorated parts attract more insects. Other kinds of spiders, like the spitting spider, use webs as weapons. The web is pulled taut to snap shut when a fly enters.

Implied Main Idea _____

_____

3. The day you learned of your acceptance to college was probably filled with great excitement. No doubt you shared the good news and your future plans with family and friends. Your thoughts may have turned to being on your own, making new friends, and developing new skills. Indeed, most people view college as a major pathway to fulfilling their highest aspirations. However, getting accepted may have caused you to wonder: What will I study? How will I decide on a major? Will I do the amount of studying that college requires? Will I be able to earn acceptable grades? (Adapted from Williams and Long, *Manage Your Life,* p. 157.)

Implied Main Idea _____

_____

4. Every year the scene is so unchanging I could act it out in my sleep. In front of the Hayden Planetarium on a muggy Saturday morning, several dozen parents gather to wave goodbye to their boys as the bus ferries them off for eight weeks of camp. First-time campers are clutchy. Old-timers are cocky. My own sons fret at length about carsickness. Then the parents give the kids a final hug and shuffle sullenly back to their depopulated urban nests. But not this year. When the bus pulled out of the planetarium's circular driveway four Saturdays ago, at last removing the waving boys at the tinted windows completely from our view, one parent interrupted the usual

hush by very tentatively* starting to clap. Then other parents joined in, first clapping and finally laughing uproariously. (Frank Rich, "Back to Camp," *New York Times*, July 22, 1995, p. 19.)

Implied Main Idea _____

_____

5. In the nineteenth century, when white settlers moved into territory inhabited by Navajo and other tribal peoples, the settlers took much more than they needed simply to survive. They cut open the earth to remove tons of minerals, cut down forests for lumber to build homes, dammed the rivers, and plowed the soil to grow crops to sell at distant markets. The Navajo did not understand why white people urged them to adopt these practices and improve their lives by creating material wealth. When told he must grow crops for profit, a member of the Comanche tribe (who, like the Navajo, believed in the order of the natural environment) replied, "The Earth is my mother. Do you give me an iron plow to wound my mother's breast? Shall I take a scythe* and cut my mother's hair?" (Norton et al., *A People and a Nation*, p. 499.)

Implied Main Idea _____

_____

CHECK YOUR UNDERSTANDING
Explain the difference between effective and ineffective inferences.
_____
_____
_____

 # Implied Main Ideas in Longer Readings

Longer readings, particularly those in textbooks, generally include thesis statements that express the main idea of the entire reading.

---

*tentatively: hesitantly, shyly.
*scythe: a sharp curved knife used to cut wheat.

However, even writers of textbooks occasionally imply a thesis statement rather than explicitly state it. When this happens, you need to respond much as you did to paragraphs without a topic sentence. Look at what the author actually says and ask what inference can be drawn from those statements. That inference is your *implied thesis statement.*

To illustrate, here's a reading that lacks a thesis statement, yet still suggests a main idea.

J. Edgar Hoover and the FBI

1 Established in 1908, the Federal Bureau of Investigation (FBI) was initially quite restricted in its ability to fight crime. It could investigate only a few offenses like bankruptcy fraud and antitrust violations, and it could not cross state lines in pursuit of felons. It was the passage of the Mann Act in 1910 that began the Bureau's rise to real power. According to the act, the Bureau could now cross state lines in pursuit of women being used for "immoral purposes" such as prostitution. Prior to the Mann Act, the Bureau had been powerless once a felon crossed a state line; now at least the FBI could pursue those engaged in immoral acts.

2 It was, however, the appointment of J. Edgar Hoover in 1924 that truly transformed the Bureau. Hoover insisted that all FBI agents had to have college degrees and undergo intensive training at a special school for FBI agents. He also lobbied* long and hard for legislation that would allow the Bureau to cross state lines in pursuit of all criminals. He got his wish in 1934 with the Fugitive Felon Act, which made it illegal for a felon to escape by crossing state lines. Thanks to Hoover's intensive efforts, the way was now open for the FBI to become a crack crime-fighting force with real power.

3 And fight crime the agency did. Its agents played key roles in the investigation and capture of notorious criminals in the thirties, among them John Dillinger, Clyde Barrow, Bonnie Parker, Baby Face Nelson, Pretty Boy Floyd, and the boss of all bosses— Al Capone.

4 In 1939, impressed by the FBI's performance under Hoover, President Franklin D. Roosevelt assigned the Bureau full responsibility for investigating matters related to the possibility of espionage by the German government. In effect, Roosevelt gave Hoover a mandate* to investigate any groups he considered suspicious.

---

*lobbied: worked to influence government officials.
*mandate: legal right.

This new responsibility led to the investigation and arrest of several spies. Unfortunately, J. Edgar Hoover did not limit himself to wartime spying activities. Instead, he continued his investigations long after World War II had ended and Germany had been defeated.

5   Suspicious by nature, Hoover saw enemies of the United States everywhere, and his investigations cast a wide net. In secret, the agency went after the leaders of student and civil rights groups. Even esteemed civil rights leader Martin Luther King Jr. was under constant surveillance by the FBI. Investigation techniques during this period included forging documents, burglarizing offices, opening private mail, conducting illegal wiretaps, and spreading false rumors about sexual or political misconduct. It wasn't until Hoover's death in 1972 that the FBI's secret files on America's supposed "enemies" were made public and these investigations shut down. (Source of information: Adler, *Criminal Justice*, pp. 146–147.)

Look for a sentence or group of sentences that sum up this reading, and you're not going to find any. There is no one thesis statement that sums up J. Edgar Hoover's positive *and* negative effects on the FBI. It's up to the reader to infer one like the following: "J. Edgar Hoover was a powerful influence on the FBI. Although he did some good, he also tarnished the agency's reputation and image."

This implied thesis statement neatly fits the contents of the reading without relying on any information not supplied by the author. It is also not contradicted by anything said in the reading itself. In short, it meets the criteria of an effective inference.

EXERCISE 5

DIRECTIONS Read the following selections. Then circle the letter of the statement that most effectively sums up the implied main idea of the entire reading.

The Hermits of Harlem

1 On March 21, 1947, a man called the 122nd Street police station in New York City and claimed that there was a dead body at 2078 Fifth Avenue. The police were familiar with the house, a decaying three-story brownstone in a rundown part of Harlem. It was the home of Langley and Homer Collyer, two lonely recluses*

---

*recluses: people who live alone, cut off from others.

famous in the neighborhood for their odd but seemingly harm-less ways.

2   Homer was blind and crippled by rheumatism. Distrustful of doctors, he wouldn't let anybody but Langley come near him. Using his dead father's medical books, Langley devised a number of odd cures for his brother's ailments, including massive doses of orange juice and peanut butter. When he wasn't dabbling in medicine, Langley liked to invent things, like machines to clean the inside of pianos or intricately wired burglar alarms.

3   When the police responded to the call by breaking into the Collyers' home, they were astonished and horrified. The room was filled from floor to ceiling with objects of every shape, size, and kind. It took them several hours to cross the few feet to where the dead body of Homer lay, shrouded in an ancient checkered bathrobe. There was no sign of Langley, so authorities began to search for him.

4   When they found him, he was wearing a strange collection of clothes that included an old jacket, a red flannel bathrobe, several pairs of trousers, and blue overalls. An onion sack was tied around his neck; another was draped over his shoulders. Langley had died some time *before* his brother. He had suffocated under a huge pile of garbage that had cascaded down upon him.

5   On several occasions, thieves had tried to break in to steal the fortune that was rumored to be kept in the house. Langley had responded by building booby traps, intricate systems of trip wires and ropes that would bring tons of rubbish crashing down on any unwary intruder. But in the dim light of his junk-filled home, he had sprung one of his own traps and died some days before his brother. Homer, blind, paralyzed, and totally dependent on Langley, had starved to death.[1]

Implied Main Idea ⓐ In the end, the Collyer brothers' eccentric and reclusive ways led to their death.

b. The Collyer brothers' deaths were probably suicides.

c. The Collyer brothers have become more famous in death than they ever were in life.

EXPLANATION In this case, *a* is the most appropriate inference because statements in the reading suggest that the brothers' eccentricity contributed to their deaths. It was, for example, a trap of

---

[1]Adams and Riley, "Hermits of Harlem," *Facts and Fallacies*, p. 226.

Langley's own devising that killed him. However, there is no evidence that either of the brothers chose to die and the only reference to the brothers' fame is to how well known they were in the neighborhood.

1. Frustration

1   **External frustrations** are based on conditions outside of the individual that impede progress toward a goal. All the following are external frustrations: getting stuck with a flat tire, having a marriage proposal rejected, finding the cupboard bare when you go to get your poor dog a bone, finding the refrigerator bare when you go to get your poor tummy a T-bone, finding the refrigerator gone when you return home, being chased out of the house by your starving dog. In other words, external frustrations are based on *delay, failure, rejection, loss,* or another direct blocking of motives.

2   **Personal frustrations** are based on personal characteristics. If you are four feet tall and aspire to be a professional basketball player, you very likely will be frustrated. If you want to go to medical school, but can earn only D grades, you will likewise be frustrated. In both examples, frustration is actually based on personal limitations. Yet failure may be *perceived* as externally caused.

3   Whatever the type of frustration, if it persists over time, it's likely to lead to aggression. The frustration–aggression link is so common, in fact, that experiments are hardly necessary to show it. A glance at almost any newspaper will provide examples such as the following:

> ### Justifiable Autocide
> BURIEN, Washington (AP)—Barbara Smith committed the assault, but police aren't likely to press charges. Her victim was a 1964 Oldsmobile that failed to start once too often.
>
> When Officer Jim Fuda arrived at the scene, he found one beat-up car, a broken baseball bat, and a satisfied 23-year-old Seattle woman.
>
> "I feel good," Ms. Smith reportedly told the officer. "That car's been giving me misery for years and I killed it."
>
> (As quoted in Coon, *Essentials of Psychology*, p. 419.)

Implied Main Idea   a. External frustration is the more painful type of frustration, and it frequently leads to aggressive feelings and actions.

b. Although there are two different types of frustration, both can, if they persist, lead to aggressive behavior.

c. Experiencing personal frustration is more psychologically wounding than the effects of external frustration.

2. **When Diets Don't Work, Some Turn to Surgery**

1 Although she had tried all her life to lose weight, by the time she was thirty-one, five-foot-four-inch pop singer Carnie Wilson weighed 300 pounds. She was so overweight that she had little energy to pursue her career. She also suffered from a dangerous condition called sleep apnea. "I would wake myself up choking about fifteen times a night, gasping for air, my heart racing. I wasn't breathing. It was the fat choking my airway. I was tired all the time, and I was borderline diabetic. I had hypertension, my triglycerides were really high, and my cholesterol was like 270 or 280. Oh, God, and the joint pain—it was impossible. I was having trouble walking. I was short of breath all the time. I could not support the weight any more. My body was giving out. I was thirty-one, and the doctors told me I could have a heart attack at any time."

2 But then former television actress Roseanne told Carnie about the weight-loss surgery that had helped her trim down. Carnie researched her options, consulted doctors, and chose to undergo a gastric bypass. This operation reduces the stomach to little more than a small pouch, and the small intestine is rerouted to limit the absorption of nutrients. Following her 1999 surgery, Carnie was able to eat only a few bites of food at a time. A year and a half later, she was down to 150 pounds. Today, she promotes weight-loss surgery in advertisements. She says that without her surgery, she would have swelled to 400 or 500 pounds, and she doesn't think she would have lived another ten years. Now, though, she says, "I feel alive. I feel healthy and inspired and attractive and light on my feet. I don't feel weighted down or sick or unhealthy or abnormal . . . or gross."

3 Not only has Carnie's progress been the topic of many a newspaper and magazine article, but she also allowed the operation to be televised over the Internet, where about 2.5 million people watched. Since then, Randy Jackson, a judge on *American Idol*, says of his weight-loss surgery: "I've tried a lot of diets, almost all of them, and this is the only thing that's been good for me." Viewers of the *Today* show watched weatherman Al Roker, who weighed 320 pounds before his 2002 gastric bypass operation, shrink in size before their eyes. Other celebrities, too, including actor Michael Genadry of the TV series *Ed*, vampire novelist Anne Rice, and blues singer Etta James, have told the world about their weight-loss success following the procedure.

4 Not surprisingly, ordinary overweight Americans have been listening to the celebrity endorsements, and some, the ones who are desperate and financially able, have chosen to have their

stomachs stapled shut. But their decision may not be wise, no matter what the celebrities say. After all, one in every 200 people dies from this operation. Many others develop hernias, blood clots, and infections. While it's true that losing weight reduces some health problems, it may actually trade one set of complications for others just as serious.

5   Those who make it through gastric bypass surgery still face a sometimes grueling, physical battle. They can no longer eat fatty or fried foods. Nor can they eat sugar and refined foods. Because the top portion of the small intestine has been bypassed and the body can no longer easily digest these kinds of foods, ingesting them leads to "dumping," which takes the form of violent vomiting, dizziness, cramps, or diarrhea. Carnie Wilson, who dumped hard five times following her surgery, said, "It's the most horrible feeling I can imagine. . . . You feel like you're dying."

6   Because the operation makes it more difficult for the body to absorb calcium, those who have had a gastric bypass must take calcium supplements for the rest of their lives to avoid osteoporosis. Iron absorption, too, is reduced, so patients have to take iron supplements to ward off anemia. Many need to have their blood drawn and analyzed every six months to watch for potential problems. Doctors are concerned that the risk for adolescents is even greater because their bodies are not fully developed.

7   But health risks aren't the only dangers that come with stomach stapling. Psychologists point out that such surgery does nothing to cure people of their emotional issues, and this is particularly true for teenagers. Dr. Jenn Berman, a California psychotherapist, says, "When a teen is overweight or obese, many times it's because [he or she] never learned emotional coping skills and turned to food [as comfort] instead. When you take that one coping skill away, it can be dangerous because the tendency is to look for another one. As harmful as overeating can be, it's way down the list compared to drugs, alcohol, and acting out sexually. Kids aren't prepared to deal with such an extremely drastic change." Plus, adults and teens often have a tough time adjusting to their new bodies, even if they now possess the bodies they've always wanted. Carnie Wilson says, "Your body changes from week to week. Your body gets way ahead of your mind. You look in the mirror, and you think: Who am I? It brings up a lot of issues." (Sources of information: Stephanie Booth, "Teenage Waist-land," *Salon*, March 4, 2004, www.salon.com/mwt/feature/2004/03/16/gastric_bypass/ index_np.html; Douglas Kalajian, "The Downsizing of Carnie Wilson," *The Palm Beach Post*, June 11, 2002, 1D; Tanya Barrientos,

"Popular Weight-Loss Surgery on Rise Despite Risks," *The Philadelphia Inquirer,* February 20, 2004.)

Implied Main Idea   a. Celebrities willing to share their personal stories of weight loss have helped many obese teenagers.

b. Despite the celebrity endorsements, gastric bypass surgery for the obese is not without its drawbacks.

c. To spend large sums of money on gastric bypass surgery, instead of dieting, is disgraceful.

d. Gastric bypass surgery is a solution to obesity that only the rich can afford.

◼ EXERCISE 6

DIRECTIONS Read each selection. Then write the implied main idea in the blanks that follow.

1. Defining the Government's Role in Health Care

1   The process of defining Washington's role in the U.S. health care system began after the Civil War, when Congress authorized a network of hospitals for disabled Union veterans. The system of federally funded medical facilities steadily expanded in the twentieth century to serve veterans of World War I, World War II, and later conflicts.

2   Efforts to extend the government's health care role even further met bitter opposition from the medical profession. The Sheppard-Towner Act of 1921 appropriated $1.2 million for rural prenatal and infant-care centers run by public health nurses. However, the male-dominated American Medical Association (AMA) objected to this infringement on its monopoly, and Congress killed the program in 1929. Efforts to include health insurance in the Social Security Act of 1935 failed in the face of opposition from the AMA and private insurers. President Truman proposed a comprehensive medical insurance plan to Congress in 1945, but the AMA again fought back, stigmatizing* the plan as an encroaching wedge of "socialized medicine."

3   Medicare and Medicaid (1965), which provide health insurance for the elderly, the disabled, and the poor, broke this logjam.

---

*stigmatizing: branding as disgraceful.

Nevertheless, lobbyists for the AMA, hospitals, and private insurance companies succeeded in limiting Washington's function to that of bill payer, with no role in shaping the health care system or, most important, in containing costs. The new programs assured millions of Americans better health care, but they proved very expensive. From 1970 to 1990, Medicare costs ballooned from $7.6 billion to $111 billion, and Medicaid from $6.3 billion to $79 billion. As the population aged, long-term care for older adults became an especially pricey component.

4   Rising costs made up only part of a larger tangle of problems. While America boasted the world's best health care, its benefits were unevenly distributed. Inner-city minorities and rural communities often lacked adequate care. Life expectancy, infant mortality, and other health indexes varied significantly along racial, regional, and income lines. The 1989 infant-mortality rate, for example, stood at 8.2 per 1,000 live births for whites and 17.7 for blacks. Although many workers belonged to prepaid health systems, millions of Americans lacked health insurance. (Adapted from Boyer, *Promises to Keep*, p. 206.)

Implied Main Idea _____

_____

2. Classrooms Across Cultures

1 The average performance of U.S. students on tests of reading, math, and other basic academic skills has tended to fall short of that of youngsters in other countries, especially Asian countries (International Association for the Evaluation of Education Achievement, 1999). In one comparison study, Harold Stevenson (1992) followed a sample of pupils in Taiwan, Japan, and the United States from first grade, in 1980, to eleventh grade, in 1991. In the first grade, the Asian students scored no higher than their U.S. peers on tests of mathematical aptitude and skills, nor did they enjoy math more. However, by the fifth grade the U.S. students had fallen far behind. Corresponding differences were seen in reading skills.

2   Important potential causes of these differences were found in the classroom itself. In a typical U.S. classroom session, teachers talked to students as a group; then students worked at their desks independently. Reinforcement or other feedback about performance on their work was usually delayed until the next day or, often, not provided at all. In contrast, the typical Japanese classroom placed greater emphasis on cooperative work between stu-

dents (Kristof, 1997). Teachers provided more immediate feedback on a one-to-one basis. And there was an emphasis on creating teams of students with varying abilities, an arrangement in which faster learners help teach slower ones.

3   However, before concluding that the differences in performance are the result of social factors alone, we must consider another important distinction: The Japanese children practiced more. They spent more days in school during the year and, on average, spent more hours doing homework. Interestingly, they were also given longer recesses than U.S. students and had more opportunities to get away from the classroom during a typical school day.

4   Although the significance of these cultural differences in learning and teaching is not yet clear, the educational community in the United States is paying attention to them. Indeed, psychologists and educators are considering how principles of learning can be applied to improve education (Bransford, Brown, & Cocking, 1999; Woolfolk-Hoy, 1999). For example, anecdotal and experimental evidence suggests that some of the most successful educational techniques are those that apply basic principles of operant conditioning,* offering frequent testing, positive reinforcement for correct performance and immediate corrective feedback following mistakes (Kass, 1999; Oppel, 2000; Walberg, 1987). (Bernstein and Nash, *Essentials of Psychology,* pp. 171–172.)

Implied Main Idea ————————————————————————————

————————————————————————————————————

 # Inferring Supporting Details

Until now, you have been drawing inferences solely to determine the author's implied main idea. But that's not the only reason to draw inferences. Writers seldom put down on paper every single piece of information necessary to understand their meaning. They almost always rely on their readers to infer some of the supporting details essential to understanding what they read. Look, for example, at this passage. Ask yourself what connection you need to infer to follow the author's train of thought from sentence 1 to sentence 2.

---

*operant conditioning: process of behavior modification in which a specific behavior is increased or decreased through positive or negative reinforcement.

[1]In the 1962 case *Robinson v. California,* the Supreme Court made the Eighth Amendment's protection against the imposition of "cruel and unusual punishment" applicable to the states. [2]But beyond that the punishment must fit the crime, the justices did little to explain what the terms *cruel* and *unusual* meant. [3]Lawrence Robinson had been convicted under a statute that made it a misdemeanor to be addicted to narcotics. [4]Robinson was not under the influence of narcotics at the time of his arrest, nor were any narcotics found on him. [5]The police officer made the arrest after observing needle marks on Robinson's arms. [6]Likening this situation to being punished for having an illness, the Court argued that even one day in jail would be excessive. (Gitelson et al., *American Government,* p. 107.)

In sentence 1, the authors tell us that in the case *Robinson v. California,* the Supreme Court applied the Eighth Amendment's protection to the states. They then tell us that the judge's decision did not nail down the meaning of the terms *cruel* and *unusual.* Even though you may not have realized it, already at the very beginning of the passage, you are expected to infer a supporting detail implied but not stated by the author. To connect sentences 1 and 2, readers have to infer that *in their decision,* "the justices did little to explain what the terms *cruel* and *unusual* meant." The author does not explicitly make that connection for his readers. They are expected to supply it.

In addition to making connections, writers often expect readers to infer the implicit consequences of an action, activity, or idea. Look, for example, at sentences 4 and 5 in the following paragraph. Sentence 4 describes a rebellion. However, the author never tells you directly how the rebellion turned out. Instead, he offers the last sentence as a clue to the implied result or outcome.

[1]The bacteria that caused a fourteenth-century plague known as the Black Death appear to have started their deadly course in the Gobi desert in the 1320s and began moving west along trade routes. [2]By 1347 the plague had reached Italy, and by 1348 it had spread throughout Europe. [3]Within two years, it had killed one-third of Europe's population and caused a devastating labor shortage. [4]Throughout the remainder of the fourteenth century, the workers who were left rebelled against low wages and unfair treatment. [5]As a result, the standard of living for those who had survived the plague improved significantly.

From sentence 5, readers can (and should) infer that the rebellions were generally successful. After all, the workers' standard of living improved, and that never would have happened had the rebellions been crushed.

But writers don't expect you to infer just results or consequences. They also expect you to infer causes. For example, in the preceding passage, the author does not expressly tell readers why fourteenth-century workers had the courage to rebel. The cause of their rebellion is implicit in the previous sentence, where we learn that the plague had left Europe with a "devastating labor shortage." Workers knew they couldn't be replaced easily and felt they were in a better position to make demands. Keep in mind, though, that the cause is not spelled out in the paragraph. Readers have to infer it.

Inferring Supporting Details in Longer Readings

Writers also expect readers to infer supporting details in readings that go beyond a paragraph. Actually, inferring the connections that link paragraphs is essential to understanding multiparagraph readings. Look, for example, at these two paragraphs from a reading discussing the reality and the myth of frontiersman Davy Crockett.

The Walt Disney television version of Davy Crockett, *Davy Crockett, Indian Fighter,* became a runaway hit in 1954 when an unknown actor named Fess Parker donned Crockett's trademark coonskin cap and played him on television. The show spawned several movies—and millions of coonskin caps—among them the 1960 epic *The Alamo,* starring Richard Nixon supporter John Wayne. Wayne even helped pay for a movie ad that showed Crockett at the Alamo. The caption for the ad openly alluded to rumors that John F. Kennedy, Nixon's opponent in the presidential race, had a ghostwriter for his Pulitzer Prize–winning book, *Profiles in Courage:* "There were no ghostwriters at the Alamo, only Men."

But Wayne, who had died of lung cancer in 1979, must have spun in his grave when Paul Andrew Hutton's 1989 essay, "Davy Crockett: An Exposition of Hero Worship," was published. In it, Hutton argued that young men volunteering for the Vietnam War had been inspired by their twin heroes, John F. Kennedy and Davy Crockett. According to Hutton, when Kennedy "issued a clarion call to fight for freedom in a distant land," young men answered the call because "they knew full well what he was talking about, for they had been brought up on those same *liberal* values by Disney's Davy Crockett." (Source of information: Allen Barra, "American Idols," Salon.com, April 10, 2004.)

To move smoothly between these two paragraphs, readers are expected to infer several supporting details. They need, that is, to infer a cause and effect relationship: John Wayne, a staunch supporter of Republican Richard Nixon, would have spun in his grave *because* he would have hated the idea of Crockett being linked to Kennedy, the man who challenged and beat his political favorite. But here again, the author does not include that information in the supporting details. Readers have to supply it by drawing an effective inference.

EXERCISE 7

DIRECTIONS Read the paragraph. Then circle the letter of the correct inference.

EXAMPLE Dr. C. James Mahoney seemed incredulous* as he sat cuddling a four-month-old chimpanzee named Cory. But the reports were true. The highly regarded New York University primate research center* at which the veterinarian had worked for eighteen years was being taken over by a New Mexico foundation charged by federal officials with a long list of violations of animal-welfare laws. The primate center and its 225 chimpanzees were added last week to the holdings of the Coulston Foundation, a research group that already owns or leases 540 other chimpanzees for medical tests. The foundation, based in Alamogordo, New Mexico, now has control of well over half of the chimpanzees used in medical research in the United States. Critics, including Dr. Jane Goodall, who pioneered studies of the endangered species in the wild, claim that the foundation, already cited for the deaths of at least five chimpanzees, cannot possibly care for more. (Andrew C. Revkin, "A Furor Over Chimps," *New York Times*, August 13, 1995, p. 2.)

To understand this passage, readers need to infer that

a. Dr. Mahoney was incredulous because he was going to be unemployed after working in the same place for eighteen years.

(b.) Dr. Mahoney was incredulous because he couldn't believe his chimps were going to be handed over to a place with such a poor history of chimp care.

c. Dr. Mahoney was incredulous because he couldn't believe he was going to be parted from his favorite chimpanzee, whom he had raised from infancy.

---

*incredulous: stunned, disbelieving.
*primate research center: center that studies the behavior of animals closely related to humans.

EXPLANATION In this case, answer *b* is the only inference that fits the passage. The first sentence points out that Dr. Mahoney was incredulous. Because the third sentence refers immediately to the foundation with violations against the animal-welfare laws, we can infer a cause and effect relationship. Dr. Mahoney is "incredulous" because the chimpanzees are being taken over by a foundation that has not taken good care of chimps in the past.

1. In the nineteenth century, questions about natural resources caught Americans between the desire for progress and the fear of spoiling the land. By the late 1870s and early 1880s, people eager to protect the natural landscape began to coalesce* into a conservation* movement. Prominent* among them was western naturalist John Muir, who helped establish Yosemite National Park in 1890. The next year, under pressure from Muir and others, Congress authorized President Benjamin Harrison to create forest reserves—public land protected from cutting by private interests. Such policies met with strong objections. Lumber companies, lumber dealers, and railroads were joined in their opposition by householders accustomed to cutting timber freely for fuel and building materials. Public opinion on conservation also split along sectional lines. Most supporters of regulation came from the eastern states. In the East, resources had already become less plentiful. Opposition was loudest in the West, where people were still eager to take advantage of nature's bounty.* (Norton et al., *A People and a Nation,* p. 509.)

   To understand this passage, readers need to infer that

   a. easterners have always been more careful about the environment than westerners.

   b. easterners were beginning to see firsthand that natural resources could run out, and that made them conservation conscious.

   c. westerners have always mistrusted causes promoted by easterners who knew little or nothing about the natural world.

2. In 1947, Jackie Robinson became the first black player in baseball's major leagues. A year later, President Truman desegregated the armed forces. And in 1950, Thurgood Marshall, a young lawyer working for the NAACP's Legal Defense Fund, won three cases that

---

*coalesce: to come or grow together.
*conservation: the act of protecting or preserving.
*prominent: famous.
*bounty: goodness, riches.

desegregated graduate programs in colleges. Still, in 1952 America's public schools remained segregated. Even when several of the NAACP's class-action lawsuits (all of which argued for integrated schools and were consolidated in the case *Brown v. Board of Education*) worked their way up to the Supreme Court at the end of 1952, the judges were too divided to come to a decision. Of the nine justices, Chief Justice Fred Vinson, in particular, was opposed to overturning *Plessy v. Ferguson,* an 1896 Supreme Court decision that allowed "separate but equal" schools. The Court tabled the case for a year. Near the end of that year, though, Vinson died of a heart attack. Three weeks later, President Dwight Eisenhower nominated Vinson's replacement, Earl Warren, a three-time governor of California with a passionate commitment to the rights of the individual.* Warren went to work on the three justices still inclined to uphold *Plessy.* Then the Court heard the arguments again at the end of 1953, and on May 17, 1954, the Supreme Court announced its unanimous opinion that segregated U.S. schools were unconstitutional. Segregation laws in twenty-one states, which affected about twelve million children of both sexes, were swept away. (Source of information: Justin Ewers, "Making History," *U.S. News & World Report,* March 22, 2004, pp. 76–80.)

To understand this passage, readers need to infer that

a. Supreme Court Justice Earl Warren played a critical role in the desegregation of America's schools.

b. with or without Supreme Court Justice Earl Warren, *Brown v. Board of Education* would have become the law of the land.

c. even if Chief Justice Fred Vinson had not died, the desegregating of schools was an idea whose time had come.

3. On television dramas, surgery is portrayed as an intense situation where the silence is broken only by the sounds of beeping monitors, whooshing machines, and the surgeon's clipped requests for instruments. In reality, though, operating rooms are usually filled with the sound of music. Doctors say that listening to music relaxes everyone on the surgical team and diminishes tension. And all surgical team members agree that music seems to have a therapeutic effect on the surgeon's ability to function under high stress. Research conducted at the State University of New York–Buffalo concurs.

---

*Oddly enough, Earl Warren is also famous for vigorously demanding the evacuation of Japanese-Americans from the West Coast during World War II. When his involvement in the internment of Japanese-Americans became widely known, he initially defended his actions. But in his autobiography, he calls it an error.

Researchers found that when surgeons like the music being played, it positively affects their heart rate and blood pressure, lowers stress, and improves performance. Hospitals have begun installing high-quality sound systems and an assortment of CDs in operating rooms. At Milwaukee's St. Francis Hospital, for example, surgeons not only indicate the surgical equipment and supplies they'll need, but they also specify the type of music they'd like to hear while they work. (Source of information: Bruce Goldfarb, "Surgery Teams Orchestrate Better When They Listen to Music," *USA Today*, March 31, 2004, p. 9D.)

To understand this passage, readers need to infer that

a. hospital administrators don't take seriously the idea that music is beneficial to the surgeon during surgery.

b. hospital administrators share the opinion that surgical teams perform better if there is music in the background.

c. researchers at the State University of New York studied how factors other than music affected a surgeon's performance.

4. A child prodigy is more than just a very smart kid; the standard definition of a prodigy is a child who by age ten displays a mastery of a field usually undertaken only by adults. Prodigies are the kids who amaze us by winning chess tournaments, playing musical instruments with sophisticated skill, and solving advanced math problems—all while they are still in elementary school. As a result, scientists have begun to ask: Are these young wonders born, or are they made? Is their gift a miracle of nature, or is it somehow brought about by the parents, teachers, and counselors in their environment? Up to now, research has been inconclusive. One 1997 study of the National Taiwan Normal University found that more than 75 percent of the prodigies studied were first-born children in small families. In addition, research conducted by psychologist Ellen Winner revealed that the parents of gifted children read to them, take them to museums, and praise their achievements. Other research, conducted by psychologist Michael O'Boyle, who scanned the brains of children gifted in mathematics, has shown that while brains of prodigies are not physically different from those of other kids, prodigies are able to use areas of the brain that are almost completely inactive in average children. In particular, prodigies seem to have a natural ability to switch more quickly between the right and left hemispheres of the brain. They also concentrate more readily and work more quickly than the average child. (Source of information: Andrew Marshall, "Small Wonders," *Time Asia*, February 17, 2003, www.time.com/time/asia/covers/501030217/story.html.)

To understand this passage, readers need to infer that

a. the research conducted by psychologist Ellen Winner also took place at a university in Taiwan.

b. the research conducted by psychologist Ellen Winner also focused on determining whether child prodigies are born or created.

c. the research conducted by psychologist Ellen Winner also took place in 1997.

 Drawing Logical Conclusions

It's time to point out that readers truly intent on mastering an author's message don't limit themselves to drawing just the inferences intended by the author. To deepen their understanding, readers frequently elaborate on an author's ideas by drawing conclusions that follow from the reading but were probably never consciously intended by the author. This next passage and the two conclusions that follow provide an example.

Exit exams are tests that high school students in some states must take to successfully pass a course or earn a diploma. Although exit exams have numerous supporters, they have come under persistent fire where diplomas are concerned. In Massachusetts, for instance, state officials had to quell a rebellion of school superintendents who wanted to award diplomas to 4,800 students who had failed the exam. In Florida, protestors demanded that the governor give diplomas to 14,000 seniors who had failed the exit exam. Given all this controversy, the question that has to be answered is, "What's wrong with exit exams?" After all, high school exit exams ensure that a diploma accurately indicates how much information students have actually absorbed from their courses. This is important because it's widely assumed that grade inflation is rampant in some schools. Thus the passing grades that allow students to get a diploma are not necessarily proof that they have mastered the course material. However, when that diploma is backed up by an exit exam, we can be sure students have mastered the courses identified on their transcripts. By the same token, exit exams should help reassure prospective employers who have begun to lose faith in the diploma as proof of achievement. In short, the presence of an exit exam grade on a student's transcript will add value to the diploma.

In this case, the implied main idea is something like this: "Exit exams are a good idea and school administrators should not cave in to the pressure to abandon them." The author does not say this explicitly. Instead, she implies her main idea by offering reasons why exit exams are valuable for documenting achievement.

However, based on what the author says, you can also draw two conclusions that she does not address: (1) the author would probably agree with legislation that made high school exit exams mandatory throughout the nation, and (2) the author would probably be unwilling to sign a petition demanding that students who failed their exit exams be allowed to get diplomas anyway. Based on what the author actually says, these are legitimate or logical conclusions. Both follow from what the author says about exit exams even though nothing in the paragraph explicitly addresses either conclusion.

Far less logical would be the following conclusion: "The author believes that the school superintendents should have been allowed to give diplomas to the 14,000 students who failed in Florida." Under some special conditions, the author might well agree, but given the usual circumstances, she would probably be against such petitions because she argues so forcefully in favor of exit exams.

CHECK YOUR UNDERSTANDING

How do the inferences in this section (pp. 320–321) differ from those described in the preceding section?

_____

_____

■ EXERCISE 8

DIRECTIONS Circle the letter of the conclusion that can be drawn from the passage.

EXAMPLE Some 6,000 languages are spoken in the world today, but about 2,400 of them are dying out because the number of speakers is rapidly declining. About 500 of these languages are already spoken by fewer than 100 people. Experts estimate that over the next 100 years, fully 90 percent of all current languages will be either totally or virtually extinct, replaced by "mega-languages" such as English, Spanish, French, or Arabic. Just as we become alarmed when a species of plant or animal nears the brink of extinction, we should be equally concerned about languages that might become extinct. In the same way that we lose something when a particular plant or animal dies out, we lose an entire system of knowledge when a language dies. All kinds of information not fully translatable into other tongues die with it. In addition, the loss of a language can rob individuals of their culture and, consequently, their very identities. Anthropologist Wade Davis has said, "When you strip away language and the culture it embodies, what you have left is alienation,* despair, and tremendous levels of anger." The plight of many Native Americans, who were forced by the U.S. government to speak English, is a good example of how individuals suffer when their language is taken away from them. (Sources of information: Thomas Hayden, "Losing Our Voices," *U.S. News & World Report,* May 26, 2003, p. 42, www.usnews.com/usnews/issue/030526/misc/26tongue.htm; Margit Waas, "Taking Note of Language Extinction," originally published in *Applied Linguistics* 18(1):101–103, 1997, www.colorado.edu/iec/alis/articles/langext.htm.)

Which conclusion follows from the reading?

a. The author probably speaks several different languages.

b. The author probably opposes teaching English to citizens of other countries.

(c.) The author would probably support efforts to create text and audio computer files of endangered languages.

EXPLANATION Answer *a* won't do because there is nothing in the passage to indicate how many languages the author does or does not speak. Answer *b* has to be eliminated because the author does not indicate that English shouldn't be taught to citizens of other countries. On the contrary, since language is said to carry with it an entire culture, she suggests that preserving English, and any other language, by keeping it alive is a good thing. Thus answer *c* is the only conclusion that follows logically from the paragraph. A writer worried about what's being lost when a language dies out is very likely to conclude that preserving text on computer files is a good thing to do.

1. In his book *After Virtue,* philosopher Alisdaire MacIntyre argues that virtue is the product of social training. From MacIntyre's point of view, virtue can be acquired only in a community where the young

---

*alienation: the condition of being withdrawn or unresponsive.

are consciously initiated into the reigning social values, including what it means to be a good person. MacIntyre interprets the word *community* in its broadest sense, making it refer to families, schools, religious institutions, political groups, and even avenues of entertainment. From his perspective, it's important that these aspects of the community be respected because it is their authority that persuades the child to accept their teachings and pursue the path of virtue. Far from simplistic in his thinking, MacIntyre recognizes that communities are historical entities that can change over time. It follows, then, that the virtuous life can also be redefined as the character of the community undergoes historical change.

Which conclusion follows from the reading?

a. MacIntyre is probably a modern-day disciple of Plato, who believed that virtue was inborn in special people who had a natural knowledge of perfection.

b. MacIntyre is following in the footsteps of St. Augustine, who believed that virtue is a gift of God.

c. MacIntyre would probably take the side of Aristotle, who believed that virtuous behavior is not inborn but the result of training.

2. Periodically, the price of gasoline soars and infuriated Americans blame Congress, the White House, and the Organization of Petroleum Exporting Countries (OPEC). According to an editorial in the *Miami Herald,* however, if Americans want to know who is really responsible for high gas prices, they should look in the mirror. "The real cause of gas-pump sticker shock," says the *Herald,* "is American consumers' addiction to the automobile and the lifestyle it allows." The editorialist goes on to point out that far too many Americans act as if they are entitled to own big, gas-guzzling cars and oversized pickup trucks, which together accounted for *half* of all vehicles sold in this country in 2003. The result? America has an insatiable* appetite for oil, and OPEC simply takes advantage of our dependence on its product. Rather than demanding lower gas prices, says the *Herald,* Americans should be driving as little as possible and insisting that their leaders do more to make mass transportation available, reliable, and affordable. (Source of information: "Gas-Guzzling Americans Drive Oil Prices Higher," *The Charlotte Observer,* April 4, 2004, p. 5E.)

Which conclusion follows from the reading?

a. The *Miami Herald* editorialist quoted in the passage would heartily agree with President George W. Bush, who wants the

---

*insatiable: never satisfied.

Senate to adopt an energy bill permitting oil drilling in the Arctic National Wildlife Refuge.

b. The *Miami Herald* editorialist is likely to endorse policies designed to force OPEC to lower its prices so that gas and oil will be available at cheaper prices.

c. The *Miami Herald* editorialist is likely to be strongly in favor of legislation that improves the quality of mass transportation across the country.

3. America lost three million private-sector jobs between 2000 and 2004, and experts estimate that about one million of these jobs were outsourced, or transferred, to workers in countries like China and India, where labor costs for even highly skilled positions are much lower than labor costs in the United States. According to AFL-CIO president John J. Sweeney, this practice of shipping jobs overseas is the reason why out-of-work Americans are having a hard time finding employment. The loss of good manufacturing jobs, in particular, has ripped apart communities and permanently lowered U.S. living standards. Laid-off workers often have no choice but to take low-wage jobs that bring many families down to the poverty line. Not surprisingly, many workers believe it is unethical for companies to rob people of jobs, exploit foreign labor, and then sell the goods produced abroad back to Americans. Companies like Boeing, however, argue that they have no choice but to send work to other parts of the globe. Boeing's executives say that the company has had to move jobs to places like South Africa, China, and Russia to keep production costs low, remain competitive, and increase profits. Like Boeing, at least 40 percent of *Fortune* 1000 companies have either moved U.S. jobs overseas or are planning to do so. Some point out that Americans have been buying products labeled "Made in Taiwan" or "Made in China" for decades. (Sources of information: John J. Sweeney, "Outsourcing Robs U.S. Jobs," *USA Today,* March 31, 2004, p. 22A; Paul J. Lim, "Lost in the Outsourcing Debate," *U.S. News & World Report,* March 30, 2004; John Cook and Paul Nyhan, "Outsourcing's Long-Term Effects on U.S. Jobs at Issue," *Seattle Post-Intelligencer,* March 10, 2004.)

Which conclusion follows from the reading?

a. John J. Sweeney is probably a supporter of President George W. Bush, who advocates tax breaks for companies with overseas manufacturing plants.

b. John J. Sweeney would be likely to support a bill that limits tax breaks for those that rely heavily on outsourcing rather than employing a largely American work force.

c. John J. Sweeney would agree with Federal Reserve Board governor Ben Bernanke, who argues that the sluggish growth in new jobs is due to American workers' increased productivity.

4. Almost all college and professional sports organizations prohibit athletes from using certain performance-enhancing drugs. The National Football League (NFL), for example, forbids players from taking at least seventy different substances, including steroids, and imposes stiff penalties for using drugs. Because of stiff penalties like the ones the NFL imposes, most athletes choose not to take illegal performance-enhancing drugs. However, many athletes are still using *legal* performance-enhancing substances to get an edge on their competitors. Some, for instance, take creatine, a natural substance that increases the production of energy in the muscles. Others take androstenedione, a drug that works like a steroid to increase performance. St. Louis Cardinals baseball player Mark McGuire was using it in 1998 when he broke the home-run record.

Players use supplements, of course, for their own personal benefit. They want to get as far as they can by winning places on professional teams with lucrative contracts and then breaking records. But athletes also argue that pressure from coaches, fans, and the media to deliver thrilling performances encourages them to do whatever they can to improve their game. "The drug use," says William Kraemer, a professor of exercise physiology at the University of Connecticut, "is a reflection of what the consumer wants. Put it this way: Would people come to see the Indianapolis 500 if the cars only went 55 miles per hour?" But others argue that any use of performance-enhancing substances, legal or illegal, is unethical. Critics of supplements say that even the legal ones give the athletes who take them an unfair advantage and force *all* athletes to take them just to keep up. Critics also point out that drug use in professional and collegiate sports has led adolescents to believe that they should use supplements. Despite warnings from the medical community, up to 11 percent of high school boys have taken performance enhancers. This statistic has led many people—including President George W. Bush, who called on major league sports to implement harsh drug policies in his 2004 State of the Union address—to conclude that adult players, who serve as role models to young athletes, behave immorally when they take supplements of any kind. (Sources of information: David Schrag, "Supplements Create Risks to Users," *University Wire*, January 20, 2004; Mark Emmons, "Why They Choose to Use: Steroids Speak to Athletes' Fears and Greed," *Mercury News*–San Jose, November 11, 2003, www.mercurynews.com/mld/mercurynews/sports/7233767.htm.)

Which conclusion follows from the reading?

a. President George W. Bush would probably agree that a baseball player who used steroids yet broke the record for the most home runs in one season should still be elected to baseball's Hall of Fame because it's performance, not character, that counts.

b. President George W. Bush would most likely say that USA Track and Field officials, who want to place a lifetime ban and a fine of up to $100,000 on any athlete who tests positive for steroids, are being too harsh.

c. President George W. Bush would probably support legislation, introduced by U.S. senators Joseph Biden and Orrin Hatch, to make androstenedione illegal under the federal Controlled Substances Act.

■ DIGGING DEEPER

LOOKING AHEAD Page 296 introduced the idea of citizen participation in government decision making. However, that passage was limited to procedures called *initiative* and *referendum.* The woman described here, Doris Haddock, found her own way to make public her feelings on campaign finance reform.

DORIS HADDOCK'S RECIPE FOR POLITICAL REFORM

1 In 1960, when Doris Haddock learned of a plan to test hydrogen bombs in Alaska, she and her husband piled into an overcrowded Volkswagen bus and headed north to the small native fishing village that would have been destroyed by the tests. Doris and her fellow activists also appealed in person and in letters to U.S. senators and representatives. The determined opposition of Doris and her companions ultimately put a stop to the tests.

2 For the next few decades, Doris took up other causes. She fought the interstate highway system that threatened to destroy her hometown of Dublin, New Hampshire. She worked hard to get respite services for the families caring for Alzheimer's patients. In 1984, at seventy-four, she joined a group of other retired women and formed a "Tuesday Academy" for practicing ballet and studying international topics of importance.

3 Then, in 1995, she heard that the Senate had failed to pass a campaign finance reform bill sponsored by Senators John McCain and Russ Feingold. Doris was deeply distressed by the news. It seemed to her that the rich were taking over a country she so deeply loved. When she confided her feelings to a friend, the friend challenged her to do something about it. Doris, now a widow and eighty-five, took up the challenge. She and other members of the Tuesday Academy spent the next two years organizing tens of thousands of nationwide petitions that demanded campaign finance reform. She also stood in parking lots around New Hampshire, in sun and in rain, talking to people about the issue and gathering signatures. But when the petitions were sent to her senators, one replied with a form letter that said spending money was a form of political speech protected by the Constitution's guarantee of free speech. The other senator just didn't answer.

4 Deeply disappointed by this response, Doris concluded that she was no longer a valued participant in the American political process. In her mind, she had been replaced by wealthy campaign contributors. Doris, though, was never a woman to give up easily, Determined

as ever, she decided to take to the road and bring her case directly to the American people. While walking across the United States, she planned to talk to people along the way and try to raise awareness about how democracy was being undermined by the members of Congress who were more beholden to big corporations and wealthy donors than to ordinary voters. Her intention was to create grass-roots support for the idea of campaign finance reform.

5   In 1998, although she was eighty-eight years old and suffering from bad knees, a bad back, arthritis, and emphysema from fifty years of smoking, she went into training for her journey. She walked ten miles a day wearing a heavy backpack; practiced sleeping on the ground; mapped out her route, and mailed thousands of letters of introduction to police chiefs and churches along her chosen path.

6   On January 1, 1999, at eighty-nine, Doris began her walk in Pasadena, California. She walked ten miles a day, making speeches about the corruption caused by "big money" in America's election campaigns and encouraging people to lodge some form of protest with members of Congress. Along the way, volunteers provided her with food and lodging, and the people she met, who had begun to refer to her as "Granny D," expressed their support and admiration for her efforts and spurred her on. As people learned about her walk, announcements of her next stop spread from town to town all across the country. In Arizona, Doris had to be hospitalized for dehydration and pneumonia. But she recovered and kept going, wearing out four pairs of shoes during her journey. On February 29, 2000, fourteen months after she began, the ninety-year-old great-grandmother ended her 3,200-mile walk in Washington, DC. She was met there by 2,200 people, including several dozen members of Congress, who walked the final miles with her.

7   Even after such a debilitating journey, Granny D took little time off to rest. She spent the next few years traveling and making speeches. In 2001, she walked continuously around the U.S. Capitol building for seven days, in subfreezing winds and rain, during the McCain–Feingold debate. And in October 2003 at ninety-four, still convinced of the power of one individual to change what's wrong, Doris launched yet another road trip, this one in a camper. Her mission: to encourage America's sixty-four million working women to vote. "You can't sit around and be a couch potato and get anywhere," Granny D told one interviewer. "That isn't a life. I say get a life. Don't be afraid to get involved."* (Sources of information: "Fact Sheet: Doris 'Granny D' Haddock," www.grannyd.com/fact.htm;

*True to her word, Doris Haddock decided in 2004 to run for the U.S. Senate.

Scott Baldauf, "Granny D Goes to Washington," *The Christian Science Monitor,* June 30, 1999; Charles Osgood and Byron Pitts, "Granny D Marches Across America in Support of Government by the People," *CBS News Sunday Morning,* March 5, 2000.)

Sharpening Your Skills

DIRECTIONS Answer the following questions by circling the letter of the correct response or filling in the blanks.

1. Based on the context, *grass-roots support* in paragraph 4 refers to
   a. people who are high up on the social ladder.
   b. government officials.
   c. ordinary people rather than politicians.

2. In paragraph 7, *debilitating* in sentence 1 means

   _____

3. Which statement most effectively expresses the implied main idea of this reading?
   a. Even in old age, Doris Haddock remains an active crusader for political reform who believes citizens need to take responsibility for their government.
   b. Doris Haddock is a passionate political activist who hopes her trek across the United States will encourage others to follow her example and walk to spread the message about campaign finance reform.
   c. Politically active for most of her life, Doris Haddock wanted to make one last political gesture before death caught up with her.
   d. Doris Haddock's heroic trek is admirable, but it did little or nothing to bring about any real campaign finance reform.

4. How do you think Doris Haddock feels about the argument that spending money in a political campaign is part of the "Constitution's guarantee of free speech" (paragraph 3)?

   _____

   _____

5. What is the implied main idea of paragraph 4?

   _____

   _____

6. What organizational pattern connects paragraphs 3 and 4?

    a. comparison and contrast

    b. cause and effect

    c. time order

    d. definition

7. What kind of transition opens paragraph 5?

    a. contrast

    b. comparison

    c. time order

    d. cause and effect

8. In paragraph 5, which supporting detail do readers need to supply?

    a. Doris Haddock was stronger than she looked.

    b. Doris Haddock liked to push herself to her limits, and the cross-country walk gave her the chance to train hard.

    c. Doris Haddock was knowledgeable about camping.

    d. Doris Haddock knew in advance that the trip was going to be hard on her, and she was training to improve her strength and endurance.

9. What would you infer Doris Haddock thinks about the fact that many Americans do not vote?

    _____

    _____

10. Which conclusion can be drawn from this reading?

    a. Doris Haddock is the kind of person likely to favor expressions like "You can't fight City Hall."

    b. Doris Haddock would be likely to agree with a statement like the following: "Our democratic system is currently in perfect working order; it just needs to stay that way."

    c. Doris Haddock probably agrees with John Locke, who said, "New opinions are always suspected, and usually opposed. . . ."

    d. Doris Haddock is likely to agree wholeheartedly with Abraham Lincoln, who said, "This country, with its institutions, belongs to the people who inhabit it. Whenever they shall grow weary of the existing government, they can exercise their constitutional right of amending it. . . ."

WORD NOTES: PUN INTENDED

The word *pun* was defined on page 296. Thus you already know that puns are plays on words. Sometimes puns employ different senses of the same word; for example: A young student asked his English teacher, "What's the matter, aren't you feeling well?" "Tense," she said, and he responded, "Present, I think." The joke here (and puns are never knee-slappingly hilarious) is that the teacher uses the word *tense* to suggest a state of mind, and the student responds as if the teacher had used the word to describe different verb forms.

Sometimes puns rely on words that sound like or resemble other words and thereby suggest some association with the person or situation at the heart of the pun; for example: "Erwin Rommel's favorite song must have been "Tanks for the Memories." Erwin Rommel was a famous German general known for his military tactics and his role in a plot to assassinate his commander-in-chief, Adolf Hitler. The pun here is that the song title resembles a real song, "Thanks for the Memories," only the punster known as "pun-jab" uses his punning version of that tune to remind readers of Rommel's military background.

What puns appear to be at work in this sentence: "It's a little known fact that the computer dates back to ancient times. Few people know that it was Eve who had the first byte, and it was already an Apple."

You can find more about all kinds of puns in all kinds of disciplines at www.bigpuns.com.

Students who want to do a more in-depth review of inferences with the help of **Getting Focused,** the companion software accompanying this text, should look at "Question 4: Does the Author Expect You to Read Between the Lines?"

To get more practice drawing inferences and conclusions, go to **laflemm.com** and click on "Reading for Thinking: Online Practice." Complete and correct Practices 4 and 5 for inferences, and 13 and 14 for drawing conclusions.

Test 1: Reviewing the Key Points

DIRECTIONS Answer the following questions by circling the correct response or filling in the blanks.

1. Readers who cannot locate a sentence or statement that sums up a passage or reading should be ready to do what?

   _____

2. Effective inferences should be based on or follow from _____

   _____. They should not

   rely too heavily on _____.

3. Ineffective inferences tend to rely too heavily on _____

   _____.

4. *True* or *False.* Only main ideas need to be implied. All other essential information will appear on the page.

5. *True* or *False.* Good readers draw only those inferences intended by the author.

To correct your test, turn to the answer key on page 643.

◣▬● Test 2: Recognizing Effective Inferences

DIRECTIONS Read each paragraph. Then circle the letter of the best inference.

1. Every year desperate, distraught cancer victims travel to the Philippines in the hopes of being cured by people who call themselves "psychic surgeons." These so-called surgeons claim to heal the sick without the use of a knife or anesthesia, and many victims of serious illness look to them for a cure. But curing the sick is not what these surgeons are about. When they operate, they palm* bits of chicken and goat hearts; then they pretend to pull a piece of disease-ridden tissue out of the patient's body. If a crowd is present, and it usually is, the surgeons briefly display the lump of animal tissue and pronounce the poor patient cured. Not surprisingly, psychic surgeons cannot point to many real cures; nevertheless, the desperate and dying still seek them out.

Implied Main Idea   a. More people than ever before are flocking to psychic surgeons.

b. Psychic surgeons are complete frauds.

c. When people are desperate, they are inclined to abandon their skepticism.

2. Do you like to watch colorful birds? Then keep your eyes peeled for the gorgeous indigo bunting, with its marbled mix of green, yellow, and blue feathers. Well, at least the male is a fabulous creature; the female is a rather drab brown. If your tastes run to splashes of pure brilliant color, then scan the woods for the scarlet tanager, whose fire-engine-red color is interrupted only by pure black wings. Unless, of course, you're looking at a female, who's a bit on the dowdy side. If you prefer your birds even more flamboyant,* then keep your eyes peeled for the Halloween-colored Baltimore oriole, who likes to hang out around swampy areas. The female is a bit bolder and more inclined to appear at bird feeders. Unfortunately, she's—you guessed it—a drab brown.

Implied Main Idea   a. Bird watching has become a more popular hobby than ever before, but unfortunately, it still has a nerdy image.

b. Although female birds are likely to be less colorful than males, they are a good deal more aggressive.

c. Among certain birds, only the males are colorful.

---

*palm: conceal in one's hand.
*flamboyant: showy, outrageous.

3. For a long time, scientists have speculated that birds might actually be descended from dinosaurs; but they haven't had any proof, at least not until recently. In 1998, diggers in China's fossil-rich earth found dinosaur bones bearing what appeared to be feather-like markings. According to paleontologist Philip Currie, the fossils are the evidence needed to prove the dinosaur–bird connection. However, Larry Martin, a paleontologist at the University of Kansas, is less convinced that the impressions on the bones came from feathers. Still, he, like almost everyone else who tries to reconstruct the past, is anxious to see the new fossils when they go on display. From his point of view, seeing just may be believing.

Implied Main Idea a. Although not everyone is convinced, there is now some real evidence suggesting that birds descended from dinosaurs.

b. Thanks to the discovery of dinosaur bones in China, it's now definite that birds descended from dinosaurs.

c. The fossil record suggests that dinosaurs were the descendants of birds.

4. Writer and feminist Gloria Steinem became a Playboy Bunny to give readers an inside look at what female employees of the Playboy Clubs had to go through to please the boss as well as the customers. The journalist Carol Lynn Mithers posed as a man to get a job on a sports magazine and published the results in a *Village Voice* article called "My Life as a Man." Anchorman Walter Cronkite voted under false names twice in the same election to expose election fraud. *Miami Herald* reporters went undercover to expose housing discrimination. CBS's *60 Minutes* set up a bar called the Mirage, staffed it with undercover journalists, and watched as various city officials demanded bribes for their services. The *Chicago Sun-Times* sent female journalists into downtown Chicago clinics that performed costly abortions on women who were not pregnant. In 1992, ABC News's *Prime Time Live* used undercover reporters and hidden cameras to document charges that some Food Lion grocery stores sold tainted meat and spoiled fish. In 1999, another *Prime Time Live* reporter posed as a telephone psychic to expose the fraudulent practices of the psychic hotline industry. (Source of information: Joe Saltzman, "A Chill Settles Over Investigative Journalism," *USA Today*, July 1997, p. 29.)

Implied Main Idea a. Investigative journalists of the past have used deception to expose corruption.

b. No ethical journalist would use deception to get a story.

    c. Since Food Lion sued and won its case against the journalists who exposed some unsafe practices in Food Lion stores, investigative journalism has been on the decline.

5. Between 1845 and 1846, Ireland was hit by a blight that attacked its staple crop, potatoes. As the potatoes rotted in the fields, close to one million people died from starvation, malnutrition, and disease, and an additional million were forced to flee their starving country. Between 1847 and 1854, the United States opened its doors to 1.2 million Irish immigrants. Yet, fearful of this large, new population, many Americans looked on the suffering Irish arrivals with suspicion. All too often, Irish immigrants were confronted by signs that read "No Irish Need Apply," and many wondered if they hadn't made a terrible mistake.

Implied Main Idea   a. When Irish immigrants arrived in America between 1847 and 1854, they were blamed for everything from poverty to unemployment.

    b. To escape the catastrophic effects of the potato blight of 1845, many Irish immigrants fled to the United States, but they did not receive an especially warm welcome.

    c. Throughout history, the United States has opened its arms to immigrants from other countries, and this policy should never change.

Test 3: Recognizing Effective Inferences

Copyright © Laraine Flemming. All rights reserved.

DIRECTIONS Read each paragraph. Then circle the letter of the best inference.

1. In one 1970s experiment conducted by psychologist Leonard Bickman, a male who wore either a suit and tie, a milk company uniform, or what appeared to be a security guard's uniform approached pedestrians on a Brooklyn street and asked them to pick up some litter, give some change to a man who needed it for a parking meter, or move to a different location. When the man was wearing a guard's uniform, 36 percent of the people approached did as they were asked. When the man was wearing a suit and tie, 20 percent complied. But when he was wearing the milk company uniform, only 14 percent complied with the request. Similarly, in a 1988 study, a female dressed in a dark blue uniform; a business suit; or stained T-shirt, pants, and tennis shoes approached pedestrians in a St. Louis shopping center. The woman would point at her accomplice and say, "This fellow is overparked at the meter and doesn't have any change. Give him a nickel." When the woman was wearing a uniform, 72 percent of those asked complied with her request. When she was wearing the business suit, 48 percent of people did as they were asked. But when she was wearing the T-shirt and pants, only 52 percent complied. In 1993, when communication researcher Chris Segrin analyzed nineteen similar experiments, he found that all had yielded similar results. (Adapted from Remland, *Nonverbal Communication in Everyday Life,* pp. 266–267.)

Implied Main Idea   a. The results of several studies suggest that people like, trust, and respect individuals who wear uniforms.

   b. The results of several studies suggest that we are more likely to comply with the requests of people in official uniforms or business attire.

   c. Several studies suggest that we respond positively to those who dress the way we do.

   d. New studies about the effect of clothing on behavior suggest that most people are naturally compliant, no matter what the person giving the orders is wearing.

2. Some people choose to handle conflict by engaging in **avoidance,** or not confronting the conflict at all. They simply put up with the situation, no matter how unpleasant it may be. While seemingly unproductive, avoidance may actually be useful if the situation is short-term or of minor importance. If, however, the problem is really

bothering you or is persistent, then it should be dealt with. Avoiding the issue often uses up a great deal of energy without resolving the aggravating situation. Very seldom do avoiders feel that they have been in a win-win situation. Avoiders usually lose a chunk of their self-respect since they so clearly downplay their own concerns in favor of the other person's. (Berko et al., *Communicating,* p. 248.)

Implied Main Idea a. Meeting problems head-on is the only way to solve them.

b. Most people handle conflict by engaging in avoidance; unfortunately, it's a strategy that never works.

c. Although avoiding conflict can be effective in some situations, it's an ineffective strategy when the problem is persistent.

d. People who use the strategy of avoidance to manage conflict always end up with low self-esteem.

3. For generations, Smokey the Bear has warned Americans that forest fires are tragic and should be prevented, and it's true that fires often destroy large areas of natural vegetation. However, fires also produce new growth. The ash that results from a fire enriches the soil. Fire also stimulates the release of new seeds. Lodgepole pine cones, for instance, release new seeds only when temperatures greater than 113°F melt the waxy coating that encases them. Fire also burns away trees' leaves and branches, allowing sunlight, which is necessary for seed growth, to reach the forest floor. In addition, wildfires strengthen existing growth. They eliminate dead material that accumulates around live growth. Wildfires also help weed out smaller plants. This removal of both live and dead vegetation reduces the remaining plants' competition for water, sun bik light, nutrients, and space, allowing them to grow stronger.

Implied Main Idea a. Odd as it may seem, fire is an effective fertilizer.

b. Wildfires are certainly hazardous, but they are also beneficial.

c. The National Park Service should do more to promote fires in our national forests.

d. Smokey the Bear has been an invaluable public relations tool in the ongoing battle against practices that cause forest fires.

4. According to the National Alliance for Youth, 15 percent of youth sports events involve some kind of verbal or physical abuse from competitive parents or coaches. To combat increasing instances of "sideline rage," some youth sports leagues require parents to attend classes or workshops on appropriate fan behavior. Some leagues even insist that parents sign a pledge of good conduct. If parents fail to attend the workshop or sign the pledge, their children cannot play on the team. The Positive Coaching Alliance holds similar workshops all over the country to teach coaches how to handle players' parents or referees. Other youth sports leagues are simply creating new rules that prohibit spectators from yelling from the stands at participants. Some of these leagues even fine anyone who shouts out criticism of coaches, players, or referees. In addition, many state legislatures have recently passed or are now considering bills that impose more severe punishments on anyone who attacks a referee at a sporting event. The Illinois legislature, for example, mandated a minimum $1,000 fine for battery* of a sports official.

Implied Main Idea a. Parents who live through their children are likely to interfere if their children are not on the winning side in competitive games.

b. A number of measures are now being aimed at curbing the parental "sideline rage" that has become a serious problem at sports events for kids.

c. When it comes to "sideline rage," the parents are much worse than the coaches.

d. Several state legislatures are enacting laws designed to curb bad behavior on the part of coaches and parents.

---

*battery: physical abuse.

Test 4: Drawing an Effective Inference

DIRECTIONS Write a sentence that expresses the implied main idea of the passage.

1. When the Barbie doll first appeared in prefeminist 1959, she had large breasts, a tiny waist, rounded hips, shapely legs, and little feet in high-heeled shoes. She wore heavy make-up, and her gaze was shy and downcast. She was available in only two career options: airline stewardess or nurse. In the 1960s era of women's liberation, though, Barbie had her own car and her own house, and a Barbie Goes to College play set became available. In 1967, her face was updated to sport a more youthful, model-like appearance with a direct gaze. In the 1970s, Barbie's career options expanded to include doctor and Olympic medalist, and in 1977, she got another facelift that left her with a softer, friendlier look, a wide smile, and bright eyes. During the 1980s and 1990s, when girls were encouraged to grow up to be independent wage earners, Barbie's options increased even more to include professions such as business executive, aerobics instructor, and firefighter. Today, Barbie has a thicker waist, slimmer hips, and smaller breasts, and she comes in black, Asian, and Latina versions.

Implied Main Idea _____

_____

2. In 1984, Congress passed a law prohibiting anyone from selling one of his or her organs to a person in need of a transplant. Since then, however, the number of people on waiting lists to receive an organ has risen steadily, and now, about 6,000 individuals die every year because the need for organs greatly exceeds the number donated. As a possible solution, the American Medical Association has begun encouraging transplant centers and organ procurement organizations to study whether more people would donate organs if they or their loved ones received a small financial reward for doing so. The question is: Is this practice ethical? Dr. Gregory W. Rutecki of The Center for Bioethics and Human Dignity believes that it is not. According to Dr. Rutecki, "Introducing money into an enterprise that has until now been solely characterized by acts of selfless goodwill is crass and . . . can lead to abuse." Dr. Rutecki argues that even modest financial incentives would quickly deteriorate into an organ black market, where human body parts are sold to the highest bidder. He is also concerned that the introduction of money could compromise the ethics of "informed consent," a decision to donate that is made with an understanding of all the risks involved. Poor people, in particular, would be likely to feel coerced into donating organs. Then there is the possibility of severe abuse within a system that permits financial compensation. Ruthless people might actually begin stealing body parts from living individuals to sell. According to Dr. Rutecki, motivating potential donors with money could lead to nightmarish consequences, so it is *not* the solution to the organ shortage problem.

Implied Main Idea _____

_____

3. Over billions of years, the human body has evolved to function and to thrive in a gravitational environment. When astronauts spend extended periods of time in outer space, where there is no gravity, they lose muscle mass. That's because weightlessness allows many muscles in the body to go unused. Without the constant pull of gravity to work against, the muscles become very weak. Astronauts who spend months aboard a space station can barely stand when they return to Earth. Their heart muscles deteriorate, too. They also lose bone mass, so their skeletal system is weakened. The redistribution of fluids in a zero-gravity environment also results in fluid loss. In addition, the immune system does not function as effectively.

Implied Main Idea _____

_____

4. Yoga, a series of deep-breathing and stretching movements, relaxes the body by slowing heartbeat and respiration, and by lowering blood pressure. Yoga also massages the lymph system. This stimulates the elimination of waste products from the body. Yoga seems to improve cardiovascular circulation in cardiac patients, too. It relieves the insomnia and mood swings of menopausal women and often reduces the pain of many people who suffer from backaches. In addition, the stretches and poses of yoga improve balance, flexibility, strength, and endurance. As a result, more and more athletes and exercise buffs are adding yoga to their fitness routines.

Implied Main Idea _____

_____

5. Most scientists would agree that animals experience fear. Many mammals, for example, exhibit the "fight or flight" response when confronted by a predator. More and more scientists are also now

claiming that many mammals feel grief as well. Elephants, for instance, seem to mourn over dead or dying family members for days. Chimpanzees who lose a relative sometimes exhibit signs of depression and even refuse to eat. Scientists have also found evidence that animals might be capable of love and affection. Two whales that mate, for example, stroke each other with their flippers and swim slowly side by side. In addition, many creatures are clearly capable of feeling playful happiness. Mammals such as dolphins frolic and chase each other, especially when they're young. Scientists claim that young dolphins are not just developing adult skills. They are displaying feelings of joy in the fun they're having.

Implied Main Idea _____

_____

Test 5: Inferring Supporting Details

DIRECTIONS Read each paragraph. Then answer the questions about supporting details by filling in the blanks.

1. Next time you hear complaints about how long it takes the Food and Drug Administration to approve a new drug, you might want to remind the person complaining about the 1950s thalidomide scandal. The drug known as thalidomide was produced by a small German pharmaceutical firm called Chemie Grunenthal, and it appeared on the market around 1957. Sold as a tranquilizer and a treatment for morning sickness, thalidomide was inadequately tested. Yet assured by the drug's makers that it was safe, doctors prescribed it and thousands of patients, most of them pregnant women, dutifully ingested it. Then in the early 1960s, hospitals in Germany, the United States, Canada, Great Britain, and the Scandinavian countries began to report the birth of babies with horrifying deformities. The infants had hands but no arms, feet but no legs. However, it wasn't until Dr. William McBride, a physician in Australia, made the connection between thalidomide and the babies' deformities that the drug was finally removed from the market. But that was in 1961. By that time, twelve thousand deformed infants had already been born. Astonishing as it might seem in light of its tragic past, thalidomide actually made a comeback in the 1990s when it was discovered that the drug might be useful in the treatment of leprosy and AIDS.

Implied Supporting Detail The author does not say what caused twelve thousand deformed infants to be born. Instead she expects readers to infer that _____

_____.

2. In 1963, Martin Luther King Jr. sought to increase the support of the movement for civil rights. In May, he helped organize demonstrations for the end of segregation in Birmingham, Alabama. The protesters found the perfect enemy in Birmingham's police commissioner, Eugene "Bull" Connor, whose beefy features and snarling demeanor made him a living symbol of everything evil. Connor's police used clubs, dogs, and fire hoses to chase and arrest the demonstrators. President John F. Kennedy watched the police dogs in action on television with the rest of the country and confessed that the brutality made him sick. He later observed that "the civil rights movement should thank God for Bull Connor. He's helped it as much as Abraham Lincoln." As a result of the demonstrations, the president sent the head of the Justice Department's

civil rights division to Birmingham to try to work out an arrangement that would permit desegregation of lunch counters, drinking fountains, and bathrooms. The president also made several calls to business leaders himself, and they finally agreed to his terms. (Schaller et al., *Present Tense,* p. 235.)

Implied Supporting Detail The authors never explain why President Kennedy thought Bull Connor actually helped the civil rights movement. Instead, they expect you to infer that Connor helped the movement by _____

_____.

3. During a national address focusing on civil rights, President John F. Kennedy acknowledged that the nation faced a moral crisis. He rejected the notion that the United States could be the land of the free "except for the Negroes." Reversing his earlier reluctance to request civil rights legislation, he announced that he would send Congress a major civil rights bill. The law would guarantee service to all Americans regardless of race in public accommodations— hotels, restaurants, theaters, retail stores, and similar establishments. Moreover, it would grant the federal government greater authority to pursue lawsuits against segregation in public education and increase the Justice Department's powers to protect the voting rights of racial minorities. (Schaller et al., *Present Tense,* p. 236.)

Implied Supporting Detail The authors do not specifically define the moral crisis facing the nation. Instead they expect readers to infer that _____

_____.

was the cause of a moral crisis in America.

4. On Christmas Day, 1859, the ship HMS *Lightning* arrived at Melbourne, Australia, with about a dozen wild European rabbits bound for an estate in western Victoria. Within three years, the rabbits had started to spread beyond western Victoria, after a bushfire destroyed the fences enclosing one colony. From a slow start, the spread of the rabbits picked up speed during the 1870s, and by 1900 the rabbit was the most serious agricultural pest ever known in Australia. Rabbits eat grass, the same grass used by sheep and cattle, and so quickly the cry went up: "Get rid of the rabbit!" The subsequent history of control attempts in Australia is a sad tale of ecological ignorance. Millions of rabbits were poisoned and shot at great expense with absolutely no effect on their numbers. Nowhere else has the introduction of an exotic species had such an enormous

impact and spotlighted the folly of such introduction experiments. (Adapted from Krebs, *The Message of Ecology,* p. 8.)

Implied Although the author does not specifically say how the rabbits got
Supporting Detail off the estate, he expects readers to infer that they _____

_____.

Test 6: Drawing Your Own Conclusions

DIRECTIONS Answer the following questions by circling the letter of the correct response.

1. Research has shown that people are more likely to help others when they're in a good mood. Psychologists have named this tendency the *good mood effect*. In one experiment conducted over the course of a year, pedestrians in Minneapolis were stopped and asked to participate in a survey. When researchers examined the responses in light of the weather conditions, they found that people answered more questions on sunny days than on cloudy ones. In another experiment, researchers found that the more the sun was shining, the larger the tips left by restaurant customers. Yet another experiment focused on pedestrians at a shopping mall, who were asked to change a dollar. Researchers discovered that when the request occurred outside a bakery or coffee shop, where strong, pleasant odors like freshly baked chocolate chip cookies or freshly brewed French roast coffee were in the air, people were more likely to help than they were if the request was made in a place with no pleasant smells emerging from it. (Source of information: Brehm and Kassim, *Social Psychology*, 5th ed., pp. 367–368.)

   Which conclusion follows from the passage?

   a. If you're trying to raise money for your favorite charity, you would be better off stationing yourself outside a doughnut shop than in front of your neighborhood cleaners.

   b. Someone who tries to raise money for charity by standing in front of the local police station in hopes of donations will never collect a dime.

   c. If you want to raise money for your local basketball team, you should probably go door to door accompanied by two of the team members.

2. Several states in America are converting one lane of some of our nation's busiest highways into a toll lane. These pay-as-you-go routes allow drivers to buy their way out of traffic jams and sail past nonpaying motorists stuck in congestion. Some states are allowing private companies to build the new toll lanes in exchange for the revenue generated from them. Other states are simply designating existing lanes as toll lanes. However, many people consider this trend unfair. Several driver advocacy groups claim that tolls amount to yet another tax on people who have no choice but to drive. As AAA spokesperson Mantill Williams put it, "Our overall

philosophy is tolls are a regressive* tax on motorists." Others have dubbed the new routes "Lexus Lanes"* and criticize them as a luxury for only those who can afford to pay. Advocates of toll lanes, however, say that they are just like any other convenience that some people choose to pay for and some people don't. "It offers a model of personal choice for drivers," says John Horsley of the American Association of State Highway and Transportation Officials. "If you're willing to pay a bit more, you can get there faster." (Source of information: Fred Bayles, "Toll Lanes: A Freer Ride for a Price," *USA Today,* April 8, 2004, p. A3.)

Which conclusion follows from the passage?

a. John Horsley would probably support a transportation bill before Congress that allows states to add toll lanes with special privileges to portions of interstate highways.

b. Mantill Williams is likely to agree with those who think toll lanes are a great way of giving more flexibility and more options to state governments.

c. The author of this passage is firmly opposed to adding toll lanes to our nation's busy highways.

3. Is it ethical to keep animals in zoos? Some animal rights groups say no. They believe that animals have a right to be free and conclude, therefore, that *all* zoos are wrong because they deprive creatures of their freedom. Those in favor of zoos, however, argue that the need for species conservation outweighs the cost to individual animals. They justify the existence of zoos because of the role they play in the preservation of animal populations, particularly through captive breeding programs. Furthermore, they maintain that the alternative to zoos—letting species simply dwindle or perish altogether in the wild—is the less ethical choice. However, Dr. Michael Hutchins of the Department of Conservation and Science for the American Zoo and Aquarium Association believes that even zoos that focus on conservation may not be doing enough to justify keeping animals in captivity. According to Dr. Hutchins, "A strong commitment to individual animal welfare is equally important." Many agree with Dr. Hutchins that zoos behave ethically *only* if they work toward the dual goals of conserving species while providing high-quality care in as natural an environment as possible. (Source of information: Bridget M. Keuhn, "Is It Ethical to

---

*regressive: decreasing proportionately as the amount taxed increases.
*The Lexus is an expensive car; thus the new routes help those who can buy expensive cars is the implication.

Keep Animals in Zoos?" *Journal of the American Veterinary Medical Association,* December 1, 2002, www.avma.org/onlnews/javma/dec02/021201d.asp.)

Which conclusion follows from the passage?

a. Dr. Michael Hutchins probably agrees that it is perfectly acceptable for traveling circuses to include animals in their acts.

b. Dr. Michael Hutchins would be likely to defend researchers who keep animals in laboratories in order to conduct experiments on them.

c. In all likelihood, Dr. Michael Hutchins would be willing to donate or raise funds for zoo renovation projects devoted to recreating an animal's natural habitat in the wild.

4. Dov Charney, the founder and CEO of American Apparel, has decided that the company he owns, American Apparel, will not make profit the only measure of success. Charney does not outsource production of T-shirts and casual wear. Everything the company sells is designed and produced in a downtown Los Angeles building, which houses 760 mostly Hispanic workers, all of whom earn on average eleven dollars an hour. Charney's workers also receive health insurance, a paid vacation, and, if they need them, free English classes. His employees can, if they wish, also take yoga and sign up for a massage. In other words, Dov Charney's workers are better off than the majority of textile workers in Los Angeles. According to the Department of Labor, only a third of the city's 5,000 garment factories comply with federal and state labor laws concerning the minimum wage and overtime pay. Charney doesn't just comply with the law, he goes above and beyond in an effort to make his workers happy and productive. You would think, then, that he would be the idol of the anti-sweatshop movement. But think again. Richard Appelbaum, a University of Santa Barbara sociologist and the coauthor of a book on sweatshops called *Behind the Label,* believes that Charney's workers still need a union even if they say they don't want one. Appelbaum argues that the American Apparel workers are dependent on Charney's goodwill, and that's a dangerous position to be in. In Appelbaum's eyes, a union would protect them from changes in Charney's mood or fortunes. Charney strongly disagrees, of course, and his employees don't publicly express any interest in collective bargaining of any kind. But that hasn't discouraged union advocates, who still believe that American Apparel needs a union. (Source of information: Linda Baker. "Made in the U.S. of A.," February 11, 2004, Salon.com.)

Which conclusion follows from the passage?

a. Dov Charney would do anything to make a profit.

b. Richard Appelbaum would not insist that workers at American Apparel need a union if Charney raised workers' wages to twelve dollars an hour.

c. Richard Appelbaum would probably say that all workers, even those with a generous boss, need a union.

Test 7: Recognizing Implied Main Ideas in Longer Readings

DIRECTIONS Circle the letter of the statement that best expresses the implied main idea.

1. Explaining the Growth of the Bureaucracy*

1   What accounts for the growth of bureaucracies and bureaucrats since the late 1800s? Was all this growth the result of bureaucratic incompetence and unresponsiveness? Many observers believe that the growth can be attributed directly to the expansion of the nation itself. There are a great many more of us—more than 248 million in 1990, compared with fewer than 5 million in the 1790s—and we are living closer together. Not only do the residents of cities and suburbs require many more services than did the predominantly rural dwellers of the early 1800s, but the challenges of urban and industrial life have intensified and outstripped the capacity of families or local and state governments to cope with them. Thus the American people have increasingly turned to their national government for help.

2   There is considerable evidence that the growth of bureaucracies is "of our own making." Public opinion polls indicate widespread public support for expanding federal involvement in a variety of areas. Even when public support for new programs is low, pollsters find Americans unwilling to eliminate or reduce existing programs. Furthermore, the public's expectations about the quality of service it should receive are constantly rising. The public wants government to be more responsive, responsible, and compassionate in administering public programs. Officials have reacted to these pressures by establishing new programs and maintaining and improving existing ones.

3   The federal bureaucracy has also expanded in response to sudden changes in economic, social, cultural, and political conditions. During the Great Depression and World War II, for example, the federal bureaucracy grew to meet the challenges these situations created. Washington became more and more involved in programs providing financial aid and employment to the poor. It increased its regulation of important industries and during the war imposed controls over much of the American economy. As part of the general war effort, the federal government also built

---

*bureaucracy: management of a government through bureaus or departments staffed by nonelected officials.

roads and hospitals and mobilized the entire population. When these crises ended, the public was reluctant to give up many of the federal welfare and economic programs implemented during the time of emergency. (Gitelson et al., *American Government*, p. 358.)

Implied Main Idea   a. Bureaucracies are simply a fact of modern life, and there is no escaping them.

b. At least three different factors account for the growth of bureaucracies.

c. The expansion of government programs has encouraged the growth of bureaucracies and tripled the number of bureaucrats.

2. Holiday Cheer

1 The observance of public school holidays began at the end of the nineteenth century. The goal of school holidays, at that time at least, was to bring people together. Holiday celebrations in the schools—particularly Christmas—were meant to unite a nation of immigrants. But as Bob Dylan would say, "The Times They Are a-Changin'."

2 In Chicago, the principal of the Walt Disney Magnet School saw his attempt at holiday harmony backfire. This elementary school has a mix of students, including black, Asian, Muslim, Hispanic, Yugoslavian, Romanian, and Jewish children, so the principal tried to tone down Christmas by issuing a ban on Santa Claus and any other symbols or activities associated with "a specific religious tradition." Teachers protested—one gave the principal a copy of *How the Grinch Stole Christmas*—and the head of the school board overturned the ban. With Christmas parties, decorations, and carols in full swing throughout the school, Essam Ammar, a Muslim parent, asked, "How am I going to raise my children as proud Muslims with all this going on?"

3 As passions intensify over how to celebrate the holiday season, some parents are demanding that a wide variety of other religious and ethnic holidays, including the Hindu Diwali festival, Hanukkah, and Kwanzaa, get equal time with Christmas. Others protest any diminution* of Christmas traditions, such as bans on trees and Santa Claus, in some communities. At the moment, there seems to be no resolution in sight.

———————
*diminution: act of decreasing.

Implied Main Idea a. Celebrating the holiday season in public schools began as an effort to bring together people who might otherwise stay separated.

      b. School is no place to celebrate holidays if those holidays cause conflict.

      c. Observing the holidays in public schools has become far more complicated than it once was as different ethnic groups compete to celebrate their particular holidays.

Test 8: Inferring Implied Main Ideas in Longer Readings

DIRECTIONS Read the selection and then write the implied main idea on the blanks.

1. Improving Your Memory

1 Do you, like just about everyone else, want to improve your memory? Well, the good news is that you can. All you have to do is put the following advice into practice, and you'll see immediate results.

2 For example, remembering when Christopher Columbus discovered America is easy enough if you use visualization. You could, for example, imagine Columbus standing on the beach with his ships in the harbor in the background. Fortunately, unrealistic images work just as well or better, and you could imagine Columbus's boat having the large numerals *1492* printed on its side, or Columbus reviewing his account books after the trip and seeing in dismay that the trip cost him $1,492. You could even envisage something still more fanciful: Since 1492 sounds like the phrase "for tea, nightie two," you might imagine Columbus serving tea in his nightie to two Indians on the beach. A weird image like this is often easier to remember than a realistic one because its silliness makes it more distinct (Levin, 1985).

3 Visual imagery also works well for remembering single terms, such as unfamiliar words in a foreign language. The French word for snail, *l'escargot*, can be remembered easily if you form an image of what the word sounds like in English—"less cargo"—and picture an event related to this English equivalent, such as workmen dumping snails overboard to achieve "less cargo" on a boat. The biological term *mitosis* (which refers to cell division) sounds like the phrase "my toes itch," so it is easier to remember if you picture a single cell dividing while scratching its imaginary toes.

4 Another device for memory improvement is called the method of loci, or locations. With this method, you purposely associate objects or terms with a highly familiar place or building. Suppose you have to remember the names of all the instruments in a standard symphony orchestra. Using the method of loci, choose a familiar place, such as the neighborhood in which you live, and imagine leaving one of the instruments at the doorstep of each house or business in the neighborhood. To remember the instruments, simply take an imaginary walk through the neighborhood, mentally picking up each instrument as you come upon it.

5 Research on loci has found the method effective for remembering a wide variety of information (Christen and Bjork, 1976). The same loci, or locations, can work repeatedly on many sets of terms or objects without one set interfering with another. After memorizing the musical instruments in the previous example, you could still use your neighborhood to remember the names of exotic fruit, without fear of accidentally "seeing" a musical instrument by mistake. Loci can also help in recalling terms that are not physical objects, such as scientific concepts. Simply imagine the terms in some visual form, such as written on cards, or, better yet, visualize concrete objects that rhyme with each term and leave these around the mental neighborhood.

6 Imagery and visual loci work for two reasons (Pressley and McDaniel, 1988). First, they force you to organize new information, even if the organization is self-imposed. Second, they encourage you to elaborate mentally on new information. In "placing" musical instruments around the neighborhood, you have to think about what each instrument looks like and how it relates to the others in a symphony. These mental processes are essential for moving information into long-term memory. (Adapted from Seifert, *Educational Psychology*, pp. 199–201.)

Implied Main Idea _____

_____

2. **Remembrance of Things Past**

1 A whiff of perfume, the top of a baby's head, freshly cut grass, a locker room, the musty odor of a basement, the floury aroma of a bakery, the smell of mothballs in the attic, and the leathery scent of a new car—each may trigger what Diane Ackerman (1990) has called "aromatic memories." Frank Schab (1990) tested this theory in a series of experiments. In one, subjects were given a list of adjectives and instructed to write an antonym, or word opposite in meaning, for each adjective. In half of the sessions, the sweet smell of chocolate was blown into the room. The next day, subjects were asked to list as many of the antonyms as they could—again, in the presence or absence of the chocolate aroma. As it turned out, the most words were recalled when the smell of chocolate was present at both the learning and the recall sessions. The reason? The smell was stored in the memory right along with the words, so it later served as a retrieval cue.

2 The retrieval of memories is influenced by factors other than smell. In an unusual study, Duncan Godden and Alan Baddeley

(1975) presented deep-sea divers with a list of words in one of two settings: fifteen feet underwater or on the beach. Then they tested the divers' recall in the same or another setting. Illustrating what is called *context-dependent memory,* the divers recalled 40 percent more words when the material was learned and retrieved in the same context. The practical implications are intriguing. For example, recall may be improved if material is retrieved in the same room in which it was initially learned (Smith, 1979).

3   Indeed, context seems to activate memory even in three-month-old infants. In a series of studies, Carolyn Rovee-Collier and her colleagues (1992) trained infants to shake an overhead mobile equipped with colorful blocks and bells by kicking a leg that was attached to the mobile by a ribbon. The infants were later more likely to recall what they learned (in other words, to kick) when tested in the same crib and looking at the same visual cues than when there were differences. Apparently, it is possible to jog one's memory by reinstating the initial context of an experience. This explains why I will often march into my secretary's office for something, go blank, forget why I was there, return in defeat to my office, look around, and ZAP!, suddenly recall what it was I needed.

4   Studies also reveal that it is often easier to recall something when our state of mind is the same at testing as it was while we were learning. If information is acquired when you are happy, sad, drunk, sober, calm, or aroused, that information is more likely to be retrieved under the same conditions (Bower, 1981; Eich, 1980; Eich et al., 1994). The one key complicating factor is that the mood we're in leads us to evoke memories that fit our current mood. When we are happy, the good times are most easy to recall; but when we feel depressed or anxious, our minds become flooded with negative events of the past (Blaney, 1986; Ucros, 1989). (Adapted from Brehm and Kassin, *Social Psychology,* p. 231.)

Implied Main Idea ————————————————————————

————————————————————————

Test 9: Taking Stock

DIRECTIONS Read each passage. Then answer the questions by filling in the blanks or circling the letter of the correct response.

1. [1]After a 1997 study published by the *New England Journal of Medicine* revealed that drivers are four times more likely to be involved in accidents while talking on cell phones, states such as New York decided to ban hand-held cell phones and permit motorists to use only hands-free models. [2]Do hands-free phones solve the problem of driver distraction? [3]Over the last several years, psychologist David Strayer and his colleagues at the University of Utah have conducted several experiments to study the consequences of talking on cell phones while driving. [4]In 2001, they found that people who were talking on both hand-held and hands-free cell phones while reacting to traffic signals were likely to react slower than people who were not on the phone. [5]In another study, published in 2003 in the *Journal of Experimental Psychology: Applied,* researchers placed 110 volunteers in a driver training situation that mimicked the inside of a car and was enclosed by screens that displayed realistic-looking surroundings. [6]Some of the participants talked on hands-free cell phones to other students while they simulated driving on a highway and in a city in heavy traffic. [7]These participants exhibited a slower reaction time than students who did not talk on cell phones. [8]They took longer to brake and longer to accelerate, moved their eyes less, and paid less attention to their environment. [9]They did not remember elements of their surroundings as accurately as participants without cell phones. [10]Three of the cell phone users even rear-ended a simulated car in front of them. (Sources of information: Ellen Goodman, "The $64,000 Question: Just How Dangerous Is Car-Phoning?" *The Boston Globe*, July 10, 2001, p. A9; University of Utah News and Public Relations, "Cell Phone Users Drive 'Blind,'" January 27, 2003, www.utah.edu/unews/releases/03/jan/cellphone.html.)

   1. What is the implied main idea?

   _____

   _____

   2. What kind of transition opens sentence 3? _____

   3. How would you define the word *simulated* in sentence 6?

   _____

4. The author expects the reader to infer that New York's decision to ban hand-held cell phones was

a. pure coincidence and not related to the 1997 study mentioned in the first sentence.

b. a result of the 1997 study mentioned in the first sentence.

c. a plan that had been in the making long before the 1997 study mentioned in the first sentence.

5. How might David Strayer respond to claims that the New York legislation had solved the problem of cell phones being a distraction while driving?

_____

_____

2. [1]In the Middle Ages some time around 1347, a disastrous plague known as the Black Death swept through western Europe. [2]Estimates suggest that the plague killed close to one-third of the population by the time it passed out of Europe. [3]In France, the death rate was so high, Cardinal Clement VI had to consecrate the Rhone River so corpses could be allowed to sink into its waters and disappear. [4]France had neither time nor room to provide a proper burial. [5]In the seventeenth century a smallpox epidemic decimated the Native-American tribes in the New World. [6]The first major outbreak of the disease struck the Northeast Atlantic coast between 1616 and 1619, leaving the Massachusetts and Algonquin tribes reduced from 30,000 people to 300. [7]In 1918, a deadly flu epidemic roamed around the world, taking a terrifying toll wherever it appeared. [8]In a single year, it killed more Americans than died in battle in World Wars I and II, the Korean war, and the Vietnam war. [9]Although official estimates suggest that twenty million people died as a result, the true number can never be known since medical facilities were in such chaos, it was difficult to keep accurate records. (Sources of information: James Surowiecki, "The High Cost of Illness," *The New Yorker,* May 12, 2003; Gina Kolata, *Flu.* New York: Farrar and Straus, 1999; boisestate.edu/westernciv/plague; www.thefurtrapper.com.)

1. What is the implied main idea?

_____

_____

2. How would you define *decimated* in sentence 5?

_____

3. Sentences 5, 7, and 8 open with what kind of transition?

_____

4. To make sense out of sentence 4, readers have to infer what answer to this question: Why did France lack time and room?

_____

5. In her book *Flu,* which describes the effects of the 1918 flu epidemic mentioned in the passage, author Gina Kolata uses the word "obsessed" to describe researchers determined to track down the virus that caused that flu. Based on the passage, what do you think is the motive for their obsession?

_____

C H A P T E R 7

Defining the Terms *Fact* and *Opinion*

In this chapter, you'll learn

- **how to tell the difference between** *fact* **and** *opinion.*

- **how to recognize statements that mix opinion with fact.**

- **how to distinguish between** *informed* **and** *uninformed* **opinions.**

- **how to identify opinions backed by** *circular reasoning* **and** *irrelevant facts.*

- **how textbooks often include opinions as well as facts.**

T he goal of Chapter 7 is to ensure that you fully understand the terms *fact* and *opinion.* After you know exactly what the two terms mean, you'll be in a good position

**to evaluate how well or how poorly writers use facts to
buttress, or support, opinions they want readers to share.**

 # Facts Versus Opinions

Statements of **fact** provide information about people, places, events,
and ideas that can be **verified,** or checked, for accuracy. Facts do
not reveal the author's personal perspective, or point of view. The
following are all statements of fact:

- American Samoa consists of seven islands in the South Pacific.
- The Treaty of Versailles ended World War I.
- For his work on atomic structure, scientist Niels Bohr was
  awarded the 1922 Nobel Prize in physics.
- John Wilkes Booth assassinated Abraham Lincoln on April 14,
  1865.
- In February 1903 more than 1,200 Mexican and Japanese farm
  workers organized the Japanese-Mexican Labor Association.

These facts can be checked in encyclopedias or in other reference
books in libraries anywhere in the world, and they will always
be the same. Facts do not vary with place or person. Whether you
live in Dayton, Ohio, or Fairbanks, Alaska, if you look up Martin
Luther King Jr.'s date of birth, it will always be the same: January
15, 1929.

Troubling Facts

Because facts can be checked, they are generally not subject to
question or argument. However, statements of fact can be questioned if they are not widely known. For example, it's a fact that
Muhammad, the Arab prophet who founded Islam, preached several sermons that focused on the rights of women. But since that
fact is not widely known, it's likely to be questioned.

Then, too, facts can and do change over time as new discoveries
come to light or methods of research improve. This is especially true
in fields like science, history, and medicine, where information is
considered factual only insofar as it is based on existing knowledge.
As scientists and historians gain more precise knowledge of the

world, the facts on which they base their theories sometimes undergo dramatic change.

For example, it was once considered a fact that the Sun revolved around the Earth. But in the sixteenth century, a Polish astronomer named Nicolaus Copernicus used the laws of planetary motion to challenge that "fact." Copernicus proved that, *in fact,* the Earth revolves around the Sun.

Generally, however, facts are fixed pieces of information. They often consist of dates, names, and numbers that cannot be affected by the writer's background or training. Facts can be verified, or checked, and *proved* accurate or inaccurate, true or false, to the satisfaction of most people. Thus, unless they are newly discovered, they are not often the subject of disagreement.

Statements of Fact

- can be checked for accuracy or correctness.
- can be proven true or false.
- are not affected by the writer's background or training.
- rely heavily on names, dates, and numbers.
- are not usually the subject of disagreement unless they are not widely known.

Calling It a Fact Doesn't Necessarily Make It One

Because people tend to accept facts without giving them too much thought, some writers and speakers preface opinions with the phrase "the fact is," as in the following sentence: "*The fact is* that Richard Nixon, had he not resigned, would have been impeached." Despite the opening phrase, this statement really is an opinion, and not everyone would agree with it. In effect, what the author tries to do is bully you into agreeing that the statement is an indisputable, or unquestionable, fact when it's anything but. Similarly, beware of expressions like "it's a well known fact that . . . ," "in point of fact," and "without a doubt." Writers sometimes use this kind of confident language to discourage readers from evaluating opinions disguised as facts.

Finding Facts on the World Wide Web

If you are using a search engine like Google to locate facts via the World Wide Web, always double-check the results of your search. This advice is doubly important if the website addresses you explore don't end in the letters *edu, gov,* or *org,* endings that indicate large (and generally reliable) institutions.

One of the wonderful things about the Internet is that it allows ordinary people to share their knowledge or expertise with others. However, many of these amateur experts, while knowledgeable, don't necessarily have a team of editors to verify their information. Thus they unwittingly can and occasionally do misinform.

One recent website search, performed by the author of this text, revealed—to the author's amazement—that Frances Hodgson Burnett, the creator of a famous children's book, *The Secret Garden,* had an amazingly long life. According to one website, Burnett was born in 1849 and died in 1974, making her 125 years old at the time of death. Now this "fact" is impressive. Unfortunately, it's also inaccurate. Burnett was born in 1849, but she actually died in 1924, a fact confirmed by a quick search of *several sites* related to Burnett's life and work. Someone managing the website had missed the error. Where the Web is concerned, this kind of error is not all that unusual. Books, particularly reference books, have usually been double-checked by teams of people. Websites, however, are sometimes the product of one or two overworked souls, who can and sometimes do make mistakes. Unfortunately, they don't have a copyeditor and proofreader waiting in the wings to spot the errors. Thus the error remains until some sharp-eyed researcher or reader spots it and notifies the appropriate website manager.

The World Wide Web is a wonderful source for researching all kinds of things, including factual information. But you should always check several sites to confirm the accuracy of your facts.

Opinions

Statements of **opinion** reflect the writer's perspective on the subject being discussed. Shaped by an author's personal experience, training, and background, opinions about the same subject can vary from person to person, group to group, and place to place. For an illustration, ask a group of teenagers how they feel about high school dress codes. Then ask their parents. Don't be surprised if you uncover a marked difference of opinion.

Unlike facts, opinions cannot be verified by using outside sources. They are too **subjective**—too personal—to be checked in reference books or historical records. The following are all statements of opinion:

- Jennifer Lopez is an artist of extraordinary talent.
- Thanks to cellist Yo-Yo Ma, the glorious music of Argentinian Astor Piazzolla is now more widely known.
- Pet owners deserve legal punishment if their animals do someone harm.
- This country needs stricter gun control laws.
- Young women under the age of thirty are not generally inclined to call themselves feminists.

Because opinions are so heavily influenced by one's training, knowledge, and experience, it's impossible to talk about them as accurate or inaccurate, right or wrong. For example, if you own a dog and firmly believe that dogs make more desirable pets than cats, no cat lover can *prove* you wrong because you're expressing an opinion, not stating a fact.

Evaluating Opinions

Saying that everyone has the right to an opinion doesn't mean that opinions can't be judged or evaluated. They most certainly can. Critical readers want and need to distinguish between informed and uninformed opinions. **Informed opinions** are well argued. They are backed by reasons and/or evidence. **Uninformed opinions,** in contrast, are unsupported by evidence or backed by inappropriate reasons. Once you can distinguish between the two, you'll be surprised at how often writers give their opinions without bothering to support them. So yes, the old saying is true: Everyone has the right to an opinion. But it's also true that every opinion does not deserve the same consideration or respect. (For more on informed and uninformed opinions, see pages 368–371.)

Opinions on the Web

As you know from page 361, you should double-check any facts you locate on the Web. For different reasons, the same is true for opinions. After all, anyone can put an opinion on the Web. Just think of the many *Web logs* or *blogs*, personal websites where people express their opinions on any range of topics from politics to movies.

Opinions on the Web aren't necessarily evaluated by anyone else except the person holding them. This means that those opinions don't have to be informed by logic or research. In fact, the Web is where you will find people willing to express an opinion without even pretending to cite evidence or outline their logic. They feel they don't have to. Convinced of their own rightness, they often don't even acknowledge that someone else might hold a different opinion.

The following chapters discuss more fully how to evaluate persuasive writing that puts forth an opinion. The advice in those chapters applies as much or more to the Web as it does to books, magazines, and newspapers. Any opinion on the Web needs to be very carefully evaluated before you decide to make it your own.

Statements of Opinion

- can be evaluated but cannot be verified for accuracy or correctness.

- cannot be proven true or false, right or wrong (although they can be termed ethical or unethical, moral or immoral).

- are shaped by the writer's knowledge, background, or training.

- often communicate value judgments, indicating that the author thinks something is right or wrong, good or bad.

In addition to the characteristics listed in the preceding box, the language a writer uses is another important clue to the presence of opinions.

The Language of Opinions

- Statements of opinion often include verbs or adverbs such as *suggests, appears, seems, might, could* or *should be, possibly, probably, likely, apparently, presumably, arguably, allegedly, supposedly.*

- Statements of opinion often make comparisons using words such as *more, most, better, best, greatest, finest.*

- Statements of opinion sometimes include words that make value judgments: *beautiful, perfect, significant, interesting, critical, key,* and *crucial.*
- Opinions are frequently prefaced, or introduced, with phrases such as *one interpretation of, another possibility is, this study suggests, in all likelihood, it would seem, arguably, supposedly.*

CHECK YOUR UNDERSTANDING

What's the essential difference between facts and opinions?

_____

_____

_____

EXERCISE 1

DIRECTIONS Label each statement *F* for fact or *O* for opinion.

_____ **1.** All this uproar about animal rights is nonsense. Animals don't have rights.

_____ **2.** In 1909, Ernest Rutherford showed that atoms were mostly space.

_____ **3.** When it was under Spanish control, the city of Los Angeles was called *El Pueblo de Nuestra Señora la Reina de los Angeles del Río de Porciúncula,* which means "The Town of Our Lady the Queen of the Angels by the Little Portion River."[1]

_____ **4.** For a brief time, 2004 presidential candidate Howard Dean of Vermont seemed to breathe new life into the Democratic party.

_____ **5.** Martin Luther King Jr.'s "Letter from Birmingham Jail" was published in 1963 by the American Friends Service Committee, a Quaker organization.

_____ **6.** Teenagers today are obsessed with money and success. They don't care about making the world a better place.

_____ **7.** The atomic weight of carbon is closer to 12 than to 14.

---
[1]Bill Bryson, *Made in America,* New York: William Morrow and Company, 1994, p. 106.

_____ **8.** Women's stomachs are less effective than men's when it comes to absorbing alcohol and neutralizing* its effects.

_____ **9.** Singer Robi Rosa is as talented as he is headstrong.

_____ **10.** Queen Victoria of England died on January 22, 1901; at her death, she had been queen for almost sixty-four years.

Blending Fact and Opinion

Reading critically would probably be a good deal easier if authors kept statements of fact and opinion neatly divided. But they don't. Whether consciously or unconsciously, writers of all kinds—and textbook authors are no exception—can't always avoid coloring a fact with an opinion. Your job as a critical reader is to make sure you recognize when and where fact and opinion blend together. Then you won't mistakenly accept as fact an opinion you haven't consciously thought through or considered. Take, for example, the following sentence:

> At least thirty-eight states have sensibly decided to give terminally ill patients the right to refuse medical treatment.

At a quick glance, this sentence might appear to be a statement of fact. After all, it's easy enough to verify how many states have given terminally ill patients the right to reject medical treatment. But think again about the author's use of the word _sensibly._ This is a word with positive **connotations,** or associations. Use it to describe someone, and chances are he or she would be pleased. What the author has done in the above sentence is to include her opinion of the action taken by those thirty-eight states. That makes the statement a blend of both fact and opinion.

Now what about the next sentence? How would you label it—fact, opinion, or a blend of both?

> In 1944, Russian troops entered eastern Czechoslovakia, and the nightmare of life under Communist rule began.

The first part of this sentence is a fairly obvious statement of fact. Any encyclopedia can tell you when Russian troops entered Czechoslovakia. But what about the phrase _nightmare of life under Communist rule?_ Do you detect any trace of opinion in those words? If you said yes, you're well on your way to being a critical reader. People who took part in or supported the Communist regime in Czechoslovakia would probably not agree that life under Communist rule

_____
*neutralizing: making harmless or without effect.

was a nightmare. What we have here is another example of a statement that blends fact and opinion.

 # Connotative Language Is a Clue

To discover when writers have mixed a pinch of opinion in with their facts, you'll need to be alert to **charged,** or **connotative, language**—language that carries with it strong positive or negative associations. Writers dealing in pure fact tend to rely heavily on **denotative language.** They employ words that suggest little more than their **denotation,** or dictionary definitions. Words like *table, chair,* and *rock,* for example, carry little or no emotional impact. Thus they are considered far more denotative than connotative.

Changing the Connotation with the Context

Change the **context,** or setting, of a word, and it can become more connotative than denotative. For example, the word *stories* in the following sentence evokes little more than its denotation.

> *Aesop's Fables* is a collection of *stories* written by a Greek storyteller.

However, look what happens when the context of the word *stories* changes:

> In an effort to deny Jean a promotion, a jealous coworker spread *stories* about her character.

With this change in context, the word *stories* no longer refers to "an account of events"; instead, it becomes a synonym for *lies* and takes on a negative connotation. This example illustrates a key point about labeling language connotative or denotative: *Context is crucial.* Don't assume that a word that is denotative in one sentence is always lacking an emotional charge. A word can be connotative or denotative, depending on the setting in which it appears.

CHECK YOUR UNDERSTANDING
Explain how an author can mix an opinion in with a fact.

◄ EXERCISE 2

DIRECTIONS Read each sentence and look carefully at the italicized word or words. Then fill in the blank with one of the following letters:

D for dictionary meaning only
C+ for positive connotation
C– for negative connotation

D   **EXAMPLE** *Twentieth-century author* Gertrude Stein spent most of her life in France.

EXPLANATION The phrase *twentieth-century author* does not carry with it any positive or negative associations. It simply identifies the time in which Stein lived.

_____ 1. Displaying his usual blend of *stamina, strength,* and *determination,* Lance Armstrong won his sixth Tour de France bicycle race in 2004.

_____ 2. "Zulu" is a *general name* for some 2.5 million Bantu-speaking peoples who live in South Africa.

_____ 3. The Amazon River is the *second longest river* after the Nile.

_____ 4. Nuclear weapons are the *plague of this century.*

_____ 5. In the nineteenth century, Marshall "Wild Bill" Hickok was *fearless* in his pursuit of outlaws.

_____ 6. *Famed revolutionary hero* Emiliano Zapata was *beloved* by the poor of Mexico.

_____ 7. Gospel music is the kind of *intense joyful music* that *makes the spirit sing.*

_____ 8. Francisco Goya was a Spanish painter of the *late eighteenth and early nineteenth centuries.*

_____ 9. John James Audubon was a nineteenth-century *painter and naturalist.**

_____ 10. John D. Rockefeller, founder of the Standard Oil Company, was famous for his charity work, but he was also known as a *robber baron* whose business methods were remarkably *ruthless.*

◄ EXERCISE 3

DIRECTIONS Some of the following statements are purely factual. Others blend fact and opinion. Label the statements that are pure

---

*naturalist: person who studies nature.

fact with an *F.* For the statements that blend fact and opinion, put a *B* in the blanks. For those sentences you mark with a *B,* underline the word or words that led you to your conclusion.

B

EXAMPLE Singer Ednita Nazario's 1999 splendid album "Corazon" was produced by Dolores del Infante, an alias for Latin singer Robi Rosa.

EXPLANATION In this statement, the author provides factual information about the album, but the word "splendid" announces the author's opinion of the music.

_____ 1. According to the Television Advertising Bureau, an extraordinary 98.2 percent of all American households have a television set.

_____ 2. Psychiatrist Bruno Bettelheim spent decades studying fairy tales and their effect on children.

_____ 3. An astounding number of people have tattoos covering 98 percent of their body.

_____ 4. Amazingly, Diane Nash was only twenty-two years old when she led the campaign to desegregate the lunch counters in Nashville, Tennessee.

_____ 5. Jerry Garcia, the long-time lead singer for the Grateful Dead, died on August 9, 1995.

_____ 6. Juan Rodríguez Cabrillo explored the coast of California in 1542.

_____ 7. At the end of World War I, victorious Britain and France greedily divided up the Turkish Empire.

_____ 8. Highly acclaimed for her book about the Vietnam war, *Fire in the Lake,* writer Frances FitzGerald returned to the subject of Vietnam in *Vietnam: Spirits of the Earth,* published in 2002.

_____ 9. After World War II, Great Britain turned Palestine over to the United Nations, which in November 1947 voted to create the State of Israel.

_____ 10. In 1908, the phenomenal Jack Johnson became the first African American to win the world heavyweight championship.

Informed Versus Uninformed Opinions

While everybody has a right to an opinion, it doesn't follow that every opinion deserves the same degree of attention or respect. Imagine, for example, that a friend saw you taking an aspirin for a headache and told you that chewing a clove of garlic was a far better remedy. When you asked why, he shrugged and said: "I don't know. I heard it someplace." Given this lack of explanation, argument, or evidence, it's unlikely that you would start chewing garlic cloves to cure a headache. Uninformed opinions—opinions lacking sufficient reasons or evidence—usually do fail to persuade.

More likely to convince are informed opinions backed by logic or evidence. For an example, look at this paragraph, which opens by expressing an opinion about the Internet's darker side.

> Although the Internet provides us with a convenient way to conduct research and to shop, it also has a darker side. Every day, hundreds of people report that they are victims of online stalking. In 2000, police arrested John Edward Robinson, the first Internet serial killer, who murdered at least five women he met and corresponded with online. In 1999, the FBI investigated 1,500 online child solicitation* cases, a number more than double that of the previous year. Criminals are also using the Internet to steal credit card numbers, thereby costing cardholders and issuers hundreds of millions of dollars per year. Online identity theft is a growing problem, too. Law-enforcement officials say that it's the fastest-growing financial crime; in 1999, the Social Security Administration received more than 30,000 complaints of misused social security numbers, which can be bought and sold via the Internet. Still other criminals are using the Internet for adoption fraud. For example, Internet adoption broker Tina Johnson caused much heartache and created an international dispute in 2001 when she took money from two couples in two different countries for the adoption of the same infant twin girls.

In this example, the author opens with an opinion—that the Internet, whatever its advantages, also has a "darker side." Aware, however, that not everyone might agree, she adds a significant number of facts and reasons designed to make her opinion convincing. Among other things, we learn that on a daily basis hundreds of people report they are the victims of online stalkers. We also hear about an Internet serial killer and about criminals' use of the Internet to steal credit card and Social Security numbers. All these supporting details are factual. One way or another, they can be verified. By the end of the passage, it's clear that we are dealing with an informed opinion, one worthy of serious consideration.

---

*solicitation: approaching someone for sexual purposes.

Recognizing Circular Reasoning

The paragraph about the Internet offers a good example of an informed opinion. Would you say the same about the next passage?

> We Americans like to brag about progress, but, in fact, life was better in the nineteenth century than it is now. People were happier and more at peace with themselves. There just wasn't the same kind of anxiety and tension that there is today. If we had a chance, we would probably all get into a time machine and go backward, rather than forward. All of our highly touted technological progress has not brought us an increased measure of contentment.

The author of this paragraph believes life was better a century ago. However, she—like our friend who prescribes garlic for headaches—offers no solid evidence to back up that opinion. The author could have quoted from journals, letters, or interviews; cited statistics; or even mentioned that there was hardly any divorce a century ago. But instead of offering support that might justify her opinion, the author simply makes the same claim over and over in different words. This tactic, called **circular reasoning,** is typical of writers given to promoting uninformed opinions. Lacking evidence, they rely on repetition. In response to circular reasoning, critical readers rightly become skeptical, or suspicious, of the opinion being expressed.

CHECK YOUR UNDERSTANDING

Explain and give an example of circular reasoning.

_____

_____

_____

Identifying Irrelevant Facts

Authors who haven't completely thought out the basis for their opinions are also given to supplying **irrelevant,** or unrelated, facts. Look, for example, at the following:

> Health care workers must be tested for the virus that causes AIDS. To date, more than 100,000 people have died from AIDS-related illnesses. In addition, current figures from the national

Centers for Disease Control and Prevention show that thousands more are already infected with HIV, the virus that causes AIDS, and will probably develop full-blown AIDS.

To make her opinion about AIDS testing convincing, the author needs factual statements that support a cause-and-effect connection between infected health care workers and the spread of the virus that causes AIDS. Such facts would be relevant and would help justify her opinion.

But those are not the facts the author supplies. Instead, she offers two facts proving that AIDS is a serious epidemic. Unfortunately, these facts are irrelevant to her opinion about mandatory testing. Critical readers would not be convinced.

Looking for Relevant Facts

In judging opinions, critical readers are always on the lookout for **relevant facts** that have a direct connection to the opinion being expressed. Consider, for example, the following passage:

> The Italian government takes excellent care of Italy's mothers. Pregnant women in Italy are guaranteed paid leaves, combined with free medical care. According to a 1971 law, pregnant women must be allowed to stay at home during the last two months of pregnancy, and new mothers can stay at home for the first three months following their babies' birth. During this five-month period, the government guarantees women who worked before their pregnancy 80 percent of their former salaries.

Here the author offers readers an opinion about how the Italian government treats mothers. (Note the connotations of the word *excellent*.) In support of this point of view, the passage supplies specific facts describing the financial and medical aid offered to mothers by the Italian government. Unlike the facts in the previous paragraph on testing health care workers, the facts in this passage are relevant, or related, to the author's claim.

CHECK YOUR UNDERSTANDING

Explain the difference between relevant and irrelevant facts.

_____

_____

EXERCISE 4

DIRECTIONS Read each passage. Then in the blank at the end, label each either *U* for uninformed or *I* for informed. If you label the passage uninformed, circle the appropriate letter to indicate if the author relied on circular reasoning or irrelevant facts.

EXAMPLE Even as millions of television viewers tune in week after week to the phenomenon known as reality TV, critics and the media bash popular series like *Survivor, The Bachelor, Who Wants to Marry My Dad,* and *Joe Millionaire* for trying to pass off voyeurism,* humiliation, and cruelty as entertainment. But have these people ever really watched a reality show? If they had, they would see that the popular shows have legitimate appeal. Unlike cop drama clones and boring sitcoms, reality TV offers exciting and compelling human stories. In fact, the joys and sorrows of reality show participants provoke strong emotional responses in viewers. How many of the network's stale, scripted shows manage to elicit pity, anger, fear, sorrow, amusement—or sometimes even all of these—in the way a reality TV show can? Many reality shows also serve up some useful social criticism. They zoom in on humanity's weaknesses and flaws, offering indirect but instructive truths in the process. *Survivor,* for example, points out the dark side of team playing—it's not always what corporate America says it is. Dating reality shows cut to the heart of what *really* matters to many people in the choice of a mate. In a way, reality TV shows have come to serve a communal purpose. They inspire us to watch together and to discuss what we see. When was the last time an episode of *Everybody Loves Raymond* or *E.R.* inspired this type of meaningful dialogue? (Source of information: James Poniewozik, "Why Reality Is Good for Us," *Time,* February 17, 2003, pp. 65+.)

____*I*____

a. circular reasoning

b. irrelevant facts

EXPLANATION This is an informed opinion because the author supplies a series of reasons in order to make her opinion persuasive.

1. Professional-wrestling television shows are not appropriate for children. These programs are not intended for younger viewers. Yet

---

*voyeurism: the act of watching others as a way of achieving pleasure.

about one million kids under the age of twelve are watching TV wrestling. Parents who let their young children watch these shows don't realize the harm they are causing. They need to think about the long-term damage their kids could suffer and to be more cautious about the potential risks. Kids must be encouraged to choose among the many other TV shows that are more appropriate for young children. They should certainly not be allowed, never mind encouraged, to watch wrestling, which teaches impressionable young kids all the wrong lessons about life and how it should be lived.

———

a. circular reasoning

b. irrelevant facts

2. Every American should seriously consider buying one of the new hybrid gasoline-electric cars. Thousands of people have already bought a Honda Insight or a Toyota Prius, both of which cost around $20,000. The demand for these cars, which combine a small gasoline engine with an electric motor, already exceeds production. Within the next two years, various auto manufacturers plan to introduce a hybrid sport utility vehicle, a hybrid minivan, and a hybrid truck. It's clear that hybrid vehicles are a growing trend, and one day in the near future, there should be one in every American garage. Fortunately, there are signs that hybrid autos are catching on and becoming trendy among celebrities. Anxious to imitate their idols, ordinary Americans will probably follow suit.

———

a. circular reasoning

b. irrelevant facts

3. The career of legendary queen of salsa Celia Cruz (1924–2003) was both long and influential. During her half-century career, Cruz recorded more than seventy albums and traveled all over the world, entertaining four generations of fans with her extraordinary voice and flamboyant performances. More than anything else, she helped define salsa, an Afro-Cuban musical style characterized by Latin rhythms. Cruz also received numerous awards and honors—including the prestigious National Medal of Arts, a Grammy Award, and an honorary doctorate degree from Yale University—all in recognition of her contributions. Perhaps most important, Cruz is credited with breaking down racial and cultural barriers by winning

a mainstream audience over to Latin music. Twenty of her albums went gold, selling more than 500,000 copies each. Because her music appeals to a wide range of people and because she took such pride and joy in her Cuban heritage, she served as a passionate ambassador of Hispanic culture. Proud of her accomplishments, Cruz always credited them to her father, saying "In a sense, I have fulfilled my father's wish to be a teacher as through my music, I teach generations of people about my culture."

———

a. circular reasoning

b. irrelevant facts

4. Although the so-called Mozart effect has been widely accepted by many educators, parents, legislators, and music marketers, new evidence indicates that it may not exist. In 1993, researchers at the University of Wisconsin claimed that college students who listened to ten minutes of a Mozart sonata prior to taking a spatial-reasoning test significantly improved their ability to perform tasks such as cutting and folding paper. This study gave birth to the belief that listening to Mozart's music helps increase intelligence. However, researchers have not been able to duplicate the results of this first experiment. As a matter of fact, a Harvard University graduate analyzed the conclusions of sixteen similar studies and found no scientific proof that music increased IQ or improved academic performance. Researchers at Appalachian State University and two Canadian universities have come to the same conclusion.

———

a. circular reasoning

b. irrelevant facts

5. When the threat of bioterrorism became very real in the fall of 2001, some companies began to market home-testing kits for the detection of substances tainted by anthrax, a deadly respiratory disease spread by bacteria. Costing from twenty to twenty-five dollars, the kits were available primarily over the Internet. Alarmed by the public's positive response to the kits, members of several different consumer groups issued warnings against their purchase, and for good reason. Testing for anthrax should not be done by individuals. Even when the government tested buildings for the presence of anthrax, the results of those tests were not always accurate. In the case of a test performed at one site, for example, the results were initially negative. But later tests showed that there were actually

anthrax spores present. The government has the capability to test and retest, using a variety of different and more refined methods, to double- and even triple-check for accuracy. Average homeowners, however, do not have such resources at their disposal. Ordinary people are likely to perform the test and take the results as accurate. Yet there is always the possibility of a false positive that indicates anthrax is present when it isn't; or, even worse, a false negative, suggesting the house is safe from disease when it's not. Performing the same test two or three different times is probably not the solution either. Often what's needed is a more sophisticated screening device, precisely the kind available in laboratories but not available to the ordinary consumer.

———

a. circular reasoning

b. irrelevant facts

 ## Fact and Opinion in Textbooks

Many students assume that textbook writers restrict themselves to facts and avoid presenting opinions. Although that may be true for some science texts, it's not true for textbooks in general, particularly in the areas of psychology, history, and government. Look, for example, at the following passage. Do you detect the presence of an opinion?

 Presidents are not just celebrities, they are the American version of royalty. Lacking a royal family, Americans look to the president to symbolize the uniqueness of their government. (Gitelson et al., *American Government*, p. 311.)

If you said the entire passage was an opinion, you'd be right. There's no way to verify how *all* Americans feel about the role of the president. And a good many may have no interest in royalty, so why would they look for a substitute?

As the excerpt illustrates, textbooks do, indeed, offer opinions. However, that's not a failing as long as the authors offer support for the opinions expressed in their writing.

Here, for example, is another textbook excerpt. The authors open with an opinion about the American military's attempt to manage news during the Gulf War. Note, however, that the opinion is not left unsupported. On the contrary, a specific example follows right on its heels.

Opinion

*Example
offered as
support*

Part of the strategy [during the first Gulf War] was to "spin" the news so that U.S. successes were emphasized and losses minimized. When announcing that eleven marines had been killed in action, for example, the military first showed twenty minutes of footage on Iraqi bridges and buildings being blown up, and the American deaths were treated virtually as an afterthought. The strategy, which worked, was to force nightly news programs to divide their attention between the bad news—eleven killed at the outset of a potentially difficult ground war—and the good news—visually spectacular footage of a truck traveling across a bridge seconds before the bridge blew up. (Johnson et al., *American Government*, p. 354.)

The two examples cited here should make it clear that opinions are not limited to the editorial pages of newspapers. They also turn up in textbooks, which means you need to be alert to the ways in which an author can mix a personal point of view in with what seem to be pure facts.

EXERCISE 5

DIRECTIONS Read each textbook passage. Fill in the blank at the end with an *F* to indicate that the passage is purely factual or a *B* to indicate that opinions are blended in with the facts.

1. While well over 80 percent of the people vote in many European elections, only about half of the people vote in American presidential elections (and a much smaller percentage vote in congressional elections). Many observers blame this low turnout on voter apathy* and urge the government and private groups to mount campaigns to get out the vote.

   But . . . voting is only one way of participating in politics. It is important (we could hardly call ourselves a democracy if nobody voted), but it is not all-important. Joining civic associations, supporting social movements, writing to legislators, fighting city hall—all of these and other activities are ways of participating in politics. It is possible that, by these measures, Americans participate in politics *more* than most Europeans—or anybody else for that matter. Moreover, it is possible that low rates of registration indicate that people are reasonably well satisfied with how the country is governed. If 100 percent of all adult Americans registered and voted, . . . it could

   ---
   *apathy: lack of interest or feeling.

mean that people are deeply upset about how things are run. (Wilson and Dilulio, *American Government*, pp. 145–146.)

———

2. Louis XVI died on the scaffold on January 21, 1793. On February 1, the National Convention* declared war on the British Empire and the Dutch Republic. Already fighting the two powers, Austria and Prussia,* which after France had the mightiest of eighteenth-century armies, the Convention now added to its enemies . . . the two powers that led the world in shipping, finance, and credit. The Convention had no choice; war with the Dutch and British became unavoidable late in 1792, when the French not only invaded Belgium but proclaimed assistance to revolutionists of all countries. The Dutch and British governments . . . received from the execution of Louis XVI a moral issue on which to rally support in their countries. A wave of horror . . . united European opinion against the regicides* in France. (Adapted from Palmer, *Twelve Who Ruled*, pp. 22–23.)

———

3. Methaqualone was first synthesized in 1951 in India, where it was introduced as an antimalarial drug but found to be ineffective. At the same time, its sedating effects resulted in its introduction in Great Britain as a safe, nonbarbiturate sleeping pill. The substance subsequently found its way into street abuse; a similar sequence of events occurred in Germany and Japan. In 1965, methaqualone was introduced into the United States as the prescription drugs Sopors and Quaalude. It was not listed as a scheduled (controlled) drug. By the early 1970s, "ludes" and "sopors" were part of the drug culture. Physicians overprescribed the drug for anxiety and insomnia, believing that it was safer than barbiturates. Thus the supplies for street sales came primarily from legitimate sources. (Adapted from Abadinksy, *Organized Crime*, p. 383.)

———

4. Author and pastor Charles Swindoll is credited with saying, "The longer I live, the more I realize the impact of attitude on life." Swindoll is convinced that attitude is more important than appearance,

---

*National Convention: the ruling body in France after the revolution of 1789.
*Prussia: former kingdom of north central Europe including present-day northern Germany.
*regicides: the killers of a king.

giftedness, or skill. For example, people who go through life with a positive mental attitude see daily obstacles as opportunities rather than roadblocks and are therefore more likely to achieve their personal and professional goals. People who filter daily experiences through a negative attitude tend to focus on what is going wrong and find it difficult to achieve contentment or satisfaction in any aspect of their lives. It makes no difference how attractive, intelligent, or skilled they are; their attitude holds them back. (Reece and Brandt, *Effective Human Relations in Organizations,* p. 149.)

———

 5. Filipinos began settling in the Yakima Valley around 1918–1920. The majority of those who settled there became agricultural laborers. By the late 1920s, there were many who worked on truck farms, in orchards, and in packinghouses. Some leased plots for independent farming. . . . If Filipinos were going to settle in the Yakima Valley, they had to secure work within agriculture; Yakima was a single-economy region.

By 1927 Filipinos had engendered the resentment of many whites who viewed them as competitive sources of labor. So deep was the anti-Filipino animosity that mob attacks took place the same year. Filipinos were attacked wherever vigilante groups encountered them. Some Filipinos were even assaulted in their homes, while others were forcibly rounded up and placed on outbound trains. (Chan et al., eds., *Peoples of Color in the American West,* p. 243.)

———

■ DIGGING DEEPER

LOOKING AHEAD If it surprised you to discover that textbooks are richer in opinions than you once thought, you may be equally surprised to learn that some textbooks are subjected to censorship by competing groups, each of whom believes that certain images, words, or ideas must be eliminated from all reading materials lest they do significant harm to students exposed to them.

POLICING THE LANGUAGE

1 For her 2003 book, *The Language Police: How Pressure Groups Restrict What Students Learn,* writer and educational consultant Diane Ravitch created what she called "A Glossary of Banned Words, Usages, Stereotypes, and Topics." A little more than thirty pages, the list actually would have been a good deal longer had Ravitch been able to obtain bias guidelines from every publisher, state testing agency, and professional association. But she was not. Although such guidelines are widely used by the publishers of elementary and high school textbooks and tests, they are a closely guarded secret because, as the author points out, the word *censorship* has negative connotations. No one wants to admit engaging in it. Thus most of the written guidelines Ravitch was able to gather have euphemistic titles like "Principles for Bias, Sensitivity, and Language Simplification." Such titles imply—as they were meant to—that nothing is being censored. Instead, the publisher or professional association involved is simply being "sensitive" to the harm that might be inflicted if kids were allowed to encounter such words or images in textbooks. In reality, though, such groups are afraid of coming under attack from religious groups, feminists, advocates for the handicapped, educational reformers, and multiculturalists among others, who have managed to exert a powerful influence on elementary and high school publishing.

2 What are some of these distressing words that made the banned list? Anyone imagining a host of obscenities and racial epithets obviously hasn't the faintest idea of how easily ordinary—and seemingly unobjectionable—language can damage youthful minds. The apparently harmless word *bookworm,* for example, made Ravitch's list. It's objectionable because it could discourage students from becoming avid readers. The terms *boyish figure* and *boys' night out* are also banned for being sexist. *Yacht* and *polo* need to be eliminated because they are elitist and refer to activities

most people aren't rich enough to pursue. Like words, some topics breed trouble, and the following all appear on Ravitch's list of likely suspects: *evolution, bodily functions, situation ethics, suicide, divorce,* and *crimes that have gone unpunished.*

3   In California, the decades-old children's story "The Little Engine That Could" was rejected because the little engine was openly identified as male and thus could be considered a symbol of sexism. On a standardized test, the New York State Education Department omitted references to *Jews* in Isaac Bashevis Singer's story about growing up in pre–World War II Poland, presumably because references to a person's ethnic background are considered insulting. It didn't seem to matter to those censoring the test that Singer is famous for his stories, not just of life in general, but of Jewish life in particular. Similarly, a passage in which Annie Dillard wrote about being a white child going to an all-black library was revised to eliminate all references to race, even though Dillard's purpose was to highlight her childhood feelings about race.

4   According to Ravitch, her awakening to the excessive control exerted over elementary and high school textbooks and tests came when she was involved in a national testing project. When test makers attempted to include a short informational passage about peanuts in a proposed national test of fourth graders, it was rejected by the "bias and sensitivity review panel" because the peanuts were described as "nutritious" and the passage failed to take into account that for people who are allergic to peanuts, the nuts are deadly. Another passage on quilting in the nineteenth century got eliminated because it showed women in what was considered a stereotypical context—involved in sewing. To those "sensitive" to the stereotype, it apparently did not matter that such a situation was completely realistic and appropriate for nineteenth-century women. From Ravitch's perspective, one of the "stranger recommendations of the bias and sensitivity panel working on the national tests involved the rejection of a passage about a blind hiker who scaled Mount McKinley, the highest peak in North America." This passage did not make the grade for two reasons: (1) Its emphasis on hiking and climbing suggested a regional bias; and (2) it suggested that, in the context of hiking, blind people are at a disadvantage because they cannot see the terrain. For bias hunters, these two reasons made the passage unacceptable.

5   But Ravitch does not include all these examples simply to draw attention to them. On the contrary, she is on a mission. She openly calls the presence of such censorship in schools a "huge

scandal in American education" and insists that "no one asked the rest of us whether we want to live in a society in which everything objectionable to every contending party has been expunged from our reading materials."

6   Ravitch and her many supporters, who also want to end the reign of the language police, are not making a case for textbooks and tests that approve of ethnic slurs or sexist insults. Instead, they argue that religiously removing all controversial topics or language from high school textbooks and tests has several consequences, all of them bad. (1) Often an author's work is gutted of meaning. Leave out, for instance, Singer's reference to Jews and you lose his reason for writing. (2) History and science are misrepresented. If we eliminate references to women doing women's work in the nineteenth century, we lose sight of a crucial aspect of that era. It was a world divided into two spheres of influence: The domestic sphere belonged to women; all the rest belonged to men. By the same token, eliminate references to the theory of evolution and we disregard the assumptions shared by most members of the current scientific community. (3) The text becomes devoid of reality and forfeits both the interest and the respect of student readers. If the books they read purify the reality they know, high school students are unlikely to take their textbooks seriously. Thus a history book that refuses to acknowledge the horrors of past wars or the tragedies that have resulted from racial or religious hatred is likely to make students think that history has nothing to do with the real world and is, therefore, not worthy of serious attention.

7   To quote Diane Ravitch, "How boring for students to be restricted only to stories that shatter their self-esteem or that purge complexity and unpleasant reality from history and current events. How weird for them to see television programs and movies that present life and all its confusing and sometimes unpleasant fullness, then to read textbooks in which language, ideas, and behavior have been scrubbed of anything that might give offense." How weird indeed! (Sources of information: Ravitch, *The Language Police;* Diane Ravitch, "You Can't Say That," *The Wall Street Journal,* February 13, 2004, Editorial Page. If you want to see other examples of censorship gathered by Ravitch, log on to www.languagepolice.com.)

Sharpening Your Skills

DIRECTIONS   Answer the following questions by filling in the blanks or circling the letter of the correct response.

1. What question based on the title would you use to guide your reading?

   _____

2. In your own words, what is the main idea of this reading?

   _____

   _____

3. In paragraph 2, what is the function of sentence 3?

   a. It's a topic sentence.

   b. It's a major detail.

   c. It's a minor detail.

   d. It's a transitional sentence.

4. Does paragraph 3 open with a fact or an opinion?

   _____

5. What's the implied main idea of paragraph 3?

   _____

   _____

6. In paragraph 4, the references to peanuts, quilting, and mountain climbing are supporting details that help make what point?

   _____

7. The first two transitions in paragraph 5 tell readers to expect

   a. more of the same.

   b. a contrasting position.

   c. a sequence of events.

   d. the effects of the event described.

8. In paragraph 6, what transition reverses the point of view expressed in the opening sentence?

   _____

9. Circle the letter of the conclusion that follows from this reading.

   a. Although Diane Ravitch is personally upset by censorship from pressure groups, she would not encourage parents to write letters of complaint.

    b. Diane Ravitch hopes her book will get the public's attention and force publishers of elementary and high school texts to stop caving in to pressure groups.

    c. Diane Ravitch is probably an atheist.

    d. Diane Ravitch is a supporter of home schooling.

10. Based on the reading, what conclusion would you draw about the author's position on textbook censorship?

    a. The author seems to agree with Ravitch.

    b. The author seems to disagree with Ravitch.

    c. The author doesn't reveal her personal point of view.

How did you arrive at your conclusion?

_____

_____

_____

WORD NOTES: SEARCHING FOR TRUTH

The discussion of fact and opinion on page 359 introduced a form of the verb *verify*, meaning "to prove true." *Verify* is an important word to add to your vocabulary. However, you should also consider learning some of its synonyms. Learning groups of words related in meaning is a good way to rapidly enlarge your vocabulary.

1. **Confirm:** to remove all doubts, as in "Can you *confirm* the receipt of my proposal?"

2. **Corroborate:** to strengthen through statements supplied by another, as in "No one was alive to *corroborate* the testimony of the accused."

3. **Substantiate:** to establish something by means of factual evidence, as in "The historian's position had now been firmly *substantiated* by the discovery of both diaries and letters."

4. **Authenticate:** to prove genuine, as in "The museum was swindled when it paid for the sculpture before it was *authenticated*."

Now fill in the blanks with one of the four words defined above.

1. Because the professor's long-time assistant was able to

   _____ his statements, the police were willing to let him go.

2. The art historian was unable to _____ the painting as a genuine Picasso.

3. The secretary called to _____ the arrival of the package.

4. Researchers have been able to _____ long-standing rumors about Thomas Jefferson's affair with his slave, Sally Hemmings.

Students who want to do a more in-depth review of fact and opinion with the help of **Getting Focused,** the companion software accompanying this text, should look at "Question 8: Does the Author Balance Fact and Opinion?"

Test 1: Reviewing the Key Points

DIRECTIONS Answer the following questions by circling the correct response or filling in the blanks.

1. The true test of a fact is whether it can be _____.

2. Opinions can't be _____, but they can be _____

   _____.

3. *True* or *False.* The World Wide Web is a better source of factual information than reference books are.

4. *True* or *False.* Writers always keep their facts and opinions separate from one another.

5. Connotative language carries with it strong _____.

6. Denotative language relies strictly on the _____.

7. *True* or *False.* Changing the context of a word can make it more denotative or connotative.

8. *True* or *False.* Textbooks report facts; they do not include opinions.

9. Facts or reasons offered in support of an opinion need to be

   _____.

10. When writers use circular reasoning, they usually lack _____

    so instead they rely on _____.

To correct your test, turn to the answer key on page 643.

Test 2: Distinguishing Between Fact and Opinion

DIRECTIONS Label each of the following statements *F* for fact, *O* for opinion, or *B* for both.

_____ 1. As George Orwell so correctly said, "The greatest enemy of clear language is insincerity."

_____ 2. Among people suffering from depression, one portion of the brain is significantly smaller than the other.

_____ 3. The planet Neptune was discovered in 1846 by the German astronomer Johann G. Galle.

_____ 4. The assassination in Dallas, Texas, of John Fitzgerald Kennedy, the thirty-fifth president of the United States, was among the most tragic acts of the twentieth century.

_____ 5. The Mexican revolutionary Emiliano Zapata (1879–1919) had a profound influence on modern Mexico.

_____ 6. Louise Brown, the world's first test-tube baby, was born on July 25, 1978.

_____ 7. We should return to the days when films were made in black and white rather than color.

_____ 8. Mexico's oil reserves are the seventh largest in the world.

_____ 9. Physical competence produces psychological competence. (M. Burch Tracy Ford, head of Miss Porter's School in Farmington, Conn.)

_____ 10. According to the Centers for Disease Control and Prevention in Atlanta, Georgia, foodborne diseases cause approximately 325,000 hospitalizations and 5,000 deaths per year.

Test 3: Recognizing Informed and Uninformed Opinions

DIRECTIONS Label each passage with either an *I* for informed opinion or a *U* for uninformed opinion.

1. On March 12, 2003, death row inmate Delma Banks Jr.[2] had eaten his last meal and was ten minutes away from being executed when the U.S. Supreme Court spared him by agreeing to review his case. The Court's decision suggests that, in Banks's case at least, justice has been served, and Banks will get a chance to prove his innocence. There is very little evidence that Banks, who was convicted for killing a sixteen-year-old boy in 1980, actually committed the crime. Physical evidence is lacking, and the key witnesses in his trial were two drug addicts, who testified against Banks in exchange for having charges against themselves dropped. During his trial, Banks's defense attorney did an ineffective job. For example, he made no objection to the racist tactics prosecutors used to select the all-white jury that decided the fate of his black client. Banks had no prior criminal record and always insisted that he was innocent. According to the three former federal judges who urged the Supreme Court to intervene, Banks's case puts into question the very "integrity of the administration of the death penalty in this country." (Source of information: Bob Herbert, "Pull the Plug," *New York Times*, April 24, 2003, www.nytimes.com/2003/04/24/opinion/24HERB.html.)

_____

2. Even though Elvis Presley died on August 16, 1977, he is certainly not forgotten. On the contrary, the legend of Elvis lives on. To honor the twentieth anniversary of his death, RCA released a four-volume CD, *Elvis Presley Platinum: A Life in Music.* It was so popular that record stores couldn't keep it on the shelves. In honor of that same anniversary, more than fifty thousand fans descended on Graceland, Elvis's Tennessee home. In 1997 and 1998, the San José Ballet toured the country performing a ballet in the singer's honor, calling it *Blue Suede Shoes* after one of Presley's earliest and biggest hits. Sightings of Elvis, real and bogus, continue to be reported to this day; in fact, an up-to-date list can be found at http://honorelvis.com/sightings. Anyone who needs further proof that for many "The King" lives on in memory need only type his name

_____

[2]On February 24, 2004, the U.S. Supreme Court threw out the death sentence of Texas inmate Delma Banks Jr. and granted him the right to further appeal his conviction.

into a search engine and sit back to watch the results pile up to somewhere well over a million.

———

3. Parents who allow their little girls to enter beauty pageants for children should think twice about what they are doing. Beauty pageants for women are bad enough but beauty pageants for children are simply disgraceful. How can these pageants do anything but cause harm to parents and children alike? Instead of celebrating and publicizing these pint-sized beauty queens, the media should point out how damaging such competitions are to vulnerable little girls, who have not yet established a sure sense of their own self-worth. State legislatures should ban pageants for anyone under the age of eighteen as a way of discouraging those ambitious parents who don't have the sense to protect their own children from harm.

———

4. Hunters like to claim that they were among the first environmentalists, but nothing could be further from the truth. Hunting benefits only those men and women who like to kill living creatures for sport. Oddly enough, environmental groups like the National Audubon Society and the Sierra Club support hunting, but that should not encourage anyone else to do so. The only way animals should be hunted is with a camera, never with a gun.

———

5. The label *organic* doesn't necessarily mean that food has been grown or raised without pesticides and man-made fertilizers. Currently, what's considered organic in one state may not be in another. Some states' certification programs allow organic produce to be grown with certain fertilizers and insecticides that other states specifically prohibit. Moreover, twenty states have no rules whatsoever governing organic food. "As it now stands, in an unregulated state there's nothing to stop some farmers from just sticking an organic label on their tomatoes, say, and putting them out for sale without ever having followed any organic principles," observes Katherine DiMatteo, executive director of the national Organic Trade Association. (Adapted from Jennifer Reid Holman, "Can You Trust Organic?" *Self*, November 1997, p. 163.)

———

Test 4: Recognizing Circular Reasoning and Irrelevant Facts

DIRECTIONS Circle the appropriate letter to indicate if the passage expresses an informed opinion, uses circular reasoning, or cites an irrelevant fact or facts.

1. The one-cent penny still serves several necessary roles, so Americans should not eliminate this coin. First of all, rendering the penny obsolete would hurt the poor. Because merchants usually round up to the nearest nickel on cash purchases, lower-income Americans, who conduct most of their business using cash, would wind up paying more. The nonprofit organization Americans for Common Cents claims that rounding will cost consumers an additional $600 million a year. Those who advocate keeping the penny also say that eliminating it would hurt charities because they collect millions of dollars in donated pennies. Finally, the penny should remain in circulation because Americans are fond of it. According to Americans for Common Cents, polls consistently show that up to 65 percent of Americans oppose getting rid of this coin.

   a. The passage expresses an informed opinion.

   b. The passage relies on circular reasoning.

   c. The passage cites an irrelevant fact or facts.

2. Local, state, and federal governments violate citizens' right to privacy when they post public records on the Internet. Easy access to the personal information contained in voter registration records, property tax rolls, and court records should alarm every American. Putting such data online simply makes public records *too* public. It's become much too easy to obtain personal information that should be kept private. Websites that post such information are a disservice to the people of this country. That's why governments should not improve the public's access to sensitive records by putting them online.

   a. The passage expresses an informed opinion.

   b. The passage relies on circular reasoning.

   c. The passage cites an irrelevant fact or facts.

3. In the United States, being able to speak Spanish can be an advantage personally and professionally. The Hispanic population is growing rapidly. Currently, 3.5 million Hispanics reside in this country. In many communities, their numbers have doubled in the

last decade, and in many cities and counties, even in states like Kansas, Hispanics now account for almost half of the population. Thirty-two percent of all California residents are now Hispanic. With this many Spanish-speaking neighbors, English-speaking citizens will see the Spanish language entering more and more into pop culture like television commercials and music. The ability to speak Spanish will also be a tremendous asset in the workplace as increasing numbers of businesses seek to hire bilingual employees who can communicate with Hispanic customers. In particular, professionals who interact with the public on a daily basis—such as law-enforcement officers and nurses—will benefit from having knowledge of Spanish.

a. The passage expresses an informed opinion.

b. The passage relies on circular reasoning.

c. The passage cites an irrelevant fact or facts.

4. The underpaid and underappreciated officials who referee National Football League (NFL) games deserve a raise in salary. Referees see to it that the rules and regulations of the game are enforced. Without them, the game could turn into a dangerous free-for-all. Yet, in general, their job is a thankless one that earns them insults and worse from the players and boos from the crowd. A bit more money in referees' paychecks seems necessary to offset the drawbacks of their thankless job. This seems only fair since 41 percent of Americans, according to a Peter Harris Research Group survey, say that their favorite leisure activity is watching football.

a. The passage expresses an informed opinion.

b. The passage relies on circular reasoning.

c. The passage cites an irrelevant fact or facts.

5. The laws that prohibit convicted felons who have served out their sentences from voting are both inconsistent and unfair. As the *New York Times* has pointed out, the laws vary significantly from state to state. In some states, for instance, felons on parole can't vote, but those on probation can. In other states, felons can apply to have their voting rights restored. However, local governments can, without giving a reason, deny the application. Unfortunately, the states that do restore felons' voting rights once their time has been served are not always efficient when it comes to notifying the men and women leaving prison about their rights. Some supporters of Al Gore insist that the removal of suspected felons from the voter rolls in Florida tipped the 2000 election scales in the direction of George W. Bush. Recently, two different courts of appeals ruled that taking

away voting rights from those who have served time for a felony may well violate the Voting Rights Act of 1965.* The courts of appeals are correct. Released prisoners have served their time. They have paid their debt to society. Disenfranchising them is not only undemocratic, it also completely undermines the notion that people who have committed a serious crime can be rehabilitated. In effect, the refusal to return the vote to those who have committed yet paid for a crime suggests that there is no such thing as an ex-felon. On the contrary, it suggests the opposite: Once a felon, always a felon. This is hardly the message we should be sending to those men and women struggling to once again become productive citizens.

a. The passage expresses an informed opinion.

b. The passage relies on circular reasoning.

c. The passage cites an irrelevant fact or facts.

---

*On August 6, 1965, President Lyndon Johnson signed into law legislation designed to protect voters from discrimination by state governments inclined to express prejudice by placing restrictions or limitations on voting rights.

Test 5: Taking Stock

DIRECTIONS Read the passage. Then answer the questions by filling in the blanks or circling the letter of the correct response.

Saving the Manatees

1 Since 1967, the manatee, a gentle marine mammal that lives in Florida waters, has been on the federal government's endangered species list. Yet between 1974 and 2002, biologists still counted as many as 4,673 manatee deaths. During that time, predictions that the manatee would soon become extinct prompted animal advocates, like members of the Save the Manatee Club and the Sierra Club, to insist on greater protections. Beginning in 1978, the Florida legislature responded by passing laws establishing areas where boating is banned or restricted, lowering boat speed limits in areas populated by manatees, and limiting permits for waterfront development. While these laws seem to have helped the manatees, they have also created conflict between environmentalists and Florida residents whose lifestyles and livelihoods have been adversely affected.

2 Laws designed to protect manatees seem to have reduced the number of deaths. Manatees swim from the ocean into warmer rivers during the winter months; therefore, many of them are injured or killed in collisions with boats. Limiting boaters' speeds and prohibiting them from entering areas where manatees tend to congregate have lowered the mortality rate. In 1972, the first aerial population survey indicated that there were only 600 to 800 manatees; several censuses in the 1990s, though, indicated that their numbers had increased to between 1,500 and 2,500. In January 2001, a survey conducted by Florida's Marine Research Institute counted 3,276 manatees, far more than expected. In 2003, the Florida Fish and Wildlife Conservation Commission counted 3,113 manatees.

3 While these statistics are good news to the manatees' protectors, they have also served as ammunition for those who advocate removing the manatee from the endangered species list and reevaluating manatee protections. Many Floridians oppose the current restrictions because of the personal and economic effects they have had on the state's human residents. Not only do the laws restrict boaters and fishermen, but they also prevent property owners and developers from using their lands as they see fit. Thus, all these groups have argued against manatee protection measures, seeing them as a hindrance to personal freedom. (Sources of information:

Craig Pittman, "Fury Over a Gentle Giant," *Smithsonian*, February 2004, pp. 54–60; "Synoptic Surveys: 1991–2004," Save the Manatee Club, www.savethemanatee.org/population4a.htm.)

1. What question based on the title could help you focus your reading?

   _____

2. In your own words, what is the main idea of the entire reading?

   _____

   _____

3. Based on the context, the word *hindrance* in paragraph 3 means
   a. help.
   b. obstacle.
   c. guarantee.
   d. erase.

4. Which pattern(s) organize the details in paragraph 1?
   a. definition
   b. time order
   c. comparison and contrast
   d. cause and effect
   e. classification

5. Which pattern(s) organize the details in paragraph 2?
   a. definition
   b. time order
   c. comparison and contrast
   d. cause and effect
   e. classification

6. Sentence 1 in paragraph 1 is
   a. a fact.
   b. an opinion.
   c. a blend of fact and opinion.

7. The last sentence in paragraph 1 is
   a. a fact.
   b. an opinion.
   c. a blend of fact and opinion.

8. In the first sentence of paragraph 2, the word *seem* suggests

a. a fact.

b. an opinion.

9. The word *ammunition* in paragraph 3 suggests that the controversy over protecting the manatees

a. is not emotionally charged.

b. involves people who are generally friends with one another.

c. has a high level of hostility.

10. In paragraph 3, the author expects readers to draw which inference from sentence 1?

a. Advocates of removing the manatee from the endangered species list don't consider the statistics accurate.

b. Advocates of removing the manatee from the endangered species list will argue that the statistics prove the manatees are no longer in danger of extinction.

c. Advocates of removing the manatee from the endangered species list believe those statistics favor the cause of the manatees' protectors.

C H A P T E R 8

Identifying Purpose and Tone

 In this chapter, you'll learn

- how *informative* writing and *persuasive* writing differ.

- why discovering the author's purpose is essential to critical reading.

- how the title and the source of a reading help you predict the writer's purpose.

- how thesis statements help you confirm or revise your prediction.

- how tone relates to purpose.

- how to recognize an ironic tone.

Most writing falls into three categories: (1) writing meant to inform, (2) writing designed to persuade, and (3) writing intended purely to entertain. Because we're focusing on critical reading issues, such as evaluating evidence and separating fact from opinion, this chapter is

solely concerned with writing meant to inform or to persuade. Determining whether a writer intends to inform or to persuade can sometimes be difficult whereas writing bent on entertaining is pretty easy to recognize. The only possible complication or difficulty might be that you don't share the author's sense of humor.

Understanding the Difference Between Informative Writing and Persuasive Writing

To be a good critical reader, you need a clear understanding of how informative writing and persuasive writing differ.

Informative Writing

The goal of **informative writing** is to make the audience more knowledgeable about a particular subject. Informative writing usually leans heavily on factual information and doesn't promote any one opinion. If anything, informative writing is likely to offer competing opinions on the same subject while the author remains objective, or impartial, refusing to champion one opinion over another.

Here's a good example of writing meant primarily to inform.

Two factors in the development of obesity in children are beyond human control. These two factors are heredity and age. Like it or not, thinness and fatness do run in families. Overweight children tend to have overweight parents and underweight parents tend to have underweight children (LeBow, 1984). In addition, most people inevitably put on fat more during certain periods of life than during others. Late childhood and early puberty form one of these periods; at this time, most children gain fat tissue out of proportion to increases in other tissues, such as muscle and bone. (Adapted from Seifert and Hoffnung, *Child and Adolescent Development*, p. 390.)

In this example, the topic is obesity in children, and the authors briefly describe two of its causes: heredity and age. Notice, however, that they do not express a point of view about the subject. Nor do the authors suggest that readers should adopt a particular point of view. Their primary purpose is to dispense information, not to persuade.

Persuasive Writing

Persuasive writing promotes a particular point of view; its goal is to make readers share the author's position or perspective. While writers intent on persuasion often pair their opinions with facts, the facts are carefully chosen. They are there to convince readers that the author is right. Although authors writing to persuade sometimes present opposing points of view, they do so in order to discredit the opposition and show readers why these contradictory opinions contain flaws of some sort and aren't worthy of serious consideration. Unlike those with an informative purpose, authors of persuasive writing don't present themselves as objective. Although the best of them try to keep an open mind and treat opposing positions fairly, they are still committed to their own views and write in the hope that you will share them. Here, to illustrate, is a passage written with a persuasive intent.

Four women widowed by the September 11 terrorist attacks—Kristen Breitweiser, Patty Casazza, Lorie Van Auken, and Mindy Kleinberg—have demonstrated the power of ordinary citizens to influence a huge bureaucracy*—the federal government. By tirelessly organizing protests and rallies, lobbying members of Congress, meeting with White House officials, gathering documents, and just plain refusing to give up, they have shown Americans the power of determined political activism. By demanding that agencies like the FBI and CIA explain how terrorists could have found the country so unprepared, these four widows have reminded the government of its responsibilities to its citizens. The four women have also modeled the kind of vigilance that citizens of a democracy should exercise. Kristen Breitweiser has admitted that, prior to September 11, she never read newspaper articles about the Middle East, Osama bin Laden, or Al-Qaeda. Now she realizes that she—and her fellow citizens—should have been keeping themselves informed about world affairs. Perhaps the most important thing that these women have done, though, is to lay the groundwork for a safer future. Through the commission they helped bring into being, all Americans have learned what needs to be done to make sure a tragedy like September 11 never happens

---

*bureaucracy: an institution with many different levels and departments.

again. (Source of information: Sheryl Gay Stolberg, "9/11 Widows Skillfully Applied the Power of a Question: Why?" *New York Times,* April 1, 2004, p. A1, www.nytimes.com/2004/04/01/national/01FAMI.html.)

The author of this passage has a strong conviction. He believes that the four widows who prodded Congress into forming a commission to investigate 9/11 did the country a great service. In an effort to persuade readers to share his point of view, he offers several reasons designed to convince.

CHECK YOUR UNDERSTANDING

See how well you can sum up the differences between informative writing and persuasive writing.

Informative Writing	**Persuasive Writing**

The Importance of Purpose

Identifying the primary **purpose,** or reason for writing, is important because the author's purpose determines how critically you need to read. After all, your time is limited. You can't possibly check every source or ponder everything you read. With purely informational writing, you can relax a bit and read to understand the author's message. Just make sure that the writer is objectively describing events or ideas without telling you how to interpret or view them. In fact, a writer whose primary purpose is to inform is very likely to give you different explanations of the same events so that you can develop your own opinions.

However, the more an author leans toward persuasion, the more consistently you must *evaluate* what you read, considering the amount and kind of evidence offered. Because persuasive writing tries to affect how you think, feel, and behave, you need to look for reasons, check facts, and consider the effect of word choice before you let yourself be influenced.

In a very real way, the author's purpose shapes or determines your reading response. The clearer it becomes that an author is intent on persuasion, the more willing you must be to do a close and critical reading in an effort to determine the author's **bias,** or personal leaning.

Determining the Primary Purpose

To be sure, a good deal of writing blends information and persuasion. For example, a writer who wants to inform her readers about changes that have taken place in Berlin, Germany, since the Berlin Wall* came down also needs to persuade readers that her account is accurate and trustworthy. Similarly, an author may wish to convince his readers that they should give more money to AIDS research. But to make that position persuasive, he will probably inform them about current funding.

As a critical reader, you should always try to determine an author's **primary,** or major, purpose. Be aware, however, that it's not always possible to be absolutely certain whether a writer meant to inform *or* to persuade. Some writers inform and persuade in equal measure.

CHECK YOUR UNDERSTANDING
In your own words, why is knowing the author's purpose important?
_____
_____
_____
_____

*Berlin Wall: the wall that divided East and West Berlin. It was erected by the Communist government to keep East Germans from fleeing to democratic West Germany.

Predicting Purpose

The only way to truly identify an author's purpose is to read what he or she has to say. However, even before you begin reading, there are two very important clues you can use to predict the author's purpose—the source of the reading and the author's background.

The Source Is a Clue to Purpose

The source, or location, of a reading is often a solid clue to purpose. Technical manuals, guidebooks, science texts and journals, reference books, dictionaries, reports of scientific experiments, and newspaper accounts of current events are usually written primarily to inform. Writing drawn from these sources usually does not promote any one particular point of view, but instead offers an *objective*, or impersonal, account of both people and events.

Unlike the preceding sources, editorials, opinion pieces, letters to the editor, and book, movie, and theater reviews in both newspapers and magazines are all likely to promote one particular point of view over other, competing points of view. The same applies to pamphlets published by political parties or special-interest groups, books and articles challenging or revising commonly held beliefs or theories, biographies of famous people, and journals promoting particular causes. All these sources are likely to feature persuasive writing.

Check the Author's Background

Information about the author's background is not always available to you. But when it is, it can be a useful clue to purpose. For example, a government official who represents the U.S. Department of Health and Human Services and reports on the use of antibiotics in poultry raising is less likely to have a persuasive intent than the president of the New England Poultry Association. If a writer represents a group that could benefit from what he or she claims, then you should suspect a persuasive purpose. You might be wrong, but the chances are good that you will be right.

EXERCISE 1

DIRECTIONS What follows is a list of possible sources for written material. Next to each item on the list is a blank. Put a *P* in the blank if you think the source is likely to contain persuasive writing. If you think it's likely to contain informative writing, put an *I* in the blank.

_*P*___ **EXAMPLE** A letter to the editor of the *Pittsburgh Post Gazette* responding to news that researchers had unveiled genetically engineered mice able to run faster and longer than naturally bred mice.

_*I*___ A front page article about the attempts of several states to eliminate, revise, or maintain bilingual education programs.

EXPLANATION Like editorials, letters to the editor express an opinion, often one that is passionately held by a writer who would like to sway the minds of others. Front page articles, in contrast, are supposed to report on, rather than judge, the events described.

_____ **1.** An article about Cuban leader Fidel Castro appearing in the *Encyclopaedia Britannica*

_____ **2.** An article about Fidel Castro appearing on the front page of the *New York Times*

_____ **3.** A biography of Fidel Castro titled *The Man Who Destroyed Cuba*

_____ **4.** A book titled *A Field Guide to American Houses*

_____ **5.** A government pamphlet titled *Historic Buildings in the Southern States*

_____ **6.** A book review of a work titled *The Triumph of American Architecture*

_____ **7.** A government report on global warming

_____ **8.** A letter about global warming written to the editor of the *Atlanta Times*

_____ **9.** A book titled *The Field Guide to North American Birds*

_____ **10.** An article about the disappearance of songbirds appearing in a journal titled *Save the Earth Now*

Titles Also Provide Clues

Another clue to purpose is the title of a reading. Titles that simply describe a state of affairs—"Teamwork Used to Teach Math"—usually signal that the writer just wants to inform readers without necessarily persuading them. Titles that express an opinion are quite a different matter. A title like "Teamwork and Mathematics Don't Mix" should immediately suggest to you that the author's primary purpose is persuasion.

Sometimes, of course, the title is no help whatsoever in determining the author's purpose. For example, titles like "A Look at the Nation" or "Family Affairs" don't reveal the author's purpose.

EXERCISE 2

DIRECTIONS Read each pair of titles. If the title suggests the writer wants mainly to inform, put an *I* in the blank. If it suggests persuasion, fill in the blank with a *P*.

EXAMPLE

a. Bilingual Education Is on the Rise ___*I*___
b. Congress Should Pass "English Only" Legislation ___*P*___

EXPLANATION The first title simply describes a state of affairs without passing any judgment. The second title takes a definite stand, indicating that the writer wants readers to be persuaded.

1. a. Against Assisted Death _____

   b. Assisted Death in the Netherlands _____

2. a. Support for Same-Sex Schools Is Increasing _____

   b. It Will Take More Than Same-Sex Schools to Get Rid of Gender Bias _____

3. a. Women Don't Belong in the Military _____

   b. Women in the Military _____

4. a. Astrology: The Science of Crackpots* _____

   b. Understanding Astrology _____

5. a. The Science of Cloning _____

   b. Let's Be Cautious About Cloning _____

EXERCISE 3

DIRECTIONS Try your hand at creating titles that express your intent. Make title *a* a statement that suggests your purpose is to inform. Title *b* should reveal your intention to persuade.

————————
*crackpots: persons with odd ideas.

EXAMPLE

Topic   Animal Rights

a. *The History of the Animal Rights Movement in America*

b. *Animals Don't Have Rights; People Do*

EXPLANATION Title *a* suggests the writer is intent on describing the animal rights movement whereas title *b* suggests the author wants to discourage support for the movement.

1. **Topic**   The Super Bowl

    a. _____

    b. _____

2. **Topic**   School Prayer

    a. _____

    b. _____

3. **Topic**   Online Courtships

    a. _____

    b. _____

4. **Topic**   Divorce

    a. _____

    b. _____

5. **Topic**   Cloning

    a. _____

    b. _____

 # The Main Idea Is the Clincher

The title, source, and any available information about the author's background can frequently suggest his or her purpose. But it's the author's stated or implied main idea that is the clincher, or deciding factor. It will tell you whether your initial prediction about purpose is accurate or in need of revision.

Main Ideas in Informative Writing

In writing meant to inform, authors describe, but they do not judge or evaluate, events, people, or ideas. Here, for example, the writer describes an author's beliefs about Greek culture.

> In *Black Athena*, Martin Bernal argues that the Greeks were deeply indebted to the Egyptians for almost every aspect of their culture.

Based on this thesis statement, which does not in any way evaluate Bernal's work, experienced critical readers would assume the author intends to describe Martin Bernal's book without making any claims about its value. While the remainder of the reading could prove them wrong—critical readers continuously test and revise their expectations—it's more than likely that their first response will prove correct.

Main Ideas in Persuasive Writing

Writers intent on persuasion will usually state or imply a main idea that identifies some action that needs to be taken, some belief that should be held, or some value judgment that should be shared. Here is an example.

> Martin Bernal has expended enormous energy on *Black Athena*, but he is absolutely wrong to assert, as he does, that he has rewritten the history of the eastern Mediterranean. (Emily Vermeule, "The World Turned Upside Down," *New York Review of Books*, March 26, 1992, p. 43.)

Faced with this thesis statement, most critical readers would correctly assume that the author wants readers to share her opinion of *Black Athena*.

Look now at the next two thesis statements. Which one do you think suggests that the author's goal is to persuade? Put a *P* in the blank next to that statement.

_____ **1.** A number of factors cause children to become obese, or seriously overweight.

_____ **2.** Because obesity is a serious health problem, parents need to pay close attention to what their children eat.

If you filled in the blank next to statement 2, you correctly recognized that the first statement did not encourage readers to pass any judgment or take any action. Statement 2, in contrast, strongly suggests that readers should share the author's feelings about the obesity of children—it's a serious health problem. It also encourages parents to act on those feelings by keeping a close watch on their children's diet. This is the kind of thesis statement that tells readers to look for and evaluate the author's evidence for such a claim.

⬛ EXERCISE 4

DIRECTIONS Read each pair of thesis statements. Write an *I* in the blank if the writer intends mainly to inform. Write a *P* if the statement encourages readers to share the writer's point of view.

EXAMPLE

a. In the 1990s, lawsuits involving bias in the workplace tripled after the government enacted new anti-discrimination legislation.

 I

b. In the United States, lawsuits have begun to replace logic and common sense; it's time to put an end to frivolous litigation.

 P

EXPLANATION Statement *a* simply identifies an existing state of affairs, while statement *b* calls readers to action.

1. a. In 1996, Buck and Luther, two Atlantic bottlenose dolphins, were retired from Navy service with full honors. To prepare them for a return to the sea, the Navy sent them to a retraining center in Florida. But some person or group set the dolphins free before retraining was completed, and the two dolphins barely survived their punishing first few weeks at sea.

 _____

b. It's sad but true that we humans often hurt wild animals in our attempts to help them. When two Atlantic bottlenose dolphins, Buck and Luther, were retired from Navy service, they were sent to a retraining center in preparation for their return to the ocean and life on their own. Unfortunately, some misguided animal lovers decided to speed up the process and liberated the dolphins before they were ready. As a result, Buck and Luther barely survived their newfound freedom.

——

2. a. The Tuskegee Study of Untreated Syphilis in the Negro Male was begun in 1932, when the U.S. Public Health Service began tracking 399 black men with syphilis. The study's stated purpose was to chart the natural history of the disease without recourse to any treatment, but the men recruited for the study were never told its true purpose.

——

   b. In May of 1997, President Clinton apologized on behalf of the nation to the survivors of the Tuskegee Study of Untreated Syphilis in the Negro Male. But his apology can never erase the horrible stain that experiment left on America's history.

——

3. a. The study of working-class women by sociologists Elaine Wethington and Ronald Kessler has been widely discussed and highly publicized. However, when closely examined, it's clear that their work brings little or nothing new to the debate about women and work.

——

   b. Sociologists Elaine Wethington of Cornell University and Ronald Kessler of University of Michigan found that women who worked at low-wage, part-time jobs were more stressed than women who worked full time.

——

4. a. Radon, particularly in combination with smoking, poses an important public health risk and it should be recognized as such.

——

   b. Research strongly suggests that radon, a naturally occurring radioactive gas, which collects in many homes, is linked to more than 20,000 deaths from lung cancer.[1]

——

———
[1]"Researcher Links Radon to 21,000 Deaths a Year," *New Haven Register,* February 20, 1998, p. F1.

5. a. Now that scientists have found the hormone that triggers hunger, they should take the next step and discover how this hormone can be controlled. Such a discovery would be an enormous advance in the war against obesity.

———

b. Based on research at the University of Texas Southwestern Medical Center, scientists believe they have found the hormone that triggers feelings of hunger.

———

 # The Effect of Purpose on Tone

Tone in writing is much like tone of voice in speech. It's the emotion or attitude created by the writer's choice of words, content, and style. Good writers know how to create and vary tone. Good readers recognize how tone can help identify purpose.

Tone in Informative Writing

Critical readers know that informative writing is likely to have a cool, objective, or neutral tone, the kind of tone that relies heavily on denotative language and doesn't try to affect readers' emotions. In informative writing, the tone is unlikely to reveal the author's personal feelings about the topic discussed.

Look, for example, at the following passage from page 396, written solely to inform. Notice the absence of charged language. Note, too, that the authors' personal feelings are not revealed.

 Two factors in the development of obesity in children are beyond human control. These two factors are heredity and age. Like it or not, thinness and fatness do run in families. Overweight children tend to have overweight parents, and underweight children tend to have underweight parents (LeBow, 1984). In addition, most people inevitably put on fat more during certain periods of life than during others. Late childhood and early puberty form one of these periods; at this time, most children gain fat tissue out of proportion to increases in other tissues, such as muscle and bone. (Seifert and Hoffnung, *Child and Adolescent Development,* p. 390.)

In this passage, the authors simply want to tell readers about the two factors in obesity that are beyond human control, and their tone matches their purpose. It's objective and to the point.

Tone in Persuasive Writing

In persuasive writing, tone can vary enormously. Although it can be cool and reserved, it's more likely to express some emotion. Tone in persuasive writing can be coaxing, admiring, enthusiastic, rude, even sarcastic. How, for example, would you describe the tone of the following passage?

> I have been fat all my life and I am thoroughly sick of apologizing for it. This is my declaration of independence from all you skinny people out there who have insisted how much better off I would be if I lost a few pounds. Tragically, we live in a culture that celebrates the thin and denigrates* the fat. This state of affairs leads to the kind of desperate and dangerous dieting I have engaged in for most of my adult life. And I am not alone in this obsession with losing weight. At some time in their lives, at least 80 percent of the American population has dieted to lose weight, even though studies show the majority of diets fail (Fett and Dick, 91). We would probably all be a lot better off if we spent time improving our souls instead of our bodies. No matter what we do, our bodies will decay; our souls will not.

At the beginning of the paragraph, judging by the words alone, it appears that the author wants only to inform readers about his own miserable dieting experience. He seems to focus solely on himself. He doesn't express any wish to affect other people's lives. But the passionate and angry tone is a dead giveaway to the author's real purpose, which is more persuasive than informative. By the end of the passage, it's clear the author wants us to believe that we should stop thinking so much about dieting and instead spend more time concentrating on our spiritual well-being.

Checking the match between tone and purpose is important. Informative writing that suddenly becomes angry and emotional in tone may be more persuasive in intent than you initially realized. Or, it may be that the writer honestly intends to inform, but his or her bias interferes with the writer's ability to stay fair and balanced. Whatever you do, *don't think of tone as verbal decoration*. For writers, it's a tool to create meaning. For readers, it's a crucial clue to

---

*denigrates: criticizes, demeans.

the author's primary purpose. Tone also tells you how willing the author might be to at least acknowledge another point of view.

Words Useful for Describing Tone

admiring	insulted
amused	insulting
annoyed	ironic (saying the opposite of
angry	what is intended)
anxious	joyful
appalled	mistrustful
astonished	nostalgic (looking fondly
awed (filled with wonder)	toward the past)
bullying	outraged
cautious	passionate
confident	playful
contemptuous	puzzled
critical	regretful
cynical	sad
disgusted	sarcastic
disrespectful	shocked
dumbfounded (very surprised)	solemn
embarrassed	soothing
engaged (deeply involved)	sorrowful
enthusiastic	sure
horrified	surprised
humorous	trusting

EXERCISE 5

DIRECTIONS After reading each selection, identify the author's purpose. Then circle the letter of the word or phrase that best fits the author's tone.

EXAMPLE Jazz singer Ella Fitzgerald was a quiet and humble woman who experienced little of the love she sang about so exquisitely for more than fifty years. Her voice, even in later years when she suffered from crippling arthritis, was always filled with a clear, light energy that could set the toes of even the stodgiest* listeners tapping. Although Fitzgerald, an African American, came of age in

---

*stodgiest: lacking in life, without energy.

an era when racism was rampant, whatever bitterness she felt never spilled over into her music. She sang the lyrics of a white Cole Porter or a black Duke Ellington with the same impossible-to-imitate ease and grace, earning every one of the awards heaped on her in her later years. When she performed with Duke Ellington at Carnegie Hall in 1958, critics called Fitzgerald "The First Lady of Song." Although she died in 1996, no one has come along to challenge her title, and Ella Fitzgerald is still jazz's first lady.

Purpose   a. to inform

           (b.) to persuade

Tone   a. coolly annoyed

           (b.) enthusiastic and admiring

           c. emotionally neutral

EXPLANATION Throughout the passage, the author describes Ella Fitzgerald in strong, positively charged language, creating an enthusiastic and admiring tone that encourages readers to share the admiration. The purpose, therefore, is persuasive.

1. As a mail carrier for more than twenty years, I can tell you firsthand that we are much maligned members of the population. Customers see only the flaws in mail delivery. They never appreciate the huge effort that makes service both speedy and efficient. For an absurdly small price, you can send mail anywhere in the country, from Hawaii to Alaska. You'd think this would impress most people, but no. Instead of thanking us for services rendered, they whine and complain about the few times mail gets lost. And just because a few members of the postal service have engaged in violent behavior, people now use the insulting expression *going postal* to refer to unexpected outbreaks of violence brought on by stress. This phrase unfairly insults the rest of us hardworking employees who do our jobs without complaint day in and day out.

Purpose   a. to inform

           b. to persuade

Tone   a. comical

           b. insulted

           c. emotionally neutral

2. In his book *An Anthropologist on Mars*, the renowned neurologist*
Dr. Oliver Sacks gives readers an important and insightful perspective on injuries and disorders of the brain. According to
Dr. Sacks, some injuries and disorders result in greater creativity
and achievement. With compassionate insight, Dr. Sacks describes,
for example, a painter who becomes colorblind through a car accident. Initially in despair, the painter eventually started painting stunning black-and-white canvases that won him more critical acclaim
than he had received before his mishap.

As in his previous works, Dr. Sacks gives readers an unexpected
perspective on disease and injury. In *An Anthropologist on Mars*, he
once again makes us rethink and reconsider our most cherished
beliefs about health and illness. His book should be required reading for anyone interested in the power of human beings to adapt to
and ultimately overcome loss.

Purpose a. to inform

   b. to persuade

Tone a. admiring

   b. cautious

   c. emotionally neutral

3. Deep processing, which is effective for many kinds of learning,
involves analyzing information in terms of its meaning. If, for instance, you want to learn a new word, it frequently helps to break
the word down into meaningful parts. For example, to remember the
meaning of *taciturn* ("inclined to silence; not liking to speak"), you
might think about it as being partially made up of the more common
word *tacit*, meaning "unspoken." Or, perhaps you've never quite
managed to remember the difference between *libel* and *slander*. If
you think about the fact that *libel* appears to contain the same word-
root found in *library*, that will make it easier to remember that *libel*
means "making false statements harmful to a person's reputation"
in writing [think how libraries are filled with writing] while *slander*
refers to making those kinds of statements *orally*. (Adapted from
Gamon and Bragdon, *Learn Faster & Remember More*, p. 159.)

Purpose a. to inform

   b. to persuade

---

*neurologist: a doctor who specializes in the workings and diseases of the nerv-
ous system.

Tone a. outraged

     b. relaxed and friendly

     c. emotionally neutral

4. Jazz pianist Michel Petrucciani, who died in 1999 at the age of thirty-one, was only about four feet tall. But he was a giant when he sat in front of a piano. The childhood victim of a disease that turned his bones so brittle they could barely support his tiny body, Petrucciani couldn't go out and play like other kids. Instead, he stayed home, playing the piano and listening to the music of jazz and swing greats like Dexter Gordon, Benny Goodman, and Miles Davis. For Petrucciani—who remained upbeat, determined, and feisty* until the day of his death—disease had forced him to turn to music. Ironically, he was grateful for that. The world, in turn, should be grateful for the music this young man produced. Although Petrucciani's music never quite loses its jazz edge, it's also lush and lyrical, filled with a sense of passionate longing. Petrucciani died with a small but loyal following, yet if there is any justice in the world, that following will grow. One only has to listen to the artist play songs like "Miles Davis Licks" and "Bimini" to know immediately that his talent was both rare and great.

Purpose a. to inform

      b. to persuade

Tone a. solemn and serious

     b. emotionally neutral

     c. enthusiastic and admiring

5. Owners of sport utility vehicles (SUVs) should show their patriotism by getting rid of their gas-guzzling cars. SUV ownership contributes to this country's unhealthy dependence on foreign oil. Just look at the Ford Excursion, a nine-foot-long, four-ton monster that gobbles up an entire gallon of gas to travel a mere twelve miles. SUV owners use more than their fair share of oil and keep America beholden to the Middle East for fuel. SUVs also contribute to the destruction of our planet's environment. Over its lifetime, the Ford Excursion spews seventy tons of carbon dioxide—the main cause of global warming—into the atmosphere. As a result, environmental groups like the Sierra Club have nicknamed the Excursion the "Ford Valdez" after the *Exxon Valdez,* an oil tanker that dumped 11 million gallons of oil into the ocean.

*feisty: combative.

Purpose a. to inform

b. to persuade

Tone a. irritated

b. casual

c. emotionally neutral

CHECK YOUR UNDERSTANDING

Define the term *tone* and explain its relationship to purpose.

_____

_____

_____

Learning to Recognize Irony

No discussion of tone would be complete without some mention of **irony**—the practice of saying one thing while implying exactly the opposite. This might sound confusing at first, but like most of us, you've probably used irony more than once in your life. Haven't you ever had a really horrible day and said to someone, "Boy, what a great day this was!" Or, seeing a friend wearing a sad expression, maybe you said, "Gee, you look happy."

If either of these examples sounds familiar, then you know more about irony than you think, and you're prepared for writers who assume an ironic tone like the one used in the following passage.

> The school board has decided to reduce the school budget once again. But why take half measures? Why not eliminate the budget altogether and close our schools? After all, a little learning is a dangerous thing. Better to keep our children totally ignorant and out of harm's way.

The author of this paragraph doesn't want his readers to take what he says *literally*, or at face value. After all, who would seriously suggest that keeping children ignorant is a good idea? The author's point is just the opposite of what he actually says. He doesn't want the school budget further reduced. But instead of saying that directly, he makes an outrageous suggestion that draws attention to where the cuts could lead.

When writers present what seems to be an outrageous or impossible opinion as if it were obvious common sense, critical readers assume the writer is being ironic, and they respond by inferring a message directly opposed to the author's actual words. As you might expect, *an ironic tone is a good indicator of a persuasive purpose.*

CHECK YOUR UNDERSTANDING

What is irony?

_____

_____

_____

EXERCISE 6

DIRECTIONS Read each passage and circle the letter that best identifies the author's tone.

1. According to the American Association of Furriers, wearing fur coats is once again back in fashion. Now that's good news for the thousands of mink, rabbits, foxes, and raccoons that are brutally slaughtered so that fashionable men and women can sport a trendy fur coat or hat. No doubt these animals are honored to suffer and die for the sake of human vanity.

Tone a. anxious

   b. comical

   c. emotionally neutral

   d. ironic

2. When the voters of Michigan sent Charles Diggs Jr. to the United States House of Representatives in 1954, he became the first black congressman in the state's history. He was not, however, the first black congressman in the United States. During the period of Reconstruction, from 1865 to 1877, the United States government tried to rebuild the South after the political and economic devastation of the Civil War. Black citizens held prominent government positions throughout the nation, including the posts of mayor, governor, lieutenant governor, state supreme court justice, U.S.

senator, and U.S. congressman. (Juan Williams, *Eyes on the Prize.* New York: Penguin, 1987, p. 49.)

Tone a. outraged

b. lighthearted

c. emotionally neutral

d. ironic

3. It is refreshing to note that many right-thinking citizens are calling for a ban on the celebration of Halloween because the holiday encourages devil worship. Hallelujah? It doesn't take the intellect of a TV evangelist to see that the wearing of "Casper the Friendly Ghost" costumes leads children to the wanton embrace of Beelzebub.* And it is a known fact that candy corn is the first step toward addiction. Only the devil (or an underemployed dentist) would knowingly offer popcorn balls to innocent children. But why stop at Halloween? Many other holidays conceal wickedness behind a vicious veil of greeting cards and Bob Hope TV specials. (Steve Ruebal, "Toss Out Halloween? Let's Not Stop There," *USA Today,* October 29, 1991, p. 11A.)

Tone a. confident

b. ironic

c. emotionally neutral

d. friendly

4. According to one of your readers, insufficient attention has been paid to the possibility that men are also victims of domestic violence. It is his opinion that men are, in fact, just as likely to be victimized by women as women are by men. The difference is that men, for fear of looking unmasculine, fail to report it. Well, I'm just all broken up at the thought of this new social problem. I can imagine how horrible it is for a 220-pound male to be terrorized by a 120-pound female. The poor thing must live in terror at the thought of her menacing approach. A man like that is certainly as much in need of our sympathy as are the women who end up hospitalized or worse in the wake of a domestic dispute.

Tone a. ironic

b. friendly

c. emotionally neutral

d. sympathetic

---

*Beelzebub: another name for the devil.

5. On December 1, 1955, Rosa Parks left the Montgomery Fair department store late in the afternoon for her regular bus ride home. All thirty-six seats of the bus she boarded were soon filled, with twenty-two Negroes seated from the rear and fourteen whites from the front. Driver J. P. Blake, seeing a white man standing in the front of the bus, called out for the four passengers on the row just behind the whites to stand up and move to the back. Nothing happened. Blake finally had to get out of the driver's seat to speak more firmly to the four Negroes. "You better make it light on yourselves and let me have those seats," he said. At this, three of the Negroes moved to stand in the back of the bus, but Parks responded that she was not in the white section and didn't think she ought to move. She was in no-man's-land. Blake said that the white section was where he said it was, and he was telling Parks that she was in it. As he saw the law, the whole idea of no-man's-land was to give the driver some discretion* to keep the races out of each other's way. He was doing just that. When Parks refused again, he advised her that the same city law that allowed him to regulate no-man's-land also gave him emergency police power to enforce the segregation codes. He would arrest Parks himself if he had to. Parks replied that he should do what he had to do; she was not moving. She spoke so softly that Blake would not have been able to hear her above the drone of normal bus noise. But the bus was silent. Blake notified Parks that she was officially under arrest. (Taylor Branch, *Parting the Waters.* New York: Simon & Schuster, 1988, p. 128.)

Tone a. ironic

b. admiring

c. emotionally neutral

d. irritable

---

*discretion: ability or power to decide.

Clues to Purpose

Informative Writing

- is found in textbooks, newspapers, lab reports, research findings, case studies, and reference works.
- employs a title that simply names or describes a topic.
- includes a main idea that describes a situation, event, person, concept, or experience without making a judgment or offering an evaluation.
- relies more on denotative than connotative language.
- relies mainly on facts and gives opinions largely to illustrate what others think.
- takes an emotionally neutral tone.
- remains objective and reveals little or nothing about the author's personal feelings.
- includes pros and cons of the same issue.

Persuasive Writing

- is found in newspaper editorials, political pamphlets, opinion pieces, and articles or books written to explain the author's position on current or past events.
- employs a title that suggests a point of view.
- states or suggests a main idea identifying an action that needs to be taken or a belief that should be held—or at the very least considered.
- often relies heavily on connotative language.
- relies a good deal on opinion and uses facts mainly to serve opinions.
- often expresses a strong emotional tone that reveals the author's personal feelings.
- includes only the reasons for taking an action or explains why arguments against it are not sound.
- can employ irony.
- Uses rhetorical questions,* which require no answers.

---

*What kind of person would harm an innocent child? For more on rhetorical questions, see page 448.

■ **DIGGING DEEPER**

LOOKING AHEAD The following reading introduces a topic briefly referred to in the chapter—bilingual education. Authors Kevin Ryan and James M. Cooper provide you with a good deal more information about bilingual education and the controversies surrounding it.

BILINGUAL EDUCATION

1 Congress passed the Bilingual Education Act in 1968 and subsequently amended it a number of times to provide federal funds to develop bilingual programs. Much of the expansion of bilingual programs in the 1970s can be attributed to a series of court cases, the most notable of which was the 1974 U.S. Supreme Court case

Lau v. Nichols of *Lau* v. *Nichols.* The case involved a class action suit* on behalf of Chinese-speaking students in San Francisco, but it had implications for all of the nation's non-English-speaking children. The Court found that "where inability to speak and understand the English language excludes national origin–minority group children from effective participation in the educational program offered by a school district, the district must take affirmative steps to rectify the language deficiency in order to open its instructional program to these students." Basing its ruling on the Civil Rights Act of 1964, the Court held that the San Francisco school system unlawfully discriminated on the basis of national origin when it failed to cope with the children's language problems.

2 Although the *Lau* case did not mandate bilingual education as the means to solve the problem, subsequent state cases did order bilingual programs. With the advice of an expert panel, the U.S. Office of Civil Rights suggested guidelines for school districts to follow, the so-called Lau Remedies. The guidelines "specified that language minority students should be taught academics in their primary home language until they could effectively benefit from English language instruction."

Bilingual Education Models

Our common language is . . . English. And our common task is to ensure that our non-English-speaking children learn this common language.
—*WILLIAM BENNETT*
Former U.S. Secretary of Education

3 Students with a native language other than English have two goals in school: learning English and mastering content. [Four] types or models of **bilingual education** programs have been

---

*class action suit: a lawsuit in which the person (or group) bringing the suit represents others who have suffered similar treatment.

Different models

designed to help them reach these goals. In the *immersion* model, students learn everything in English. Teachers using immersion programs generally strive to deliver lessons in simple and understandable language that allows students to internalize English while learning academic subjects. The extreme case of immersion is called *submersion,* wherein students must "sink or swim" until they learn English. Sometimes students are pulled out for English as a Second Language (ESL) programs, which provide them with instruction in English geared toward language acquisition.

4   The *transitional* model provides intensive English-language instruction, but students get some portion of their academic instruction in their native language. The goal is to prepare students for regular classes in English without letting them fall behind in subject areas. In theory, students transition out of these programs within a few years.

5   *Maintenance* or *developmental* bilingual education aims to preserve and build on students' native-language skills as they continue to acquire English as a second language.

Controversies

California and Arizona abandon bilingual education

6   Choosing the best method for educating students who need to learn English has become a divisive political battle. The transitional and maintenance models of bilingual education are in growing jeopardy, as first California, then Arizona, and now other states threaten these bilingual programs. In 1998, California voters passed Proposition 227, which called for LEP [Limited English Proficient] students to be taught in a special English-immersion program in which nearly all instruction is in English, in most cases for no more than a year, before moving into mainstream English classrooms. Proposition 227 basically ended transitional and maintenance models of bilingual education in California, except when sufficient numbers of parents specifically request that their children continue in them. Many parents, administrators, and teachers are concerned that all children, not just LEP students, will be affected as mainstream teachers grapple with students who may be unprepared to deal with grade-level work in English after one year in immersion.

7   The legality of Proposition 227 was challenged in the courts, but in 2001 a federal appeals court upheld the law. By 2001, English-language learners in California elementary and middle schools had improved their overall scores on state standardized tests for the third year in a row, but the scores for high school students had stalled. Supporters of Proposition 227 argue that the test scores improved as a result of the law being implemented.

Bilingual education supporters, on the other hand, point out that average scores have risen for all students and that the rate of increase in scores for LEP students still lags behind those of English-speaking students.

8   Although some educators believe students who use English as a second language should be educated in their native language as well, critics insist such an approach doesn't work. The critics believe the best path to academic achievement for language-minority students in most cases is to learn English and learn it quickly. Too many bilingual programs, they say, place LEP students into slower learning tracks where they rarely learn sufficient English and from which they may never emerge. These critics basically support an immersion model of bilingual education but oppose the transitional and maintenance models. However, supporters of transitional and maintenance models argue that students can best keep up academically with their English-speaking peers if they are taught at least partly in their native languages while learning English.

Bilingual critics support immersion model

9   In the early 1970s, language-minority speakers and their advocates fought for bilingual education as their right, but today many of them are expressing doubts about the effectiveness of bilingual programs. Civil rights and cultural issues are giving way to concerns that non-native English speakers are just not sufficiently mastering the English language. Advocates say, it is not fair to blame bilingual education for the slow progress some students are making. They cite research indicating that instruction in the native language concurrent with English instruction actually enhances the acquisition of English. The problem is not bilingual education, they say, it's that becoming proficient in any second language takes longer than just one or two years. They also point out that there is a shortage of well-qualified, fully bilingual teachers, so in many cases the problem with bilingual classes is not the curriculum but the quality of instruction. Some school systems have used teacher aides who speak the child's language to help connect the child and the school. The use of bilingual peer tutors may also help provide a greater sense of stability.

Many still support bilingual education

10   Despite this controversy, many school districts are in desperate need of bilingual teachers, particularly those who speak Spanish and Asian languages. If you speak a second language or still have time to include learning a language in your college program, you could help meet a serious educational need and, at the same time, greatly enhance your employment opportunities. Speaking a foreign language, especially Spanish, is also an asset for the regular classroom teacher who may have Spanish-speaking students in class. (Ryan and Cooper, *Those Who Can, Teach,* pp. 53–57.)

Need for bilingual teachers

Sharpening Your Skills

DIRECTIONS Answer the following questions by circling the letter of the correct response or filling in the blanks.

1. Which statement best expresses the main idea of the entire reading?

   a. Several types of bilingual education currently exist to help students reach their educational goals; the three most popular are immersion, submersion, and transitional. Each has its own strengths and weaknesses.

   b. In an effort to improve the education of non-native speakers, Congress passed the Bilingual Education Act in 1968, but bilingual education remains a source of controversy to this day.

   c. Research suggests that students from other countries learn English more quickly through the immersion method.

   d. The problem with bilingual instruction is not the curriculum but the quality of the instruction.

2. Which of the following statements more effectively paraphrases the Supreme Court's decision (*Lau v. Nichols*) on equality of education?

   a. Students who have not mastered English are required by law to attend bilingual classes until they pass an exam that indicates their mastery of English.

   b. If students have not mastered English, giving them the same books, classrooms, teachers, and course work cannot be considered equal treatment.

   c. Students who have not mastered English should be allotted additional time to complete assignments and exams.

3. In paragraph 3, which sentence is the topic sentence?

   a. sentence 1

   b. sentence 2

   c. sentence 3

4. How would you label this sentence from paragraph 6: "In 1998, California voters passed Proposition 227, which called for LEP students to be taught in a special English-immersion program in which nearly all instruction is in English, in most cases for no more than a year, before moving into mainstream English classrooms"?

   a. major detail

   b. minor detail

5. How would you label this sentence from paragraph 6: "Proposition 227 basically ended transitional and maintenance models of bilingual education in California, except when sufficient numbers of parents specifically request that their children continue in them."

   a. major detail

   b. minor detail

6. Which patterns of organization can you see at work in paragraphs 3 and 4?

   a. cause and effect; definition

   b. classification; definition

   c. time order; comparison and contrast

7. Label the following statements *F* for fact, *O* for opinion, or *B* for a blend of the two.

   a. Congress passed the Bilingual Education Act in 1968 and subsequently amended it a number of times to provide federal funds to develop bilingual programs.

   ⎯⎯⎯

   b. Students with a native language other than English have two goals in school—learning English and mastering content.

   ⎯⎯⎯

8. How would you describe the authors' tone?

   ⎯⎯⎯⎯⎯⎯⎯⎯⎯⎯⎯⎯⎯⎯⎯⎯⎯⎯⎯⎯⎯⎯⎯⎯⎯⎯⎯⎯

9. The authors' purpose is

   a. to inform.

   b. to persuade.

10. From this reading, you could correctly draw which conclusion?

    a. The authors believe bilingual programs can be improved and become more successful.

    b. The authors no longer believe in bilingual education programs. They are convinced that total immersion is the only effective method of teaching a second language.

    c. The authors consider access to bilingual education to be a civil rights issue.

    d. The authors would not encourage schools to spend money on bilingual education.

WORD NOTES: TYPES OF IRONY

The word *irony,* defined on page 413 as the practice of "saying one thing while implying exactly the opposite," is a widely used term and like so many other words, its meaning can vary with context. For an example, take a look at the word *ironic* in the following sentence: "Isn't it a bit *ironic* for you to simultaneously imitate and criticize your best friend's behavior?" In this sentence, the word *ironic* indicates that a particular action is exactly the opposite of what one would expect under the circumstances. This is another common meaning for the words *irony* and *ironic.*

You also need to know that the word *irony* is closely related in meaning to *sarcasm.* In both irony and sarcasm, what is said is actually the opposite of what is meant. The difference is that *irony* is used to make a point whereas *sarcasm* is used strictly to insult or hurt (which may be one good reason why sarcastic people don't have a lot of friends).

Dramatic Irony

In your literature or drama classes, you may have also been introduced to the phrase *dramatic irony.* The phrase refers to a device playwrights use when they create characters who know less than their audience. All through the famous play *Oedipus Rex,* for example, the audience knows that disaster will strike when King Oedipus finds out the truth about his birth, but the king himself remains completely unaware of his doom until it's too late.

Socratic Irony

Take a philosophy course and you could also be introduced to the term *Socratic irony.* According to the Greek philosopher Plato, his teacher, Socrates, would first claim ignorance and then ask a series of questions, designed to lead his students to the point he wanted to make: "I know nothing of it, but I wonder 'what is the nature of love?'" This method is called Socratic irony, in part because it is based—like irony in general—on a contradiction. Socrates claimed not to know anything but was, in fact, leading his students toward the very conclusion he had in mind.

Students who want to do a more in-depth review of paragraph essentials with the help of **Getting Focused,** the companion software accompanying this text, should look at "Question 9: What Tone Does the Author Use?" and "Question 10: What's the Author's Purpose?"

To get more practice identifying tone and purpose, go to **laflemm.com** and click on "Reading for Thinking: Online Practice." Complete and correct Practice 6.

Test 1: Reviewing the Key Points

DIRECTIONS Answer the following questions by filling in the blanks.

1. What is the goal of informative writing?

   _____

2. Informative writing is likely to offer _____ on the same subject.

3. What is the goal of persuasive writing?

   _____

4. Identifying the primary purpose is important because the author's purpose determines _____.

5. Even before you begin reading, you can use two clues to predict the author's purpose. These two clues are _____ and _____.

6. When trying to determine purpose, the _____ is the clincher, or deciding factor.

7. In informative writing, the author _____ but does not _____ people, events, or ideas.

8. Informative writing relies more on _____ language, whereas persuasive writing relies more on _____ language.

9. Tone is the _____ an author expresses through words.

10. In contrast to persuasive writing, the tone in informative writing is unlikely to _____.

To correct your test, turn to the answer key on page 644.

Test 2: Identifying Purpose and Tone

DIRECTIONS Circle the appropriate letters to identify the author's purpose and tone.

1. In areas with a large Mexican population, politicians running for office are likely to talk about amnesty for the millions of illegal immigrants currently living in the United States. However, it's time that they did more than talk, since the number of Mexican men and women living here illegally is growing at a rapid rate.* The majority are productive, law-abiding people, who simply want to earn a better standard of living for themselves and their families. In many cases, they have already endured great hardship just to get to this country. Once here, they are often forced by unscrupulous employers to accept low wages and poor working conditions because they fear being deported. Granting them amnesty would give illegal immigrants the right to complain and the right to demand fair working conditions. It is the compassionate and humane thing to do. The idea should not be abandoned once the campaign speeches are over and the votes have been counted.

The author's primary purpose is

a. to inform.

b. to persuade.

The author's tone is

a. emotionally neutral.

b. casual.

c. arrogant.

d. sympathetic.

2. From 1972 through 1996, the South was more Republican than the nation as a whole. The proportion of white southerners describing themselves to pollsters as "strongly Democratic" fell from more than one-third in 1952 to about one-seventh in 1984. There has been a corresponding increase in "independents." As it turns out, southern white independents have voted overwhelmingly Republican in recent presidential elections. If you lump independents together with the parties for which they actually vote, the party alignment among white southerners has gone from six-to-one Democratic in 1952 to about fifty-fifty Democrats and Republicans. If this contin-

---

*Recent figures put the number of illegal immigrants somewhere between seven and nine million, with 70 percent coming from Mexico.

ues, it will constitute a major realignment in a region of the country that is rapidly growing in population and political clout. (Wilson and Dilulio, *American Government,* p. 161.)

The author's primary purpose is

a. to inform.

b. to persuade.

The author's tone is

a. emotionally neutral.

b. critical.

c. solemn.

d. surprised.

3. Oregon and Washington have proven that voting by mail is superior to the old method of voting in a polling place. First of all, surveys clearly show that voting by mail is an option people want. Seventy percent of Oregonians and 65 percent of Washingtonians prefer voting by mail. They like the convenience of a mail-in ballot that allows them to integrate voting more easily into their busy lives. Furthermore, voters feel that voting by mail allows them to make more informed choices. For example, one Washington survey revealed that residents believe they make better decisions because they can take more time with their ballot at home rather than rushing to complete it in a voting booth. Not surprisingly, the benefits of voting by mail have produced a dramatic increase in voter turnout during elections. For instance, almost 80 percent of registered voters in Oregon submitted a ballot in the 2000 presidential election, compared to a nationwide average of 51 percent voter turnout. Other states should follow the example set by Washington and Oregon.

The author's primary purpose is

a. to inform.

b. to persuade.

The author's tone is

a. anxious.

b. emotionally neutral.

c. confident.

d. sarcastic.

4. The United States had been fighting Japan in World War II for almost four years when President Harry Truman decided to use the

atomic bomb to bring the war to an end. On Monday, August 6, 1945, at approximately 8:11 a.m., an American B-29 bomber named the *Enola Gay* dropped an atomic bomb over the southwestern Japanese port of Hiroshima from an altitude of 31,600 feet. At 2,000 feet, the bomb exploded, producing first a blinding fireball and then a huge mushroom cloud that billowed miles into the sky. The explosion obliterated everything within a one-mile radius, killing 75,000 people instantly. About 25,000 more people would die later from the effects of the radiation. Still Japan did not surrender. So, three days later, on August 9, 1945, at 11:00 a.m., the United States dropped a second atomic bomb on Nagasaki, a Japanese city 186 miles southwest of Hiroshima. More than 35,000 Japanese perished immediately in the blast. On August 14, the Japanese accepted America's terms for surrender, and President Truman announced the end of World War II.

The author's primary purpose is

a. to inform.

b. to persuade.

The author's tone is

a. emotionally neutral.

b. fearful.

c. furious.

d. sad.

5. The Apollo Space Program of the 1960s and 1970s was responsible for a series of moon landings. In 1967, the project got off to a tragic start when fire killed three astronauts during a preflight test on the launch pad. The tragedy, however, did not put an end to the space program. In 1968 and 1969 a series of successful missions took astronauts into space for six to ten days at a time. Apollo missions 7, 8, 9, and 10 tested the equipment and operations necessary for placing men on the moon's surface. On July 20, 1969, the *Apollo 11* mission fulfilled its purpose when astronauts Neil Armstrong and Buzz Aldrin did what had once seemed impossible: They walked on the moon while people all over the world stayed glued to their television sets and watched in awe. A second lunar landing occurred that same year as part of the *Apollo 12* mission. In 1970, *Apollo 13* was supposed to result in a third landing. However, damage to the spacecraft caused the mission to be aborted, and the astronauts barely made it safely back to Earth. Near tragedy, however, did not prove a permanent obstacle. In 1971 and 1972, four more Apollo flights produced four more lunar landings. *Apollo 14, 15,*

16, and *17* astronauts walked on the moon, performed scientific experiments, collected samples of moon rocks, and took photographs.

The author's primary purpose is

a. to inform.

b. to persuade.

The author's tone is

a. emotionally neutral.

b. skeptical.

c. critical.

d. admiring.

Test 3: Recognizing Purpose and Tone

DIRECTIONS Read each passage. Then answer the accompanying questions by circling the appropriate letter or letters.

1. The Disappointed Electorate

1 Barriers such as preregistration requirements and long ballots reduce the numbers of citizens who vote. But another obstacle is the myth of broken promises. Many Americans do not take part in elections because they do not believe that government in general and elected officials in particular can solve the country's problems. They also question the honesty and integrity of many political leaders.

2 This lack of confidence in government is relatively new. The Vietnam War in the 1960s undermined confidence in government, and the Watergate scandal and the resignation of President Richard Nixon diminished it still further in the early 1970s. In 1999, President Bill Clinton was impeached by the House of Representatives and became only the second president in our history to be tried for misconduct by the Senate. Although he was acquitted of all charges brought against him, the events surrounding the impeachment and the Senate trial were seen as bringing discredit not only on President Clinton but also on the political and governmental system in general. . . . The highly controversial election of President George W. Bush, who received a majority of the electoral college vote but lost in the popular vote to Democratic candidate Al Gore by over 500,000 votes, also weakened many Americans' confidence in the political process.

3 In this atmosphere of cynicism, many potential voters doubt that their vote matters and simply stay home on election day. Several studies have clearly documented the reasons for failure to vote. First, many people believe that government cannot solve the nation's problems. In addition, . . . people are less likely than before to strongly identify with one political party, an identification that once got out the vote. Finally, some people have even begun to question whether it makes any difference who wins elections.

4 Should we be concerned about the disappointed voter? Some observers say yes, arguing that low turnout undermines representative government, which, they argue, depends on full electoral participation. Others disagree, suggesting that people who are ill informed may make poor choices when they vote. It has even been argued that low levels of voter turnout are a sign of a healthy

system—that is, they show that people are satisfied with their government. (Gitelson et al., *American Government,* p. 207.)

1. The author's primary purpose is

    a. to inform.

    b. to persuade.

2. The author's tone is

    a. admiring.

    b. critical.

    c. emotionally neutral.

    d. puzzled.

2. **Asia's Dynamic and Distinctive Media Scene**

1   . . . Asia is where much of communication began—paper was invented there and the first newspaper appeared hundreds of years ago. That legacy, however, was lost to history and has little to do with the modern Asian media. The emerging media of East Asia, like their counterparts in the West, deliver information and news, convey opinion, offer entertainment, and provide a market-place for goods and services through advertising, but their editorial voices and other content differ greatly [from the U.S. media].

2   These differences are philosophical. While media in the United States and elsewhere in the West are the product of Western enlightenment with an emphasis on freedom and individual rights, the media of much of Asia are influenced by Confucian philosophy, which stresses consensus* and cooperation. As one study puts it, "Thus what may look the same is actually quite different in function."

3   The consensus model of Asian media has meant more cooperation with government than is the case in the West, where conflict and adversarial disputes are more often the case. That means, in many countries, the kind of investigative reporting that embarrasses government or business, which is so common in the West, is not welcomed. In some instances, in Singapore, for example, the restrictive media system has little formal censorship, though journalists often engage in self-censorship. Malaysia's Mohammed Mahatir and Singapore's long-time leader Lee Kwan Yew (now a senior minister in the government) oppose Western-style freedoms and any absolute notion of freedom of the press. They argue that

---

*consensus: agreement among many different individuals or groups.

Western values have led to a breakup of families and a disruption of government. Singapore and some other countries keep a tight leash on their press in an otherwise free-market economy and sometimes penalize foreign media who "abuse their welcome." For example, both *Time* and the *Wall Street Journal* have been banned and fined in Singapore for reporting on the government and military in unflattering articles.

4   Outsiders in several Asian countries cover international news at their own peril and sometimes are expelled for angering local authorities. Asia's media scene, like that of Western Europe and North America, is highly diverse and complex, ranging from national dailies in Japan, with millions of readers, to a vast array of magazines, television programming, a movie industry, advertising and public relations enterprises, and various new media cyberspace ventures. At the same time, rural Asia relies on community radio and small, often poor vernacular* newspapers and broadsheets.* As in other parts of the world, there are vast differences between urban and rural communication in Asia. (DeFleur and Dennis, *Understanding Mass Communication*, pp. 248–250.)

1. The author's primary purpose is

   a. to inform.

   b. to persuade.

2. The author's tone is

   a. deeply concerned.

   b. light-hearted and humorous.

   c. emotionally neutral.

   d. critical.

3. Presidential Access

1   Technically, the White House Office is part of the Executive Office of the President, but in an important sense the two organizations are separate. The White House Office is composed of staff members who are located in the White House and serve the president's political needs. Smaller than the Executive Office of the President, it is nevertheless a sizable organization in its own right—for example, in the Clinton administration, it employed more than 400 people. The White House Office includes assistants, special assistants, counselors, special counselors, and consultants with

---

*vernacular: everyday, as opposed to literary, language.
*broadsheets: public notices.

varying titles who function almost totally in the service of the president. Originally, the staff's function was limited to coordinating executive branch activities, but presidents, frustrated by their inability to control the bureaucracy, have increasingly come to rely on the White House Office to develop and implement policy initiatives. Indeed, cabinet secretaries, much to their chagrin, often find that policies affecting their departments are developed in the White House Office.

2   The actual structure of the office depends on the president's organizational preferences. Some presidents have favored a rather loose structure in which several aides report directly to the president. Sometimes referred to as the "wheel," this highly personalized approach is designed to assure the president access to information.

3   Most modern presidents, however, have favored a tight structure, with staff responsibilities and reporting procedures clearly detailed, and subordinates reporting to a chief of staff. Under this organizational style, which resembles a pyramid, only one or two key aides have access to the president. Eisenhower, with his military background, preferred this type of arrangement and delegated much authority to his chief aide, Sherman Adams. Nothing could come to the president unless it was initialed by Adams. Carrying the pyramid style a step further, Nixon used his chief of staff, H. R. "Bob" Haldeman, and his domestic adviser, John Ehrlichman, to seal him off from the rest of the government. Haldeman had such tight control over the president's daily schedule that not even members of the president's family could see him without Haldeman's permission.

4   Pyramid structures can reduce the president's burden, allowing him to concentrate on those issues that truly require his time. But the relief may come at some cost. The top aides may limit their communications to what the president wants to hear, cutting off dissenting viewpoints. And they may make important decisions before the questions reach the president. As two critics have observed, "presidential assistants can become assistant presidents." (Gitelson et al., *American Government,* pp. 322–323.)

1. The primary purpose of this reading is

    a. to inform.

    b. to persuade.

2. The author's tone is

    a. critical.

   b. skeptical.

   c. admiring.

   d. emotionally neutral.

4. *Juku,* Japanese for "Cram School"

1 On a brisk Saturday morning, while most of their friends were relaxing at home, sixteen-year-old Jerry Lee and eight other Asian teenagers huddled over their notebooks and calculators for a full day of math and English lessons.

2   During the week they all attend public schools in the city. But every Saturday, they go to a Korean *hagwon,* or cram school, to spend up to seven hours immersed in the finer points of linear algebra or Raymond Chandler.*

3   "I complain, but my mom says I have to go," said Jerry, a Stuyvesant High School student from Sunnyside, Queens, who has already scored a 1520 on the Scholastic Aptitude Test for college but is shooting for a perfect 1600. "It's like a habit now."

4   Long a tradition in the Far East, where the competition to get into a top university borders on the fanatic, the cram schools of Asia have begun to appear in this country too, in Queens and New Jersey and Los Angeles and elsewhere, following the migration of many Koreans, Japanese, and Chinese over the last two decades.

5   In the last ten years, the cram schools—called *juku* in Japanese and *buxiban* in Chinese—have become a flourishing industry, thriving on immigrant parents' determination to have their children succeed. Only a handful of cram schools existed here when the *hagwon* that Jerry attends, the Elite Academy, opened in 1986. Today, the Korean-language yellow pages list about three dozen Asian cram schools in the New York area. In Los Angeles, the Chinese yellow pages list about forty.

6   While the pressure to get into a good school is not nearly so extreme in the United States, the cram schools, such as the ambitiously named Nobel Education Institute in Arcadia, a heavily Asian suburb of Los Angeles, have nonetheless found a burgeoning* niche* in Asian communities. Chinese and Korean newspapers bulge with cram school advertisements. Some schools simply print lists of their graduates who have been accepted to New York

---

*Raymond Chandler (1888–1959): considered by many to be the finest mystery writer of all time; the creator of fictional detective Philip Marlowe.
*burgeoning: growing, flourishing.
*niche: corner, place.

City's specialized high schools, as well as to Harvard, Stanford, and MIT.

7   For many busy parents, the schools have become a kind of academic baby-sitting service. But most see them as a way of ensuring that their children excel in spite of the public schools that they perceive as lax* and unchallenging compared with those in Asia. (Ashley Dunn, "Cram Schools: Immigrants' Tools for Success," *New York Times*, January 28, 1995, p. 1.)

1. The author's primary purpose is

  a. to inform.

  b. to persuade.

2. The author's tone is

  a. admiring.

  b. critical.

  c. ironic.

  d. emotionally neutral.

5. What Is History?

1 In the United States, authors and publishers decide *what* will be included in a history textbook and *how* it will be presented. Then when the time comes to choose a particular book for middle and high school students, a school district's teachers and administrators are typically the only ones involved in the selection process. In Japan, however, the procedure is different. All history textbooks used there must be screened and approved by the Ministry of Education. Then each school must select and use one of the seven or eight textbooks on the list authorized by the government.

2   Japan's system of textbook selection has been in place since 1903. It is only during the last thirty years, though, that it has sparked any controversy. During this time, there have been repeated clashes over how to interpret Japan's role in World War II. The first skirmish in the battle took place in 1965 when the prominent historian Saburo Ienaga wrote a book that spoke openly about Japanese aggression and brutality during the Second World War. The book was promptly eliminated from the list of texts approved by the Ministry of Education, which claimed that Ienaga's book cited too many examples of Japan's "dark side" dur-

---

*lax: lacking in strictness or firmness.

ing the war. Outraged by what he perceived to be outright censorship, Ienaga filed a lawsuit claiming that the government's textbook approval process was unconstitutional and illegal.

3   Ultimately, Japan's Supreme Court voted to uphold the Ministry's right to screen and approve, or censor, textbooks; however, it requested that the government not tamper with a book's content. In 1982, the media devoted extensive coverage to another battle between Ienaga and the Ministry of Education when the government ordered the author to soften some of the wording in his book. For example, he was required to describe the Japanese army's invasion of China as an "advance into" China rather than an act of "aggression." The Chinese and Korean governments subsequently accused Japan of distorting wartime history. As a result, by the late 1990s, Ienaga and his supporters had succeeded in getting approval for history textbooks that included factual details about anti-Japanese resistance movements in Korea; forced suicides in Okinawa; and the Japanese Army's Unit 731, which conducted medical experiments on prisoners of war.

4   Many of Japan's conservatives, however, were outraged by textbook references to the country's "dark history." They claimed that such brutal descriptions of Japanese history only made Japanese schoolchildren anxious and uncomfortable. By early 2000, the Japanese Society for History Textbook Reform set out to "correct history" by writing *The New History Textbook,* which offered a "positive view" of Japan's past. Although this "corrected" history was placed on the government's approved list, it was immediately criticized for minimizing, even covering up historical facts. For example, it claimed that Japan's goal in starting wars was the liberation of Asia rather than colonialism.* The book understandably incited angry indignation from China and Korea. It even sparked one anti-Japan protest in Korea, because it did not deal frankly with the atrocities Japan had committed during World War II. In 2002, when *The New History Textbook* was made available for adoption, almost all Japan's school districts rejected it.

5   Although the subject of how best to approach the "dark" side of American history has come up in the past, the debate has never been as public, intense, and angry as it is currently in Japan. Still, scholars in the United States have suggested that Americans should learn from the Japanese debate because textbooks can have such a powerful influence on the perception of a history. As

---

*colonialism: one country's controlling of other countries in order to profit from them.

Frances FitzGerald has pointed out in *America Revised,* where kids are concerned, history textbooks report "the truth of things."

6   Children and teenagers frequently accept textbook information without questioning it and what they learn from those books shapes their beliefs and views, not just about their country but also about other countries as well. It's for precisely this reason that Japan's neighbors, some of whom have been invaded by its military, objected to the government's version of events. They were afraid that Japanese schoolchildren would grow up without a clear understanding of what Japan had done in the past, particularly during World War II.

7   The Japanese controversy and the positions it implies—a sanitized version of history versus one that admits past mistakes—could prove highly instructive for U.S. students, parents, and educators. All three groups need to seriously consider the versions of history that appear in middle and high school textbooks and look closely at the stories they tell. Do these historical narratives give students a full and detailed view of the United States's handling of domestic and international issues? Or, do they suggest that the United States has seldom, if ever, made mistakes in governing its people or in handling its international affairs? After all, history is not a factual list of dates and events. It is an interpretation of how and why events have unfolded in a particular way. (Source of information: Kathleen Woods Masalski, "Examining the Japanese History Textbook Controversies," *Japan Digest* (Indiana University), November 2001, www.indiana.edu/~japan/ Digests/textbook.html.)

1. The author's primary purpose is

   a. to inform.

   b. to persuade.

2. The author's tone is

   a. outraged.

   b. concerned.

   c. emotionally neutral.

   d. admiring.

Test 4: Taking Stock

DIRECTIONS Read each passage. Then answer the questions by circling the letter of the correct response(s) or filling in the blanks.

1. Fix Roads Now

1 [1]Far too many of America's roads and highways are a mess. [2]They are crumbling and marred by potholes, and many are simply inadequate for the huge number of vehicles that travel them every day. [3]As a result, unsafe driving conditions and congestion are costing lives. [4]Already, nearly 43,000 deaths occur on our roads every year. [5]If no improvements are made, that number is expected to rise to almost 52,000 per year by 2009.

2 [1]Poor road conditions and congestion are also costing Americans a good deal of money. [2]Highway deaths and injuries waste about $230 billion a year in medical expenses, lost wages, and travel delays. [3]Highway accidents are a major source of legal and insurance expenses. [4]Traffic jams slow the delivery of goods and services and often prevent people from getting to work on time. [5]It's been estimated that bad roads rob the U.S. economy of $70 billion per year.

3 [1]Unsafe roads also reduce our quality of life. [2]Accidents cause pain, suffering, and long-term disability. [3]Congested highways increase commute times and shorten time spent with our families. [4]Bumper-to-bumper traffic slows us down and increases our anxiety, contributing to tension and stress-related diseases. [5]And one thing Americans do not need is more stress. (Source of information: Kit Bond, "Roads Are a Good Investment," *USA Today,* February 18, 2004, p. A10.)

1. Which statement best sums up the main idea?

   a. America's roads and highways are ancient.

   b. America's highways are the cause of countless accidents and injuries.

   c. America's roadways need to be improved and repaired as quickly as possible.

   d. America's roads and highways are worse than those in other countries.

2. The author's main idea is

   a. stated.

   b. implied.

3. The author's primary purpose is

a. to inform.

b. to persuade.

4. Which type of transition opens sentence 3 in paragraph 1?

a. time order

b. cause and effect

c. comparison

d. contrast

5. How would you paraphrase the topic sentence in paragraph 2?

_____

_____

6. Which of the following sentences is a major detail?

a. And one thing Americans do not need is more stress.

b. Highway deaths and injuries waste about $230 billion a year in medical expenses, lost work, and travel delays.

7. What cycle of causes and effects does the author expect you to infer from the following sentence: "Bumper-to-bumper traffic slows us down and increases our anxiety, contributing to tension and stress-related diseases."

_____

_____

8. Which pattern or patterns organize this reading?

a. definition

b. time order

c. comparison and contrast

d. cause and effect

e. classification

9. How would you describe the author's tone?

a. humorous

b. sad

c. critical

d. objective

10. Which of these conclusions follows from the reading?

a. The author would applaud a federal program dedicated to highway repair.

b. The author believes that America's highways were poorly constructed when first built.

c. The author believes that America's highways cannot be repaired; they must be replaced.

d. The author would not support any federally funded program, even if it was devoted to improving the roadways.

2. And the Winner Is Google

1 [1]When searching the World Wide Web, computer users can choose from a number of different search engines, or tools for finding and compiling a list of relevant websites. [2]A few of the most popular search engines are Yahoo!, Lycos, Infoseek, AltaVista, and Google. [3]The most successful of these is Google, which now handles more queries than its rivals do—and for good reason. [4]Google has become the dominant search engine because it is more effective and efficient than any of the others.

2 [1]True, Google and the other search engines function in much the same way. [2]They all send "spiders" or "robots" out to crawl through cyberspace from link to link. [3]At each website, they gather information about what's there by indexing all the words. [4]Then when someone requests information on a topic by typing in keywords, search engines assemble a list based on the index they have created. [5]Google, however, is different from the others in one aspect. [6]As it assesses each website, it notes how many other Web pages provide links to those pages. [7]Then when it provides search results, Google presents them in rank order, with the most-linked-to ones at the top.

3 [1]Because of this special ranking feature, Google's results are more accurate and of higher quality than those of other search engines. [2]Search engines often return hundreds of thousands of responses for just one keyword or phrase. [3]Most search engines make no attempt, though, to sift through the results in order to identify what might be useless. [4]Unlike its rivals, Google is based on the democratic idea that the best sites are the ones linked to the most, which is generally correct. [5]Therefore, inherent* in what Google presents in response to a query is a consensus about

—————
*inherent: natural to.

which sites are truly worthwhile. [6]In Google's search results, "junk" is usually sifted to the bottom, leaving the most valuable sites at the top of the list.

4   [1]In addition to being more relevant and more useful, Google's results are also more comprehensive and arrive faster. [2]The size of its database,* unlike some compiled by other search engines, continues to expand. [3]In 2002, for example, it indexed the information of more than 3 billion Web pages, far more than any other search engine. [4]Studies show that Google consistently produces more search results than its competitors and also finds more unique hits—results found by it and it alone—than any of the others. [5]Plus, it's known for being lightning fast; searches typically take under 20 seconds to complete.

5   [1]For all these reasons, the amazing Google has rightly become the leader of the pack. [2]Its method is so superior that circa 2001, the verb *to google* entered the English language. [3]Clearly, no matter what information researchers seek, Google can help them find it. (Source of information: Joel Achenbach, "Search for Tomorrow," *The Washington Post*, February 15, 2004, p. D01.)

1. Which statement best sums up the main idea?

a. Currently, Google is considered the best search engine on the Web.

b. Among search engines, Google is highly favored by those who use the Web for serious research.

c. When you need to search the Web for information, you can use different search engines.

d. The World Wide Web offers an amazing wealth of information for researchers.

2. The author's main idea is

a. stated.

b. implied.

3. The author's primary purpose is

a. to inform.

b. to persuade.

4. Which pattern or patterns organize this reading?

a. definition

b. time order

*database: pool of information.

    c. comparison and contrast

    d. cause and effect

    e. classification

5. Which statement most effectively sums up the implied main idea of paragraph 2?

    a. Like other search engines, Google sends out "spiders" that crawl from site to site.

    b. Web search engines all work in a similar way.

    c. While it's true that search engines all work in pretty much the same way, Google has a key feature that the others do not.

    d. Unlike other search engines, Google uses "spiders" to crawl through cyberspace link by link; then it makes a list of the most popular sites.

6. Which statement most effectively paraphrases the topic sentence in paragraph 3?

    a. Like other search engines, Google uses just one or two keywords to return hundreds of thousands of responses.

    b. With a Google search, the best sites appear at the top of the list, whereas the least useful sites appear at the bottom.

    c. The ability to rank results makes Google a more effective search engine.

7. In paragraph 2, which type of transition opens sentence 5?

    a. cause and effect

    b. comparison

    c. contrast

    d. addition

8. Paragraph 4 includes two kinds of transition. They are

    a. addition and reversal

    b. time order and comparison

    c. addition and time order

9. How would you describe the author's tone?

    a. sarcastic

    b. admiring

c. angry

d. shocked

10. From this reading, you could correctly draw which conclusion?

a. People who use the Web for research want to get a list that includes as many different sites as possible.

b. People who use the Web for research do not want to sift through ten useless sites in an effort to find two good ones.

c. People who use the Web for research do not particularly care if a search engine is slow as long as it gives them good results.

d. None of the other search engines will ever be able to overtake Google in popularity.

C H A P T E R   9

Recognizing and Evaluating Bias

 In this chapter, you'll learn

- **how to spot bias in informative writing.**

- **how to determine the degree of bias in persuasive writing.**

- **how to evaluate bias in persuasive writing.**

Chapter 9 focuses on the subject of *bias*. You'll learn how a writer's personal feelings can find their way into informative writing despite his or her best efforts to remain emotionally uninvolved or objective. You'll also learn how to recognize when bias is clouding a writer's judgment or ability to be fair. When that happens, critical readers take note and reserve judgment until they can become better informed.

Bias and Context

The word *bias* has a bad reputation. We frequently use it to suggest that someone has a closed mind and cannot or will not listen to opposing points of view. But *bias* merely refers to a point of view or personal leaning. In other words, expressing a bias isn't necessarily bad.

Because of our background, experience, and training, most of us have personal opinions that influence how we see and interpret the world around us. Thus how critical readers respond to bias depends a good deal on context, on where that bias appears. It also depends on how strongly the bias is expressed.

For example, unless they are writing for the editorial page, newspaper reporters are expected to describe events as objectively as possible. If reporters describe events in highly connotative or emotionally charged language that reveals a personal point of view, they are doing readers a disservice. In other words, their biases are inappropriate in that context.

In contrast, newspaper editorials are supposed to express a personal bias. That's one of the reasons we read them. We want, for example, to get columnists Maureen Dowd's and Bob Herbert's perspectives on some current issue or event. However, even writers determined to persuade should offer readers a fair and reasonable argument. If a writer is so committed to one point of view that he or she cannot be logical or fair, then the degree of bias is excessive, and we need to be wary of accepting that writer's point of view without casting around for other opinions.

In sum, then, all writers have biases, and there's nothing wrong with revealing them in the appropriate context. What's important is that writers not let bias interfere with their ability to be logical and fair.

Recognizing Bias in Informative Writing

Writers whose primary goal is to inform rather than to persuade usually work hard to keep their biases to themselves. For example, the author of a modern American history textbook might be a long-time Republican who considers Democrat Lyndon Baines Johnson one of history's worst presidents. Yet in writing a chapter about Johnson's presidency, he should control his inclination to criticize

Johnson's record. Like writers of reference works, authors of text-books are expected to provide an impersonal and objective account of events and allow students to form their own opinions.

Pure Information Is Hard to Find

Writers are only human. Try as they might, they can't always eliminate every shred of personal bias from their writing. Although the overall tone of a passage may be emotionally neutral, the connotations of individual words or phrases can still suggest a personal bias or leaning. Note, for example, the italicized words in the following paragraph. These words have negative connotations and suggest that the authors do not admire the way former president Harry Truman handled foreign policy.

President Truman . . . had a personality that tended to increase international tensions. Whereas Roosevelt had been ingratiating,* patient, and evasive, Truman was *brash,* *impatient,* and direct. *He seldom displayed the appreciation of subtleties so essential to successful diplomacy.* In his first meeting with V. M. Molotov, the Soviet commissar of foreign affairs, Truman sharply *berated** the Soviet Union* for violating the Yalta accords,* a charge Molotov denied. When Truman *shot back* that the Soviets should honor their agreements, Molotov stormed out of the room. The president was pleased with his "tough method." "I gave it to him straight 'one-two to the jaw.'" This *simplistic display of toughness* became a trademark of American Cold War* diplomacy.* (Norton et al., *A People and a Nation,* p. 488.)

The authors of this textbook passage don't seem to be fans of Harry Truman. After all, would a fan refer to Truman's "simplistic display of toughness"? But what about the next passage? Do you think the writer is also a critic of Harry Truman? Or is he a fan?

On his first day in office, Harry Truman remarked to a newspaperman, "Did you ever have a bull or a load of hay fall on you?

---

*ingratiating: eager to please.
*brash: hasty and unthinking.
*berated: criticized harshly at length.
*Soviet Union: the former name of fifteen separate republics governed by the Communist party, also called "Soviet Russia."
*Yalta accords: agreements made at the end of World War II in the city of Yalta, located near the Black Sea.
*Cold War: a period of hostile rivalry between the United States and Communist Russia.
*diplomacy: the conduct of relations between nations by government officials.

If you ever did, you know how I felt last night." Yet President Truman's *native intelligence enabled him to grasp quickly the situation into which he was so suddenly thrown,* and on which he had not been briefed by Roosevelt. He had to have a few boon* companions from Missouri around the White House for relaxation, but *he won the friendship and respect of gentlemen in politics* such as Dean Acheson, soldiers such as General Marshall, and foreign statesmen such as Clement Attlee. He made good cabinet, judicial, and ambassadorial appointments; *he kept a firm hand* on the new Department of Defense and the foreign service; and, *with more fateful decisions than almost any president in our time, he made the fewest mistakes.* Truman was always folksy, always the politician, *but nobody can reasonably deny that he attained the stature of a statesman.* (Morison, *The Oxford History of the American People,* p. 1051.)

Unlike the authors of the first passage, the author of this paragraph admires Harry Truman and his record as president. As you can see, his choice of words encourages readers to do the same.

When they recognize bias in writing meant to inform, critical readers don't throw up their hands in horror and refuse to read further. Instead, they identify the author's particular leaning and make sure that they don't absorb it right along with the author's description of events or ideas.

What's Left Out *Is* Significant

Sometimes the intrusion of bias in informative writing is obvious in the author's choice of words. But bias can also be more subtle. Sometimes writers reveal bias not by what they say but by what they leave out. For instance, a history writer who records only the successful or praiseworthy actions of President Franklin Delano Roosevelt but leaves out Roosevelt's order to intern, or imprison, Japanese-Americans during World War II reveals a bias in favor of Roosevelt. Anytime an author describes a person or position where opposing points of view are possible without mentioning—or just barely acknowledging—the opposition, your critical antennae should go up. The writer's purpose may be informative, but you, the reader, are still not getting the whole story.

*boon: in this context, good-natured, jolly.

CHECK YOUR UNDERSTANDING

Explain why context is important to evaluating bias.

_____

_____

Rhetorical Questions Can Reveal a Hidden Bias

As you may know from composition class, rhetoric is the art of using language to persuade. Thus it probably comes as no surprise that **rhetorical questions**—questions that do not require or call for a reply—are a signal of both persuasive intent and personal bias. You can certainly expect rhetorical questions to turn up in persuasive writing, but they can also appear in writing that is meant to inform. They are a tip-off to the unexpected presence of bias. Here's an example.

> Given that more teenagers than ever before are grappling with problems such as depression, alcoholism, and drug abuse, desperate parents are looking for help. Many are turning to wilderness programs, which promise to change the attitude and behavior of the young people by exposing them to and training them for life in the outdoors. Most of these programs are in western states like Idaho and Utah. Some are on farms or in deserts. Almost all share the same premise—sustained exposure to a natural world where kids have to fend for themselves can provide troubled young boys and girls with new skills and increased self-confidence. Yet promising as these programs may sound, they raise a crucial question: Is the wilderness—with its inherent, overwhelming, and often uncontrollable dangers—really the place to heal the psyches of troubled children?

Up until the last sentence, this passage is mainly informative. The author describes the purpose, location, and theory behind wilderness programs. But in the final sentence, she uses a rhetorical question that reveals her bias. The question, with its emphasis on nature's dangers, is phrased in a way that ensures only one answer—a definite no. Because it doesn't really expect any answer except the one suggested, the rhetorical question reveals a persuasive purpose and personal bias not apparent in the other sentences.

When authors ask questions that don't require an answer, those questions are rhetorical, and you need to be aware of the bias such questions reveal.

Informative Writing Lacking in Bias

- employs an emotionally neutral tone throughout.
- describes both sides of an issue equally without evaluating or judging either side.
- includes no personal opinions or value judgments from the author.
- includes little or no connotative language.

Informative Writing That Reflects a Bias

- may use charged language that interrupts an emotionally neutral tone.
- gives an author's personal opinion.
- emphasizes either positive *or* negative views of a subject but doesn't give equal space to both sides.
- uses rhetorical questions.

EXERCISE 1

DIRECTIONS Each of the following passages comes from a source where one would expect the author to eliminate any evidence of bias. Read each one. Then circle the appropriate letters to indicate whether the author or authors have eliminated all evidence of bias.

EXAMPLE

Trial Elements

1 A trial is often compared to a boxing match. Both are contests between *adversaries,* persons who oppose or fight one another. In a trial, the adversaries are called **litigants** and, rather than hitting each other, they challenge each other's evidence and testimony. For this reason, an American trial is often labeled an **adversary proceeding.** The judge acts as a referee and interprets the rules of the "match."

2   The person who files suit in a civil case is called a **plaintiff.** In a criminal trial, the prosecution brings the charges. The United

States attorney is the prosecutor in federal cases. In state trials, the prosecutor may be known as the state's attorney, county prosecutor, or district attorney. The person being sued or charged with the crime is the **defendant.**

3   Every trial has two purposes: to establish the facts of the case and to find the law that applies. The role of the jury is to decide questions of fact. (Adapted from Hardy, *Government in America*, p. 502.)

Presence of Bias   a. The author is describing the elements of a trial and clearly favors our legal system.

b. The author is describing the elements of a trial and is clearly critical of our system.

c. It's impossible to determine the author's personal feelings.

> **EXPLANATION** Drawn from a textbook, this selection does not reveal any bias for or against our legal system. The language remains almost completely denotative, and there is no evidence whatsoever of the author's personal opinion.

1. The Presidency of John F. Kennedy

1 John F. Kennedy's ambitious social program, the New Frontier, promised more than Kennedy could deliver: an end to racial discrimination, federal aid to education, medical care for the elderly, and government action to halt the recession* the country was suffering. Only eight months into his first year, it was evident that Kennedy lacked the ability to move Congress, which was dominated by conservative Republicans and southern Democrats. Long-time members of Congress saw him and his administration as publicity hungry. Some feared the president would seek federal aid to parochial schools. The result was the defeat of federal aid to education and of a Kennedy-sponsored boost in the minimum wage.

2   Still struggling to appease conservative members of Congress, the new president pursued civil rights with a notable lack of vigor. Kennedy did establish the President's Committee on Equal Employment Opportunity to eliminate racial discrimination in government hiring. But he waited until late 1962 before honoring a 1960 campaign pledge to issue an executive order forbidding segregation in federally subsidized housing. Meanwhile, he appointed

---

*recession: economic downturn.

five die-hard segregationists to the federal bench in the Deep South. The struggle for racial equality was the most important domestic issue of the time, and Kennedy's performance disheartened* civil rights advocates. (Adapted from Norton et al., *A People and a Nation,* p. 991.)

Presence of Bias a. The authors are admirers of John F. Kennedy.

b. The authors are critical of John F. Kennedy.

c. It's impossible to determine the authors' personal feelings.

2. The Civil Rights Act of 1964

1 In 1961, a new administration, headed by President John F. Kennedy, came to power. At first Kennedy did not seem to be committed to civil rights. His stance changed as the movement gained momentum and as more and more whites became aware of the abuse being heaped on sit-in demonstrators, freedom riders (who tested unlawful segregation on interstate bus routes), and those who were trying to help blacks register to vote in southern states. Volunteers were being jailed, beaten, and killed for advocating activities among blacks that whites took for granted.

2 In late 1962, President Kennedy ordered federal troops to ensure the safety of James Meredith, the first black to attend the University of Mississippi. In early 1963, Kennedy enforced the desegregation of the University of Alabama. In April 1963, television viewers were shocked to see civil rights marchers in Birmingham, Alabama, attacked with dogs, fire hoses, and cattle prods. (The idea of the Birmingham march was to provoke confrontations with white officials in an effort to compel the national government to intervene on behalf of blacks.) Finally, in June 1963, Kennedy asked Congress for legislation that would outlaw segregation in public accommodations.

3 Two months later, Martin Luther King Jr. joined in a march on Washington, DC. The organizers called the protest "A March for Jobs and Freedom," signaling the economic goals of black America. More than 250,000 people, black and white, gathered peaceably at the Lincoln Memorial to hear King speak. "I have a dream," the great preacher extemporized,* "that my four little children will one day live in a nation where they will not be judged by the color of their skin but by the content of their character."

---

*disheartened: disappointed.
*extemporized: spoke without practice or preparation.

4   Congress had not yet enacted Kennedy's public accommodations bill when he was assassinated on November 22, 1963. His
successor, Lyndon B. Johnson, considered civil rights his top legislative priority. Within months, Congress enacted the Civil Rights
Act of 1964, which included a vital provision barring segregation
in most public accommodations. This congressional action was, in
part, a reaction to Kennedy's death. But it was also almost certainly a response to the brutal treatment of blacks throughout the
South. (Janda et al., *The Challenge of Democracy*, pp. 549–550.)

Presence of Bias   a. The authors are admirers of John F. Kennedy.

b. The authors are critical of John F. Kennedy.

c. It's impossible to determine the authors' personal feelings.

3. **Lowell, Robert** (1917–1977)   American poet from a famous
aristocratic American family; regarded by most critics as the best
English language poet of his generation and by certain readers as
beyond criticism altogether. For better or for worse, Lowell was the
modern poet-as-film-star: his private affairs were apparently
carried out mainly in public (this is miscalled "confessionalism"):
his themes included the personalities and behavior of his relatives, his various marriages and liaisons,* the (presumably) affective disorder* which landed him in hospital many times, and
so on. Lowell was extremely gifted but the conventional view
of his development, even where it judges the most recent poems
as failures, is not quite correct, for it mistakes potential for
achievement, and overrates him. (Adapted from Martin Seymour-
Smith, *Who's Who in Twentieth-Century Literature.* New York:
McGraw-Hill, 1976, p. 216.)

Presence of Bias   a. The author admires Robert Lowell.

b. The author is critical of Robert Lowell.

c. It's impossible to determine the author's personal feelings.

4. **The Animal Rights Movement**

1 Opposition to animal research has a long history, going back at
least as far as the antivivisectionist* movement of the nineteenth

---

*liaisons: love affairs.
*affective disorder: a disorder that involves extreme shifts in emotion, in Lowell's
case from great enthusiasm to deep depression.
*antivivisectionist: person opposed to the cutting of living animals for scientific
purposes.

century. In recent years the growth of the animal rights movement was spurred by a book called *Animal Liberation* (1975), by Australian philosopher Peter Singer. Singer argued that many uses of animals by humans—for food, for clothing, and as captive research subjects—reflected "speciesism": the exploitation of certain species (nonhuman animals) for the benefit of another (humans). Because animals, like humans, can feel pain, Singer argued, they are entitled to just as much consideration as humans are.

2   In Singer's view, speciesism is a form of discrimination that is just as evil as racism and sexism. "Would the experimenter be prepared to perform his experiment on a human infant?" Singer asks. "If not, then his readiness to use nonhumans is simple discrimination" (Singer, 1976, p. 156).

3   Many animal rights supporters have advanced their views in books and articles and have worked for laws and regulations that would ensure the humane treatment of animals. Others have resorted to acts of terrorism in the name of animal rights (Jasper & Nelkin, 1992). Some activists have invaded animal laboratories, destroyed equipment, stolen data, and let the animals out of their cages. Animal rights activists have also staged dramatic demonstrations . . . in an attempt to convince the public of what they see as the cruelty of animal research.

4   The animal rights movement has been accused by researchers of painting a distorted picture of animal research. In fact, most animal research is neither cruel nor painful, and the large majority of animal researchers are concerned about animal welfare (Novak, 1991). When researchers employ surgical procedures with animals, they almost always use anesthesia to eliminate pain. Many animal rights supporters acknowledge such humane practices but believe that animal research remains unnecessarily intrusive. But the moral fervor of other animal rights advocates has led them to engage in misleading portrayals of scientists as sadists and laboratories as torture chambers. (Rubin et al., *Psychology*, pp. 68–69.)

Presence of Bias   a. The authors support the animal rights movement.

b. The authors are critical of the animal rights movement.

c. It's impossible to determine the authors' personal feelings.

5. **Frida Kahlo**

1   The Mexican artist Frida Kahlo (1907–1954) was born Magdalena Carmen Frida Kahlo Calderónin Coyoacán. Although she began

her education intending to be a physician, she was forced to change her mind when she suffered a terrible accident at the age of eighteen. The accident left her so debilitated that a life devoted to medicine would have been far too strenuous for her to pursue.

2   While she was recovering from the accident, Kahlo began painting. In 1928, she approached famed muralist Diego Rivera (1886–1957) and asked for his opinion of her work. Rivera thought she had talent and encouraged her. One year later, the two were married. Their relationship, however, was stormy, and they were divorced in 1939, only to remarry the following year.

3   Kahlo's first public exhibition took place in 1938. In 1939, her work was exhibited in a Paris exhibition called "Mexique." As a result of the exhibition, one of her works, a self-portrait, was purchased for the famed French museum the Louvre. Although her problems with Rivera and her constant physical pain—her body had never completely recovered from the accident—encouraged Kahlo's growing dependency on alcohol, Kahlo continued to paint, further developing her brand of colorful, personalized surrealism.* However, she did not have a major exhibition in her own country until 1953, one year before her death. Overshadowed in her lifetime by her famous husband, Kahlo overtook him in death, so much so that her name has become better known than his. Yet in comparing the works of the two artists, a key question emerges. Does Kahlo's fame rest on the quality of her work or on the current tendency to celebrate women artists whatever their degree of talent? (Christopher Fresa, *Modern Painters.* Cleveland: Bogus Publications, 1999, p. 200.)

Presence of Bias a. The author admires Kahlo's work.

b. The author thinks Kahlo's work is overrated.

c. It's impossible to determine the author's bias.

 # Responding to Bias in Persuasive Writing

We don't expect to find bias in informative writing, and encountering it usually comes as a surprise. Persuasive writing, in contrast, raises different expectations. We expect writers to be personally engaged—to tell us about the personal reasons, experiences, or feel-

---

*surrealism: a movement in art and literature emphasizing the expression of the imagination as it might appear in dreams, with the emphasis on free association rather than logic and reason.

ings that led them to their points of view. In short, we expect persuasive writing to reveal a bias. What we don't expect, even in persuasive writing, is that writers are imprisoned or blinded by their biases. Despite their personal feelings, we expect them to acknowledge opposing points of view and to treat those points of view fairly. A writer who fails to acknowledge opposing points of view or, even worse, ridicules or insults them should not be completely trusted. Yes, the writer may sound confident and convincing, but critical readers are not impressed. They don't assume that a confident tone is always based on solid evidence, and they demand to know a bit more before deciding to support or share the writer's point of view.

Acceptable Versus Unacceptable Bias

To understand the difference between acceptable and excessive or unacceptable bias in persuasive writing, compare the following passages.

> After reading about courses teaching television literacy,* I must say I am appalled by the sheer idiocy that abounds on so many college campuses today. What should instructors do if they discover that students have trouble reading their textbooks because they have spent too much time watching television? What else? Give those same students more television to watch. That way, teachers can avoid making demands on students *and* avoid doing their job. All they need to do is flip on the television set and call themselves "media specialists."

The author of this passage expresses a strong bias against courses in television literacy. But the problem with the passage is not the author's bias. The problem is that the author doesn't explain or defend those feelings. Instead, in a tone of outraged irony, he ridicules the opposing point of view. In this case, the author's bias interferes with his ability to treat fairly those who hold an opposing point of view. This degree of bias is unacceptable. It is so excessive it interferes with the writer's ability to persuade.

To see how an author can express a bias and still be persuasive, read the following passage. Although the author freely admits her bias, she still keeps an open mind and points out not just what's wrong about opposing points of view, but what's right as well.

---

*television literacy: the condition of being educated or knowledgeable on the subject of television.

I must admit to being troubled by courses that make commercials and soap operas the focus of study. Although I agree that TV programming plays a powerful role in most people's lives and that its influence over our minds and imaginations should be critically examined, I'm not sure courses in television literacy are the answer. A better alternative would be to make television viewing a small portion of a course on critical reading and thinking. Then students could apply their critical skills to both television scripts and images. This approach would eliminate what seems to be a legitimate objection to courses in television literacy—that they encourage students to do more of what they already do: Watch too much TV.

In this passage, the author expresses a definite bias: She is not in favor of courses "that make commercials and soap operas the focus of study." Still, that bias does not prevent her from giving the opposing point of view its due. She admits that the influence of television "should be critically examined," and she suggests an alternative to courses in television literacy: critical thinking or reading courses that would allot a small portion of time to analyzing scripts and images.

To evaluate bias in persuasive writing, look over the following list. Anytime you encounter a writer intent on persuasion, make sure you can say no to these five questions.

Questions to Help Evaluate Bias in Persuasive Writing

1. Does the author use a tone that drips with sarcasm or seethes with anger?

2. Does the author insist that an opposing point of view is not possible for sane people? (For *sane*, you can also substitute words like *patriotic, honest,* and *ethical*.)

3. Does the author rely more on insulting the opposition than on explaining the merits of his or her point of view?

4. Does the author insist that opposing points of view have no value or merit *without* explaining why those opposing views are mistaken or inaccurate?

5. Does the author make use of circular reasoning or irrelevant facts? (See Chapter 7.)

If you answer yes to even one of the five questions, you need to find a more balanced discussion of the issue at hand before taking sides.

CHECK YOUR UNDERSTANDING

Explain the difference between acceptable and excessive bias.

_____

_____

EXERCISE 2

DIRECTIONS Each of the two selections expresses a bias, but only one expresses such a strong bias that critical readers might be suspicious of the author's ability to fairly evaluate opposing points of view. Put a check (✓) in the blank if you think the author is biased but fair. Put a *B* in the blank if you think the author is too biased to be fair toward opposing points of view.

1. Jefferson's Bible

1 While serving as third president of the United States, Thomas Jefferson began a project to revise the Bible. Jefferson studied the Scriptures every day and selected what he considered to be the Bible's best and most authentic material. Concentrating on the New Testament—specifically the Gospels of Matthew, Mark, and Luke—Jefferson literally cut out his favorite passages (which he said were like "diamonds in a dunghill") with a razor and pasted them together to create his own version. In doing so, he censored out any mention of Jesus as God or the Son of God. He also eliminated all miracles and supernatural events.

2 For example, his version does not include any reference to the immaculate conception* of Jesus by Mary, the miracles attributed to Jesus, or the Resurrection. Jefferson's version ends with Jesus's burial. Jefferson told one correspondent that the material he discarded was all "ignorance . . ., superstitions, fanaticism, and fabrications." The material he chose is mainly composed of parables

_____

*immaculate conception: According to the Bible, the Virgin Mary conceived without the stain of original sin.

and sayings that focus on the morals and ethics Jesus preached and demonstrated. According to one scholar, Jefferson "made a Socrates out of Jesus."

3   Jefferson never intended for anyone to see this new version. However, it was discovered in 1886 and published by the Government Printing Office from 1904 to 1957. The book was distributed to all new congressional members during that time. In 2001, the book was reissued by Beacon Press as *The Jefferson Bible: The Life and Morals of Jesus of Nazareth.* Since its publication, some scholars and religious leaders have denounced Thomas Jefferson's revision of the New Testament as "sheer audacity." These critics object to Jefferson's project of cutting and pasting together what he considered to be the best and most authentic passages of Scripture. They say his tampering with a sacred work mocks the Christian faith.

4   Although understandable, this criticism of Jefferson is not really fair. Jefferson did not rewrite the Bible; he merely selected those passages that were, to him, most meaningful. What Jefferson did was no different from highlighting, underlining, or annotating the Bible to mark favorite passages, something many Christians have done for years in their personal copies. Furthermore, Jefferson did not intend for his version of the Bible to be published. He intended to keep it to himself for private study and reflection. Remember it was discovered and printed only after his death.

5   The point is that Jefferson did not try to convince anyone else to accept his personal beliefs. Throughout his career Jefferson fought for religious freedom for all Americans, and we still possess this freedom today. Therefore, it's not fair to attack Jefferson for exercising the same right we enjoy. On the contrary, we should view his version of the Bible as an important historical document, one that helps us better understand this very important and influential founding father.

———

2. Hunters Are Wildlife's Best Friends

1   I am a hunter. I feed my family with the game I kill. All Americans eat dead stuff, but our meat is better, and it is harvested with a responsible connection to the Earth. This is true conservation—the wise use.

2   Our time-honored tradition continues because, in the face of global habitat destruction, those of us who cherish wildlife have

demanded restrictions on its harvest, based on a sound and proven scientific equation of sustained-yield management.

3   We save and guard habitat and manage wildlife not for our freezers or shooting opportunities but rather for the future of this most valuable resource. The condition of wildlife and the ground that supports it are a barometer by which the quality of our lives is based.

4   Read this very carefully, because these game laws and restrictions are self-imposed, insisted on, policed and financed by us hunters to the tune of billions of dollars a year.

5   The lies of the animal rights freaks are perpetrated for the single cause of greed. They are to animals what Jim Bakker* was to religion. After deceiving millions of Americans out of millions of dollars, they have yet to save any animals.

6   Look closely at their shameful agenda and track record. These zealots* hate Americans who eat turkey on Thanksgiving. They are also extremely dangerous, having bombed medical testing labs, destroyed family-run farms, and even been convicted of animal abuse on occasion, grandstanding their lies at the expense of real animals' welfare. They recently committed their most repulsive act yet when one group proclaimed that the heinous crimes charged to accused mass murderer Jeffrey Dahmer were the exact same crimes as the preparation of a chicken for the grill. No clear-thinking American could possibly stand behind such statements.

7   If you truly appreciate wild animals, these people must be stopped and hunters' dedicated efforts must be supported. Sure, we have bad guys. But those who conduct legal banking businesses should never be lumped together with bank robbers. Poachers are the bad guys, and hunters despise them as our number one enemy.

8   When responsible citizens are genuinely concerned about the well-being and future of wildlife, they do their homework and discover the truth. Our Ted Nugent World Bowhunters organization is dedicated to this truth and to sharing the wonderment of the great out-of-doors with our families and friends. (Ted Nugent, "Hunters Are Wildlife's Best Friends," *USA Today,* October 3, 1991.)

----

*Jim Bakker: a television evangelist who served time in prison for improper use of funds collected for religious purposes.
*zealots: people so committed to a cause they lack all reason or compassion.

Bias and Careless Thinking

Writers whose bias keeps them from considering opposing points of view are inclined to use circular reasoning and irrelevant facts (see pages 368–371). They don't do this because they're dishonest. They are just so certain of their own rightness they don't always think about convincing others. Sure that they—and only they—are right, they fail to thoroughly explain their positions.

In addition to using circular reasoning and irrelevant facts, writers blinded by bias also tend to engage in two other kinds of careless thinking—*slippery slope* and *personal attack*.

Slippery Slope

Writers who engage in *slippery slope* thinking insist that taking even one step in a particular direction will invariably lead to another series of steps that will end in disaster. Here's an example:

> If we ban handguns, the next step will be the banning of rifles, and then people who hunt for food will no longer be able to feed their families.

Writers who use slippery slope thinking assume that events similar in nature follow one another without reference to any specific context or condition. They ignore the fact that events usually arise in response to or as a result of particular circumstances. For example, many people want to ban handguns because statistics show a connection between handguns in the home and violent crime, both in and outside the home. That same connection does not exist between hunting rifles and crime. Thus it makes no sense to claim that banning handguns will automatically lead to banning rifles. Handguns and rifles are similar kinds of weapons, but they are used in very different ways and under very different circumstances.

Personal Attacks

Be wary of writers who respond to opposing points of view by personally attacking the opposition. In the following passage, note how the author attacks her opponent's character rather than his point of view.

Once again, David DeGrecco, columnist for the *New Jersey Sun,* has presented his tired old case for gun control. As usual, DeGrecco serves up the argument that gun control laws can help eliminate some of the violence plaguing city streets across the country. Outspoken as usual, DeGrecco is curiously silent about his recent bout with criminal behavior. Less than two weeks ago, he and several others were arrested for demonstrating at the opening of a nuclear power plant. For one so determined to bring law and order to our streets, DeGrecco does not seem to mind breaking a few laws himself.

Here the author is obviously biased against the gun control laws championed by David DeGrecco. That's certainly her right. Still, to be persuasive, she needs to challenge what the columnist claims— that gun control laws can help eliminate violence. But instead of doing that, she attacks the man personally, pointing out that he was recently jailed. Yet DeGrecco's position on nuclear power has nothing to do with the issue at hand—gun control. This, then, is another instance of bias clouding the writer's ability to respond fairly and respectfully to opposing points of view.

EXERCISE 3

DIRECTIONS Each of the following readings expresses a strong bias for or against a particular position. But in some cases the author has fallen victim to the two errors in reasoning described above. Identify those errors by putting an *S* (for slippery slope) or a *P* (for personal attack) in the blank. If the passage does not contain either error, put a check (✓) in the blank.

1. No Sexual Harassment Equals No Soldiers

1 Over the years, there's been a good deal of attention focused on sexual harassment in the military, and rightly so. No one wants to see officers in charge of young female recruits abuse their power by sexually harassing those in their care. However, supporters of women in the military are making a crucial mistake when they try to eliminate sexism in the military and at the same time insist that women should go into combat right alongside men.

2 To be a warrior means that a soldier has to revert to a more primitive mode of behavior and thought. It means that one has to assume a kill-or-be-killed mentality that allows little room for compassion or thought. It is very difficult, perhaps impossible, to encourage this mindset in men and at the same time expect them

to fight side by side with women without reverting to a more primitive mode of behavior. As Fred C. Ikle, an undersecretary of
defense in the Reagan administration, expressed it, "You can't cultivate the necessary commitment to physical violence and fully
protect against the risk of harassment. Military life may . . . foster
the attitudes that tend toward rape, such as aggression and
single-minded assertion."[1]

3   Viewed from this perspective, efforts to eliminate sexual harassment could have disastrous consequences during wartime, particularly if women are allowed into combat. Committed to being
respectful toward women, male soldiers will also feel that they
must rein in their aggression in the presence of women. As a
result, they will hold back during combat training and eventually
during combat itself. Our country will lose its military strength
and its position as a world power.

-----

2. Egg Donation May Not Be Such a Miracle for Donors

1   Because so many couples desperately want a child and can't have
one, the search for women willing to donate their eggs for in vitro
fertilization* has become a big business. Although many people
consider in vitro fertilization a wondrous miracle, I must admit to
being skeptical about the use of egg donors. The couple who gains
a child, thanks to a donor, may be rightly jubilant; the donor,
however, may be taking more risks than she realizes.

2   For starters, the egg donation process is not particularly pleasant. To prepare, women take daily hormone injections which force
the maturation of ten to twenty eggs instead of the normal one or
two. As a result of the injections, donors often suffer cramping
and mood swings. Sometimes their ovaries become dangerously
enlarged. At this time, there have been no signs of long-term side
effects on donors, but it is possible that the injections may increase the possibility of ovarian cancer. No one really knows for
sure what the long-term effects are mainly because in vitro fertilization hasn't been around for very long.

3   Those who favor the use of egg donors argue that the women
are being well paid for the risks they take. Unfortunately, the
issue of payment only points to another objection. Clinics and
hospitals pay donors as much as $5,000 for their eggs. In the face

-----

[1]Richard Rayner, "The Warrior Besieged," *New York Times,* June 22, 1997, p. 29.
*in vitro fertilization: *in vitro* literally means "in glass": the term refers to the
process of creating life in an artificial setting outside the human body.

of such a sum, women who are young or poor—or in many cases both—can be lured by the money into ignoring the risks. As Diana Aronson, the executive director of Resolve, the national support group for infertile couples, points out: Large sums of money offered donors can lead to "inappropriate assessment of risk. If you're a college student, four cycles at $5,000 each may pay for . . . college"[2] and if you're a poor, unmarried mother, $5,000 will pay the rent for months.

4   Yes, egg donation may well provide infertile couples with the baby they so desperately desire, but someone else may be paying a terrible price for their joy. Couples desiring to use egg donation should ask themselves whether they are willing to let another human being take serious health risks so that they can become parents.

———

3. **Attica Still Haunts Us**

1 The worst prison insurrection in U.S. history occurred at the Attica Correctional Facility near Buffalo, New York, in September 1971. The atmosphere at the prison had been tense due to overcrowded and deteriorating conditions. Then, on September 9, a guard broke up a scuffle between two inmates, who were put into isolation cells as a result. A rumor that the inmates were being tortured spread throughout the facility. The next day, a group of inmates armed with baseball bats, pipes, chairs, and knives seized control of an exercise yard and took forty guards hostage. They demanded, among other things, better conditions and am-nesty for crimes committed during the revolt. They also insisted that New York's governor, Nelson Rockefeller, come to the prison to address the problem. Governor Rockefeller refused. Three days after the riot began, he authorized state police to regain control of the facility by force if necessary.

2   On September 13, police armed with tear gas and shotguns stormed the prison, firing more than 2,000 rounds of ammuni-tion in six minutes. Eleven hostages and thirty-two inmates were killed as a direct result of the police attack, although ini-tially it was thought that the deaths were a result of prisoners' violence. When the prison's guards were again in control, they stripped, beat, and tortured inmates. They were especially bru-tal with the riot's leaders. In the first hours after regaining

———

[2]Marie McCullough, "Life for Sale: Market for Women's Eggs Is Heating Up," *Philadelphia Inquirer,* March 8, 1998, pp. A1 and A19.

control of the prison, police also denied medical care to the wounded. As a result, in 1974, lawyers filed a class-action lawsuit on behalf of the 1,280 prisoners who were harassed during the attack.

3   But it wasn't until August of 2000 that the State of New York finally settled the suit filed on behalf of the 1,280 prisoners incarcerated at the Attica Correctional Facility during the riot. Those men still alive received a group settlement of $8 million for the suffering they endured as a result of the prison insurrection. And make no mistake, they deserve every penny of that settlement and a good deal more. Prior to the revolt, inmates had endured appallingly inhumane conditions at the facility. They had been permitted a shower just once a week and given a roll of toilet paper just once a month. Their food was poor in quality and badly prepared. Requests for meals reflecting religious preferences were routinely denied. Because the prison's capacity had been exceeded by more than 40 percent, prisoners were also subjected to terrible overcrowding. When the inmates finally seized control of an exercise yard and took the guards hostage, Nelson Rockefeller flatly refused to address what were very legitimate grievances. Determined to present himself as tough on crime and criminals, Rockefeller ordered a poorly executed assault on the prison, which left more than forty people dead.

4   Given the circumstances, it's hard to understand critics who claim the Attica settlement was unjust. Clearly, those opposing the $8 million award for damages have no compassion for prisoners, who apparently don't deserve to be treated like human beings. For critics of the Attica award, there is no such thing as rehabilitation in prison. Their motto is: "Lock 'em up and throw away the key."

———

4. Same-Sex Schools: Are They Really a Step Forward for Girls?

1   On March 2, 2004, the Bush administration announced plans to relax restrictions on single-sex public schools and classrooms. The announcement came after almost thirty years of determined efforts by the federal government to enforce coeducation in public schools. Thanks to new regulations drafted by the U.S. Department of Education, it will be much easier to establish and maintain single-sex schools at taxpayers' expense.

2   This move on Washington's part will undoubtedly delight those who have been insisting, for more than a decade, that girls in par-

ticular would do better in school if boys were not present. The movement in favor of single-sex education for girls started in 1992 when the American Association of University Women published the report "How Schools Shortchange Girls." As the title indicates, the study strongly suggested that public schools do not do enough to ensure that boys and girls get equal treatment. Much was made of the fact that, according to the study at least, teachers tend to call on boys more often than girls. For those educators convinced by this lone study, easing the restrictions on single-sex schools is an undisguised blessing.

3   However, there are at least two good reasons why single-sex schools, particularly for girls, are anything but a blessing. As Feminist Majority Foundation president Eleanor Smeal points out, the loosening of restrictions on single-sex schools offers no special benefit to girls. Like other feminists, Smeal believes that separating students by gender encourages sexism among boys and does not adequately prepare girls for jobs in integrated workplaces.

4   When it comes to preparation for the future, Smeal is 100 percent correct in her criticism. Girls need to have boys in the classroom. If they don't learn how to work and to compete with boys while in school, where the stakes aren't so high, how will they compete after graduation in the workplace? Imagine, for example, that a young woman, who has never been in intellectual competition with men, enters a management meeting where only men are present. Is she going to be able to hold her own, or is she going to become anxious and tongue-tied because her male colleagues don't use a "nurturing" style, purportedly employed more by women than by men?

5   Then, too, where does this isolation by gender end? Can we expect women who have gone to single-sex schools to demand that places of employment also be segregated? Probably. Once we agree that women should study only with one another, a segregated workplace can't be far behind.

CHECK YOUR UNDERSTANDING

Explain the errors in logic described in Chapter 9: slippery slope thinking and personal attacks.

_____

_____

■ **DIGGING DEEPER**

LOOKING AHEAD The authors of the passages on pages 455–456 questioned the value of making television the subject of serious study. The author of this next selection, however, clearly thinks that television talk shows merit serious attention. Although talk shows may give ordinary people a chance at the fifteen minutes of fame artist Andy Warhol claimed everyone gets sooner or later, that fame can sometimes come at a price.

THE ETHICS OF TELEVISION TALK SHOWS

1   Television talk shows differ in significant ways from radio talk shows. The most important difference is that television talk shows have a visual component that is lacking in radio. The television shows are usually taped before a live audience, members of which are often allowed to participate in the program. After the program's guests are presented on stage and after their problems are exposed or their stories told, the program host often seizes a microphone and gallops into the audience. Individuals are singled out here and there for their comments about what they have just seen and heard. Two key ethical issues raised by these talk shows are *content* and *procedures*.

Content

2   Geraldo Rivera, Sally Jessy Raphael, Montel Williams, Rikki Lake, Maury Povich, Jenny Jones, and Jerry Springer are among those who have [or had] television talk shows available via syndication in almost every major market. Among the topics discussed on these programs on a typical autumn Friday in 1997 were the following: gossip, plastic-surgery woes, crime stories on television news, hair makeovers, and paternity tests. As long as the gossip isn't malicious, an ethicist could not find much to strenuously object to in this collection of programs. However, on Tuesday of the following week, the overall nature of the programs' content had changed. Viewers were able to tune in programs on serial killers, drugs, former lovers, a sex survey, erotomania, dangerous teens, unfulfilled wishes, and lovers. Talk show critics argue that this latter list of program topics more accurately reflects the overall nature of these programs.

3   As is the case with radio talk shows, the television "talk culture is spectacularly ill-suited to dealing with complicated subjects." Therefore, "the plot is always the same. People with

problems—'husband says she looks like a cow,' 'pressured to lose her virginity or else,' 'mate wants more sex than I do,' 'boy crazy,' 'dresses like a tramp'"—are subjected to relentless preaching by the host and the studio audience." With few exceptions, the guests are often poor and have little education. The subjects under discussion are often lurid,* if not bizarre. Some critics feel that this sort of public humiliation of guests borders on class exploitation and has important ethical implications. Should these programs be capitalizing on people who are "so needy—of social support, of education, of material resources and self-esteem—that they mistake being the center of attention for being actually loved and respected?" Rousseau's* philosophy advocates treating others with compassion and seeking to promote harmony among all those involved. Do television talk shows of the sort described promote that goal?

4   As theater, these talk shows are fairly entertaining, but as serious program material—and they are taken seriously by many viewers—they fail to provide much positive benefit to either participants or audience. Although television talk show guests have more on-air time than radio call-in participants, there is still precious little time to present a problem in its full context before advice is shouted to the guests by audience members, all of whom are strangers and none of whom is a qualified advice giver. On television talk shows, on-stage guests do get Andy Warhol's 15 minutes of fame,* but selected audience members get only about 15 seconds. What positive outcomes can result from such exchanges?

5   A Pennsylvania State University researcher who studied daytime talk shows concluded that they "do more harm than good." Most of these shows "are simply mouthing mantras* of pop-therapy. . . . Strangers get to give advice without being responsible for its effect. The central distortion that these shows propound is that they give useful therapy to guests and useful advice to the audience." St. Thomas Aquinas* reminds us that the best actions are those guided by prudence,* justice, temperance,* and courage. Can any of these virtues be said to be at work on television talk shows?

---

*lurid: marked by sensationalism.
*Jean-Jacques Rousseau (1712–1778): French philosopher who believed that humanity, although basically good, was corrupted by society.
*15 minutes of fame: pop artist Andy Warhol (1928–1987) claimed that everyone gets fifteen minutes of fame, suggesting that fame is both fleeting and superficial.
*mantras: commonly repeated words or phrases used in meditation practice.
*St. Thomas Aquinas (1225–1274): Italian philosopher and theologian whose teachings combined reason and faith.
*prudence: good judgment.
*temperance: moderation.

6   The content of these television talk shows, then, is an important ethical issue. Why must private lives be made public? Of
what use are these programs to participants if no sound, reasonable, problem solution is offered them? Why are commercial
breaks inserted at precisely the moment someone in the audience
begins to question the whole process or takes the issue in a direction not approved of by the host? It is not difficult to see how "the
national conversation has been coarsened, cheapened, reduced to
name-calling and finger-pointing, and bumper-sticker sloganeer-
ing" by television talk shows.

Procedures

7 If the content of television talk shows were not troubling enough,
the way some of these shows "ambush" their guests raises additional ethical concerns. A 1995 study by the Kaiser Family Foundation found that "America's television talk show hosts score an
average of sixteen 'ambush disclosures' an hour on guests. . . .
Often guests have little or no control about the disclosure." The
study analyzed 200 videotapes of daytime talk shows and found
what most already know: "Hosts and guests talk mostly about
family, personal relationships, and sex." The study found that
"the most common disclosures per hour were: five of a sexual
nature, four about a personal attribute such as addiction, three
about abuse, two about an embarrassing situation, and two about
criminal activity."

8   Ambush disclosures can sometimes have decidedly negative
consequences. One legendary talk show moment featured a brawl
between white skinheads and the black civil rights activist Roy
Innis. On another show, this one about domestic violence, chairs
were thrown, and the host, Geraldo Rivera, suffered a broken
nose. Another famous talk show moment came when a male
guest on the *Jenny Jones Show* was told he would meet a secret
admirer. The guest "was humiliated when the admirer turned out
to be a homosexual man. The guest was charged with murdering
the admirer [three days after] the taping."

9   Clearly, the "ambush" nature of these programs raises serious
ethical concerns. Lawrence Kohlberg's moral development philosophy notes that the most mature level of ethical decision making is
one where all involved are treated with dignity and are recognized
as having certain rights, especially when actions involve them as
individuals and concern personal matters. Do television talk
shows operate on Kohlberg's highest level of ethical decision making? Is the dignity of each guest respected? Are guests properly
informed about what might happen on the show?

10   For his part, Geraldo Rivera took steps in early 1998 to clean up his journalistic image. After eleven seasons of serving up "daily dosages of urban blight and occasional fisticuffs," the *Geraldo Rivera Show* was scheduled to leave the air. Rivera struck a deal with NBC that was reportedly worth $40 million. He planned to return to the mainstream of network news, but, as of early 1999, had not done so. Before his syndicated talk show, he spent some time as a journalist with ABC News, but was fired in 1985.

11   Jenny Jones remained unrepentant. In her autobiography, *Jenny Jones, My Story,* published in 1997, she was unapologetic for her syndicated talk show, "a favored target of critics, part of the . . . trash TV trend where family feuds, makeovers . . . dominate daytime." Jones says her detractors "never want to write about how the show, and she personally, helps many people." Critics often take an elitist view of her show, she says, noting that she does not exploit her guests or look down on them. "They're the same people I run into when I go shop at Kmart, which I do," she says. (Leslie, *Mass Communication Ethics,* pp. 263–266.)

Sharpening Your Skills

DIRECTIONS Answer the following questions by filling in the blanks or circling the letter of the correct response.

1. Which statement best expresses the main idea of the entire reading?
   a. Television talk shows differ from radio talk shows.
   b. Television has a visual component lacking in radio.
   c. The content and procedures of television talk shows raise some crucial ethical issues.
   d. Television talk shows exploit people who lack money and education.

2. The author does not specifically define "ambush disclosures." However, you can infer a definition. Write that definition below.

   _____

   _____

3. According to the author, which of the following is *not* one of the ethical issues raised by television talk shows?
   a. Television talk shows exploit people who are poor and lacking in education.

b. Television talk shows only pretend to solve serious and complicated problems.

c. Television talk shows insult the intelligence of viewers.

d. The "ambush" methods of television talk shows can have violent consequences.

4. The author alludes, or refers, to the ideas of two famous philosophers, Jean-Jacques Rousseau and St. Thomas Aquinas. What is the purpose of these references?

a. To show how television talk shows do not fulfill the teachings of these philosophers.

b. To show how television talk shows fulfill the teachings of these philosophers.

c. To show the superiority of radio talk show hosts when it comes to commonsense solutions to life's problems.

d. To illustrate how the world has changed since these philosophers were alive.

5. Which of the following is *not* a rhetorical question?

a. What positive outcomes can result from such exchanges? (paragraph 4)

b. Can any of these virtues be said to be at work on television talk shows? (paragraph 5)

c. Why must private lives be made public? (paragraph 6)

6. How do you think the author feels about former talk show host Geraldo Rivera?

_____

_____

7. In her autobiography, Jenny Jones mentions that she shops at Kmart. What conclusion does she want readers to draw from that piece of information?

_____

8. How would you describe the author's tone?

a. neutral

b. heated

c. light-hearted

d. skeptical

9. Which statement more effectively describes the author's bias?

   a. The author is in favor of television talk shows because they put the spotlight on people whose lives are often ignored.

   b. The author is very critical of television talk shows.

   c. It's impossible to determine the author's bias.

10. What do you think is the author's purpose?

   a. to inform

   b. to persuade

Explain the basis for your answer.

_____

_____

_____

_____

WORD NOTES: BERATING SYNONYMS

On page 446, you learned the meaning of the word *berate*—to criticize harshly and at length. This is yet another word with some useful synonyms that should be added to your vocabulary.

1. **Upbraid:** to criticize or reproach with good reason, as in "The court *upbraided* her for fleeing the country after she had been allowed to go free on bail."

2. **Revile:** to criticize or reproach using abusive language, as in "Those who had collaborated with the Nazis were *reviled* by their neighbors after the war ended."

3. **Rail:** to criticize or reproach with language that is harsh but not necessarily abusive, as in "It does not pay to *rail* at one's fate; a better strategy is to do something that will change it."

4. **Vituperate:** to criticize with abusive language. *Note:* The word *vituperate* appears more frequently as a noun or an adjective than a verb, as in (1) "The king was not touched by the *vituperation* heaped on him by his hungry subjects";

and (2) "In arguments, she tends to use the kind of *vituperative* language that only makes matters worse."

Pay attention to the subtle differences among these four words as you use them to fill in the blanks. *Note:* You will have to change the endings.

1. The young mother _____ her tiny daughter for running into the street.

2. There's really no point in _____ at the Internal Revenue Service. Taxes are like death; they are simply part of life.

3. When his neighbors found out he had been a member of the Ku Klux Klan, he was _____ for it.

4. The level of _____ in his speech was terrifying; it was hard to believe that one human being could be filled with so much hate.

Now it's your turn to use the words in sentences.

1. upbraid: _____

_____

2. revile: _____

_____

3. rail: _____

_____

4. vituperation: _____

_____

To get more practice recognizing and evaluating bias, go to **laflemm.com** and click on "Reading for Thinking: Online Practice." Complete and correct Practices 9–12.

Test 1: Reviewing the Key Points

DIRECTIONS Answer the following questions by filling in the blanks or circling the correct response.

1. *True* or *False*. Writers whose primary purpose is to inform never allow themselves to reveal a personal bias or leaning.

2. Sometimes writers reveal bias not by what they say but by

   _____.

3. Bias in persuasive writing is bad or excessive when the writers are

   unable to _____.

4. *True* or *False*. There is no point in looking for evidence of bias in a textbook. Textbooks don't express a bias.

5. Rhetorical questions are _____.

6. If you spot one or more rhetorical questions in informative writing,

   there is a good chance that the author _____.

7. Which of the following statements does *not* describe informative writing?
   a. Informative writing uses mostly connotative language.
   b. Informative writing presents both sides of an issue.
   c. Informative writing avoids presenting the author's personal opinions on the subject.
   d. Informative writing doesn't often ask rhetorical questions.

8. Even writers who openly express a bias should not _____.

   They should still be able to _____ opposing points of view.

9. Writers who engage in slippery slope thinking insist that

   _____.

10. A writer who can't make a logical argument against an opposing point of view often attacks the _____ instead of the position.

> **To correct your test, turn to the answer key on page 644.**

Test 2: Recognizing Bias

DIRECTIONS Each of the following passages appears in a source where one would expect to find no evidence of bias. However, some of the passages do reveal a bias. Read each one. Then circle the appropriate letter to indicate what the passage does or does not reveal about the author's bias.

1. **Donoso, José (1924–1996)**   Born in Santiago, Chile, to a prominent family, José Donoso quit school at age nineteen and traveled in South America, where he worked on sheep farms and as a dockhand. Later, he went to school in the United States and received a B.A from Princeton University in 1951. Donoso spent the next decade working as a teacher and journalist in Chile, writing profusely. In 1955, Donoso published his first book, *Veraneo y otros cuentos* (*Summer Vacation and Other Stories*), which received the Municipal Literary Prize; one year later, he published *Dos cuentos* (1956; *Two Short Stories*), and in 1957 his first novel, *Coronación* (*Coronation*), appeared to much critical acclaim. *Coronación* describes the moral collapse of an aristocratic family, a recurrent theme in Donoso's work. Marrying Maria Pilar Serrano, a Bolivian painter, in 1961, Donoso began writing what is often considered his masterpiece, *El obsceno pájaro de la noche* (1970: *The Obscene Bird of Night*). He also renewed his friendship with Mexican novelist Carlos Fuentes, whom he had met in grade school. While spending some time at Fuentes's home, he completed *El lugar sin límites* (1966; *Hell Has No Limits*) and *Este Domingo* (1966; *This Sunday*), grim novels of psychological desolation and anguish. (Appiah and Gates, *The Dictionary of Global Culture*, p. 185.)

   a. The authors admire Donoso's work.

   b. The authors are critical of Donoso's work.

   c. It's impossible to determine the authors' personal feelings.

2. **Christoph Gottwald (1954–),**   German Novelist and Poet. Because he got his start writing mysteries popular with everyone but the critics, Gottwald's emergence as a serious novelist has been shamelessly ignored. Yet his 1997 novel *Endstation Palma*, reminiscent of Heinrich Böll's early work, is worthy of serious critical attention. Using themes he probed previously in novels like *Cologne Crackup* (1980) and *Lifelong Pizza* (1994), Gottwald

again explores the inability of language to communicate our deepest needs, often with tragic results. Abandoning the comic detachment he used so brilliantly in his first two books, the novelist now assumes the voice of a man passionately committed to his subject and tortured by the strength of his own emotions. A conservative voice in a literary world desperate to be trendy, Gottwald may not get the audience he deserves, either in Germany or America. However, his fiction—in contrast to the work of his more highly praised and less talented contemporaries—will be read by future generations, long after more acclaimed novelists have been properly consigned to the trashbin of history. (Wordsmith, *Twentieth Century Comparative Literature*, p. 20.)

a. The author admires Gottwald's work.

b. The author is critical of Gottwald's work.

c. It's impossible to determine the author's personal feelings.

3. **Litigation**

Though it is expensive and time-consuming, litigation can bring about remarkable political change. Perhaps the outstanding example is the use of the courts by the National Association for the Advancement of Colored People (NAACP) in the 1940s and 1950s. In a series of cases, culminating in the *Brown v. Board of Education* decision in 1954, NAACP lawyers argued and the Supreme Court affirmed that school segregation was illegal in the United States. Women's groups, consumer groups, environmental groups, religious groups, and others have followed the lead of the civil rights movement in taking their causes to the courts. Corporations and trade associations have also engaged in litigation. However, the high cost restrains many groups. One interest group, the Women's Equity League, was unable to appeal a court ruling against it in an important case because it could not afford the $40,000 necessary to pay for copies of the trial transcript. (Gitelson et al., *American Government*, p. 228.)

a. The authors are supporters of litigation as an instrument of social change.

b. The authors are critical of litigation as an instrument of social change.

c. It's impossible to determine the authors' personal feelings.

4. Sigmund Freud

1 Sigmund Freud (1885–1939), the father of psychoanalytic theory, grew up in a middle-class Jewish family in Vienna, Austria, where he spent most of his life. As a young man, Freud received a medical degree and opened a practice as a neurologist. Among his patients were many cases of *hysteria,* an emotional disorder characterized by physical symptoms such as twitches, paralysis, and even blindness without any discernible* physical basis. Freud's work with these patients gradually led him to conclude that repressed memories and wishes underlie emotional disorders and that personality involves a perpetual conflict among forces within ourselves.

2 Freud's early writings were denounced by other scientists. In his later years, however, Freud began to receive the recognition he deserved for his courageous exploration of the human mind. When the Nazis invaded Austria in 1938, Freud was persuaded to move to England. He died a year later. (Rubin et al., *Psychology,* p. 395.)

a. The authors admire the work of Sigmund Freud.

b. The authors are critical of Freud's work.

c. It's impossible to determine the authors' personal feelings about Freud's work.

5. Jewish Refugees from the Holocaust

By World War II's end, about six million Jews had been forced into concentration camps and had been systematically killed by firing squads, unspeakable tortures, and gas chambers. The Nazis also exterminated as many as 250,000 gypsies and about 60,000 gay men. During the depression, the United States and other nations had refused to relax their immigration restrictions to save Jews fleeing persecution. The American Federation of Labor and Senator William Borah of Idaho, among others, argued that new immigrants would compete with American workers for scarce jobs, and public opinion polls supported their position. This fear of economic competition was fed by anti-Semitism. Bureaucrats applied the rules so strictly—requiring legal documents that fleeing Jews could not possibly provide—that otherwise-qualified refugees were kept out of the country. From 1933 to 1945, less than 40 percent

*discernible: visible to the eye or accessible to the understanding.

of the German-Austrian immigration quota was filled. (Norton et al., *A People and a Nation,* p. 543.)

a. The authors believe that World War II immigration restrictions were necessary at the time.

b. The authors are highly critical of World War II immigration restrictions.

c. It's impossible to determine the authors' personal feelings.

Test 3: Taking Stock

DIRECTIONS Read the passage. Then answer the questions by filling in the blanks or circling the letter of the correct response.

Identity Theft

1   In 2001, Wanda, a 39-year-old Navy wife in Virginia Beach, received a call from a bank asking her to make a payment on a delinquent $15,000 loan. Wanda had never taken out a loan, but the bank had not made a mistake. As it turned out, a woman had stolen Wanda's personal information and used it to obtain credit. Wanda found out she had $17,000 in unpaid debts and a bad credit record. In short, she was the victim of "identity theft," a crime that involves pilfering someone's personal information and using it to obtain fraudulent credit cards and loans. Because identity theft is a growing problem with serious consequences, Americans need to change some of their habits or risk becoming victims like Wanda.

2   Stealing someone's identity is not all that difficult. Thieves just need to get their hands on an individual's name, Social Security number, and date of birth—the required information for getting credit. While the assumption is that criminals find this information on the Internet, they actually rely more on low-tech methods. The trash, for example, is a gold mine for documents containing personal information, so many identity thieves go "dumpster-diving" in search of discarded tax forms, legal documents, and hospital records. Others rob postal drop boxes to get information from individuals' correspondence. Some set up bogus websites that lure victims into providing personal data. Still others pay company employees to steal customers' records. As one identity thief put it, "All you need is some idiot, some young kid working at a hospital or bank who's not happy with his job, who's not making enough money. He'll sell you Social Security numbers." After gathering the necessary details, an identity thief can apply for a credit card, even listing his or her own name as an additional cardholder on the account. When the cards arrive, the thief begins spending.

3   According to the Federal Trade Commission (FTC), in 2002, about 7 million American consumers were victims of identity theft, and the number of complaints received by the agency has nearly doubled every year for the past three years. The growing number of such cases is producing severe consequences for both businesses and individuals. The FTC estimates that identity theft costs nearly $53 *billion* every year. Because federal law protects

them from fraudulent use of credit cards, consumers are usually not responsible for thieves' purchases. However, even if cardholders' liability is only $50, they may be forced to spend thousands more to undo the damage to their credit histories. Most victims of identity theft must devote many frustrating hours to sorting out the mess, dealing with angry creditors and restoring their reputations as trustworthy consumers.

4   Businesses and government agencies have tried to combat this problem in a number of ways. Congress recently made identity theft a separate crime. The FTC created and maintains an identity theft database that provides information to law-enforcement agencies about perpetrators, victims, and potential witnesses. The three major credit-reporting companies—Equifax, Experian, and TransUnion—have begun sharing fraud notifications with each other. In addition, some state legislators are trying to pass new laws to limit the appearance of Social Security numbers on identification cards and other public documents. They are also seeking to double the maximum prison time, from 10 to 20 years, for identity theft.

5   However, everyone involved agrees that not enough is being done. Individuals and businesses criticize law-enforcement agencies for letting jurisdiction* issues hamper investigations and for focusing only on the larger cases while letting the smaller ones languish. As security issues analyst Avivah Litan points out, fewer than 1 in 700 instances of identity theft ends with the offender's conviction. Therefore, says Litan, many thieves have learned that identity theft is a "lucrative, low-risk crime."

6   Others, in contrast, blame organizations for not doing more to safeguard the information they collect. Hospitals and universities, for example, aren't required by federal law—as financial services and insurance companies are—to protect information. Still others blame credit card companies for their lax security practices. According to Ed Mierzwinski of the U.S. Public Interest Research Group, "There's so much money to be made that [credit card] companies don't care if they lose some money to identity theft." As a result, says Mierzwinski, "They don't have passwords that are changed often enough. They don't have audit trails,* . . . and they make credit too easy to get." He also criticizes the U.S. Congress, which "has made identity theft a crime for the criminal,

*jurisdiction: area of control or authority.
*audit trails: lists of documents that would allow the company to trace illegal credit back to the thief.

but it hasn't gone after the companies who aid and abet identity theft."

7   Then, too, consumers themselves contribute to the problem. In 1999, Americans made $1.1 billion worth of credit card purchases. The average American uses several cards and carries an average of $5,800 in credit card debt from month to month. The median total outstanding debt of households rose 9.6 percent between 1998 and 2001. In 2003, 1.6 million people filed for bankruptcy. Clearly, people are living well beyond their means, and most of them are teetering on the brink of financial disaster.

8   Still, consumers can take a few steps to protect themselves. For instance, if your Social Security number appears on your driver's license, have the state issue an alternate number. Also, don't print your Social Security number on checks, and do not share it with anyone unless absolutely necessary. Rip up the credit card solicitations you receive in the mail so that no one can get them from the garbage and fill them out. Before throwing them away, shred all documents that contain vital personal information. Obtain a copy of your credit report at least once a year to check for suspicious activity. Don't leave mail in your mailbox with the red flag up. As FTC Identity Theft Program manager Joanna Crane says, "To prevent [identity theft] from ever happening at all, you have to be extremely vigilant." (Sources of information: Stephen Mihm, "Dumpster-Diving for Your Identity," *The New York Times Magazine,* December 21, 2003, p. 42; Neal Conan, "Analysis: Identity Theft," *Talk of the Nation (NPR),* November 26, 2002.)

1. In your own words, what is the main idea of the entire reading?

_____

_____

2. Which statement best sums up the main idea of paragraph 2?

a. Dumpsters contain all the information an identity thief needs to commit crimes.

b. It is relatively easy to steal identities.

c. People can protect themselves from identity thieves in a number of ways.

d. Credit cards are much too easy to obtain.

3. How would you label the following supporting detail from paragraph 2? "The trash, for example, is a gold mine for documents containing personal information, so many identity thieves go 'dumpster-diving' in search of tax forms, legal documents, and hospital records."

   a. major

   b. minor

4. Which pattern or patterns organize the details in paragraph 3?

   a. definition

   b. time order

   c. comparison and contrast

   d. cause and effect

   e. classification

5. What conclusion follows from the reading?

   a. The thief who stole Wanda's identity was caught and sentenced to jail time.

   b. The author of the reading considers identity theft a difficult problem that has no solution.

   c. The author of the reading was once a victim of identity theft.

   d. Currently, the best hope for avoiding identity theft is in the hands of the consumer rather than the government or legal system.

6. From the information in paragraph 5, a reader might logically draw the conclusion that Avivah Litan would be most likely to

   a. support legislators' attempts to increase the maximum prison time for convicted identity thieves.

   b. support the enactment of legislation forcing credit card companies to tighten their security.

   c. advocate training consumers to limit credit card spending.

7. In paragraph 7, the author suggests that American consumers are part of the problem because they are so in debt. This criticism relies heavily on which of the following?

   a. circular reasoning

   b. personal attacks

   c. slippery slope thinking

   d. irrelevant evidence

8. From the information in paragraph 8, a reader might logically draw the conclusion that Joanna Crane

   a. believes very little can be done to put a stop to identity theft.

   b. would support laws that make credit much harder to get.

   c. would probably agree that every business and household should have a paper shredder.

9. The author's purpose is

   a. to inform.

   b. to persuade.

10. How would you describe the author's bias?

   a. The author is critical of how little is being done by institutions to protect consumers from identity theft.

   b. The author thinks consumers are at least partially responsible for identity theft.

   c. It is impossible to determine the author's personal bias.

C H A P T E R 10

Understanding and Evaluating Arguments

In this chapter, you'll learn

- why the ability to analyze arguments is a key critical reading skill.

- how to identify the essential elements of an argument.

- how to recognize some common errors that undermine or weaken an argument.

You may not realize it, but arguments are everywhere. The candidate who says "vote for me" offers an argument explaining why. The salesperson who wants to sell you a new DVD player is quick to describe the advantages of the latest models. Even a neighbor who wants to sell you her used car will try to convince you that you're getting a real bargain.

The point of these examples is simple: You need to be in a position to analyze and evaluate the competing arguments that confront you practically every day. Once you are able to do that, you can make informed decisions about which arguments are convincing and which ones are not. Then you can decide with confidence whether you want to share—or at least consider—the other person's point of view.

What's the Point of the Argument?

The starting point of an argument is the opinion, belief, or claim the author of the argument wants readers to accept or at least seriously consider. Whenever you encounter an argument in your reading, the first thing to do is decide what opinion, belief, or claim the author thinks you should share. In other words, you need to discover the main idea or central point of the author's argument. Discovering that point will be easier once you are familiar with the three kinds of statements—condition, value, and policy—likely to be at the heart of written arguments. What follows are the three types of statements, along with a description of the evidence they usually require.

Statements of Condition

These statements assert that a particular condition or state of affairs exists or existed. Although these statements are based more on fact than opinion, they usually identify a state of affairs not likely to be well known by readers and thus in need of proof. The following would all be considered statements of condition.

1. Unlike most other crimes, drug offenses are subject to three jurisdictions: local, state, and federal.
2. The family as we know it has not been in existence for very long.
3. Although Henry David Thoreau celebrated solitude in his now classic book *Walden,* he actually spent very little time alone.
4. Romantic love is a very modern concept.

Although reasons are essential in any argument, statements of condition usually rely heavily on sound factual evidence.

Statements of Value

Statements of value express approval or disapproval. Frequently, they contrast two people, ideas, or objects and suggest that one is better or worse than the other. The following are all statements of value.

1. Among all the sports, boxing is the most dangerous and dehumanizing.
2. Lyndon Baines Johnson was a better president than most people realize.
3. The Electoral College has outlived its usefulness.
4. Given the outbreaks of mad cow disease, the government needs to do a better job overseeing the inspection of beef.

Although statements of value can and do require facts, they typically need examples and reasons as well. For instance, to talk about the "state of decline" in U.S. education, a writer would probably have to offer statistics proving an earlier superiority and more statistics or examples illustrating the current decline.

Statements of Policy

Statements of policy insist that a particular action should or should not be taken in response to a specific condition or situation. These policy statements often include words like *must, need, should, would,* or *ought.* The following are all statements of policy.

1. The Internet needs to be censored so that children do not have access to pornographic material.
2. Shoeless Joe Jackson* should be admitted to the Baseball Hall of Fame.
3. College athletes who do not maintain a B average should be prohibited from playing any team sports.
4. Consumers should have the right to take legal action against HMOs that provide inadequate medical care.

With statements of policy, factual evidence is important, but sound reasons that answer the question *why* are also essential.

Can different types of argument statements be combined? The answer is most definitely yes. Here's an example: "Despite the cloud of

---

*Shoeless Joe Jackson: a famous baseball player who many think was unfairly implicated in the Black Sox baseball scandal of the 1919 World Series.

shame surrounding his name, Shoeless Joe Jackson was never convicted of any crime. As one of the most talented players in the history of baseball, he should be admitted to the Baseball Hall of Fame." In this case, we have a statement of condition (Jackson was never convicted of a crime). But we also have a statement of value (he was one of the most talented players in the history of baseball), and a statement of policy (he should be admitted to the Baseball Hall of Fame).

When you analyze an argument, be on the lookout for statements that describe an existing condition, assign value, or urge a policy or action. Such statements, separately or combined, are usually central to an author's argument.

CHECK YOUR UNDERSTANDING

Describe the three types of statements likely to be at the center of an argument.

1. Statements of condition: _____

_____

2. Statements of value: _____

_____

3. Statements of policy: _____

_____

EXERCISE 1

DIRECTIONS Read each passage. Paraphrase the main idea or point of the argument. Then circle the appropriate letter to identify it as a statement of policy, value, or condition.

EXAMPLE

Does the Punishment Fit the Crime?

1 In 1984, lawmakers wanted to send a tough message on the sale of drugs. As part of a bill called the Sentencing Reform Act, Congress assigned mandatory minimum sentences for all drug offenses taking place near schools. Offenders could get anywhere from five to twenty years based on the amount of drugs involved. With time, additional mandatory minimums became part of the

legal system, including the "three strikes you're out" provision that specified life sentences for repeat drug offenders. While mandatory minimum sentences are still seen by some to be a solution to drug use in the United States, there are several reasons why the courts need to reconsider the effectiveness of mandatory minimum sentences.

2   Thanks in large part to mandatory minimum sentencing, jails are currently packed. A federal penitentiary like Leavenworth, built to house 1,200 prisoners, has occasionally housed as many as 1,700, creating overcrowded conditions that breed violence and riots. State correctional facilities are also overflowing, so much so that violent criminals are sometimes released in order to make room for nonviolent drug offenders. In 2003, the number of imprisoned drug offenders was an astonishing 330,000. This figure is larger than the number of people imprisoned for all crimes in 1970.

3   The group Families Against Mandatory Minimums (FAMM) regularly lobbies Congress for the repeal of mandatory minimums, citing cases like that of Michael T. Irish, a first offender sentenced to twelve years in federal prison for helping unload hashish from a boat, or Charles Dulap, imprisoned for eight years in federal prison for the crime of renting a truck used by a friend to import marijuana. FAMM was founded over a decade ago by Julie Stewart, who hadn't been particularly interested in the subject of mandatory minimum sentencing until her brother was imprisoned for five years after he was caught growing marijuana seedlings. It was Stewart who came up with FAMM's motto, "Let the Punishment Fit the Crime." (Source of information: Eric Schlosser, *Reefer Madness,* New York: Houghton Mifflin, 2003, pp. 53–55.)

a. In your own words, what is the point of the author's argument?

The courts need to change the laws requiring mandatory

minimum sentences.

b. That point is a statement of

a. condition.

b. value.

c. policy.

EXPLANATION Because the author supports a particular action—the court's reconsideration of mandatory minimum sentences—*c* is the best answer.

1. Parents with a computer in the house should purchase software that filters, or blocks out, objectionable websites. Although most parents do not turn their kids loose in front of a computer and let them surf the Web on their own, even devoted parents cannot be with their children all the time. This means that impressionable kids can find their way to inappropriate, even dangerous websites. Kids can, for example, access websites featuring pornographic pictures and text. Children with access to the Web can also come into contact with people who want to seduce and abuse them. To avoid these very real dangers, parents need to purchase one of the many software programs that effectively locks kids out of all sexually explicit websites. There is also software that blocks access to expressly racist or anti-Semitic* sites. Parents might think about purchasing this type of software as well. While such websites may not endanger children's bodies, they can certainly harm their minds.

   a. In your own words, what is the point of the author's argument?

   _____

   _____

   b. That point is a statement of
      a. condition.
      b. value.
      c. policy.

2. In far too many cases, students' grades have become so inflated that they're virtually meaningless. A whopping 83 percent of high school seniors who took the Scholastic Aptitude Test (SAT) in 1993 claimed to be A or B students, while only 28 percent of their 1972 counterparts made the same claim. It's nice to think that the nation's kids are just getting smarter. However, we'd have to overlook the fact that, during the same period, the average SAT score actually *fell* from 937 to 902. And what happens to all those stellar* students when they get to college? Well, they are likely to receive more inflated grades. The old "gentleman's C,"* earned by those who put forth only minimum effort, has become the "average person's B." Even elite, demanding schools like Harvard are doling out A's and B's to those who do little more than show up for class. The C grade no

---

*anti-Semitic: prejudiced against all people of the Jewish faith.
*stellar: excellent.
*gentleman's C: An old expression indicating that the sons of the wealthy or well-placed need not worry about achieving a grade higher than a "C," because they had money and position to back them up.

longer seems to exist. That's why graduate schools and employers have begun interpreting applicants' grade point averages much differently. They know that A sometimes stands for "average."

a. In your own words, what is the point of the author's argument?

_____

_____

b. That point is a statement of
   a. condition.
   b. value.
   c. policy.

3. Retrieving Forgotten Heroes

1 Although some of the names of heroes of the civil rights movement have become household words—who hasn't heard of Martin Luther King Jr.?—others have remained relatively unknown, and it's time that we draw attention to their many contributions. Most of us know, for example, about Rosa Parks and how her refusal to move to the back of the bus and give up her seat to a white passenger helped spark the historic bus boycott in Montgomery, Alabama. Fewer people know that in 1944, a young black woman named Irene Morgan boarded a Greyhound bus to Gloucester County, Virginia. Weak from recent surgery, Morgan also refused to move to the back of the bus when told to do so. The police were called and she was arrested. Convicted of her "crime," Morgan appealed her decision and made legal history when Thurgood Marshall[1] argued her case before the Supreme Court and won.

2 Also relatively unknown is Fred L. Shuttlesworth. As pastor of the First Baptist Church in Birmingham, Alabama, Shuttlesworth organized the demonstrations and marches that helped win civil rights for African-Americans. Shuttlesworth was a tireless organizer with superhuman courage. Racists bombed his house and beat him bloody numerous times, but Shuttlesworth was unstoppable. He provided shelter to civil rights workers and preached unending opposition to any form of discrimination.

3 Twenty-one-year-old student activist Robert Zellner was recruited to the civil rights movement by Martin Luther King himself. Zellner went on to become the first white field secretary in the largely black organization Student Non-Violent Coordinating

---

[1]Marshall later became the first African-American to sit on the Supreme Court.

Committee (SNCC). At demonstrations or sit-ins, Zellner always carried a Bible to indicate that his protests were meant to be peaceful, but that didn't save him from several brutal beatings. On one march to a voter registration office, Zellner was called a traitor to his race and beaten to the ground. In a sadly ironic twist, he was then jailed for being part of an "illegal" demonstration. A hero in his own right, Zellner never abandoned the cause of civil rights and he is still active as a speaker on college campuses. Yet his name is not widely known. (Source of information: Taylor Branch, *Parting the Waters: America in the King Years, 1954–63,* New York: Simon and Schuster, 1988, p. 513.)

a. In your own words, what is the point of the author's argument?

_____

_____

b. That point is a statement of
   a. condition.
   b. value.
   c. policy.

4. *Empress of Ireland*

1 Most people know about the early twentieth-century maritime disasters the *Titanic* and the *Lusitania.* The *Titanic* was a British luxury ocean liner that accidentally hit an iceberg during its very first voyage from England to New York. When it sank on April 15, 1912, more than 1,500 of the 2,200 people on board lost their lives. The British ocean liner *Lusitania* was torpedoed and sunk by a German submarine off the coast of Ireland on May 7, 1915. When the ship went down, 1,198 died. Few people, however, realize that sandwiched between these two high-profile sinkings was a third one every bit as tragic. On May 29, 1914, the *Empress of Ireland,* a luxury liner that made regular voyages between England and Canada, sank off the coast of Quebec. Of the 1,477 people aboard, 1,012 were killed.

2 On the day it sank, the *Empress of Ireland* had just left Quebec and was steaming down the St. Lawrence River toward open ocean water. Another ship, the Norwegian *Storstad,* was steaming downriver. The river was shrouded in fog; nonetheless, the two ships sighted each other at about 2:00 a.m. Aboard the *Empress of Ireland,* Captain Henry Kendall made adjustments to

his ship's course, estimating that his changes would allow the ships to pass each other at a comfortable distance. Moments after Kendall altered his course, however, the *Storstad* completely disappeared in the fog. Concerned about the lack of visibility and the other ship's proximity, the captain blew the liner's whistle three times to indicate to the *Storstad* that he had ordered a reversal of the engines to slow his ship down. But when the Norwegian ship materialized again, it was heading straight for the side of the *Empress of Ireland.* Captain Kendall knew instantly that a collision was unavoidable, and he immediately ordered a sharp turn in hopes of reducing the *Storstad*'s impact to just a glancing blow.

3   Unfortunately, though, when the *Storstad* hit the *Empress of Ireland,* its bow went between the liner's steel ribs, delivering a fatal wound. Water poured in so fast that most of the liner's sleeping passengers had no chance to escape. Just ten minutes after impact, the ship lay on her side, with hundreds of passengers locked in her hull. Only fourteen minutes after the collision, the *Empress of Ireland* sank into the icy waters of the St. Lawrence. It was the worst disaster in Canadian history. (Source of information: www.pbs.org/lostliners/empress.html.)

a. In your own words, what is the point of the author's argument?

_____

_____

b. That point is a statement of
   a. condition.
   b. value.
   c. policy.

 # Four Common Types of Support

Writers who want their arguments to be taken seriously know they have to do more than state their opinion. To be persuasive, they also have to provide their readers with support. In response, critical readers need to recognize and evaluate that support, deciding if it is both relevant and up to date. Four common types of support are likely to be used in an argument: reasons, examples and illustrations, expert opinions, and research results.

Reasons

Reasons are probably the most common method of support used by authors who want to argue a point. In the following passage, the author hopes to convince readers that cockfighting should be outlawed in the three states that still permit it.

> Cockfighting has been outlawed in forty-eight states. In the two remaining states—New Mexico and Louisiana—people can still legally participate in this violent pastime. It's high time that those states, too, end the brutality by passing laws to make cockfighting a crime. Cockfighting is one of the worst forms of animal cruelty. Participants strap razor-sharp spurs to two roosters' legs, feed them stimulants, and then toss the birds into a pit, where they tear each other apart until one dies a bloody death.
>
> Besides being cruel to animals, cockfights encourage illegal and violent behavior. They are notorious arenas of illegal gambling and drug trafficking, firearms dealing, and fighting. Shootings have even occurred when the violence in the ring spills over into the crowd. Raids of cockfights often result in many arrests. In a very real way, cockfights reinforce the idea that violence is a source of amusement. Perhaps worst of all, they send that very same message to children whose parents allow them to witness these fights. The parents apparently consider them nothing more than good, clean fun.

To persuade readers to share her point of view, the author of this passage provides four specific reasons: (1) cockfighting is cruel to animals, (2) it encourages illegal and even violent behavior, (3) it reinforces the idea that violence is a source of amusement, and (4) it sends that message to children. By means of these four reasons, the author hopes that readers will begin to share, or at least to seriously consider, her point of view.

Examples and Illustrations

Particularly when arguing general statements of value—for example, boxing is dangerous, pesticides cause health problems, or Isaac Newton was an eccentric* genius—writers are likely to cite examples, illustrations, or even personal experiences as proof of their point. Look at how the following author uses examples to persuade readers that plastic litter is not just unsightly, but also deadly.

*eccentric: odd, weird.

As litter, plastic is unsightly and deadly. Birds and small animals die after getting stuck in plastic six-pack beverage rings. Pelicans accidentally hang themselves with discarded plastic fishing line. Turtles choke on plastic bags or starve when their stomachs become clogged with hard-to-excrete crumbled plastic. Sea lions poke their heads into plastic rings and have their jaws locked permanently shut. Authorities estimate that plastic refuse annually kills up to two million birds and at least 100,000 mammals. (Gary Turbak, "Plastic: 60 Billion Pounds of Trouble," *The American Legion Magazine.*[2])

Here's a case where the author piles example upon example in an effort to convince readers that plastic can be lethal.

Expert Opinions

In order to persuade, writers often call on one or more experts who support their position. In the following passage, for instance, the author suggests that cloning geniuses may not be a good idea. To make her point, she gives a reason *and* cites an expert.

With the birth of Dolly, the first successfully cloned sheep, some have suggested that we can now consider the human gene pool a natural resource. We can clone a Nobel Prize–winning writer like Toni Morrison or a star athlete like Michael Jordan and thereby create a population of gifted and talented people. What could be wrong with that? Well, in the long run, probably a lot.

There's simply no guarantee that the clones would be everything the originals were. After all, genes don't tell the whole story, and the clone of a prizewinning scientist, if neglected as a child, might well end up a disturbed genius, no matter what the original gene source. As John Paris, professor of bioethics at Boston College, so correctly says on the subject of cloning, "Choosing personal characteristics as if they were the options on a car is an invitation to misadventure. (Source of information: Jeffrey Kluger, "Will We Follow the Sheep?" *Time*, March 10, 1997, p. 71.)

In this case, the author doesn't just let her argument rest solely on her own reasoning. She also makes it clear that at least one knowledgeable expert is very much on her side.

---

[2]Also used in Rosen and Behrens, *The Allyn and Bacon Handbook.*

Research Results

In the same way they use experts, writers who want to persuade are likely to use the results of research—studies, polls, questionnaires, and surveys—to argue a point. In the following passage, for example, the author uses an expert and a study to support a statement of condition: There's a quiet revolution taking place among Amish women.

> In a tiny shop built on the side of a farmhouse in Pennsylvania's Lancaster County, Katie Stoltzfus sells Amish* dolls, wooden toys, and quilts. Does she ever. Her shop had "a couple of hundred thousand" dollars in sales last year, says the forty-four-year-old Amish entrepreneur and mother of nine. Mrs. Stoltzfus's success underscores a quiet revolution taking place among the Amish. Amish women, despite their image as shy farm wives, now run about 20 percent of the one thousand businesses in Lancaster County, according to a study by Donald B. Kraybill, a professor of sociology at Elizabethtown College in Elizabethtown, Pennsylvania. "These women are interacting more with outsiders, assuming managerial functions they never had before, and gaining more power within their community because of their access to money," says Professor Kraybill, who recently wrote a book about Amish enterprises. (Timothy Aeppel, "More Amish Women Are Tending to Business," *Wall Street Journal,* February 8, 1996, p. B1.)

To make sure that readers seriously consider his position, the author cites a study and identifies the person who conducted the study, making it clear that his opinion is grounded in solid research.

CHECK YOUR UNDERSTANDING
Name the four types of support common to written arguments.

1. _____ 3. _____

2. _____ 4. _____

---

*Amish: a religious group that generally avoids contact with the modern world and its modern machinery.

EXERCISE 2

DIRECTIONS Each group of statements opens with an opinion or a claim that needs to be argued. Circle the letters of the two sentences that help argue that point.

EXAMPLE Eyewitness testimony is far from reliable.

(a.) The testimony of eyewitnesses can often be influenced by the desire to please those in authority.

(b.) Studies of eyewitness testimony reveal an astonishingly high number of errors.

c. Eyewitness testimony carries a great deal of weight with most juries.

EXPLANATION Statements *a* and *b* both undermine the reliability of eyewitnesses and thereby provide reasons why eyewitness testimony cannot always be considered reliable. Statement *c*, however, is not relevant, or related, to the claim made about eyewitness testimony.

1. Uniforms should be mandatory* for all high school students.

    a. Most students hate the idea of wearing a uniform.

    b. Parents on a strict budget would no longer have to worry about being able to provide expensive back-to-school wardrobes.

    c. If uniforms were mandatory in high school, students would not waste precious time worrying about something as unessential as fashion.

2. All zoos should be abolished.

    a. Zoos only encourage the notion that animals are on Earth for the amusement of humans.

    b. If all zoos were closed, no one has any idea what would happen to the animals now living in them.

    c. Although many zoos have improved the living conditions for the animals they possess, those animals still lack the freedom they have in the wild.

———
*mandatory: required or commanded by authority.

3. Because the deer population is sky-high, hunters should be allowed to shoot more deer per season.

   a. Desperate for food, deer are foraging by the roadside, where many are hit by cars, another indication that their population has to be reduced.

   b. With the exception of hunting, there doesn't seem to be any practical way to slow down the growth in the deer population.

   c. Most hunters have a great respect for the animals they kill.

4. Parents need to limit the amount of television their children watch.

   a. Unlike reading, watching television does not encourage a child to think imaginatively.

   b. Children who watch a lot of television are consistently exposed to violence and can easily become too accepting of it.

   c. Programs for children dominate Saturday morning television.

■ EXERCISE 3

DIRECTIONS Read each passage. Then answer the questions that follow.

EXAMPLE Unfortunately, some people still believe that African-Americans endured slavery without protest. But nothing could be further from the truth. In 1800, for example, Gabriel Prosser organized an army of a thousand slaves to march on Richmond. However, a state militia had been alerted by a spy, and the rebellion was put down. Prosser was ultimately executed for refusing to give evidence against his co-conspirators. In 1822, Denmark Vesey plotted to march on Charleston, but he, too, was betrayed by an informer. Probably the most serious revolt occurred in 1831 under Nat Turner. It resulted in the execution of Turner and more than a hundred black rebels.

a. What is the point of the author's argument?

   It's simply not true that African-Americans endured slavery

   without protest.

b. Paraphrase the examples used to support that point.

   1. In 1800, Gabriel Prosser organized an army of slaves to

      march on Richmond.

> *2. In 1822, Denmark Vesey plotted to take over Charleston.*
>
> *3. In 1831, Nat Turner and 100 rebels revolted.*

EXPLANATION In this case, the author uses three examples to make her point: African-Americans did not endure slavery without protest.

1. The fact that more women are lawfully arming themselves should be good news for everyone concerned with violence against women. Since the publication of Betty Friedan's *The Feminine Mystique*, feminists have been urging women to be independent and self-sufficient. What better evidence that women have "arrived" than that they no longer have to rely exclusively on the police (still mostly male) for protection? Feminists should applaud every woman who is skilled in handgun use. (Talk about controlling your own body.) Liberation from fear when walking on a dark street, driving on a country road late at night, or withdrawing cash from a bank machine is more important on a daily basis to most women than smashing any glass ceiling in the workplace. (Laura Ingraham, "Armed and Empowered," *Pittsburgh Post-Gazette*, May 19, 1998, p. E3.)

   a. What is the point of the author's argument?

   _____

   _____

   b. Paraphrase the reasons used to support that point.

   _____

   _____

   _____

2. All states should consider limiting tractor-trailer traffic on crowded highways. Over the past twenty years, the number of tractor-trailers on our nation's roads and interstates has doubled to 2.6 million, and that number is still increasing. By 2020, the number of trucks is expected to have doubled again. At the same time, though, the capacity of our roads and highways has either remained the same or expanded only a little. Put these two factors together and it becomes clear that the growing number of trucks is increasing the danger of accidents. Already, around 4,500 drivers and passengers die every year in truck-car accidents because smaller, lighter cars are easily crushed by the much bigger rigs, and that fatality rate will only con-

tinue to rise as the number of trucks increases. Obviously, the solution to this problem is to limit trucks to traveling in truck-only lanes and to prohibit them from traveling during rush hours. By restricting truckers in these ways, state officials can make the roads safer for everyone. (Source of information: Fred Bayles, "More Big Trucks Mixing with Cars Worries Officials," *USA Today,* February 9, 2004.)

a. What is the point of the author's argument?

_____

_____

b. Paraphrase the reasons used to support that point.

_____

_____

_____

3. It's never too late to get physically fit. A 1999 study published in the *New England Journal of Medicine* showed that taking up weight training can reverse some of the effects of aging. In the experiment, nursing home residents ranging in age from eighty-six to ninety-five participated in a supervised, eight-week weight-training program. All of these elderly people increased their strength and improved their balance. Another more recent study conducted by the University of Pennsylvania Medical School has shown that elderly people who take up weight training can improve their bone density and reduce arthritic pain.

a. What is the point of the author's argument?

_____

_____

b. Paraphrase the results of the studies used to support that point.

_____

_____

_____

4. Almost every college student has experienced prefinals terror—the horrible anxiety that puts your stomach on a roller coaster and your brain in a blender. Few escape those final-exam jitters because

everyone knows just how much is riding on that one exam, often more than half of the course grade. Yet therein lies the crux* of the problem. Infrequent high-stakes exams don't encourage students to do their best work. More frequent tests—given, say, every two or three weeks—would be a much more effective method of discovering how well students are or are not mastering course concepts. With more frequent testing, students would be less anxious when they take exams; thus anxiety would no longer interfere with exam performance. More frequent testing also encourages students to review on a regular basis, something that a one-shot final exam does not do. Lots of tests also mean lots of feedback, and students would know early on in the course what terms or concepts required additional explanation and review. They wouldn't have to wait until the end of the semester to find out that they had misunderstood, or missed altogether, a critical point or theory.

a. What is the point of the author's argument?

_____

_____

b. Paraphrase the reasons used to support that point.

_____

_____

_____

 Flawed Arguments

The preceding section of this chapter introduced four types of evidence likely to appear as support in an argument. In this section, you'll learn about the flaws or errors you should check for in each one.

Irrelevant Reasons

In their haste to prove a point, authors sometimes include reasons that aren't truly relevant, or related, to their claim. Here, for example, is an argument flawed by an irrelevant reason.

_____

*crux: core, heart, key point.

The 1996 tragedy on Mount Everest in which eight people died in a single day is proof enough that amateurs should not be scaling the world's highest mountain. Even with the most skillful and reliable guides, amateurs with little or no mountaineering experience cannot possibly know how to respond to the sudden storms that strike the mountain without warning. Dependent on their guides for every move they make, amateur climbers can easily lose sight of the guides when a heavy storm hits. Left to their own devices, they are more than likely to make a mistake, one that will harm themselves or others. Besides, rich people—the climb can cost anywhere from $30,000 to $60,000—shouldn't be encouraged to think that money buys everything. As F. Scott Fitzgerald so powerfully illustrated in *The Great Gatsby,* it's precisely that attitude that often leads to tragedy and death.

The point of this passage is clear-cut: Amateurs should not be climbing Mount Everest. In support of that claim, the author does offer a relevant reason. Mount Everest can be the scene of sudden storms that leave amateur climbers stranded, separated from their guides, and likely to harm themselves or others. But tucked away in the passage is a far less relevant reason: Rich people should not be allowed to think money buys everything. Well, maybe they shouldn't. Yet that particular reason, along with the allusion, or reference, to *The Great Gatsby,* is not related to the author's claim. Neither one clarifies why amateurs and the world's tallest mountain don't mix. This is the point that needs to be argued.

Circular Reasoning

As you know from Chapter 7, writers sometimes engage in circular reasoning. They offer an opinion and follow it with a reason that says the same thing in different words. Unfortunately, circular reasoning is not that unusual—particularly when an author is utterly convinced of his or her own rightness. In the following passage, for example, the writer believes that health care workers should be tested for AIDS. He's so convinced he's right that he's forgotten to give his readers a reason why the testing should be done. Instead, he repeats his opening point as if it were a reason for his claim.

Health care workers, from hospital technicians to doctors, should be forced to undergo AIDS testing, and the results should be published. Although there has been much talk about this subject, too little has been done, and the public has suffered because of it. We need to institute a program of mandatory testing as soon as possible.

Hasty Generalizations

Generalizations, or broad general statements, by definition cover a lot of territory. They are used to sum up and express a wide variety of individual events or experiences. When generalizations appear in arguments, the rule of thumb is simple: The broader and more wide ranging the generalization, the more examples writers need to supply in order to be convincing. If an author generalizes about a large group on the basis of one or even two examples, you need to think twice before making the author's opinion your own.

In the following passage, the author makes a general statement about all HMOs. Unfortunately, that statement is based on one lone example, a fact that seriously weakens his argument.

> HMOs are not giving consumers adequate health care. Instead, budgeting considerations are consistently allowed to outweigh the patients' need for treatment. In one case, a child with a horribly deformed cleft palate was denied adequate cosmetic surgery because the child's HMO considered the surgery unnecessary, yet the child had trouble eating and drinking. (Source of information: Howard Fineman, "HMOs Under the Knife," *Newsweek*, July 27, 1998, p. 21.)

Unidentified Experts

In the passage about cloning on page 494, it makes sense for the author to quote a bioethicist in support of her opinion. After all, a bioethicist specializes in the study of moral and ethical issues that result from biological discoveries and applications. However, critical readers are rightly suspicious of allusions to unidentified experts, who may or may not be qualified to offer an opinion. Consider, for example, the "expert" cited in the following passage.

> Despite the doom-and-gloom sayers who constantly worry about the state of the environment, the Earth is actually in pretty good shape. As Dr. Paul Benjamin recently pointed out, "Nature is perfectly capable of taking care of herself; she's been doing it for hundreds of years."

The author uses Dr. Paul Benjamin to support her claim that environmentalists anxious about the Earth's future are dead wrong. Yet for all we know, Dr. Benjamin might be a dentist, and a dental degree does not qualify him as an environmental expert. Without some knowledge of Dr. Benjamin's **credentials,** or qualifications, we shouldn't be swayed by his opinion. It also wouldn't hurt to know more about Dr. Benjamin's personal background and biases. If, for example, he's worked for a company cited for abuses to the environment, his ability to stay objective, or neutral, is suspect.

Inappropriate Experts

Occasionally, a writer might also attempt to support an argument by citing a famous person who doesn't truly qualify as an expert in the area under discussion.

> We should abolish NATO and end foreign aid. After all, didn't George Washington tell us to avoid entangling ourselves in the affairs of other nations? Even today, we should let his wisdom be our guide and steer clear of foreign involvements that drain our energy and our resources.

During the eighteenth century, George Washington may well have qualified as an expert in foreign affairs. But to cite him as an authority on modern problems is a mistake. It is doubtful that Washington could have imagined America's current status as an international power. Because his opinion could not be considered adequately informed, critical readers would not be impressed by references to his name and authority.

Unidentified Research

In the following passage, the author relies on some "studies" to prove a statement of policy: Pornography should be more strictly censored. But to be convincing as support, scientific research needs **attribution;** in short, readers need to know who conducted the research. References to unnamed studies like the one in this passage should arouse skepticism in critical readers.

> Because pornography puts womens' lives in danger, it must be more strictly censored. Studies have shown again and again that pornography is directly related to the number of rapes and assaults on women. As if that weren't enough, by repeatedly presenting women as sexual objects, pornography encourages sexual discrimination, a cause-and-effect relationship noted by several prominent researchers.

Authors may identify a study in the text itself or in a footnote that refers readers to a list of sources at the back of the book. Where a study is identified doesn't matter. What matters is that the author provides readers with enough information to check the source of the supposed evidence.

Dated Research

It also helps to know *when* the study was conducted; a writer who uses out-of-date studies rightfully runs the risk of losing readers' confidence. Take, for example, the following passage.

> The threat of radon gas is not as serious as we have been led to believe. In 1954, a team of government researchers studying the effects of radon in the home found no relationship between high levels of the gas in private dwellings and the incidence of lung cancer.

Here we have an author trying to prove a point about radon gas with a more than half-century-old study. To be considered effective evidence for an opinion, scientific research should be considerably more up-to-date.

CHECK YOUR UNDERSTANDING		
Complete the following chart by describing the types of errors that can occur in arguments.		

Type of Support	Possible Error	Definition of Error
Reasons	Irrelevant reasons	
	Circular reasoning	
Examples and Illustrations	Hasty generalizations	
Expert Opinion	Unidentified experts	
	Inappropriate experts	
Research Results	Unidentified research	
	Dated research	

EXERCISE 4

DIRECTIONS Identify the error in reasoning by circling the appropriate letter.

EXAMPLE These days it's difficult to avoid the fact that the United States is in the grip of a serious health problem: More than 60 percent of the population is overweight. As a result, many men and women are at increased risk of serious diseases ranging from colon cancer to diabetes. But if you count up the calories in, say, an oversized cheeseburger or a slice of double-cheese pizza, is it any wonder? Fast food companies arose to meet a real need; Americans were pressed for time and often had to eat their meals on the run. But instead of making those meals healthy as well as profitable, the fast food industry decided it was better if they used cooking methods that shortened preparation time and, not incidentally, increased profits. Thus Americans were consuming, without their knowledge, high-calorie meals that didn't cost all that much in dollars but were actually very expensive in terms of health risks. No wonder people like Caesar Barber are suing fast food companies. As Professor James Darwin has pointed out, when it comes to America's health problems, the fast food industry has a lot to answer for.

a. irrelevant reason

b. circular reasoning

c. hasty generalization

(d.) unidentified or inappropriate expert

e. unidentified or dated research

EXPLANATION In this case, *d* is the correct answer because the author uses the words of Professor James Darwin to support his case. We, however, know nothing about Professor Darwin's area of expertise. Thus we cannot tell if he is qualified to decide what the fast food industry does or does not have to answer for.

1. If you have a grass lawn surrounding your house, you are probably contributing to this country's environmental problems. For one thing, you could be using fertilizers and pesticides that can damage the soil structure, pollute wells, and kill wildlife. Homeowners with lawns actually use more fertilizers annually than the entire country of India puts on its crops. They also apply up to ten times more pesticides than U.S. farmers do. Unfortunately, research has proven that these chemicals wash off yards and pollute water supplies, thus contaminating the food chain. Lawn mowers cause another

environmental problem. They produce as much air pollution in one hour as a car produces in a 350-mile drive. In addition, grass clippings are choking already-overflowing landfills. Yard waste, most of which is cut grass, is the second largest component of the 160 million tons of solid waste we dump into landfills every year. If that weren't enough, your lawn may be contributing to the destruction of plant and animal species. When developers building new houses bulldoze complex habitats and replace them with houses and grass, many plants and animals are killed or starved out.

a. irrelevant reason

b. circular reasoning

c. hasty generalization

d. unidentified or inappropriate expert

e. unidentified or dated research

2. The U.S. government needs to invest more money to improve and expand this country's rail service. In particular, Congress should commit to developing a national intercity network of high-speed trains. An intermodal transportation system (one that includes rail along with highways and airlines) is essential to keeping Americans moving in the event of a crisis. During a national emergency that disrupts one mode of transportation, the others should be able to absorb the traffic and allow people to continue to travel. For example, when airplanes were grounded for several days following terrorist attacks in September 2001, people relied on Amtrak passenger trains to get them where they needed to be. Without the trains, our nation would have been paralyzed. Furthermore, we need a rail system like those in European countries such as France and Germany. Railroad transportation is an important public service, and it needs to be kept efficient and up-to-date.

a. irrelevant reason

b. circular reasoning

c. hasty generalization

d. unidentified or inappropriate expert

e. unidentified or dated research

3. Thousands of people who need organ transplants die every year because too few people agree to donate organs. Consequently, some people have begun to argue for tempting donors or their families with financial incentives in the form of either cash payments or tax credits. This is a terrible idea. Under no circumstances should we

institute a system that permits the exchange of money for organs. Individuals or their families should not be allowed to gain financially from helping people who need transplants. Indeed, putting price tags on human organs is an appalling solution to the problem of an inadequate organ supply. We may need more donors to solve this crisis, but buying organs is just not the right way to address the shortage.

a. irrelevant reason

b. circular reasoning

c. hasty generalization

d. unidentified or inappropriate expert

e. unidentified or dated research

4. It just may be nature itself—not humans burning fossil fuels—that is causing global warming. Naturally occurring gases, such as water vapor, methane, nitrous oxide, and ozone, contribute to the so-called greenhouse effect that has raised Earth's temperature 30 degrees since the "Little Ice Age" of the seventeenth and eighteenth centuries. The oceans, too, seem to be partly responsible for the overall increase in our planet's temperature. From 1958 to 1978, Dane Chang and his colleagues at Hill Laboratories carefully studied the correlation between ocean temperatures and levels of carbon dioxide, the gas that causes global warming. These researchers found that increases in ocean temperature follow a rise in the atmosphere's carbon dioxide level. Such studies would seem to indicate that natural factors are producing our warmer climate.

a. irrelevant reason

b. circular reasoning

c. hasty generalization

d. unidentified or inappropriate expert

e. unidentified or dated research

5. A growing number of school districts are banning the childhood game of dodge ball from physical education classes and rightly so. The game is simply too aggressive and can cause serious harm. In one California incident, a child playing dodge ball was knocked to the ground by the ball's impact. Dodge ball is also not especially good exercise, particularly for those who are overweight. The slowest and heaviest children usually get knocked out of the game quickly. They then spend the rest of the game on the sidelines while the more athletic kids keep playing. It doesn't take a highly trained

psychologist to realize that this experience cannot be good for an overweight child's self-esteem or self-image.

a. irrelevant reason

b. circular reasoning

c. hasty generalization

d. unidentified or inappropriate expert

e. unidentified or dated research

◼ EXERCISE 5

DIRECTIONS Read each selection and answer the questions by circling the appropriate letters or filling in the blanks.

EXAMPLE

The Scopes Trial Revisited

1   The 1925 Scopes trial, also known as the Monkey Trial, got its name from John Scopes, a Tennessee high school teacher who was tried and found guilty of breaking Tennessee's newly created Butler Act. The act forbade the teaching of Darwin's* theory of evolution, which argued that fossil evidence showed how humans had developed from lower forms of animal life—an idea that directly challenged the Christian view of creation. Ultimately, Scopes was charged with teaching theories that denied the biblical version of human creation.

2   Scopes's conviction was eventually overturned by the Supreme Court. Yet even before his conviction was struck down, his trial had done what seemed to be irreparable damage to the creationist notion that humans, unlike animals, were created by God. Scopes's defense attorney was the brilliant, witty, and eloquent Clarence Darrow, who mercilessly grilled his client's accusers. Darrow was particularly hard on the leading prosecutor, William Jennings Bryan, repeatedly posing questions that left Bryan embarrassed and stumbling for answers.

3   Regardless of the outcome of the Scopes trial, the controversy over how to teach human origins in the schools has never really gone away. Periodically it is stirred up again, as it was in Kansas in 1999, when the state school board removed the theory of evolution from the high school curriculum. It was reinstated in

---

*Charles Darwin (1809–1882): the naturalist whose books *Origin of Species* and *The Descent of Man* scandalized the public by insisting there was concrete evidence to support the notion of humans' evolution from lower species.

2001, leaving some parents irate and determined to pull their children out of school and teach them at home. It would seem, then, that no school board's decision about how to teach the origins of humanity can leave everyone satisfied. Still, there is another possibility to consider: Schools could teach both theories so that neither group, creationist or evolutionist, feels slighted.

4   And there does seem to be some support for this more flexible position. A 1999 Gallup poll, for example, found that 68 percent of American adults believe children should learn both theories. Another poll came up with similar results. Then, too, don't parents have the right to determine what their children learn in school? Parents who want their kids to learn about creationism should not have their wishes denied; nor, for that matter, should parents who want their kids to learn about evolution. Both sides can be made happy if schools would present the evidence for both theories and let students decide which makes more sense to them.

5   An essential goal of education is to teach students to think critically. We want, that is, for them to know how to evaluate evidence and arrive at an informed decision. What better way to encourage critical thinking than to lay all the evidence for both sides of this controversy before students. Then they can decide which theory of human origins they choose to believe.

1. What is the author's point?

Schools should teach both evolution and creationism.

2. Identify the three reasons used to support that point.

a. *Polls suggest that a majority of parents want their children to learn both theories.*

b. *Parents should have the right to decide what their children are taught.*

c. *Teaching both theories would encourage critical thinking.*

3. Which of the following does the author offer in support of her conclusion?

a. specific illustration

b. results of research

c. expert opinion

4. Which error in reasoning can you detect in paragraph 4?

   a. irrelevant reason

   b. circular reasoning

   c. hasty generalization

   d. unidentified or inappropriate expert

   (e.) unidentified or dated research

> **EXPLANATION** In this example the author presents readers with a statement of policy. To convince them, she identifies three reasons why her proposal makes sense. Her evidence, however, is a bit shaky. You can tell that by the presence of a rhetorical question in paragraph 4, where she doesn't allow for the suggestion that maybe parents shouldn't be permitted to determine and select curriculum. Even less convincing is her claim (paragraph 4) that "another poll" also found that a majority of adults want both theories taught. Unfortunately, who conducted the poll as well as when it took place remain a mystery. This is a good example of unidentified research.

1. Who Really Benefits from the Lottery?

1 In a recent editorial published in this newspaper, an argument was put forth in favor of a state-run lottery. According to the author of the editorial, there are many benefits to a state-run lottery and apparently no drawbacks. Now, the writer may honestly believe that a lottery would be a boon to everyone in the state, but I would argue that legalized gambling is a disaster waiting to happen.

2   Knowingly or unknowingly—and it doesn't matter which—state governments encourage addictive gambling when they promote lotteries. According to the American Psychiatric Association, addictive, or problem, gambling is a mental illness. Although treatable, it's still an illness, and it can lead to a host of social problems such as bankruptcy, theft, domestic violence, and job loss. Needless to say, these social problems can, in the end, prove costly to states hoping to benefit from lottery revenues. In promoting lotteries, the state, in essence, collects money from gambling with one hand and pays out double that amount in social services with the other. Advocates of state-run lotteries should consider that fact when they justify the lotteries by claiming they are a source of revenue for social programs. That logic may seem sound, but it doesn't add up on paper when the costs of addictive gambling are taken into account.

3   For example, a 1995 study by the Wisconsin Policy Research Institute estimated that each problem gambler cost the state

around $9,500 per year in social services and business losses. The total loss to the state was about $307 million per year.[3] Another study indicates that around one in four problem gamblers has a history of substance abuse. This is yet another reason why state governments should not encourage gambling.

4   As Dr. Benjamin Martino has pointed out, legalized gambling blurs an important moral distinction: the distinction between honestly earned money and "ill-gotten" gains. Money from gambling is ill-gotten because it is not connected with any honest labor that benefits society. When we sanction* legalized gambling, we approve of bestowing wealth on people who have not worked for it. Given the number of ways in which legalized gambling hurts a society, how can any state government see fit to promote it?

1. What is the author's point?

_____

_____

2. Identify the four reasons used to support that point.

a. _____

_____

b. _____

_____

c. _____

_____

d. _____

_____

3. In addition to these four reasons, which of the following does the author offer in support of his conclusions?

a. specific illustration

b. results of research

c. expert opinion

_____

[3]Chester Hartman, "Lotteries Victimize the Poor and Minorities." *New Haven Register,* August 3, 1998, p. 17.
*sanction: approve.

4. Which error or errors in reasoning can you detect in paragraphs 3 and 4?

   a. irrelevant reason

   b. circular reasoning

   c. hasty generalization

   d. unidentified or inappropriate expert

   e. unidentified or dated research

2. Speed-Cams: More for Profit Than Safety

1 In more than sixty cities across the United States, law-enforcement officials are installing traffic cameras that photograph drivers who speed or violate other rules of the road. These devices, also known as "speed-cams" and "red-light cameras," are controlled by a computer and a companion metal detector installed under the pavement. When the metal detector calculates that a car is moving too fast, it signals the camera to snap a photo of the vehicle's license plate. A police officer then reviews these records and issues a citation to the driver. Many Americans are rightly outraged by these "robocops" on our roads. In fact, several states have decided *not* to implement this technology. States currently using these cameras should follow suit and remove the devices immediately.

2 First of all, these cameras don't really deter speeders. Unless it's dark enough so that you see a flash in your rearview mirror, odds are you won't know you've been caught by a speed-cam. If you don't realize you've been caught, you're not likely to slow down. Then, too, there have to be other, less intrusive ways of ensuring motorists' safety. While some states photograph only the rear of the car, others—including Arizona, California, and Colorado— photograph the driver too. This type of electronic monitoring should concern every citizen of this country, and we should not allow our government to take pictures of us without our consent.

3 Their unreliability is another reason to scrap the cameras. These technological marvels can, in fact, malfunction and fail. In San Diego, speed-cam sensors clocked drivers going much faster than they really were. As a result, the city disconnected its cameras in July 2001. This example proves once and for all that these machines cannot be counted on to take accurate measurements and create error-free records.

4 Finally, opponents of speed-cams object to them because private companies handle the picture-taking with only a minimum of police involvement. More to the point, these companies base their profits on the number of tickets issued. Sometimes those profits

amount to as much as $70 per ticket. Cities, too, are raking in increased revenues from fines paid by violators. In 2003, the British government pulled in more than $50 million in fines from one speed-cam. In the same year, Washington, DC, issued $34 million worth of speed-cam-based tickets. This kind of revenue without a corresponding increase in human resource costs is certainly one of the technology's most attractive features, causing some critics to argue that city governments are more interested in profit than public safety.

5   But supporters of speed-cams also need to know that in 2003 the Australian government had to freeze $6 million in fines because of a speed-cam snafu. A truck was issued a camera-generated ticket for going twenty miles faster than the truck's engine could actually go. This kind of error suggests that speed-cams are subject to serious errors and cannot be relied on.

1. What is the author's point?

_____

_____

2. Identify the three reasons used to support that point.

a. _____

_____

b. _____

_____

c. _____

_____

3. In addition to these three reasons, which of the following does the author use as support?

a. specific illustration

b. results of research

c. expert opinion

4. Which error or errors in reasoning can you detect in paragraph 3?

a. irrelevant reason

b. circular reasoning

    c. hasty generalization

    d. unidentified or inappropriate expert

    e. unidentified or dated research

3. Grooming Counts or Does It?

1 Many companies have established rigid grooming standards for their employees. Walt Disney World, for example, insists that employees follow established guidelines for hairstyle, jewelry, makeup, and facial hair. Airlines also require flight attendants to meet certain weight restrictions. Federal Express (FedEx) and United Parcel Service (UPS), too, impose grooming standards that limit the length of men's hair. Currently, however, some of these policies are being justifiably challenged in courts by workers who claim that the standards infringe on their religious rights. At issue is whether employers have the right to enforce rigid grooming rules on workers whose appearance expresses their religious beliefs or their cultural heritage.

2 According to the Equal Employment Opportunity Commission (EEOC), no company is allowed to prevent its employees from expressing religious beliefs through their appearance. The EEOC claims that forbidding such expressions of religious belief violates the Civil Rights Act. Both FedEx and UPS, for example, have fired drivers who refused to cut off their dreadlocks—long, thick strands of knotted or braided hair associated with Rastafarianism.* Similarly, several police officers employed by the Dallas Police Department were reprimanded or fired for wearing dreadlocks. In these cases and others, the EEOC and the Justice Department's Civil Rights Division have interceded on behalf of the employees.

3 The question of civil rights aside, employers also need to keep in mind that an employee's appearance seldom interferes with his or her ability to do the job. In other words, employers can afford to be more tolerant. Chris Warden, for example, was terminated from his job as a FedEx driver for wearing dreadlocks even though his manager's evaluations called him a superior employee. Warden's case proves that wearing dreadlocks does not affect an individual's job performance and therefore should not be a cause of dismissal.

4 As the multicultural population of the United States continues to grow, companies will be challenged more often for their insistence on strict grooming policies. It's high time employers

---

*Rastafarianism: a religious and political movement originating in the 1930s in Jamaica.

embraced diversity and redefined outdated notions about what is "reasonable" and "acceptable." (Source of information: David France, "Law: The Dreadlock Deadlock," *Newsweek*, September 10, 2001, p. 54.)

1. What is the author's point?

_____

_____

2. Identify the two reasons used to support that point.

a. _____

_____

b. _____

_____

3. In addition to these two reasons, which of the following does the author use as support?

a. specific illustration

b. results of research

c. expert opinion

4. Which error or errors in reasoning can you detect in paragraph 3?

a. irrelevant reason

b. circular reasoning

c. hasty generalization

d. unidentified or inappropriate expert

e. unidentified or dated research

4. **Could El Al Be a Model?**

1 Officials of Israel's El Al Airline say that the four suicide hijackings that occurred in the United States on September 11, 2001, could never have occurred on their airplanes. They may be right. El Al has the most elaborate, thorough, and successful security system in the entire airline industry.

2   El Al's rigorous system of luggage screening prevents bombs and weapons from getting on board an airplane. Before being loaded onto an aircraft, all suitcases and bags are put into a

pressurized box that will recognize and detonate any explosives inside. Bags transferring from flights are subjected to the same screening, and bags that cannot be matched to a passenger are not permitted on board. El Al also subjects passengers themselves to a time-consuming and controversial[4] screening process, used to ensure that potential terrorists will not board a plane. Even before a traveler arrives at the airport, his or her name has already been compared to a computerized list of terrorist suspects compiled by law-enforcement agencies around the world.

3   If a would-be hijacker manages to foil this system and board the plane, he or she faces still another security measure: undercover agents who travel on every flight. These armed agents, who look and behave like ordinary travelers, are stationed in aisle seats, where they watch for trouble. They are ready to defend passengers and protect the plane from a terrorist takeover. In addition to the presence of undercover agents, most of El Al's pilots are well educated and have advanced degrees.

4   El Al is based in a country torn for years by conflict and violence, yet it keeps travelers safe. In fact, the sole hijacking of an El Al plane occurred in 1968, at a time when the current security measures were not in place. (Source of information: Vivienne Walt, "Unfriendly Skies Are No Match for El Al," *USA Today*, October 1, 2001, p. 1D.)

1. What is the author's point?

_____

_____

2. Identify the three reasons used to support that point.

a. _____

_____

b. _____

_____

c. _____

_____

---

[4]Critics of El Al's policies have complained that the screening process smacks of racial profiling.

3. In addition to these three reasons, which of the following does the author use as support?

   a. specific illustration

   b. results of research

   c. expert opinion

4. Which error or errors in reasoning can you detect in paragraph 3?

   a. irrelevant reason

   b. circular reasoning

   c. hasty generalization

   d. unidentified or inappropriate expert

   e. unidentified or dated research

 # Identifying the Opposing Point of View

By definition, a solid argument includes a point of view or position and some form of support. However, arguments that revolve around a statement of policy or value are very likely to include both an opposing point of view and the author's response to it.

Here again is the article on mandatory minimum sentences (pp. 487–488), only now it contains an opposing point of view along with the author's response.

Does the Punishment Fit the Crime?

1   In 1984, lawmakers wanted to send a tough message on the sale of drugs. As part of a bill called the Sentencing Reform Act, Congress assigned mandatory minimum sentences for all drug offenses taking place near schools. Offenders could get anywhere from five to twenty years based on the amount of drugs involved. With time, additional mandatory minimums became part of the legal system, including the "three strikes you're out" provision that specified life sentences for repeat drug offenders. While mandatory minimum sentences are still seen by some to be a solution to drug use in the United States, there are several reasons why the courts need to reconsider the effectiveness of these mandatory minimum sentences.

2   Thanks in large part to mandatory minimum sentencing, jails are currently packed. A federal penitentiary like Leavenworth, built to house 1,200 prisoners, has occasionally housed as many

as 1,700, creating overcrowded conditions that breed violence and riots. State correctional facilities are filled to overflowing, so much so that violent criminals are sometimes released in order to make room for nonviolent drug offenders. In 2003, the number of imprisoned drug offenders was an astonishing 330,000. This figure is larger than the number of people imprisoned for all crimes in 1970.

3   The group Families Against Mandatory Minimums (FAMM) regularly lobbies Congress for the repeal of mandatory minimums, citing cases like that of Michael T. Irish, a first offender sentenced to twelve years in federal prison for helping unload hashish from a boat, or Charles Dulap, imprisoned for eight years in federal prison for the crime of renting a truck used by a friend to import marijuana. FAMM was founded over a decade ago by Julie Stewart, who hadn't been particularly interested in the subject of mandatory minimum sentencing until her brother was imprisoned for five years after he was caught growing marijuana seedlings. It was Stewart who came up with FAMM's motto, "Let the Punishment Fit the Crime."

4   According, however, to someone like Deborah Daniels, who was U.S. attorney in the Southern District of Indiana from 1988 to 1993, the punishment usually does fit the crime. This is so even in cases like that of non-violent offender Mark Young,* who got a life sentence for playing the role of middleman in a drug-trafficking scheme. Daniels insists that mandatory minimum sentences are essential if the United States wants to encourage other countries to wage war on drugs. In her mind, mandatory minimum sentences set the right example.

5   Daniels doesn't seem to recognize that there is no proven cause-and-effect relationship between mandatory minimum sentences and drug trafficking in other countries, where drug exports rise and fall based on a variety of factors (e.g., government corruption, state of the economy, ease of access to drugs). All these factors have little or nothing to do with any sentencing example set by the United States.

6   What Daniels also doesn't acknowledge is how mandatory minimum sentences have been used to wring information from those threatened with stiff sentences. Since it is now the prosecutor, rather than the judge, who can demand a specific sentence, some prosecutors have used that power to get information about others allegedly involved in drug trafficking. Not surprisingly, the legal rewards for providing information have created a brand

---

*Young had two prior convictions, one for trying to fill a fake prescription and one for possession of amphetamines.

new black market—the buying and selling of drug deals. Thus a defendant who hopes to avoid lengthy jail time can buy, for the right amount of cash, information about alleged drug deals. In fact, some professional informers charge as much as $25,000 for a drug lead that might help diminish a lengthy mandatory minimum sentence. As members of FAMM regularly point out, mandatory minimum sentences are not only more than likely to be out of proportion to the crime, but they also encourage false testimony and the growth of an illegal market for drug information.

In this illustration, the author's argument has expanded to include an opposing point of view—Attorney Deborah Daniels believes that mandatory minimum sentences set an example for other countries involved in a war on drugs—and a response. There's no evidence of a cause-and-effect connection between mandatory minimum sentences and the willingness of other countries to wage that war.

EXERCISE 6

DIRECTIONS Read each argument. Then answer the questions that follow.

EXAMPLE

Home Schooling Isn't Really School

1   As a public school teacher, I have to admit I cringe every time I hear the phrase "home schooling." I know that many parents believe they are helping their children by teaching them at home. But in my experience, home schooling may do more harm than good.

2   Children who enter my class after a long period of home schooling usually have huge gaps in their education. True, they often read and write better than the average fifth grader, and their spelling is good. But they know very little about the social sciences, and science itself seems to be a foreign word.

3   In addition, children who have been schooled at home frequently have difficulty working with other children. Unused to the give-and-take of group interactions, they quickly show their discomfort or displeasure. Their response is understandable since they have spent years at home in a class of one or two at most.

4   I know that many parents believe that home schooling protects their children from dangerous or corrupting ideas and experiences. To some degree, they are probably correct in that assumption. Unfortunately, the protection home schooling provides may cost too heavy an intellectual price. In general, parents do not

have the necessary training or background to give their children the wide-ranging and up-to-date education they need. And certainly parents cannot provide the kind of peer socialization found in schools outside the home.

1. What is the point of the author's argument?

Home schooling may do more harm than good.

2. What two reasons does the author give in support of that point?

a. *Children can end up with big gaps in their education.*

b. *Children schooled at home usually have difficulty working in groups.*

3. Identify the opposing point of view mentioned in the reading.

Parents believe that they are protecting their children from bad experiences and inappropriate ideas.

4. Paraphrase the author's response.

The protection costs too much socially and intellectually.

EXPLANATION As is often the case, the author states the point of the argument at the beginning of the reading—home schooling can do more harm than good—and then follows with two reasons for that position. Although the answer to a possible objection appears at the end, this is not necessarily standard. Answers to objections can just as easily be sprinkled throughout.

1. The Benefits of Home Schooling

1 Although it has been harshly criticized by many—often by those who have a vested interest* in supporting the status quo*—home schooling just may be the answer to our current educational crisis.

2   At home, children can learn one-on-one or in small groups. If they need some additional explanation or instruction, the home

---

*vested interest: having a special reason to promote or protect that which gives one a personal advantage.
*status quo: existing state of affairs.

tutor can readily supply it. In public schools, in contrast, children often sit in classrooms with twenty or thirty other students. Such class numbers make it almost impossible for teachers to give students the individual attention they so frequently need. There are so many competing voices and questions, a teacher can't possibly respond to all of them. Someone has to go consciously unattended or unconsciously ignored.

3   Another advantage of home schooling is that it allows children to learn in a comforting, familiar environment, lacking in distractions. Any parent who has ever delivered a weeping child to the door of his or her classroom knows full well how terrifying some children find the classroom atmosphere with its noisy hubbub. Children who learn at home aren't distracted by their surroundings, nor are they inhibited by the presence of other children who might unthinkingly laugh at their mistakes.

4   Critics who claim that home schooling can't provide children with the breadth of knowledge they need always assume that the parents don't have the necessary qualifications. Yet of the parents I know personally who teach their children at home, two have a master's degree in physics, another a doctorate in psychology, and still another is a former elementary teacher with ten years of teaching experience to her credit. Parents who take on the responsibility of home schooling do not do so lightly. They know full well that they must provide their children with an education that prepares them for the world they will eventually enter.

1. What is the point of the author's argument?

_____

_____

2. Identify the two reasons used to support that point.

a. _____

_____

b. _____

_____

3. Identify the opposing point of view mentioned in the reading.

_____

_____

4. Paraphrase the author's response.

_____

_____

2. Teacher Performance Linked to Pay

1 In January 2004, The Teaching Commission, a blue-ribbon panel of nineteen leaders in government, business, philanthropy, and education that was chaired by former IBM chairman Louis V. Gerstner Jr., released its report on improving education in America's schools. Among the commission's conclusions was the controversial recommendation that each teacher's pay be determined by student performance. Although immediately opposed by many teachers and teachers' organizations, this suggestion should be implemented in our schools. The recommendation makes sense for a number of reasons. For one, compensating teachers based on classroom results would replace an archaic, eighty-year-old system that pays a good teacher the same as a poor one. Currently, teachers' salaries are based only on years of experience, so an ineffective teacher who has taught for twenty years earns far more than a newer but far more effective one. According to The Teaching Commission, this system "does nothing to reward excellence." In other words, it would be fairer to the hardest-working teachers to reward them with bigger paychecks.

2   Opponents of performance-based pay argue that such a plan ignores the many factors affecting student performance, such as poverty or family background, that are outside teacher control. The commission, however, has recommended that teacher evaluations be designed to take such factors into account. What's more, commission members argue that many other professions use performance-based pay plans. Gerstner said, "Lawyers do it, engineers do it, business people do it. All professional people ultimately come up with methodology to judge the difference between great performance and mediocre performance. Just because it's hard doesn't mean we can't do it."

3   In fact, The Teaching Commission believes that tying teachers' salaries to performance will help raise their overall professional status. Unfortunately, teaching is often viewed as a second-rate occupation. The commission believes, though, that if teachers were compensated like professionals in other fields and were less limited by antiquated, experience-based pay scales, the highest-performing teachers would garner more respect for their efforts.

Plus, bright and more talented individuals might be attracted to the profession.

4   The end result would be an increase in student achievement. Incentives could make teachers' work more difficult, but they would be rewarded for achieving better results. They would be more inclined to do whatever it takes to help their students learn; therefore, students stand to benefit the most. (Sources of information: The Teaching Commission, "Teaching at Risk: Blue-Ribbon Panel Calls for Overhaul of Teacher Education and Compensation to Recruit and Retain Talent in America's Public Schools," Press Release, January 14, 2004, www.theteachingcommission.org/ press/2004_01_14_01.html; "Teacher Pay Tied to Student Progress?" CNN.com, January 14, 2004, www.cnn.com/2004/ EDUCATION/01/14/teacher.salaries.ap/.)

1. What is the point of the author's argument?

_____

_____

2. Identify the four reasons used to support that point.

a. _____

_____

b. _____

_____

c. _____

_____

d. _____

_____

3. Identify the opposing point of view mentioned in the reading.

_____

_____

4. Paraphrase the author's response.

_____

_____

■ **DIGGING DEEPER**

LOOKING AHEAD The author of the reading on page 505 was convinced that the fast food industry had a lot to answer for when it came to the issue of obesity in the United States. The author of this reading has a different point of view.

Eat French Fries at Your Peril

1 Flush from their victories against the tobacco companies, some lawyers and activists have decided to take on another public health enemy—the fast food industry. The plan is to sue the companies selling the high-calorie foods that contribute to one of America's major health problems—obesity. Currently, 61 percent of the adults in the United States are overweight while the number of overweight children has tripled in the last twenty years. As some would have it, fast food is to blame.

2   From the point of view, for example, of John Banzhaf, a George Washington University law professor who helped wage war on the tobacco companies, the fast food industry, from McDonald's to Pizza Hut, has not adequately warned the public about the calories and fat their products contain. If they did, the logic goes, Americans would be more inclined to renounce fat-filled delicacies like cheeseburgers with fries. Without doubt, Banzhaf's position has earned some support from books like Marion Nestle's *Food Politics* and Eric Schlosser's *Fast Food Nation*. Both authors suggest that the way fast food companies manufacture and market products has contributed to the staggering increase in obesity. It should come as no surprise, then, that lawyers are gearing up to sue companies selling foods like pizza, french fries, and hamburgers. The talk is about suing to recover the cost of treating diseases related to being overweight, like high blood pressure and diabetes. The hoped-for end result is that the fast food industry will decide not only to decrease the amount of fat and calories in their products but also to increase prices so that it is not as easy for consumers to grab a loaded-with-fat burger.

3   Yet while only the most die-hard fan of french fries would claim that companies are committed to performing a public service by offering good fast food at low prices, it's also true that litigation, relatively successful against the tobacco industry, may well be the wrong approach. Fast food companies, after all, are quite different from the tobacco companies, which have decided, by and large, to give in to the court of public opinion and settle the lawsuits they

once fought so vigorously. Tobacco companies could not change their product to make it safer. Fast food companies, in contrast, have options. As Eric Schlosser, one of the industry's strongest critics, says: "Fast food companies could actually change their behavior rather easily. . . . Fast food companies could just change the recipe to grilling instead of deep-frying and have a profound impact on the healthiness of what they're selling."

4   In addition, when it comes to showing a direct cause-and-effect relationship, those trying to pin their obesity on fast food will have a tough row to hoe. Obesity is considered to be 60 percent environmental and 40 percent genetic. In other words, obesity runs in families. Someone like fifty-six-year-old Caesar Barber, who at five ten and 270 pounds has filed a class-action suit against McDonald's, Burger King, Wendy's, and KFC, will have a tough time proving his claim that eating fast food is the primary cause of his obesity and resulting health problems. Unless he can prove that key point, it may not matter that, as Barber said when interviewed on ABC's *Good Morning America,* "They [the companies] never explained to me what I was eating."

5   Remember, too, that the general public was behind the plaintiffs of the class-action suit against the tobacco companies. There is, however, no guarantee that suits against the fast food companies will have the same support. For one thing, if the suits are successful, the fast food industry will undoubtedly change how it makes and markets its products. The industry, for sure, will pass the extra cost on to consumers, who are unlikely to be grateful about that benefit of litigation. It's also true that some overweight people are tired of being told that "thinner is better." They might not look kindly on the notion that the fast food industry has inflicted obesity on the overweight consumer. They are more likely to argue that being obese should be an acceptable body type variation.

6   John Doyle, cofounder of the Center for Consumer Freedom, a restaurant industry group, also makes an argument that most Americans will find compelling. Doyle's position is that people should be smart and savvy enough to recognize that foods like cheese, hamburgers, and french fries are high in both calories and fat. In short, people need to take responsibility for what they eat—no one is forcing them to feast on french fries. Anyone who does is probably going to gain weight, and that's their fault. It most certainly is not the fault of companies who make and serve french fries. Doyle has a point. After all, does anyone really need to be told that a double cheeseburger is loaded with fat? (Sources

of information: Geraldine Sealey, "Whopper of a Lawsuit: Fast Food Chains Blamed for Obesity, Illnesses," ABCNews.com, July 26, 2002; Megan McArdle, "Can We Sue?" May 24, 2002, http://archive.salon.com/2002/5/24/fastfoodlaw.)

Sharpening Your Skills

DIRECTIONS Answer the following questions by filling in the blanks or circling the letter of the correct response.

1. In your own words, what is the main idea of the entire reading?

   _____

   _____

2. In paragraph 3, the primary organizational pattern is
   a. definition.
   b. cause and effect.
   c. comparison and contrast.
   d. classification.

3. Which transition in paragraph 3 is an obvious clue to the pattern?

   _____

4. In paragraph 4, Caesar Barber's lawsuit against several fast food companies is used to make which point?
   a. Few people are willing to file a class-action suit against the fast food industry.
   b. People who sue the fast food companies may have difficulty proving fast food was the sole source of their health problems.
   c. More and more people are filing lawsuits blaming the fast food industry for everything from obesity to diabetes.

5. In paragraph 5, the first transition in the paragraph signals _____, whereas the second transition signals

   _____.

6. The author offers four reasons why using lawsuits to attack the fast food industry may not work. Please paraphrase the first two.

   _____

   _____

7. The first sentence of paragraph 6 is

   a. a fact.

   b. an opinion.

   c. a blend of fact and opinion.

8. What is the author's purpose?

   a. to inform

   b. to persuade

9. How would you describe the author's tone?

   a. skeptical

   b. neutral

   c. outraged

   d. friendly

10. Based on what the author says, you could draw which conclusion?

   a. If consumers were disappointed after buying pills advertised as capable of making body fat melt away, the author would probably suggest that they sue the company who made the pills.

   b. If consumers were disappointed by pills advertised as capable of melting away body fat and wanted to sue the company that made the pills, the author would probably tell them they should have known better than to buy the pills in the first place.

   c. If consumers were disappointed after buying pills that were advertised as capable of making body fat melt away, the author would probably advise them not to expect results in so short a time.

WORD NOTES: SPEAKING OF SANCTIONS

Page 511 introduced the verb *sanction,* meaning "to approve." Similarly, the noun *sanction* can mean "permission" or "approval." However, the word *sanction* has an additional definition that you should be aware of because it often turns up in the news. In its plural form, the word refers to penalties or actions used to bring about a change in a nation's behavior. For example, economic *sanctions* were in place against Iraq for a number of years; the goal of those penalties was to exact more responsible behavior from former Iraqi leader Saddam Hussein.

The following sentences use the word *sanction* in different ways. For each sentence, give the correct meaning.

1. How can you *sanction* such obviously unethical practices?

_____

2. The economic *sanctions* against the government of South Africa were harshly criticized by the corporations who had a vested interest in free trade.

_____

Now it's your turn to create two different sentences, each one illustrating a different use of the word *sanction.*

1. _____

_____

2. _____

_____

Students who want to do an in-depth review of the steps in analyzing arguments with the help of **Getting Focused,** the companion software accompanying this text, should look at "Question 11: Is the Author's Argument Sound?"

To get more practice analyzing arguments, go to **laflemm.com** and click on "Reading for Thinking: Online Practice." Complete and correct Practices 7 and 8.

Test 1: Reviewing the Key Points

DIRECTIONS Answer the following questions by filling in the blanks or circling the letter of the correct response.

1. Every argument begins with _____.

2. Which one of the following statements is *not* likely to be at the heart of an argument?

   a. statement of negation

   b. statement of condition

   c. statement of value

   d. statement of policy

3. Writers who want their arguments to be seriously considered know they have to provide the appropriate support. Critical readers, in turn, know that they have to _____ and _____ that support.

4. When an argument is based on a statement of _____ or a statement of _____, it's also likely to contain a response to the opposition.

5. In their haste to prove a point, writers sometimes include reasons that are not _____ to their claim.

6. A writer who offers an opinion and supports it by saying the same thing in different words is guilty of using _____.

7. Writers who offer one example to prove a broad general claim are guilty of drawing _____.

8. A writer who uses expert opinion should give readers an idea of the expert's _____.

9. Writers who use research to support their claims need to provide some form of _____ so that readers know who conducted it.

10. Writers who use research also need to make sure that the research cited is not so _____ that it may no longer be applicable.

To correct your test, turn to the answer key on page 644.

Test 2: Analyzing Arguments

DIRECTIONS Read each argument and answer the questions that follow by filling in the blanks or circling the letter of the correct response. *Note:* The author may or may not respond to opposition and the argument may or may not include an error.

1. Kids and Sports

1   For many parents, competitive team sports like Little League Baseball and Peewee Football are an essential part of childhood. Thus they are anxious for their kids to try out and "make the team." Supposedly, competitive sports build physical strength. Even more important—or so the argument goes—playing competitive sports early on in childhood builds character. Still, parents intent on making sure their kids learn how to compete might want to rethink the notion that sports in which somebody has to win or lose are important to a young child's development. Competitive sports for preteen kids have some important disadvantages; these disadvantages need to be considered before parents push kids onto a playing field where the winner takes all.

2   Here's one thing that should be considered: Competitive sports can unduly stress a child's still developing body. Football, basketball, baseball, and even tennis are physically demanding. They put a very heavy strain on the body. This is particulary true if muscles or bones are still developing. Now, a ten-year-old who is just playing for the fun of it will probably not repeat a movement or motion that hurts, but what if that same child is playing for a trophy? Is he or she going to stop throwing that tough-to-hit curve ball just because there is a little pain involved? It's not likely. Unfortunately, the end result can be lifelong damage to a shoulder or an arm. Thomas Tutko, author of the book *Winning Is Everything and Other Myths,* argues that kids should not be playing physically demanding sports before the age of fourteen. From Tutko's perspective, playing competitive sports before that age is simply too "traumatic," both physically and psychologically.

3   In his book *No Contest: The Case Against Competition,* author and researcher Alfie Kohn emphasizes that the psychological effects of competitive sports on those still too young to play them may be worse than the physical injuries that can ensue. Kohn's book summarizes the results of several hundred studies focusing on the effects of competition both on and off the playing field. Whether in the context of sports or the classroom, Kohn contends that competition "undermines self-esteem, poisons our relation-

ships, and holds us back from doing our best."[5] Clearly, Kohn would not support the notion of competition as a character builder for children. If anything, he sees it as a character destroyer, even if those competing are grownups.

4   To be fair to those who insist there's no point to playing basketball, football, or baseball unless you keep score, these are games where the score counts. However, the position argued here is not that competitive sports should be abandoned; rather, they should be postponed until the child is ready to be not just a winner, but a loser as well. A fifteen-year-old is probably able to accept the simple fact that, at some time in life, everyone loses at something. But does a nine-year-old have to learn this lesson? In their early years, kids should concentrate on achieving their personal best. Are they running faster, jumping higher, or throwing faster than they did the last time around? Those are the questions they should be asking themselves, not who won and who lost.

1. What is the author's point?

_____

_____

2. Identify the two reasons used to support that point.

a. _____

_____

b. _____

_____

3. Does the author include any of the following?

a. examples or illustrations

b. research results

c. expert opinion

4. Does the author respond to any opposing point of view? _____
If so, fill in the blanks that follow.

Opposition   _____

_____

---

[5]A. Kohn, "No Win Situations," *Women's Sports & Fitness,* July/August 1990, pp. 56–58.

Response _____

_____

5. Circle one or more of the appropriate letters to indicate the presence or absence of errors in the author's argument.

a. irrelevant reason

b. circular reasoning

c. hasty generalization

d. unidentified or inappropriate expert

e. unidentified or dated research

f. no errors

2. Access to Adoption Files

1 As of November 1, 2004, adoptees and birth parents living in the province of Alberta, Canada, will have the legal right to obtain information about one another. Initially, either party will have the right to veto access, but after 2005, neither will have veto power over access to adoption records. With the exception of losing the right to veto, this policy should also be uniformly accepted in the United States, where access to adoption records is still hotly disputed with the dispute resulting in a hodgepodge of policies that vary from state to state. In some states, adoptees are allowed no information or "nonidentifying information." This information is limited to age, physical characteristics, talents, hobbies, and basic medical data. But the amount of even that information depends on the agency or court that releases it.

2 Over the years, many adoptees have rightly protested this situation, causing some states to modify their rules for access. But the decision about access to adoption records should not be left up to the individual states. Instead, Congress should step in and enact legislation that gives adopted children the right to discover their parents and their history, both personal and medical.

3 After all, restricting access to adoption files makes the search more difficult, but it does not necessarily stop adoptees—and less frequently birth parents—from searching. Those men and women desperate for information will, if they can afford it, hire a detective to find out what they are driven to know.

4 The truth is that many adoptees feel guilty about being put up for adoption. They assume that they did something wrong, something that made them so unlovable their parents were forced to give them up. These men and women need to know the real

causes for their adoption. It helps an adoptee to know, for example, that his mother gave him up for adoption because she was too young to support him, not because she didn't love him. Such knowledge helps relieve the burden of guilt some adoptees carry around their entire lives.

5   There are also physical—rather than psychological—reasons why adoptees need access to their files. To take proper care of their health, they need to know what diseases they might have inherited. In more extreme cases, knowledge about biological parents can mean the difference between life and death. Sometimes adoptees are in need of an organ transplant, and they require an organ that comes from a natural relative. If all their relatives are unknown, these adopted men and women are at a terrible disadvantage—one that could cost them their lives.

6   Some parents who have given up their children for adoption resent the idea of opening up adoption files. They feel that their right to privacy will be threatened. Yet this objection is based on the assumption that adopted children want to hunt down their parents and intrude on their lives. But, as study after study shows, adoptees only want to know who their biological parents are. In some cases, they may even want to meet them, but they do not want to push their way into the lives of people who will not accept them. Giving the adopted person access to files does not mean that the parent or parents forsake all rights to privacy. It only means that the adopted child can attempt to make contact if he or she wishes, and the parents can refuse or accept as they see fit.

1. What is the author's point?

_____

_____

2. Identify the three reasons used to support that point.

a. _____

_____

b. _____

_____

c. _____

_____

3. Does the author include any of the following?

a. examples or illustrations

b. research results

c. expert opinion

4. Does the author respond to any opposing point of view? _____
If so, fill in the blanks that follow.

Opposition _____

_____

Response _____

_____

5. Circle one or more of the appropriate letters to indicate the presence or absence of errors in the author's argument.

a. irrelevant reason

b. circular reasoning

c. hasty generalization

d. unidentified or inappropriate expert

e. unidentified or dated research

f. no errors

Test 3: Analyzing Arguments

DIRECTIONS Read each argument and answer the questions that follow by filling in the blanks or circling the letter of the correct response. *Note:* The author may or may not respond to opposition and the argument may or may not include an error.

1. Banning Peanuts

1 There was a time when the peanut butter and jelly sandwich was a staple of the school lunchbox. Often it was the one food that fussy children would willingly eat, and parents were grateful it existed, even if they personally found the combination distasteful. The popularity of peanut butter and jelly sandwiches, however, is a thing of the past as schools from New York to California have stopped serving them in the cafeteria. Many school officials have also asked parents not to put peanut products of any kind into their kids' lunches.

2 If the ban on peanuts sounds silly to you, then you obviously don't know an important fact: Based on 2000 U.S. Census data, the Food Allergy and Anaphylaxis* Network (FAAN) estimates that 1 in every 125 children is affected by peanut allergy. Other studies also strongly indicate that the number of children with allergies is increasing at alarming rates. The need for a ban on peanuts in the schools is not a trivial issue. It's a matter of life or death.

3 In November of 1998, seventeen-year-old Mariya Spektor of Niskayuna, New York, died after she unknowingly ate some cereal that had peanut oil in it. In the very same month, twelve-year-old Kristine Kastner of Mercer Island, Washington, died after she ate a chocolate chip cookie that had finely minced peanuts in it. The reality is that children can and do die if they unwittingly ingest peanut products, and neither parents nor educators can afford to take the chance that this might happen.

4 Critics of the ban, among them some members of FAAN, worry that the peanut ban pits parent against parent, especially when desperate parents reduce the issue to "My kid's life or your kid's peanut butter sandwich." Still, opponents of the ban argue that there are other ways to handle the problem. They emphasize self-management on the part of the child along with special lunch zones where peanuts are, or are not, allowed.

5 Such suggestions, however, overlook a couple of crucial points. Labels don't always make it easy to discover exactly what's in the food being consumed. Then too, kids will be kids. Tell them to

*anaphylaxis: hypersensitivity to a foreign substance.

stay in one area of the cafeteria while avoiding another and they will do the exact opposite. Thus if peanuts in any form are allowed in school, there's always the possibility that a child with an allergy will ingest a snack that might prove deadly. Naturally, a child allergic to peanuts is not going to bite into a peanut butter and jelly sandwich, but that same child might well munch on a chocolate chip cookie containing peanuts, not realizing that nuts are in the cookie.

6   Parents of children allergic to peanuts are aware that many do not want peanut products banned from schools. One of those parents is Mark LoPresti of Grand Island, New York. LoPresti has a three-year-old son who is severely allergic to peanuts, and the father acknowledges the ban can create problems. Still he is fiercely determined that peanuts must be banned when his son is ready to go to school. As LoPresti puts it, "I'm not going to sacrifice my son's life for the right to have a peanut butter sandwich." It's hard not to sympathize with LoPresti's point of view. When it comes to the ban on peanut products in schools, an old adage seems to apply: "It's better to be safe than sorry." (Sources of information: Carrie Hodges, "Peanut Ban Spreads to Cafeteria," *USA Today,* December 3, 1998, p. 17a; www.canoe.ca/Health 9902/16_allergy.html.)

1. What is the author's point?

_____

_____

2. Identify the reason used to support that point.

_____

_____

3. Does the author include any of the following?
   a. examples or illustrations
   b. research results
   c. expert opinion

4. Does the author respond to any opposing point of view? _____
   If so, fill in the blanks that follow.

Opposition   _____

_____

Response _____

_____

5. Circle one or more of the appropriate letters to indicate the presence or absence of errors in the author's argument.

a. irrelevant reason

b. circular reasoning

c. hasty generalization

d. unidentified or inappropriate expert

e. unidentified or dated research

f. no errors

2. Protecting Our Children from Pornography

1 In December 2000 Congress enacted the Children's Internet Protection Act (CIPA), which requires schools and libraries to have in place software filters that block computer access to sites featuring obscenity or pornography and are, therefore, harmful to minors. Libraries or schools that did not have such filters in place by 2002 faced the loss of government subsidies. This legislation seemed eminently sensible. It seemed almost impossible that anyone would quarrel with it. Yet, in fact, there was immediate opposition from the American Civil Liberties Union and, in particular, the American Library Association. Stranger still, a lower court actually sided with the American Library Association in a suit challenging the constitutionality of applying CIPA to libraries. Fortunately, on June 23, 2003, the Supreme Court struck down the lower court's ruling. But even though the issue has come to a legal resolution, the question remains: How is it that sensible people take it upon themselves to challenge legislation that does nothing more than protect innocent children?

2   More than 75 percent of the nation's public libraries offer Internet access. Thanks to that access, any twelve-year-old—unless filters are in place—can reach sites featuring hardcore sex scenes. Even worse, kids can get into chatrooms where they might make contact with sex offenders or child molesters. Children should not be exposed to such websites or chatrooms. As Dr. Melanie Powers has pointed out, even one experience with a pornographic site can do irreparable damage to a child's psyche.

3   Opponents of the filters on library computers argue that they also block access to constitutionally protected free speech and unfairly infringe upon the right of adults to have access to infor-

mation not considered illegal in any way. But this complaint is sheer nonsense. Adults who want access to sites filtered out by the software can ask that it be temporarily dismantled. This is a right that is actually guaranteed by the CIPA legislation.

4   Libraries routinely enact the role of censor when they refuse to stock their shelves with pornographic books, magazines, or videos, and you won't find copies of *Hustler* or *Penthouse* tucked away in the magazine rack of your local library. Nor for that matter will you find a copy of *Deep Throat* in the video department. Yet no one claims that this act of censorship infringes on the right to free speech. Why shouldn't the same principle apply to the Internet? Libraries don't stock pornography; therefore, why shouldn't they exclude pornographic sites from their offerings to the public?

5   Our libraries need to be open to everyone. But by allowing children access to any website available on the Internet, we are turning our libraries into adult bookstores and doing what real adult bookstores cannot do for fear of legal retribution. Libraries that don't use software filters are exposing vulnerable children to pornographic material that might well do them terrible, even lethal, harm. (Sources of information: www.net/services/cipa; www.cnn.com/2003/law/06/24/scotus.internetporn.library./

1. What is the author's point?

_____

_____

2. Identify the two reasons used to support that point.

a. _____

_____

b. _____

_____

3. Does the author include any of the following?

    a. examples or illustrations

    b. research results

    c. expert opinion

4. Does the author respond to any opposing point of view? _____
If so, fill in the blanks that follow.

Opposition _____

_____

Response _____

_____

5. Circle one or more of the appropriate letters to indicate the presence or absence of errors in the author's argument.

a. irrelevant reason

b. circular reasoning

c. hasty generalization

d. unidentified or inappropriate expert

e. unidentified or dated research

f. no errors

3. Dangerous Self-Esteem

1   For years now, we have heard that high self-esteem is a prerequisite for achievement. As a result, many students work in classrooms where posters proclaim "we applaud ourselves." Exactly for what isn't always made clear. In elementary school, students complete sentences that begin "I am special because. . . ." According to what has become established educational wisdom, children who are praised, even for their mistakes, will become confident, successful adults. In response to that wisdom, some states (California for one) have established educational task forces on—you guessed it—promoting self-esteem. Yet now there is some evidence that self-esteem, if it's not backed by real achievements, might be dangerous.

2   As psychologist Brad Bushman of the University of Michigan puts it, kids who develop unrealistically high opinions of themselves can, when brought face to face with a more realistic version of who they are, become "potentially dangerous." Bushman, along with Ray Baumeister of Case Western Reserve University, conducted a study of unrealistic self-esteem and found that students inflated by self-esteem not based on real achievement were likely to react with hostility or aggression when confronted by a world that fails to mirror their sense of importance.

3   The findings of Bushman and Baumeister have also been echoed by James Gilligan of Harvard Medical School. Gilligan,

a long-time researcher into the causes of violence, agrees that inflated self-esteem with no basis in fact can be dangerous. Clinical psychologist Robert Brooks of Harvard concurs as well. According to Brooks, if teaching self-esteem is done inappropriately, "you can raise a generation of kids who cannot tolerate frustration."

4   Those who argue that the failure to teach self-esteem will cause a generation of children to grow up feeling worthless are missing the point. Schools and parents should continue to praise children for a job or task well done. No one is saying that they shouldn't. But self-esteem has to be based on real achievement, not on empty praise that encourages a child to believe everything he or she does is perfect, despite evidence to the contrary.

5   In the end, inflated self-esteem not based on any real accomplishment may well do more harm than good. Unfortunately, the tendency of some young people to become aggressive whenever the world does not reflect their own inflated sense of self-importance is proof positive that an entire generation of young people will never amount to anything. Raised by self-indulgent parents who threw traditional values out the window because they had to "do their own thing," these kids never had a chance to become responsible adults. One can only fear for our society once it is in their hands. (Source of information: Sharon Begley, "You're OK, I'm Terrific," *Newsweek*, July 13, 1998, p. 69.)

1. What is the author's point?

_____

_____

2. Identify the reason used to support that point.

_____

_____

3. Does the author include any of the following?

    a. examples or illustrations

    b. research results

    c. expert opinion

4. Does the author respond to any opposing point of view? _____
If so, fill in the blanks that follow.

Opposition   _____

_____

Response   _____

_____

5. Circle one or more of the appropriate letters to indicate the presence or absence of errors in the author's argument.

a. irrelevant reason

b. circular reasoning

c. hasty generalization

d. unidentified or inappropriate expert

e. unidentified or dated research

f. no errors

4. In Praise of Bilingualism

1   Lack of English skills is the main reason why minority students fall behind in school. For those who care about the education of America's young people, that should be reason enough to promote bilingual education. But for those who are still not convinced, let me offer the results of some significant research and lay to rest commonly expressed worries about the effect of bilingual education on the acquisition of English.

2   Research on the effects of bilingual education shows that bilingualism does not interfere with performance in either language (Hakata & Garera, 1989). Thus it makes no sense to argue that non-native speakers should not have bilingual instruction because it will interfere with their acquisition of English. This claim is not grounded in any factual evidence.

3   Instead of discouraging bilingual education by trying to eliminate funding for it, we should encourage it because research suggests that the ability to speak two languages improves cognitive flexibility* and the ability to think creatively (Diaz, 1983). This may be one reason why most other industrialized countries insist that their students master *at least* one other language. They know what we in the United States ignore: Bilingualism enlarges a person's capacity for understanding the world by giving him or her two different languages of interpretation. As linguist Benjamin

_____

*cognitive flexibility: ease and quickness of thinking.

Whorf established decades ago in his now classic article "Science and Linguistics," "We dissect nature along lines laid down by one native language. . . . The world's presented in a kaleidoscopic* flux* of impression which has to be organized by our minds—and this means largely by the linguistic systems in our minds."[6]

4   The child—or for that matter, the adult—who can speak two languages has more tools for understanding the world than we who are limited solely to English.

1. What is the author's point?

_____

_____

2. Identify the two reasons used to support that point.

a. _____

_____

b. _____

_____

3. Does the author include any of the following?

a. examples or illustrations

b. research results

c. expert opinion

4. Does the author respond to any opposing point of view? _____
If so, fill in the blanks that follow.

Opposition   _____

_____

Response   _____

_____

———————
*kaleidoscopic: like a child's toy that constantly changes patterns and colors.
*flux: change, movement.
[6]Edward T. Hall, *The Silent Language*. New York: Anchor Books, 1973, p. 123.

5. Circle one or more of the appropriate letters to indicate the presence or absence of errors in the author's argument.

a. irrelevant reason

b. circular reasoning

c. hasty generalization

d. unidentified or inappropriate expert

e. unidentified or dated research

f. no errors

Test 4: Analyzing Arguments

DIRECTIONS Read each argument and answer the questions that follow by filling in the blanks or circling the letter of the correct response. *Note:* The author may or may not respond to opposition and the argument may or may not include an error.

1. Double Punishment Not an Answer

1   The Higher Education Act (HEA) was signed into law over three decades ago by President Lyndon Baines Johnson. Its purpose was to make advanced education a reality for students who, without financial aid, might not be able to attend college. But since 1998 more than 140,000 students have not received any aid because they answered yes to question 35 on the application form: "Have you ever been convicted of possessing or selling drugs?" In 2003 alone, a little over 29,000 students found themselves without financial aid because of their response to that one question. For good reason, some members of Congress are sponsoring H.R. 685, a bill that would repeal the 1998 revision of the Higher Education Act.

2   For one thing, federal financial aid is not denied to people who commit far more serious crimes. The form does not ask about the applicant's overall criminal record, so those people who have been convicted of non-drug-related crimes can still receive financial aid. As one expert put it, "You can murder your grandmother and get financial aid, but you can't smoke a joint. You are denied aid even if you are convicted of a [drug] misdemeanor with no jail time. It is inequitable."

3   Furthermore, the criminal justice system has already punished the prospective student as a result of his or her conviction. Michael Cunningham, for example, was convicted of possessing a gram of marijuana. He paid the fine, completed his community service sentence, and now lives with the consequences of having a criminal record. Does it seem right that he was also forced to quit school because he was denied the $3,000 in financial aid he needed for his tuition? Mr. Cunningham's example is proof enough that this new legislation only serves to further penalize those who have already paid their debt to society.

4   Supporters of the law argue that it's a tough but necessary component of the war on drugs. They claim that the prospect of being denied financial aid will deter young people from getting involved with drugs. However, the law ignores the fact that people make mistakes but can still repent and change. Besides, most

young people who experiment with drugs are just not thinking ahead three or four years to when they might need funds for college. Chances are that the law's ability to deter people from drug use is being overestimated.

5   Finally, this law is not even what its sponsor wanted. U.S. Representative Mark Souder, a Republican from Indiana, said, "It hasn't worked out at all the way I intended." He meant for the financial aid denial to apply only to those who were convicted of drug use while either applying for or actually receiving assistance. He says he did not mean to penalize those who honestly admitted to a prior conviction.

6   Obviously, this law robs students of much-needed aid and should be eliminated. The war on drugs will not be won by throwing extra obstacles in the paths of people who seek to better themselves by attending college. (Sources of information: Michael Kranish, "Truth and Its Consequences," *Boston Sunday Globe,* September 9, 2001, pp. E1–E2; www.dailylobo.com/news/2003/02/21/opinion/editorial.DrugPolicyLimits.A10.)

1. What is the author's point?

_____

_____

2. Identify the four reasons used to support that point.

a. _____

_____

b. _____

_____

c. _____

_____

d. _____

_____

3. Does the author include any of the following?

a. examples or illustrations

b. research results

c. expert opinion

4. Does the author respond to any opposing point of view ? _____
If so, fill in the blanks that follow.

Opposition _____

_____

Response _____

_____

5. Circle one or more of the appropriate letters to indicate the presence or absence of errors in the author's argument.

a. irrelevant reason

b. circular reasoning

c. hasty generalization

d. unidentified or inappropriate expert

e. unidentified or dated research

f. no errors

2. More Homework May Not Pave the Road to Success

1 Local communities across the nation are pressuring schools to boost test scores so kids can get into and do well in college. In response to that pressure, teachers are piling on the homework, starting in elementary school. A University of Michigan study found that in 1997, children ages nine to eleven were averaging three and a half hours of homework a week—a figure that is steadily increasing. At Farmland Elementary School in Rockville, fifth graders are being assigned up to an hour and a half of homework every day. Even six-year-olds are getting nightly homework assignments. Fortunately, more parents and education professionals are beginning to question the value of homework for younger children and are insisting that schools follow the PTA recommendation of ten minutes of homework per grade level.

2 First of all, it's clear that homework assignments for elementary school children do not improve academic performance. A 1999 study conducted by Sandra Hofferth, a scientist at the University of Michigan's Institute for Social Research, found no link between heavy homework assignments and improved grades. Harris Cooper, Ph.D., the chairman of the Psychological Sciences Department at the University of Missouri at Columbia, is one of the top authorities

on homework. Cooper claims that for kids in elementary school, "The effect of homework on achievement is trivial, if it exists at all."

3   While it's true that many parents and educators consider assignments that encourage creative thinking to be valuable, these are not the assignments children are getting for homework. Instead, they are being asked to complete dull textbook assignments that do not develop imagination or creativity.

4   Too much homework is also likely to generate angry, tearful battles at home because children dislike the dull assignments and try to avoid doing them. Parents, in turn, must force their kids to sit down and do the work, all of which creates a tension-filled home environment. In the long run, children will only begin to dislike school and schoolwork even more. Furthermore, Boston school board president General Francis A. Walker pointed out in 1900 that homework harms children's health. Around the same time, many educators believed that homework caused tuberculosis, nervous conditions, and heart disease in youth.

5   Excessive homework also interferes with extracurricular activities, which are just as important as academic studies. Many children today are involved in sports, hobbies, and music lessons. After-school assignments make it difficult for kids to engage in these activities, which teach valuable life skills that are just as important as formal academic knowledge. Children also need time just to be kids. They need to play with their friends and have leisure time with their families. As child psychiatrist Stanley I. Greenspan, M.D., pointed out in his book *The Irreducible Needs of Children*, a child needs a variety of nonacademic activities to grow into a whole person. That's why school districts should follow the lead of the East Porter County School Board in Indiana. In 1998, the board adopted a policy requiring school personnel to coordinate assignments so that students do not have to devote their entire evening to homework.

6   The drawbacks to homework outweigh the benefits. Let's stop pretending that it's helping kids achieve and keep schoolwork in the schools. (Source of information: Stephanie Dunnewind, "Homework Overload?" *The Seattle Times*, November 16, 2002, p. 12.)

1. What is the author's point?

_____

_____

2. Identify the four reasons used to support that point.

a. _____

_____

b. _____

_____

c. _____

_____

d. _____

_____

3. Does the author include any of the following?

a. examples or illustrations

b. research results

c. expert opinion

4. Does the author respond to any opposing point of view? _____
If so, fill in the blanks that follow.

Opposition _____

_____

Response _____

_____

5. Circle one or more of the appropriate letters to indicate the presence or absence of errors in the author's argument.

a. irrelevant reason

b. circular reasoning

c. hasty generalization

d. unidentified or inappropriate expert

e. unidentified or dated research

f. no errors

3. Serving the Nation: A Universal Call

1 Israel requires all of its young men to serve three years of mandatory military service. The Israeli Defense Force drafts women, too,

but not for combat positions. Sweden does not have a professional army. Instead, all of its younger men train for military service and then remain in the reserves until age forty-seven. The United States would do well to follow suit and require all of its young men and women to serve in the military for one or two years after leaving high school.

2   Opponents of compulsory service object, saying that universal conscription* would cost too much. They argue that Americans won't permit an increase in taxes to fund a significantly larger military. However, these critics forget that freedom is not free. All Americans should have the opportunity to serve their country. Also, learning to defend one's homeland is a patriotic obligation. Therefore, young people should be proud to devote a short time of their lives to fulfill an important civic responsibility.

3   This country needs compulsory military service in order to train its citizens to combat terrorism and to give them the skills to respond to threats and attacks of any kind. After World War II in 1945, President Truman noted that America's "geographic security is gone—gone with the advent of the atomic bomb, the rocket, and modern airborne armies." Yet fewer than 6 percent of Americans under the age of sixty-five know anything about military service. The rest of the population relies on a relatively small number of servicemen and women to protect them. This is a dangerous state of affairs given that the twenty-first century has ushered in a new age of warfare, one that often takes the form of attacks on inno- cent civilians. Americans can no longer be complacent or expect others to guard their safety. All citizens need to learn the special- ized communication, emergency response, and civil defense skills necessary for combating various kinds of threats to the nation's security.

4   Mandatory military service would also help close the social gap that currently divides Americans from one another. According to journalism professor and naval reservist Philip Meyer, "One of the unplanned consequences of the military draft was a great leveling effect, where social-class distinctions were set aside." Unfortu- nately, once World War II came to an end, that leveling effect was no longer so powerful, and the country began to divide into sepa- rate and often unequal social groups. If all young men and women were once again required to serve together as equals, democratic ideals would be reinforced, and divisions between people of differ- ent classes would be narrowed.

---

*conscription: drafting for military service.

5   In an era when America is threatened by suicide bombers and bioterrorism, it makes sense for all citizens to participate in basic military training. One to two years of service is a small price to pay for a stronger defense and greater national unity.

1. What is the author's point?

_____

_____

2. Identify the two reasons used to support that point.

a. _____

_____

b. _____

_____

3. Does the author include any of the following?

a. examples or illustrations

b. research results

c. expert opinion

4. Does the author respond to any opposing point of view? _____
If so, fill in the blanks that follow.

Opposition   _____

_____

Response   _____

_____

5. Circle one or more of the appropriate letters to indicate the presence or absence of errors in the author's argument.

a. irrelevant reason

b. circular reasoning

c. hasty generalization

d. unidentified or inappropriate expert

e. unidentified or dated research

f. no errors

4. Information About Anthrax Helps Calm Panic

1 In the autumn of 2001, a wave of anthrax contaminations raised the possibility that America might be subjected to biological warfare. And it's certainly true that disease-causing microorganisms can be used as instruments of terror. Yet despite constant media speculation that our country's enemies might drop deadly anthrax bacteria from the skies or dump it into our waters, this particular biological weapon could probably not be used on a massive scale. No matter what the media hype, there are three reasons why large-scale bioterrorism with anthrax would be difficult to achieve.

2   First of all, infecting large numbers of people would require specific types and large amounts of the deadly microorganism. Killer forms of anthrax, for example, must be manufactured in a laboratory by people who know which strains can be developed into lethal weapons. Then, once a fatal strain is actually produced, it must still be delivered in large enough quantities to infect a person. A toxic dose of anthrax is defined as 8,000 to 10,000 spores. Also, this quantity must be inhaled in order to fatally infect an individual. It has to be inhaled because anthrax-induced infections of the skin are fatal in only about 25 percent of cases.

3   Distributing anthrax on a large scale is another problem terrorists would face. For example, lethal anthrax spores would have to be ground finely enough to be inhaled. Each spore would have to be no larger than five microns. If the spores were dropped from airplanes, the wind would disperse them. This would make it unlikely that one individual could inhale enough to cause a fatal infection. Indoors, filters in buildings' ventilation systems would cleanse the majority of spores from the air.

4   Third, health care professionals can treat anthrax infections with an arsenal of antibiotics. As talk show host Oprah Winfrey has assured the public, "There are plenty of drugs that can be used safely and effectively." So far, she claims, no anthrax strains have shown any resistance to antibiotics like penicillin and the tetracyclines. According to U.S. Secretary of Health and Human Services Tommy Thompson, eight staging areas around the country are each stocked with fifty tons of medical supplies, including vaccines, antibiotics, gas masks, and ventilators. These supplies can be moved within hours to the site of a bioterrorist attack.

5   Yes, the American public should stay informed about the possible dangers of a bioterrorist attack. But people should not panic or let fear restrict their movements. Biological weapons are a reality, yet the likelihood of a successful large-scale attack is very slight. (Source of information: www.thezephyr.com/anthrax.htm.)

1. What is the author's point?

_____

_____

2. Identify the three reasons used to support that point.

a. _____

_____

b. _____

_____

c. _____

_____

3. Does the author include any of the following?

a. examples or illustrations

b. research results

c. expert opinion

4. Does the author respond to any opposing point of view? _____
If so, fill in the blanks that follow.

Opposition   _____

_____

Response   _____

_____

5. Circle one or more of the appropriate letters to indicate the presence or absence of errors in the author's argument.

a. irrelevant reason

b. circular reasoning

c. hasty generalization

d. unidentified or inappropriate expert

e. unidentified or dated research

f. no errors

Test 5: Taking Stock

DIRECTIONS Read the passage. Then answer the questions by filling in the blanks or circling the letter of the correct response.

The Sport of Boxing Needs a Fighting Chance

1 Boxing, according to fight promoter Lou DiBella, "is dirty from top to bottom. The sport is dying. It's like a cancer patient on chemo." It wasn't always so. At one time, boxing was very popular; throughout the early- to mid-twentieth century, when Joe Louis, Muhammad Ali, Joe Frazier, and George Foreman were fighting, it seemed like everyone was a boxing fan. People crowded around radios to hear announcers describe bouts, and boxers were admired for their skill and heroism. The sport has inspired many great writers (Ernest Hemingway, Jack London, and Joyce Carol Oates), filmmakers (*Rocky, Raging Bull,* and *Champion*), and even musicians (Bob Dylan). Today, however, even the best boxers are seen as celebrities who earn millions of dollars rather than superb athletes dedicated to their sport. The World Heavyweight title is no longer a position of respect and glory. One case in point is ex-champion and convicted rapist Mike Tyson, who is frequently in trouble with the law.

2   Of course, boxing still has die-hard supporters who love the sport for its grace and excitement. "Boxing is the raw, narrative drama of physical conflict with a hero and a loser," says writer Jack Newfield. "On its rare best nights, fights like the ones between Ali and Frazier . . . reveal character and will and bravery that can be as uplifting as a symphony or a play." And many fans still agree with former heavyweight champion George Foreman that "boxing is the sport that all other sports aspire to be."

3   Yet even supporters like Newfield have referred to the current state of boxing as a "slum" and a "sewer." They acknowledge that the sport is declining because of its corruption and its lack of uniform rules and standards. Cleaning up boxing and restoring it to its former glory days will require remedying two serious problems.

4   First and foremost, the sport must free itself of rampant corruption. For years, boxing has been plagued by bribes and fixed fights, and undercover FBI investigations have resulted in charges of money laundering, racketeering, fraud, conspiracy, and tax evasion. In a recent investigation, boxer Mitchell Rose told FBI agents that employees of Top Rank, boxing's second-largest promotional company, offered him $5,000 to throw his 1995 fight with Eric

"Butterbean" Esch. When he refused the bribe and won the fight, Rose was blacklisted. In 2001, a grand jury indicted Thomas Williams for accepting payment to take a dive against Richie Melito. Boxer Shelby Gross claims to have been offered $10,000 to lose to Melito, but he says he rejected the bribe.

5   Forged records and deliberate mismatches, too, have blighted the sport. Boxing's managers and promoters stand to make huge profits on events, so they are inclined to embellish boxers' records to generate more audience interest in a particular match. For example, when promoter Don King arranged Mike Tyson's first fight after Tyson's release from prison, he chose Peter McNeely, a boxer with a fake record of 36–1 to be Tyson's opponent. King's plan to engineer an explosive comeback for Tyson was almost too successful. McNeely was such a weak opponent, it took Tyson only ninety seconds to demolish McNeely in the ring, and matches that short are not crowd-pleasers. FBI stings have also produced forged medical records that have allowed boxers to continue to fight and earn managers and promoters large sums of money while sacrificing their own health.

6   Even when the fights are legitimate, boxing's judging is often disgraceful. While sports like basketball and baseball have quantifiable measures for winning, the outcome of a boxing match, as for a figure skating routine, is subjective—dependent on the opinion of those doing the judging. Jack Newfield says that, in many cases, promoters pay the judges, including their travel expenses. "[The judges] know which fighter is under an exclusive contract to that promoter. They don't have to be told that if they favor that promoter's employee, they will get future assignments from that promoter. Can you imagine a baseball owner picking and paying the home-plate umpire in a World Series game?" Lou DiBella, senior vice president of HBO Boxing and TVKO, agrees: "Judges know the unspoken agenda. It's the equivalent of George Steinbrenner picking the umpires for a playoff game with the Red Sox." Consequently, many decisions in championship fights are indefensible, and not surprisingly, such biased and unfair decisions demoralize fighters.

7   To combat all these abuses, the U.S. Congress has enacted several laws, including the Professional Boxing Safety Act of 1996 and the Muhammad Ali Boxing Reform Act of 2002. In April 2004, the U.S. Senate passed a bill to establish the United States Boxing Administration (USBA). The bill's sponsor, Senator John McCain, said, "Without the adoption and implementation of minimum uniform federal standards, I fear that the sport of boxing will continue its downward spiral into irrelevance." Not everyone

agrees with the idea of creating a national commission. Among them is promoter Murad Muhammad, who says, "You can't change one hundred years of tradition." However, Mr. Muhammad has had charges of assault and battery and defamation of character filed against him, so his opinion doesn't merit serious consideration. Most fans agree that the USBA can strengthen and enforce existing boxing laws, reduce arbitrary practices, and provide uniformity in ranking criteria and contractual guidelines.

8   The USBA also needs to correct boxing's second major problem: the mistreatment of the boxers themselves. The USBA can establish and enforce uniform health and safety standards and create a centralized medical registry to protect boxers from injury or death. Since 1970, about fifty professional fighters have actually died in the ring. The most recent tragedy happened in 2003 when thirty-four-year-old Brad Rone, who had high blood pressure and was out of shape but needed money, was allowed to fight in Utah and ended up dying of heart failure after the first round. Clearly, better oversight for boxers' physical welfare is needed, and a national regulatory agency could demand that boxers like Rone pass complete physical examinations before entering a ring.

9   In addition to the creation of the USBA, boxers themselves should seize more power and authority by creating an association, or union, to look out for their financial interests. Right now, a boxer's adviser and representative is his manager, which is akin to a baseball coach doubling as a financial adviser to a pitcher or an outfielder. It's no wonder that the majority of boxers make very little money and have no financial contracts, no pension plans, and no insurance. Just as baseball players have a union that negotiates on their behalf, boxers should organize themselves so that they can have similar protections.

10   In an effort to resuscitate a dying sport, Jack Newfield has created a Bill of Rights for Boxers that proposes, among other things, a national commission and a labor union to end the abuses. "Boxing has become like a gruesome car wreck," wrote Newfield. "I can keep watching only if I'm pulling a victim out to safety. . . . The best way I can display my respect for [boxers] is to try to clean up their polluted and toxic environment." (Sources of information: Jack Newfield, "Should We Let Boxing Die?" *Parade,* May 2, 2004, pp. 6–7; Jack Newfield, "The Shame of Boxing," *The Nation,* November 12, 2001, www.thenation.com/doc.mhtml? i20011112&s=newfield; Rebecca Hanks, "McCain Gives Boxing Fighting Chance," U.S. Senate Committee on Commerce, Science, and Transportation Press Release, April 1, 2004, http:// commerce.senate.gov/newsroom/printable.cfm?id=219936.)

1. Use context clues to define the word *rampant* in paragraph 4.

_____

2. In your own words, what is the main idea of the entire reading?

_____

_____

3. What does the author's reference to Mike Tyson illustrate?

_____

4. What pattern organizes paragraph 6?

_____

5. Which statement best sums up the main idea of paragraph 9?
   a. Boxers need a union to protect their interests.
   b. Boxers aren't very smart when it comes to financial matters.
   c. Boxers and baseball players have a lot in common.
   d. Boxers are not treated very well by their managers.

6. What opposing point of view does the author mention?

_____

7. How does the author respond to the opposition?

_____

8. Would you say the author's response reveals
   a. no bias.
   b. acceptable bias.
   c. excessive bias.
   Please explain.

_____

9. From Lou DiBella's statement in paragraph 6, a reader might logically draw which conclusion?

   a. Lou DiBella wouldn't disagree with Jack Newfield's analogy comparing boxing to a "gruesome car wreck" (paragraph 10).

   b. Lou DiBella would be unlikely to support Senator John McCain's bill to create the United States Boxing Administration.

   c. Lou DiBella is probably one of the people responsible for the corruption in the sport of boxing.

   d. Lou DiBella is probably a good friend of boxing promoter Murad Muhammad, who is mentioned in paragraph 7.

10. What conclusion can be drawn from the reading?

   a. Boxing promoters and managers want to reform boxing and make it a safer sport.

   b. Boxing promoters and managers don't care whether boxing is made safer or stays exactly the same.

   c. Boxing promoters and managers will probably fight many of the changes reformers like Newfield want to make.

Putting It All Together

This section of *Reading for Thinking* lets you bring together everything you have learned about comprehension and critical reading. It also offers you the opportunity to deepen your understanding of some topics introduced in the preceding chapters.

The readings that follow are accompanied by discussion questions and writing assignments, which ask you to do what up till now you've seen others do—argue a point of view. These questions and assignments are important because *Reading for Thinking* is not concerned solely with teaching you to understand and evaluate the ideas of others. Ultimately, its goal is to encourage you to confidently express and argue your own particular point of view.

■ **READING 1**

BECOMING AN ETHICAL THINKER
Joseph Turow

LOOKING AHEAD Several of the readings in the preceding chapters dealt with questions of ethics. There was a good reason for this. All the critical thinking strategies outlined in this book can help you in making ethical decisions about whether a particular idea or action is right or wrong. In other words, actively concerning yourself with ethics will not only make you a better person but also a better critical thinker. In this reading, textbook author Joseph Turow reviews some key theories about ethical behavior that have stood the test of time.

PRE-READING AND FOCUS STRATEGIES

1. Although the language is straightforward and direct, some of the concepts in this reading may be new to you, which means you should do a detailed survey of the material. In addition to the headings, read the first and last sentences of every paragraph. Quickly read through the list of ethical approaches summarized in the chart at the end of the reading.

2. The reading uses a lot of marginal annotation. Pre-read the annotations carefully. Then when you read the entire selection, make sure to compare the text definitions with the annotations in the margin. Sometimes they are slightly different, so comparing them will give you a deeper understanding of a key term.

3. The headings in this reading mention five different ethics theories. After you finish a section, see if you can paraphrase the ethical theory described. Then try to come up with an example of that theory as it would be practically applied.

4. A chart summarizing the theories completes the reading. To review when you finish, cover up the columns under the headings—*Philosopher, Central Tenet,* and *Example of Application.* See if you can remember how to fill in the three columns for each ethical approach. Put a check mark next to the ones you can't recall and reread those sections to find out what you missed.

WORD WATCH Some of the more difficult words in this reading are defined below. Watch for these words as you read. The number in parentheses indicates the paragraph in which they appear. An asterisk marks their first appearance in the reading.

raunchy (7): crude, vulgar

innuendo (7): sexual suggestion

impunity (11): without fear of punishment

autonomy (12): independence

contemporary (13): modern

inherent (18): characteristic or typical

---

1 **ETHICS** IS A SYSTEM OF PRINCIPLES ABOUT WHAT IS RIGHT THAT guides a person's actions. Ethics has come to be recognized as the study of concepts such as *ought, should,* and *duty.* The term **moral** tends to be attached to activities that are either good or bad and the rules that we develop to deal with those activities. Some prefer to think of *morals* as being culturally transmitted indicators of right and wrong, whereas *ethics* is merely a way to determine what we ought to do.

ethics A system of principles about what is right that guides a person's actions.

moral Describes activities that are either good or bad and the rules that we develop to cover those activities.

2 In the same way, the term *immorality* is most often associated with the Judeo-Christian concept of sin, and sin is most often equated with evil. The term *unethical* is more acceptable in modern culture because it tends not to carry the connotation of evil-doing. Instead, it most often connotes wrongdoing (rather than doing right). To be *ethical* or *unethical* rather than *moral* or *immoral* is more a reflection of modern connotation than representative of any real difference in meaning.

Classical Ethics

3 Over the centuries, philosophers have developed various approaches to understanding what is ethical and what is not. By applying one or more of these classical approaches to ethics, we can better evaluate—from an ethics standpoint, at least—our behavior and the behavior of others. The five ethical approaches [are as] follows: *the Golden Mean, the categorical imperative, the principle of utility, the Judeo-Christian ethic,* and *the veil of ignorance.* . . . Let's look at them one at a time.

Golden Mean Aristotle's belief that an individual who combines both intellectual and moral virtues while following reason can be happy, and that an individual's acts are right and virtuous if they are the mean of two extremes.

4 *The Golden Mean* The Greek philosopher Aristotle believed that an individual who combines both intellectual and moral virtues while following reason can be happy. An individual's acts are right and virtuous if they are the mean of two extremes. This idea led to the development of Aristotle's **Golden Mean,** which represents the average of the extreme actions between the intellectual and moral virtues. While Aristotle was certainly not the first to develop the

saying "moderation in all things," he was certainly one of its major proponents.

5   Aristotle reasoned that an individual could be happy if he or she chose the average path between the two extremes that would lead him or her on the best course. Yet he also stated that each person should seek his or her own Golden Mean; each person is different, and what might be too much for one person could possibly be too little for another. While Aristotle believed in the Golden Mean, he also believed that an individual could make the correct ethical choice only if she or he had the proper qualities of intelligence.

6   To apply Aristotle's Golden Mean, begin by identifying ethical extremes and then seek a balance between the two. For those who are prone to one extreme, the balance comes from leaning toward the other extreme. The farther away you are, the more you must lean.

7   Consider an everyday example. Alex has a tendency to want to sexually harass his female coworkers by using lewd language and telling raunchy* jokes that make them quite uncomfortable. According to the Golden Mean approach, Alex should address his unethical behavior by forcing himself toward the other extreme—that is, by making sure he never uses any language that has even a hint of sexual suggestiveness. If a bit of innuendo* does escape from his lips every now and then under these circumstances, that will not be a problem, according to the Golden Mean. . . .

Judeo-Christian ethic or the **Golden Rule** The admonition to "do unto others as you would have them do unto you."

8   *The Judeo-Christian Ethic* The **Judeo-Christian ethic,** also known as the **Golden Rule,** refers to the admonition to "do unto others as you would have them do unto you." This was neither the first nor the last time this maxim was proposed as an ethical guideline. Kung Fu Tzu (Confucius) presented his version five hundred years before the birth of Christ as a proscription: "Do not do to others what you would not want done to you."

categorical imperative Emmanuel Kant's theory that individuals should follow ethical principles as if these principles could be applied in any situation, so that an individual would act only in ways in which she or he would want everyone else to act, all the time.

9   Continuing with our earlier example, following this rule might mean that Alex would simply stop harassing his female coworkers because when he thinks about it, he realizes that he would not want them harassing him. The same would be true about producers of sex and violence on TV: They would recognize that they wouldn't want their children being bombarded with such materials, so they would stop bombarding other people's kids with them.

10   *The Categorical Imperative* German philosopher Emmanuel Kant developed his theory of the **categorical imperative,** which holds that individuals should follow ethical principles as if these princi-

ples could be applied in any situation. "We should act in such a way that we could wish the maxim of our action to become a universal law." That way, Kant believed, we would be able to develop rules of order, or duties. The word *maxim,* in this sense, means the principle on which the action was based—the type of principle that people formulate in determining their conduct. So, if a person won't lie out of principle, he or she should be willing to apply that principle as a law, universally. Many have pointed out that this is simply a reformulation of the Golden Rule, and it's easy to see why.

11   Under the categorical imperative, an individual would act only in ways in which he or she would want everyone else to act, all the time. Thus, it would be permissible for us to lie only if we wished everyone to lie all the time. We could murder with impunity* only if we would allow others to do so. Kant reasoned that rational beings wouldn't tolerate a state of existence in which everyone could lie or kill without compunction. And, of course, that's true. How could we live in a society in which we would expect a lie for every question we asked, or one in which murder were the rule rather than the exception?

12   As part of his method for recognizing moral duties under the categorical imperative, Kant insisted that all human beings were owed a minimum of respect simply because they were human beings and capable of reason—in the same way as other natural rights philosophers believed that we are all born with "certain inalienable rights." Only if we demonstrate that we do not deserve to be respected do we relinquish that right. In other words, every person's autonomy* should be respected except in cases in which the exercise of that autonomy conflicts with the public good (as represented by the laws of the state).

13   A contemporary* example relating to the categorical imperative involves invading other people's private information. If we as individuals would not want such a thing to happen to us, we should then act toward other people in the same way. Similarly, executives working for media firms that have the capability of secretly collecting information from people who visit their websites should ask whether they would want that done to them. If they followed the categorical imperative, they would use an "opt in" approach to information collection. That is, they would ask everyone for permission to collect and use the data, just as they might want to be asked.

14   *The Principle of Utility* British philosopher John Stuart Mill believed in **the principle of utility**—so called because it promoted

the principle of utility John Stuart Mill's theory promoting an action based on its utility, or usefulness; often rephrased as "the greatest good for the greatest number." The basis of utilitarianism is the idea that the rightness or wrongness of any action can be judged entirely in terms of its consequences.

15 an action based on its utility, or usefulness. In fact, the now-familiar phrase "the greatest good for the greatest number" is the foundation of utilitarian philosophy.

The basis of utilitarianism is a single, guiding precept: The rightness or wrongness of any action can be judged entirely in terms of its consequences. Motives are therefore irrelevant—completely the opposite of Kant's theory of the categorical imperative. Mill believed that good consequences give pleasure, whereas bad consequences result in pain. (This became known as the "pleasure-pain principle.") According to utilitarianism, the right course of action is the one that promotes the greatest pleasure or minimizes the most pain for those involved in the decision-making.

16 According to this principle, a person or company would have to evaluate the costs and benefits of harassing coworkers, televising violent programs, or secretly collecting information from friends or customers. If the individual or the company determine that more pain than benefit would result from doing these things, they should stop. For example, an online store might conclude that collecting and storing personal information from adults without their permission could lead to bad feelings if customers found out, and therefore could cause it to lose those customers. The result might be that the store would set up a procedure to get permission from its customers after informing them what data it would collect and how it would use that data.

veil of ignorance John Rawls's theory holds that, in any given situation, justice emerges only when all parties are treated without social differentiation; from this perspective, fairness is the fundamental idea in the concept of justice.

17 *The Veil of Ignorance* Philosopher John Rawls's theory of the **veil of ignorance** holds that, in any given situation, justice emerges only when all parties are treated without social differentiation. From this perspective, fairness is the fundamental idea in the concept of justice.

18 In such a situation of equality, a journalist would determine the just thing to do by determining the fairest option, and would make the ethical decision without considering his or her own personal interests. All people going behind this veil of ignorance would have to forget who they are and what their own values and ideologies are, and step into the shoes of the others involved in the ethical situation. Behind this veil of ignorance, journalists would be more objective in their reporting because their inherent* biases would not come into play, as the person reporting the story would put aside his or her own values and ideas.

19 Journalists can use Rawls's idea of the veil of ignorance to write a truly fair story. Reporters who cover the same beat day after day can start to make assumptions about people and use those assumptions in the stories they write. But journalists who go behind the veil of ignorance should try to look at the story as if

they were coming into contact with the people involved for the first time and should bury any preconceived notions about the people. This is a very idealistic look at journalism, but Rawls argues that journalists who use his suggestions will probably be better and fairer journalists.

Making Ethical Decisions

20 Every day you will find yourself in situations in which ethical decisions need to be made. . . . How will you make these decisions? What sort of moral reasoning process should you follow . . . [in order to be] a good citizen?

21   Bob Steele, a senior faculty member at the Poynter Institute, outlines a model that [amateurs] and professionals alike can use to evaluate and examine their decisions and to make good ethical decisions. Steele is concerned specifically with journalism, but the ethical-thinking process that he suggests can work for all sorts of professions.

22   He says, *ask yourself these ten questions:*

1. What do I know? What do I need to know?

2. What are my ethical concerns?

3. What is my . . . purpose?

4. What organizational policies and professional guidelines should I consider?

5. How can I include other people, with different perspectives and diverse ideas, in the decision-making process?

6. Who are the stakeholders—those affected by my decision? What are their motivations? Which are legitimate?

7. What if the roles were reversed? How would I feel if I were in the shoes of one of the stakeholders?

8. What are the possible consequences of my actions in the short term? in the long term?

9. What are my alternatives to maximize my truth-telling responsibility and minimize harm?

10. Can I clearly and fully justify my thinking and my decision to my colleagues? to the stakeholders? to the public?

Classical Ethics Recap

Approach	Philosopher	Central Tenet	Example of Application
The Golden Mean	Aristotle	Any ethical choice always lies between two extremes. Individuals should identify the extremes faced in any situation, and then seek a balance between them. For those prone to one extreme, the balance comes from leaning toward the other extreme.	A TV network program director may try to get the producers of a particularly violent program to reduce the amount of mayhem on their show by telling them to cut out all violent car chases and fights. The program director realizes that the program's creators won't fully adhere to this extreme order. He believes in the Golden Mean, however: If he pushes them toward the other extreme, maybe they will end up in the appropriate middle when it comes to using violent action on the show.
The Judeo-Christian Ethic/The Golden Rule	Kung Fu Tzu (Confucius)	"Do unto others as you would have them do unto you," or, "Do not do to others what you would not want done to you."	Alex has a tendency to want to sexually harass his female coworkers by using lewd language and telling raunchy jokes that make them quite uncomfortable. If Alex applied the Judeo-Christian ethic, he would simply stop harassing his female coworkers because when he thinks about it, he realizes that he would not want them harassing him.

The Categorical Imperative	Emmanuel Kant	"We should act in such a way that we could wish the maxim of our action to become a universal law."	Executives working for . . . firms that have the capability of secretly collecting information from people who visit their websites would have to ask whether they would want that done to them. If they followed the categorical imperative, they . . . would ask everyone for permission to collect and use the data, just as they would want to be asked.
The Principle of Utility	John Stuart Mill	"The greatest good for the greatest number" is the foundation of utilitarian philosophy.	An online store might conclude that collecting and storing personal information from adults without their permission could lead to bad feelings if customers found out and therefore could cause it to lose those customers. The result might be that the store would set up a procedure to get permission from its customers, arguing that the data collected would expand consumers' choices.
The Veil of Ignorance	John Rawls	In any given situation, justice emerges only when all parties are treated without social differentiation.	Reporters who cover the same beat day after day can start to make assumptions about people and use those assumptions in the

Classical Ethics Recap—Continued

Approach	Philosopher	Central Tenet	Example of Application
		Fairness is the fundamental idea in the concept of justice.	stories they write. But journalists who go behind the veil of ignorance should try to look at the story as if they were coming into contact with the people involved for the first time and should bury any preconceived notions. This is a very idealistic notion of journalism, but Rawls argues that journalists who use his suggestions will probably be better and fairer journalists.

Adapted from Joseph Turow, *Media Today: An Introduction to Mass Communication,* 2nd ed. Boston: Houghton Mifflin, 2003, pp. 115–119.

PUTTING IT ALL TOGETHER DIRECTIONS Answer the following questions by circling the letter of the correct response or filling in the blanks.

Vocabulary **1.** What's the author's definition of *maxim?* _____

_____

Main Idea **2.** Which statement most effectively paraphrases the main idea of the entire reading?

a. Over the course of time, five ways of evaluating ethical decisions have evolved, but only two of them are still in use.

b. Ethical decision making is absolutely crucial to living a decent life.

c. Five methods of evaluating ethical behavior have evolved over time, and knowing something about each can help us evaluate behavior from an ethical point of view.

d. Over the centuries, five different approaches to ethics have evolved. Among them, Aristotle's notion of the "Golden Mean" is the most widely understood and applied, perhaps because it is the easiest to comprehend.

Supporting Details **3.** Which of the following philosophers is *not* used to explain the main idea?

    a. Aristotle

    b. Kant

    c. Nietzsche

    d. John Stuart Mill

Transitions **4.** The transition that opens paragraph 2 suggests that which of the following patterns organizes paragraphs 1 and 2?

    a. cause and effect

    b. comparison and contrast

    c. definition

    d. time order

Purpose **5.** What is the author's purpose?

    a. to inform

    b. to persuade

Drawing Your Own Conclusions **6.** Read the following description and circle the appropriate letter to indicate which ethical principle is being applied.

Gina was in a hurry and wanted to take a shortcut to work, which would mean ignoring the "Do not walk on the grass" sign and running across the beautifully kept lawn of the local library. She had one foot on the lawn when she thought to herself, "If everyone did this, the lawn could be destroyed." That thought made her continue her mad dash along the sidewalk rather than across the lawn.

Gina applied which ethical principle?

    a. Aristotle's Golden Mean

    b. Kant's categorical imperative

    c. Judeo-Christian Golden Rule

7. Read the following description. Then circle the appropriate letter to identify the ethical principle David is applying.

David is a very self-absorbed young man. In meetings of the college council, he tends to interrupt the other members in order to express his opinions. As a result, council members have bitterly complained to David directly and criticized him harshly behind his back. Aware of how angry he has made people, David is trying hard to change. Now he never interrupts anyone. On the contrary, he waits until everyone else seems to have voiced an opinion. And before speaking, he always prefaces his comments by asking if anyone else wants to say anything.

a. Aristotle's Golden Mean

b. Kant's categorical imperative

c. Judeo-Christian ethic

8. In terms of what you know about the difference between fact and opinion, is it possible to claim that Aristotle's ethical approach is, *in fact*, better than Kant's? Please explain your answer.

_____

_____

9. Would you say that the author's tone is emotionally neutral or emotionally charged? Please explain your answer.

_____

_____

10. Explain why you think the author does *or* does not express a bias in favor of one particular ethical system.

_____

_____

■   **VOICING YOUR OPINION** Do you think it's important to evaluate your personal behavior in terms of ethical standards? Why or why not? Do you think most of the people you know evaluate their behavior in ethical terms?

_____

_____

_____

■   **THINKING THROUGH WRITING** Write a paper that (1) identifies which of the five approaches described you favor, (2) summarizes the approach you prefer, and (3) illustrates that approach with a specific example.

■ **READING 2**

CONFORMITY, COMPLIANCE, AND OBEDIENCE
Douglas Bernstein and Peggy Nash

LOOKING AHEAD The following reading by textbook authors Douglas Bernstein and Peggy Nash explores some of the reasons people conform, or change their behavior, in order to fit in and be accepted by a group. It also suggests that there are times when a willingness to comply with a request or obey a command can be a bad thing, bad not just for ourselves but for others as well.

PRE-READING AND FOCUS STRATEGIES

1. This reading is packed with information, so get as much out of your survey as you possibly can. Read the marginal annotations along with the first and last sentences of every paragraph. In addition, study the accompanying figure and its caption.

2. The title makes a distinction among *conformity, compliance,* and *obedience.* Read to understand precisely how the authors define and differentiate among the three terms.

3. The reading's title definitely suggests a comparison and contrast pattern of organization. However, the comparison and contrast pattern is often accompanied by cause and effect; see if the authors describe the causes and effects of compliance, conformity, and obedience.

4. Many of the headings pose questions. The question-as-heading format is useful to readers. It tells them that they should be able to answer the question after reading the section.

WORD WATCH Some of the more difficult words in this reading are defined below. Watch for these words as you read. The number in parentheses indicates the paragraph in which they appear. An asterisk marks their first appearance in the reading.

---

norms (4): accepted rules of behavior

ambiguity (10): a situation or condition open to more than one interpretation

genocide (13): the planned murder of an entire national, racial, or religious group

hypothetical (16): possible but not yet realized

---

1 SUPPOSE YOU ARE WITH THREE FRIENDS. ONE SAYS THAT Franklin Roosevelt was the greatest president in the history of the United States. You think that the greatest president was Abraham Lincoln, but before you can say anything, another friend agrees that it was Roosevelt, and then the other one does, too. What would you do? Disagree with all three? Maintain your opinion but keep quiet? Change your mind?

conformity The changing of one's behavior or beliefs to match those of others, generally as a result of real or imagined, though unspoken, group pressure.

2 When people change their behavior or beliefs to match those of other members of a group, they are said to conform. **Conformity** occurs as a result of *unspoken* group pressure, real or imagined (Cialdini & Trost, 1998). You probably have experienced group pressure when everyone around you stands to applaud a performance you thought was not that great. You may conform by standing as well, though no one told you to do so; the group's behavior creates a silent, but influential, pressure to follow suit.

compliance The adjustment of one's behavior because of a direct request.

3 **Compliance,** in contrast, occurs when people adjust their behavior because of a request, such as "Please pass the salt." When the last holdouts for conviction on a jury give in to other jurors' browbeating, they have complied with overt social pressure.

4 Conformity and compliance are usually generated by a group's spoken or unspoken norms.* In a classic experiment, Muzafer Sherif (1937) charted the formation of a group norm by taking advantage of the perceptual illusion whereby a stationary point of light in a completely dark room appears to move. Estimates of how far the light seems to move tend to stay the same over time if the observer is alone in the room. But when Sherif tested several people at once, asking each person to say aloud how far the light moved on repeated trials, their estimates tended to converge; they had established a group norm. Even more important, when individuals who had been in the group were later tested alone, they continued to be influenced by this norm.

5 In another classic experiment, Solomon Asch (1956) explored what people do when faced with a norm that is obviously wrong. The participants in this experiment saw a standard line like the one in Figure 1(A); then they saw a display like that in Figure 1(B). Their task was to pick out the line in the display that was the same length as the one they had first been shown.

6 Each participant performed this task in a small group of people who appeared to be fellow participants, but who were actually working for the experimenter. There were two conditions. In the control condition, the real participant responded first. In the experimental condition, the participant did not respond until after the other people did. The experimenter's assistants chose the correct response on

(A) STANDARD LINE

(B) TEST LINES

Figure 1: Types of Stimulus Lines Used in Experiments by Asch

Participants in Asch's experiments saw a new set of lines like these on each trial. The middle line in Part B matches the one in Part A, but when several of Asch's (1955) assistants chose an incorrect line, so did many of the participants. Try recreating this experiment with four friends. Privately ask three of them to choose the line on the left when you show this drawing to all four, and then see if the fourth person conforms to the group norm. If not, do you think it was something about the person, the length of the incorrect line chosen, or both that led to noncomformity? Would conformity be more likely if the first three people were to choose the line on the right?

six trials, but on the other twelve trials they all gave the same, obviously incorrect, response. So, on twelve trials, each participant was confronted with a "social reality" created by a group norm that conflicted with the physical reality created by what the person could clearly see. Only 5 percent of the participants in the control condition ever made a mistake on this easy perceptual task. However, among participants who heard the others' responses before giving their own, about 70 percent made at least one error by conforming to the group norm. A recent analysis of 133 studies conducted in 17 countries reveals that conformity in Asch-type situations has declined somewhat in the United States since the 1950s, but that it still occurs. It is especially likely in collectivist cultures, where conformity to group norms is emphasized (P. B. Smith & Bond, 1999).

7   *Why Do People Conform?* Why did so many people in Asch's experiment give incorrect responses when they were capable of near-perfect performance? One possibility, called *public conformity,* is that they gave an answer they did not believe in simply because it was the socially desirable thing to do. Another possibility is called *private acceptance,* meaning that the participants, using the other people's responses as legitimate evidence about reality, were convinced that their own perceptions were wrong, and actually changed their minds. Morton Deutsch and Harold Gerard (1955) reasoned that if conformity disappeared when people gave their responses without identifying themselves, then Asch's findings must reflect public conformity, not private acceptance. In fact, conformity does decrease when people respond privately instead of publicly, but it is not eliminated (Deutsch & Gerard, 1955). People sometimes publicly produce responses that they do not believe in, but hearing other people's responses also influences their private beliefs (Moscovici, 1985).

8   Why are group norms so powerful? Research suggests three influential factors (Cialdini & Trost, 1998). First, people are motivated to be correct, and norms provide information about what is right and wrong. This factor may help explain why some extremely disturbed or distressed people consider stories about suicide to be "social proof" that self-destruction is a reasonable way out of their problems (Cialdini, 1993). Second, people want to be liked by other group members. Finally, norms guide the distribution of social reward and punishment (Cialdini, 1995). From childhood on, people in many cultures learn that going along with group norms is good and earns rewards. These positive outcomes presumably help compensate for not always saying or doing exactly what we please. People also learn that breaking a norm may bring punishment,

ranging from scoldings for small transgressions to imprisonment for violation of norms that have been translated into laws.

9 *When Do People Conform?* People do not always conform to group influence. In the Asch studies, for example, nearly 30 percent of the participants did not go along with the assistants' obviously wrong judgments. Countless experiments have probed the question of what combinations of people and circumstances do and do not lead to conformity.

10 *Ambiguity,** for example, is important in determining how much conformity will occur. As the physical reality of a situation becomes less certain, people rely more and more on others' opinions, and conformity to a group norm becomes increasingly likely (Aronson, Wilson, & Akert, 1999). You can demonstrate this aspect of conformity on any street corner. First, create an ambiguous situation by having several people look at the sky or the top of a building. When passersby ask what is going on, be sure everyone excitedly reports seeing something interesting but fleeting—perhaps a faint light or a tiny, shiny object. If you are especially successful, conforming newcomers will begin persuading other passersby that there is something fascinating to be seen.

11 If ambiguity contributes so much to conformity, though, why did so many of Asch's participants conform to a judgment that was clearly wrong? The answer has to do with the *unanimity* of the group's judgment and the *size of the majority* expressing it. Specifically, people experience intense pressure to conform as long as the majority is unanimous. If even one other person in the group disagrees with the majority view, conformity drops greatly. For example, when Asch (1951) arranged for just one assistant to disagree with the others, fewer than 10 percent of the real participants conformed. Once unanimity is broken, it becomes much easier to disagree with the majority, even if the other nonconformist does not agree with the person's own view (J. C. Turner, 1991). Conformity also depends on the size of the majority. Asch (1955) demonstrated this phenomenon by varying the number of assistants in the group from one to fifteen. Conformity to incorrect norms grew as the number of people in the group increased. However, most of the growth in conformity occurred as the size of the majority rose from one to about three or four members. Psychologists believe that this effect occurs because pressure to conform has already reached a peak after someone has heard three or four people agree. Hearing more people confirm the majority view thus has little additional social impact (Latané, 1981).

Applying Psychology

SIGN HERE, PLEASE Have you ever been asked to sign a petition in favor of a political, social, or economic cause? Supporters of such causes know that those who comply with this small request are the best people to contact later with requests to do more. Complying with larger requests is made more likely because it is consistent with the signer's initial commitment to the cause. If you were contacted after signing a petition, did you agree to donate money or become a volunteer?

12   *Gender* has also been studied as a factor influencing conformity. Early research on conformity suggested that women conform more than men, but this difference stemmed mainly from the fact that the tasks used in those experiments were often more familiar to men than to women. Indeed, people are especially likely to conform when they are faced with an unfamiliar situation (Cialdini & Trost, 1998). However, no male-female differences in conformity have been found in subsequent research using materials that are equally familiar to both genders (Maupin & Fisher, 1989).

13   *Inducing Compliance* In the experiments just described, the participants experienced psychological pressure to conform to the views or actions of others, even though no one specifically asked them to do so. In contrast, *compliance* involves changing what you say or do because of a direct request. How is compliance brought about? Many people believe that the direct approach is always best: If you want something, ask for it. But salespeople, political strategists, social psychologists, and other experts have learned that often the best way to get something is to ask for something else. Three examples of this strategy are the foot-in-the-door technique, the door-in-the-face procedure, and the low-ball approach.

14   The *foot-in-the-door technique* consists of getting a person to agree to small requests and then working up to larger ones. In the original experiment on this strategy, homeowners were asked to do one of two things. Some were asked to allow placement of a large, unattractive "Drive Carefully" sign on their front lawn. Approximately 17 percent of the people approached in this way complied with the request. In the foot-in-the-door condition, however, homeowners were first asked only to sign a petition supporting laws aimed at reducing traffic accidents. Several weeks later, when a different person asked these same homeowners to put the "Drive Carefully" sign on their lawns, 55 percent of them complied (Freedman & Fraser, 1966).

15   Why should the granting of small favors lead to granting larger ones? First, people are usually far more likely to comply with a request that costs little in time, money, effort, or inconvenience. Second, complying with a small request makes people think of themselves as being committed to the cause or issue involved (Cialdini, 1995). In the study just described, participants who signed the petition might have thought, "I must care enough about traffic safety to do something about it." Compliance with the higher-cost request (displaying the sign) increased because it was consistent with these people's self-perceptions and past actions (Eisenberg et al., 1987).

16   The foot-in-the-door technique can be very effective. Steven Sherman (1980) created a 700 percent increase in the rate at which people volunteered to work for a charity simply by first getting them to say that in a hypothetical* situation, they would volunteer if asked. For some businesses, the foot in the door is a request that potential customers merely answer a few questions; the request to buy something comes later. Others offer a small gift, or "door opener," as salespeople call it. Acceptance of the gift not only gives the salesperson a foot in the door but may also invoke the reciprocity norm: Many people who get something free feel obligated to reciprocate by buying something (Cialdini, 1993).

17   The second approach, known as the *door-in-the-face procedure,* also effectively obtains compliance (Cialdini, 1995). This strategy begins with a request for a favor that is likely to be denied. The person making the request then concedes that the initial favor was excessive and substitutes a lesser alternative—which is what he or she really wanted in the first place! Because the person appears willing to compromise, and because the new request seems small in comparison with the first one, it is more likely to be granted than if it had been made at the outset. The door-in-the-face strategy is at the heart of bargaining among political groups and between labor and management.

18   The third technique, called the *low-ball approach,* is commonly used by car dealers and other businesses (Cialdini & Trost, 1998). The first step in this strategy is to get a person's oral commitment to do something, such as to purchase a car. Once this commitment is made, the cost of fulfilling it is increased, often because of an "error" in computing the car's price. Why do buyers end up paying much more than originally planned for "low-balled" items? Apparently, once people commit themselves to do something, they feel obligated to follow through, especially when the person who obtains the initial commitment also makes the higher-cost request (Burger & Petty, 1981).

Obedience

obedience A form of compliance in which people comply with a demand from an authority figure.

19   Compliance involves a change in behavior in response to an explicit request. In the case of **obedience,** the behavior change comes in response to a demand from an authority figure (Lutsky, 1995). In the 1960s, Stanley Milgram developed a laboratory procedure to study obedience. In his first experiment he used newspaper ads to recruit forty male volunteers between the ages of twenty and fifty from the local community. Among the participants were professionals, white-collar businessmen, and unskilled workers (Milgram, 1963).

20   Imagine you are one of the people who answered the ad. When you arrive for the experiment, you join a fifty-year-old gentleman who has also volunteered and has been scheduled for the same session. The experimenter explains that the purpose of the experiment is to examine the effects of punishment on learning. One of you—the "teacher"—will help the learner remember a list of words by administering electric shock whenever the learner makes a mistake. Then the experimenter turns to you and asks you to draw one of two cards out of a hat. Your card says, "TEACHER." You think to yourself that this must be your lucky day.

21   Now the learner is taken into another room and strapped into a chair. Electrodes are attached to his arm. You are shown a shock generator with thirty switches. The experimenter explains that the switch on the far left administers a mild, 15-volt shock and that each succeeding switch increases the shock by 15 volts. The one on the far right delivers 450 volts. The far left section of the shock generator is labeled "Slight shock." Looking across the panel, you see "Moderate shock," "Very strong shock," and at the far right, "Danger—severe shock." The last two switches are ominously labeled "XXX." The experimenter explains that you, the teacher, will begin by reading a list of word pairs to the learner. Then you will go through the list again, presenting just one word of each pair. The learner will have to say which word went with it. After the first mistake, you are to throw the switch to deliver 15 volts of shock. Each time the learner makes another mistake, you are to increase the shock by 15 volts.

22   You begin, following the experimenter's instructions. But after the learner makes his fifth mistake and you throw the switch to give him 75 volts, you hear a loud moan. At 90 volts, the learner cries out in pain. At 150 volts, he screams and asks to be let out of the experiment. You look to the experimenter, who says, "Proceed with the next word."

23   No shock was actually delivered in Milgram's experiments. The "learner" was always an employee of the experimenter, and the moans and other sounds of pain came from a prerecorded tape. But you do not know that. What would you do in this situation? Suppose you continue and eventually deliver 180 volts. The learner screams that he cannot stand the pain any longer and starts banging on the wall. The experimenter says, "You have no other choice; you must go on." Would you continue? Would you keep going even when the learner begged to be let out of the experiment and then fell silent? Would you administer 450 volts of potentially deadly shock to an innocent stranger just because an experimenter demands that you do so?

Results of Milgram's obedience experiment When Milgram asked a group of undergraduates and a group of psychiatrists to predict how participants in his experiment would respond, they estimated that fewer than 2 percent would go all the way to 450 volts. In fact, 65 percent of the participants did so. What do you think you would have done in this situation?

24   Only 5 participants in Milgram's experiment stopped before 300 volts, and 26 out of 40 (65 percent) went all the way to the 450-volt level. The decision to continue was difficult and stressful for the participants. Many protested repeatedly. But each time the experimenter told them to continue, they did so. Here is a partial transcript of what a typical participant said:

> [After throwing the 180-volt switch]: He can't stand it. I'm not going to kill that man in there. Do you hear him hollering? He's hollering. He can't stand it. What if something happens to him? I'm not going to get that man sick in there. He's hollering in there. Do you know what I mean? I mean, I refuse to take responsibility. He's getting hurt in there. . . . Too many left here. Geez, if he gets them wrong. There are too many of them left. I mean, who is going to take responsibility if anything happens to that gentleman?
>
>   [After the experimenter accepts responsibility]: All right. . . .
>
>   [After administering 240 volts]: Oh, no, you mean I've got to keep going up the scale? No sir, I'm not going to kill that man. I'm not going to give him 450 volts.
>
>   [After the experimenter says, "The experiment requires that you go on"]: I know it does, but that man is hollering in there, sir.

This participant administered shocks up to 450 volts (Milgram, 1974).

Factors Affecting Obedience

25   Milgram had not expected so many people to deliver such apparently intense shocks. Was there something about his procedure that produced such a high level of obedience? To find out, Milgram and other researchers varied the original procedure in numerous ways. The overall level of obedience to an authority figure was usually quite high, but the degree of obedience was affected by several characteristics of the situation and procedure.

Proximity and obedience In variations on his original experiment, Milgram found that close physical proximity to an authority figure enhanced participants' obedience to that authority (Milgram, 1965). This principle is employed in the military, where no one is ever far away from the authority of a higher-ranking person.

26   *Prestige* One possibility is that the experimenter's status as a Yale University professor helped produce high levels of obedience in Milgram's original experiment. To test the effects of status and prestige, Milgram rented an office in a run-down building in Bridgeport, Connecticut. He then placed a newspaper ad for research sponsored by a private firm. There was no mention of Yale. In all other ways, the experimental procedure was identical to the original.

27   Under these less prestigious circumstances, the level of obedience dropped, but not as much as Milgram expected: 48 percent

of the participants continued to the maximum level of shock, compared with 65 percent in the original study. Milgram concluded that people are willing to obey orders to do great harm to another even when the authority making the demand is not a particularly reputable or distinguished person.

28 *Presence of Others Who Disobey* To assess how the presence of other people might affect obedience, Milgram (1965) created a situation in which there were three teachers. Teacher 1 (an employee of the experimenter) read the words to the learner. Teacher 2 (also an employee) stated whether or not the learner's response was correct. Teacher 3 (the actual participant) delivered the shock when the learner made mistakes. At 150 volts, when the learner began to complain that the shock was too painful, Teacher 1 refused to participate any longer and left the room. The experimenter asked him to come back, but he refused. The experimenter then instructed Teachers 2 and 3 to continue by themselves. The experiment continued for several more trials. However, at 210 volts, Teacher 2 said that the learner was suffering too much and also refused to participate further. The experimenter then told Teacher 3 (the actual participant) to continue the procedure. In this case, only 10 percent of the participants (compared with 65 percent in the original study) continued to deliver shocks all the way up to 450 volts. In line with research on conformity, the presence of others who disobey appears to be the most powerful factor reducing obedience.

29 *Personality Characteristics* Were the participants in Milgram's original experiment heartless creatures who would have given strong shocks even if there had been no pressure on them to do so? Quite the opposite; most of them were nice people who were influenced by experimental situations to behave in apparently antisocial ways. In a later demonstration of the same phenomenon, college students playing the role of prison guards behaved with aggressive heartlessness toward other students who were playing the role of prisoners (Zimbardo, 1973).

30   Still, not everyone is equally obedient to authority. For example, people who display what we described earlier as authoritarianism are more likely than others to comply with an experimenter's request to shock the learner. The same tends to be true of people who are "*externals*" (T. Blass, 2000). . . . Such people believe that what happens to them is controlled by factors outside themselves. . . .

In Review: Types of Social Influence

Type	Definition	Key Findings
Conformity	A change in behavior or beliefs to match those of others	In cases of ambiguity, people develop a group norm and then adhere to it. Conformity occurs because people want to be right, because they want to be liked by others, and because conformity to group norms is usually reinforced. Conformity usually increases with the ambiguity of the situation, as well as with the unanimity and size of the majority.
Compliance	A change in behavior or beliefs because of a request	Compliance increases with the foot-in-the-door technique, which begins with a small request and works up to a larger one. The door-in-the-face procedure can also be used. After making a large request that is denied, the person substitutes a less extreme alternative that was desired all along. The low-ball approach also elicits compliance. An oral commitment for something is first obtained; then the person claims that only a higher-cost version of the original request will suffice.
Obedience	A change in behavior in response to an explicit demand, typically from an acknowledged authority figure	People may inflict great harm on others when an authority demands that they do so. Even when people obey orders to harm another person, they often agonize over the decision. People are most likely to disobey orders to harm someone else when they see another person disobey.

Evaluating Obedience Research

31 Milgram's obedience studies were conducted more than forty years ago. How relevant are they today? Consider this fact: The U.S. Federal Aviation Authority attributes many commercial airplane accidents to "Captainitis." This phenomenon occurs when the captain of an airliner makes an obvious error, but none of the other crew members are willing to challenge the captain's authority by pointing out the error. As a result, planes have crashed and many people have died (Kanki & Foushee, 1990). Obedience to authority may also explain why a few years ago, many travelers at the airport in Frankfurt, Germany, followed an airport official's incorrect instructions to move *toward* a fire that had broken out rather than *away* from it. Several of those travelers died in the fire. These tragic events suggest that Milgram's findings are still relevant and important (Saks, 1992). Indeed, the results of his experiments have been confirmed in recent years in several Western countries, with female as well as male participants (T. Blass, 2000; P. B. Smith & Bond, 1999). Nevertheless, debate continues over the ethics and meaning of Milgram's work.

32 *Questions About Ethics* Although the "learners" in Milgram's experiment suffered no discomfort, the participants did. Milgram (1963) observed participants "sweat, stutter, tremble, groan, bite their lips, and dig their fingernails into their flesh." Against the potential harm inflicted by Milgram's experiments stand the potential gains. For example, people who learn about Milgram's work often take his findings into account when deciding how to act in social situations (S. J. Sherman, 1980). But even if social value has come from Milgram's studies, a question remains: Was it ethical for Milgram to treat his participants as he did?

Linkages Is it ethical to deceive people to learn about their social behavior?

33 In the years before his death in 1984, Milgram defended his experiments (e.g., Milgram, 1977). He argued that the way he dealt with his participants after the experiments prevented any lasting harm. For example, he explained to them that the learner did not experience any shock, and the learner came in and chatted with each participant. And on a later questionnaire, 84 percent of the participants said that they had learned something important about themselves and that the experience had been worthwhile. Thus, Milgram argued, the experience was actually a positive one. Still, the committees charged with protecting human participants in research today would be unlikely to approve Milgram's experiments, and less controversial ways to study obedience have now been developed (Meeus & Raaijmakers, 1995).

34 *Questions About Meaning* Do Milgram's dramatic results mean that most people are putty in the hands of authority figures and that most of us would blindly follow inhumane orders from our leaders? Some critics have argued that Milgram's results cannot be interpreted in this way because his participants knew they were in an experiment and may simply have been playing a cooperative role. If so, the specific social influence processes identified in his studies may not explain obedience in the real world . . . (Lutsky, 1995). Most psychologists believe, however, that Milgram did demonstrate a basic truth about human behavior—namely, that under certain circumstances people are capable of unspeakable acts of brutality toward other people. Sadly, examples abound. One of the most horrifying aspects of Nazi atrocities against the Jews—and of more recent attempts at genocide* against ethnic groups in Eastern Europe and Africa—is that the perpetrators are not necessarily demented, sadistic fiends. Most of them are normal people who, because of the situations they face, are influenced to behave in a demented and fiendish manner.

Douglas Bernstein and Peggy Nash, *Essentials of Psychology*, Boston: Houghton Mifflin, 2001, pp. 305–312.

PUTTING IT ALL TOGETHER | **DIRECTIONS** Answer the following questions by circling the letter of the correct response or filling in the blanks.

Context Clues and Word Parts **1.** In the last sentence of paragraph 8, the authors use the word *transgressions*. Based on the context and on word part analysis (*trans* = across and *gress* = move or go), how would you define this word?

_____

Main Idea **2.** Which of the following statements most effectively paraphrases the main idea of the entire reading?

a. Many people are all too ready to conform to the group or comply with the wishes of others, so much so that they forget about their own needs entirely.

b. Both conformity and compliance are common responses to group pressure; however, most people know where to draw the line when it comes to obeying the wishes of others.

c. While compliance and conformity also carry certain risks, it is blind obedience that is most dangerous.

d. According to research, conformity, compliance, and obedience are all triggered by several different factors, and there is no one specific cause for any of the three.

Patterns 3. Paragraphs 9–12 are organized according to which pattern?

    a. comparison and contrast

    b. cause and effect

    c. time order

    d. definition

Inferences 4. What is the implied main idea of paragraphs 7 and 8?

_____

_____

5. What would you say is the implied answer to the question posed at the top of paragraph 15?

_____

6. In paragraph 31, the author does not explicitly state the cause and effect relationship between obedience and authority and the behavior of those who walked toward the fire instead of away from it. What cause and effect relationship is implied?

_____

Purpose 7. What is the author's purpose?

    a. to inform

    b. to persuade

Drawing 8. a. A group of students has gathered to discuss how college students
Your Own   can take a more active role in shaping their education. When a
Conclusions   rather timid-looking student with a slight stutter says that he thinks faculty evaluations should be administered, published, and circulated to help students choose instructors for courses, an attractive and articulate young woman announces that the idea is ridiculous. In a confident voice, she says, "Students will just use the evaluations to air grievances." From her point of view, the evaluations won't be objective. As soon as she finishes, several other members of the group chime in in agreement with her position while some others nod assent. The one student who disagrees with the group and agrees with the timid man wants to speak up and defend the need for faculty evaluations. Given the circumstances, is it likely that she will? Please explain.

_____

_____

b. A group of people has gathered for what has been described as a new kind of therapy designed to bolster self-esteem. The leader of the group is an expensively dressed man who has been introduced as Doctor Paul. At the start of the session, the leader announces that the only way self-esteem can be increased is if a person first willingly admits his or her weaknesses. Then the leader asks for volunteers to share what they feel are their personal deficiencies. One young woman volunteers, but as she begins to speak, the doctor starts to badger her, telling her that she is not being truly forthcoming. In response, the woman appears ready to cry. Most of the other group members stare fixedly at the floor, but one young man looks at the leader and says in a confident, even tone, "No one is going to be forthcoming in the face of such badgering." The woman being badgered stops hanging her head and seems ready to protest her treatment as well. Given the circumstances, is it likely that she will? Please explain.

_____

_____

Bias 9. Which statement best describes the authors' position on the Milgram experiments, described in paragraphs 19–34.

    a. The authors are critical of the experiments.

    b. The authors believe the Milgram experiments made an important contribution to the study of human behavior.

    c. The authors reveal no evidence of personal bias.

Argument 10. What opinion did Stanley Milgram express when his experiments came under attack?

_____

What reason or reasons did he give in support of that opinion?

_____

_____

VOICING YOUR OPINION If you were part of an experiment in which you were asked to inflict pain on someone for the good of scientific progress, do you think you would have done what so many participants in the Milgram experiment did, or would you have defied authority? Please explain.

_____

_____

_____

■   **THINKING**   Briefly summarize the Milgram experiments and then explain
  THROUGH   whether, from the point of view of John Stuart Mill, the experiments
  WRITING   would be considered ethical (see pages 563–564 to review the central ideas of Mill's approach). Finally, describe your own view of the
experiments, explaining why you do or do not consider them
ethical.

■ READING 3
CULTURE AND COMMUNICATION
Joseph DeVito

LOOKING AHEAD Our culture, which is made up of what we believe, how we behave, and what we value, profoundly affects how well we do or do not communicate with one another. In the following selection, author and teacher Joseph DeVito describes some of the specific ways in which culture can encourage or discourage our ability to communicate.

PRE-READING AND FOCUS STRATEGIES

1. Use the title to pose a question that can guide your reading: In what ways can culture affect communication?

2. The reading covers some familiar territory and while it's detailed in coverage, it uses many illustrations that you may have encountered in everyday life. Thus you can do a more abbreviated survey. Read the title, the opening and concluding paragraphs, and the first sentence of each remaining paragraph. Remember to pose questions and make predictions based on the headings and you are ready to start reading.

3. Many of the key terms in this reading are compared and contrasted. Use the margins to record similarities and differences.

WORD WATCH Some of the more difficult words in this reading are defined below. Watch for these words as you read. The number in parentheses indicates the paragraph in which they appear. An asterisk marks their first appearance in the reading.

---

idiom (4): form of language unique to a region or group

hedonism (6): making the pursuit of pleasurable experience the main goal in life

orientation (17): leaning, direction

transactions (18): exchanges or activities

explicit (18): direct or stated

precedence (19): priority, first claim

semantics (36): study of meaning

syntax (36): word order

nuances (37): implications

perception (38): understanding, way of seeing

1 *CULTURE* REFERS TO THE RELATIVELY SPECIALIZED LIFESTYLE of a group of people—consisting of their values, beliefs, artifacts, ways of behaving, and ways of communicating. Included in culture would be all that members of a social group have produced and developed—their language, modes of thinking, art, laws, and religion.

Thinking Ahead
Why is culture so important in interpersonal communication?

2 Culture is not synonymous with race or nationality. However, members of a particular race or country are often taught similar beliefs, attitudes, and values. This similarity makes it possible to speak of "Hispanic culture" or "African American culture." But, lest we be guilty of stereotyping, recognize that within any large culture—especially a culture based on race or nationality—there will be enormous differences. The Kansas farmer and the Wall Street executive may both be, say, German American, but they may differ widely in their attitudes and beliefs and in their general lifestyle. In some ways the Kansas farmer may be closer in attitudes and values to the Chinese farmer than to the Wall Street executive.

3 Culture is passed on from one generation to the next through communication, not through genes. Thus culture does not refer to color of skin or shape of eyes since these are passed on through genes, not communication. Culture does refer to beliefs in a supreme being, to attitudes toward success and happiness, and to the values placed on friendship, love, family, or money, since these are transmitted through communication.

4 Culture is transmitted from one generation to another through **enculturation,** a process by which you learn the culture into which you're born (your native culture). Parents, peer groups, schools, religious institutions, and government agencies are the main teachers of culture. One new instrument for spreading culture is the Internet. Because the Internet, although world wide, is so dominated by the United States and by the English language and idiom,* the culture of the Internet is dominated by the culture of the United States. "Some countries," notes one media watcher, "already unhappy with the encroachment of American culture—from jeans to Mickey Mouse to movies and TV programs—are worried that their cultures will be further eroded by an American dominance in cyberspace" (Pollack 1995, D1).

5 A different process of learning culture is **acculturation,** the process by which you learn the rules and norms of a culture different from your native culture. Through acculturation, your original or native culture is modified through direct contact with (or exposure to) a new and different culture. For example, when immigrants settle in the United States, the host country, their

own culture becomes influenced by the host culture. Gradually, the values, ways of behaving, and beliefs of the host culture become more and more a part of the immigrants' culture. At the same time, the host culture changes, too, as it interacts with the immigrants' culture. Generally, however, the culture of the immigrant changes more. The reasons for this are that the host country's members far outnumber the immigrant group, and the media are largely dominated by and reflect the values and customs of the host culture. . . .

6   Research shows that your cultural values will influence your interpersonal communications . . . as well as your decision making, assessments of coworkers, teamwork, trust in others, the importance you place on cultural diversity in the workplace, and your attitudes toward the role of women in the workplace (Stephens and Greer 1995, Bochner and Hesketh 1994). For example, your beliefs and values about gender equality will influence the way in which you communicate with and about the opposite sex. Your group and individual orientation will influence how you perform in work teams and how you deal with your peers at school and at work. Your degree of hedonism* will influence the kinds of interactions you engage in, the books you read, the television programs you watch. . . .

Thinking Back
How has your culture influenced what you believe?

How Cultures Differ

Thinking Ahead
How comfortable are you with the beliefs your culture teaches about the importance of the individual versus the group or about the differences between men and women?

7 Cultures differ in at least four major ways that are especially important for communication. Here we discuss power distances, masculine and feminine orientation, collectivism and individualism, and high and low context (Gudykunst 1991, Hall and Hall, 1987, Hofstede 1997). As you review these several differences, recognize that the differences are matters of degree. Characteristics are not in one culture and absent in the other but are present to different degrees in both.

8 *Power Distances* In some cultures power is concentrated in the hands of a few, and there is a great difference in the power held by these people and that held by the ordinary citizen. These are called high power distance cultures; examples are Mexico, Brazil, India, and the Philippines (Hofstede 1983, 1997). In low power distance cultures, power is more evenly distributed throughout the citizenry; examples include Denmark, New Zealand, Sweden, and to a lesser extent the United States. These differences impact on interpersonal communication and relationships in a variety of ways.

9   Friendship and dating relationships will be influenced by the power distance between groups (Andersen 1991). For example, in India (high power distance), friendships and romantic relationships are expected to take place within your cultural class; in Sweden (low power distance), a person is expected to select friends and romantic partners not on the basis of class or culture, but on individual factors such as personality, appearance, and the like.

10   In low power distance cultures there is a general feeling of equality which is consistent with acting assertively, and so you're expected to confront a friend, partner, or supervisor assertively (Borden 1991). In high power distance cultures, direct confrontation and assertiveness may be viewed negatively, especially if directed at a superior.

11   In high power distance cultures you're taught to have great respect for authority; people in these cultures see authority as desirable and beneficial, and challenges to authority are generally not welcomed (Westwood, Tang, and Kirkbride 1992, Bochner and Hesketh 1994). In low power distance cultures, there's a certain distrust for authority; it's seen as a kind of necessary evil that should be limited as much as possible. This difference in attitudes toward authority can be seen right in the classroom. In high power distance cultures there's a great power distance between students and teachers; students are expected to be modest, polite, and totally respectful. In low power distance cultures students are expected to demonstrate their knowledge and command of the subject matter, participate in discussions with the teacher, and even challenge the teacher, something many high power distance culture members wouldn't even think of doing. The same differences can be seen in patient-doctor communication. Patients from high power distance cultures are less likely to challenge their doctor or admit that they don't understand the medical terminology than would patients in low power distance cultures.

12   High power distance cultures rely more on symbols of power. For example, titles (Dr., Professor, Chef, Inspector) are more important in high power distance cultures. Failure to include these in forms of address is a serious breach of etiquette. Low power distance cultures rely less on symbols of power, and less of a problem is created if you fail to use a respectful title (Victor 1992). But even in low power distance cultures you may create problems if, for example, you call a medical doctor, police captain, military officer, or professor Ms. or Mr.

13   In the United States, two people quickly move from Title plus Last Name (Mr. or Ms. Smith) to First Name (Pat). Similarly, in low power distance cultures less of a problem is created if you're too informal or if you presume to exchange first names before sufficient interaction has taken place. In high power distance cultures too great an informality—especially between those differing greatly in power—would be a serious breach of etiquette. Again, in even the lowest power distance culture, you may still create problems if you call your English professor Pat.

14   *Masculine and Feminine Cultures* A popular classification of cultures is in terms of their masculinity and femininity (Hofstede 1997). In a highly "masculine" culture men are viewed as assertive, oriented to material success, and strong; women on the other hand are viewed as modest, focused on the quality of life, and tender. In a highly "feminine" culture, both men and women are encouraged to be modest, oriented to maintaining the quality of life, and tender. The ten countries with the highest masculinity score (beginning with the highest) are Japan, Austria, Venezuela, Italy, Switzerland, Mexico, Ireland, Jamaica, Great Britain, and Germany. The ten countries with the highest femininity score (beginning with the highest) are Sweden, Norway, Netherlands, Denmark, Costa Rica, Yugoslavia, Finland, Chile, Portugal, and Thailand. Out of 53 countries ranked, the United States ranks 15th most masculine (Hofstede 1997).

15   **Masculine cultures** emphasize success and socialize their people to be assertive, ambitious, and competitive. Members of masculine cultures are thus more likely to confront conflicts directly and to competitively fight out any differences; they're more likely to emphasize win-lose conflict strategies. **Feminine cultures** emphasize the quality of life and socialize their people to be modest and to emphasize close interpersonal relationships. Members of feminine cultures are thus more likely to emphasize compromise and negotiation in resolving conflicts; they're more likely to seek win-win solutions.

16   Organizations can also be viewed in terms of masculinity or femininity. Masculine organizations emphasize competitiveness and aggressiveness. They emphasize the bottom line and reward their workers on the basis of their contribution to the organization. Feminine organizations are less competitive and less aggressive. They're more likely to emphasize worker satisfaction and reward their workers on the basis of need; those who have large families, for example, may get better raises than the single people, even if the singles have contributed more to the organization.

17 *Individual and Collective Orientation* Cultures differ in the extent to which they promote individual values (for example, power, achievement, hedonism, and stimulation) versus collectivist values (for example, benevolence, tradition, and conformity). The countries with the highest individualist orientation* (beginning with the highest) are the United States, Australia, Great Britain, Canada, Netherlands, New Zealand, Italy, Belgium, Denmark, Sweden, France, and Ireland. Countries with the highest collectivist orientation (beginning with the highest) are Guatemala, Ecuador, Panama, Venezuela, Colombia, Indonesia, Pakistan, Costa Rica, Peru, Taiwan, and South Korea (Hofstede 1983, 1997, Hatfield and Rapson 1996, Kapoor, Wolfe, and Blue 1995). With a few notable exceptions, the individualist countries are wealthy and the collectivist countries are poor. For example, Japan and Hong Kong—which score in the middle—are wealthier than many of the most individualist countries. The following self-test will help you examine your own orientation toward individualism or collectivism.

Test Yourself: Are You an Individualist or a Collectivist?

18 Respond to each of the following statements in terms of how true they are of your behavior and thinking: 1 = almost always true, 2 = more often true than false, 3 = true about half the time and false about half the time, 4 = more often false than true, and 5 = almost always false.

1. My own goals, rather than the goals of my group (for example, my extended family, my organization), are the more important.
2. I feel responsible for myself and to my own conscience rather than for the entire group and to the group's values and rules.
3. Success to me depends on my contribution to the group effort and the group's success rather than to my own individual success or to surpassing others.
4. I make a clear distinction between who is the leader and who are the followers and similarly make a clear distinction between members of my own cultural group and outsiders.
5. In business transactions* personal relationships are extremely important, so I would spend considerable time getting to know people with whom I do business.

6. In my communications I prefer a direct and explicit* communication style; I believe in "telling it like it is," even if it hurts.

To compute your individualist-collectivist score, follow these steps:

1. Reverse the scores for items 3 and 5 (if your response was 1 reverse it to a 5, if your response was 2 reverse it to a 4, if your response was 3 keep it as 3, if your response was 4 reverse it to a 2, if your response was 5 reverse it to a 1).

2. Add your scores for all 6 items, being sure to use the reverse scores for items 3 and 5 in your calculations. Your score should be between 6 (indicating a highly individualist orientation) to 30 (indicating a highly collectivist orientation).

3. Position your score on the following scale:

6 _____ 15 _____ 30
highly   about equally individualist   highly
individualist   and collectivist   collectivist

Does this scale and score accurately measure the way in which you see yourself on this dimension? Is this orientation going to help you achieve your personal and professional goals? Might it hinder you?

19   One of the major differences between these two orientations is in the extent to which an individual's goals or the group's goals are given precedence.* Individual and collective tendencies are, of course, not mutually exclusive; this is not an all-or-none orientation but rather one of emphasis. You probably have both tendencies. Thus, you may, for example, compete with other members of your basketball team for most baskets or most valuable player award (and thus emphasize individual goals). At the same time, however, you will—in a game—act in a way that will benefit the entire team (and thus emphasize group goals). In actual practice both individual and collective tendencies will help you and your team each achieve your goals. Yet most people and most cultures have a dominant orientation; they're more individually oriented (they see themselves as independent) or more collectively oriented (they see themselves as interdependent) in most situations, most of the time (cf. Singelis 1994).

20   At some instances, however, these tendencies may come into conflict. For example, do you shoot for the basket and try to raise your own individual score or do you pass the ball to another player who is better positioned to score and thus benefit the team as a whole? You make this distinction in popular talk when you call someone a team player (collectivist orientation) or an individual player (individualist orientation).

21   In an **individualist culture** members are responsible for themselves and perhaps their immediate family. In a **collectivist culture** members are responsible for the entire group.

22   In an individualist culture success is measured by the extent to which you surpass other members of your group; you would take pride in standing out from the crowd. Your heroes—in the media, for example—are likely to be those who are unique and who stand apart. In a collectivist culture success is measured by your contribution to the achievements of the group as a whole; you would take pride in your similarity to other members of your group. Your heroes, in contrast, are more likely to be team players who do not stand out from the rest of the group's members. Not surprisingly, advertisements in individualist cultures emphasize individual preferences and benefits, independence, and personal success; advertisements in collectivist cultures emphasize group benefits, family integrity, and group harmony (Han and Shavitt 1994).

23   In an individualist culture you're responsible to your own conscience, and responsibility is largely an individual matter; in a collectivistic culture you're responsible to the rules of the social group, and responsibility for an accomplishment or a failure is shared by all members. Competition is fostered in individualist cultures while cooperation is promoted in collectivist cultures.

24   In an individualist culture you might compete for leadership in a small group setting, and there would likely be a very clear distinction between leaders and members. In a collectivist culture leadership would be shared and rotated; there is likely to be little distinction between leader and members. These orientations will also influence the kinds of communication members consider appropriate in an organizational context. For example, individualist members will favor clarity and directness while collectivists will favor "face-saving" and the avoidance of hurting others or arousing negative evaluations (Kim and Sharkey 1995).

25   Distinctions between in-group members and out-group members are extremely important in collectivist cultures. In individualist

cultures, where the person's individuality is prized, the distinction is likely to be less important.

26 *High- and Low-Context Cultures* Cultures also differ in the extent to which information is made explicit or is assumed to be in the context or in the persons communicating. A **high-context culture** is one in which much of the information in communication is in the context or in the person—for example, information that was shared through previous communications, through assumptions about each other, and through shared experiences. The information is thus known by all participants but isn't explicitly stated in the verbal messages. A **low-context culture** is one in which most of the information is explicitly stated in the verbal message. In formal transactions it would be stated in written (or contract) form.

27 To further appreciate the distinction between high and low context, consider giving directions ("Where's the voter registration center?") to someone who knows the neighborhood and to a newcomer to your city. With someone who knows the neighborhood (a high-context situation), you can assume that she or he knows the local landmarks. So you can give directions such as "next to the laundromat on Main Street" or "the corner of Albany and Elm." With the newcomer (a low-context situation), you can't assume that she or he shares any information with you. So you would have to use only those directions that a stranger would understand, for example, "make a left at the next stop sign" or "go two blocks and then turn right."

28 High-context cultures are also collectivist cultures (Gudykunst, Ting-Toomey, and Chua 1988; Gudykunst and Kim 1992). These cultures (Japanese, Arabic, Latin American, Thai, Korean, Apache, and Mexican are examples) place great emphasis on personal relationships and oral agreements (Victor 1992). Low-context cultures are also individualist cultures. These cultures (German, Swedish, Norwegian, and American are examples) place less emphasis on personal relationships and more emphasis on verbalized, explicit explanation, and on written contracts in business transactions. The characteristics of individual-collective and high- and low-context cultures discussed here are summarized in Table 3.1.

29 Members of high-context cultures spend lots of time getting to know each other interpersonally and socially before any important transactions take place. Because of this prior personal knowledge, a great deal of information is shared by the members and therefore does not have to be explicitly stated. Members of low-context

Table 3.1 Differences in Individual (Low-Context)
and Collective (High-Context) Cultures

In every culture there will be variations in each of these characteristics. View these, therefore, as general tendencies rather than absolutes. Further, the increased mobility, changing immigration patterns, and the exposure to media from different parts of the world will gradually decrease the differences between these two orientations. This table is based on the work of Hall (1983) and Hall and Hall (1987) and the interpretations by Gudykunst (1991) and Victor (1992).

Individual (Low-Context) Cultures	Collective (High-Context) Cultures
Your own goals are most important	The group's goals are most important
You're responsible for yourself and to your own conscience	You're responsible for the entire group and to the group's values and rules
Success depends on your surpassing others	Success depends on your contribution to the group
Competition is emphasized	Cooperation is emphasized
Clear distinction is made between leaders and members	Little distinction is made between leaders and members; leadership would normally be shared
In-group versus out-group distinctions are of little importance	In-group versus out-group distinctions are of great importance
Information is made explicit; little is left unsaid	Information is often left implicit and much is often omitted from explicit statement
Personal relationships are less important; hence, little time is spent getting to know each other in meetings and conferences	Personal relationships are extremely important; hence, much time is spent getting to know each other in meetings and conferences
Directness is valued; face-saving is seldom thought of	Indirectness is valued and face-saving is a major consideration

cultures spend much less time getting to know each other and hence don't have that shared knowledge. As a result everything has to be stated explicitly.

30   This difference between high- and low-context orientation is partly responsible for the differences observed in Japanese and American business groups. . . . The Japanese spend lots of time

getting to know each other before conducting actual business, whereas Americans get down to business very quickly. The Japanese (and other high-context cultures) want to get to know each other because important information isn't made explicit. They have to know you so they can read your nonverbals, for example (Sanders, Wiseman, and Matz 1991). Americans can get right down to business because all important information will be stated explicitly.

31   To high-context cultural members what is omitted or assumed is a vital part of the communication transaction. Silence, for example, is highly valued (Basso 1972). To low-context cultural members what is omitted creates ambiguity, but this ambiguity is simply something that will be eliminated by explicit and direct communication. To high-context cultural members ambiguity is something to be avoided; it's a sign that the interpersonal and social interactions have not proved sufficient to establish a shared base of information (Gudykunst 1983).

32   When this simple difference isn't understood, intercultural misunderstandings can easily result. For example, the directness characteristic of the low-context culture may prove insulting, insensitive, or unnecessary to the high-context cultural member. Conversely, to the low-context member, the high-context cultural member may appear vague, underhanded, or dishonest in his or her reluctance to be explicit or engage in communication that a low-context member would consider open and direct.

Thinking Back 33   Another frequent source of intercultural misunderstanding that can be traced to the differences in high and low context can be seen in face-saving (Hall and Hall 1987). High-context cultures place much more emphasis on face-saving. For example, they're more likely to avoid argument for fear of causing others to lose face; on the other hand, low-context members (with their individualistic orientation) will use argument to win a point. Similarly, in high-context cultures criticism should only take place in private. Low-context cultures may not make this public-private distinction. Low-context managers who criticize high-context workers in public will find that their criticism causes interpersonal problems and does little to resolve the original difficulty that led to the criticism in the first place (Victor 1992).

Can you recall an example of how one of these cultural differences (power distance, masculine-feminine, individual-collective, and high-low context) influenced an interpersonal interaction?

Thinking Ahead
How does your culture influence what you do when you talk with an older and higher status person or with someone with whom you want to establish a romantic relationship?

34   Members of high-context cultures are reluctant to say no for fear of offending and causing the person to lose face. Thus, it's necessary to be able to read in the Japanese executive's "yes" when it means yes and when it means no. The difference isn't in the words used but in the way in which they're used.

Theories of Culture and Communication

35 Here are several attempts to explain the interaction of culture and communication, to formulate a theory of culture and communication. Although none provides a complete explanation, each provides some understanding of how some part of culture interacts with some part of communication.

36 *Language Relativity* The general idea that language influences thought and ultimately behavior got its strongest expression from linguistic anthropologists. In the late 1920s and throughout the 1930s, the view was formulated that the characteristics of language influence the way you think (Carroll 1956, Fishman 1960, Hoijer 1954, Miller and McNeill 1969, Sapir 1929). Since the languages of the world differ greatly in semantics* and syntax,* it was argued that people speaking widely different languages would also differ in how they viewed and thought about the world. This view became known as the *linguistic relativity hypothesis.*

37 Subsequent research and theory, however, did not support the extreme claims made by linguistic relativity researchers (Pinker 1994). A more modified hypothesis seems currently supported: The language you speak helps to highlight what you see and how you talk about it. For example, if you speak a language that is rich in color terms (English is a good example), you would find it easier to highlight and talk about nuances* of color than would someone from a culture which has fewer color terms (some cultures distinguish only two or three or four parts of the color spectrum). But this does not mean that people see the world differently; only that their language helps (or doesn't help) them to focus on certain variations in nature and makes it easier (or more difficult) to talk about them. Nor does it mean that people speaking widely differing languages are doomed to misunderstanding each other. Translation enables us to understand a great deal of the meaning in a foreign language message. We also have our communication skills; we can ask for clarification, for additional examples, for restatement. We can listen actively, give feedforward and feedback, use perception checking.

38 Language differences do not make for very important differences in perception,* thought, or behavior. Difficulties in intercultural understanding are more often due to ineffective communication than to differences in languages.

39 *Uncertainty Reduction* All communication interactions involve uncertainty and ambiguity. Not surprisingly, uncertainty and ambiguity are greater when there are large cultural differences

(Berger and Bradac 1982, Gudykunst 1989, 1994). Because of this greater uncertainty in intercultural communication, time and effort are needed to reduce it and to thus communicate meaningfully. Reducing your uncertainty about another person will not only make your communication more effective, but will also increase your liking for the person (Douglas 1994). In situations of great uncertainty the techniques of effective communication (for example, active listening, perception checking, being specific, and seeking feedback) take on special importance.

40   Active listening and perception checking techniques, for example, help you to check on the accuracy of your perceptions and allow you the opportunity to revise and amend any incorrect perceptions. Being specific reduces ambiguity and the chances of misunderstandings. Misunderstanding is a lot more likely when talking about "neglect" (a highly abstract concept) than when talking about "forgetting your last birthday" (a specific event).

41   Seeking feedback helps you to correct any possible misconceptions almost immediately. Seek feedback on whether you're making yourself clear ("Does that make sense?" "Do you see where to put the widget?") as well as on whether you understand what the other person is saying ("Do you mean that you'll never speak with them again? Do you mean that literally?")

42   Although you're always in danger of misperceiving and misevaluating another person, you're in special danger in intercultural situations. Therefore, try to resist your natural tendency to judge others quickly and permanently. A judgment made early is likely to be based on too little information. Because of this, flexibility and a willingness to revise opinions are essential intercultural skills.

Joseph A. DeVito, *The Interpersonal Communication Book,*
9th edition, Pearson Education, pp. 40–49.

PUTTING IT ALL TOGETHER   DIRECTIONS   Answer the following questions by circling the letter of the correct response or filling in the blanks.

Context   **1.** Based on the context, how would you define the word *breach* in paragraph 12?

_____

Main Idea   **2.** Which of the following statements best expresses the main idea of the entire reading?

    a. People belonging to different cultures find it almost impossible to communicate with one another.

b. The distribution of power is a key feature that distinguishes one culture from another.

c. All cultures can be divided into two groups, high and low context. High context cultures try to make everything explicit and unambiguous, whereas low context cultures value ambiguity.

d. The four features frequently used to characterize culture differences also play a powerful role in how people communicate with one another.

Vocabulary **3.** In your own words, explain the difference between *enculturation* and *acculturation*.

_____

_____

Topic **4.** Which sentence in paragraph 2 is the topic sentence?
Sentence
    a. sentence 1

    b. sentence 2

    c. sentence 3

    d. sentence 4

Patterns of **5.** Which patterns organize the information in the section titled "Power
Organization Distances" (paragraphs 8–13)?

_____

Inferences **6.** What is the implied main idea of paragraph 12?

_____

Drawing **7.** Based on what you read in the section titled "Power Distances,"
Your Own how do you think a foreign exchange student from India might
Conclusions react if a professor from the United States said the student should feel free to address her by her first name?

_____

Explain your answer based on the reading.

_____

Do you think a student from Sweden would have the same or a similar reaction?

_____

Explain your answer based on the reading.

_____

8. A young scientist raised in a highly masculine culture is attending a conference on global warming, and he strongly disagrees with the speaker who has just given a paper. How do you think he will handle his disagreement?

a. He will wait and try to discuss his disagreement with the speaker after the discussion is over.

b. He will raise his hand and point out where the speaker went wrong.

c. He will keep his disagreement to himself.

d. He will discuss his point of view with some of the other people attending and see what they think.

Explain your answer based on the reading.

_____

Purpose 9. What is the author's purpose?

a. to inform

b. to persuade

Bias 10. How would you describe the author's attitude?

a. The author favors individualist values over collectivist ones.

b. The author thinks collectivist values are preferable to individualist ones.

c. It's impossible to determine the author's personal bias.

■ **VOICING YOUR OPINION** In your own life, which persons, groups, or institutions (e.g., school, religious organizations, etc.) were particularly influential when it came to instilling in you the values of your culture? Why were they so influential? Do you think you share the values of your culture or do you consider yourself something of an outsider?

_____

_____

_____

■   **THINKING THROUGH WRITING**

1. Write a paper that first describes what you consider to be three predominant cultural values in the United States. Then describe which people, groups, or institutions made you aware of these values and their importance. Give several illustrations of how you came to absorb or at least understand the cultural values mentioned in part one of your paper. If, for example, you believe that independent thought or a sense of individuality is a central part of this country's cultural heritage, then you need to describe how, say, your third-grade teacher always counseled his students to march to their own drum and be true to themselves.

   You can organize your paper in two different ways. You can either first identify the values and then illustrate how you came to recognize their importance. Or else you can go back and forth between the values and the process of *enculturation* or, if you were born someplace else, the process of *acculturation.*

2. If you are a foreign student, describe the ease or difficulty you had when first confronted with the cultural values of this country.

■ **READING 4**

TALL TALES OF APPALACHIA
John O'Brien

LOOKING AHEAD The author of this reading was unhappy when he heard about the plan for a reality television program called *The Real Beverly Hillbillies.* From his point of view, such a show would encourage the stereotyping of Appalachia's inhabitants, something that he believed had already been done far too often with disastrous and painful results.

PRE-READING AND FOCUS STRATEGIES

1. This is an editorial from a newspaper. Thus the material is somewhat easier to understand, so adjust your survey accordingly, reading only the first sentence of every paragraph.

2. The title is an important clue to meaning. "Tall Tales" are stories that aren't true. As you read, try to identify exactly which tall tales the author has in mind. By the same token, pay close attention to any references to the real story behind the tall tales.

WORD WATCH Some of the more difficult words in this reading are defined below. Watch for these words as you read. The number in parentheses indicates the paragraph in which they appear. An asterisk marks their first appearance in the reading.

---

vagaries (5): changes, ups and downs

Gothic (5): dark and horror-filled

marginal (6): unimportant, on the sidelines

---

1 GREEN BANK, W.VA. — CBS IS DEVELOPING A REALITY TV SERIES modeled after *The Beverly Hillbillies,* the sixties sitcom. A poor family from a remote corner of southern Appalachia will be transported to a California mansion, the ensuing comic antics shown to America. Well, as a West Virginia farmer might say, that's a load of fertilizer. Having spent virtually my entire life in West Virginia, I can say with some authority that the strange, woebegone place called Appalachia and the hillbillies who inhabit it are a

myth—one devised a century ago to justify outsiders' condescension and exploitation.

2   In the 1870s, there was no "Appalachia." At that time, this mountainous stretch of the country from West Virginia to northern Georgia was one of the most prosperous agricultural areas in America. The people here drew upon their English, German, and Scotch-Irish roots to create a variety of vibrant, peaceful cultures. But in the 1880s that started to change. Outsiders came, ones who didn't care about the thriving farms. They wanted raw materials for their factories, and the mountains had them. Our mountains were covered with the largest and oldest hardwood forest that people had ever seen. The coal deposits were the richest in the world. Industrialization came here like a cyclone roaring through the mountains. People like my ancestors were bullied, threatened, and cheated out of their land. By 1920, timber companies had cut the entire forest. Most of the profits left the state along with the timber and coal.

3   As the mountains were denuded, the industrialists portrayed the families they were robbing as "backward people" and themselves as the prophets of progress. The missionaries who often accepted large donations from the industrialists exaggerated the "otherness" of these strange people. "Local color"* writers made brief visits to the mountains, then wrote fanciful books about the queer, violent mountain folk. As realistic as Harlequin romances, local color books like Mary Murfree's *In the "Stranger People's" Country* were read and reviewed as journalistic accounts.

4   College professors began to use them as textbooks in sociology classes. The news media took its part with the infamous Hatfield-McCoy feud in the 1880s and 1890s—a conflict that as Altina L. Waller wrote in her book, *Feud,* was not really a family feud, but a war between coal mining interests and local interests. Corrupt politicians took isolated incidents and described them as a hillbilly feud. Reporters from the big cities wrote about "white savages" and "West Virginia barbarians." (*The New York Times,* for example, said of people in eastern Kentucky: "They are remarkably good shots and effective assassins," adding that they "are so accustomed to murder that they do not look upon it with the horror with which it is regarded in civilized communities.") Then, in 1897, the president of Berea College in Kentucky, William Goodell Frost, desperately trying to raise money for his failing institution, created a fund-raising campaign based on the

*local color: a literary movement that tried to preserve the customs and dialects of regions profoundly altered by the Civil War.

idea of saving the people in the Appalachians from themselves. In an *Atlantic Monthly* article, Frost described the southern Appalachians as our "contemporary ancestors" waking up from a Rip van Winkle-type sleep and in need of help in joining modern America. Frost's article made mythic Appalachia and its backward hillbillies a permanent fixture in America's imaginary landscape.

5   Many in the southern Appalachians are certainly poor, but the poverty grew out of the vagaries* of the coal market and outsiders' control of resources. Industrialists and others, however, blamed the people for their own poverty, and this myth continues because it is entertaining to the Americans beyond the mountains. Some of the region's middle-class writers continue to churn out Gothic* hillbilly tales, the descendants of local color stories.

6   This mythology has even been accepted by the people living here. Not long ago, one of the student counselors at West Virginia University told me that the most persistent problem she encounters is a lack of self-esteem. Bright, capable young men and women do not think they belong in college because they are hillbillies. I have taught at a small private college in West Virginia. Ninety percent of the students were from out of state. The few West Virginians on campus huddled together in their own corner of the student union. They had become marginal* people in their own state.

7   My own father spent his life backing up, apologizing for the space he took up in the world. He took the hillbilly stereotype to heart and all of his life believed that he was backward and inferior—a despair I, too, have been trying to escape all of my life. The reality show that CBS is considering not only exploits my part of the world, it also separates struggling Appalachians from the rest of the American poor. If a television network proposed a "real life" show treating poor African-Americans, Latinos, American Indians, Asians, or Jews as curiosities, they, and all Americans of good will, would be justifiably outraged. Many of us in the southern Appalachians are outraged too. That's why coal miners from the southern Appalachians plan to protest *The Real Beverly Hillbillies* outside the shareholders' meeting on May 21 of CBS's parent, Viacom. It's time the people of the southern Appalachians stood up for themselves.

John O'Brien, "Tall Tales of Appalachia,"
New York Times, May 10, 2003, p. A21.

PUTTING IT ALL TOGETHER DIRECTIONS Answer the following questions by circling the letter of the correct response or filling in the blanks.

Context Clues 1. Given the context, it's likely that *woebegone* in the last sentence of paragraph 1 means

    a. cheerful.

    b. pitiful.

    c. strong.

    d. light-hearted.

Main Idea 2. Which statement most effectively paraphrases the main idea of the entire reading?

    a. The reigning stereotype of Appalachia hits too close to home to be funny.

    b. Television has seen to it that those who live in Appalachia are treated as comic figures worthy only of ridicule.

    c. The image of Appalachia as a weird place inhabited by backward people was created by late-nineteenth-century industrialists, who wanted to rob the region of its resources.

    d. No television program can adequately reflect the complexity of life in Appalachia; therefore, few creators of television fare even try to go beyond the traditional stereotype of the feuding hillbilly.

Transition 3. Paragraph 2 contains a transitional sentence that signals both contrast and time order. Write that sentence in the blank.

_____

Supporting Details 4. Who was Mary Murfree, and why is she mentioned (paragraph 3) in the reading?

_____

_____

5. Why is the *New York Times* mentioned (paragraph 4) in the reading?

_____

_____

Inference 6. The author says that local color writers' descriptions of Appalachia were "as realistic as Harlequin romances." Harlequin romance novels are famous for being badly written and for reusing the same boy-meets-girl plot countless times. What does the author want to suggest by using this allusion?

_____

_____

7. In paragraph 4, the author describes how the president of Berea College in Kentucky alluded to "a Rip van Winkle-type sleep." Rip van Winkle is a character in a Washington Irving* short story about a man who goes to sleep and doesn't wake up for twenty years. When he does, he's shocked by all the changes in the world around him. What did the president of Berea College want to suggest by referring to Rip Van Winkle?

_____

_____

Purpose 8. What is the author's purpose?

    a. to inform

    b. to persuade

Tone 9. How would you describe the author's tone?

    a. outraged

    b. ironic

    c. cautious

    d. objective

Drawing 10. Suppose someone said to the author, "Oh for goodness sake, *Your Own* lighten up. It's only a reality television show." Based on the read-*Conclusions* ing, how do you think the author would respond?

_____

_____

_____

▪ **VOICING** Having read this editorial, do you think you would be comfortable **YOUR** watching a program that made fun of "hillbillies," or would you be **OPINION** likely to boycott it and encourage your friends to do the same? Please explain your answer.

_____

_____

_____

_____

*Washington Irving (1783–1859): American writer; author of such famous short stories as "Rip Van Winkle" and "The Legend of Sleepy Hollow."

■ **THINKING** Write a two-part paper in which you first summarize John O'Brien's
THROUGH reasons for protesting against a planned television program that
WRITING makes fun of life in Appalachia. Then express your opinion as to
whether this makes sense, being sure to give reasons why you feel
as you do.

■ **READING 5**

FIVE WAYS TO DEAL WITH CONFLICT AND THE ART OF APOLOGIZING
Roy Berko, Andrew D. Wolvin, and Darlyn R. Wolvin

LOOKING AHEAD This reading describes five different methods of responding to conflict. As you read, see if you recognize yourself in any of the descriptions.

PRE-READING AND FOCUS STRATEGIES

1. Since you, like most people, probably already know something about conflict and the different ways of dealing with it, pre-read only the first sentence of every paragraph.

2. The title tells you that there are five approaches to conflict. It is an obvious signal that you need to read the text in order to identify and to describe each approach.

3. The authors make it easy for you to identify the five approaches by printing the names in boldface. As soon as you spot them, slow down and pay close attention to how the authors define each approach. Jot your own version of the definitions in the margins.

4. The title suggests there is an "art" to apologizing. Look for and pay special attention to those passages that describe when and how to apologize.

WORD WATCH Some of the more difficult words in this reading are defined below. Watch for these words as you read. The number in parentheses indicates the paragraph in which they appear. An asterisk marks the first appearance in the reading.

ramifications (1): consequences

habitual (1): regular, automatic

status quo (2): existing situation

equitable (7): fair

1 PEOPLE REACT DIFFERENTLY IN DEALING WITH CONFLICT. SOME people pull back, some attack, and others take responsibility for themselves and their needs. Most of us use a primary style for con-

fronting conflict. Knowing your style and its ramifications* can be helpful in determining whether you are pleased with your conflict style. If you are not, you may need to acquire the skills to make a change in your habitual* pattern. The styles of conflict management are (1) avoidance, (2) accommodation/smoothing over, (3) compromise, (4) competition/aggression, and (5) integration.

Avoidance

2 Some people choose to confront conflict by engaging in **conflict avoidance**—not confronting the conflict. They sidestep, postpone, or ignore the issue. They simply put up with the status quo,* no matter how unpleasant. While seemingly unproductive, avoidance may actually be a good style if the situation is a short-term one or of minor importance. If, however, the problem is really bothering you or is persistent, then it should be dealt with. Avoiding the issue often uses up a great deal of energy without resolving the aggravating situation. Very seldom do avoiders feel that they have been in a win-win situation. Avoiders usually lose a chunk of their self-respect since they so clearly downplay their own concerns in favor of the other person's. Avoiders frequently were brought up in environments in which they were told to be nice and not to argue, and eventually bad things would go away. Or they were brought up in homes where verbal or physical abuse was present, and to avoid these types of reactions, they hid from conflict.

Accommodation/Smoothing Over

3 People who attempt to manage conflict through **conflict accommodation** put the needs of others ahead of their own, thereby giving in. Accommodators meet the needs of others and don't assert their own. In this situation, the accommodator often feels like the "good person" for having given the other person his own way. This is perfectly acceptable if the other person's needs really are more important. But unfortunately, accommodators tend to follow the pattern no matter what the situation. Thus, they often are taken advantage of, and they seldom get their needs met. Accommodators commonly come from backgrounds where they were exposed to a martyr who gave and gave and got little but put on a happy face. They also tend to be people who have little self-respect and try to earn praise by being nice to everyone.

4   A form of accommodation known as **conflict smoothing over** seeks above all else to preserve the image that everything is okay. Through smoothing over, people sometimes get what they want,

but just as often they do not. Usually they feel they have more to say and have not totally satisfied themselves.

5 As with avoidance and accommodation, smoothing over occasionally can be useful. If, for example, the relationship between two people is more important than the subject they happen to be disagreeing about, then smoothing over may be the best approach. Keep in mind, however, that smoothing over does not solve the conflict; it just pushes it aside. It may very well recur in the future.

6 Those who use this technique as their normal means of confronting conflict often come from backgrounds in which the idea was stressed that being nice was the best way to be liked and popular. And being liked and popular was more important than satisfying their needs.

Compromise

7 **Conflict compromise** brings concerns out into the open in an attempt to satisfy the needs of both parties. It usually means "trading some of what you want for some of what I want. It's meeting each other halfway." The definition of the word *compromise,* however, indicates the potential weakness of this approach, for it means that both individuals give in at least to some degree to reach a solution. As a result, neither usually completely achieves what she or he wants. This is not to say that compromise is an inherently poor method of conflict management. It is not, but it can lead to frustration unless both participants are willing to continue to work until both of their needs are being met. Those who are effective compromisers normally have had experience with negotiations and know that you have to give to get, but you don't have to give until it hurts. Those who tend to be weak in working toward a fair and equitable* compromise believe that getting something is better than getting nothing at all. Therefore, they are willing to settle for anything, no matter how little.

Competition/Aggression

8 The main element in **conflict competition** is power. Its purpose is to "get another person to comply with or accept your point of view, or to do something that person may not want to do." Someone has to win, and someone has to lose. This forcing mode, unfortunately, has been the European-American way of operation in many situations—in athletic events, business deals, and interpersonal relations. Indeed, many people do not seem to be happy unless they are clear winners. Realize that if someone wins,

someone else must lose. The overaggressive driver must force the other car off the road.

9   The value of winning at all costs is debatable. Sometimes, even though we win, we lose in the long run. The hatred of a child for a parent caused by continuous losing, or the negative work environment resulting from a supervisor who must always be on top, may be much worse than the occasional loss of a battle. In dealing with persons from other cultures, European Americans sometimes are perceived as being pushy and aggressive. Many sales, friendships, and relationships have been lost based on the win-at-all-costs philosophy. Many of the aggressive behaviors in the personal lives of professional athletes are directly credited to their not being able to leave their win-at-all-costs attitude on the athletic field.

Integration

10   Communicators who handle their conflicts through **conflict integration** are concerned about their own needs as well as those of the other person. But unlike compromisers, they will not settle for only a partially satisfying solution. Integrators keep in mind that both parties can participate in a win-win resolution and are willing to collaborate. Thus, the most important aspect of integration is the realization that the relationship, the value of self-worth, and the issue are important. For this reason, integrative solutions often take a good deal of time and energy.

11   People who are competitive, who are communication-apprehensive, or who are nonassertive find it nearly impossible to use an integrative style of negotiation. They feel that they must win, or that they cannot stand up for their rights, or that they have no right to negotiate. In contrast, people who tend to have assertiveness skills and value the nature of relationships usually attempt to work toward integration.

12   Avoidance, accommodation, and smoothing over are all nonassertive acts; the person's needs are not met. Competition is an aggressive act in that the person gets his needs met at the expense of another person. Integration is assertive since the objective is to get one's needs met without taking away the rights of someone else. Compromise, depending on how it is acted out, can be either nonassertive or assertive.

Apologizing

13   Have you ever angrily said something to another person? Have you offended someone by being sarcastic or joking around when your remark was perceived to be serious and not funny? Have you

ever acted inappropriately toward someone whom you really like? If the answer to any of these is "yes," the question is, what did you do about it?

14   We all have said or done something we know has hurt or offended a personal friend, a significant other, or even a stranger. For many people brought up in the culture of the United States, one key to getting along with people is knowing when and how to **apologize,** to say you are sorry. How we react to having offended someone has a great deal to do with our background. If you've been brought up to fight for being right, not to give in, or to hold a grudge, you are not likely to consider apologizing. If you've been brought up to believe that the feelings of others supersede your own feelings, then making an apology is probably an automatic reaction.

15   Questions arise as to when it is appropriate to apologize and how to do it. For many people it is both hard to know when to apologize and difficult to apologize. You may be ashamed of your negative actions or have too much pride to admit to another that you did something wrong. Sometimes, even though you may want to apologize, you just may not know how. But remember that apologizing often solves the small problems and keeps them from getting bigger.

16   Traditionally, an apology basically has three stages. First, the person who has done the wrong should state exactly what he or she did. For example, the person could say, "I yelled at you after you told me that the idea I had presented at the meeting was wrong." Second, the perpetrator explains why he or she took the action. For example, the person could say, "I spent a lot of time on that solution, and I felt I had to defend myself." Third, a statement of remorse is made. For instance, the person could say, "I was upset, but I shouldn't have yelled. It didn't do anything to help deal with the task on which we were working." The reason the second step is optional is that you may not know why you took the action, or an explanation may incite further anxiety. If either of these situations is the case, it may be wise to skip that part of the process.

17   Does the process sound too formulaic or unnatural? It may well be, especially if you aren't in the habit of apologizing, but it lays out a pattern for verbalization that can and does work. Once you adopt the style, you may make adjustments to fit your own personality and situations, but at least you now have a format for the apology process.

18   The person who has been wronged may reject your apology. That is not your problem. If you offer an apology, and the apology

is sincerely worded and felt, then whether the other person accepts or rejects the action is not the issue. You have fulfilled your obligation. You have recognized that what you did or said was wrong and have taken an action to let the other person know that you are remorseful. You can only be responsible for one person's actions, your own. You cannot make the other person act as you would like him or her to act. Therefore, acceptance of the apology is out of your hands. Don't go into the process of apologizing to receive forgiveness. Go in accepting that you are doing the right thing and that's your purpose.

19   Here are some additional tips that may make it easier to say you're sorry:

Take responsibility. The starting point of any change of behavior is self-admission. Admit to yourself that you have offended someone. You may know this right away, the other person's reaction may let you know you have done something hurtful, someone else might alert you to the situation, or you may realize it yourself at a later time. However you find out, you must admit that you have done wrong and accept responsibility for your actions or you won't be prone to take action.

Explain. Recognize that your actions caused a problem for the other person. If you can do so, and it is appropriate, explain why you acted as you did. For example, if you were angry and blurted out something, you might say, "I was really having a bad day, and what I said wasn't really aimed at you. I was mad at myself, and I took my anger out on you. I'm sorry."

Show your regret. The other person needs to see that you are aware that what you did was wrong. That is, if you think you were wrong, say that you are sorry or ashamed with a statement such as "I felt bad the minute I told your secret. You trusted me, and I betrayed your trust. I shouldn't have done that." This, of course, is only appropriate if you are regretful. If not, the apology will sound phony and may cause a bigger conflict.

Repair the damage. To be complete, an apology should attempt to correct the injury. If you damaged someone's property, offer to fix it. If the damage is emotional, you might ask, "I'm really sorry. What can I do to make it up to you?" There may be nothing concrete you can do, but the offer is usually enough and shows your sincerity. You might follow up by saying something appropriate, such as "I'll try to keep my mouth shut in the future. In the meantime, let me buy you a cup of coffee."

Use good timing. If possible, apologize right away for little things. For example, if you bump into someone, say you're sorry right away. However, if you have done something more serious, like insult a friend out of anger, you may need some time to figure out exactly what to say. A quick apology might not give you time to realize what you've done, why you did it, and what the ramifications might be.

Choose an appropriate conduit. What's the best conduit for an apology? Letters, e-mail, voice mail, the phone, and speaking face to face are all message channels that are available. The first three are definitely impersonal. Using them may be easier and might save you from facing the person directly, but they are usually not as effective as other channels. Resort to using them only if there is no way to meet face to face. If a person lives far away, then there may be no choice. If that's the case, using the phone is probably a better alternative than a written presentation. At least hearing the tone of your voice can be a clue to the honesty of your message. If you do apologize by voice mail, [one authority advises that] "it is best to plan exactly what you want to say, and keep it to thirty seconds, never more than a minute." Long, rambling messages quickly lose their impact.

20   A face-to-face apology is often best because you can display your honesty. It can be a humbling experience as you must see the other person's expressions, show yours, and probably hear a verbal reply. As one expert states, it is worth the anxiety since "you will be respected by the person [whom] you are addressing as well as by yourself more if you are able and willing to make your apology in this manner [face to face]. Smiles, laughter, hugs, handshakes, and other displays of appreciation and affection are added benefits for both parties that are all possible when apologizing this way!"

21   *It's not about who "won" or who "lost."* Remember, life is not a war unless you or the other person makes it a war. Stubborn pride often leads to a loss of friends and can result in physical confrontations. "An apology is a tool to affirm the primacy of our connection with others."

Roy Berko, Andrew D. Wolvin, and Darlyn R. Wolvin, *Communicating.*
Boston: Houghton Mifflin, 2004, pp. 185–192.

PUTTING IT ALL TOGETHER **DIRECTIONS** Answer the following questions by filling in the blanks or circling the letter of the correct response.

Main Idea and Paraphrasing **1.** Paraphrase the two main ideas developed in this reading.

a. _____

_____

b. _____

_____

2. Paraphrase the authors' explanation of conflict avoidance.

_____

_____

3. In your own words, what's the drawback commonly associated with compromise as a response to conflict?

_____

_____

Supporting Details **4.** Would you call the detail about professional athletes (paragraph 9) a major or minor detail? _____

Explain your answer. _____

_____

Pattern of Organization **5.** Which overall pattern organizes the information in paragraph 16 of the reading? _____

Drawing Your Own Conclusions **6.** Frank and Evelyn are arguing over Frank's failure to complete his part of their shared research paper. Frank is insisting that his share of the paper was much more than Evelyn's and therefore he can't be blamed for not getting it done on time. Evelyn listens to his explanation and says, "I know I yelled at you and I shouldn't have but I was anxious about the paper and your behavior seemed irresponsible. Perhaps I overreacted, but I'll lose my scholarship if I don't get an A on this paper." Frank responds by saying, "You shouldn't have yelled at me. I am overworked as it is and I'm doing

more than my fair share." Frank is engaging in _____

behavior while Evelyn is trying to _____.

7. Make up an example of someone engaging in conflict accommodation.

_____

_____

_____

_____

Purpose **8.** What is the authors' purpose?

    a. to inform

    b. to persuade

Connotation and Denotation **9.** In which direction does the authors' language lean?

    a. The authors' language leans toward the highly connotative.

    b. The authors' language leans toward the highly denotative.

    c. The authors strike a balance between connotative and denotative language.

Bias **10.** Do the authors seem to favor any one style of conflict management over the other? _____

Explain why you answered yes or no.

_____

_____

■ **VOICING YOUR OPINION** How would you describe your own style of dealing with conflict? How does your style match the authors' descriptions? Does it fit right in, or do you need a new category?

_____

_____

_____

■ **THINKING THROUGH WRITING** Write two summaries of the reading, reducing it to no more than a total of twenty to twenty-five sentences. The first summary should explain the five approaches to conflict, the second should describe the process and benefits of making an apology.

■ **READING 6**

EXTREME PHILANTHROPY
Stephanie Strom

LOOKING AHEAD As you know from a previous reading, human organs for transplant are in short supply. But if everyone had the attitude described in the following reading, the problem could be solved in a very short time.

PRE-READING AND FOCUS STRATEGIES

1. Given that this selection is from a newspaper rather than a text-book, your pre-reading can be fairly quick. Get an overview by reading the first sentence of every paragraph.

2. Note the title and use it to focus your reading by asking, "What kind of philanthropy might be labeled extreme?"

3. Several different names are mentioned and repeated throughout. As you read, make sure you understand why the author describes these people and what they have in common.

WORD WATCH Some of the more difficult words in this reading are defined below. Watch for these words as you read. The number in parentheses indicates the paragraph in which they appear. An asterisk marks their first appearance in the reading.

---

altruistic (2): thinking of others first

literally (2): in actuality

designations (7): specifications

profile (7): description of specific characteristics

---

1   A LITTLE MORE THAN TWO YEARS AGO, HAROLD S. MINTZ, A salesman, gave one of his kidneys to a total stranger. "The first thing they do is send you to see a psychiatrist," said Mr. Mintz, who lives in the Washington area. "I thought that was hilarious, but it made sense. I mean, what kind of nut puts up his hand and says 'I want to give away body parts'?"

2   The number of organ donations from the living surpassed those from the dead, and has for the past two years. The vast majority of such good samaritans act to help a relative or close friend, but transplant centers report an increasing number of "altruistic*

618 ■ READING 6

donors"—that is, people who want to give of themselves, literally,* to whomever doctors decide is in need. Cathy Paykin, transplant programs director at the National Kidney Foundation, said the first publicly acknowledged instance of donor altruism occurred in 1999, when a nurse allowed doctors at Johns Hopkins University to remove a kidney using the then new method of laparoscopy.

3   Last week, the subject was in the news again, after Zell Kravinsky, a Jenkintown, PA, real-estate developer obsessed with philanthropy—he reportedly canceled his family's cable television service so he could donate more money—gave away one of his kidneys. . . .

4   Nationally, more than 80,000 people are waiting for an organ— a number that is expected to hit 100,000 by 2010. Two–thirds of them, more than 55,000, are waiting for a kidney, and altruistic donations are unlikely to shorten the line much, said Ms. Paykin. "It is definitely increasing, but is it increasing to the point where it will make a difference in the waiting list?" she said. "I doubt it."

5   The United Network for Organ Sharing, which tracks data on organ donation, lists 134 altruistic kidney donors since 1998, and eleven partial liver donors. Typically, less than 5 percent of those who offer their organs are accepted. Most are rejected for medical reasons. Since the University of Washington Medical Center in Seattle started taking altruistic donors in 2001, for instance, it has recovered organs from four. "It's really a very small percentage who qualify," said Dr. Connie Davis, medical director of the kidney and kidney–pancreatic transplant program at the university. "You have to be in better than average shape mentally and physically."

6   Those who qualify must then go through a process that can take several months. Christine Karg-Palreiro, a thirty-eight-year-old civil engineer, had planned to donate a kidney to a colleague, and went ahead with the surgery even after it turned out she was not a match for him. The surgery took place two days after the attacks of September 11, 2001, and today Ms. Karg-Palreiro has five small scars to show for it, as well as an anonymous thank you note from the recipient. "Giving a kidney is the coolest thing I've ever done and if I had a spare, I'd do it again," Ms. Karg-Palreiro said. She has long been a blood donor, as are many altruistic organ donors, and she has also signed up to donate bone marrow.

7   Mr. Kravinsky also went through with his surgery, and his kidney was, as he wished, given to a black person, though experts say federal laws would seem to prohibit such designations.* Donors may specify a certain person they want to receive their organs, but they are prohibited from discriminating against

classes of people. "What they cannot do is say 'I don't want it to go to someone who's short or tall or skinny or fat,'" said Brian Broznick, president and chief executive of the Center for Organ Recovery and Education in Pittsburgh. "To me, what he reportedly asked for would be discrimination, and I don't think it should be allowed." Dr. Radi Zaki, the transplant surgeon who handled Mr. Kravinsky's surgery at Einstein Medical Center, said a five-member ethics committee had selected the recipient, not his patient. "The designation of the kidney was completely out of his hands," Dr. Zaki said. Mr. Kravinsky's kidney ended up going to a woman with much the same profile* he had demanded, but Dr. Zaki said that was because the hospital is in a largely African-American neighborhood.

8   Harold Mintz's kidney went to a refugee from Ethiopia who had settled in Washington and is an accountant. "We get together two or three times a year," he said. "I send my kidney a birthday card every year." Mr. Mintz, who is forty-five, attributed his desire to make such a personal gift to two things: the death of his father from cancer thirteen years ago and an encounter at a mall with an elderly couple who had set up a table with a sign taped to it asking for help in saving their daughter's life. "Their daughter had leukemia and they wanted people to go to their church to see if they could find a match," Mr. Mintz said. "So instead of chocolate and flowers, I paid $60 to get typed and tested." His blood type didn't match, and he later read the young woman's obituary.

9   Years later, after hearing about the Washington Regional Transplant Consortium, the first transplant organization to actively recruit what it calls "nondesignated" donors, he decided to volunteer a kidney, overcoming the resistance of his wife and his own concern about what would happen if his daughter ever needed a kidney and he was the only match in the family. Mr. Mintz said he does not expect his story to inspire legions of people to volunteer their kidneys to strangers, but he hopes that it might make more people willing to give up organs for friends and relatives. "When people hear what I did, they think I'm a hero or something, but that's not the case," he said. "I have good days and bad days like anybody, but if you can help somebody, especially somebody you know, I just want you to know that it's possible."

Stephanie Strom, "Ideas & Trends:
Extreme Philanthropy . . . ,"
New York Times, July 27, 2003.

PUTTING IT ALL TOGETHER <mark>DIRECTIONS</mark> Answer the following questions by circling the letter of the correct response or filling in the blanks.

Main Idea 1. Which statement best expresses the main idea of the entire reading?

    a. Although people who donate an organ to complete strangers are greatly admired, they are also viewed with suspicion. They are considered too good to be true, and some people wonder if they have taken altruism just a little too far.

    b. More people should be willing to donate a kidney to strangers. If altruistic donors were more common, we could ease the suffering many people must endure while they wait for transplants, sometimes in vain.

    c. Some people are so committed to the notion of helping others that they are willing to donate a kidney to strangers.

    d. People who donate a kidney to strangers may one day regret their generosity if their remaining kidney malfunctions.

Supporting Details 2. Dr. Radi Jaki is mentioned to make which point?

    a. Some people care more about others than they do about themselves.

    b. An organ donor is prohibited from designating the recipient and discriminating against a particular group.

    c. Altruistic donors will never be able to eliminate the organ shortage.

Transition 3. The transition opening paragraph 9 suggests which pattern of organization?

    a. definition

    b. time order

    c. comparison and contrast

    d. cause and effect

Inference 4. Why is the detail about Zell Kravinsky's canceling of his cable service included in paragraph 3?

_____

5. What connection does the author expect readers to make between the little girl who died of leukemia and Harold Mintz's decision to donate a kidney?

_____

_____

Purpose **6.** What is the author's primary purpose?

    a. to inform

    b. to persuade

Tone **7.** How would you describe the author's tone?

    a. objective

    b. concerned

    c. skeptical

    d. astonished

Fact and Opinion **8.** Would you say that the reading is

    a. more fact than opinion?

    b. more opinion than fact?

    c. a balance of fact and opinion?

Drawing Your Own Conclusions **9.** According to the reading, "The number of organ donations from the living surpassed those from the dead, and has for the past two years." What does that suggest about the campaign to get people to sign donor cards giving permission for organs to be harvested after their deaths?

_____

_____

Bias **10.** Which statement best describes the author's position?

    a. The author is skeptical of the motives behind altruists' donations of kidney to strangers.

    b. The author admires those willing to give a kidney to a stranger.

    c. The author does not reveal any bias.

▪ **VOICING YOUR OPINION** What do you think of altruistic donors? Which ethical principle (see pp. 561–564) do you think drives their behavior? Do you consider their actions admirable or crazy? Please explain your answer.

_____

_____

_____

▪ **THINKING THROUGH WRITING** Signing a donor card so that organs can be harvested after death is not a particularly difficult thing to do. But few do it. Similarly, if doctors would ask next of kin to allow healthy organs to be used to save a life, the organ shortage might well disappear. Yet few doctors do. Write a paper explaining the following statement: "Although there are two relatively easy ways to remedy the shortage of human organs available for transplant, neither has become common practice." Your job is to explain why this is so.

■ **READING 7**

UNDERSTANDING CULTURAL METAPHORS
Martin J. Gannon

LOOKING AHEAD In his book *Understanding Global Cultures,* author Martin J. Gannon explains how different cultures can be understood through a close examination of some central institution, phenomenon, or activity, which serves as a metaphor* for the larger culture. In Spain, for example, it is the bullfight; for Mexico the fiesta; and for Japan the garden. What follows is the introduction to Gannon's book in which he explains the connection between culture and comprehension.

PRE-READING AND FOCUS STRATEGIES

1. The author likes to make his key points in general and specific terms. Thus you can probably limit your pre-reading to the first sentence of every paragraph.

2. Since the title says "Understanding Cultural Metaphors," read to answer two basic questions: (1) What are cultural metaphors? (2) Why is understanding them so important?

3. The author repeatedly begins with a generalization and then follows with a specific illustration. Underline the author's generalizations. Then mark the passage to clearly indicate the specific examples by using a symbol like *ex, e.g.,* or *ill.*

WORD WATCH Some of the more difficult words in this reading are defined below. Watch for these words as you read. The number in parentheses indicates the paragraph in which they appear. An asterisk marks their first appearance in the reading.

metaphor: comparison of unlike things that reveals a hidden similarity

integrate (3): connect, make sense of

subservience (5): obedience

pedagogical (6): related to teaching

warped (6): deformed

narrative (7): story

substantive (10): of major importance

disproportionately (11): not in line with actual numbers

respective (11): relating to the order of two or more persons regarded individually

condescending (13): arrogant

1 IN 1990, I WAS PRIVILEGED TO ATTEND A 10-DAY CROSS-CULTURAL training program led by Professor Richard Brislin at the East-West Center, University of Hawaii at Manoa. All 35 attendees were professionals involved in cultural studies in some way, and they included professors from a diverse range of disciplines and immigration officials of several nations. During the course of the program, a well-known cross-cultural training exercise, *The Albatross* (Gotchenour, 1977), was conducted that proved to be very insightful. Perhaps because of my background as a professor of management, I immediately wrote a case study about the experience and have used it more than 100 times in a variety of settings involving students and managers. The reader is invited to read this case study and answer the questions after it before I provide any additional details.

I recently participated in a cross-cultural training session at the East-West Center, Hawaii. There were six male volunteers (including me) and six female volunteers. We walked into a room where a man was dressed in Eastern or Asian garb but in a somewhat indistinguishable manner; he could have been a king or a Buddhist monk. A woman sat beside him, and she was also dressed in a similar indistinguishable fashion.

There was no talking whatsoever in this training session, which lasted for about 10 minutes. The "king" beckoned the males to sit on chairs, after which he indicated that the females should sit at their feet. He then greeted each male silently and in standing position; he clasped each male by the arms and then gently rubbed his hands on the male's sides. The males did as the king instructed, but there was some nervousness and laughter, although no talking. The king then bowed to each female.

Next, the king presented a large vase of water to each male, and he drank of it. The king then did the same thing with each female.

The king and queen then walked before the volunteers, peering intently at the females. After a minute or two, the king put on a satisfied look and made a noise as if satisfied. He then looked at the queen, who nodded in agreement. The queen then took the hand of one female in order to lead her to a sitting position on the ground between the king and queen. Next, the king and queen tried to push the female's head toward the ground as she sat on the ground between them (they were on chairs), but she resisted. They tried once again, but she still resisted. The training session then ended.

Instructions: Each small group should appoint a recorder/secretary to report back to the larger group. Time limit is 10 minutes. Please answer the following questions:

What kind of a culture is this? Please describe.

How would you interpret the differential treatment of males and females in this culture?

2   There were about six subgroups per session over the approximate 100 sessions, so there have been approximately 600 interpretations. In 9 of 10 instances, the subgroup describes the culture in the following manner: a male-dominated traditional culture, probably Asian or African or Middle Eastern, ritualistic, and conservative. Sometimes, the subgroup tries to identify the religion involved, and Buddhism or Islam is cited frequently. And, although almost all subgroups feel that females are in a subordinate role, a few believe that females have a high status clearly separate from that of the dominant males.

3   In fact, this is an earth-worshipping culture in which males are clearly subordinate to females, and the only way to integrate* all of the information provided is to use this framework. For example, the male leader was not being friendly when he patted the males; rather, he was checking for weapons, as males tend to have too much testosterone and too strong a tendency to engage in immature fighting. Similarly, the females were seated in the place of honor (nearest to the ground), and the males were relegated to the bleachers. The males drank first to test for poison, thus ensuring the safety of the females. Even the "king," whose ambiguous position is highlighted by the quotation marks, must ask permission of the female leader before selecting a favored female, who was placed nearest the ground for the ritual in an honored position between the two leaders. Frequently, I ask why a particular female was chosen, and rarely does anyone guess the reason: A visual inspection indicated that she had the largest feet, an obvious sign of importance in an earth-worshipping culture. In many cultures, the number three is used, and it was being used in this ritual until the favored female resisted.

4   This exercise is usually sufficient to make the point that having a framework is very useful in understanding any culture. If the trainees had been told that the culture was earth-worshipping, they could have integrated the various stimuli that were over-

whelming them. Furthermore, the feedback session after the training proved to be insightful, as the young woman selected for the ritual was asked why she resisted.

5   At this time, I usually profile this young woman, a very accomplished cultural anthropologist who has devoted her career to the study of village life around the world. She was in her mid-thirties, well published and tenured at a good university, attractive, and divorced but without children. Her response focused on the maltreatment that she had experienced at the hands of various men in her life and on her resolve never to allow such maltreatment to occur again. Thus, she had interpreted the ritual as a form of subservience* to men, as the "king" was pushing her head toward the ground, as was the "queen," but she did not mention this fact.

6   My pedagogical* point is that this young woman, given her educational training and work experiences in different villages, was as knowledgeable as or more knowledgeable than any professional in the room, but her perspective—warped* by unpleasant experiences with men—had led her to react emotionally, even to the extent that she was not able to think about an alternative framework, such as an earth-worshipping culture. I also point out that I felt overwhelmed during the training and had no idea what was going on.

7   As this narrative* suggests, culture counts, and it counts quite a bit. To give but one example, Geert Hofstede (1991) completed a questionnaire study at the IBM Corporation involving 117,000 of its managers and employees in 53 countries, in which he demonstrated that national culture explained 50 percent of the differences in attitudes. In fact, culture explained more of the difference than did professional role, age, gender, or race. A comparable but earlier study of 3,600 managers in 14 countries placed this figure at 30 percent (Haire, Ghiselli, & Porter, 1966). Given such studies, it seems that culture influences between 25 percent and 50 percent of our attitudes, whereas other aspects of work force diversity, such as social class, ethnicity, race, sex, and age, account for the remainder of these attitudinal differences.

8   But the case study also highlights other critical aspects of culture, which operate subtly, often on the unconscious or semiconscious level. Culture has been aptly compared to a computer program that, once activated by a few commands or stimuli, begins to operate automatically and seemingly in an independent manner (Fisher, 1988; Hall, 1966; Hofstede, 1991). Clearly, such automaticity occurred in the case study, but unfortunately, the stimuli were not properly matched to the cultural framework

because of the negative relationships with males that this young woman had experienced.

9   Frequently, when a foreigner violates a key cultural value, he or she is not even aware of the violation, and no one brings the matter to his or her attention. The foreigner is then isolated and begins to experience negative feelings. As one American business-man in Asia aptly pointed out, one of the central problems of doing business cross-culturally is that once a visitor makes a major cultural mistake, it is frequently impossible to rectify it, and it may well take several months to realize that polite rejections really signify isolation and banishment. Sometimes, a foreigner makes such a mistake and eventually leaves the country without even realizing or identifying what he or she had done.

10   Even genuinely small cultural mistakes can have enormous consequences. Many Germans, for instance, do not like to converse too much during meals. A German will ordinarily begin the meal by taking a sip of beer or soda and then pick up the knife and fork and hold them throughout the meal, putting them down only when he or she has finished eating. For many Germans, eating is a serious business, not to be disturbed by trivial comments and animated conversation. On the other hand, many Italians tend to talk constantly during meals and wave their hands repeatedly. As a result, a German and an Italian dining with one another may feel aggrieved by each other's behavior, and much time is wasted negotiating acceptable rules of behavior that could otherwise be spent on substantive* issues, including the development of trust.

11   Furthermore, whereas technological and societal changes have been rapid in recent decades, cultures tend to change only slowly, typically at a snail's pace, and the influence of culture persists for centuries even after mass immigrations take place. The American Irish have the "gift of the gab," befitting a cultural heritage that has a strong oral tradition, and they are disproportionately* represented in fields such as trial law and politics, where this gift is an asset. . . . The English and the French in Canada think and feel differently in large part because of their respective* cultural heritages, and these differences have threatened the very existence of the country.

12   Individuals from English-speaking countries are at a particular disadvantage culturally because the people of many non-English-speaking countries use both English and their own native languages. It is common for English-speaking visitors to a non-English-speaking country to assume cultural similarity when dissimilarity is really the norm. Today, approximately 800 million individuals speak English, which has become the international

business language, thus creating both opportunities and pitfalls for natives of English-speaking countries.

13   However, it should be noted that knowing a country's language, although clearly helpful, is no guarantee of understanding its cultural mindset, and some of the most difficult problems have been created by individuals who have a high level of fluency but a low level of cultural understanding. Glen Fisher (1988), a former foreign service officer, describes a situation in Latin America in which the American team's efforts were seriously hampered because of the condescending* attitude of one member whose fluency in Spanish was excellent. Fortunately, another member of the team helped to save the day because she showed a genuine interest in the culture and its people, even though she was just beginning to learn how to speak Spanish. Moreover, members of a culture tend to assume that highly fluent visitors know the customs and rules of behavior, and these visitors are judged severely when violations occur.

14   Americans are at a particular disadvantage in trying to understand the mind-sets of other cultures because, at least until recently, they did not travel abroad in great numbers. Even today, American travelers follow a frantic schedule, sometimes visiting Hong Kong, Thailand, Japan, and Taiwan within the space of two weeks. To expect these American travelers to understand these cultures in such a short period of time is unrealistic. Even fewer Americans spend any time residing in foreign countries, and when doing so, they tend to isolate themselves from the natives in their "golden ghettoes." By contrast, Europeans speak two or more languages, including English, and they experience great cultural diversity simply by traveling a few hundred miles from one country to another. Many Asians, because of their knowledge of the English language and education in Europe and the United States, are similar to these Europeans in terms of cultural sophistication.

15   This book describes a new method, the *cultural metaphor,* for understanding easily and quickly the cultural mindset of a nation and comparing it to those of other nations. In essence, the method involves identifying some phenomenon, activity, or institution of a nation's culture that all or most of its members consider to be very important and with which they identify closely. The characteristics of the metaphor then become the basis for describing and understanding the essential features of the society.

16   For example, the Italians invented the opera and love it passionately. Five key characteristics of the opera are the overture, spectacle and pageantry, exteriority, voice, . . . and the interaction between the lead singers and the chorus. . . . We [can] use these

features to describe Italy and its cultural mind-set. Thus the metaphor is a guide, map, or beacon light that helps the foreigner understand quickly what members of a society consider very important. This knowledge should help him or her to be comfortable in the society and to avoid making cultural mistakes. However, the cultural metaphor is only a starting point, and it is subject to change as the individual's firsthand knowledge increases.

Martin J. Gannon. *Understanding Global Cultures.* Thousand Oaks, CA: Sage Publications, 2002, pp. 1–8.

PUTTING IT ALL TOGETHER   DIRECTIONS Answer the following questions by circling the letter of the correct response or filling in the blanks.

Using Context **1.** Based on how it's used in paragraph 9, how would you define the word *rectify*?

_____

Main Idea **2.** Which statement best sums up the main idea of the entire reading?

    a. Visitors often unknowingly make terrible and largely unforgivable social errors because they don't know enough about the culture of the country they are visiting.

    b. Recognizing and analyzing cultural metaphors can help us understand the mind-set of other countries and give us a framework for understanding unfamiliar behavior.

    c. Americans are especially bad at recognizing the mind-set of another culture.

    d. Understanding cultural metaphors will be of little value if we don't understand the language in which those metaphors are expressed.

Supporting Details **3.** The case study at the beginning of the reading helps the author make which point?

    a. Misunderstandings occur all the time between people of different cultures.

    b. We need a cultural framework to adequately interpret behavior.

    c. Earth-worshipping cultures often place power in the hands of women.

    d. The lessons of personal experience are more important than formal education.

4. The study at IBM described in paragraph 7 is included to make what point?

_____

Purpose **5.** What is the author's purpose?

      a. to inform

      b. to persuade

Argument **6.** In paragraph 10, the author offers what opinion?

_____

7. What evidence does the author offer in support of that opinion?

_____

_____

Do you consider the evidence adequate? Why or why not?

_____

Tone **8.** How would you describe the author's tone?

      a. puzzled

      b. confident

      c. comical

      d. objective

9. In paragraph 8, the author describes a metaphor, or implied comparison, that compares _____ to _____.

Which statement best expresses the point of that metaphor?

a. Cultural training often controls behavior on a completely unconscious level, making our behavior almost automatic and somewhat beyond control.

b. Cultural training is hard to challenge because it starts in early childhood and after a certain point we are no longer aware of it.

c. Because of new computer technology, culture is not as influential as it once was.

Drawing **10.** Do you think the opening case study cited by this author could be a
Your Own   cause for ethical concern as the Milgram experiments (p. 581) were?
Conclusions

_____

_____

■   **VOICING** In his opening case study, the author describes the behavior of a
    YOUR cultural anthropologist. Do you think she should have reacted less
OPINION "emotionally"? Do you think the author is critical of her behavior?
        Why or why not?

_____

_____

_____

■ **THINKING** Write a short paper explaining which U.S. institution, activity, or
  THROUGH event reveals so much about American society that it could func-
  WRITING tion as a cultural metaphor. Make sure to explain why you chose
        this particular activity, event, or institution. While writing your
        paper, see if you can guess what the author selected as a cultural
        metaphor for the United States.

■ **READING 8**

THE ROLE OF THE GROUP IN JAPAN
Martin J. Gannon

LOOKING AHEAD Reading 2 suggested that people in the U.S. can go overboard when it comes to following the dictates of a group. The Japanese, however, might question now ethical it is to deviate from the group. What we call excessive conformity, they might call a virtue.

PRE-READING AND FOCUS STRATEGIES

1. Turn the title into a question, "What is the role of the group in Japan?"

2. Because there is a lot of information in this reading and much of it is likely to be unfamiliar, pre-read the first and last sentences of every paragraph before you start reading all of it.

3. Be on the lookout for contrasts between Japan and the United States.

4. Mark any particularly difficult passage for a second, sentence-by-sentence reading.

WORD WATCH Some of the more difficult words in this reading are defined below. Watch for these words as you read. The number in parentheses indicates the paragraph in which they appear. An asterisk marks their first appearance in the reading.

---

identification (4): a feeling of belonging

distinctive (6): noticeable, striking

entrepreneurial (8): related to starting a business

allocation (9): distribution

charismatic (10): exerting a powerful attraction

laterally (11): sideways

relativism (18): making decisions based on specific situations

validity (18): accuracy, truthfulness

delineated (19): defined, spelled out

---

1 THE JAPANESE EMPHASIS ON THE GROUP IS QUITE APPARENT and permeates practically every aspect of Japanese life. It can be seen in the educational system, the structure of business organization and work, and the political system, to name just a few.

2   At school, the children are identified by their class. For example, in junior high school, a student might say, "I belong to *ichinen ni kumi*," or Year 1 Class 2. (Each grade is composed of approximately six classes.) For the next three years, that student will spend every day with the other 40 to 50 students in his or her class and will identify himself or herself with that group. A well-known Japanese proverb, "The protruding nail will be hammered," aptly explains the behavior of individual students. Adhering to this proverb does not pose a problem for most students, who have learned that security, acceptance, and love flow from the group. In fact, most students display a sense of belonging that would be envied by many of their counterparts in the West, who often feel alienated and alone.

3   On the other hand, life can be intolerable for the rare student who does not fit comfortably in a group. Fellow students relentlessly bully, pick on, tease, and persecute this individual. This phenomenon, *ijime*, usually translated as bullying, leads to several deaths every year. If the nonconforming student has any friends, they quickly desert him or her for fear of being excluded from the group, which is the worst fate that can befall a Japanese child or adult.

4   Students achieve group identification* not only with their class but also with their school, particularly at the college level. The university one attends frequently determines one's future career prospects, because the top businesses hire primarily, if not exclusively, from the top universities. Ties made in college days are important in Japanese life, and throughout their lives, Japanese will identify themselves with the university they attended.

5   In Japan, a job means identification with a larger entity, through which one gains pride and the feeling of being part of something significant. An individual's prestige is tied directly to the prestige of his or her employer. The company is not typically viewed as an entity trying to take advantage of its employees in order to make profits, but as a provider of individual security and welfare. When a Japanese person is asked what he or she does, he or she usually responds with the name of the company for whom he or she works, and not the job he or she performs. By contrast, Americans will normally respond to the question of what they do by mentioning the occupation or job first, and they may not even divulge the name of the company. The Japanese worker or manager usually perceives his or her company and other institutions with a strong sense of "we" versus "they." Approximately 30 percent of the Japanese managers and workers, primarily those working for the larger firms, actually are guaranteed lifetime

employment until the age of 55, after which they can work for the larger firm's subcontractors until age 70, but at a reduced salary. This guarantee strengthens the feeling of identification with the firm. And even when a firm is not financially able to make such a guarantee, which is occurring much more frequently in recent years, its owners tend to feel far more obliged to their employees than do their American counterparts. Even in the United States, Japanese firms will frequently retrain their American employees during an economic downturn rather than lay them off or fire them, as is the norm among American-owned firms.

6   Also, the distinctive* structure of the business firm that is found in Japan supposedly fosters group identification. Prior to World War II, much of Japanese industry was organized into six huge *zaibatsus,* or family-owned companies, each of which consisted of approximately 300 companies and their suppliers. Each *zaibatsu* combined the activities of many subcontractors with whom it had long-term contracts, a manufacturing organization, a major financial institution, and an export-import organization. Such a form of organization is outlawed in the United States and other developed countries, and it was actually forbidden by law in Japan after World War II. However, a nonfamily variant of the *zaibatsu,* the *keiretsu,* has emerged and become prominent.

7   American and European managers frequently complain bitterly about the operations of the *keiretsus,* because they have a great amount of power over many activities in the marketplace, and they can persuade Japanese distributors not to carry the products of the foreign companies. Ironically, however, the most dynamic and prosperous companies in the Japanese economy tend to be those that are not members of *keiretsus* (Tasker, 1987). Similarly, although foreign executives have argued that the Japanese Ministry of Trade and Industry (MITI) has unfairly supported rising industries such as personal computing and high-definition television through its various policies and regulations, some of Japan's most profitable corporations, such as Honda and Sony, have become successful without its help; MITI actually advised Mr. Honda, the car company's founder, to go into another line of business.

8   Since 1990, there has been an increase in entrepreneurial* activities among younger managers, some of whom have started their own firms rather than accept employment in established firms. Such entrepreneurial efforts will increase as the world economy becomes more global. But identification with the company will probably remain much stronger in Japan than in the United States.

9   Furthermore, the organizational structure and work allocation* in Japanese firms also emphasize the group. Work is often assigned to various office groups and is viewed essentially as a group effort. Frequently, there are no formal job descriptions existing separate from work groups. A company will sometimes reward the office group, and not the individual, for work well done. Even the physical arrangement of the office emphasizes the group mentality: The manager will sit in front of the workers in a classroom-style setting, and they will work in subgroups with their own supervisors. If the work group is small, everyone will sit around a table, with the most senior members closer to the manager. As a general rule, the Japanese do not allow a manager to have his or her own office and, even if the work requires that he or she be given one, tend not to prefer this arrangement.

10   Japanese groups abound in society—women's associations, youth groups, PTA, and hobby groups, to name just a few. Political parties and ministerial bureaucracies often divide into opposing factions. The new charismatic* religions, such as *Soka Gakkai,* are composed of small groups that mesh together. In sightseeing, the Japanese tendency to perform activities in a group is particularly evident, because they tend to wear the same types of clothes and behave as if they were one.

11   Decision making in Japan also reflects this emphasis upon the group. For example, in a Japanese company, a business proposal is usually initiated at the middle or lower levels of management. The written proposal, called *ringi-sho,* is distributed laterally* and then upward. Each person who reviews it must impress his or her personal seal of approval. Making decisions requires a great deal of time, largely because a good amount of informal discussion has preceded the drawing up of the *ringi-sho.* In spite of its time-consuming nature, the consensus approach to decision making does have important merits. Once the decision is made, it can be implemented quickly and with force because it has the backing of everyone in the department. By contrast, American managers frequently make decisions quickly, but a great amount of time and effort is required for implementation, often because only a few key people have actually been involved in the decision-making process itself.

12   A particularly telling contrast occurred when Travelers Group and Nikko Securities were contemplating a joint venture. After Sandy Weill of Travelers and his Japanese counterparts agreed on the basic issues, Mr. Weill placed a conference call to New York to obtain board approval, which he secured in 30 minutes. Conversely, the Nikko board required 12 days of briefings and discussion to approve a decision that had been resolved in their favor.

13   Just like the water droplet the individual is significant only insofar as he or she represents the group. If individuals disagree with one another, the overall interest of the group comes before their needs. Cooperativeness, reasonableness, and understanding of others are the virtues most admired in an individual. Harmony is sought, and conflict is avoided if at all possible.

14   The extent to which the individual is responsible to the group, and the group responsible for the actions of the individual, is illustrated by the following incident. An American teacher was accompanying an eighth-grade Japanese class on its annual field trip to Kyoto when one of the Japanese teachers kindly informed her that the students would be required to sit in the school auditorium for one hour upon returning from Kyoto. When the American teacher inquired as to why, he responded that one of the students had been 10 minutes late to the school meeting earlier this morning; therefore, all would be punished.

15   Like the water that flows in the garden, the Japanese people prefer to flow with the tide. In contrast to the West, observers have noted the relative absence among the Japanese of abstract principles, moral absolutes, and definitive judgments based on universal standards. The Japanese think more in terms of concrete situations and complex human relations; therefore, whereas to Westerners, the Japanese may seem to lack principle, to the Japanese, Westerners may seem harsh and self-righteous in their judgments, and lacking in human feeling.

16   As Ellen Frost (1987) points out, many Japanese refer to this difference by saying that the Japanese are "wet" people, whereas Westerners are "dry." She elaborates as follows:

> By "dry" they mean that Westerners attach more importance to abstract principles, logic and rationality than to human feeling. Thus, Westerners are said to view all social relations, including marriage, as formal contracts which, once they no longer satisfy individual needs, can be terminated. Their ideas of morality are generalized and absolute, with little regard for the particular human context. . . . By contrast, the "wet" Japanese are said to attach great importance to the emotional realities of the particular human circumstances. They avoid absolutes, rely on subtlety and intuition, and consider sensitivity to human feelings all-important. They notice small signs of insult or disfavor and take them deeply to heart. They harbor feelings of loyalty for years, perhaps for life, and for that reason are believed to be more trustworthy. (p. 85)

17   The term *naniwa bushi* exemplifies this wet quality. In modern use, the term is applied to people who are open-minded, generous, and capable of appreciating another person's position, even when that position is neither logical nor rational. A negotiator who

adopts a rigid position, recites a familiar catalog of grievances, and appears to have no understanding of Japanese concerns is said to lack *naniwa bushi*. Such a person is judged to be neither effective nor trustworthy. Some Japanese feel that many Westerners adopt such a negotiating style, which seems to be one of the reasons why difficulties occur between them. Thus, it seems logical that Japan does not have clearly identifiable political parties, as in the case of the United States, but a loose arrangement of powerful interest groups that negotiate their differences using *naniwa bushi*.

18   Some see the Japanese identification with nature as the explanation for the origin of the relativism* of Japanese attitudes. Others point to the influence of Chinese thought, with its situational approach to applying principles. Whereas in the West, the division was between good and evil, in China the division was between yin and yang, two complementary life forces. Thus, the Japanese tend to see situations more in terms of tones of gray, whereas Americans see them as black and white. However, others suggest that this relativism stems from child-rearing techniques. . . . Probably all of these explanations are interrelated and have some validity.*

19   The emphasis upon situational ethics is illustrated in the Japanese legal system. If the convicted shows that he or she is genuinely repentant for what he or she has done, then it is highly likely that the person will receive a more lenient sentence. Furthermore, the laws passed by the Japanese Diet or Central Government are structured loosely so that the courts can interpret them in ways that different situations demand. By contrast, the American Congress attempts to write laws in such a way that all possible issues are spelled out carefully, and, as a result, judges must operate within relatively strict limits. Furthermore, the Japanese orientation toward harmony and group loyalty means that conflict resolution is valued, not the individualistic assertion of legal rights. For example, in the hamlet of Kurusu, conflict over the building of a factory received national attention from the media, and two years later, shame still pervaded the community. Consequently, the legal system and Japanese values reinforce the emphasis on group consensus or solutions prior to coming to court. The opposite situation exists in the United States, because individuals involved in legal disputes are aware that judges must interpret laws that are already delineated* finely.

20   This practice does not mean that the Japanese do not have a sense of right and wrong. It is simply that they place greater emphasis on the particular situation and human intentions than Westerners do. Lacking a Judeo-Christian heritage, Japanese do

not possess a feeling that certain areas of life are obviously sinful. The major issue is whether an action harms others and has a disruptive effect on the group and community. Many experts assert that the Japanese are motivated primarily by a sense of shame to correct a problem when such disruption occurs, whereas individualistic Westerners are motivated mostly by a sense of guilt at their failure to fulfill responsibilities. Such an orientation is particularly evident in their attitudes toward sex and drinking.

21   As Diana Rowland (1985, p. 115) explains, sex is viewed not as sinful but as just one of the more pleasurable necessities of life. In Japan, sex is not associated with love as strongly as it is in Western culture but, rather, is seen as being related more to desire. Traditionally, marriages were arranged, and even today, both families and companies act as intermediaries. Hitachi, for example, has a "Tie the Knot" Office that matches their male and female employees, many of whom eventually marry (Jordan, 1997). For many Japanese, marriages were not designed to be the sole means of satisfying sexual needs. Therefore, extramarital affairs were not censored. In practice, however, a double standard existed; men were free to keep a mistress (or mistresses) and seek sexual pleasure in any way they chose, whereas women were supposed to toe the line of marriage. One Japanese wife explained to an American friend:

> Why should the wife care if her husband goes off to "play"? It doesn't mean anything. She knows he will never leave her. In fact, I think the bond in a Japanese marriage is much stronger than that in the West. A Japanese woman would not consider divorcing her husband over such a trivial matter.

22   However, this attitude may be changing because of the rise of AIDS. Also, the divorce rate is increasing, and many women are marrying later in life. Still, this attitude confirms the fact that situational ethics is important to the Japanese.

23   Drinking and even drunkenness are good-naturedly tolerated, and even encouraged. In fact, almost anything one does while drunk, except driving, is considered forgivable. Intoxication allows the Japanese to express themselves freely without fear of repercussion, and it is normal for members of a Japanese work group to spend several hours after work drinking and eating as a group before catching a late bus home. However, Western women sometimes find this behavior difficult to accept, even when a Japanese man is very polite when not drinking. In one celebrated instance, a British female high school teacher finally lost patience with a Japanese coworker who had repeatedly harassed her while he was

drinking, and "decked" him at an office party. However, although Japanese may indulge in unruly behavior while drinking, they rarely engage in displays of hostility and violence.

Martin J. Gannon, *Understanding Global Cultures.*
Thousand Oaks, CA: Sage Publications, 2002, pp. 44–49.

PUTTING IT ALL TOGETHER DIRECTIONS Answer the following questions by circling the letter of the correct response or filling in the blanks.

Vocabulary in Context

1. Based on the context in which it appears, how would you define the phrase *moral absolutes* in paragraph 15?

_____

2. How would you define *definitive judgments* from the same paragraph?

_____

Main Idea

3. Which of the following statements best paraphrases the main idea of the entire reading?

a. The Japanese, unlike Americans, think of the group before they consider the individual, and that can create problems for U.S. businesses in Japan.

b. In contrast to life in the United States, the notion of a group identity is central to all aspects of Japanese life.

c. Unlike Americans who let personal ambition rule their professional lives, the Japanese are inclined to think of the company more than they do of personal advancement.

d. Because of their concern for the group over the individual, Japanese society has not remained economically competitive.

Supporting Details

4. In your own words explain why the Japanese think of themselves as "wet" and Westerners as "dry."

_____

_____

5. In paragraph 13, the author uses a simile* (a comparison using "like" or "as") that compares the _____ to a _____.

What is the point of the simile?

_____

_____

*For more on similes and metaphors, see **laflemm.com,** Reading for Thinking: Online Practice.

6. In paragraph 15, the author uses a simile to compare _____

to _____.

Patterns of Organization
7. What three patterns of organization are at work in paragraph 17?

_____

Purpose
8. What is the author's purpose?

a. to inform

b. to persuade

Drawing Your Own Conclusions
9. The manager of a Japanese firm has just found out that he can get a better job at a new American company that has recently set up shop in Tokyo. However, if he leaves his current firm to take a job that can advance his career and pay him more, he will be leaving in the middle of an important project, which may not get done in time without his presence. Based on what you learned from this reading, what is he likely to do and why?

_____

_____

Bias
10. Which statement best describes the author's position?

a. The author thinks the Japanese strong group identification is better than the American emphasis on individualism.

b. The author thinks the Japanese strong group identification could use a dose of American individualism.

c. It's impossible to determine the author's personal bias.

■ **VOICING YOUR OPINION** When it comes to emphasizing the group over the individual, do you think it would be good for American society to be more like Japanese society? Why or why not?

_____

_____

_____

■ **THINKING THROUGH WRITING** Write a paper explaining which approach you favor and why: the ethical approach favored by American society, based on strict, unyielding principles of right or wrong, or the situational ethics of the Japanese as they are described in this reading.

Answer Key for Reviewing the Key Points, Chapters 1–10

Reviewing the Key Points 1:   Getting a Head Start on Academic Success (p. 42)

1. False
2. how, why, what
3. You can write while reading.
4. They give your mind a chance for in-depth processing of information and help you maintain concentration.
5. Recitation tells you how well you have (or have not) understood the material.
6. boldface, italics, repetition, marginal annotations
7. contrast, example, restatement, general knowledge
8. False
9. a partial sentence
10. topic and requirements

Reviewing the Key Points 2:   Power Tools for Learning: Annotating and Paraphrasing (p. 80)

1. focus, concentration (attention or attentiveness also possible), and comprehension
2. False
3. (a) identify key points
   (b) connect the author's words to the reader's experience
   (c) identify potential test questions
4. True
5. key points
6. restate the author's ideas in your own words
7. after reading each paragraph
8. at the end of a chapter section
9. treating someone else's ideas as if they were yours
10. quoted without identifying the source

Reviewing the Key Points 3: Reviewing Paragraph Essentials (p. 151)

1. Finding the topic
2. False
3. What's the topic? and What does the author say about the topic?
4. sum up the main idea
5. True
6. The author is about to reverse or modify a previous position.
7. explain, develop, or prove an author's main idea or point
8. further develop major details, add an interesting fact or story, or provide repetition for emphasis
9. False
10. formulate potential test questions

Reviewing the Key Points 4: Understanding and Outlining Longer Readings (p. 218)

1. 6
2. True
3. True
4. False
5. first, second, finally
6. detailed and complicated; also completely unfamiliar
7. indenting
8. create a blueprint of the author's ideas
9. True
10. True

Reviewing the Key Points 5: Summarizing and Synthesizing: Two More Strategies for In-Depth Learning (p. 274)

1. one-quarter of the original text
2. False
3. True
4. True
5. False
6. False

7. makes a connection between or among the sources

8. False

9. False

10. False

Reviewing the Key Points 6: Reading Between the Lines: Drawing Inferences and Conclusions (p. 332)

1. infer the main idea

2. the author's actual words

   the reader's ideas and experiences

3. the reader's ideas and experiences

4. False

5. False

Reviewing the Key Points 7: Defining the Terms *Fact* and *Opinion* (p. 385)

1. verified

2. verified

   considered informed or uninformed; justified or unjustified

3. False

4. False

5. associations, emotions, feelings

6. dictionary meaning

7. True

8. False

9. relevant or related

10. evidence

    repetition

Reviewing the Key Points 8: Identifying Purpose and Tone (p. 425)

1. to dispense information; explain someone else's ideas or theories

2. competing points of view on the same subject

3. to convince readers to share or at least consider a particular point of view

4. how critically you need to read

5. source of the reading and the author's background

6. thesis statement or main idea

7. describes; evaluate or judge

8. denotative, connotative

9. attitude or emotion

10. be emotional, emotionally charged, or personal

Reviewing the Key Points 9:   Recognizing and Evaluating Bias (pp. 473–474)

1. False

2. what they leave out

3. give the opposition any credit

4. False

5. questions with no expectation of an answer

6. is writing to persuade

7. a

8. be blinded or wear blinkers, fairly evaluate

9. if one event takes place, more of the same will follow, and the consequences will be bad

10. the person

Reviewing the Key Points 10:   Understanding and Evaluating Arguments (pp. 529–530)

1. an opinion, a claim, or a personal point of view

2. a

3. identify, evaluate

4. policy, value

5. relevant

6. circular reasoning

7. a hasty generalization

8. credentials

9. background

10. dated

Acknowledgments

Roy Berko, Andrew D. Wolvin, and Darlyn Wolvin. From *Communicating* by Berko, Wolvin, and Wolvin, pp. 185–192, 202. Copyright © 2004. Reprinted by permission of Houghton Mifflin Company.

Douglas A. Bernstein and Peggy W. Nash. From *Essentials of Psychology* by Bernstein and Nash, pp. 171–172, 274–276, 305–312, 505–512. Copyright © 2001. Reprinted by permission of Houghton Mifflin Company.

Paul S. Boyer et al. From *Enduring Vision* by Boyer, pp. 779a–b. Reprinted by permission of Houghton Mifflin Company.

Paul S. Boyer. From *Promises to Keep* by Boyer, p. 206. Reprinted by permission of Houghton Mifflin Company.

Sharon S. Brehm and Saul M. Kassin. From *Social Psychology* by Brehm and Kassin. Copyright © 1997 by Houghton Mifflin Company. Used by permission.

David Callahan. Excerpts from *The Cheating Culture: Why More Americans Are Doing Wrong to Get Ahead*, copyright © 2004 by David Callahan, reprinted by permission of Harcourt, Inc. This material may not be reproduced in any form or by any means without the prior written permission of the publisher.

Melvin L. DeFleur and Everette E. Dennis. From *Understanding Mass Communication* by DeFleur and Dennis, pp. 248–250. Copyright © 2002. Reprinted by permission of Houghton Mifflin Company.

Joseph A. DeVito. From *The Interpersonal Communication Book*, 9/e. Published by Allyn and Bacon, Boston, MA. Copyright © 2001 by Pearson Education. Reprinted by permission of the publisher.

Ashley Dunn. "Cram Schools: Immigrants' Tools for Success" by Ashley Dunn from the *New York Times*, January 28, 1995. Copyright © 1995 by The New York Times Co. Reprinted with permission.

Mike Eskenazi. "Education/Special Report: The New Case for Latin" by Mike Eskenazi from *Time*, December 12, 2000, p. 61. Copyright © 2000 TIME Inc. Reprinted by permission.

Martin J. Gannon. From *Understanding Global Cultures: Cultural Metaphors for 40 Nations* by Martin J. Gannon, pp. 1–8, 44–49. Copyright © 2002. Reprinted by permission of Sage Publications, Inc.

Alan Gitelson, Robert L. Dudley, and Melvin J. Dubrick. From *American Government*, 5/e. Copyright © 1998 by Houghton Mifflin Company. Used by permission.

Alan Gitelson, Robert L. Dudley, and Melvin J. Dubrick. From *American Government*, 7/e. Copyright © 2004 by Houghton Mifflin Company. Used by permission.

William B. Gudykunst et al. From *Building Bridges: Personal Skills for a Changing World.* Copyright © 1995 by Houghton Mifflin Company. Used by permission.

Janet Shibley Hyde. From *Understanding Human Sexuality* by Janet Shibley Hyde. Reprinted by permission of The McGraw-Hill Companies.

Kenneth Janda, Jeffrey M. Berry, and Jerry Goldman. From *The Challenge of Democracy.* Copyright © 1995 by Houghton Mifflin Company. Used by permission.

Larry Leslie. From *Mass Communication Ethics* by Leslie, pp. 15–19, 263–266. Copyright © 2000 by Houghton Mifflin Company. Used by permission.

Paul E. Levy. From *Industrial/Organizational Psychology.* Copyright © 2002 by Houghton Mifflin Company. Used by permission.

Mary Beth Norton. From *A People and a Nation*, 5/e, by Norton et al. Copyright © 1998 by Houghton Mifflin Company. Used by permission.

Ted Nugent. From "Hunters Are Wildlife's Best Friends." *USA Today,* October 3, 1991. Reprinted by permission of the author.

John O'Brien. "Tall Tales of Appalachia" by John O'Brien from the *New York Times*, May 10, 2003. Copyright © 2003 The New York Times Co. Reprinted by permission.

William M. Pride, Robert J. Hughes, and Jack R. Kapoor. From *Business.* Copyright © 2000 by Houghton Mifflin Company. Used by permission.

Barry L. Reece and Rhonda Brandt. From *Effective Human Relations in Organizations.* Copyright © 1999 by Houghton Mifflin Company. Used by permission.

Martin S. Remland. "Nonverbal Communication in Everyday Life." Copyright © 2000 by Houghton Mifflin Company. Used by permission.

Zick Rubin, Letitia Anne Peplau, and Peter Salovey. From *Psychology.* Copyright © 1993, 1990 by Houghton Mifflin Company. Used by permission.

Kevin Ryan and James Cooper. From *Those Who Can, Teach* by Ryan and Cooper, pp. 53–57. Copyright © 2004. Reprinted by permission of Houghton Mifflin Company.

Kelvin L. Seifert, Robert Hoffnung, and Michele Hoffnung. From *Lifespan Development.* Copyright © 2000 by Houghton Mifflin Company. Used by permission.

Stephanie Strom. "Ideas & Trends: Extreme Philanthropy: Giving of Yourself, Literally, to People You've Never Met" by Stephanie Strom from the *New York Times*, July 27, 2003. Copyright © 2003 The New York Times Co. Reprinted by permission.

Joseph Turow. From *Media Today: An Introduction to Mass Communication* by Turow, pp. 115–120, 426–428. Copyright © 2003. Reprinted by permission of Houghton Mifflin Company.

James Wilson and John J. DiIulio. From *American Government* by Wilson and DiIulio, pp. 333-334. Copyright © 2004 by Houghton Mifflin Company. Used by permission.

INDEX